Behavioral Approaches to Crime and Delinquency

A Handbook of Application, Research, and Concepts

Behavioral Approaches to Crime and Delinquency
A Handbook of Application, Research, and Concepts

Edited by

EDWARD K. MORRIS and
CURTIS J. BRAUKMANN

University of Kansas
Lawrence, Kansas

PLENUM PRESS • NEW YORK AND LONDON

Library of Congress Cataloging in Publication Data

Behavioral approaches to crime and delinquency.

Bibliography: p.
Includes index.
1. Juvenile delinquency—Psychological aspects. 3. Behavior modification. 4.
Juvenile justice, Administration of. I. Morris, Edward K. II. Braukmann, Curtis J.
HV9069.B52 1987   364.2′4   87-29081
ISBN 0-306-42632-3

© 1987 Plenum Press, New York
A Division of Plenum Publishing Corporation
233 Spring Street, New York, N.Y. 10013

Printed in the United States of America

To our families

Contributors

Warren K. Bickel • Department of Psychiatry, Division of Substance Abuse, Albert Einstein College of Medicine, 1500 Waters Place, Bronx, New York

Curtis J. Braukmann • Department of Human Development, University of Kansas, Lawrence, Kansas

Barrie J. Brown • Bloomsbury Health Authority, 4 St. Pancras Way, London, England

John D. Burchard • Department of Psychology, University of Vermont, Burlington, Vermont

Terry C. Chaplin • Research Department, Mental Health Centre, Penetanguishene, Ontario, Canada

Meda Chesney-Lind • Youth Development and Research Center and Women's Studies Program, University of Hawaii at Manoa, Honolulu, Hawaii

Carl B. Clements • Department of Psychology, University of Alabama, Tuscaloosa, Alabama

William S. Davidson II • Department of Psychology, Michigan State University, East Lansing, Michigan

Mark A. Davis • Department of Psychology, Valdosta State College, Valdosta, Georgia

Lee Ellis • Department of Sociology, Minot State University, Minot, North Dakota

Linda S. Ewald • Department of Psychology, University of Hawaii at Manoa, Honolulu, Hawaii

E. Scott Geller • Department of Psychology, Virginia Polytechnic Institute and State University, Blacksburg, Virginia

Leah K. Gensheimer • Department of Psychology, Arizona State University, Tempe, Arizona

Rand Gottshalk • Department of Psychology, Michigan State University, East Lansing, Michigan

Stephen T. Higgins • Department of Psychiatry, University of Vermont School of Medicine, Burlington, Vermont

Melissa J. Himelein • Department of Psychology, University of Kentucky, Lexington, Kentucky

Robert J. Jones • Appalachian State University, BIABH Study Center, Morganton, North Carolina

Marvin D. Krohn • Department of Sociology, State University of New York, Albany, New York

Theodore W. Lane • Cumberland County Mental Health Center, Children and Youth Program, Fayetteville, North Carolina

Anne Maguire • Research Department, Mental Health Centre, Penetanguishene, Ontario, Canada

Michael J. Manos • Youth Development and Research Center, University of Hawaii at Manoa, Honolulu, Hawaii

James L. Massey • Department of Sociology, University of Georgia, Athens, Georgia

Jeffrey Mayer • Department of Psychology, Michigan State University, East Lansing, Michigan

Mary E. McCaul • Departments of Psychiatry and Behavioral Sciences, Johns Hopkins University School of Medicine/Key Medical Center, Baltimore, Maryland

Michael A. Milan • Department of Psychology, Georgia State University, Atlanta, Georgia

Edward K. Morris • Department of Human Development, University of Kansas, Lawrence, Kansas

Teru L. Morton • Vanderbilt Institute of Public Policy Studies, Vanderbilt University, Nashville, Tennessee

Janice Murakami • Department of Psychology, University of Vermont, Burlington, Vermont

Michael T. Nietzel • Department of Psychology, University of Kentucky, Lexington, Kentucky

Clifford R. O'Donnell • Department of Psychology and Youth Development and Research Center, University of Hawaii at Manoa, Honolulu, Hawaii

Jerome J. Platt • Department of Psychiatry, School of Osteopathic Medicine, University of Medicine and Dentistry of New Jersey, Camden, New Jersey

Maurice F. Prout • Department of Mental Health Sciences, Hahnemann University, Philadelphia, Pennsylvania

Vernon L. Quinsey • Research Department, Mental Health Centre, Penetanguishene, Ontario, Canada

John F. Schnelle • Department of Psychology, Middle Tennessee State University, Murfreesboro, Tennessee

Jan Sheldon • Department of Human Development and School of Law, University of Kansas, Lawrence, Kansas

William F. Skinner • Department of Sociology, University of Kentucky, Lexington, Kentucky

Maxine L. Stitzer • Departments of Psychiatry and Behavioral Sciences, Johns Hopkins University School of Medicine/Key Medical Center, Baltimore, Maryland

Douglas Upfold • Research Department, Mental Health Centre, Penetanguishene, Ontario, Canada

Montrose M. Wolf • Department of Human Development, University of Kansas, Lawrence, Kansas

William Yule • Department of Psychology, Institute of Psychiatry, University of London, London, England

Preface

The systematic application of behavioral psychology to crime and delinquency was begun only 20 years ago, yet it has already contributed significantly to our practical knowledge about prevention and correction and to our general understanding of a pressing social problem. In this handbook, we review and evaluate what has been accomplished to date, as well as what is currently at the leading edge of the field. We do so in order to present a clear, comprehensive, and systematic view of the field and to promote and encourage still more effective action and social policy reform in the future.

The chapters in this text have been written by professionals who were among the original innovators in applying behavioral psychology to crime and delinquency and who continue to make critical contributions to the field's progress, and by a new generation of energetic, young professionals who are taking the field in important and innovative directions. The contributors have attempted to review and evaluate their areas with critical dispassion, to provide thorough but not overly specialized discussion of their material, and to draw implications for how research, application, and social policy might be improved in the future. For our part as editors, we have tried to foster integration across the chapters and to provide background and conceptual material of our own.

Inevitably, some readers will judge that we have included too little material in some areas or too much in others. Where selective or differential emphasis exists, however, it is often a function of the work that is available for review and not due to known bias on our parts. This is especially true of our slightly greater attention to delinquency than to adult offending and to our emphasis on individual street crime as opposed to white-collar and organized crime. These limitations aside, we seek to offer thorough and systematic coverage of the behavioral approaches to crime and delinquency as they exist today.

Our intended audience includes advanced undergraduate and graduate students, other scholars and researchers, and those who establish policy, control resources, and direct programs for the prevention and correction of crime and delinquency. We envision, then, that the book will serve as a professional reference, as a guide for informed practitioners, and as a text for advanced courses in crime and delinquency, with special emphasis on the latter — for today's students are the future of the field. The book's audience, though, should not be restricted to those who work at the intersect of behavioral psychology, criminology, and penology alone. Rather, in our view, the applied procedures and programs, research stategies, and basic concepts described herein have broad heuristic value for those involved in preventing, correcting, and understanding crime and delinquency across an array of specialty areas and theoretical perspectives and across various levels of analysis. To be more circumspect, however, the book does not present a panacea for the problems facing the field of crime and delinquency today. What we offer are simply some useful, often powerful and far-reaching, strategies for intervention, research, and conceptual analysis that can be integrated with current justice system practices. Our goal, here, is to encourage a scientifically sound and accountable orientation toward effective and socially acceptable solutions to crime and delinquency.

Many people have contributed to this book, and acknowledgments are obviously in order. We are indebted first, of course, to the chapter authors for their fine contributions and for so graciously tolerating our editorial blue pens. In addition, we benefitted greatly from Lynda J. Powell's critical reading of the initial drafts of most chapters and her discussions with us about them; Kathleen McCandless Drake assisted here as well. We also thank Eliot Werner, Peter Strupp, Alyce Hager, William Imbornoni, and others at Plenum Press for their patience as we assembled the chapters and prepared our own. Finally, Belinda Conrad, Kathryn Keyes, Rose Roberts, and Ann Spitz also deserve our appreciation for typing, photocopying, and mailing so many manuscripts.

Our efforts were partially supported by grants from the Center for Studies of Antisocial and Violent Behavior of the National Institute of Mental Health (MH 20030 and MH 39713), which we gratefully acknowledge. The Department of Human Development at the University of Kansas also assisted in many incidental and important ways. Neither NIMH nor the department, however, is responsible for the conclusions and interpretations presented herein.

Individually, E. K. M. would like to offer his appreciation to Sidney W. Bijou, who gave him the freedom to explore areas outside of a standard curriculum and who has supported him in so many ways since; to V. Scott Johnson, who introduced him to the day-to-day workings of the Robert F. Kennedy Youth Center (Morgantown, WV) and who is a model of the toughness, sensitivity, and thoughtfulness required of applied behavior analysts in correctional settings; to Edith E. Flynn, who supported his employment at the National Clearinghouse for Criminal Justice Planning and Architecture (Champaign, IL), who gave generously of her time in independent studies to someone outside her own field, and who probably never thought her encouragement would come to this; and finally to the Departments of Human Development, Psychology, and Sociology at the University of Kansas who encouraged his teaching a course on the behavior analysis of crime and delinquency and to the students who have enrolled in that course and continue to see to its improvement.

C. J. B. is grateful to Montrose M. Wolf for a fine and extensive introduction to this area of research and scholarship and for his generous counsel and friendship over the years encompassed by this book; to Dean L. Fixsen and Elery L. Phillips for sharing their considerable expertise in the development and dissemination of behavioral procedures and programs; to Kathryn A. Ramp for a decade and a half of colleagueship in delinquency research; to William C. Williams for his fundamental and enthusiastic tutelage in behavior analysis; and, finally, to the Department of Human Development and the Bureau of Child Research at the University of Kansas and the Center for Studies of Antisocial and Violent Behavior at NIMH for opportunities to conduct research and teach in this and related areas.

For ourselves, the preparation of this handbook brought many enjoyable and gratifying opportunities to learn from one another and has contributed to our professional relationship and friendship in important ways. As for the coediting, we want to be explicit that our contributions have been equal. The handbook has no primary or secondary editor — just a joint editorship.

EDWARD K. MORRIS
CURTIS J. BRAUKMANN

Contents

3. **An Introduction to Contemporary Behaviorism: History,
    Concepts, and a System of Analysis** 61

    *Edward K. Morris, Stephen T. Higgins, Warren K. Bickel, and
    Curtis J. Braukmann*

II. BEHAVIORAL APPLICATIONS IN ADULT AND JUVENILE CORRECTIONS

4. **Probation and Parole** 109

    Michael T. Nietzel and Melissa J. Himelein

7. Token Economy Programs in Closed Institutions 195

Michael A. Milan

III. PREVENTION AND INTERVENTION IN COMMUNITY SETTINGS

8. Law Enforcement and Crime Prevention 225

John F. Schnelle, E. Scott Geller, and Mark A. Davis

IV. Special Topics in Intervention and Evaluation

12. Criminal Justice Interventions with Drug and Alcohol Abusers: The Role of Compulsory Treatment 331

Maxine L. Stitzer and Mary E. McCaul

13. The Behavioral Treatment of Rapists and Child Molesters ... 363

Vernon L. Quinsey, Terry C. Chaplin, Anne Maguire, and
Douglas Upfold

VI. PROFESSIONAL ISSUES IN BEHAVIORAL APPLICATIONS

I

INTRODUCTION

1

Behavioral Approaches to Crime and Delinquency

CURTIS J. BRAUKMANN AND EDWARD K. MORRIS

Understanding and controlling juvenile delinquency and adult crime remain elusive goals. This does not reflect disinterest of either the public, elected and appointed officials, or scholars and scientists. In the United States, as elsewhere, considerable activity pertains to preventing crime and intervening with those who commit it. At federal, state, and local levels, illegal behavior is the impetus for voluminous legislation, policymaking, and judicial deliberation as well as concentrated effort by those involved in preventive, law-enforcement, and correctional endeavors. Furthermore, criminal behavior is the object of intense study in such traditional areas of research and scholarship as psychology, sociology, political science, law, history, anthropology, and philosophy.

Given all of this activity, progress toward the ancient objectives of controlling and understanding crime and delinquency has been impressively modest. For example, although common crime-control strategies have undoubtedly improved in humaneness over the centuries, their effectiveness is still questioned: research typically does not reveal differential impacts for such correctional efforts as penal custody, parole, and probation, or such deterrent and preventive efforts as police patrols and job-training programs (Lipton, Martinson, & Wilks, 1975; Romig, 1978; Wilson & Herrnstein, 1985). Nevertheless, there are some reasons for guarded optimism, and it seems patently clear that serious crime—like such other damaging, intransigent, costly, and sometimes lethal problems as disease, natural disasters, and armed conflict—is deserving of continuing diligent efforts toward comprehension, amelioration, and prevention.

If history is a guide, the sustained search for the causes and remedies of lawbreaking will require systematic work within various approaches on conceptualization, application, and research. This handbook is about the achieved and potential contributions of the behavioral approaches, which are relatively new in the criminological and correctional arena. The book's principal emphasis is on application: the use of procedures derived from behavioral science to develop and implement programs of prevention, correction, and deterrence.

Curtis J. Braukmann and **Edward K. Morris** • Department of Human Development, University of Kansas, Lawrence, Kansas 66045.

The behavioral approaches to crime and delinquency, however, are not solely defined by intervention procedures by these procedures in combination with underlying behavior principles and metatheoretical assumptions. These approaches are also defined by "dimensions" that prescribe effective application. These dimensions—more specifically, those of applied behavior analysis (Baer, Wolf, & Risley, 1968)—are discussed in Chapter 2; the field's metatheoretical assumptions, basic principles, and intervention procedures are considered in Chapter 3. Collectively, then, the first three chapters constitute our definition of, and introduction to, the behavioral approaches to crime and delinquency.

Before considering these behavioral approaches further, we will first briefly examine the topic of crime and delinquency in order to set the stage. In so doing, and in subsequent discussions in this chapter, we will bring in themes that emerge in the chapters to follow.

CRIMINAL AND DELINQUENT BEHAVIOR

In the broadest sense, crime and delinquency refer together to all acts or omissions prohibited by public law and liable to punishment by that law. This category of behavior obviously contains extremely diverse actions that differ greatly in seriousness and dispersion. Moreover, so defined, this category varies considerably by country and region, over time, and with the age of the perpetrator.

In many places, some acts that are illegal for juveniles above some minimal age of responsibility are not so for adults. School nonattendance and consumption of alcoholic beverages are examples of such "status offenses." Furthermore, in some countries, including the United States and Great Britain, young people can be brought to court on ill-defined grounds involving no delinquency as such, because courts are concerned not only with minors' offenses but also their general welfare (Rutter & Giller, 1984).

To the extent that the category of behaviors prohibited by law is relative, the definition of crime and delinquency reflects not only societal beliefs of right and wrong but also the interests of those with the power to legislate their interests (see Sheley, 1985, pp. 44–70). Nonetheless, serious predatory acts, which include violent offenses and property crimes, such as assault and burglary, appear to be essentially "universal crimes," regarded as wrong across societies and historical periods (Wilson & Herrnstein, 1985). Such crimes appear to be those least susceptible to processing discretion (Rutter & Giller, 1984) and most worrisome to the U.S. public (Sheley, 1985), particularly the Federal Bureau of Investigation's *index* crimes—murder and nonnegligent manslaughter, aggravated assault, forcible rape, robbery, burglary, larceny, motor vehicle theft, and arson.

Predatory Crime and This Text

Much of the research and application described in this book is about preventing predation or treating persons adjudicated for it. The severity of the offenses and the intransigence of the offenders varies considerably, however. On the one hand, some of the applied and empirical work illuminated herein concerns serious adult and juvenile offenders (Milan, Chapters 6 and 7), including child molesters and rapists (Quinsey, Chaplin, Maguire, & Upfold, Chapter 13). On the other hand, much of the applied work focuses on that considerably more prevalent group of offenders with detected predatory behavior of mild to moderate gravity. Indeed, by design, some open-community work has involved youths not yet formally adjudicated (see O'Donnell, Manos, & Chesney-Lind, Chapter 9, on diversion and neighborhood programs; see Lane & Murakami, Chapter 11, concerning school-based programs).

In attending most to predatory transgressions and those who commit them, the individual chapter authors are plainly reflecting the nature of applications to date. Accordingly, their coverage does not represent a collective judgment about the limits of worthy focus. Obviously, serious criminal activity includes fraud, embezzlement, commercial price fixing, dumping of hazardous wastes, extortion, and bribery, yet little behavioral work has been directed at these and other nonstreet crimes. The nonpredatory offense category most frequently discussed in this book is illicit drug use, though some illicit drug users likewise engage routinely in predatory crime (see Stitzer & McCaul, Chapter 12).

Two other points relative to the book's focus bear noting. First, the explicit concern with lawbreaking does not imply a lack of appreciation for either primary prevention or early identification and secondary prevention efforts with elementary-school-aged children (Loeber & Dishion, 1983; Patterson, 1974). The reader interested in early identification and prevention would do well to consult Burchard and Burchard's (1987) comprehensive reference.

Second, the emphasis on those officially identified as criminal or delinquent must be considered in this light: most offenses do not result in official identification of the perpetrators, and some frequent lawbreakers apparently remain, in the short run at least, arrest-free (Elliott, Dunford, & Huizinga, 1987). Nevertheless, the association between frequency of serious criminal behavior and apprehension for significant illegal activity appears to be strong (Farrington, 1983; Rutter & Giller, 1984, pp.26–31; see Morris & Braukmann, Chapter 2, this volume).

The Correlates of Crime and This Text

Although researchers and scholars have yet to explain crime and delinquency adequately or to identify reliable ways to prevent or reduce it, they have revealed some of its correlates and epidemiological dimensions. Official data, self-reports, and victim surveys all suggest that males are more crime prone than females and that adolescents and young adults are responsible for a disproportionate amount of crime. Thus it is not surprising that the typical high-rate offender is an urban male in his teens or 20s (Wilson & Herrnstein, 1985). This group does not account for anywhere near all predatory infractions, of course. For example, there are persistent, serious offenders among females as well (Warren & Rosenbaum, 1986). Moreover, some serious crimes are relatively rare events in the lives of their perpetrators, some of whom may be behaving under acute, abnormal conditions—though these latter crimes can on occasion be among the most heinous (e.g., murder of family members by an estranged spouse).

In addition to sex and age, other correlates of significant rates of predatory offending include (1) being brought up in a troubled (e.g., cold, discordant), often large, low-income family; (2) encountering inappropriate or inadequate child-rearing practices; (3) having parents with criminal histories; (4) beginning illegal behavior at an early age; (5) having trouble in school; (6) using drugs frequently; (7) committing crimes in the company of other young men; and (8) not specializing in any type of crime (Farrington, Ohlin, & Wilson, 1986). Less persistent or serious offenders show these features to a lesser extent, of course, but age, sex, nonspecialization in offending, lawbreaking associates, drug use, and family relationship problems emerge as correlates of offending in general (e.g., Elliott, Huizinga, & Ageton, 1985; Hirschi, 1969; Rutter & Giller, 1984).

Interventions naturally conform to the demographics and correlates of offending. This is evinced throughout this book by the preponderance of interventions for males, especially those in their teens and 20s (see, for example, Chapters 5, 6, 7, 9, 11, 13, 14, 15, 18, and 19). The correlates of crime are likewise reflected in formal explanations of criminal behavior. For example, Platt and Prout (Chapter 18) suggest mechanisms by which aggressive behavior is transmitted in early social learning experiences in dysfunctional families—a theme further developed by Morton and Ewald (Chapter 10) in covering family-based interventions; Krohn, Massey, and Skinner (Chapter 17) include an account of why adolescents who commit crimes have associates who also commit crimes—some implications of which are developed by O'Donnell, Manos, and Chesney-Lind (Chapter 9); and, finally, Ellis (Chapter 19) puts forth, among other things, possible biological bases for the prevalence of young males among predatory offenders.

BEHAVIORAL APPROACHES IN GENERAL

Before specifically addressing behavioral approaches to crime and delinquency, we will first present a brief overview of behavioral approaches in general. Broadly conceived, behavioral approaches are attempts to understand, analyze, and intervene on a diverse and vast array of personal and social behaviors. These attempts at explanation, analysis, and intervention are based on established principles of behavior, well-articulated procedures for studying behavior, and evolving techniques for altering behavior. These sets of principles, analytic procedures, and change strategies have a common heritage, share underlying assumptions about behavior, and are each used in the development of the others. For example, behavior-change procedures are often initially designed on the basis of behavior principles and then selectively retained or refined on the basis of applied behavior-analytic research.

Assumptions and Principles

Among the assumptions underlying the behavioral approaches are certain theoretical ones about the nature of science. As considered at some length in Chapter 3, these assumptions have their roots in Greek philosophy and, in various and sometimes nonobvious ways, in objectivism, positivism, empiricism, associationism, evolutionary theory, and functionalism. These philosophical precursors contributed to classical behaviorism (Watson, 1913), contemporary behavior analysis (Kantor, 1959; Skinner, 1953, 1974; see also Keller & Schoenfeld, 1950), and such related perspectives as social learning theory (Bandura, 1977) and cognitive-behavioral theory (Meichenbaum & Cameron, 1982).

The assumptions of behavioral approaches are those of natural science in general, and basic behavioral principles have cumulated predominantly through an inductive process. This has meant that the principles are sufficiently general (both in the manner they are stated and in their validity) to (1) present great flexibility to those who attempt explanations of significant human behavior (cf. Wilson & Herrnstein, 1985) and (2) provide a language of great versatility that can encompass, and help to integrate, different theoretical views—an attribute noted by Krohn, Massey, and Skinner (Chapter 17) with regard to theoretical explanations of criminal activity.

Basic behavioral principles (sometimes called the principles of learning) describe lawful behavior–environment relationships that serve as the basis for understanding the content, form, and function of behavior (Catania, 1984; Millenson & Leslie, 1979; Skinner, 1953). These principles are based on decades of basic research elucidating the conditions of behavior change and maintenance. This concern with behavior change and maintenance has made the resultant principles useful springboards for the design of interventions to alter behavior (see Morris, Higgins, Bickel, & Braukmann, Chapter 3). For this reason, the behavioral orientation, unlike many other conceptual and empirical ones, has a uniquely applied focus: a strong synergism exists between its principles, fundamental research, and analytical methods, on the one hand, and the development of behavioral procedures and practical application, on the other.

Behavioral Procedures

Behavioral principles, then, have been the basis for the development of a variety of intervention procedures (see Bandura, 1969; Brigham & Catania, 1979; Kazdin, 1980; Leitenberg, 1976; O'Leary & Wilson, 1987). Among these are techniques involving differential reinforcement, environmental design, skill training, and response cost (see Morris, Higgins, Bickel, & Braukmann, Chapter 3). Behavioral interventions often include (1) the construction of new behavioral repertoires through procedures of shaping, instructing, prompting, and differential reinforcement; (2) the rearrangement of socioenvironmental contingencies, sometimes entailing incentive or "contingency management" systems such as token economies or behavioral contracts; and (3) the programming of maintenance and generalization of behavior changes outside and after the intervention. Various collective labels have been given to behavioral procedures, including *behavior modification, behavior therapy,* and *behavioral engineering.* The distinctions among these labels are not always clear, nor need they concern us here.

Of more concern, perhaps, is Phillips and Ray's (1980) observation that the boundaries of "behavioral" are somewhat unclear and increasingly permeable, with interventions that are described as "behavioral" sometimes combining ingredients from several different paradigms. Although Phillips and Ray note the advantages to this, they argue that constructs and methods from different models should not be combined without regard to assumptions, meanings, and frameworks. We concur, and accordingly articulate in Chapter 2 the dimensions of what—in the view of many in the behavioral field, including ourselves— represents the core behavioral approach to application: applied behavior analysis (Baer *et al.,* 1968). The concepts and procedures of applied behavior analysis have been demonstrated to be broadly valuable in the systematic study and development of methods to alleviate individual and societal problems.

Applied behavior analysis receives emphasis in this volume, but so do behavioral conceptualizations and interventions nominally outside the confines of this approach—see particularly Platt and Prout (Chapter 18) on cognitive-behavioral theory and interventions and Krohn, Massey, and Skinner (Chapter 17) on social learning theory in the sociological tradition. In both chapters, attention is appropriately paid to respective assumptions, meanings, and frameworks (cf. Phillips & Ray, 1980). Interested readers are referred to Wilson and Franks (1982) for exploration beyond that contained in this text of the distinctions among the related experimental-psychology models currently termed *behavioral:* applied behavior analysis, cognitive-behavior therapy, social learning theory, and neobehavioristic (S-R) theory.

Collectively, behavioral intervention procedures represent an empirically based technology for producing behavior change and promoting its generalization and maintenance. This technology, along with behavioral methods of research, has been applied to a variety of conditions and behavior problems including—in addition to criminal behavior—developmental disabilities, psychological disorders, academic difficulties, addictive behaviors, interpersonal conflicts, physical illness and handicaps, speech problems, and unemployment (see *Journal of Applied Behavior Analysis,* 1968–present; *Behavior Modification,* 1976–present; *Behavior Therapy,* 1970–present; *Behaviour Research and Therapy,* 1963–present; Journal of Behavior Therapy and Experimental Psychiatry, 1970–present; and Hersen, Eisler, and Miller's *Progress in Behavior Modification,* 1975–present).

PRELIMINARY OBSERVATIONS ON BEHAVIORAL APPROACHES TO CRIME AND DELINQUENCY

Behavioral approaches to crime and delinquency include efforts both to explain and to control offending. With regard to explanations of criminal behavior, Part V of this book, Alternative Theoretical Conceptions, includes a sampling of theoretical accounts that have made use of behavior principles (e.g., social learning theory in sociology; see Akers, 1973, 1977; Burgess & Akers, 1966). Other crime-causation descriptions that have used behavior principles—but that are not presented here, or only partially so by the renditions in Part V—include Adams (1973), Braukmann, Kirigin, and Wolf (1980), Conger (1976, 1980), Jeffery (1965, 1971), Patterson (1980), Stumphauzer (1986), and Wilson and Herrnstein (1985). Common to all these explanatory accounts is the appreciation that behavior, criminal or otherwise, is complexly affected by its various antecedents and consequences and that individual (e.g., specific learning history) and situational (e.g., social and physical context) variables are important determinants of offending.

Most of the text, however, is devoted to behavioral approaches to the control (i.e., prevention, deterrence, and remediation) of crime and delinquency and not its explanation. Behavioral approaches to intervention have been described in previous texts concerned with, for example, the design of rehabilitative milieus in adult penal institutions (Ayllon & Milan, 1979) and juvenile correctional facilities (Cohen & Filipczak, 1971), and prevention of delinquency (Wright & James, 1974), and the analysis and correction of aggression and violence (Goldstein, Carr, Davidson, & Wehr, 1981; Stuart, 1981). Other volumes have provided reviews of behavioral applications to corrections for either academicians (Trasler & Farrington, 1979) or practitioners (Bishop & Blanchard, 1973; Stumphauzer, 1986). Finally, still other books have given overviews of behavioral approaches to either crime (Nietzel, 1979) or delinquency (Stumphauzer, 1973, 1979)—as have various review articles (Braukmann, Fixsen, Phillips, & Wolf, 1975; Davidson, & Seidman, 1974; Geller, Johnson, Hamlin, & Kennedy, 1977; Morris, 1980). The present reference, however, is the most comprehensive and current of these and benefits from new contributions by authors of several of the previous publications.

The various chapters on application in this handbook describe behavioral interventions designed to change the behavior of both offenders and those who interact with them, including family members, treatment program personnel, potential victims, and police. The settings in which these interventions have been conducted range from the open community to closed institutions. Among those who have directly implemented these interventions, usually with the guidance of applied behavioral scientists, are personnel in law enforcement, corrections, and preventive agencies as well as therapists, neighborhood groups, and offenders themselves.

It should not be surprising that the behavioral applications and applied studies described herein vary considerably in comprehensiveness, sophistication, intrusiveness, and apparent effectiveness. The strengths and weaknesses of particular efforts are well described in the subsequent chapters of this book. Here, by way of broad introduction to these efforts, we offer several general observations.

Behavioral Interventions: Limitations and Merit

The first observation is that, although much has been accomplished, behavioral interventions do not offer a panacea to crime and delinquency (cf.

Ross & McKay, 1978); moreover, long-term outcomes have been somewhat limited and mixed (Braukmann & Wolf, Chapter 5; Milan, Chapter 7; Lane & Murakami, Chapter 11; Gottshalk, Davidson, Mayer, & Gensheimer, Chapter 15). Nevertheless, behavioral approaches to the study and amelioration of criminal and delinquent behavior appear to be of strong heuristic value, and they promise to offer much to correctional and preventive efforts at this juncture. For one thing, emphasis on the reliable measurement of meaningful behaviors and on the systematic study of interventions and their effective components facilitates the design of new strategies and the cumulative improvement of prevailing approaches to intervention.

Moreover, as will be clear throughout this book, much has been accomplished toward the design of environmental arrangements that, when in effect, significantly alter important behaviors of those with histories of criminal behavior. Even if long-term "cures" are often elusive, interventions that result in improved behavior while in effect are clearly important. For example, the achievement of genuine effectiveness in the short term may suggest elements valuable for effective, longer-term, minimally restrictive, prosthetic interventions (cf. Braukmann & Wolf, Chapter 5). Furthermore, if positive, rational behavior-change methods can be used in lieu of punitive, arbitrary, coercive systems of control in residential treatment settings, then resistance, alienation, and informal countertherapeutic control systems are less likely, and, accordingly, opportunities for therapeutic/educational interventions are enhanced (see Milan, Chapter 6).

Reinforcing and Humane Relationships

A second general observation is that behavioral practitioners have increasingly emphasized "consumer preference" and helping participants achieve personal goals. Furthermore, behavioral practitioners have explicitly fostered relationships between treatment providers and participants that are characterized by "warmth and empathy." Although applied behavioral researchers have frequently ignored this focus on reinforcing and humane relationships in reports of their work (Turkat & Forehand, 1980), they have nonetheless sometimes focused their research upon it (e.g., Willner et al., 1977). The humane focus of many behavioral applications—as operationalized by such participant-involvement strategies as self-government (Fixsen, Phillips, & Wolf, 1973; McNeil & Hart, 1986)—has facilitated cooperative, nonmanipulative involvement in meaningful, appropriately adjusted change strategies.

The importance of participant preference and involvement is touched upon throughout this text by, for example, Sheldon (Chapter 21) in detailing ethical and legal issues, Milan (Chapters 6 and 7) in considering institutional interventions, and Braukmann and Wolf (Chapter 5) in discussing group-home programs. As these and other chapter authors make clear, there is deep concern in the behavioral field with human rights, ethical issues, and accountability. It must be acknowledged, however, that some nominally behavioral programs have been remiss in these regards, being overly restrictive, regimented, insensitive to individual preferences and differences, and otherwise inappropriately implemented (cf. Heads, 1978).

Misconceptions and Conceptions

Our third observation is that the manner in which behavioral concepts and procedures have been presented in the past both by advocates and detractors—along with often inaccurate media presentations and the indiscriminate use of behavioral language to either identify or justify nonbehavioral interventions—has resulted in widely prevalent misconceptions, shallow understandings, and, indeed, mistrust of behavioral approaches (Morris, 1985; Saunders & Reppucci, 1978; Todd & Morris, 1983; Turkat & Forehand, 1980). For the record, again, behavioral applications do not include brain surgery, electroshock, chemotherapy, brainwashing, and seclusion. Further, the fact that a procedure or system can be conceptualized in behavioral terms does not make it behavioral in the sense we are using it (Braukmann *et al.*, 1975).

It is true, of course, that most efforts on the part of the criminal and juvenile justice systems, and other political and social systems, can be analyzed in terms of behavioral concepts. Such analyses can suggest ways in which those efforts can be made more effective and often less intrusive. Specific examples in this regard are provided in chapters by Nietzel and Himelein (Chapter 4) on probation and parole, Milan (Chapter 6) on basic procedures in institutional settings, Schnelle, Geller, and Davis (Chapter 8) on law enforcement and citizen crime prevention, Stitzer and McCaul (Chapter 12) on interventions with drug and alcohol abusers, and Burchard (Chapter 22) on social and political contingencies.

Individualized Treatment

Fourth, the application of behavioral procedures is ideally based on functional analyses, that is, on systematic examinations of what is maintaining the behavior of interest in the particular case—and not on the uncritical adoption of standard, unindividualized, or at-hand target behaviors and treatments (Emery & Marholin, 1977; Phillips & Ray, 1980; see Jones, Chapter 16, this volume). Moreover, appropriate behavioral intervention involves careful consideration of which specific skills or behaviors are (1) desirable and currently not present at sufficient strength, (2) undesirable and present at excessive strength, and/or (3) likely to have widespread effects of a durable nature if changed (for further discussion on the selection of behaviors, see Morris & Braukmann, Chapter 2).

It is evident, then, that consideration of individual differences represents the starting point for properly executed behavioral interventions. Nevertheless, behavioral practitioners have at times paid insufficient attention to the etiology or maintenance of particular behavior. Moreover, they have sometimes elected to modify behavior solely because it facilitates institutional functioning and not because it has relevance to the participant or broader society (Braukmann & Fixsen, 1975).

Some behavioral interventions have fallen short in still other ways. For one thing, the suppression of undesirable behaviors has not always been accompanied by the construction of alternative, desirable behaviors. For another, behavioral strategies have been wrongly and prematurely designed on occasion, especially early in the field's history, due to unsophisticated reliance on the direct generalization of principles from animal learning studies without further experimentation (Hersen *et al.*, 1975). Contemporary applications in the behavioral area are, however, for the most part suitably individualized. Although this is supported by the material in the book, a caveat is warranted.

Some applications described by chapter authors may not appear personalized, when in fact they were; this is especially so for applications and studies with multiple participants. This has occurred because (1) behavioral programs that serve more than one participant at a time are frequently structured, and their depiction may emphasize structural generalities to the neglect of the individualized treatment occurring; and (2) published applied research, which needs to demonstrate adequate replication for scientific conclusions, may involve nearly identical intervention procedures across several participants in a program, though this may not reflect the individually tailored nature of the treatment routinely offered in the program. In a related aside here, we note that published applied research, especially about interventions with diverse effects, may report on behaviors of less clear importance than other behaviors that were affected, simply because the former are more easily quantifiable and hence more useful for demonstrating the effectiveness of procedures (cf. Burchard & Harig, 1976).

Social Systems

Before introducing the book's sections and chapters, we would like to make one final set of observations. Behavioral approaches have for the most part been applied to selected individuals, perhaps within the context of group intervention settings, and not to social systems. Obviously, effectively changing the behavior of individuals alters, to varying extents, the systems in which they operate, particularly those relatively circumscribed systems in which they interact frequently (e.g., family, classroom, job). Interventions aimed at individuals thus should also consider these immediately surrounding interactional systems and, where possible, attempt to directly alter them, as Morton and Ewald (Chapter 10) argue in their review of family-based interventions.

Also in need of consideration is the analysis and alteration of larger social systems, from relatively localized arrangements (e.g., municipal law-enforcement agencies, individual secondary schools, prisons, neighborhoods) to more diverse and complex ones (e.g., state or federal legal, educational, and juvenile justice systems). The allure of intervention at the system level is obvious. As Hersen *et al.* (1975) have noted,

The modification of entire social systems represents a parsimonious application of behavioral principles in which large numbers of individuals are able to receive positive benefits. (p. 13)

To the extent that crime and delinquency are fostered and responded to by aspects of larger social systems (and "created" to some extent by the rule making and labeling of those systems; Becker, 1963), a macroscopic focus on modifying systems is important. Burchard (Chapter 22), for one, takes this position and makes recommendations to behavioral scientists for analyzing and intervening at the level of sociopolitical systems and social policy, for these affect whether effective prevention and treatment will occur. Put another way, given the forces of political expediency and social perceptions, simply providing empirical information based on research studies may not be sufficient to impact social policy. Social advocacy may be a necessary part of the armamentarium of the behavioral interventionist interested in system-level change (see Seekins & Fawcett, 1986).

A further comment concerning a systems perspective: Because behavioral efforts do not occur in a vacuum, behavioral practitioners need to be keenly aware of the sociopolitical contexts of their work. The social systems in which they work can be considerably biased or unfair—for example, discriminatory on racial, sexual, or age-, class-, and power-related bases. Moreover, these systems and institutions can bring administrative, economic, and other pressures to bear that can result in the compromise of personal values and the sometimes inappropriate promotion of arbitrary norms.

Some of the ethical, professional, and practical issues raised in these regards are touched upon by Sheldon (Chapter 21) and Clements (Chapter 20), who argue that behavioral psychologists must be aware of their role within larger systems and must challenge those systems when errors of commission and omission are observed. Not only must behavioral scientists be sensitive to situations where behavioral efforts may be warped by larger contexts, they must appreciate the limits of their ability to bring about constructive personal or social change in the real world of politics, bureaucratic restraints, limited resources, and resistance by program staff (Saunders & Reppucci, 1978).

AN OVERVIEW OF THE PARTS AND CHAPTERS

The reader wishing to see how the parts of the text, and the field in general, fit into a larger picture should find the following overview valuable. In it, we provide brief background material, a general description, and occasional commentary for each part and chapter of the book.

Part I: Introduction

The first part—the present and two subsequent chapters—introduces the themes, topics, and organization of the rest of the book. It provides introductory and background material on behavioral assumptions, concepts, principles, and applications. As mentioned earlier, the discussion of dimensions of behavioral applications in Chapter 2 is particularly important. That discussion touches upon such topics as single-subject research methodology, behavioral assessment, types of intervention procedures, and dissemination and quality control of programs. These assorted topics are essential for understanding and critically examining the applications and studies presented in subsequent chapters.

Part II: Behavioral Applications in Adult and Juvenile Corrections

Parts II and III present up-to-date, often critical reviews of the application of behavioral procedures in, respectively, correctional and community systems. Obviously, responses to crime and delinquency, if they are to be appropriate, must occur in many forms at many levels, as dictated by the nature of the offenses and offenders involved. This is not to say, of course, that the behavioral interventions covered herein represent all, or even necessarily sufficient, solutions across the range of appropriate entry points.

The four chapters in Part II each concern behavioral interventions within traditional adult and juvenile corrections—probation/parole, group homes, and institutions. Some of these interventions use strategies designed to change illegal behavior directly. Others use indirect strategies that involve developing skills and abilities (e.g., academic, social, and vocational) judged either to be somewhat incompatible with illegal behavior or to set the occasion for legal as opposed to illegal behavior. Perhaps the best of the described interventions embrace both direct and indirect strategies.

Probation and parole are frequent interventions because of their relative humaneness and low cost. In Chapter 4, Nietzel and Himelein trace the historical development and current dimensions of traditional probation and parole services for juveniles and adults. Against this backdrop, they describe individual- and system-level behavioral interventions. In so doing, they note the methodological problems compromising the internal and ecological validity of available behavioral research, and they suggest, accordingly, some future directions for that research. Finally, they point to pervasive factors that must be addressed if behavioral contributions to probation and parole are to be fully realized.

In Chapter 5, Braukmann and Wolf describe behaviorally based group-home programs for youthful offenders in the context of the history and current place of group homes in delinquency treatment. Primary focus is on the Teaching-Family model (Wolf, Phillips, & Fixsen, 1972), which has generated most of the extant research. The extensive available research on treatment procedures, staff training, program replication, and outcome effectiveness is described in some detail. The authors conclude with a consideration of the adaptation of the Teaching-Family model for individual, special foster care—an approach that might facilitate longer-term differential effects.

Milan contributes two chapters on applications of behavioral methods within adult and juvenile correctional institutions. In Chapter 6, he discusses the considerable research that has been conducted in secure settings concerning the effects of six classes of basic behavior change procedures (positive reinforcement, negative reinforcement, punishment, time-out and response cost, differential reinforcement and generalization training, and social skills training). In so doing, he provides informative commentary on group contingencies, "good time" programs, the side effects of various interventions, and the selection of proper treatment goals.

In Chapter 7, Milan reviews institutional token economies that have been used as major behavior rehabilitation and management systems. He describes experimental and informal analyses of the immediate in-program effects of these systems, along with evaluations of their posttreatment effects. Although he points to a number of positive results, he concludes that the potential for behavioral programs in institutions is far from realized. Milan also addresses many of the legal, ethical, and professional issues pertinent to behavioral interventions in closed settings. Finally, he joins others (e.g., Burchard & Harig, 1976; Saunders & Reppucci, 1978) in acknowledging the administrative, philosophical, political, and resource- and staff-related barriers to implementing quality programs in institutions.

Given the problems facing prison systems, it is unfortunate that, as Milan observes, little behavioral work is still ongoing in those settings. Prisons are too often characterized by a warehouse orientation, inadequate opportunities for significant instruction in functional and prosocial behavior, inmate intimidation, violence, gang control, and predominantly coercive practices. Clearly, behavioral approaches would not eliminate warehousing, violence and coercion, or the need for segregation and locks. Nonetheless, in some settings, the potential contributions of well-designed and carefully monitored behavioral programs include more meaningful and motivating, and less alienating and coercive, treatment for persons who more often than not will return to the community, perhaps the worse for the experience.

Part III: Prevention and Intervention in Community Settings

The third part of the book treats behavioral applications in community systems. Community-based interventions are recommended because of their clear value for prevention, the right of intervention participants to the least restrictive treatment environment necessary, the need to focus on the immediate social systems affecting offenders, the importance of generalization of behavior changes to the natural environment, and cost-efficiency considerations (Braukmann, Kirigin Ramp, & Wolf, 1981). The community systems considered in this part include families, schools, neighborhoods, court diversion programs, and police departments.

In Chapter 8, Schnelle, Geller, and Davis critically review behavioral efforts with regard to law enforcement and citizen crime prevention. The first half of the chapter focuses on the use of behavioral methodologies by police departments to increase efficiency and to monitor and evaluate crime management procedures. The authors review (1) behavioral evaluation research examining the effects of automobile, walking, helicopter, and directed patrols and (2) research in metropolitan police departments on behavioral procedures to increase the quality of report writing, case preparation, and investigation and apprehension activities.

The second half of Chapter 8 concerns citizen crime prevention programs. Four types of programs are considered: direct facilitation and citizen awareness efforts; property marking; security surveys for target hardening; and neighborhood patrol projects. Problems with mobilization, maintenance, proper evaluation, and effectiveness are discussed, as are ways in which behavioral approaches could directly assist in the solution of these problems.

In Chapter 9, O'Donnell, Manos, and Chesney-Lind discuss behavioral and nonbehavioral programs for diversion and neighborhood delinquency prevention, noting that the diversion of youths from court processing and institutionalization has not been especially effective. In regard to neighborhood prevention programs, O'Donnell and his colleagues describe and critically review programs that offer self-selected recreational or academic activities in high-delinquency areas, involve social workers with gangs, or provide directed services to identified high-risk juveniles. In considering the pattern of research results, the authors make several treatment and policy suggestions.

There can be little doubt that crime and delinquency have roots in family situations (Loeber & Dishion, 1983). In Chapter 10, Morton and Ewald discuss the characteristics and dynamics of dysfunctional family systems as a prelude to a review of behavioral family-based interventions for crime and delinquency. Among the interventions they describe and critique are (a) individually focused ones for such juvenile problems as fire setting, stealing, drug abuse, and running away and (b) "broad-band" efforts that include parent training, behavioral contracting, and family-systems approaches.

Morton and Ewald also describe family-based intervention and prevention efforts for crimes of familial abuse and neglect. Here, they cover both highly focused interventions as well as multifaceted ecobehavioral or integrative approaches. Overall, Morton and Ewald find considerable reason for optimism but point to needs for more basic research, emphasis on familywide interventions and evaluations, and policy-relevant study of various ways of intervening with families and individuals.

Like families, schools are basic institutions of socialization and hence are important contexts for preventive intervention. The subject of the final contribution in Part III is school-based interventions for adolescents exhibiting such problems as disobedience of school authorities, drug abuse, truancy, disorderly classroom conduct, fighting, and destruction of property. Lane and Murakami (Chapter 11) provide a context for considering such interventions by discussing the empirical and theoretical links between schools, dropping out, and delinquency, and by tracing the history of traditional special education services with regard to disciplinary-problem youths.

Within this framework, Lane and Murakami carefully review the findings on the major behavioral school-based intervention efforts, which have usually occurred in individual special classrooms in public junior and senior high schools. But the authors also describe promising behavioral work that has been directed at the larger secondary-school environment to reduce overall in-school conduct disorder, a considerable problem in large cities (Toby, 1983). In the future, these system-level efforts may benefit from fundamental research on the relationship of delinquency to the organizational and procedural characteristics of schools (see Gottfredson & Gottfredson, 1985; Rutter, Maughan, Mortimore, & Ouston, 1979).

Part IV: Special Topics in Intervention and Evaluation

This part contains a diverse set of chapters. The first two concern behavioral applications to specific types of criminal and delinquent behavior: drug abuse and sexual offending. The next two concern behavioral applications to juvenile offenders across intervention types and presenting problems: one details work occurring outside of North America, whereas the other describes a meta-analysis (i.e., a quantitative summary of research) concerning treatment effects. The final chapter presents some basic methods for—and addresses several issues surrounding—evaluation of behavioral programs in the crime and delinquency area.

In the first chapter of this section, Stitzer and McCaul (Chapter 12) describe criminal justice interventions for drug and alcohol abusers. Obviously, use of illicit drugs is in itself crime. Moreover, drug and alcohol use are related to other crimes. For example, property offenses and violent offenses are strongly related to the frequent use and sale of drugs, especially such addictive and expensive ones as heroin or cocaine (Collins, Hubbard, & Rachal, 1985). Furthermore, criminal action appears to be occasioned for some people in some circumstances by use of psychoactive substances that impair judgment, reduce inhibitions, increase confusion or paranoia, or facilitate aggressive responses— for example, alcohol use is clearly implicated in vehicular homicide and injury (Reed, 1981) and is present in many murders and rapes (Greenberg, 1981). Finally, we note that the abuse of psychoactive substances and predatory crime may have common causes (cf. Wilson & Herrnstein, 1985, pp. 355–373).

Stitzer and McCaul critically overview several criminal justice interventions targeting illicit drug use—most particularly heroin use—including supply restriction, incarceration, community supervision, and compulsory treatment participation. In so doing, they review the extant data and consider the treatment and policy implications of alternative approaches. With regard to alcohol-related crimes, the authors examine the results of programs for persons arrested for drunk driving and public drunkenness. Overall, they conclude that behaviorally based programs, differential treatment, and contingently deferred and concurrent legal sanctions could improve treatment efficacy, and generally call for more behaviorally sound programs.

In Chapter 13, Quinsey, Chaplin, Maguire, and Upfold present a detailed discussion of behavioral treatment for rapists and child molesters. The importance of effective treatment for such offenders is underscored by data suggesting that the high rate at which such offenders commit their crimes has been vastly underestimated (Abel, Mittelman, & Becker, 1985). In the context of a behavioral view of the etiology and maintenance of sex offending, Quinsey and his colleagues describe behavioral treatment, especially as it is practiced at Oak Ridge, a maximum-security hospital in Ontario, Canada. They describe assessment procedures, treatment techniques, and the positive immediate results for interventions designed to (1) increase appropriate skills and knowledge and (2) alter arousal to stimuli related to rape or child molestation. Finally, they point to problems and challenges in providing treatment within institutional programs and in conducting definitive outcome studies.

For the most part, the applied behavioral work discussed in the present text has been conducted in the United States. In Chapter 14, Yule and Brown remedy this imbalance somewhat by describing several behavioral applications with juvenile offenders outside North America. Their coverage focuses particularly on the United Kingdom, but they also discuss efforts in Holland, Belgium, New Zealand, and Australia. Most of these efforts have been in residential settings, sometimes based in part on the Teaching-Family model developed in the United States (see Braukmann & Wolf, Chapter 5). Yule and Brown note the paucity and preliminary nature of the available research outside North America and discuss constraints operating at the larger social-system levels in various countries.

In Chapter 15, Gottshalk, Davidson, Mayer, and Gensheimer describe a meta-analysis of the treatment efficacy of behavioral approaches with juvenile offenders. They searched the published literature from 1967 to 1983 for behavioral studies involving some follow-up assessment and then applied meta-analytic techniques (Glass, McGraw, & Smith, 1981; Rosenthal, 1984). The results of this empirical effort are considered carefully in a discussion that touches upon issues of generality across time and settings as well as on the power of postintervention settings to affect behavior.

The value of a meta-analysis depends, of course, on the quality of the individual studies that are included. If studies are seriously flawed, they can provide little in the way of useful information, whether they are considered individually or in aggregate. An optimal evaluation study provides knowledge about what intervention worked, to what extent, and with which participants and ideally provides some insight into why the intervention did or did not succeed.

Such evaluations are essential for a cumulative understanding of the effects of interventions, as noted by Jones in Chapter 16. He provides guidelines for the design and implementation of quality evaluations in crime and delinquency, highlighting the achieved and potential contributions of behavioral methodology to such evaluations. He argues for evaluations that (1) have an explicit theoretical framework, (2) measure program processes as well as outcomes, (3) use measures valuable to intended research consumers, (4) avoid serious threats to internal validity, and (5) address issues of "social validity" (Wolf, 1978). Jones emphasizes the importance of reliably measuring behavior, and discusses the benefits and liabilities of alternative measures of criminal behavior.

Part V: Alternative Theoretical Conceptualizations

The three chapters in this section touch on behavioral principles and concepts in considering the etiology of criminal and delinquent behavior. The first two chapters present explications that clearly fall under the rubric *behavioral*. In the first, Krohn, Massey, and Skinner (Chapter 17) describe—along with pertinent research—the sociological formulation called social learning theory (Akers, 1973, 1977), which integrates "differential association" theory (Sutherland, 1939) with basic behavioral principles (Burgess & Akers, 1966).

Social learning theory in sociology has much in common with social learning theory in psychology, especially as the latter has been developed by Bandura (1977). Both emphasize cognitive control processes, internal mediators of behavior, and learning from models. As Rosenthal (1982) observes, the social learning approach in psychology (Bandura, 1977) can be seen as falling within the more general category of cognitive-behavioral approaches, a diverse set of conceptual models and therapeutic techniques that share both the view that cognitions are major factors in maladaptive behavior and an emphasis on the modification of client cognitions using behavioral procedures (Bandura, 1977; Kendall & Hollon, 1979; Mahoney & Arnkoff, 1978; Meichenbaum, 1977; Meichenbaum & Cameron, 1982).

In Chapter 18, Platt and Prout describe cognitive-behavioral theory and interventions for crime and delinquency. They overview the development and dimensions of cognitive behavioral conceptualizations, and they describe the diverse applications of cognitive-behavioral procedures to the correction of antisocial and violent behavior. Among the cognitive-behavioral procedures they review are self-instructional training and social problem solving to improve self-regulation. Of course, emphases on problem solving and on self-direction are not restricted to behavioral approaches explicitly labeled *cognitive-behavioral* (see, for example, Braukmann & Wolf, Chapter 5).

Neither of the two previously described theory-related chapters explicitly considers biological influences on antisocial and violent behavior. The same can be said of many behavioral explanations of criminal and delinquent behavior. Accordingly, the third and final chapter in this part (Ellis, Chapter 19) was invited in an attempt to redress the neglect of biological factors. Ellis takes a strong biological view and makes the case, based on a broad range of basic research and theorizing, that neurohormonal factors appear to be involved in some predatory offending, though in complex interaction with environmental (e.g., experiential) factors. Knowledge of how people neurologically differ, he concludes, may help in the design of effective treatment and prevention.

In our view, it is obvious that nature and nurture are involved interactively in behavioral development, and it is noncontroversial that the probability of an individual behaving in socially proscribed ways in a given situation is a complex function of unique learning-history, situational, and, to some extent, biological variables (see Chapter 3 for a more expanded discussion). More controversial is the relative contribution of each class of variable in most offending behavior. Certainly, to the extent that inheritance has any role to play in the probability of criminal behavior (cf. Mednick, Gabrielli, & Hutchings, 1984), then persons with both environmentally and genetically predisposing factors would be at most risk (Rutter & Giller, 1984). Our comments here do not mean that we accept the sometimes seriously overstated cases made for biological determinism in crime and delinquency, only that biology participates in all behavior and that it thereby serves as a context for all person–environment interactions.

Part VI: Professional Issues in Behavioral Applications

The three chapters in the final section have to do with the roles and responsibilities of behavioral practitioners. In the first of the contributions, Clements (Chapter 20) addresses the functions, goals, and ethical and legal responsibilities of psychologists in adult correctional institutions. He argues that psychologists need to move beyond the role of mental health assessor and provider by taking appropriately broad and integrative views and by increasing their involvement in empirically based and well-coordinated activities of treatment, staff training, crisis intervention, planning, development, and evaluation. In discussing the opportunities and constraints for doing these things, he points to the benefit of a behavioral perspective and reviews legal issues associated with prison overcrowding, inmate classification, and treatment of the disturbed offender.

In Chapter 21, Sheldon, a lawyer and behavioral psychologist, presents a broad treatment of the closely intertwined legal and ethical issues pertinent to the behavioral treatment of adolescent and adult offenders. She addresses ethical issues surrounding informed consent, privileged communication, research procedures, and the tensions between professional employment and the protection of offender rights. The legal issues she covers touch upon program placement and release, treatment planning and provision, staff training and supervision, motivational systems, aversive techniques, involuntary servitude, search and seizure, the duty to warn third parties, and basic rights to have acceptable living conditions and to refuse treatment. Finally, she advocates the use of human rights committees and institutional review committees as protective mechanisms.

The Clements and the Sheldon chapters (Chapters 20 and 21) make clear the importance of court decisions that address the constitutional rights of adult and juvenile offenders and that set minimum criteria for treatment. Such rulings can have a system-level positive impact and have been welcomed by those in the behavioral field. Yet, as some experiences have indicated, in the short run, some judicial reforms may be mixed blessings. For example, eliminating coercive staff practices without providing for a more humane way to keep order and protect lives may inadvertently increase the informal, predatory power structure (e.g., gangs) and correspondingly require increased use of isolation to protect inmates. Behavioral approaches could potentially offer assistance in this regard by providing for positive means of establishing constructive order.

In the book's final chapter, Burchard focuses on social and political contingencies that affect the behavior of both offenders and therapists. He describes four such contingencies, which he terms the *training-school, diversion, intensive-supervision,* and *funding* contingencies. He recommends that behavioral practitioners become more involved in establishing and modifying such contingencies and discusses barriers to this. Finally, he provides examples of how behavioral practitioners may be able to have beneficial impacts at the policy level and encourages a greater emphasis on prevention.

Concluding Comments

Behavioral efforts to uncover the roots of crime and delinquency and to develop diverse means for its control have clearly provided neither a fully developed explanation of criminogenic mechanisms nor a definitive set of crime-control strategies. Yet important contributions have been made toward these ends. To the extent that behavioral methods appear to be effective, in the short term at least, the claim that "nothing works" (Martinson, 1974) is seriously misleading—though maintenance of behavior change remains a significant problem (Rutter & Giller, 1984).

What seems needed are continuing commitments to empiricism—to evaluating the effects of interventions and adjusting strategies accordingly as well as to innovative application and research informed by ongoing developments in behavioral and related areas of research, scholarship, and practice. Important contributions are likely to come from those who are well versed in the strengths and weaknesses of what has already transpired and who are well educated in both the basics and the leading edge of research, application, and conceptualization in the behavioral sciences.

More than this, though, favorable circumstances must exist for continued innovative development in the behavioral approaches to crime and delinquency. Unfortunately, the long-range prognosis concerning propitious circumstances is unclear. Necessary public support may be at risk in the present climate of general despair about intervention efforts and of advocacy for punitive justice (West, 1985). To conclude that nothing can be done because successes have come grudgingly seems defeatist and wrongheaded. Nothing *will* be done, of course, without resources and commitments to ongoing quality work and without continued investment in research and innovation and in the education of skilled scientists and practitioners.

What is needed is an enlightened perspective: an understanding that we are not going to solve our problems simply by locking all offenders up or otherwise punishing them. No doubt, as Rutter and Giller (1984) have remarked, so-called therapeutic approaches can sometimes be less appropriate than "just-deserts" punishment when, for example, they restrict the liberty of juveniles out of proportion to the seriousness of their offenses. Yet, as Rutter and Giller (1984) also have observed:

> An exclusive "crime control" or "justice" approach . . . ignores the extensive evidence that severe and persistent delinquency is often accompanied by widespread personal difficulties and disturbances which give rise to distress and social impairment for the individual, as well as "trouble" for society. (p. 322)

Clearly there is strong social importance in attempting to prevent and treat serious recidivist delinquency: as high-rate serious offenders proceed through their adult years, they are at some risk for displaying a cluster of pervasive antisocial features, including immoderate drinking, overaggressiveness, continued offending (though generally at decreasing rates; cf. Gottfredson & Hirschi, 1986) as well as chronic unemployment and desertion and nonsupport of families (McCord, 1978; Robins, 1966; West & Farrington, 1977). The associated social costs are considerable, especially given that these persons appear to be at some risk for passing on their "social disability" (Short & Strodtbeck, 1965; Wolf, Braukmann, & Kirigin Ramp, in press) to their offspring (Mednick *et al.,* 1984; Robins, 1966; Wilson & Herrnstein, 1985).

Although most youthful offenders are not serious persistent delinquents, a good portion of them continue lawbreaking, some of it serious, for several years and have considerable and long-term personal and social difficulties. Accordingly, therapeutic intervention seems important in their case as well— though not if the intervention is more restrictive than equally effective and reasonably humane alternatives or, especially, if the intervention inadvertently increases the risk that offending will persist. Interventions, therapeutic or otherwise, should be used judiciously given their track record and the limits in resources; moreover, interventions should be as near "natural" and nonintrusive as possible.

All things being equal, effective early preventive efforts are clearly preferable to later intervention. However, designing and implementing individually focused preventive programs characterized by reasonable cost-benefit ratios, sufficient ability to attract and motivate at-risk families, predictively accurate identification procedures, and adequate protection of choice and liberty remain a formidable challenge for the future. Another important challenge for the future is the design of ecological approaches to prevention and deterrence in which social systems are altered to decrease the pressures and opportunities for offending.

As more effective and humane corrective, preventive, and deterrent interventions are developed by applied behavioral researchers, careful attention will need to focus on maintaining the long-term quality of those interventions and on replicating them with equal effectiveness in contexts beyond the original one (see Morris & Braukmann, Chapter 2). In the dissemination phase of future behavioral interventions, as in the development and demonstration phases, there will need to be sustained emphasis on careful research and evaluation—a hallmark of the behavioral approaches.

References

Abel, G., Mittelman, M., & Becker, J. (1985). Sexual offender: Results of assessment and recommendation for treatment. In M. H. Ben-Aron, S. J. Hucker, & C. D. Webster (Eds.), *Clinical criminology: The assessment and treatment of criminal behaviour* (pp. 191–206). Toronto: M & M Graphics.

Adams, R. (1973). Differential association and learning principles revisited. *Social Problems, 20,* 458–470.

Akers, R. L. (1973). *Deviant behavior: A social learning approach.* Belmont, CA: Wadsworth.

Akers, R. L. (1977). *Deviant behavior: A social learning approach* (2nd ed.). Belmont, CA: Wadsworth.

Ayllon, T., & Milan, M. A. (1979). *Correctional rehabilitation and management.* New York: Wiley.

Baer, D. M., Wolf, M. M., & Risley, T. R. (1968). Some current dimensions of applied behavior analysis. *Journal of Applied Behavior Analysis, 1,* 91–97.

Bandura, A. (1969). *Principles of behavior modification.* New York: Holt, Rinehart & Winston.

Bandura, A. (1977). *Social learning theory.* Englewood Cliffs, NJ: Prentice-Hall.

Becker, H. S. (1963). *Outsiders.* New York: Free Press.

Bishop, C. H., & Blanchard, E. B. (1971). *Behavior therapy: A guide to correctional administration and programming.* Athens, GA: Institute of Government, University of Georgia.

Braukmann, C. J., & Fixsen, D. L. (1975). Behavior modification with delinquents. In M. Hersen, R. M. Eisler, & P. M. Miller (Eds.), *Progress in behavior therapy* (Vol. 1, pp. 191–231). New York: Academic Press.

Braukmann, C. J., Fixsen, D. L., Phillips, E. L., & Wolf, M. M. (1975). Behavioral approaches to treatment in the crime and delinquency field. *Criminology, 13,* 299–331.

Braukmann, C. J., Kirigin, K. A., & Wolf, M. M. (1980). Group home treatment research: Social learning and social control perspectives. In T. Hirschi & M. Gottfredson (Eds.), *Understanding crime* (pp. 117–130). Beverly Hills: Sage.

Braukmann, C. J., Kirigin Ramp, K., & Wolf, M. M. (1981). Behavioral treatment of juvenile delinquency. In S. W. Bijou & R. Ruiz (Eds.), *Behavior modification: Contributions to education* (pp. 211–231). Hillsdale, NJ: Erlbaum.

Brigham, T. A., & Catania, A. C. (Eds.). (1979). *Handbook of applied behavior research: Social and instructional processes.* New York: Wiley.

Burchard, J. D., & Burchard, S. N. (Eds.). (1987). *The prevention of delinquent behavior.* Beverly Hills: Sage.

Burchard, J. D., & Harig, P. T. (1976). Behavior modification and juvenile delinquency. In H. Leitenberg (Ed.), *Handbook of behavior modification and behavior therapy* (pp. 405–452). Englewood Cliffs, NJ: Prentice-Hall.

Burgess, R. L., & Akers, R. L. (1966). A differential association-reinforcement theory of criminal behavior. *Social Problems, 14,* 128–147.

Catania, A. C. (1984). *Learning.* Englewood Cliffs, NJ: Prentice-Hall.

Cohen, H. L., & Filipczak, J. (1971). *A new learning environment.* San Francisco: Jossey-Bass.

Collins, J. J., Hubbard, R. L., & Rachal, J. V. (1985). Expensive drug use and illegal income: A test of explanatory hypotheses. *Criminology, 23,* 743–764.

Conger, R. D. (1976). Social control and social learning models of delinquent behavior: A synthesis. *Criminology, 14,* 17–40.

Conger, R. D. (1980). Juvenile delinquency: Behavior restraint or behavior facilitation? In T. Hirschi & M. Gottfredson (Eds.), *Understanding crime* (pp. 131–142). Beverly Hills: Sage.

Davidson, W. S., & Seidman, E. (1974). Studies of behavior modification and juvenile delinquency. *Psychological Bulletin, 81,* 998–1011.

Elliott, D. S., Huizinga, D., & Ageton, S. S. (1985). *Explaining delinquency and drug use.* Beverly Hills: Sage.

Elliott, D. S., Dunford, F. W., & Huizinga, D. (1987). The identification and prediction of career offenders utilizing self-reported and offical data. In J. D. Burchard & S. N. Burchard (Eds.), *The prevention of delinquent behavior* (pp. 90–121). Beverly Hills: Sage.

Emery, R. E., & Marholin II, D. (1977). An applied behavior analysis of delinquency: The irrelevancy of relevant behavior. *American Psychologist, 32,* 860–873.

Farrington, D. P. (1983). Offending from 10 to 25 years of age. In K. T. Van Dusen & S. A. Mednick (Eds.), *Prospective studies of crime and delinquency* (pp. 17–37). Boston: Kluwer-Nijhoff.

Farrington, D. P., Ohlin, L. E., & Wilson, J. Q. (1986). *Understanding and controlling crime: Toward a new research strategy.* New York: Springer-Verlag.

Fixsen, D. L., Phillips, E. L., & Wolf, M. M. (1973). Achievement Place: Experiments in self-government with pre-delinquents. *Journal of Applied Behavior Analysis, 6,* 31–47.

Geller, E. S., Johnson, D. F., Hamlin, P. H., & Kennedy, T. D. (1977). Behavior modification in prisons: Issues, problems, and compromises. *Criminal Justice and Behavior, 4,* 11–43.

Glass, G. V., McGraw, G., & Smith, M. L. (1981). *Meta-analysis in social research.* Beverly Hills: Sage.

Gottfredson, G. D., & Gottfredson, D. C. (1985). *Victimization in schools. Law, Society, and Policy* (Vol. 2). New York: Plenum Press.

Gottfredson, M., & Hirschi, T. (1986). The true value of lambda would appear to be zero: An essay on career criminals, criminal careers, selective incapacitation, cohort studies, and related topics. *Criminology, 24,* 213–234.

Goldstein, A. P., Carr, E. G., Davidson, W. S., & Wehr, P. (1981). *In response to aggression: Methods of control and pro-social alternatives.* New York: Pergamon.

Greenberg, S. W. (1981). Alcohol and crime: A methodological critique of the literature. In J. J. Collins, Jr. (Ed.), *Drinking and crime* (pp. 70–109). New York: Guilford Press.

Heads, T. B. (1978). Ethical and legal considerations in behavior therapy. In D. Marholin (Ed.), *Child behavior therapy* (pp. 416–433). New York: Gardner.

Hersen, M., Eisler, R. M., & Miller, P. M. (1975). Historical perspectives in behavior modification: Introductory comments. In M. Hersen, R. M. Eisler, & P. M. Miller (Eds.), *Progress in behavior modification* (Vol. 1, pp. 1–17). New York: Academic Press.

Hersen, M., Eisler, R. M., & Miller, P. M. (1975–present). *Progress in behavior modification* (series). New York: Academic Press.

Hirschi, T. (1969). *Causes of delinquency.* Berkeley: University of California Press.

Jeffery, C. R. (1965). Criminal behavior and learning theory. *Journal of Criminal Law, Criminology, and Police Science, 56,* 294–300.

Jeffery, C. R. (1971). *Crime prevention through environmental design.* Beverly Hills: Sage.

Kantor, J. R. (1959). *Interbehavioral psychology.* Granville, OH: Principia.

Kazdin, A. E. (1980). *Behavior modification in applied settings.* Homewood, IL: Dorsey.

Keller, F. S., & Schoenfeld, W. N. (1950). *Principles of behavior.* New York: Appleton-Century-Crofts.

Kendall, P., & Hollon, S. (Eds.). (1979). *Cognitive-behavioral interventions: Theory, research, and procedures.* New York: Academic Press.

Leitenberg, H. (Ed.). (1976). *Handbook of behavior modification and behavior therapy.* Englewood Cliffs, NJ: Prentice-Hall.

Lipton, D., Martinson, R., & Wilks, J. (1975). *The effectiveness of correctional treatment: A survey of treatment evaluation studies.* New York: Praeger.

Loeber, R., & Dishion, T. (1983). Early predictors of male delinquency: A review. *Psychological Bulletin, 94,* 68–99.

Mahoney, M. J., & Arnkoff, D. (1978). Cognitive and self-control therapies. In S. L. Garfield & A. E. Bergin (Eds.), *Handbook of psychotherapy and behavior change: An empirical analysis* (2nd ed., pp. 689–722). New York: Wiley.

Martinson, R. (1974). What works? Questions and answers about prison reform. *Public Interest, 10,* 22–54.

McCord, J. (1978). A thirty-year follow-up of treatment effects. *American Psychologist, 33,* 284–289.

McNeil, J. K., & Hart, D. S. (1986). The effect of self-government on the aggressive behavior of institutionalized delinquent adolescents. *Criminal Justice and Behavior, 13,* 430–445.

Mednick, S. A., Gabrielli, W. F., & Hutchings, B. (1984). Genetic influences in criminal convictions: Evidence from an adoption cohort. *Science, 224,* 891–894.

Meichenbaum, D. H. (1977). *Cognitive behavior modification.* New York: Plenum Press.

Meichenbaum, D. H., & Cameron, R. (1982). Cognitive-behavior therapy. In G. T. Wilson & C. M. Franks (Eds.), *Contemporary behavior therapy: Conceptual and empirical foundations* (pp. 310–338). New York: Guilford Press.

Millenson, J. R., & Leslie, J. C. (1979). *Principles of behavior analysis*. New York: Macmillan.

Morris, E. K. (1980). Applied behavior and analysis for criminal justice practice: Some current dimensions. *Criminal Justice and Behavior, 7,* 131–145.

Morris, E. K. (1985). Public information, dissemination, and behavior analysis. *The Behavior Analyst, 8,* 95–115.

Nietzel, M. T. (1979). *Crime and its modification: A social learning perspective*. New York: Pergamon Press.

O'Leary, K. D., & Wilson, G. T. (1987). *Behavior therapy: Application and outcome* (2nd ed.). Englewood Cliffs, NJ: Prentice-Hall.

Patterson, G. R. (1974). Interventions for boys with conduct problems: Multiple settings, treatment, and criteria. *Journal of Consulting and Clinical Psychology, 42,* 471–481.

Patterson, G. R. (1980). Children who steal. In T. Hirschi & M. Gottfredson (Eds.), *Understanding crime* (pp. 73–90). Beverly Hills: Sage.

Phillips, J. S., & Ray, R. S. (1980). Behavioral approaches to childhood disorders: Review and critique. *Behavior Modification, 4,* 3–34.

Reed, D. S. (1981). Reducing the costs of drinking and driving. In M. H. Moore & D. R. Gerstein (Eds.), *Alcohol and public policy* (pp. 336–387). Washington, DC: National Academy of Sciences.

Robins, L. N. (1966). *Deviant children grown up*. Baltimore: Williams & Wilkins.

Romig, D. A. (1978). *Justice for our children*. Lexington, MA: D. C. Heath.

Rosenthal, R. (1984). *Meta-analytic procedures for social research*. Beverly Hills: Sage.

Rosenthal, T. L. (1982). Social learning theory. In G. T. Wilson & C. M. Franks (Eds.), *Contemporary behavior therapy: Conceptual and empirical foundations* (pp. 339–363). New York: Guilford Press.

Ross, R. R., & McKay, H. B. (1978). Behavioral approaches to treatments and corrections: Requiem for a panacea. *Canadian Journal of Criminology, 20,* 279–295.

Rutter, M., & Giller, H. (1984). *Juvenile delinquency: Trends and perspectives*. London: Guilford Press.

Rutter, M., Maughan, G., Mortimore, P., & Ouston, P. (1979). *Fifteen thousand hours: Secondary schools and their effects on children*. Somerset, England: Open Books.

Saunders, J. T., & Repucci, N. D. (1978). The social identity of behavior modification. In M. Hersen, R. M. Eisler, & P. M. Miller (Eds.), *Progress in behavior modification* (Vol. 6, pp. 143–158). New York: Academic Press.

Seekins, T., & Fawcett, S. B. (1986). Public policymaking and research information. *The Behavior Analyst, 9,* 35–45.

Sheley, J. F. (1985). *America's "crime problem": An introduction to criminology*. Belmont, CA: Wadsworth.

Short, J. F., & Strodtbeck, F. L. (1965). *Group process and gang delinquency*. Chicago: The University of Chicago Press.

Skinner, B. F. (1953). *Science and human behavior*. New York: Macmillan.

Skinner, B. F. (1974). *About behaviorism*. New York: Knopf.

Stuart, R. B. (1981). (Ed.). *Violent behavior: Social learning approaches to prediction, management, and treatment*. New York: Brunner/Mazel.

Stumphauzer, J. S. (1973). *Behavior therapy with delinquents*. Springfield, IL: Charles C Thomas.

Stumphauzer, J. S. (1979). *Progress in behavior therapy with delinquents*. Springfield, IL: Charles C Thomas.

Stumphauzer, J. S. (1986). *Helping delinquents change: A treatment manual of social learning approaches*. New York: Haworth.

Sutherland, E. H. (1939). *Principles of criminology* (3rd ed.). Philadelphia: Lippincott.

Toby, J. (1983). Violence in school. In M. Tonry & N. Morris (Eds.), *Crime and justice: An annual review of research* (Vol. 4, pp. 1–47). Chicago: University of Chicago Press.

Todd, J. T., & Morris, E. K. (1983). Misconception and Miseducation: Presentations of Radical Behaviorism in Psychology Textbooks. *The Behavior Analyst, 6,* 153–160.

Trasler, G. B., & Farrington, D. P. (Eds.). (1979). *Behavior modification with offenders: A criminological symposium*. Cambridge, England: Institute of Criminology.

Turkat, I. D., & Forehand, R. (1980). The future of behavior therapy. In M. Hersen, R. M. Eisler, & P. M. Miller (Eds.), *Progress in behavior modification* (Vol. 9, pp. 1–47). New York: Academic Press.

Warren, M. Q., & Rosenbaum, J. L. (1986). Criminal careers of female offenders. *Criminal Justice and Behavior, 13,* 393–418.

Watson, J. B. (1913). Psychology as the behaviorist views it. *Psychological Review, 20,* 158–177.

West, D. J. (1985). Clinical criminology under attack. In M. H. Ben-Aron, S. J. Hucker, & C. D. Webster (Eds.), *Clinical criminology: The assessment and treatment of ciminal behaviour* (pp. 1–13). Toronto: M & M Graphics.

West, D. J., & Farrington, D. P. (1977). *The delinquent way of life.* New York: Crane Russak.

Willner, A. G., Braukmann, C. J., Kirigin, K. A., Fixsen, D. L., Phillips, E. L., & Wolf, M. M. (1977). The training and validation of youth-referred social behaviors of child-care personnel. *Journal of Applied Behavior Analysis, 10,* 219–230.

Wilson, G. T., & Franks, C. M. (Eds.). (1982). *Contemporary behavior therapy: Conceptual and empirical foundations.* New York: Guilford Press.

Wilson, J. Q., & Herrnstein, R. J. (1985). *Crime and human nature.* New York: Simon & Schuster.

Wolf, M. M. (1978). Social validity: The case for subjective measurement or how applied behavior analysis is finding its heart. *Journal of Applied Behavior Analysis, 11,* 203–214.

Wolf, M. M., Phillips, E. L., & Fixsen, D. L. (1972). The Teaching-Family: A new model for the treatment of deviant child behavior in the community. In S. W. Bijou & E. L. Ribes-Inesta (Eds.), *Behavior modification: Issues and extensions* (pp. 51–62). New York: Academic Press.

Wolf, M. M., Braukmann, C. J., & Kirigin Ramp, K. A. (in press). Serious delinquent behavior as part of a significantly handicapping condition: Cures and supportive environments. *Journal of Applied Behavior Analysis.*

Wright, J., & James, R. (1974). *A behavioral approach to preventing delinquency.* Springfield, IL: Charles C Thomas.

2

The Dimensions of Applied Behavior Analysis for Crime and Delinquency

EDWARD K. MORRIS AND CURTIS J. BRAUKMANN

Understanding how applied behavior analysis pertains to crime and delinquency requires more than familiarity with the conceptual system of contemporary behaviorism or with the basic principles of behavior, or with specific behavioral procedures and programs. That understanding requires appreciation of a set of specific dimensions that reflect both a scientific concern with empirical analysis and humanistic considerations regarding improved personal and social conditions of daily life. More specifically, these dimensions represent a means for interweaving contemporary behaviorism, basic behavior principles, and applied behavioral procedures and programs with theory and practice in crime and delinquency. Finally, the dimensions present useful criteria for evaluating a wide range of correctional interventions, from traditional clinical therapy to large-scale program implementations, whether those interventions are behavioral in nature or not. In describing the dimensions of applied behavior analysis in this chapter, we hope to provide unifying themes for the behavioral applications presented throughout the rest of this book.

Applied behavior analysis is defined by seven dimensions that set forth the standards for the field more generally (see Baer, Wolf, & Risley, 1968; see also Morris, 1980). Let us begin by briefly introducing them. The first dimension is the *applied* dimension, which specifies that behavioral applications be focused on problems of relatively immediate social importance. In this regard, applied behavior analysts should be sensitive to the relationships between the behavior-change goals they select and the social and ethical concerns of a program's participants and the community at large (Kazdin, 1977a; Wolf, 1978). The second and third dimensions concern methodological criteria: the *behavioral* dimension requires that behavior be measured validly and reliably, whereas the *technological* dimension specifies that interventions be described in sufficient detail to permit replication. Fourth, the *analytic* dimension reflects the need for empirical analyses of the effects of behavioral procedures and programs. A major presumption here is that good application is also good

Edward K. Morris and **Curtis J. Braukmann** • Department of Human Development, University of Kansas, Lawrence, Kansas 66045.

research; that is, interventions are ideally evaluated through experimental analyses (Risley, 1969). The fifth and sixth dimensions concern two outcomes of applying behavioral procedures and programs: the dimension of *effectiveness* requires an examination of the social importance of intervention outcomes, whereas the dimension of *generality* emphasizes the need for maintaining treatment effects across time and promoting their spread across settings and related behaviors. The final dimension pertains to the relevance of specific interventions to an overall *conceptual system* of behavior.

These dimensions are critical to the development of effective behavioral interventions, but if these interventions are to have long-lasting and widespread effects, they must be disseminated and replicated in new settings by indigenous behavior-change agents. The means for doing so represent a new and important direction for applied behavior analysis and hence are described in a section following the seven dimensions. Effective dissemination and replication, themselves, however, cannot stand outside of the social systems in which they are to be developed. Thus, in the concluding section of this chapter, we will briefly discuss the relationship of behavioral interventions to broader social systems (see Harshbarger & Maley, 1976; Rogers-Warren & Warren, 1977).

In presenting the dimensions of applied behavior analysis, describing procedures for dissemination and replication, and pointing out the importance of social contexts, we will attempt to describe the critical aspects of applied behavior analysis for interventions into crime and delinquency as well as provide criteria for evaluating the usefulness of those interventions. In addition, we will suggest how these research, intervention, and conceptual strategies can be integrated with current justice system practice for the systematic expansion of its problem-solving capabilities; we will present an introductory sampling of behavioral interventions into crime and delinquency; and we will explain how an understanding of applied behavior analysis can bring ethical concerns into proper perspective and make misapplications less likely. Our goal is to encourage an accountable, data-based orientation that can contribute to effective, efficient, socially acceptable, and humane solutions to this critical and pressing social problem. Let us now turn directly to the dimensions of applied behavior analysis.

THE APPLIED DIMENSION

Behavior analysis is "applied" when it involves the application of behavioral principles and procedures to problems of relatively immediate social significance. In applied behavior analysis, then, the individuals, their behaviors, and the conditions under which their behaviors occur represent real-life problems that must be dealt with in an organized, timely, and nonarbitrary fashion.

Applied usually refers to the implementation of behavioral interventions that are derived from functional analyses of the presenting problems, often in accord with basic behavioral principles. But, applied behavior analysis also encompasses two additional types of activities. First, applied behavior analysis may sometimes involve purely descriptive and inferential analyses of significant social problems and processes that are not themselves intervened upon directly (e.g., process analyses of social interactions among delinquents and correctional staff; see Buehler, Patterson, & Furniss, 1966). Second, applied behavior analysis may sometimes also refer to interventions that are either not based on individual behavioral assessments or not attuned to behavioral principles (Azrin, 1977) but that may be effective nonetheless. Thus, applied behavior analysis represents a continuum that ranges from (a) descriptive analyses of socially significant problems, through (b) analyses that lead to behavioral applications, to (c) applications not based on individualized assessments or specific behavioral principles (see Deitz, 1978). Solutions to social problems may be achieved on the latter end of this continuum but are likely to be more effective, efficient, socially acceptable, and humane when they are based on accurate descriptive analyses of the problems, on sound conceptual analyses of the causes of these problems, and on the experimental analysis of the effects of behaviorally based interventions on these problems (Emery & Marholin, 1977).

Social Validity

To define behavior analysis as "applied" when it is extended to problems of relatively immediate social significance seems clear enough. But defining social significance is not a simple matter. What is socially significant, and what is not, and how that is to be determined is addressed by applied behavior analysts in their concern with "social validity" (Fuqua & Schwade, 1986; Kazdin, 1977a; Van Houten, 1979; Wolf, 1978). In general, social validity reflects an explicit sensitivity to (a) the significance of applied behavioral goals, (b) the appropriateness of behavioral procedures and programs, and (c) the importance of program effects. If the goals, procedures, and effects of an applied behavioral intervention lack social validity, then the intervention may not be acceptable or maintained once in place (e.g., Filipczak & Friedman, 1978).

The social significance of behavior *goals* will be discussed in this section of the chapter; the social importance of behavioral *effects* will be examined later. Although we will not address the social validity of behavioral *procedures* in any detail (but see Sheldon, Chapter 21), we would like to point out that it pertains to such issues as the social acceptability of (a) intervention procedures and programs, (b) research designs, and (c) cost-effectiveness. With respect to cost-effectiveness, two points deserve special mention. First, applied behavioral interventions may sometimes be more expensive than currently comparable correctional placements that offer no treatment. The added expense, however, may only be short term, for in the long run, correctional placements without treatment may be more expensive if they do not reduce the problem or if they somehow exacerbate it. Second, behavioral interventions can actually cost less than typical correctional placement because they can occur in less restrictive settings that are also less expensive to maintain (e.g., community-based group homes vs. institutional placement; see Burchard, Chapter 22). Thus applied behavior analysis offers flexibility that can be used to develop cost-reducing and effective alternatives to traditional correctional programs (e.g., Davidson & Robinson, 1975; Kirigin, Wolf, Braukmann, Fixsen, & Phillips, 1979).

The Social Significance of Behavioral Goals

To get to the major point of the applied dimension, applied behavior analysts should be sensitive to how the goals they select serve the goals of the individuals and the social systems with which they work. Applied behavior analysts may focus on the goals *they* think are relevant to a social problem, but if those (a) who actually present the problem, (b) who are its victims, or (c) who are otherwise concerned about it do not agree that a particular goal is socially significant, then the application may not provide a workable solution (Opton, 1974; Wexler, 1973). To avoid this, the social significance of behavioral goals should be evaluated from the perspective of relevant members of the community, whether they are community members at large, family members, school officials, social workers, law-enforcement officers, judges, correctional personnel, or delinquents and criminals themselves. Care must be taken, of course, in sampling for relevant members of the community and in using normative comparison data, especially in cases where the values of different social groups may be in conflict (Kimbles, 1973; Turner & Jones, 1982).

The social validation of behavioral goals has been conducted in several applied behavior analysis projects to date. For instance, delinquent youths have rated the appropriateness and desirability of behaviors displayed by teaching parents in group homes as a means for selecting behaviors to train new teaching parents (Willner *et al.,* 1977). Community members have provided social validity for the appropriateness of adolescents' conversational skills as a means for selecting skills to teach to other delinquent adolescents (Minkin *et al.,* 1976). And, social validation measures from youths, their parents, and other relevant community members and agencies have been used for evaluating the appropriateness of the overall goals of delinquency treatment programs (e.g., Braukmann *et al.,* 1975).

As mentioned before, conflicts may arise about the significance of certain behavioral goals. Also, social validity measures can be misleading, manipulated, and abused (Deitz, 1978). Such difficulties mean that a technology must be developed for properly determining and evaluating social validity (cf. Fuqua & Schwade, 1986; Van Houten, 1979). Those problems aside, applied behavior analysts should focus on socially significant behavioral goals. If they do not, then their interventions are less likely to succeed.

Levels of Behavior Analysis

The concerns of those interested in crime and delinquency, or in basic behavior-analytic research, need not be "applied" in the sense meant here;

that is, their concerns may not always have *immediate* social application. To understand the range of activity that can take place at the intersect of behavior analysis and the field of crime and delinquency, two other domains of behavior analysis need to be briefly delineated: (1) research on the basic principles of behavior and (2) research on the behavioral content of crime and delinquency. Both of these domains are closely interrelated with applied behavior analysis (cf. Baer, 1978; Skinner, 1972) and are described next, before we turn to the behavioral dimension.

Delinquent and criminal behavior is the behavior of individuals, even though these individuals may act in groups and even though the conditions responsible for the development and maintenance of their behavior may be widespread. Thus, at one level, an understanding of crime and delinquency requires an understanding of the principles of individual human behavior (Homans, 1969). For applied behavior analysts, this understanding is primarily achieved through the research paradigm called the experimental analysis of behavior (Skinner, 1966; see Catania, 1984; Millenson & Leslie, 1979), which aims to elucidate the behavioral principles describing much of the structure, function, and development of behavior. In such research, the behavior, the conditions under which it occurs, and even the organism may be selected at the convenience of the investigator, so that the best possible analysis of the principles may be achieved. This research is important to the science of behavior in general and need not have any immediate social significance, although it often will have some significance—at least subsequently.

In contrast to an analysis of the basic behavioral principles, research may also be focused on a particular content-related behavioral domain such as crime and delinquency. Here, research may target socially relevant individuals or groups (e.g., delinquents, police officers), their behavior (e.g., assault, policing strategies), and/or conditions under which their behavior occurs (e.g., neighborhoods, police precincts) but not on changing behavior directly. Knowledge of the behavioral content of crime and delinquency is requisite for effective intervention; knowing the basic principles of behavior alone would be insufficient.

Crime and delinquency research of the latter sort may be oriented toward structural or functional analyses (cf. Catania, 1973). Structural analyses describe the "what" or general form of behavior. These analyses may range from broad statistical descriptions of group behavior (e.g., patterns of delinquency across ages within urban settings, cf. Wolfgang, Figlio, & Sellin, 1972) to precise behavioral observations of one or a few individuals (e.g., patterns of youth and staff interactions in a detention facility, as in Buehler *et al.*, 1966). In contrast, functional analyses describe the "why" of the behavior–environment interaction. These analyses range from detailed studies of individuals and the conditions that influence their behavior (e.g., Bailey, Wolf, & Phillips, 1970) to controlled experimental studies addressing general cause-and-effect relationships among large samples of individuals (e.g., Powers & Witmer, 1951; Schnelle, Kirchner, Casey, Uselton, & McNees, 1977).

Structural and functional analyses in the domain of behavioral content often include analog research in which the relationships being studied occur in laboratory settings and are then extrapolated to situations existing in other environments (cf. Stumphauzer, 1970, 1972). Such research is often called for when those relationships are difficult or unethical to demonstrate in more complex settings, as in the analysis of precursors to aggression (e.g., Horton, 1970; Ribes-Inesta & Bandura, 1976; see Feldman, 1977, for a review of this type of research in crime and delinquency).

Research on behavioral content is sometimes difficult to distinguish from that on basic behavior principles (e.g., in the case of some analog studies) or from applied behavior analysis (e.g., behavioral assessments of deviant social interactions). Research on the behavioral content of crime and delinquency is, indeed, focused on socially important behavior but is distinguished from applied behavior analysis in that in the former (a) arbitrary experimental control may be imposed in arbitrary contexts by the researcher and/or (b) the results of the research do not supply an analysis that is of immediate use. Applied behavior analysis is not so simple.

THE BEHAVIORAL DIMENSION

As for the "behavioral" dimension, applied behavior analysis is focused primarily on the objective measurement of how people behave and the circumstances under which their behavior occurs. Accordingly, perhaps the most obvious characteristic of applied behavior analysis is its emphasis on the valid and reliable assessment of the behavior–environment relationships of interest. This is the field of behavioral assessment (see Hersen & Bellack, 1981; Nelson & Hayes, 1986). In what follows, we will briefly examine issues pertinent to both the validity and the reliability of behavioral assessment.

Behavioral Assessment: Validity

Most generally, the goal of behavioral assessment is to identify and measure socially significant behavior and the variables related to it in order to enhance our understanding of the problem and contribute to effective interventions. More specifically, behavioral assessment involves a process of (a) identifying target behavior(s) with appropriate measurement procedures, (b) identifying the environmental and organismic influences on this behavior, (c) selecting intervention strategies likely to succeed, and (d) evaluating the effectiveness of the intervention. The first three processes are relevant to implementing behavioral procedures and programs; the first and fourth are relevant to assessing programmatic outcome (see Jones, Chapter 16, this volume).

The development and use of behavioral assessment is grounded on four primary assumptions (see Nelson & Hayes, 1981). First, although psychometrically sound assessment tools and procedures (e.g., behavioral inventories and observations) are a prerequisite for accurate assessment, it is their usefulness in increasing both our understanding of behavior and our ability to implement effective interventions that is important in the long run. Second, the behavior being assessed is assumed to be the outcome of (a) an individual's past interactional history, as manifested in the behavior's current function in the environment, and (b) the context of the assessment. Thus the focus of assessment is on what a person does rather than on hypothetical traits a person is said to "possess." Third, behavior should be observed directly, ideally in its natural environment, but at least in analog situations. The process of assessment, of course, may alter the environment and hence the behavior of interest, in which case, unobtrusive measures can be helpful (Kazdin, 1977b). And fourth, functional relationships between behavior and its controlling variables should be sought. The last includes answers to such questions as what antecedents set the occasion for behavior, what consequences maintain it, what contextual conditions affect those interactions, and what behaviors are functionally similar (i.e., produce the same consequences) irrespective of topography? Understanding these relationships can help in the planning of effective interventions.

The emphasis on direct measurement contrasts with some psychological and sociological research strategies that rely on people's reports of what they do and why they do it. An individual's description or explanation of past, present, or future behavior is for many purposes a less then desirable substitute for the direct, reliable measurement of those interactions. What people report about their behavior may be an important source of hypotheses about how the criminal justice practitioner might proceed, but these verbal reports may correlate poorly or not at all with the behavior of interest. For example, delinquents' reports of the logic of their moral decision making may be assessed and intervened upon, and this may be important if it is the verbal report that is of interest. Changes in these verbal reports, however, may not be related to changes in delinquent activity. As a general rule, criminal justice practitioners should focus on behaviors that are the presenting problem or that are causally related to it, whether the problem is the behavior of criminals and delinquents (e.g., theft, assault, and arson) or of those who work with them (e.g., police patrolling strategies, judicial sentencing practices, the behavior of correctional personnel).

The criteria for selecting target behaviors are both conceptual and empirical (e.g., Kratochwill, 1985; Nelson & Hayes, 1981). As for the conceptual criteria, behaviors should be selected for intervention (a) that represent a physical danger to the person or others, (b) that are likely to be maintained by others following intervention, and (c) that are likely to maximize positive adaptation to the environment, flexibility of repertoire, and long-term benefits (see Goldiamond, 1974). With respect to empirical criteria, behaviors should be selected for intervention based on (a) their consistency with local norms, (b) their relevance to successful future performance, (c) their importance as rated by social validity measures, and (d) the seriousness of the prognosis if the behavior is not changed.

Although the emphasis in behavioral assessment is on direct naturalistic observation, behavioral assessment also shares a number of tools (and the means for evaluating the structural properties of those tools) with the more traditional psychometric approaches to assessment. Both may employ role playing, interviewing, questionnaires, self-ratings, ratings by others, permanent products, and standardized tests; moreover, behavioral assessment may also use traditional psychometric methods for evaluating the structural properties of assessment tools (e.g., concurrent validity, content validity, construct validity, internal consistency, test–retest reliability).

A variety of behavioral techniques are available for the direct behavioral assessment and evaluation of individuals, groups, and their environments, and the research described throughout this book provides many examples. Readers interested in additional coverage of behavioral assessment should see Ciminero, Calhoun, and Adams (1977), Cone and Hawkins (1977), Haynes (1978), Hersen and Bellack (1981), and Nelson and Hayes (1986). Those interested in more general methods of program evaluation should consult Jones (Chapter 16, this volume).

Special Problems in Crime and Delinquency Assessment

Crimes and delinquencies are behaviors that are fairly infrequent in the lives of most people—even among those labeled *delinquent* or *criminal*—and thus are not always reliably, immediately, or easily detected when they do occur. As a result, crimes and delinquencies are problems for which procedures of direct observational measurement are often not possible. Hence measures of criminal and delinquent behavior must often be derived from records kept by the police and court authorities. This is a useful, but unfortunately limited, strategy. It is limited because not all offenses are discovered, not all that are discovered are reported, not all that are reported are recorded, and agency policies affecting detection and recording may change over time and across jurisdictions (Hawkins, Cassidy, Light, & Miller, 1977; Hindelang, Hirschi, & Weis, 1981; LeFleur, 1975). Furthermore, the low frequency and delayed nature of agency record-based measures limits their use in the intrasubject research designs that are a hallmark of most behavioral research (see the analytic dimension, discussed later). Still, the collection of data from official records should not be overlooked as an important source of information.

An alternative approach to measuring crime and delinquency is the use of self-report measures. In this strategy, people are asked directly about their illegal activities. The format sometimes involves interviews and sometimes paper-and-pencil questionnaires (Kandel, 1978); respondents are assured of anonymity and confidentiality. Many self-report instruments yield acceptable test–retest reliabilities, have acceptable internal consistency (Hindelang *et al.*, 1981), and are valid in the sense that they often compare well with concurrent checks of offical records (Braukmann, Ramp, & Wolf, 1985; Elliott & Voss, 1974; Erickson & Empey, 1963; Farrington, 1973; Hirschi, 1969; Kulik, Stein, & Sarbin, 1968) and with reports and ratings of others concerning the youths' behavior (Braukmann *et al.*, 1985; Elliott & Voss, 1974; Gould, 1969; Kandel, Kessler, & Margulies, 1978) (see Hindelang *et al.*, 1981). Among the problems with most self-report instruments is an overrepresentation of minor offenses; moreover, appropriate concerns exist about under- and overreporting (Wilson & Herrnstein, 1985).

In general, difficulty in obtaining direct and reliable measures of criminal and delinquent activity has often encouraged (if not forced) applied behavior analysts to focus indirectly on crime and delinquency by targeting alternative behaviors judged to be importantly related to the problem. That is, behavioral interventions have sometimes had to focus directly on (a) the elimination of behaviors, which although not illegal, have some likelihood of getting the participant into trouble (e.g., aggressive interpersonal style), (b) the establishment of behaviors basic to many lawful extratreatment activities (e.g., skills basic to participating more effectively in noncriminal peer groups, in job situations, and in school), and (c) the establishment and elimination of behaviors necessary for the treatment program to take place (e.g., following instructions or participation in self-government) (see Braukmann, Fixsen, Phillips, & Wolf, 1975).

Again, we should note that just because analysis and intervention are forced to focus on related behaviors, this does not mean that the analysis and intervention should be restricted in focus to the verbal self-reports of offenders' motivations and cognitive-moral structures that supposedly describe and explain their deviance. It is not clear that changes in these reports will significantly alter the frequency or intensity of crime and delinquency. Indeed, correlations between self-report, attitudinal, and cognitive measures related to actual delinquent behavior can be quite low (Sowles & Gill, 1970). And, even if the verbal reports do display a substantial correlation with delinquent activity, no causation has been established; such is the nature of a correlation. Indeed, the two behaviors—the report and the delinquency—may be a function of common antecedent conditions. Correlations are not causes, even though they sometimes may reveal them.

Finally, in following any indirect approach toward assessment and intervention, applied behavior analysts in the field of crime and delinquency should accept responsibility for establishing and documenting relationships between the nondelinquent and noncriminal behaviors being targeted and subsequent reductions in criminal and delinquent activity (Baer, 1975; Emery & Marholin, 1977; Johnson, 1977). If no such relationship can be established, then the applied behavior analysis has failed in an important sense, and other behaviors and strategies must be examined.

Behavioral Assessment: Measurement Reliability

As mentioned earlier, a critical aspect of the behavioral dimension is that behavior be measured reliably. Interactions between people and their physical and social environments are what constitute the subject matter for applied behavior analysis. As such, reliable measurement of these interactions is required for accurate description and analysis.

When mechanical means of recording behavior, and the conditions under which the behavior occurs, are possible, measurement reliability may not be a serious problem. For instance, tachographs can be installed in law-enforcement vehicles to monitor car and equipment functioning (e.g., speed and use of emergency equipment; see Schnelle, Geller, & Davis, Chapter 8). Mechanical procedures, however, are often not feasible, and hence applied behavior analysts have developed direct measurement technologies that rely primarily on human observers (see Barlow & Hersen, 1984; Hartmann, 1982; Kratochwill, 1978). Granted, the use of reliable human observers is not without its problems: (1) definitional criteria applied by observers may change over time; (2) observers' scoring may vary, depending on whether their interobserver agreement is being monitored; and (3) the presence of observers may create reactive effects so that the observed behavior is not representative (Kazdin, 1977b). These problems are not generally serious, however, and they can often be solved or controlled for.

Because of the potential problems in using human observers, procedures for assessing interobserver agreement have become a requisite component of any applied behavior analysis using human data takers (see Kazdin, 1977b). If an applied behavior analysis is to be successful, there must be assurance that the success of the intervention is due to the variables actually under study and their effects on behavior, not to errors or biases of the observers. In general, two independent observers must be shown to agree sufficiently that the behaviors of interest occurred at the time specified. Thus, not only must the applied science focus on behavior, but it also must produce an explicit measure of observer agreement in order for the analysis to be acceptable. The texts referred to on behavioral assessment here also contain descriptions of procedures for establishing and assessing reliability.

THE TECHNOLOGICAL DIMENSION

The technological dimension requires that the procedures by which behavior analysis is conducted be replicable by other individuals, especially other similarly trained individuals. In other words, the salient characteristics of specific procedures, programs, and settings should be identified in a sufficiently complete and objective manner. Not only should they be described in a fashion that allows for replication, but methods should also be described for dealing with unexpected outcomes or side effects. Objective, technological descriptions are required for advancing any science—basic or applied.

In addition, to insure the replicability of behavioral interventions, explicit methods have to be developed for transferring the control of intervention programs from their original developers to individuals operating in new settings or to individuals who will be maintaining the intervention program in the original setting after the developers have departed (Fawcett, Seekins, & Braukmann, 1981). This may mean that interventions need to be packaged via written manuals, video- or audiotapes, or other forms designed to assist others in replicating the procedures. Such replicability should be assessed directly to assure that the program results in appropriate use of the technology. Replications of more complex technologies may also require extensive education of the adopters in the use of the technology, including, perhaps, direct *in vivo* teaching and ongoing quality-control supervision of the adopters by the intervention developers (Phillips, Phillips, Fixsen, & Wolf, 1974). All in all, the dissemination of empirically validated interventions will likely require a substantial and sustained effort beyond their initial research and development (Liberman, 1980). As mentioned earlier, this topic will be discussed more fully after describing the seven basic dimensions.

THE ANALYTIC DIMENSION

The analytic dimension of applied behavior analysis entails the caveat that good application also often requires good research. In other words, problem solving and decision making in the application of behavioral procedures and programs should ideally be data-based, with solutions and decisions evaluated empirically. Although the applied, behavioral, and technological dimensions must also be met in order to achieve good application, the analytic dimension provides the final sufficiency by demonstrating that changes in behavior are, indeed, the result of the interventions applied. That is, the analytic dimension requires proof by demonstration that observed changes in behavior are the reliable effects of an application and not of other conditions. This analytic requirement is especially critical during the initial development of behavioral procedures and programs. After these procedures and programs have been developed, refined, and evaluated, however, the routine experimental analysis of the intervention may not be practicable or necessary. Still, though, further implementations or replications of that intervention are probably best undertaken with ongoing empirical evaluations of the methods used and the outcomes achieved so as to ensure continued quality control.

Research Designs

If good application should also be good research, then good experimental control of the intervention and proof of its effectiveness are obviously necessary. Experimental control permits firm conclusions about the effectiveness of current programs and makes subsequent applications more effective and reliable. In applied behavior and analysis, these demonstrations are usually achieved through individual and group-replication designs. Among the most widely used and powerful of these are the reversal and multiple-baseline designs. Either may be implemented in a variety of ways, and with different control conditions, but for the purposes of illustration, we will describe only the generic models. For more in-depth presentations and analyses, see Barlow and Hersen (1984), Kazdin (1982), Jayaratne and Levy (1980), Johnston and Pennypacker (1980), Kratochwill (1978), and Sidman (1960).

The Reversal Design

Reversal designs demonstrate the effectiveness of behavioral procedures and programs by presenting and removing the intervention across several different occasions. In the simplest case of the reversal design, repeated measures of the behavior of interest are taken during a baseline (or preexperimental period), and the intervention is then applied and subsequently removed, allowing for the effects of the application and its removal to be observed. When an intervention is made that changes the rate of behavior appropriately, preliminary evidence is available that the procedure was effective. To be certain that the effect is a reliable one, however, the intervention must be removed, with a subsequent return of behavior to its baseline (or preexperimental) rate. Ideally, and ethically, the intervention should be applied another time (i.e., replicated). The reversal design is a convincing analytic procedure when it demonstrates that behavior change can be made to occur and reverse as a function of applying and removing an intervention program. Ideally, for a program to be maximally practical, behavior change should generalize and be maintained over time; in other words, the change ultimately should not reverse, which is the topic of the dimension of generality taken up later.

Demonstrations of the analytic power of the reversal design have been achieved in a variety of juvenile and criminal justice settings. As an illustrative example, Bassett, Blanchard, and Koshland (1975) used the reversal design in a prison setting to evaluate procedures designed to increase attendance at a remedial education center. Figure 1 presents a graph of the percentage of the available hours that adult prisoners spent in the center as a function of the number of "tokens" they earned for doing so. During baseline, the prisoners spent less than 20% of their time in the center. The figure shows, however, that doubling the number of points earned more than doubled attendance. Reversing these conditions back to baseline and demonstrating a concommitant drop in attendance provides further evidence that the intervention had been the cause of the change. A final reinstating of the intervention adds even more proof for the case and an even more compelling argument for the use of the intervention—attendance increased even further and was maintained for an additional 3-month period, as indicated by the last data point.

For another demonstration of the reversal design in prison settings, see Bassett and Blanchard's (1977) evaluations of the effects of supervision within a token economy system. In group-home settings with delinquents, reversal designs have been used to evaluate procedures for improving schoolwork (Bailey et al., 1970), for increasing participation in a self-government system (Fixsen, Phillips, & Wolf, 1973), and for using self-evaluation techniques in a token economy (Wood & Flynn, 1978). The design has also been used to evaluate the effectiveness of various law-enforcement patrolling strategies in reducing crime (e.g., Schnelle et al., 1978).

In each of the various phases of a reversal design, care must be taken that the phases are long enough, that the behavior within them is stable enough and without excess variability, and that evaluations of change from phase to

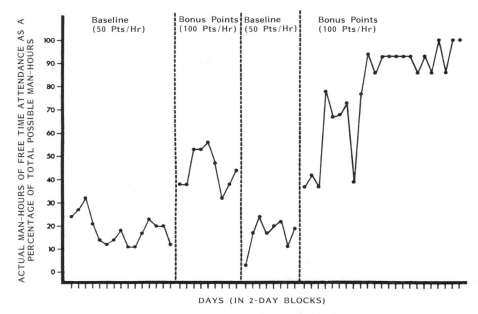

Figure 1. Percentage of free hours prisoners devoted to attending a remedial education center as a function of experimental conditions. From "Applied Behavior Analysis in a Penal Institution: Targeting 'Free World' Behaviors" by J. E. Bassett, E. B. Blanchard, and E. Koshland, 1975, *Behavior Therapy, 6,* p. 645. Copyright 1975 by Academic Press. Reprinted by permission.

phase are unambiguous. If changes are ambiguous, then the applied behavior analyst focuses on increasing the efficacy of the intervention, not on employing techniques for revealing weak effects (e.g., the use of additional subjects or statistical manipulation) (see Johnson & Pennypacker, 1980; Sidman, 1960).

The Multiple-Baseline Design

Occasions will arise when the reversal design will be inappropriate or impossible to use. For instance, an intervention (e.g., a remedial reading program) may be so effective that behavior change is relatively permanent. In addition, the particular settings and individuals involved may not allow the behavior to be returned to baseline pretreatment levels for practical reasons. Finally, and most important, altering behavior repeatedly across baseline and intervention conditions may be unethical if it involves harm. When one or more of these conditions pertain, a multiple-baseline design is an appropriate alternative.

In a multiple-baseline design, the demonstration of experimental control is achieved by taking simultaneous measures of multiple behaviors and then intervening on each of the behaviors at successive points in time. The simultaneous measurement may be of (a) different *behaviors* of an individual or group, (b) the same behavior of different *individuals* or groups, or (c) the same behavior of individuals or groups in different *settings*. After measuring baseline rates of each of the multiple behaviors, an intervention is imposed on one of them. This is done while the other behaviors continue as untreated (multiple) baseline control conditions. After demonstrating an effect on the first behavior selected, the intervention is applied to a second behavior, and then, for a convincing demonstration, to at least one more. Repeated demonstrations that each intervention alters its target behavior at the time it is applied, while the untreated baselines remain stable, provides assurance that the intervention is the primary controlling variable for the observed changes.

The multiple-baseline design has been used on numerous occasions in criminal justice practice to evaluate the effectiveness of behavioral procedures and programs. One illustrative example of a multiple-baseline across different behaviors comes from a study by Pierce and Risley (1974) in which the authors demonstrated that consistently enforced loss of recreation time for minor rule violations by adolescents in a community recreation center reduced those violations (see Fig. 2). Figure 2 presents the respective percentages of daily rule violations across three behaviors—(a) trash in game room, (b) pool rack not hung up, and (c) trash in hall—under baseline conditions of occasional rule enforcement and intervention conditions of consistent rule enforcement.

Other examples of the multiple-baseline design across different behaviors are widely available, as in, for example, a study demonstrating the efficacy of a training package for increasing conversation skills of delinquents (Minkin *et al.,* 1976). The multiple-baseline design across the same behavior of different individuals has been used to demonstrate the positive effects of training delinquent youths to negotiate conflict situations with their parents (Kifer, Lewis, Green, & Phillips, 1974) and to illustrate changes in delinquent youths' ratings of the social skills of group-home teaching parents as a function of the latter's training (Willner *et al.,* 1977). Finally, the multiple-baseline design across different settings has been used to evaluate the effects on youth behavior of sequentially introducing a token economy system across the cottages of an institution for delinquents (Hobbs & Holt, 1976) as well as to evaluate the effects of a police saturation patrol strategy across different patrol zones (Schnelle *et al.,* 1977).

Additional Designs

A number of other individual-analysis replication designs that meet the requirements of the analytic dimension are also available, many of which involve various combinations and permutations of those just discussed (see also the texts cited previously). Moreover, the application of any of these designs may also be used in parametric and component analyses. In parametric analyses, the focus is on the effectiveness of different values of the independent variables. For instance, one might want to conduct a parametric analysis to see how different numbers of law-enforcement officers in a patrol zone affect the crime rate. Or, one might conduct a parametric analysis to see

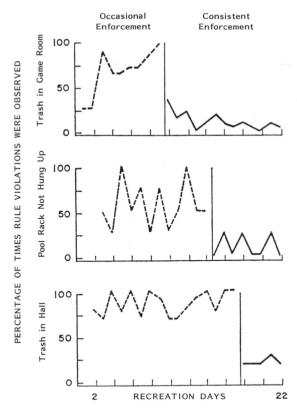

Figure 2. The percentage of time that rule violations were observed during 2-hour recreation periods by an independent observer who never enforced rule violations. Dashed lines correspond to the period when the recreation center director only occasionally enforced rule violations. Solid lines correspond to the period when he made checks every 15 minutes and enforced every violation. From "Recreation as a Reinforcer: Increasing Membership and Decreasing Disruptions in an Urban Recreation Center" by C. H. Pierce and T. R. Risley, 1974, *Journal of Applied Behavior Analysis, 7,* p. 409. Copyright 1974 by the Society for the Experimental Analysis of Behavior, Inc. Reprinted by permission.

how different point values in a token economy affect behavior (see Phillips, Phillips, Fixsen, & Wolf, 1971). In a component analysis, the effectiveness of different elements of a multicomponent applied behavioral procedure or program are evaluated (cf. Phillips, Phillips, Wolf, & Fixsen, 1973). Here, for example, one might be interested in the roles played by different elements of a furlough release program or in what aspects of foot patrol officers' behavior (e.g., visibility on the streets, contacts with key neighborhood members, and/or good public relations) contribute to their effectiveness.

Analytic Criteria

How completely and how often experimental control must be demonstrated by the analytic designs in order to achieve believable results is a problem of judgement for applied behavior analysts and their audiences (see Kazdin & Wilson, 1978). In applied behavior analysis, demonstrations of reliable effects have generally been communicated by means of graphed presentations of the data rather than through reduction and summarization by means of statistical analyses (Parsonson & Baer, 1978; Robinson & Foster, 1979). Statistical approaches to the analysis of individual (e.g., Hartmann *et al.*, 1980; Kazdin, 1984) and group behavior (e.g., Dixon & Massey, 1969; Kerlinger, 1964) are also employed, but statistical approaches also present problems of judgment for the practitioner and audience alike (e.g., Was the appropriate statistical test used? Were all the assumptions of the test met? Were enough subjects used for the results to be considered robust?).

One particular problem with group designs and their accompanying statistical analyses is that error variance may conceal individual cases for whom an application was useless or dysfunctional. In addition, rigorous between-group designs and the random assignment of subjects to treatment and control conditions are often a luxury not available or even permissible in applied settings (e.g., Baunach, 1980; Keller & Alper, 1970). Such designs and analyses, however, are critical to the analysis of large-scale demonstrations and interventions that may have an important impact on practice and policy. In any event, what is critical in the analytic dimension is the reliable experimental control of behavioral effects that meets scientific standards of acceptability. Whether the effects are reliable and large enough to have social significance is another matter—a point to be discussed in the next section.

For the applied behavior analyst working in the justice system, the analytic dimension may be the most difficult and frustrating of the seven dimensions to achieve. Sometimes believable demonstrations of cause-and-effect relationships are impossible to obtain, and often they will be inconvenient to attempt. Also, occasions will arise when such demonstrations will not be permitted by others or will be unethical to pursue (Keller & Alper, 1970). In these instances, alternative and less robust research designs will have to suffice, with the result, of course, that subsequent conclusions about causality must be made more cautiously. For example, in one descriptive analysis of the effects of a disciplinary program in a prison, a replication design could not be used because the researchers had no control over the timing of the program's implementation (Schnelle & Lee, 1974). Nevertheless, quasi-experimental and time-series analyses were conducted on retrospectively acquired data, and an effect of the program was illustrated. Whether the program was the cause of the effect, of course, could not be ascertained because the procedures could not be replicated.

Similar treatment of data have been used to evaluate the effectiveness of police intervention strategies on automobile speeding (Campbell & Ross, 1968; Glass, 1968) and to evaluate the effects of requiring breath-analyzer tests for drivers suspected of being intoxicated (Ross, Campbell, & Glass, 1970). Quasi-experimental designs (Campbell, 1969; Campbell & Stanley, 1963; Cook & Campbell, 1979), time-series analyses (Bakeman & Gottman, 1986; Jones, Vaught, & Weinrott, 1977), and more general program evaluation strategies (Attkisson, Hargreaves, Horowitz, & Sorensen, 1978; Caro, 1971; Davidson,

Koch, Lewis, & Wnesinski, 1980; Weiss, 1972; see also Jones, Chapter 16, this volume) are valuable ancillary means of program design and analysis. In the long run, however, an applied science of criminal justice will evolve more quickly and effectively when the analytic dimension demonstrating scientifically sound cause-and-effect relationships can be met. Good application, again, will likely represent good research.

THE EFFECTIVENESS DIMENSION

After applying the behavioral, technological, and analytic dimensions to problems of social significance, certain outcomes may be expected. These outcomes are related to two further dimensions of applied behavior analysis—the dimensions of effectiveness and generality. We will discuss the effectiveness dimension here and the dimension of generality in the subsequent section.

The effectiveness of an applied behavior analysis can be examined in two different ways. We have just discussed the first: whether or not the effects of a procedure or program are significant by accepted scientific standards. The second means of demonstrating effectiveness, and the one on which we focus here, is the more practical one: are the effects of an applied behavior analysis consistently reproducible enough, expedient enough, and large enough to be socially important? Even though an application may be significant by statistical and other scientific standards, if it is not also socially important, then it has failed as an applied behavior analysis. The amount of change required for social importance, then, is not just a scientific question—it is also a practical one. As such, an evaluation of effectiveness should be made by the people and agencies for whom an effect is important. As described before, evaluations of this sort are evaluations of social validity; in this case, we are concerned with the social importance of behavioral effects (see Fuqua & Schwade, 1986; Wolf, 1978).

The Social Importance of Behavioral Effects

Although the social validation of intervention effectiveness is often conducted informally, it is not yet a widespread formal practice. Several examples, however, may be described. For instance, the social validity of treatment effects has been assessed in studies designed to enhance (a) appropriate interaction skills of staff in delinquency treatment programs (Willner et al., 1977), (b) conversational skills of delinquent youths (Minkin et al., 1976), and (c) youth demeanor in youth–police interactions (Werner et al., 1975). In all of these studies, relevant consumers (e.g., youths, adult community members, and law enforcement officers) evaluated the behavioral changes resulting from the interventions. Social validity has also been used to evaluate the overall effectiveness of larger-scale delinquency treatment programs (e.g., Braukmann et al., 1975). In this case, the social validity measures were found to correlate well with the more typical analytic measures of program effectiveness (e.g., participants' police and court contacts; cf. Kirigin, Braukmann, Atwater, & Wolf, 1982).

As mentioned before, social validity measures can be misleading, manipulated, and abused. For instance, programs may be rated as being highly effective when no apparent or meaningful behavior change has occurred (e.g., Berleman, Seaburg, & Steinburn, 1972). Also, social validity may be sensitive to effects other than those related to the original goals of an application. Thus, again, care must be taken in developing social validity measures (see Fuqua & Schwade, 1986; Kazdin, 1977a; Van Houten, 1979; Wolf, 1978).

THE GENERALITY DIMENSION

Not only should effective applied behavior analyses have practical importance for socially relevant problems, but that effectiveness should also display generality. Generality (or transfer of treatment) should be displayed in one or a combination of three ways. First, behavior change should be durable and maintained over time. Obviously, the overall value of an intervention is lessened when behavior change cannot be maintained after a procedure or program has been withdrawn—if that was the purpose of the intervention. Second, behavior change should occur in settings other than those in which the program is conducted, whether or not the program remains in effect. To demonstrate change in one setting, yet not have it generalize to other settings will often mean that the effects are reduced in practical importance. For instance, intensive probation programs may be effective in reducing social conflicts between delinquents and adults in home settings but not necessarily with adults in school settings; special programs may be required for the latter (e.g., Kirigin, Phillips, Timbers, Fixsen, & Wolf, 1977; Schumaker, Hovell, & Sherman, 1977). And third, the effectiveness of an intervention should have an effect on as wide a variety of related behaviors and/or individuals as possible and even open the way for the development of new behaviors not directly targeted by the procedure or program. In general, then, applied behavior analysis with criminals and delinquents may be no better than any other approach unless its effects generalize and are maintained (Burchard, 1973; Morris, 1978).

Generality and maintenance, like the other dimensions of applied behavior analysis, must be planned for and achieved. They should not otherwise be expected to occur. Strategies for actively facilitating behavioral generalization and maintenance are not as yet completely developed, but a number of accepted and conceptually sound procedures have evolved and are described briefly later (for more extensive coverage, see Baer, 1982; Marholin & Seigel, 1978; Marholin, Seigel, & Phillips, 1976; Stokes & Baer, 1977).

Reactive Strategies

When an intervention does not produce generalization or maintenance across settings, time, or responses, two primarily reactive strategies are available. First, and most obviously, the intervention can be applied directly in the settings where generality and maintenance are not occurring. That is, behavior may be sequentially intervened upon in each setting as, for instance, might be the case in teaching delinquents the skills for socializing with adults at home and at school. Second, and related, lack of generality and maintenance can be remediated by repeating the intervention across settings and responses until generality and maintenance begin to appear in untrained settings and for untrained responses. That is, sufficient exemplars may be required before generality and maintenance occur. Here, for instance, a program for abusive parents may have to be instituted across more than one of their children and across multiple settings (e.g., home, at relatives' homes, and grocery stores) before the generality of nonabusive behavioral control strategies would be evinced.

We should not fail to realize that the behavior of some delinquents and criminals may be highly resistant to generalization and maintenance of any known form. Sometimes the environments to which these individuals must return may be intractable, and sometimes their behavior may be so excessively deviant that available intervention programs seem insufficient to the task. In these cases, applied behavior analysts will have to extend the first reactive strategy outlined before and provide long-term prosthetic and supportive environments. The behavioral technology for doing so, however, is clearly at hand.

Proactive Strategies

In addition to these reactive strategies, a number of proactive strategies are also available for directly programming generality and maintenance from the beginning; these may, of course, be instituted reactively as well. First, interventions can be implemented in which the consequences of behavior intervened upon are varied in kind or frequency, so that the behavior will remain strong in the face of environments that do not support it in a strong and diversified manner. That is, instead of using immediate and continuous consequences, the intervention could employ more "indiscriminable" contingencies that might, for instance, provide delayed or only intermittent consequences for the target behavior. Second, interventions can be applied across many settings to ensure that behavior does not become overly situation-specific. This method of "training loosely" might involve, for instance, the instruction of delinquents in social skills by multiple adult trainers in multiple settings. Third, and related, the intervention setting might include the presence of conditions that commonly occur in nontraining settings such that those additional conditions, too, contribute to the occurrence of the behavior. Intervention in the presence of "common stimuli" suggests, for instance, that if an individual with a history of assaults has difficulty handling criticism in the presence of peers, then the intervention setting (e.g., a clinic situation) should include the presence of peers.

A fourth strategy, which does not involve active programming, is to assess the environments in which generalization and maintenance are to occur in order to discover what appropriate behaviors are prompted and supported in those environments (why teach any others?) and to discern whether environmental support occurs for behaviors that are incompatible with or detrimental to those being taught—if so, then alternative behaviors might be sought. In other words, applied behavior analysts can make use of the natural contingencies endemic to the setting in which generalization and maintenance are sought (see Baer & Wolf, 1970).

Two final strategies for promoting generalization and maintenance are also largely proactive but involve the individual more directly. First, individuals who have acquired new treatment-appropriate behavioral repertoires can be taught to prompt others to maintain the repertoire as in, for instance, instructing delinquents to prompt their parents or teachers to notice and respond positively when they are behaving appropriately (see, e.g., Seymour & Stokes, 1976). This strategy involves recruiting the natural contingencies of reinforcement for support. Second, and related, instead of being taught to prompt behavior from others, people can also be taught how to prompt or suppress behavior from themselves. One part of this strategy is to teach people how to arrange their physical environments and how to organize their time in order to increase or decrease the probability of certain behaviors. For instance, youths who are having difficulty staying out of gang-related activities might be encouraged to arrange their work schedules to conflict with such activities, at least at the times those activities are most likely to be unlawful. A second part of this strategy is to teach people how to manage their troublesome behaviors with other aspects of their own behavior. Such mediated generalization might involve, for instance, teaching self-observation and self-control techniques—techniques that individuals can direct toward themselves as opposed to having others direct those techniques toward them (see, e.g., Brigham, 1978; Rachlin, 1978).

The technology of generalization and maintenance awaits further research and development but much can already be accomplished. Although applied behavioral programs may be more humane and can be made less costly than alternative correctional interventions, the long-term goal of any intervention ought to be generalized and maintained behavior change. Such change needs to be actively promoted.

THE CONCEPTUAL SYSTEM DIMENSION

Theory has not been mentioned in the description of the previous six dimensions, each of which reflects the somewhat pragmatic quality of applied behavior analysis. Undisciplined pragmatism, however, no matter how precisely technological, may yield only a bag of tricks or unrelated procedures. What is needed is a conceptual system of understanding, which can be achieved by relating these practices to a system of underlying principles and concepts that describe and explain behavior.

The conceptual system to which applied behavior analysts have most commonly adhered is the system of principles and concepts developed by behavioral psychologists over the last 70 years, most notably in radical behaviorism (see Skinner, 1953, 1966, 1974; see also Morris, Higgins, Bickel, & Braukmann, Chapter 3, this volume). These and related conceptual systems underlie most applied behavioral procedures (see Kazdin, 1978).

The value of a conceptual system is that its assumptions, concepts, and principles can relate eclectic pragmatism to empirically derived constructs, which can then be further organized into the systematic development of effective, inductively derived theory. In recent years, behaviorally based conceptual system has been increasingly interrelated with specific concerns of the criminal justice community, specifically, in the areas of sociology and social deviance (Akers, 1973; Burgess & Bushell, 1969), crime and delinquency (Braukmann, Kirigin, & Wolf, 1980; Burgess & Akers, 1966; Jeffery, 1965; Nietzel, 1979), law (Robbins & Sepler, 1978; Skinner, 1953, pp. 333–349; Wexler, 1975), crimes without victims (Stacknik, 1972), and issues related to coercion, ethics, and legal rights (Friedman, 1975; Goldiamond, 1976; Hayes & Maley, 1977; Krapfl & Vargas, 1977; Martin, 1975; Stolz, 1978; Vargas, 1975; Wexler, 1973; see Sheldon, Chapter 21, this volume). Overall, applied behavior analysis conducted within an appropriate conceptual system can contribute to and stimulate further development of behavior analysis as a natural science and as an effective applied science. The description, prediction, control, and explanation of behavior are enhanced by the adoption of an effective conceptual system, and communication among basic and applied researchers is made more effective thereby.

Perhaps a specific example is in order. The implementation of incentive or point systems to promote socially important behavior change in institutions (see Milan, Chapter 7, this volume), community-based group homes (see Braukmann & Wolf, Chapter 5, this volume), and probation programs (see Nietzel & Himelein, Chapter 4, this volume) may be described in minute and complex technological detail—so much detail, in fact, that effective communication about those systems is hindered. But, by relating those diverse and complex procedures to underlying basic behavioral principles and concepts (e.g., conditioned reinforcement, chaining, shaping, etc.; see Morris *et al.,* Chapter 3, this volume), other criminal justice practitioners may be better able to understand the underlying basis of such a behavior management system and to replicate it in varying settings, with different populations, and for a variety of different behaviors. The generic nature of applied behavioral procedures (e.g., tokens and backup reinforcers) can also be abstracted and described in terms of more general applied behavioral concepts. In the present example, the procedures might be conceptualized as a token economy system (Kazdin, 1977c).

This argument for a conceptual system does not mean that technological or "how-to" cookbooks have no place in applied behavior analysis, for such packages can be useful—indeed, they are essential. Clearly, though, relating specific instances of application and research to empirically derived principles, concepts, and theory, can aid the generalization of practitioner behavior to novel situations and advance the cumulation of knowledge (cf. Birnbrauer, 1979; Ott, 1980; see Glaser, 1977, and Empey, 1978, for similar concerns within crime and delinquency).

It is important to reemphasize that applied behavior analysis should not be a mere technology of behavior change procedures or programs (Birnbrauer, 1979; Deitz, 1978; Pierce & Epling, 1980). A successful technology should rest ultimately on an underlying body of substantiated basic science—in this case, the science of behavior. That science, though, has not at all been fully attained, and thus some effective applied behavioral technologies may rest on unknown principles (Deitz, 1978). As stated earlier in this chapter, however, technology that is not well-grounded in a conceptual system can solve many problems but may be less effective in doing so than when based on an encompassing conceptual system. Behavior change is best achieved technologically, analytically, and conceptually. When the analytic and conceptual system dimensions are achieved, then not only can applied behavior analysis produce meaningful behavior change, but it may also contribute to the general body of knowledge about behavior, just as does basic research, because researchers in both cases investigate the relationships between behavior and the conditions under which it occurs.

REPLICATION AND DISSEMINATION

To assume that the best of what is known in the behavioral and social sciences will somehow find its way into widespread practice is naive (Paine, Bellamy, & Wilcox, 1984.) Accordingly, explicit efforts are often required to disseminate effective intervention strategies and procedures. This is especially true when the intervention is a complex one, involving extensive and sophisticated treatment and system management activities. Both the developers and adopters of such interventions have to expend considerable effort in assuring quality replication and dissemination.

Developers must not only create interventions that have certain specific characteristics (see the later discussion), but they should ideally maintain sustained involvement of the transfer of their interventions to new adopters (Wolf, Braukmann, & Kirigin Ramp, 1982). Unfortunately, applied researchers are seldom active in disseminating the interventions they have developed (Kazdin, 1979; Paine et al., 1984; Stolz, 1984). This is due, in part, to the availability of resources that are often more appropriate for research and development than for dissemination; in addition, the rewards for researchers are typically for creating new knowledge and not for its careful transfer to the public arena (Fawcett et al., 1981; King, 1981).

The steps involved in high-quality dissemination begin with the research and development involved in constructing and refining a prototypical program. The program developer interested in creating a widely adoptable solution should aim for an intervention characterized by relative effectiveness, flexibility, cost efficiency, simplicity, consumer satisfaction, and compatibility with the values, experiences, and needs of those who would use the technology (cf. Fawcett *et al.*, 1981). Following the initial research and development comes the testing of the program's utility, the standardization of critical procedures, the development of implementation-assistance procedures (e.g., procedural manuals and staff-training workshops), the development of evaluation and quality-assurance procedures, the field testing of a replication program's effectiveness, broader site recruitment and dissemination using implementation-assistance and quality-assurance procedures, and the evaluation of the widespread implementation (Paine *et al.*, 1984).

The creation of effective implementation-assistance and quality-assurance procedures are of central importance here. Program developers who seek to disseminate complex behavioral interventions must be able to assure the quality and viability of the replications. This requires the development of procedures for ongoing staff training and performance monitoring, especially if the replicated intervention is multifaceted, involves people with overlapping responsibilities, and has a steady staff turnover rate. In such cases, infrequent monitoring and inadequate training can result in rapid deterioration of behavioral technologies (Bassett & Blanchard, 1977; Risley, 1975).

What is needed for quality assurance is accurate monitoring of and significant consequences for staff performance. Monitoring may involve periodic formal assessment of effectiveness as well as repeated formal and informal collection of corrective feedback from all those who significantly affect or are affected by the intervention. Given such assessments and feedback, differential consequences can be applied to the behavior of those implementing the intervention. Among the possible consequences here are professional recognition, advancement, pay raises, merit awards, and accreditation (Kirigin-Ramp, 1984).

The important role of the adopter in the dissemination of behavioral interventions has been highlighted by Stolz (1981, 1984), who observes that the dissemination of innovative behavioral techniques designed to affect significant social problems may depend on the sustained efforts of individual policymakers. This is especially so if the techniques do not easily fit within existing systems or do not match already available resources. Although noting that an explicit technology does not exist for increasing the adoption rate of innovative behavioral interventions, Stolz (1981) concluded that a key variable is the personal interaction between agency decision makers and knowledgeable colleagues who promote the use of the intervention.

Stolz (1981) also identified ten other conditions associated with the successful dissemination and adoption efforts: (a) research data show the innovation to be effective; (b) the technology meets the continuing mission of the adopting agency; (c) the potential adopter has a pressing management problem; (d) the availability of the dissemination is timely; (e) the potential adopter is able to view ongoing (model) programs; (f) the adoption is proposed by the policymakers; (g) the intervention is tailored to local conditions; (h) those who have to implement the adoption are involved in asking for it; (i) funds are available for dissemination; and (j) a key person—trained, enthusiastic, and skilled—persists in protecting the adopted program from political forces that would cause its demise. Fawcett *et al.* (1981) made similar points and likewise noted the importance of political factors, particularly an understanding of the often complex and subtle contingencies that exist in many social systems. In a similar vein, Paine *et al.* (1984) have stressed the importance of establishing strong working relationships with all those whose support is critical to program survival.

At issue here is the responsible dissemination of applied behavior analyses that represent better solutions than those already generally available. Obviously, dissemination for dissemination's sake serves no important purpose, whether in the area of crime and delinquency or elsewhere. For the most part, fortunately, programs that do not help potential adopters solve their problems are not likely to be adopted or sustained even if initially implemented (cf. Braukmann *et al.*, 1975). The larger concern here is not the premature dissemination of inappropriate interventions but the lack of widespread or adequate adoption of already useful interventions due to the absence of explicit, quality-focused dissemination.

CONCLUSION: A SYSTEMS PERSPECTIVE

In this chapter, we have described the seven dimensions of applied behavior analysis for criminal justice practice as well as critical issues related to the dissemination and replication of those practices. One last point remains to be discussed and will conclude the chapter: applied behavior analysis should be attuned to a systems or ecological frame of reference. As solutions to problems in the fields of crime and delinquency, applied behavior analyses can be viewed on two basic levels—the procedural and the programmatic. A third level, though, cannot be overlooked—one comprising the larger social system.

At the first level, specific behavioral procedures can be applied to solve specific problems and can be evaluated as to their efficacy in doing so. As shown throughout many of the chapters in this book, innumerable procedural applications have been made, and their relatively immediate effects have been examined. Many of these applications have met the standards of the dimensions outlined in this chapter. However, many have not. In some cases, the dimensions have not been fully implemented; for instance, behavioral procedures have sometimes been applied without attention to the individual differences of participants when such attention was called for. In other cases, the procedures have sometimes been applied without attempts to establish generalization and maintenance of behavior change. In addition, positive relationships have too infrequently been demonstrated between the behaviors changed and actual reductions in crime and delinquency. Furthermore, as noted in Chapter 1, behavior change has sometimes been attempted solely for the convenience of program administrators and staff but not for the benefit of the individual or group actually in need of assistance or for the benefit of society as a whole (Braukmann & Fixsen, 1975; Reppucci & Saunders, 1974).

Behavior change procedures employed in these latter instances are not being applied to socially important goals and may produce undesirable effects or no effects at all in the long run (Burchard, 1973). In these cases, the applications have not been true applied behavior analyses (Emery & Marholin, 1977), and only first-order superficial change may have been achieved (Rappoport, 1977; Watzlawick, Weakland, & Fisch, 1974; Winett & Winkler, 1972).

At the second level of application, behavioral programs are applied to more complex circumstances (e.g., institutional treatment of large numbers of delinquents). These programs, which consist of organized sets of behavioral procedures, may be evaluated for their ability to effect change over a broad spectrum of social, vocational, and academic problems. Unfortunately, however, if the procedures used in a behavioral program are oriented only to superficial, first-order changes that do not represent socially important goals, then the program is unlikely to be any more effective than any other program (Emery & Marholin, 1977). If the behavioral procedures used within a program are not applied appropriately, then no specific problem may actually be solved. In addition, various social and/or political constraints may occur at this programmatic level that can severely limit achieving important social change no matter how well the behavioral program is focused on problem resolution (Nay, 1978; Reppucci & Saunders, 1975; see Clements, Chapter 20, this volume). These social and political limitations, however, are also socially important problems, and applied behavior analysts may be able to provide solutions for them, too. Indeed, these issues are an important new area of concern for applied behavior analysts (e.g., Andrasik & McNamara, 1977; Burkhart, Behles, & Stumphauzer, 1976; Kennedy, 1976; McInnis, 1978).

A focus on the third level of application—the larger social system or context—clearly points out some of the problems that may occur at the procedural and programmatic levels of application. Whenever and wherever possible, applications should go beyond first-order change to achieve second-order change—change that actually alters systems that are the reasons for the problems in the first place (Nietzel, 1979; Rappaport, 1977; Watzlawick et al., 1974; see Burchard, Chapter 22, this volume). Applied behavior analysts should be attuned to, assess, and be prepared to confront issues at this level. Problems are not solved by first-order change that is of minor social importance and that allows the continued existence of the systems that maintain and perhaps even support the problems in the first place. In regard to crime and delinquency, problems will best be solved through second-order change that alters the social systems that foster or do not effectively discourage violent or antisocial behavior, whether external to or from within criminal justice settings. These social systems range from dyadic social interactions, to family interactions, to neighborhood organization, to law-enforcement and correctional agency practices, and even to larger social, cultural, and economic systems.

It is clear that a narrow perspective on problem solving aimed at individual delinquents or criminals, or at isolated groups thereof, outside of the social systems that develop or support their behavior, is not likely to lead to long-lasting, effective change. The ecology of the social problems must be considered (Harshbarger & Maley, 1976; Rogers-Warren & Warren, 1977; Stumphauzer, 1973). Crime and delinquency are problems as large as society itself and should be approached and analyzed as such. Applied behavior analysts can err and become part of the problem, rather than part of the solution, when they focus exclusively on first-order change (Clements, Chapter 20, this volume; Holland, 1977, 1978; Shaw, 1972).

For the most part, practical means of altering large-scale systems are beyond the capabilities of individual applied behavior analysts, though important inroads are being taken in behavioral community psychology (Glenwick & Jason, 1980; Nietzel, Winett, McDonald, & Davidson, 1977), social policymaking (see Seekins & Fawcett, 1986), and the dissemination of public information (see Morris, 1985). In any event, attention to a systems or contextual perspective—even if by necessity constrained—will be more effective than no attention to a systems perspective at all. The ideal of solving large-scale problems from a systems perspective can serve as a superordinate goal for the future. In the meantime, by adhering as much as possible to the dimensions of applied behavior analysis, we can help avoid the too-narrow use of behavioral procedures and programs and can more broadly promote the growth, effectiveness, and humaneness of the behavioral approaches to crime and delinquency.

REFERENCES

Akers, R. L. (1973). *Deviant behavior: A social learning approach*. Belmont, CA: Wadsworth.

Andrasik, F., & McNamara, J. R. (1977). Optimizing staff performance in an institutional behavior change system. *Behavior Modification, 1*, 235–248.

Attkisson, C. C., Hargreaves, W. A., Horowitz, M. J., & Sorensen, J. E. (1978). *Evaluation of human service programs*. New York: Academic Press.

Azrin, N. H. (1977). A strategy for applied research: Learning based but outcome oriented. *American Psychologist, 32*, 140–149.

Baer, D. M. (1975). In the beginning, there was the response. In E. Ramp & G. Semb (Eds.), *Behavior analysis: Areas of research and application* (pp. 16–30). Englewood Cliffs, NJ: Prentice-Hall.

Baer, D. M. (1978). On the relationship between basic and applied research. In A. C. Catania & T. A. Brigham (Eds.), *Handbook of applied behavior analysis: Social and instructional processes* (pp. 11–16). New York: Irvington.

Baer, D. M. (1982). The role of current pragmatics in the future analysis of generalization technology. In R. B. Stuart (Ed.), *Adherence, compliance, and generalization in behavioral medicine* (pp. 192–212). New York: Brunner/Mazel.

Baer, D. M., & Wolf, M. M. (1970). The entry into natural communities of reinforcement. In R. Ulrich, T. Stachnik, & J. Mabry (Eds.), *Control of human behavior* (Vol. 1, pp. 319–324). Glenview, IL: Scott, Foresman.

Baer, D. M., Wolf, M. M., & Risley, T. R. (1968). Some current dimensions of applied behavior analysis. *Journal of Applied Behavior Analysis, 1*, 91–97.

Bailey, J. S., Wolf, M. M., & Phillips, E. L. (1970). Home-based reinforcement and the modification of pre-delinquents' classroom behavior. *Journal of Applied Behavior Analysis, 3*, 223–233.

Bakeman, R., & Gottman, J. M. (1986). *Observing interaction: An introduction to sequential analysis*. New York: Cambridge University Press.

Barlow, D. H., & Hersen, M. (1984). *Single case experimental designs.* New York: Pergamon Press.

Bassett, J. E., & Blanchard, E. B. (1977). The effect of the absence of close supervision on the use of response cost in a prison token economy. *Journal of Applied Behavior Analysis, 10,* 375–379.

Bassett, J. E., Blanchard, E. B., & Koshland, E. (1975). Applied behavior analysis in a penal setting: Targeting "free world" behaviors. *Behavior Therapy, 6,* 639–648.

Baunach, P. J. (1980). Random assignment in criminal justice research: Some ethical and legal issues. *Criminology, 17,* 435–444.

Berleman, W. C., Seaberg, J. R., & Steinburn, T. W. (1972). The delinquency prevention experiment of the Seattle Atlantic Street Center: A final evaluation. *Social Science Review,* September, 323–346.

Birnbrauer, J. S. (1979). Applied behavior analysis, service, and the acquisition of knowledge. *The Behavior Analyst, 2,* 15–21.

Braukmann, C. J., & Fixsen, D. L. (1975). Behavior modification with delinquents. In M. Hersen, R. M. Eisler, & P. M. Miller (Eds.), *Progress in behavior therapy* (Vol. 1, pp. 191–231). New York: Academic Press.

Braukmann, C. J., Fixsen, D. L., Kirigin, K. A., Phillips, E. A., Phillips, E. L., & Wolf, M. M. (1975). Achievement Place: The training and certification of teaching parents. In W. S. Wood (Ed.), *Issues in evaluating behavior modification* (pp. 131–152). Champaign, IL: Research Press.

Braukmann, C. J., Fixsen, D. L., Phillips, E. L., & Wolf, M. M. (1975). Behavioral approaches to treatment in the crime and delinquency field. *Criminology, 13,* 299–331.

Braukmann, C. J., Kirigin, K. A., & Wolf, M. M. (1980). Group home treatment research: Social learning and social control perspectives. In T. Hirschi & M. Gottdfredson (Eds.), *Understanding crime* (pp. 113–130). Beverly Hills: Sage.

Braukmann, C. J., Ramp, K. A., & Wolf, M. M. (1985). *Teaching-Family model: Aftercare and site replication* (Continuation request for Grant MH39713). Lawrence, KS: University of Kansas Achievement Place Research Project.

Brigham, T. A. (1978). Self-control: Part II. In A. C. Catania & T. A. Brigham (Eds.), *Handbook of applied behavior analysis* (pp. 259–274). New York: Irvington.

Buehler, R. E., Patterson, G. R., & Furniss, J. M. (1966). The reinforcement of behavior in institutional settings. *Behavior Research and Therapy, 4,* 157–167.

Burchard, J. D. (1973). Behavior modification with delinquents: Some unforeseen contingencies. In J. S. Stumphauzer (Ed.), *Behavior therapy with delinquents* (pp. 66–74). Springfield, IL: Charles C Thomas.

Burgess, R. L., & Akers, R. L. (1966). A differential association-reinforcement theory of criminal behavior. *Social Problems, 14,* 128–147.

Burgess, R. L., & Bushell, D. (Eds.). (1969). *Behavioral sociology: The experimental analysis of social process.* New York: Columbia University Press.

Burkhart, B. R., Behles, M., & Stumphauzer, J. S. (1976). Training juvenile probation officers in behavior modification: Knowledge, attitude change, or behavioral competence? *Behavior Therapy, 7,* 47–53.

Campbell, D. T. (1969). Reforms as experiments. *American Psychologist, 24,* 409–429.

Campbell, D. T., & Ross, H. L. (1968). The Connecticut crackdown on speeding: Time series data on quasi-experimental analysis. *Law and Society Review, 3,* 33–53.

Campbell, D. T., & Stanley, J. C. (1963). *Experimental and quasi-experimental design for research.* Chicago, IL: Rand McNally.

Caro, F. G. (Ed.). (1971). *Readings in evaluation research.* New York: Sage.

Catania, A. C. (1973). The psychologies of structure, function, and development. *American Psychologist, 28,* 434–443.

Catania, A. C. (1984). *Learning.* Englewood Cliffs, NJ: Prentice-Hall.

Ciminero, A. R., Calhoun, K. S., & Adams, H. E. (1977). *Handbook of behavioral assessment.* New York: Wiley.

Cone, J. D., & Hawkins, R. P. (1977). *Behavioral assessment: New directions in clinical psychology.* New York: Bruner/Mazel.

Cook, T. D., & Campbell, D. T. (1979). *Quasi-experimentation: Design and analysis for field settings.* Chicago: Rand McNally.

Davidson, W. S., & Robinson, M. J. (1975). Community psychology and behavior modification: A community-based program for the prevention of delinquency. *Journal of Corrective Psychiatry and Behavior Therapy, 21,* 1–12.

Davidson, W. S., Koch, J. R., Lewis, R. G., & Wnesinski, M. D. (1980). *Evaluation strategies in criminal justice.* Elmsford, NY: Pergamon Press.

Deitz, S. M. (1978). Current status of applied behavior analysis: Science versus technology. *American Psychologist, 33,* 805–814.

Dixon, W. J., & Massey, F. J. (1969). *Introduction to statistical analysis.* New York: McGraw-Hill.

Elliott, D. S., & Voss, H. L. (1974). *Delinquency and dropout.* Lexington, MA: D. C. Heath.

Emery, R. E., & Marholin, D. (1977). An applied behavior analysis of delinquency. *American Psychologist, 32,* 860–873.

Empey, L. T. (1978). *American delinquency: Its meaning and construction.* Homewood, IL: Dorsey Press.

Erickson, M. L., & Empey, L. T. (1963). Court records, undetected delinquency, and decision making. *Journal of Criminal Law, Criminology, and Police Science, 54,* 456–469.

Farrington, D. (1973). Self-reports of deviant behavior: Predictive and stable? *Journal of Criminal Law, Criminology, and Police Science, 64,* 99–110.

Fawcett, S. B., Seekins, T., & Braukmann, C. J. (1981). Developing and transferring behavioral technologies for children and youth. *Children and Youth Services Review, 3,* 319–342.

Feldman, M. P. (1977). *Criminal behavior: A psychological analysis.* New York: Wiley.

Filipczak, J., & Friedman, R. M. (1978). Some controls on applied research in a public secondary school: Project PREP. In A. C. Catania & T. A. Brigham (Eds.), *Handbook of applied behavior analysis: Social and instructional processes* (pp. 563–584). New York: Irvington.

Fixsen, D. L., Phillips, E. L., & Wolf, M. M. (1973). Achievement Place: Experiments in self-government with pre-delinquents. *Journal of Applied Behavior Analysis, 6,* 31–47.

Friedman, P. R. (1975). Legal regulation of applied behavior analysis in mental institutions and prisons. *Arizona Law Review, 17,* 39–104.

Fuqua, R. W., & Schwade, J. (1986). Social validation of applied behavioral research. In A. Poling & R. W. Fuqua (Eds.), *Research methods in applied behavior analysis: Issues and advances* (pp. 265–292). New York: Plenum Press.

Glaser, D. (1977). Concern with theory in correctional evaluation research. *Crime and Delinquency, 23,* 173–179.

Glass, G. V. (1968). Analysis of data on the Connecticut speeding crackdown as a time-series quasi-experiment. *Law and Society Review, 3,* 55–76.

Glenwick, D. S., & Jason, L. A. (1980). *Behavioral community psychology: Progress and prospects.* New York: Praeger.

Goldiamond, I. (1974). Toward a constructional approach to social problems. *Behaviorism, 2,* 1–84.

Goldiamond, I. (1976). Protection of human subjects and patients. *Behaviorism, 4,* 1–42.

Gould, L. C. (1969). Who defines delinquency: A comparison of self-reported and officially reported indices of delinquency for three racial groups. *Social Problems, 16,* 325–336.

Harshbarger, D., & Maley, R. (Eds.). (1976). *Behavior analysis and systems analysis.* Kalamazoo, MI: Behaviordelia.

Hartmann, D. P. (Ed.). (1982). *Using observers to study behavior: New directions for methodology of social and behavioral science.* San Francisco: Jossey-Bass.

Hartmann, D. P., Gottman, J. M., Jones, R. R., Gardner, W., Kazdin, A. E. & Vaught, R. (1980). Interrupted time-series analysis and its application to behavioral data. *Journal of Applied Behavior Analysis, 13,* 543–559.

Hawkins, J. D., Cassidy, C. H., Light, N. B., & Miller, C. A. (1977). Interpreting official records as indicators of recidivism in evaluating delinquency prevention programs. *Criminology, 15,* 397–434.

Hayes, S. C., & Maley, R. F. (1977). Coercion: Legal and behavioral issues. *Behaviorism, 5,* 87–95.

Haynes, S. N. (1978). *Principles of behavior assessment.* New York: Gardner Press.

Hersen, M., & Bellack, A. (1981). *Behavioral assessment: A practical handbook* (2nd ed.). New York: Pergamon Press.

Hindelang, M. J., Hirschi, T., & Weis, J. G. (1981). *Measuring delinquency.* Beverly Hills: Sage.

Hirschi, T. (1969). *Causes of delinquency.* Berkeley: University of California Press.

Hobbs, T. R., & Holt, M. M. (1976). The effects of token reinforcement on the behavior of delinquents in cottage settings. *Journal of Applied Behavioral Analysis, 9,* 189–198.

Holland, J. G. (1977). Behaviorism and the social system. In N. Datan & H. W. Reese (Eds.), *Lifespan developmental psychology: Dialectical perspectives on experimental reserach* (pp. 311–316). New York: Academic Press.

Holland, J. G. (1978). Behaviorism: Part of the problem or part of the solution? *Journal of Applied Behavior Analysis, 11,* 163–174.

Homans, G. C. (1969). *The nature of social science.* New York: Harcourt, Brace, & World.

Horton, L. E. (1970). Generalization of aggressive behavior in adolescent delinquent boys. *Journal of Applied Behavior Analysis, 3,* 205–211.

Jayaratne, S., & Levy, R. L. (1980). *Empirical clinical practice.* New York: Columbia University Press.

Jeffery, C. R. (1965). Criminal behavior and learning theory. *The Journal of Criminal Law, Criminology, and Police Science, 56,* 294–300.

Johnson, V. S. (1977). Behavior modification in the correctional setting. *Criminal Justice and Behavior, 4,* 397–428.

Johnston, J. M., & Pennypacker, H. S. (1980). *Strategies and tactics of human behavioral research.* Hillsdale, NJ: Lawrence Erlbaum.

Jones, R. R., Vaught, R. S., & Weinrott, M. (1977). Time-series analysis in operant research. *Journal of Applied Behavior Analysis, 10,* 151–166.

Kandel, D. B. (Ed.). (1978). *Longitudinal research on drug use.* Washington, DC: Hemisphere.

Kandel, D. B., Kessler, R. C., & Margulies, R. Z. (1978). Antecedents of adolescent initiation into stages of drug use: A developmental analysis. In D. B. Kandel (Ed.), *Longitudinal research on drug use* (pp. 73–99). Washington, DC: Hemisphere.

Kazdin, A. E. (1977a). Assessing the clinical or applied importance of behavior change through social validation. *Behavior Modification, 1,* 427–452.

Kazdin, A. E. (1977b). Artifact, bias, and complexity of assessment: The ABC's of reliability. *Journal of Applied Behavior Analysis, 10,* 141–150.

Kazdin, A. E. (1977c). *The token economy.* New York: Plenum Press.

Kazdin, A. E. (1978). *History of behavior modification.* Baltimore, MD: University Park Press.

Kazdin, A. E. (1979). Advances in child behavior therapy: Applications and implications. *American Psychologist, 34,* 981–987.

Kazdin, A. E. (1982). *Single-case research designs: Methods for clinical and applied settings.* New York: Oxford University Press.

Kazdin, A. E. (1984). Statistical analyses for single-case experimental designs. In D. H. Barlow & M. Hersen, (Eds.), *Single-case experimental designs* (pp. 285–324). New York: Pergamon Press.

Kazdin, A. E., & Wilson, G. T. (1978). *Evaluation of behavior therapy: Issues, evidence, and research strategies.* Cambridge MA: Ballinger.

Keller, O. J., & Alper, B. S. (1970). *Half-way houses: Community-centered correction and treatment.* Lexington, MA: Heath.

Kennedy, R. E. (1976). Behavior modification in prisons. In W. E. Craighead, A. E. Kazdin, & M. J. Mahoney (Eds.), *Behavior modification: Principles, issues, and applications* (pp. 321–340). Boston: Houghton Mifflin.

Kerlinger, F. N. (1964). *Foundations of behavioral research.* New York: Holt, Rinehart & Winston.

Kifer, R. E., Lewis, M. A., Green, D. R., & Phillips, E. L. (1974). Training predelinquent youths and their parents to negotiate conflict situations. *Journal of Applied Behavior Analysis, 7,* 357–364.

Kimbles, S. L. (1973). Behavior therapy with the black delinquent. In J. S. Stumphauzer (Ed.), *Behavior therapy with delinquents* (pp. 49–53). Springfield, IL: Charles C Thomas.

King, L. (1981). Comment on "Adoption of innovations from applied behavioral research: 'Does anybody care?'" *Journal of Applied Behavior Analysis, 14,* 507–511.

Kirigin, K. A., Phillips, E. L., Timbers, G. D., Fixsen, D. L., & Wolf, M. M. (1977). Achievement Place: The modification of academic behavior problems of youths in a group home setting. In

B. C. Etzel, J. M. LeBlanc, & D. M. Baer (Eds.), *New developments in behavioral research: Theory, method, and application* (pp. 473–487). Hillsdale, NJ: Erlbaum.

Kirigin, K. A., Wolf, M. M., Braukmann, C. J., Fixsen, D. L., & Phillips, E. L. (1979). Achievement Place: A preliminary outcome evaluation. In J. S. Stumphauzer (Ed.), *Progress in behavior therapy with delinquents* (pp. 118–149). Springfield, IL: Charles C Thomas.

Kirigin, K. A., Braukmann, C. J., Atwater, J., & Wolf, M. M. (1982). An evaluation of Teaching-Family (Achievement Place) group homes for juvenile offenders. *Journal of Applied Behavior Analysis, 15,* 1–16.

Kirigin Ramp, K. (1984). Effective quality control for social service programs: One piece of the puzzle. In S. C. Paine, G. T. Bellamy, & B. Wilcox (Eds.), *Human services that work* (pp. 261–268). Baltimore: Paul H. Brookes.

Krapfl, J. E., & Vargas, E. A. (1977). *Behaviorism and ethics.* Kalamazoo, MI: Behaviordelia.

Kratochwill, T. R. (Ed.). (1978). *Single subject research: Strategies for evaluating change.* New York: Academic Press.

Kratochwill, T. R. (1985). Selection of target behaviors: Issues and directions. *Behavioral Assessment, 7,* 3–5.

Kulik, J., Stein, K., & Sarbin, T. (1968). Disclosure of delinquent behavior under conditions of anonymity and non-anonymity. *Journal of Counseling and Clinical Psychology, 32,* 375–382.

Lefleur, L. B. (1975). Biasing influences on drug arrest records: Implications for deviance research. *American Sociological Review, 40,* 88–103.

Liberman, R. P. (1980). Review of *Psychosocial treatment for chronic mental patients* by Gordon L. Paul and Robert P. Lentz. *Journal of Applied Behavior Analysis, 13,* 367–371.

Marholin, D., & Siegel, L. J. (1978). Beyond the law of effect: Programming for the maintenance of behavior change. In D. Marholin (Ed.), *Child behavior therapy* (pp. 397–415). New York: Gardner Press.

Marholin, D., Siegel, L. J., & Phillips, D. (1976). Transfer and treatment: A search for empirical procedures. In M. Hersen, R. M. Eisler, & P. M. Miller (Eds.), *Progress in behavior modification* (Vol. 3, pp. 293–342). New York: Academic Press.

Martin, R. (1975). *Legal challenges to behavior modification.* Champaign, IL: Research Press.

McInnis, T. (1978). Training and motivating staff members. In D. Marholin (Ed.), *Child behavior therapy* (pp. 434–445). New York: Gardner Press.

Millenson, J. R., & Leslie, J. C. (1979). *Principles of behavior analysis.* New York: Macmillan.

Minkin, N., Braukmann, C. J., Minkin, B. L., Timbers, G. D., Timbers, B. J., Fixsen, D. L., Phillips, E. L., & Wolf, M. M. (1976). The social validation and training of conversation skills. *Journal of Applied Behavior Analysis, 9,* 127–140.

Morris, E. K. (1978). A brief review of legal deviance: References in behavior analysis and delinquency. In D. Marholin (Ed.), *Child behavior therapy* (pp. 214–238). New York: Gardner Press.

Morris, E. K. (1980). Applied behavior analysis for criminal justice practice: Some current dimensions. *Criminal Justice and Behavior, 7,* 131–145.

Morris, E. K. (1985). Public information, dissemination, and behavior analysis. *The Behavior Analyst, 8,* 95–115.

Nay, W. R. (1978). Intra-institutional "roadblocks" to behavior modification programming. In D. Marholin (Ed.), *Child behavior therapy* (pp. 446–459). New York: Gardner Press.

Nelson, R. O., & Hayes, S. C. (1981). Nature of behavioral assessment. In M. Hersen & A. S. Bellack (Eds.), *Behavioral assessment: A practical handbook* (pp. 3–37). New York: Pergamon Press.

Nelson, R. O., & Hayes, S. C. (1986). *Conceptual foundations of behavioral assessment.* New York: Guilford.

Nietzel, M. T. (1979). *Crime and its modification: A social learning perspective.* New York: Pergamon Press.

Nietzel, M. T., Winett, R. A., McDonald, M. L., & Davidson, W. S. (1977). *Behavioral approaches to community psychology.* New York: Pergamon Press.

Opton, E. M. (1974). Psychiatric violence against persons: When therapy is punishment. *Mississippi Law Journal, 45,* 605–644.

Ott, B. D. (1980). Advocacy and instruction in behavior therapy: Examination of productivity in current dimensions. *Behavior Therapist, 3,* 23–24.

Paine, S. C., Bellamy, G. T., & Wilcox, B. (1984). *Human services that work.* Baltimore: Paul H. Brookes.

Parsonson, B. S., & Baer, D. M. (1978). The analysis and presentation of graphic data. In T. R. Kratochwill (Ed.), *Single subject research: Strategies for evaluating change* (pp. 101–165). New York: Academic Press.

Phillips, E. L., Phillips, E. A., Fixsen, D. L., & Wolf, M. M. (1971). Achievement Place: Modification of the behavior of pre-delinquent boys within a token economy. *Journal of Applied Behavior Analysis, 4,* 45–59.

Phillips, E. L., Phillips, E. A., Wolf, M. M., & Fixsen, D. L. (1973). Achievement Place: Development of the elected manager system. *Journal of Applied Behavior Analysis, 6,* 541–561.

Phillips, E. L., Phillips, E. A., Fixsen, D. L., Wolf, M. M. (1974). *The Teaching-Family handbook.* Lawrence, KS: University of Kansas Printing Service.

Pierce, W. D., & Epling, W. F. (1980). What happened to analysis in applied behavior analysis. *The Behavior Analyst, 3,* 1–9.

Pierce, C. H., & Risley, T. R. (1974). Recreation as a reinforcer: Increasing membership and decreasing disruptions in an urban recreation center. *Journal of Applied Behavior Analysis, 7,* 403–411.

Powers, E., & Witmer, H. (1951). *An experiment in the prevention of delinquency: The Cambridge-Somerville youth study.* New York: Columbia University Press.

Rachlin, H. (1978). Self-control: Part I. In A. C. Catania & T. A. Brigham (Eds.), *Handbook of applied behavior analysis* (pp. 246–258). New York: Irvington.

Rappaport, J. (1977). *Community psychology: Values, research, and action.* New York: Holt, Rinehart & Winston.

Reppucci, N. D., & Saunders, J. T. (1975). Social psychology of behavior modification. *American Psychologist, 29,* 649–660.

Ribes-Inesta, E., & Bandura, A. (Eds.). (1976). *Analysis of delinquency and aggression.* Hillsdale, NJ: Lawrence Erlbaum.

Risley, T. R. (1969). Behavior modification: An experimental-therapeutic endeavor. In L. A. Hamerlynck, P. O. Davidson, & L. E. Acker (Eds.), *Behavior modification and ideal mental health services* (pp. 37–52). Alberta, Canada: University of Calgary Press.

Risley, T. R. (1975). Certify procedures not people. In W. S. Wood (Ed.), *Issues in evaluating behavior modification* (pp. 159–181). Champaign, IL: Research Press.

Robbins, I. P., & Sepler, H. J. (1978). A behavioral analysis of legal intent. *Law and Psychology Review, 4,* 18–41.

Robinson, P. W., & Foster, D. F. (1979). *Experimental psychology: A small-N approach.* New York: Harper & Row.

Rogers-Warren, A., & Warren, S. F. (Eds.). (1977). *Ecological perspectives in behavior analysis.* Baltimore: University Park Press.

Ross, H. L., Campbell, D. T., & Glass, G. V. (1970). Determining the effects of a legal reform: The British "breathanalyzer" crackdown of 1967. *American Behavioral Scientist, 13,* 493–509.

Schnelle, J. F., & Lee, F. J. (1974). A quasi-experimental retrospective evaluation of a prior policy change. *Journal of Applied Behavior Analysis, 7,* 483–496.

Schnelle, J. F., Kirchner, R. E., Casey, J. D., Uselton, P. H., & McNees, M. P. (1977). Patrol evaluation research: A multiple-baseline analysis of saturation police patrolling during day and night hours. *Journal of Applied Behavior Analysis, 10,* 33–40.

Schnelle, J. F., Kirchner, R. E., MacRae, J. W., McNees, M. P., Eck, R. H., Snodgrass, S., Casey, J. D., & Uselton, P. H. (1978). Police evaluation research: An experimental and cost-benefit analysis of a helicopter patrol in a high crime area. *Journal of Applied Behavior Analysis, 11,* 11–21.

Schumaker, J. B., Hovell, M. F., & Sherman, J. A. (1977). An analysis of daily report cards and parent-managed privileges in the improvement of adolescents' classroom performance. *Journal of Applied Behavior Analysis, 10,* 449–464.

Seekins, T., & Fawcett, S. B. (1986). Public policymaking and research information. *The Behavior Analyst, 9,* 35–45.

Seymour, F. W., & Stokes, T. F. (1976). Self-recording in training girls to increase work and evoke staff praise in an institution for offenders. *Journal of Applied Behavior Analysis, 9,* 41–54.

Shaw, M. (1972). Ethical implications of a behavioral approach. In D. Jehu, P. Hardiker, M. Yelloly, & M. Shaw (Eds.), *Behavior modification in social work* (pp. 161–172). London: Wiley.

Sidman, M. (1960). *Tactics of scientific research.* New York: Basic Books.

Skinner, B. F. (1953). *Science and human behavior.* New York: Macmillan.

Skinner, B. F. (1966). What is the experimental analysis of behavior? *Journal of the Experimental Analysis of Behavior, 9,* 213–218.

Skinner, B. F. (1972). Some relations between behavior modification and basic research. In S. W. Bijou & E. Ribes-Inesta (Eds.), *Behavior modification: Issues and extensions* (pp. 1–6). New York: Academic Press.

Skinner, B. F. (1974). *About behaviorism.* New York: Knopf.

Sowles, R. C., & Gill, J. H. (1970). Institutional and community adjustment of delinquents following counseling. *Journal of Counsulting and Clinical Psychology, 34,* 398–402.

Stachnik, T. J. (1972). The case against criminal penalties for illicit drug use. *American Psychologist, 27,* 637–642.

Stokes, T. F., & Baer, D. M. (1977). An implicit technology of generalization. *Journal of Applied Behavior Analysis, 10,* 349–367.

Stolz, S. B. (1978). Ethics of social and educational interventions: Historical content and a behavior analysis. In A. C. Catania & T. A. Brigham (Eds.), *Handbook of applied behavior analysis: Social and instructional processes* (pp. 652–676). New York: Irvington.

Stolz, S. B. (1981). Adoption of innovations from applied behavioral research: "Does anybody care?" *Journal of Applied Behavior Analysis, 14,* 491–505.

Stolz, S. B. (1984). Dissemination of standardized human service models: A behavior analyst's perspective. In S. C. Paine, G. T. Bellamy, & B. Wilcox (Eds.), *Human services that work* (pp. 235–245). Baltimore: Paul H. Brookes.

Stumphauzer, J. S. (1970). Modification of delay choices in institutionalized youthful offenders through social reinforcement. *Psychonomic Science, 18,* 222–223.

Stumphauzer, J. S. (1972). Increased delay of gratification in young prison inmates through imitation of high-delay peer models. *Journal of Personality and Social Psychology, 21,* 10–17.

Stumphauzer, J. S. (Ed.). (1973). *Behavior therapy with delinquents.* Springfield, IL: Charles C Thomas.

Turner, S. M., & Jones, R. T. (Eds.). (1982). *Behavior modification in black populations: Psychosocial issues and empirical findings.* New York: Plenum Press.

Van Houten, R. (1979). Social validation: The evolution of standards of competency for target behaviors. *Journal of Applied Behavior Analysis, 12,* 581–591.

Vargas, E. A. (1975). Rights: A behavioristic analysis. *Behaviorism, 3,* 178–190.

Watzlawick, P., Weakland, J., & Fisch, R. (1974). *Change: Principles of problem formation and problem reduction.* New York: Norton.

Weiss, C. H. (1972). *Evaluation research.* Englewood Cliffs, NJ: Prentice-Hall.

Werner, J. S., Minkin, N., Minkin, B. L., Fixsen, D. L., Phillips, E. L., & Wolf, M. M. (1975). What should kids say to cops? An analysis of an "intervention program." *Criminal Justice and Behavior, 2,* 55–84.

Wexler, D. B. (1973). Token and taboo: Behavior modification, token economies, and the law. *California Law Review, 61,* 81–109.

Wexler, D. B. (1975). The surfacing of behavioral jurisprudence. *Behaviorism, 3,* 172–177.

Willner, A. C., Braukmann, C. J., Kirigin, K. A., Fixsen, D. L., Phillips, E. L., & Wolf, M. M. (1977). The training and validation of youth-preferred social behaviors in child-care personnel. *Journal of Applied Behavior Analysis, 10,* 219–230.

Wilson, J. Q., & Hernnstein, R. J. (1985). *Crime and human nature.* New York: Simon & Schuster.

Winett, R. A., & Winkler, R. C. (1972). Current behavior modification in the classroom: Be quiet, be docile, be still. *Journal of Applied Behavior Analysis, 5,* 499–504.

Wolf, M. M. (1978). Social validity: The case for subjective measurement. *Journal of Applied Behavior Analysis, 11,* 203–214.

Wolf, M. M., Braukmann, C. J., & Kirigin Ramp, K. (1982). Program survival: A case study in the development and maintenance of a behavioral intervention program. In B. Bolton & R. Roessler (Eds.), *Proceedings of the symposium on applied research methodology* (pp. 43–49). Fayetteville, AR: The University of Arkansas Rehabilitation Research and Training Center.

Wolfgang, M. E., Figlio, R. M., & Sellin, T. (1972). *Delinquency in a birth cohort.* Chicago: University of Chicago Press.

Wood, R., & Flynn, J. M. (1978). A self-evaluation token system versus an external evaluation token system alone in a residential setting with predelinquent youths. *Journal of Applied Behavior Analysis, 11,* 503–512.

3

An Introduction to Contemporary Behaviorism

History, Concepts, and a System of Analysis

EDWARD K. MORRIS, STEPHEN T. HIGGINS,
WARREN K. BICKEL, AND CURTIS J. BRAUKMANN

Behavioral psychology has its roots in the philosophical and psychological traditions of the ancient Greek civilization, was nurtured by the Renaissance and scientific revolution, and emerged finally as a formal system of psychology in the early decades of this century. Since its emergence, behaviorism has grown in several directions, the modern product we refer to as "contemporary behaviorism" (see Day, 1980). In contrast to this long-standing tradition, the development of the behavioral approaches to crime and delinquency is of relatively recent origin, having begun both in theory and in practice in the mid-1960s (e.g., Burgess & Akers, 1966; Jeffery, 1965; Schwitzgebel, 1964; see Morris, 1978). Thus, their philosophical and psychological lineage aside, the behavioral approaches to crime and delinquency represent only about 20 years of systematic conceptual and empirical development—a brief span of time in the history of science. To put it another way, they have a long history but a short past (cf. Ebbinghaus, 1908, p. 1).

As described throughout this book, the behavioral applications to crime and delinquency have met with some noted successes, yet much remains to be accomplished—not only in application and with respect to public policy but theoretically and conceptually as well. By focusing so much on application in this book, short shrift has seemingly been given to philosophical, theoretical, and conceptual concerns as well as to the coverage of the basic principles of behavior. Such material is not actually missing, however. To the contrary, every chapter touches in some way on these points. Nonetheless, a general

Edward K. Morris • Department of Human Development, University of Kansas, Lawrence, Kansas 66045.   **Stephen T. Higgins** • Department of Psychiatry, University of Vermont School of Medicine, Burlington, Vermont 05405.   **Warren K. Bickel** • Department of Psychiatry, Division of Substance Abuse, Albert Einstein College of Medicine, 1500 Waters Place, Bronx, New York 10461.   **Curtis J. Braukmann** • Department of Human Development, University of Kansas, Lawrence, Kansas 66045.

introduction to these matters would seem useful. Thus, in this chapter, we will offer an overview of what we take to be the core behavioral approach to crime and delinquency in a way that provides a conceptual organization for the material to follow. Our treatment will not be complete, however, because a single chapter is insufficient space for the amount of material to be covered, but where appropriate, we will offer citations and references to additional material in order to fill out that being offered here.

The present chapter is composed of two main sections. In the first, we will provide a brief overview of the history and philosophy of contemporary behaviorism. Our presentation will be somewhat different from those offered elsewhere, in large part because this history and philosophy are different in important ways from how the behavioral views are typically portrayed. In the second section of the chapter, we will present a conceptual system for the analysis of behavior that is characteristic of contemporary behaviorism. In doing so, we interweave an introduction to the basic principles of behavior and related applied behavioral procedures. Before turning to this material, though, we must first clarify some terminology.

A MATTER OF TERMINOLOGY

Although behaviorism, as a system of psychology, formally emerged about 75 years ago, it is no one thing—there have been and are many types of behavioral psychology. The general orientation of this handbook, and this chapter in particular, is most closely aligned with what we refer to as "contemporary behaviorism," which largely reflects the influence of *radical behaviorism,* but which we take to include important characteristics of *interbehavioral psychology* as well (see Morris, 1982, 1984; Morris, Higgins, & Bickel, 1982a, 1983).

As for radical behaviorism, it refers not to the science of behavior *per se,* but rather to the philosophy of that science (Skinner, 1953, 1971, 1974; see the journal, *Behaviorism,* 1972–present), where *radical* is commonly taken to mean *thoroughgoing* in the sense that behavior is at the root of, or fundamental to, everything psychological (Michael, 1985). The science of behavior, in this view, is referred to as the "experimental analysis of behavior" (see Skinner, 1966a; see, e.g., the *Journal of the Experimental Analysis of Behavior,* 1958–present), and the application of that science is called "applied behavior analysis" (Baer, Wolf, & Risley, 1968; see, e.g., the *Journal of Applied Behavior Analysis,* 1968–present; *Behavior Therapy,* 1970–present; *Behavior Modification,* 1976–present). More currently, the entire corpus of these basic and applied research programs and their attendant theoretical orientation are often referred to as the field of "behavior analysis" (see, e.g., *The Behavior Analyst,* 1977–present).

As for interbehavioral psychology, *interbehavioral* emphasizes the reciprocal and systemslike nature of all behavioral interactions (Kantor, 1959, 1971). No terminological differentiations are made among basic and applied research and conceptual analysis. (For a general overview, see Smith, Mountjoy, & Ruben, 1983; for some clinical implications and applications, see Ruben & Delprato, 1987; see also the newsletter, *The Interbehaviorist*, 1970–present).

Although contemporary behaviorism, as embodied in radical behaviorism and interbehavioral psychology, is emphasized in this chapter, this view is not the only one represented in the handbook. Basic, applied, and conceptual work is also covered from the perspectives of (a) cognitive behaviorism (Meichenbaum, 1977; Meichenbaum & Cameron, 1982; see Platt & Prout, Chapter 18, this volume); (b) psychological social learning theory (Bandura, 1969, 1977; Rosenthal, 1982; see Nietzel & Himelein, Chapter 4, this volume; Morton & Ewald, Chapter 10); (c) sociological social learning theory (Akers, 1973; see Krohn, Massey, & Skinner, Chapter 17, this volume); and (d) what might be referred to as biobehavioral psychology (Mednick & Christiansen, 1977; see Ellis, Chapter 19, this volume).

These alternative views differ in subtle and not so subtle ways from each other and especially from contemporary behaviorism. Although a discussion of this latter point takes us beyond the central intent of our introductory material here, perhaps one important distinction can be made: cognitive behaviorism, social learning theory, and biobehavioral psychology are "methodologically" behavioral, as opposed to being philosophically so (see Day, 1983; Moore, 1981). In *methodological behaviorism,* behavior is nominally the subject matter of psychology because psychology as a science requires material that can be objectively observed and directly investigated. Nonetheless, behavior is usually of secondary interest because it is generally taken to be (a) a manifestation of constructs of supposedly more primary interest, which are hypothesized to exist in dimensions other than behavior (e.g., traits, cognitive states and processes, and the mind), or (b) a manifestation of processes that are the subject matter of another science (e.g., biology) (see Kantor, 1947; Skinner, 1950). Methodological behaviorism, then, is scientific in the sense that it is objective and rigorous in its research methodology. But it is not necessarily behavioral in the sense of a commitment to a natural science of behavior, where behavior qua behavior is taken as the fundamental subject matter for the science of psychology and where constructs are directly about behavior that emerges from person–environment interactions—and nothing else.

This tension between contemporary behaviorism and methodological behaviorism is also at the heart of differences between contemporary behaviorism and most of the rest of psychology. Although not the focus of the material to follow, these differences are necessarily touched on in our presentation of the historical and philosophical background to contemporary behaviorism.

HISTORICAL AND PHILOSOPHICAL BACKGROUND

The history and philosophy of contemporary behaviorism is a difficult and complex subject matter whose systematic treatment goes beyond what can reasonably be accomplished in what follows. Nevertheless, we can introduce the material by way of a broad overview. For more thorough treatments available elsewhere, perhaps the two best are (a) Kantor's (1963, 1969) texts on the scientific evolution of psychology, which focus on the historical development of a natural science of behavior, and (b) Day's (1980) chapter, "The Historical Antecedents of Contemporary Behaviorism," which covers the philosophical lineage of radical behaviorism more specifically. Other scholarly treatments to be recommended are Zuriff's (1985) *Behaviorism: A Conceptual Reconstruction,* Smith's (1986) *Behaviorism and Logical Positivism: A Reassessment of the Alliance,* Boakes's (1984) *From Darwin to Behaviorism,* O'Donnell's (1985) *The Origins of Behaviorism: American Psychology, 1870–1920,* Keller's (1973) *The Definition of Psychology,* and Kazdin's (1978) *History of Behavior Modification.* In this section of the chapter, we will borrow from these sources in introducing an abbreviated version of the history and philosophy of contemporary behaviorism.

Classical Greek Philosophy

The philosophical beginnings of contemporary behaviorism lie in ancient Greek civilization (ca. 600–100 B.C.) and more specifically in the flourishing of the Hellenic culture (450–300 B.C.) and in the systematic treatment given to psychology by Aristotle (384–322) (see Kantor, 1963, pp. 61–151). The most important contribution to contemporary behaviorism from this era was perhaps the *naturalism* of classical Greek philosophy. Put broadly, this view is embodied in two assumptions: (a) that nature is a proper subject matter for scientific investigation and (b) that out of such investigation would come descriptions of natural laws concerning the subject matter. More centrally, naturalism holds that nothing exists outside of nature—nothing has supernatural or more than natural significance.

This perspective is consonant with contemporary behaviorism's view (a) that behavior is the proper subject matter for a natural science of psychology, (b) that the study of behavior will yield natural laws descriptive of it (cf. Grunbaum, 1952; Homans, 1969), and (c) that nothing in psychology exists outside of behavior, whether behavior be public or private (e.g., covert or within the skin; see Moore, 1980; Skinner, 1945). In this view, behavior is the unique, emergent property of person–environment interactions and, as such, may be studied in relation to (a) a person's biological structure and functioning, which is largely the province of physiological psychology, or to (b) a person's environment, which has largely been the focus of behavioral psychology. Both physiological and behavioral psychology are fundamental for understanding behavior, but each develops its independent natural laws, neither set of which explains nor should contradict the subject matter of the other.

This naturalistic Greek philosophy contrasts with the idealism and mentalism that would soon come to infuse philosophical psychology and which remains pervasive today. This change was wrought from disruptive cultural, social, and economic factors in the ancient world that led to a turning inward toward personal concerns and the rise of new theological views that were antithetical to a science of behavior. Moreover, naturalistic Greek thinking, notably that of Plato and Aristotle, was reinterpreted to support an idealized concept of the soul and mind that is now deeply ingrained in Western philosophical thought, especially in the dichotomy between mind and body. With the decline of the Hellenic civilization and later that of the Roman empire, so, too, declined scientific perspectives on behavior (Kantor, 1963). A culture more compatible with, and nurturant of, a naturalistic psychology would not occur again for more than a thousand years.

Modern Philosophy

When the rekindling of naturalistic psychology began again, it was as part of the general emergence of modern philosophy during the Renaissance and the soon-to-come scientific revolution. Credit for the role of modern philosophy in psychology is usually given to Rene Descartes (1596–1650), in large part through distinctions he drew between mind and body. From here on, psychology would develop to some degree along two separate lines—one interested in the immaterial mind and the other interested in the material body. Neither line of development, however, characterizes contemporary behaviorism, for contemporary behaviorism is neither mentalistic nor physiologically reductionistic. Descartes also posited that only humans have minds but that their bodies and behaviors, and those of nonhumans, could be conceived of mechanistically; that is, the workings of behavior could be accounted for in terms of mechanical cause-and-effect principles. In this, Descartes and the early philosophical materialists (e.g., La Mettrie, 1709–1751; Cabinis, 1757–1808) contributed to psychology not only Cartesian dualism but also the beginnings of a reflexive, stimulus response (S-R), mechanistic account of behavior.

Contemporary behaviorism is commonly understood as being mechanistic in its adherence to a reflexive, S-R account of behavior, but this is a mistaken impression. First, at the level of behavior, the unconditioned S-R reflex relationship (e.g., the knee-jerk reaction), referred to as "respondent" behavior in contemporary behaviorism, comprises but a minor part of human activity of psychological interest. Reflex or respondent (or classical) conditioning plays a slightly larger role but pales in comparison to what is generally taken to be the other major class of behavior—*operant* behavior, which also encompasses what is typically referred to as "purposeful" or "intentional" behavior (see Day, 1976a; Skinner, 1974).

Second, contemporary behaviorism is not philosophically mechanistic (Ringen, 1976) but rather is contextualistic in world view (Hayes, 1986; Reese, 1982; see Pepper, 1942, pp. 323–379), especially in its interbehavioral manifestations (Morris, 1982, 1984). In contrast to linear cause-and-effect (S-R) mechanistic thinking, contextualism holds (a) to an integrated-field view in which the form of a response has no immutable function but is rather just one of a number of participants in a field of factors that comprise behavior; (b) to strong, reciprocal, dynamic interactions between person and environment; and

(c) to "historical causation," which stresses the evolutionary nature of current functional relationships between behavior and environment. In contextualism, then, a person's response is understood in terms of its interrelationships with the other factors in the integrated field, its functional interdependence with them, and its historical context—all of which give it "meaning."

British Empiricism and Associationism

British *empiricism* emerged, partially, as a philosophical movement in opposition to another of Descartes's views, held as well by Immanuel Kant (1724–1804)—that humans are born with innate ideas about the universe and that subsequent knowledge was, in large part, derived rationally and deductively therefrom. In contrast, the British empiricist view, typically attributed to John Locke (1632–1704), was that ideas are not innate but instead come from experience; the mind was, so to speak, a tabula rasa. Empiricism took a variety of forms in the hands of other British and Scottish philosophers, most notably Thomas Hobbes (1588–1679), David Hume (1711–1776), David Hartley (1705–1757), James Mill (1773–1836), and John Stuart Mill (1806–1873), but the role of experience was always primary.

Contrary to some misunderstandings of empiricism and the metaphor of the tabula rasa (now, the "black box"), empiricist logic does not rule out the effects of biological factors on behavior—likewise, neither does contemporary behaviorism. As for the British empiricists, Locke himself took some innate factors as givens (e.g., native curiosity). His empiricist point was simply that what is important psychologically is not given at birth. Likewise, in contemporary behaviorism, biology is accorded its place as a participant in all behavior and as a source of individual differences, both within and across people, but not as a source of behavior by itself. Behavior emerges from organism–environment interactions, and the laws of behavior describe relationships between responding and the environment. In this sense, biology is the context for, not the cause of, behavior.

An additional feature of much of British and Scottish empiricism was its *associationism:* Whereas simple ideas came from experience, complex ideas were derived from the association of simple ideas. Controversies arose, of course, about the quantitative and qualitative differences between simple and complex ideas and about what constituted the basic elemental ideas that were associated. Likewise, within contemporary behaviorism, similar discussions abound as to the proper level of analysis and unit of behavior—issues that have concerned the field since its inception (Skinner, 1935) and that remain critical today (see Thompson & Zeiler, 1986).

Although contemporary behaviorism has some associationistic characteristics, it is not philosophically associationistic in outlook (Branch, 1977). Associationism implies a molecular view that suggests that fundamental, atomic units of response and environment exist and may be identified *a priori* on the basis of their form or structure alone and that their contiguity multiplied out somehow produces and explains more complex behavior. In contrast, contemporary behaviorism adheres to a molar perspective in which the units of behavior cannot be identified *a priori* and in which complex behavior is not merely the accumulation of simpler, discrete stimulus-response associations (Lubinski & Thompson, 1986). Rather, behavior is defined in terms of interrelated functional classes of stimuli and responses (Skinner, 1935; see Meehl, 1986) and is not restricted by temporal contiguity but rather is enriched by accepting action-at-a-temporal-distance (Marr, 1983). Contemporary behaviorism is, of course, largely analytic in research strategy and tactics, but this does not mean it is "elementaristic" or reductionistic. Little psychological sense accrues to associationism and its related molecular views, for it is at the molar level that human activity takes on psychological significance (see Day, 1980, on the gestaltlike, purposive nature of contemporary behaviorism; cf. Krechevesky, 1939; Verplanck, 1954).

Psychological Science

Like the other sciences before it, psychology eventually separated itself from pure philosophy. The views of Descartes and others gave way to experimental as opposed to philosophical claims about human action. The first stirrings of this activity occurred in experimental sensory physiology, for it was in sensation and perception that the mind and experience were said to interact. Of fundamental importance here was the work of Hermann von Helmholtz (1821–1894; see von Helmholtz, 1857/1962) and Gustav Fechner (1801–1887; see Fechner, 1860/1966), the latter of whom is considered the founder of psychophysics (see Boring, 1950).

Experimental sensory physiology burgeoned during the 1880s, but without a unifying philosophical commitment for its many unrelated findings. The first systematization of this work, both empirically and philosophically, is typically accredited to Wilhelm Wundt (1832–1920; see Wundt, 1910), who is also regarded as the founder of experimental psychology. Later, Wundt's views would be developed into the first school of psychology—*structuralism*—by his student in the United States, Edward B. Titchener (1867–1927; see Titchener, 1899).

Wundt's structural psychology may be characterized in three ways: (1) the subject matter of psychology was the mind—the immediate experience of sensations and feelings; (2) his experimental method was introspection—the *having* or observing of immediate experience; and (3) the problem of psychology was to analyze experience into its elemental units, to examine the nature of the interconnections, and to determine the laws of the interconnections. This was the working out of associationism in detail.

Structuralism and Functionalism

Wundt's primary concerns were structural: what was the mind constructed of, and how? In contrast, Wundt's rival in the United States, William James (1842–1910; see James, 1890), proposed that what was important about the mind was not its structure but rather its function, that is, what use or purpose it served. Thus, with James at Harvard University comes the founding of *functionalism;* at the University of Chicago, these views would be expanded upon by John Dewey (1859–1952; see Dewey, 1896; Dewey & Bentley, 1949) and George Herbert Mead (1863–1931; see Mead, 1934). Functionalism was focally interested in the utility, adaptiveness, and practical consequences of the mind and consciousness and much less in their structure. In an analogous sense, this is the orientation of contemporary behaviorism—it is interested less in the structural characteristics of responding and more in its function.

This dichotomy between structure and function underlies several unfortunate misunderstandings in psychology, then as now. In any case, what really is at issue is not the inherent correctness of structural or functional views but the nature of questions asked about behavior and the use to which the answers are put. Essentially, structuralism asks *what* questions, whereas functionalism asks *why* questions. With respect to the mind, *what* questions about its structure are orthogonal to *why* questions about its function. The same is true of behavior, that is, behavior may be studied to reveal features of its structure (i.e., its form or topography) or features of its function (i.e., the variables to which it is lawfully related) (see Catania, 1973, 1978). Contemporary behaviorism focuses on function, eschewing the possibility of a fundamental understanding of behavior based on its structure alone. To know what people do is not to know why they do it. The latter—response function—is best understood on the basis of the interrelationships between responding and the context in which it occurs.

Functionalism entered psychology from the philosophies of James, Dewey, and Mead through James R. Angell (1869–1949; see Angell, 1904) and Harvey Carr (1873–1954; see Carr, 1925) at the University of Chicago. As a school of psychology, functionalism was not well organized. Thus, although important in counteracting structuralism, it perhaps served more as foundation for the *classical behaviorism* of John B. Watson (1878–1956; see Watson, 1913). The emergence of classical behaviorism, though, was strongly intertwined with and influenced by earlier traditions in experimental medicine, the Darwinian revolution, and the biological sciences, for which we turn back to the 1800s.

Darwin, Natural Selection, and Animal Behavior

Contemporary behaviorism is actually less a product of early experimental psychology than of developments in the biological sciences, largely related to the work of Charles Darwin (1809–1882). Darwin's development of evolutionary theory and his thesis concerning natural selection were an impetus both to functionalism and to the eventual emergence of classical behaviorism. Moreover, evolutionary thinking is today at the heart of much of contemporary behaviorism (Skinner, 1981). An additional, related influence was that of

Claude Bernard (1813–1878; see Bernard, 1965), whose work in experimental medicine reflects well some of the conceptual and logical characteristics of current experimental practices in contemporary behaviorism (Thompson, 1984).

The influence of Darwin's work in biology and on the general intellectual milieu of the times is well known. With respect to the science of behavior, the primary issue had to do with the continuity of mind. Prior to Darwin, non-human animals were commonly assumed to be without minds. Darwin, however, made the case not only for evolutionary continuity in biological structure and functioning across species (Darwin, 1859, 1871) but also for continuity in mental structure and functioning, which meant across the minds of humans and nonhumans (Darwin, 1872). Darwin's views thus set the occasion for investigations aimed at affirming or disaffirming the continuity of mind across species.

But how was the mind to be studied? It could not be studied directly because of its immaterial nature. For humans, verbal reports of introspectively observed material could be obtained, and these were generally taken to suffice (Titchener, 1899; Wundt, 1910). With nonhumans, however, verbal reports were not to be had; only nonverbal behavior could be studied, and hence that is what was studied. Still, behavior was not a subject matter in its own right, but rather the basis on which inferences could be made about animal minds: this is methodological behaviorism.

The study of nonhuman behavior in this context emerged formally as comparative psychology, beginning with the work of George John Romanes (1848–1894; see Romanes, 1882). Romanes argued that nonhuman minds could be known by inference: If nonhumans and humans displayed similar behavior (e.g., fear or problem solving), then the supposedly concomitant subjective mental states of humans could be inferred to exist in nonhumans as well. Romanes's inferences, though, were flawed by his logical fallacy of affirming the consequent (see Morris, Higgins, & Bickel, 1982b); moreover, his observations were criticized for being too anecdotal in nature. C. Lloyd Morgan (1852–1936; see Morgan, 1894) and others called for parsimony in these matters, arguing basically that if nonhuman behavior could be explained on simpler grounds (e.g., conditioning), then those explanations were to be preferred to the more complex ones (e.g., in terms of mind and consciousness). The comparative physiologist, Jaques Loeb (1859–1924; see Loeb, 1900, 1916), went a step further and called for the restriction of concepts such as the mind, intelligence, and consciousness to what would later be called "operational definitions"—objective, a priori, positively agreed-upon definitions (e.g., consciousness can be presumed when respondent conditioning can be observed). These considerations aside, the mind was not foresaken; it was just approached with increasing care.

From Morgan and through Loeb, comparative psychology quickly advanced in its experimental procedures, research practices, and conceptual development. These contributions and those of Claude Bernard in experimental medicine (Bernard, 1865; see Thompson, 1984) can be seen in several ways in contemporary behaviorism as well, several of which have come to define central characteristics of the approach, as we will describe below.

Continuity in Behavior

First, contemporary behaviorism concurs with continuity across species with respect to biology and behavior. As general modes of adaptation, the behavioral processes (e.g., respondent and operant conditioning) and basic behavioral relationships (e.g., unconditioned respondent behavior and unconditioned reinforcement) are taken to be products of phylogenic selection and to hold across species to one degree or another. No tabula rasa exists here.

The literature on the experimental analysis of human behavior supports this assumption of continuity in many respects, at least in continuity from other species to humans (see, e.g., Higgins & Morris, 1984), though perhaps not always from humans to other species (see Lowe, 1979). Accepting continuity in behavioral processes, though, is not the same as holding that behavior itself is continuous across species: cross-species differences obviously exist in biological interaction with the behavioral processes (e.g., biology is context for behavior), in basic unconditioned behavioral relationships (e.g., preparedness; see Logue, 1979; Seligman & Hagar, 1972), and in the contributions of the behavioral processes and the unconditioned relationships (see Reese, 1986; Schwartz, 1974). Furthermore, the possibility exists that some behavioral processes may apply only to humans (e.g., with respect to verbal behavior, see Lowe, 1979; Skinner, 1938, p. 424). None of these possibilities takes behavior out of the realm of natural science; these are empirical not philosophical matters (see *The Experimental Analysis of Human Behavior Bulletin,* 1983–present).

Parsimony

Contemporary behaviorism adheres to one sense of parsimony embodied in naturalism: It seeks explanations of behavior at the level of behavior itself. This analytic strategy does not deny the occurrence of behavioral relationships referred to by such terms as *consciousness, personality, intentionality,* or *responsibility.* Although subjective, these terms describe important characteristics of human behavior described by members of our linguistic community (see Deitz & Arrington, 1984; Morris, 1985a; Skinner, 1945). The use of these terms in contemporary behaviorism, though, is restricted to description and not applied to explanation (though even then such terms are generally eschewed because of the excess mentalistic connotation often conveyed; see Hineline, 1980). Thus, for example, the labels *antisocial personality* and *conscience* may be taken to describe certain person–environment interactions, but they cannot in turn be taken to refer to hypothetical causal constructs said to explain those interactions. That would reify the descriptions and be tautological. Instead, the interactions described as antisocial personality and conscience need explaining at the level of behavior, taking into account the behavioral processes involved and the historical and current contexts in which they occur. In an interesting sense, explanations of a behavioral nature are more complex than those that appeal to hypothetical constructs; the latter are simple in comparison and free for the asking. That is, antisocial behavior and feelings of guilt are easy to explain in terms of hypothetical personality structures and cognitive states, whereas, in contrast, the behavior and the feeling, the specific conditions under which they occur, and the historical and current context of which they are a function are much more difficult to analyze, especially after the fact.

Research Methodology

As mentioned earlier, contemporary behaviorism owes more of its historical and philosophical background to the biological sciences than to institutionalized scientific psychology. This point is made especially clear with respect to research methodology. To be specific, the research logics that emerged from Claude Bernard's experimental medicine and Loeb's work in general physiology are strikingly similar to those employed today in the experimental analysis of behavior and in applied behavior analysis. Loeb exerted a strong influence on W. J. Crozier's (1892–1955) approach to general physiology (see Crozier & Hoagland, 1934); Crozier, in turn, directly influenced B. F. Skinner, whose research he supervised at Harvard University during the late 1920s (Day, 1980, pp. 223–225; Kazdin, 1978, pp. 92–93; cf. McKearney, 1977).

To put these matters succinctly, the experimental and applied analyses of behavior are committed to (a) taking behavior as a subject matter in its own right, rather than as a manifestation of something else; (b) describing functional relationships between responding and the conditions under which it occurs—for it is from these relationships that theory is inductively derived (see Turner, 1967); and (c) employing experimental control over individual cases of these functional relationships where variability is taken as lawful and its causes determinable, as opposed to being to some degree random and in need of statistical control. These views were elaborated on by Skinner (1950, 1956) and are now oft-defining characteristics of contemporary behaviorism (see Johnston & Pennypacker, 1980; Sidman, 1960).

As a brief aside, these views about the analysis of behavior hold when the interest is in describing lawful relationships or principles that operate at the level of the behavior of individuals as well as discovering and refining effective applied behavioral procedures. Different research methods are, of course, called for in answering other types of questions about behavior. Questions of an actuarial nature especially require group statistical methods (see Gottshalk, Davidson, Mayer, & Gensheimer, Chapter 15; Jones, Chapter 16, both in this volume). At issue is the match between the questions asked and methods used, not the inherent appropriateness or inappropriateness of one strategy or the other (cf. Johnston & Pennypacker, 1980; Michael, 1974, 1985, pp. 110–114).

Selection by Consequences

In that evolution proceeds through the natural selection of biological characteristics via their effect upon reproduction, Darwin gave credence to a form of causation in biology that might be called "selection by consequences." In this case, the selection occurs through "contingencies of survival" that occur over the lifetime of a species. Such causation is analogous to perhaps the most fundamental principle in contemporary behaviorism—reinforcement. Reinforcement is a form of behavioral adaptation that occurs in the lifetime of the individual, where the consequence of a response affects its strength in the behavioral repertoire (and under what circumstances). Skinner has written extensively on the parallels between the contingencies of survival and the contingencies of reinforcement as well as on how the former influence the latter (Skinner, 1966b, 1975, 1981). In addition, he has also noted an important sense in which cultural practices, and indeed entire cultures, evolve through a similar process (Skinner, 1971).

Evolutionary thinking was also to have another earlier influence, this time on philosophy, in ways important to contemporary behaviorism, and especially in its contextualistic world view—*pragmatism*.

Pragmatism

Earlier, we mentioned William James and the founding of the functionalist school of psychology, which stood in contrast to structuralism. James's functionalism yielded a secondary but central contribution to contemporary behaviorism—the philosophy of knowledge known as pragmatism (James, 1907; see Day, 1980, pp. 234–237). In the hands of James, and as influenced by the biological concept of adaptiveness, pragmatism asserts that knowledge is relative and that absolute truth impossible to obtain. Put more simply, knowing is human behavior, and human behavior is adaptive in relationship to its historical and current context. Thus knowing the "truth" can never get outside of itself for some absolute evaluation because that, too, is behavior that is adaptive—and so forth.

Under this functionalist epistemology, the criterion for truth in contemporary behaviorism is different from Loeb's operationism and what would later emerge as the criterion of truth-by-agreement in logical positivism. Given that what is "true" in pragmatism cannot stand independently from the behavior of the scientist, the truth criterion in contemporary behaviorism becomes a pragmatic one—effective action. In other words, what is true is that which affords the most effective description, prediction, and control of behavior; as for control, what is at issue is what controls behavior—not control invoked for control's sake. These are the criteria against which competing views—both behavioral and nonbehavioral—must be judged. Truth is always empirical, never given. Pragmatism, of course, is more complex than this, and the interested reader might consult James (1907), Pierce (1940), Rucker (1969), and Scheffler (1974) for more detailed accounts.

Conclusion

As summarized here, comparative psychology was an active research enterprise in the years leading up to the emergence of J. B. Watson's classical behaviorism. This work contributed conceptually to behaviorism as a system of psychology; it contributed methodologically to research strategies and tactics; and it contributed empirically through work from many different quarters. Two of the latter are especially important. From the work of the Russian reflexologists, Vladamir Bechterev (1857–1927) and Ivan P. Pavlov (1849–1936), Watson drew his basic behavioral process—the conditioned reflex (i.e., respondent behavior) (Bechterev, 1913; Pavlov, 1927). And, from the work of C. Lloyd Morgan and Edward L. Thorndike (1874–1949; see Thorndike, 1911) came research on the importance of the consequences of behavior—the law of effect (i.e., the reinforcement of operant behavior), which would influence post-Watsonian behaviorism. Let us now finally turn to Watson's views.

Classical Behaviorism and Beyond

Classical behaviorism was born of many of the characteristics described thus far, especially naturalism, evolutionary theory, comparative psychology, and functionalism. Classical behaviorism, though, is not identical with contemporary behaviorism, largely due to differences with respect to operationism (e.g., classical behaviorism's sometime adherence to methodological behaviorism), the principles of behavior (i.e., classical behaviorism's adherence to respondent processes only), and analyses of specific sorts of human behaviors (e.g., thinking as only subvocal speech). Nonetheless, the emergence of classical behaviorism through the work and promotion of John B. Watson (Watson, 1913, 1919, 1924) represented a major change in psychology. Here, for the first time, was a modern, self-styled, objective, and functional psychology that eschewed mentalism, that emphasized a naturalistic approach to psychology, and that took behavior to be its subject matter.

The details of Watson's career and his psychology and of the emergence of classical behaviorism are widely available, though often oversimplified and misleading (Todd & Morris, 1986); thus several comments are in order. First, Watson was better prepared for his undertaking than is generally assumed. To begin with, he was well trained in functionalist philosophy and psychology at the University of Chicago as well as in anatomy and physiology. Moreover, as a comparative psychologist, he was among the leaders of his generation. Second, Watson's supposedly bold claims in support of environmentalism have mostly been taken out of context from the rest of his writing and from the general character of the psychology of that era. Much of his earliest work in comparative psychology was strongly ethological in nature, and his later statements about the power of the environment in molding human character were often well qualified, and at least no stronger than assertions made by others with countervailing views.

Perhaps one of the more interesting aspects of Watson's classical behaviorism, from the standpoint of philosophy, was Watson's seemingly equivocal adherence to a thoroughly naturalistic versus a methodological behaviorism. The formalization and development of the latter were influenced strongly through certain moves in philosophy at this time.

Operationism and Positivism

Operational definitions of the sort promoted by Loeb became an institutional characteristic of science through the influence of the logical positivist movement in European philosophy during the 1920s (i.e., the Vienna Circle); they also quickly infused psychology during the 1930s (see Moore, 1975, 1985; Smith, 1986). The message seemed clear at the time: If psychology wanted to be a real science, it would have to develop objective definitions for its subjective terms and otherwise exclude that which was essentially subjective and private from its subject matter because it was unamenable to the objective criterion of truth-by-agreement. Operationism could only be applied to what was publicly observable, and anything private or subjective had to be recast in operational terms.

The methodological behaviorism spawned from this movement became a dominating force in American psychology but has had several unfortunate effects (see Moore, 1981). First, operational definitions and positivist philosophy became so narrow that terms lost the character of what they originally referred to (e.g., the meaning of *intelligence* is not effectively captured by the following sentence: Intelligence is what intelligence tests measure). Second, although ostensively objective, the movement did not satisfactorily resolve the mind–body problem because the mind was still taken to stand in some immaterial relationship to behavior—but to be outside the realm of scientific psychology. And third, too much of this movement ignores the involvement of the scientist in science. Science is the behavior of scientists, and the behavior of scientists is a function of the same sorts of variables as is any other behavior. These are matters of epistemology that cannot be glossed over with the patina of objectivism (Day, 1983; Moore, 1981).

Much of psychology has continued in the mold of this sort of operationism and positivism, but not without protest, most commonly from phenomenologists, humanists, gestalt psychologists, and psychoanalysts. And, contrary to common assumption, contemporary behaviorism is also critical of this approach. In contrast to the operationism of the logical positivists, that of contemporary behaviorism has evolved in part from the positivism of Ernst Mach (1838–1926; see Mach, 1983/1960). In this view, the problem is not how to make subjective terms objective by *a priori* operational definitions but rather to discover and describe the circumstances that lead people to talk in subjective terms or about that which is private (i.e., to find out what controls their speaking in subjective terms). The epistemological issue, then, is linguistic, and not a matter of logic (Deitz & Arrington, 1984; Skinner, 1945). In contemporary behaviorism, the referents of subjective terms descriptive of behavior (e.g., *antisocial personality, conscience, mentally ill,* or *cognitive dysfunction*) are for the most part taken to be the behaviors of people in context. The problem is how to account for the variables affecting a term's use; that, when accomplished, is the operational definition of the term.

In summary, contemporary behaviorism does not rule out that which is subjective and private (e.g., behavior within the skin) from potential scientific analysis. It simply accepts them as behavior–environment relationships that are sometimes private (inaccessibility or phenomenally), difficult to talk about, and even more difficult to analyze (see Moore, 1975, 1985; Skinner, 1945, 1957). This brief rendering of contemporary behaviorism's version of operationism and positivist philosophy does a disservice to its epistemology, but at least the view can be seen to be more phenomenological and less scientistic than typically thought (for further discussion, see Day, 1969a, 1980, pp. 225–137; Giorgi, 1975; Marr, 1985; Skinner, 1945, 1957; see also Arrington & Deitz, 1986; Day, 1969b; Deitz & Arrington, 1986; and Morris, 1985a, for contemporary behaviorism's relationship to the analytic philosophy of Ludwig Wittgenstein, 1889–1951; Wittgenstein, 1953; see also Malcolm, 1977).

Neobehaviorism

Methodological behaviorism has remained a dominant force in psychology. After Watson, came the neobehavioristic learning theories of the 1930s and 1940s. Edwin Tolman (1886–1961) developed his purposive behaviorism in an attempt to provide objective accounts of purpose and intention through the use of intervening variables (e.g., expectations and cognitive maps) (Tolman, 1932). Clark Hull (1884–1952) proposed a drive-reduction theory of learning in which hypothetical constructs (e.g., drives) mediated the relationships between behavior and environment (Hull, 1952).

From these neobehavioral theories emerged psychological social learning theories of human behavior. The first of these attempted to operationalize psychodynamic psychology in terms of Hullian principles and concepts in what was called psychodynamic (or dynamic) social learning theory (e.g., Dollard & Miller, 1950; Miller & Dollard, 1941; Sears, Maccoby, & Levin, 1957). A second version of social learning theory followed Tolman's more cognitive orientation, in what is now referred to as cognitive social learning theory (e.g., Bandura, 1969, 1977; see Platt & Prout, Chapter 18, this volume). These theories, and others, continue in the mold of a methodological behaviorism in which behavior exists primarily as an index of hypothetical constructs of more central interest that are, in themselves, unamenable to direct analysis. Contemporary behaviorism represents one of the few alternatives to these views.

Conclusion

Contemporary behaviorism reflects the continued evolution of that which came before it, though not in ways conventionally thought. The perspective we have offered on contemporary behaviorism is different from that often attributed to behaviorism in general (see Morris, 1985b; Todd & Morris, 1983). Typically, behaviorism is presented as mechanistic, solely S-R in process, formal and associationistic, narrowly operational, and without concern for the private and subjective. In contrast, contemporary behaviorism is contextual and pragmatic in world view, adaptive and evolutional in nature, functional and holistic in analysis, and, in a way, phenomenological and capable of confronting what is private and subjective—yet at the same time being naturalistic. Readers interested in pursuing the philosophical implications of these views are encouraged to turn to the citations provided before or to the original sources themselves (see, e.g., Kantor, 1924, 1926, 1945, 1947, 1950, 1953, 1959, 1971, 1981, 1982, 1984; Skinner, 1945, 1953, 1957, 1969, 1971, 1974).

A CONCEPTUAL SYSTEM OF ANALYSIS

Now that we have introduced the history and philosophy of contemporary behaviorism, we turn to a conceptual system for the analysis of behavior that stems from the views presented thus far, especially as contemporary behaviorism interrelates radical behaviorism and interbehavioral psychology (Morris, 1982, 1984). In presenting this material, we hope also to facilitate the reading of subsequent chapters by briefly introducing the principles of behavior and, where appropriate, mentioning the related applied behavioral procedures. Our intent, here, is not to provide a theory of crime and delinquency (e.g., Burgess & Akers, 1966; see Braukmann, Kirigin, & Wolf, 1980) but rather to discuss the stuff of which a theory might be made.

To forecast slightly, in the conceptual system we offer, human behavior is analyzed and synthesized in terms of an integrated field of five factors: (a) the person as a biological entity and as contributor of response forms and functions to behavioral interactions; (b) the environment as a structural entity and as contributor of stimulus forms and functions to behavioral interactions; (c) the media of contact between the person and environment (e.g., light and sound waves); (d) the historical context of person–environment interactions, through which current stimulus and response functions have evolved; and (e) the current setting, both biological and environmental, which influences which of the evolved person–environment interactions can and will occur on a particular occasion. Each of the five factors varies on many dimensions of form and function and, as a group, they interact dynamically. Moreover, each is necessary for an analysis of behavior—no one factor is a sole cause. In what follows, we describe the conceptual system composed of these factors (with the exception of the media, which are taken as given), how they interrelate, and how they provide a unifying view of human behavior.

As for the behavioral principles and applied behavioral procedures, we will offer a brief introduction to some of the basic terms and concepts. Unfortunately, in doing so, we will seemingly present the principles and procedures as being rather simplified in content and rigor and lacking in important nuances and technical complexity. In actuality, the principles and procedures are quite the opposite; that they seem otherwise is the fault of abbreviation on our part. For more thorough accounts of this material and for a better sense of the current state of the science, both basic and applied, readers might consult the journals cited in the introductory section of the chapter, but let us offer a few additional references. For systematic introductions to the basic principles, we recommend Holland and Skinner (1961), Keller (1969), Reynolds (1975), and Whaley and Malott (1971); for intermediate level texts, see Catania (1984), Fantino and Logan (1979), and Millenson and Leslie (1979); for higher level analyses, see Honig (1966) and Honig and Staddon (1977); and for advanced professional reviews, see the two series, *Advances in Analysis of Behavior* (Harzem & Zeiler, 1981; Zeiler & Harzem, 1979, 1983) and *Quantitative Analyses of Behavior* (Commons, Herrnstein, & Rachlin, 1982a; Commons, Herrnstein, & Wagner, 1982b, 1985; Commons, Kacelnik, & Shettleworth, in press; Commons, Mazur, Nevin, & Rachlin, 1987; Commons & Nevin, 1981).

For material in applied behavior analysis, we recommend Cooper, Heron, and Heward (1987), Kazdin (1984), and Martin and Pear (1983) for introductions; Catania and Brigham (1978) and Leitenberg (1976) for intermediate level analyses; and *Progress in Behavior Modification* (e.g., Hersen, Eisler, & Miller, 1982) and the *Annual Review of Behavior Therapy: Theory and Practice* (e.g., Franks, Wilson, Kendall, & Brownell, 1984) for ongoing professional reviews. For coverage of applied behavioral procedures and programs related to crime and delinquency, see Nietzel (1979) on crime and Stumphauzer (1973, 1979, 1986) on delinquency. Still more specific material on crime and delinquency is available in Ayllon and Milan (1979), Bishop and Blanchard (1971), Cohen and Filipzak (1971), Goldstein, Carr, Davidson, and Wehr (1981), Goldstein and Glick (1987), Ribes-Inesta and Bandura (1976), Schwartz and Goldiamond (1975), Stuart (1981), and Tharp and Wetzel (1969). Finally, this handbook's individual chapters offer comprehensive overviews of applied behavioral procedures and programs and should obviously be consulted as well. Indeed, in the material to follow, we cite specific chapters that are particularly illustrative of the material being introduced. All of this is said by way of an overview; now let us begin with the first of the four factors in the conceptual system of analysis being offered.

The Person

People and their behaviors may be conceptualized and described at three different levels: (a) in terms of the person's biological structure, (b) in terms of the person's response forms, and (c) in terms of the person's response functions. Each level represents a viable subject matter for scientific inquiry, but the last—response function—is of focal interest because it is here that people interact with the environment in ways that comprise what is most interesting and important in the account of behavior. Because all three levels are necessarily a part of behavior, however, we start with the first.

Biological Structure

For our purposes, the person's "biological structure" refers essentially to anatomical, physiological, and neurological structure and functioning. The biological structure is a product of the interaction among three specific subfactors: (a) phylogenic evolution, (b) ontogenic conditions of prenatal development (e.g., parental alcohol consumption), and (c) the physical postnatal conditions of development (e.g., nutrition, disease, poisoning, and injury). These subfactors are not static but are in continuous, reciprocal interaction (see Gollin, 1981). The biological structure is forever changing, thereby affecting both response form and function.

Biological Structure and Response Form. With respect to the effects of the biological structure on response form, the ever-changing matrix of biological factors defines the limits and capabilities of what a person can and cannot physically accomplish. Individual variability exists, of course, in the imposition of the biological structure on response form, both across individuals and within individuals over time. The importance of this source of variability, however, is not easily determined. As for such socially complex behaviors as crime and delinquency, the problem has remained a difficult empirical and conceptual issue for many years (Gould, 1981; see, e.g., Yochelson & Samenow, 1976; Borgaonkar & Shah, 1974) and has been the source of heated scientific and idiological debates over the relative contributions of nature and nurture to behavior (see, e.g., Lewontin, Rose, & Kamin, 1984; Wilson & Herrnstein, 1985). The resolution of this issue does not seem imminent, however; indeed, the problem may be intractable given the questions being asked (Anastasi & Foley, 1948).

Biological Structure and Response Function. With respect to the effects of the biological structure on response function, the phylogenic contributions establish the ways in which a person's behavior adapts to and interacts with the environment. These general response functions are affected in three ways by phylogeny (see Skinner, 1966b, 1975, 1977).

First, and most generally, people inherit behavioral modes of adaptation that are respondent and operant in nature. In respondent functioning, behavior reflects the interaction between respondent (reflex) responding and antecedent environmental events said to *elicit* the responses. These antecedents are technically referred to as eliciting stimuli. Respondents are reflexive and autonomic in nature (e.g., eye blinks and knee jerks), though they may be more extended and "instinctive" as well (e.g., pain-elicited aggression). In contrast, in operant functioning, behavior reflects the interaction between operant responses and consequent environmental events, the latter of which increase or decrease the rate of responding; these events are called reinforcing and punishing stimuli, respectively. Operant responding, too, comes under the influence of antecedent environmental events that are said to "set the occasion" for the response as a function of their relationship to behavioral consequences; these are technically referred to as discriminative stimuli. Operants represent the greater part of human behavior and all of that which may be called purposeful or intentional (Day, 1976a; Skinner, 1971, 1974).

The second way in which phylogeny operates is to establish certain *unconditioned* respondent and operant relationships, that is, relationships established through natural selection and hence likely to have been important for survival. In respondent behavior, unconditioned stimuli may elicit respondents without prior conditioning. In operant behavior, unconditioned (or primary) reinforcers and unconditioned punishers affect the subsequent occurrence of the responses they follow without appreciable prior environmental interaction. For example, under appropriate conditions of deprivation, food, liquid, and other biological necessities function as primary or unconditioned reinforcers; likewise, conditions that are physically harmful typically function as primary or unconditioned punishers. The functions of these unconditioned consequences have clear and obvious influences on the survival of the species as well as of the individual.

The third way in which phylogeny affects behavior is through the inherited processes of respondent and operant conditioning. These processes represent most directly the means by which a person's behavior adapts to, and interacts with, the environment on a moment-to-moment basis. In respondent behavior, relationships between unconditioned eliciting stimuli and neutral stimuli can impart a conditioned eliciting stimulus function to the latter; such stimuli are called conditioned (eliciting) stimuli. The responses these conditioned eliciting stimuli produce are called conditioned respondents (e.g., the conditioning of fear of strangers).

In the operant case, relationships between unconditioned reinforcers and neutral stimuli can impart a conditioned reinforcing function to the latter; such stimuli are then called conditioned (or *secondary*) reinforcers (e.g., money or signs of social approval from peers). Conditioned punishers (e.g., social disapproval) result from similar relationships between neutral stimuli and unconditioned punishers. In addition, other relationships among reinforcement, punishment, and neutral stimuli can impart a discriminative function to stimuli that, when they occur, evoke behavior that in the past has led to those consequences (e.g., the presence of another person as discriminative for approach or avoidance). As for operant behavior itself, most all of it appears to be acquired and maintained in the lifetime of an individual.

For contemporary behaviorism, the biological structure is primarily of interest in its role as a context for behavior: The biological structure is a contextual condition that determines what behavior can or cannot physically occur at a particular time, given that the potential for behavior has already been established by the historical context (see subsequent sections of this chapter). The effects of the biological structure are dynamic and hence exert different effects at different times, sometimes over the span of many years (e.g., physical maturation) and sometimes more briefly (e.g., the effects of drugs). As a physical context for behavior, however, the biological structure does not "cause" behavior nor does it directly affect the basic behavioral principles *per se*. What it affects is the possible physical occurrence of behavior (e.g., anatomically, physiologically, and neurologically) as well as the extent and strength of specific relationships into which behavior may enter with respect to the environment. In our later section on the current context, we will discuss the behavioral effects of biological variables that interact more directly with behavior.

Response Form

The second level at which people may be conceptualized and described is in terms of their behavior's response form, structure, or topography, that is, in terms of the physical characteristics of responding. All human responses have a form or structure that may be described (or potentially described) by physical measurement alone. A formal analysis, as such, entails objective, physical descriptions of activities, both simple and complex.

Such descriptions, of course, are difficult or impossible to obtain when the responses entailed occur within the skin (e.g., respondent aspects of emotion or operant aspects of "mental" arithmetic). The problem of obtaining truth-by-agreement about such covert events has led the strict operationist to put them aside. Within the epistemology of contemporary behaviorism, however, private events remain an important part of the subject matter, and to dismiss them out of hand would lead to certain embarrassing gaps in the analysis of behavior (Skinner, 1957, Chapter 19). The privacy of these responses, nonetheless, presents serious problems with respect to how we learn to talk about them (Skinner, 1945), our reliability in reporting their occurrence (Skinner, 1974, Chapter 1), and their causal status for other responses (Branch, 1987; Day, 1976b; Hayes & Brownstein, 1986; Moore, 1980). In general, the contemporary behavioral view is that covert responding is simply a part of more behavior to analyze, not a special source of autonomous personal control—at least not anymore than any other behavior is a source of control for other responding. How we can act on or analyze such activity effectively is the problem—and a serious one.

In any event, whether public or private, the analysis of response forms is not unimportant to understanding behavior, nor is it incompatible with an analysis of response functions (Catania, 1973, 1978). Analyses of response forms are useful in gaining a more complete understanding of behavior and its development and for the proper remediation of behavior when it is deviant (see Wahler & Fox, 1981a). Both the analysis of form and the analysis of function are legitimate means for understanding behavior; one approach need not have priority over the other, depending on the problem at hand (see Morris & Braukmann, Chapter 2, this volume). Response form and function represent relatively distinct sets of problems and issues, just as do the respective fields of anatomy and physiology in biology. Form and function, however, are interlocked in that they are mutually determined by the progressive interactions between people and their environments over time (Catania, 1973, 1978). In fact, structure and function are in continuous interaction and development (Bijou & Baer, 1978).

Nonetheless, contemporary behaviorism has favored the analysis of response functions as compared to response form because of its interest in *why* questions about behavior—why a person does such and such (e.g., engage in crime). The analysis of behavioral structure (the *what*) alone cannot answer this question because response form is without inherent function (Baer, 1981). Response function depends on the other factors to which responding is related—the environment, the media, and the historical and current context. Response functions are to be analyzed directly, which is our next topic.

Response Function

The third level at which people may be conceptualized and described is in terms of their behavior's response functions, that is, in terms of an analysis of responding according to its interactions with the other factors. At this level of analysis, we come to speak of the meaning of behavior within its overall context. Response functions are the *whys* of, or reasons for, behavior. For example, when we say that a person purchases a gun (a response form) for self-protection (a response function) in avoiding or escaping certain situations, we are describing, in part, a function or meaning of a response form; the function of purchasing guns, of course, is not inherently for self-protection.

Two points bear mention here. First, response functions cannot be defined independently of the other factors in the field; thus, contemporary behaviorism holds to a "context theory" of meaning. Personal experience within a particular cultural setting can, of course, provide a reasonable basis for making accurate guesses about the function of a particular response form (e.g., a smile), but a response form alone has no inevitable response function. Second, response form–function relationships are typically multiple: (a) one response form may have different functions for different individuals or for the same individual at the same or different times (e.g., physical aggression in self-defense versus that involved in assault and battery) and (b) one response function may be served simultaneously by a variety of different response forms. As an example of the latter, some high-school students may act out in class, whereas others work studiously (two response forms), yet both responses may serve the same function in that they are related to a common consequence, for instance, teacher attention. Also, different response forms (e.g., acting out and working) may occur with the same students at different times, yet for essentially the same reason (e.g., teacher attention; see Mayer, Butterworth, Nafpaktitis, & Sulzer-Azaroff, 1983).

This general analysis of response functions provides a conceptually useful perspective on behavior, yet is often impractical because of the myriad of interrelationships between response form and function. The principles of behavior, however, yield a parsimonious and heuristic organization of these complexities. As described previously, behavior can be organized into two broad functional categories—respondents and operants. Both are reciprocally defined in terms of the stimulus functions that affect their occurrence—in the case of respondents, antecedent eliciting stimuli, and in the case of operants, consequent reinforcing and punishing stimuli and antecedent discriminative stimuli.

Just as with the relationships between response form and function presented before, two comparable sets of interrelationships should also be noted. First, respondents and operants cannot be identified unequivocally without taking into account the conditions under which they occur. Second, a multiplicity of form–function relationships may also be described, although these of course hold within the constraints of the biological structure (Logue, 1979; Reese, 1986; Seligman & Hager, 1972). One response form may be either a respondent or an operant across individuals or within individuals over time. For example, a student may cry and gasp respondently because of an upset stomach. Crying and gasping, however, may also be operant if what controls their occurrence is the consequence of days off from school. Also, respondent and operant response functions can be served by a variety of response forms. Respondents may come in the form of simple unconditioned and conditioned reflexes (e.g., blushing when teased) or more complex sequences of behavior (e.g., unconditioned aggressive behavior upon the occasion of punishment or omitted reinforcement). Operants come in an almost infinite variety of forms.

The Environment

In the analysis just presented, we briefly introduced some of the basic principles of behavior in terms of respondent and operant behaviors and their related stimulus functions (e.g., eliciting, reinforcing, punishing, and discriminative stimuli). We did not, however, introduce any applied behavioral procedures. This is so because applied behavior analysts do not intervene directly on people and rarely on the physical form of their responses. Rather, applied behavior analysts are concerned with the variables of which responding is a function and can be made a function of. These variables are typically in the external environment.

Clearly, an individual's biological structure can be altered, but such intervention is usually not possible in most social settings and, even if it were, the control would likely be arbitrary and unrelated to the conditions that impart and maintain behavior in the first place. Such interventions (e.g., pharmacological) may, of course, be important and necessary at times, but they are not applied behavior analyses of the problems at hand (see Morris, 1980; Morris & Braukmann, Chapter 2, this volume). Given this orientation, no applied behavioral procedures exist to be described in the preceding section on the person. Instead, they have been developed in relationship to the environment and the historical and current context of behavior, and thus they will be introduced in each of the three remaining subsections of the chapter.

The environment may be parsed in several ways, but, for our purposes, we will distinguish between (a) the environment that affects behavior directly through its physical characteristics and concommitant stimulus functions and (b) the environment that serves, in part, as context for the functional relationships between stimulus and response functions. The latter will be addressed in the section on the current context. The former is the focus of what we present here. The analysis of the environment with which the person interacts will be analyzed at three levels corresponding to those at which the person was analyzed. These levels are the environmental structure, stimulus form, and stimulus function.

Environmental Structure

The structure of the environment plays a role in the analysis of behavior analogous to that of biological structure: It refers to the physical construction of the environment in which behavior occurs and may be examined in terms of the ways it came to exist and what has become of it since. Of more interest is the role it plays in limiting and allowing the physical occurrence of behavior. The size of a jail cell or the architectural arrangement of a housing project can have profound effects on what behaviors can and cannot occur (see Harries, 1980; Jeffery, 1971), and there is no reason to overlook such effects (cf. Harshbarger & Maley, 1974; Rogers-Warren & Warren, 1977). Nonetheless, the environmental structure is not a psychological cause of behavior, nor does it directly affect the basic principles of behavior, even though it may profoundly influence what behavior can occur. In our later discussion of the function of the current context, we will discuss how the environment is implicated in the behavioral principles.

Stimulus Form

The second level of analysis of the environment is that of stimulus form (or topography), which is analogous to response form in that the concern is with a formal or topographical description. Like responses, all stimuli have forms that may be described (or potentially described) in terms of their physical measurement. And likewise, an important part of the environment exists within a person's skin. Such private stimuli exist in biological (e.g., a toothache) and behavioral dimensions (e.g., visual imagining or covert verbal responses as potential stimuli for subsequent responding), which may or may not take on stimulus functions for other behavior. For instance, clients (e.g., spouse abusers) can be taught to use verbal problem-solving or decision-making strategies with others as acceptable, alternative means of achieving useful consequences (e.g., financial and child-rearing practices); these strategies can then be turned on oneself and applied just as one might use them with another person to solve a problem or make a decision (see Morton & Ewald, Chapter 10; Platt & Prout, Chapter 18, both in this volume). In acknowledging the environment within the skin, however, we are not thereby acknowledging another set of processes or structures than what is already known about behavior. The primary concern remains with the interactions between stimulus functions and response functions and the location of some of their correlated forms (Branch, 1987). All the problems of privacy discussed earlier still hold, so that effective action is difficult to achieve anywhere but in the environment outside the skin, where the general source of covert behavioral relations ultimately lies and which in the long run supports the covert behavior (see Hayes & Brownstein, 1986; Moore, 1980).

A formal, purely descriptive analysis of the stimulus environment may be conducted for the range of all possible environmental organic and inorganic events with which behavior interacts, extending from relatively discrete instances (e.g., money) to more complex categories (e.g., overheard conversations). Although the analysis of stimulus forms is important to understanding behavior, such analyses alone are generally insufficient for understanding the relationships between responding and the environment, that is, how a stimulus functions to affect responding. For that, the functions of stimuli must be considered directly.

Stimulus Functions

The third level of analysis of the environment lies at the heart of contemporary behaviorism: The environment needs to be understood in terms of its stimulus functions for a person's corresponding response functions. When we describe how the environment affects behavior, we are describing its stimulus function. For instance, if we say that firearms can be used for self-protection or assault, we are describing two different stimulus functions for the firearms. Neither of these functions is inherent, but one may be more probable than the other, depending on the circumstances.

As with the case with response functions, two sets of interrelationships should be noted. First, stimulus functions are defined by their interrelationships with the other factors in the behavioral field, especially response functions, and not on the basis of their form alone. Second, a multiplicity of form–function relationships may be described. One stimulus may have different functions for different individuals at the same time or for the same individual at the same or different times. Firearms, for instance, have different stimulus functions when used for murder or for hunting. In addition, one stimulus function (e.g., a murder weapon) may be served through a wide variety of forms.

Like the concept of response function, that of stimulus function is a valuable analytic tool for the analysis of behavior as well, but it, too, presents difficulties in that a myriad of form–function relationships can occur. Again, however, we may turn to the principles of behavior for some parsimonious and practical organization: The functions of the environment may be defined in terms of their generic effects on responding, that is, in terms of their eliciting, reinforcing, punishing, and discriminative functions.

In a manner also analogous to our description of the interrelationships between response forms and functions, two sets of interrelationships should be noted here as well. First, these stimulus functions cannot be defined without taking into account the response functions and other factors with which they interact. Stimuli function as eliciting stimuli with respect to respondents and as reinforcing, punishing, and discriminative stimuli with respect to operants. Second, a multiplicity of form–function relationships can occur, which again hold within the limits of the biological structure (see Logue, 1979; Reese, 1986; Seligman & Hager, 1972). A particular stimulus form may be eliciting, reinforcing, punishing, or discriminative for different individuals or for the same individual at the same or different times. For example, positive comments from high-school principals may be reinforcing or punishing to students, depending on their prior interactions with authority figures, the presence of peers, and importance of other resources controlled by principals. No stimulus has an inherent function by itself. Finally, eliciting, reinforcing, punishing, and discriminative functions can be served by a large number of stimulus forms. Because stimulus functions are central to much of behavior, we will discuss each of them in more detail next and, in the process, introduce some of the major applied behavioral procedures.

Eliciting Stimuli. As mentioned before, the eliciting function of stimuli occurs with respect to respondents—these stimuli are said to elicit such responding. Eliciting stimuli may be either unconditioned or conditioned and so, too, may be the behaviors they elicit. Moreover, the function of eliciting stimuli may generalize across formally similar stimuli. For instance, respondent concomitants of emotional behaviors elicited by an altercation with someone might be elicited at a later time by people who are similar in dress and age. Although powerfully felt (e.g., emotionally), the eliciting function of stimuli for respondent behaviors seem not to play a major role in complex human social behavior, especially that related to crime and delinquency. Most of the latter is operant in nature.

The last point aside, some important behavioral procedures are based on the process of elicitation. For instance, in the treatment of rapists and child molesters, preliminary assessments of sexual deviance are often made by measuring changes in sexual arousal elicited by pictures of potential victims. These, then, become the baseline against which to measure the success of subsequent interventions (see Quinsey, Chaplin, Maguire, & Upfold, Chapter 13, this volume).

Reinforcing Stimuli. In operant behavior, response consequences may increase or decrease the subsequent rate of responding. Consequences that increase the rate are termed reinforcers, and may be either positive or negative. Those that add something to a person's environment (e.g., social attention) and that thereby increase the rate of behavior (e.g., social interaction) on which they are contingent are called positive reinforcers; the process is called positive reinforcement. Response consequences that entail removing something (e.g., threats of physical harm) from a person's environment and that thereby increase the rate of behavior (e.g., submission) on which they are contingent are called negative reinforcers; the process is called negative reinforcement. Behavior maintained by negative reinforcement is typically referred to as avoidance and escape responding. Avoidance responses postpone the delivery of negative reinforcers (i.e., punishers or aversive stimuli), whereas escape responses remove aversive events that are ongoing.

Reinforcement is necessary to maintain operant behavior, but not every response has to be reinforced: Reinforcement may be intermittent, yet maintain responding (see Ferster & Skinner, 1957; Zeiler, 1984)—indeed, quite powerfully so. Intermittent reinforcement can be arranged in many ways, and *schedule of reinforcement* specifies how reinforcers are related to responses. The schedule of reinforcement is a critical determinant of the overall rate of behavior, the pattern in which responding is distributed across time, and the behavior's resistance to extinction. Most human social behavior occurs within extremely complex schedules of reinforcement based on fixed and variable numbers of responses emitted, fixed and variable temporal relationships, and the intermingling of the two, either concurrently or successively. With respect to applications in crime and delinquency, considerations of the schedules of reinforcement probably occur most frequently with respect to (a) the schedule of "token" delivery in token economies and the schedules by which the tokens are backed up with other reinforcers (see Milan, Chapter 7, this volume) and (b) the deliberate weaning of behavior from "rich" schedules to those more commonly encountered in the natural environment in attempts to promote response generalization (see Morris & Braukmann, Chapter 2, this volume).

As alluded to before, schedules of reinforcement may run concurrently. Indeed, human behavior is under many simultaneous schedules—never just one—thereby adding to the complex texture of person–environment interactions. Responding on concurrent schedules, though, is a lawful phenomena, just as it is on single schedules: Research on *choice* shows that the relative distribution of responses on, and time spent in, a schedule generally matches the reinforcement rate as well as other characteristics of reinforcement (e.g., magnitude, presence of aversive stimuli) (Pierce & Epling, 1983). The characterization of reinforcement in terms of the "matching law" seems a considerably more realistic picture of behavior in the natural environment than that of single schedules alone. Moreover, it shows clearly that the rate of a behavior can be changed indirectly by changing the parameters of reinforcement on schedules operating elsewhere (i.e., by changing the relative distribution of reinforcement; Epling & Pierce, 1983; McDowell, 1982). In general, the effectiveness of reinforcement is context dependent on other sources and amounts of reinforcement (see Wilson & Herrnstein, 1985).

The direct use of positive reinforcement in the behavioral approaches to crime and delinquency is ubiquitous and is to be found in all the subsequent chapters describing applied behavioral procedures and programs (see Milan, Chapter 6, this volume, for commentary on negative reinforcement). For example, reinforcement (or contingency) contracting is used with family members for behavior incompatible with stealing (see Morton & Ewald, Chapter 10, this volume), with probationers and parolees for behavior incompatible with drug use (see Nietzel & Himelein, Chapter 4, this volume), with delinquents in group homes for social and academic skills (see Braukmann & Wolf, Chapter 5, this volume), and with youths and adults in closed institutions across a wide variety of social, educational, and vocational activities (see Milan, Chapters 6 and 7, this volume).

Punishing Stimuli. Like reinforcement, punishment also involves response consequences, but in this case, the consequences decrease the rate of behavior. This effect is achieved either through the presentation of stimuli (e.g., criticism from peers) in what might be called positive punishment or through the termination or reduction of stimuli (e.g., loss of money through fines) in what might be called negative punishment. The same considerations of the scheduling and concurrent nature of reinforcement apply generally here as well.

In applied behavior analysis, the use of procedures that directly reduce response rates (i.e., punishment) is avoided when possible. Therapeutically speaking, the reasons for this are many, but among the more important ones are the following. First, punishment cannot be used effectively when the probability of detecting punishable behavior is low, as it typically is with crime and delinquency (Baer, 1975; see Morris & Braukmann, Chapter 2, this volume). Second, punishment does not build functional behavior, which is the usual goal of applied behavioral programs (see Goldiamond, 1974). And third, punishment can produce undesirable side effects such as emotional responses and aggression and will engender escape and avoidance responding (see Newsom, Favell, & Rincover, 1983). Punishment procedures are typically used only after nonpunitive procedures have failed and, even then, only in concert with positive procedures for establishing and maintaining other behaviors. Unfortunately, under certain conditions, punishment may be necessary and appropriate, but careful scrutiny must attend its use (see Axelrod & Apsche, 1983). The legal and ethical issues involved here are complex, and the reader should consult Sheldon (Chapter 21; see also Clements, Chapter 20, both in this volume; Martin, 1975; Stolz, 1978).

The therapeutic use of punishment contingencies in the behavioral approaches to crime and delinquency occurs across a range of settings. For instance, the direct use of punishment is found in applying aversive consequences for deviant sexual interests so as to reduce the latter (see Quinsey *et al.*, Chapter 13, this volume). Punishment through response cost (e.g., increased effort or loss of reinforcers) is observed in programs making access to illicit drugs more difficult by restricting their supply and in programs that increase monetary fines for driving under the influence of alcohol (see Stitzer & McCaul, Chapter 12; see also Milan, Chapter 6, both in this volume). And punishment through time-out (from positive reinforcement) has been employed to decrease rule violations and aggressive and antisocial behaviors (see Milan, Chapter 6, this volume).

Discriminative Stimuli. Operant behavior is defined with respect to its consequences (e.g., reinforcement and punishment). However, through those consequences, the antecedents of operant behavior also take on control. Stimuli come to set the occasion for operant responding when the probability of reinforcement is higher in their presence than in their absence (e.g., convenience store robberies may occur frequently at night, as opposed to in daylight, because of the cover of darkness and fewer witnesses). After some exposure to this arrangement, the response rate will be higher in the presence of the discriminative stimulus than in its absence. Responses under the control of discriminative stimuli are called discriminated operants.

Similar to the antecedent control of respondent behavior, generalization is a characteristic of discriminative control over operant behavior. As with respondent generalization, the probability of a discriminated operant's occurring in the presence of other stimuli depends upon the physical similarity between stimuli—the greater the similarity, the more probable the response (e.g., uniformed law-enforcement officers never encountered before will have similar effects to those previously encountered). Stimulus generalization may also occur on the basis of functional stimulus equivalence, but that is discussed later.

Operant behavior is ultimately a function of its consequences, and, hence, response consequences are the foci of most applied behavioral procedures and programs. However, most operants are also discriminated operants. As such, the influence of this behavioral relation plays a role in the analysis and intervention into crime and delinquency. For instance, the presence of foot patrols, as opposed to patrol cars, can increase reported crime; providing checklists for patrol officers increases the probability of adequately and accurately filed crime reports and case preparation materials; and warning signs and labels can reduce shoplifting (see Schnelle, Geller, & Davis, Chapter 8, this volume).

The discriminative control of operant behavior is ubiquitous—human behavior is unlikely to occur outside the concurrent functioning of discriminative stimuli. These stimuli are defined by their functional relationships to behavior and only by those relationships. Occasionally, though, specific classes of discriminative stimuli are identified by their content; the most common are instructions and models. Instruction following and the imitation of models, though, do not involve new principles of behavior; rather, they identify important content-related relationships between behavior and the environment that can be engendered by means other than direct experience with the contingencies described or modeled.

Instructions are a convenient method for engendering new responses in verbally competent individuals, given, of course, that the prerequisite behaviors are available. When the prerequisites are intact, an instruction to make the response and some specifications about how to do so may be all that is necessary to establish new behaviors. For responding to be maintained, however, reinforcement must follow from the naturally existing contingencies for the instructed response or from the instruction giver for rule following. The latter—rule-governed behavior—has many complex properties, some not necessarily the same as behavior that develops directly from differential reinforcement contingencies (i.e., contingency-shaped behavior; see Skinner 1969, pp. 133–171), even though the form of the responses may appear identical (see Catania, Matthews, & Shimoff, 1982; Matthews, Shimoff, Catania, & Sagvolden, 1977). Moreover, the rules in rule-governed behavior may operate not as simple discriminative stimuli but may take on contextual properties as well (see later section on the current context).

Rule-governed behavior obviously involves verbal processes as well as behavior described as cognitive in nature and, hence, is important to applied behavior analysis and especially to those versions of behavior therapy that involve extensive verbal counseling (see Ferster, 1979; Krumboltz & Thoresen, 1969; Zettle & Hayes, 1982). For instance, procedures that either explicitly or implicitly establish rule-governed behavior (and self-control via rule stating) can be found in applications for truancy (e.g., "paradoxical instructions," see Nietzel & Himelein, Chapter 4, this volume), sexual deviance (see Quinsey *et al.*, Chapter 13, this volume), job-finding skills (Nietzel & Himelein, Chapter 4, this volume), and self-government systems within group homes (see Braukmann & Wolf, Chapter 5, this volume). Rule-governed behavior is also, in part, what is established in educational components of programs for sex offenders (e.g., information on male and female sexuality; see Quinsey *et al.*, Chapter 13, this volume), for driver education components in treating drinkers (e.g., information on the effects of alcohol; see Stitzer & McCaul, Chapter 12, this volume), and for imparting skills to group home teaching parents (see Braukmann & Wolf, Chapter 5, this volume).

Modeling is a second convenient means for engendering new behavior and involves the demonstration of a response by one person (the modeler) and its imitation by a second (see Krohn, Massey, & Skinner, Chapter 17, this volume). Imitation, like rule-governed behavior, becomes a generalized class of responding that is readily engaged in, yet is still operant and as such is controlled by its consequences, their schedule of delivery, and related discriminative stimuli. Like rule-governed behavior, too, imitation is complex and controversial and subject to a variety of interpretations (e.g., Bandura, 1977, pp. 22–50; Deguchi, 1984; see Platt & Prout, Chapter 18, this volume). Controversy aside, the use of models (live and video) and the use of reinforcement of imitation are common among the behavioral approaches to crime and delinquency, especially those that focus on social skills training, such as those for appropriate heterosexual interactions (see Quinsey *et al.*, Chapter 13, this volume), interpersonal skills within families (see Nietzel & Himelein, Chapter 4, this volume), and staff teaching procedures in group home settings (see Braukmann & Wolf, Chapter 5, this volume) (see Milan, Chapter 6, this volume, for a general review of social skills training).

Summary. The relationships between responding and its consequences and antecedents are referred to in general as the "contingencies of reinforcement." In describing the temporal and functional relationships into which responses and the environment enter, we have only been able to offer a superficial analysis of the extent and complexity of these relationships. People are always responding in one way or another, thereby continuously producing consequences in the presence of antecedents on a moment-to-moment basis. Sometimes, the contingencies of reinforcement will be relatively simple, as in the effects of one person on another and those specified by classroom rules, whereas at other times they will be more complex, as in family interaction patterns. The contingencies also operate on larger organizational levels, as in those within correctional institutions, both on correctional staff and inmates, alike; moreover, they are readily apparent in social policies that determine resource allocation in statewide correctional programs; and they operate across the culture as a whole, as in the contingencies that maintain various sex-role patterns and stereotypes related to sexual discrimination and abuse.

Applied behavior analysts working in the areas of crime and delinquency attempt to intervene and alter these contingencies, though they are more successful with the less complex cases. They have developed programs to improve the contingencies of reinforcement at an interpersonal level (e.g., altering child effects on adult behavior; see Polirstok & Greer, 1977; cf. Bell & Harper, 1977), within classrooms (e.g., behavioral contracting; see Lane & Murakami, Chapter 11, this volume), and in family interaction patterns (e.g., family management practices; Patterson, 1982; see Morton & Ewald, Chapter 10, this volume), group homes and prisons (e.g., token economies; see Braukmann & Wolf, Chapter 5, this volume; Clements, Chapter 20, this volume; Milan, Chapter 7, this volume), the sociopolitical community (e.g., social policy changes; see Burchard, Chapter 22, this volume; Nietzel & Himelein, Chapter 4, this volume), and subcomponents of the culture at large (e.g., changes in social networks; see O'Donnell, Manos, & Chesney-Lind, Chapter 9, this volume; see also discussions of systems and ecological approaches and behavioral community psychology in Morton & Ewald, Chapter 10, and in Schnelle, Geller, & Davis, Chapter 8, both in this volume). The contingencies of reinforcement, then, operate at varying levels, and need to be intervened upon at the appropriate level to achieve the most effective action possible.

The Historical Context

The historical context refers to a person's past interactions with the environment, and encompasses phylogenic, ontogenic, and interactional histories. Together, these are the sources of the current functional relationships between responding and the environment (i.e., the current response and stimulus functions). Historical causation, then, operates to impart interdependent functions (or meanings) to the person's environment and to a person's responding, and does so in two ways—phylogenically and interactionally (see Morris, Johnson, Powell, & Todd, 1987).

Phylogenic History

The role of phylogenic history as a contextual condition affecting person–environment interactions has already been discussed in the earlier section on the phylogenic contributions to the biological structure. As stated there, and to repeat, the phylogenic history is the source of (a) the person's biological structure and functioning, (b) the unconditioned relationships in respondent behavior and operant behavior, and (c) the processes of respondent and operant conditioning.

Interactional History

More interesting and more accessible to professionals involved in crime and delinquency is the interactional history between responding and the environment across an individual's lifetime. People's interactional histories are the sources of the acquired functional relationships into which their responses and the environment enter and are an important source of between-person individual differences and within-person variability over time in those relationships. With respect to the principles of behavior, this primarily involves the development of stimulus and response functions. More specifically, historical causation is both the source of conditioned respondents and operants and of the conditioned functions of eliciting, reinforcing, punishing, and discriminative stimuli.

Respondent Behavior and Elicitation. In respondent behavior, *respondent conditioning* produces conditioned eliciting stimuli and their co-related conditioned respondents. Establishing a conditioned respondent involves two components. First, the unconditioned eliciting stimulus and the to-be-conditioned eliciting stimulus must be presented in close temporal relationship, with the former typically preceding the latter. Second, the probability of the unconditioned eliciting stimulus must be greater following the conditioned eliciting stimulus than at other times. For a conditioned-reflex relation to remain intact, these conditions must be intermittently maintained. If not, then the conditioned eliciting stimulus and conditioned response will undergo respondent extinction.

The stimuli that function as conditioned elicitors and the responses that are conditioned respondents will differ across people as the result of different interactional histories and will differ within people over time due to continual changes in their histories. Interestingly, the heart of the behavioral approaches to the treatment of crime and delinquency is the altering of behavioral interactions by allowing or imposing new, therapeutic histories. Thus, for instance, covert sensitization programs that seek to suppress the respondents involved in sexual arousal to imagined inappropriate stimuli (e.g., children) by pairing them with unconditioned stimuli (e.g., noxious odors) that elicit incompatible respondents (see Nietzel & Himelein, Chapter 4, this volume; Quinsey *et al.*, Chapter 13, this volume) are essentially programs that impose a new interactional history with the intent of altering future interactions.

Operant Behavior, Reinforcement, Punishment, and Discriminative Stimulus Control. In operant behavior, interactional history produces (a) new and differentiated operant responding through the *operant conditioning* of operant responses, (b) conditioned reinforcers, punishers, and discriminative stimuli, and (c) the loss of these behavior–environment relationships through *operant extinction* and punishment. With respect to extinction, this occurs when reinforcement is no longer forthcoming or when a break occurs in the contingency between a particular class of responses and its consequences.

Much of operant behavior is acquired through *shaping* as well as through the manipulation of antecedent stimuli, such as in instructions and modeling. As for shaping, this involves the differential reinforcement of successive approximations to a new response. The process is begun by reinforcing a response already in an individual's repertoire that in some way approximates the new response (e.g., effective interpersonal skills). Then, when another response even closer to the criterion is emitted, it, too, is reinforced, and so on. Subsequently, the new response is arrived at. *Chaining* is another method for building behaviors and can be used effectively with complex behavior that can be broken down into a series of steps (e.g., vocational training of mechanical skills). The response is trained by first establishing either the initial response in the chain, the *forward chaining* procedure, or the final response, the *backward chaining* procedure, and then proceeding with the others in a serial fashion.

Not only does behavior become elaborated and strengthened in operant conditioning, but it comes under the control of new conditioned reinforcers and punishers as well as discriminative stimuli. Within applied behavior analysis, most of the focus is on constructing new behaviors, making weak behaviors more probable, and bringing other behaviors under the control of already functional and existing consequences. Relatively less effort has gone into constructing new reinforcers (e.g., motives), yet the control of behaviors by deviant reinforcers (e.g., inflicting pain) or the lack of control by nondeviant reinforcers (e.g., parental attention) is a major problem in the development and maintenance of antisocial behaviors. Clearly, many applied behavior programs in crime and delinquency do build new reinforcers and punishers but often only implicitly. For an explicit example, however, see Braukmann and Wolf's (Chapter 5, this volume) description of the development of positive youth–staff relationships in group homes for delinquents. Part of the rationale for this component of their program is that once the positive relationship is established, it can then be used to establish new behavior and maintain old behavior by more natural, less arbitrary means than, for instance, with a token economy. Moreover, diminution of the relationship as a consequence of delinquent behavior becomes a negative reinforcer for behavior incompatible with delinquency—this is akin to the development of "conscience."

Perspectives on Historical Causation: Traits and Situations

Although historical causation is fundamental to contemporary behaviorism, it is not always a readily explicit characteristic of the approach. Because of misunderstandings this oversight creates, we explicate further, especially where historical causation helps resolve some long-standing problems in the trait–situationism controversy, with implications as well for the nature–nurture debate.

In an important sense, people are "active" participants in their interactions with their environments. That is, their behavior represents a strong, mutual interdependence that is affected as much by its historically derived response functions for the environment as it is by the environment's historically derived stimulus functions for responding. Because these relationships differ from one person to another, applied behavioral procedures and programs must often be individualized, both with respect to what aspects of the response repertoire need to be strengthened or weakened and with respect to what will be effective eliciting, reinforcing, punishing, and discriminative stimuli in the procedures and programs that are implemented (see Sheldon, Chapter 21, this volume).

The interactional nature of contemporary behaviorism is illustrated by this emphasis on the role of the historical context in the simultaneous development of stimulus and response functions. In saying that people are "active" contributors to their behaviors through their interactional histories, however, we do not mean to imply that people are autonomous agents in control of their behaviors. Likewise, however, neither are we asserting that the environment is an ultimate autonomous cause, though, for practical purposes, applied behavior analysts adopt this latter perspective because, pragmatically speaking, the environment is typically all that can be altered to affect behavior. The tension between these views of causality is at the heart of the trait–situationism debate, which shares some logical characteristics and flaws with the nature–nurture issue, both of which are clarified when approached from an interactional, field-theoretic perspective; hence we elaborate briefly.

Within the view we have presented, stimulus functions and response functions develop simultaneously and are defined with respect to one another. As such, stimulus functions have no more control over behavior than do response functions—the two are interdependently and mutually defining. A situation does not compel a response to occur except through a person's historically derived response functions for that situation; and a person does not compel a response to occur except through the situation's historically derived stimulus functions for that response—everything else being equal. Thus situations do not possess independent or inherent power to control behavior any more than persons possess independent power to control behavior through their personal traits. Both are the products of interactional histories unique to each individual; hence the phenomenological character of contemporary behaviorism (see Day, 1969b).

Interactions may display those qualities commonly attributed to personal or situational control depending on how they are viewed or investigated (Bowers, 1973), but those attributions are often shorthand conventions derived from an overemphasis on mechanistic and reductionistic thinking as opposed to a contextual world view. Still, summarizing the effects of interactional history and of the currently evolved stimulus and response functions in trait or situational terms, respectively, is not inherently objectionable. What is objectionable is to reify those terms so that they become causal agents. Predictions about behavior can be made on the basis of information about the person and on the basis of information about the situation, but the ability to do so does not thereby give causal power to either source. To assert that such power exists anywhere moves the analysis of behavior away from the interactional account it requires.

People react differently to seemingly identical aspects of their environments, and they react identically to very different aspects of the environments—both of which change over time. Historical causation is difficult to appreciate as the source of these differences because it is hard to see (as is evolution). Because of this, explanations of behavior often become couched in terms of various constructs, including not only traits, but also misused senses of the terms *expectations, locus of control,* and *self-efficacy.* These constructs, however, are no more than shorthand descriptions of the effects of historical causation (see Biglan, 1987; Morris, 1985c). As mentioned before, applied behavior analysis seeks to change deviant functional relationships between responding and the environment by providing "prosthetic" histories. Through such changes, behavior changes, and so does what people report as changes in their expectations, locus of control, and self-efficacy. The latter correlate with changed response–environment relationships—they are not necessarily its causes.

This argument is not an argument against the role that one of a person's responses (e.g., statement of expectations) may play as the environment for another of that person's responses (see Morton & Ewald, Chapter 10; Nietzel & Himelein, Chapter 4; Platt & Prout, Chapter 18, all in this volume). People commonly react to what they themselves do and say, both publicly and privately, yet this remains within the realm of the functional relationships between responding and the environment (Hayes & Brownstein, 1986). No new stuff is involved—we are still speaking of response–environment relationships, not a new source of control.

The Current Context

The historical context imparts functions to stimuli and to responses—without it, there would be no behavior. Given a historical context, however, the particular stimulus and response functions (a) that *will* occur on any one occasion and (b) that *can* occur depend on the structure and function of current context—all causes have contexts. We will deal with the latter first (see Morris *et al.,* 1987).

The Structure of the Current Context

The structure of the current context and its influence on behavior has already been discussed under the topics of the biological and the environmental structure. In both cases, these factors affect what behaviors can and cannot occur on a particular occasion. To reiterate briefly, the biological structure (i.e., anatomical, physiological, and neurological) affects what a person can and cannot physically accomplish. Differences obviously exist across people in these regards and within them over time. For instance, differences across individuals in physiogonomy (e.g., mesomorphs and endomorphs) will affect what general activities they are likely to excel in and be reinforced for; changes in body constitution across a lifetime will likewise affect behavior. In addition, more transient organismic factors, such as physical injury or the effects of drugs, will have local effects on what current and subsequent interactions can occur. These influences notwithstanding, we want to be clear that biology does not "cause" behavior in any psychological sense but, rather, that it is the context that influences what response forms can and cannot physically occur.

The environmental structure (i.e., the physical ecology) operates in a similar fashion but through factors external to an individual's biological constitution. The physical construction of the environment places obvious limits on what behaviors can and cannot occur. The environment in this sense is also not usefully considered as a psychological cause of behavior, though clearly it is important as context and should not be overlooked in developing procedures for the prevention of crime and delinquency (see Harries, 1980; Jeffery, 1979).

The Function of the Current Context

Whereas the historical context determines what functional relations *may* exist between behavior and environment and the structure of the current context (i.e., biological and environmental) influences which of those functions *can* occur, the current context also operates functionally to determine which of those relationships *will* occur, given that they may and can. The sources of the function of the current context, like its structure, may again be taken to reside in either biology or environment. Now, however, the focus is on the function of the current context, not on its structure.

The Function of the Current Biological Context. Not only does the biological context affect what people can and cannot do, but it also affects whether or not they will do something, given that they could. These contextual conditions may affect unconditioned relationships in either respondent or operant behavior as well as relationships that have been conditioned.

With respect to respondent behavior, for instance, the strength of both unconditioned and conditioned stimulus and response functions is, for instance, affected (a) by the number of prior elicitations (reflex fatigue) and their rapidity (refractory phase), (b) by the concurrent presentations of other eliciting stimuli (e.g., facilitation and inhibition), and (c) by the occurrence of other conditions (e.g., deprivation of unconditioned reinforcers and punishers). Eliciting stimuli, whether conditioned or unconditioned, have no immutable function based on their form alone. Their function is derived in part from their current context (see Balsam & Tomie, 1985).

With respect to operant behavior, the strength of the unconditioned and conditioned stimulus and response functions is affected by the current context in much the same way as in the case of respondent behavior. When the relationships involve the functioning of *unconditioned* reinforcers and punishers, the relevant contextual variables are referred to as establishing operations, and are said to have two effects (Michael, 1982). First, the deprivation of a primary reinforcer (e.g., food or sexual contact) establishes the presentation of the stimulus as a reinforcer and, second, it increases the probability of behavior that in the past has led to that reinforcement; the latter has the characteristics of an emotional predisposition. Likewise, the presentation of a punishing stimulus establishes the removal of the stimulus as a reinforcer and increases the probability of behavior that in the past has led to that removal. Moreover, still other operations have similar or related effects; for instance, drugs, illness, and fatigue all affect the functional relationships between response and environment—they alter both response functions and stimulus functions (e.g., how one perceives the world and what it means to us).

As for *conditioned* relationships in operant behavior, similar variables are at work. For instance, the strength of conditioned reinforcers and related discriminative stimuli are affected by establishinglike operations. Money, for instance, which is a conditioned reinforcer, will be differentially effective as a reinforcer as a function of unemployment or a recent lottery win; social reinforcers are a function of their relative deprivation and satiation (see Gewirtz, 1972). Conditioned reinforcers, punishers, and discriminative stimuli are also affected by other contextual conditions. These conditions may involve (a) relatively simple conditional discriminative control (e.g., the presence of a police officer can alter the function of an unlocked car), (b) complex contextual control involved in stimulus equivalence relations (e.g., the substitutability of various stimulus forms for one stimulus function, as in the equating of tokens in a token economy with backup reinforcement; see Sidman, 1986), (c) contingency-specifying stimuli (e.g., descriptive statements and rules that describe the function of certain behavioral consequences; Schlinger & Blakely, 1987; see Michael, 1982, on "establishing stimuli"), and (d) on a more molar level, schedules of reinforcement, which themselves in proper combination can make reinforcers out of punishers (Morse & Kelleher, 1977).

One example of the importance of context comes from recent analyses and interventions into deviant social systems (Wahler, 1980). Here, for instance, an examination of the encounters between socially isolated mothers and out-of-home relatives and welfare workers showed that the nature of these encounters altered the function of nagging by the mothers' children that occurred later in the day. Encounters that were aversive made the children's nagging aversive to the mother and led to abusive treatment of the children, whereas when the social encounters were not aversive, the very same child behavior (i.e., nagging) did not predispose abusive behavior by the mothers (see Wahler & Fox, 1981b; Wahler & Graves, 1983).

Conclusions

Like the historical context, current contextual conditions are not always contiguous with behavior or easily observed. As such, both produce sometimes difficult-to-understand individual differences and variability. These contextual conditions are ubiquitous, however, and applied behavioral procedures and programs that take these contextual conditions into account are more effective for doing so.

CONCLUDING COMMENTS

In Chapter 1, we provided an introduction to the behavioral approaches to crime and delinquency. In doing so, we first discussed the general nature of crime and delinquency, especially predatory crime and its correlates and epidemiological dimensions, and we introduced some applied behavioral procedures and programs. Second, we offered several preliminary observations about the behavioral approaches with respect to (a) their limitations and merit, (b) the reinforcing and humane nature of the relationships between applied behavior analysts and those with whom they work, (c) some misconceptions about the approach, (d) the importance of individualized treatment, and (e) considerations of the social context in which behavioral procedures and programs are implemented. And third, we presented an overview of the chapters to follow.

In Chapter 2, we offered three central considerations for the effective implementation of applied behavioral procedures and programs. First, and most prominently, we highlighted the seven dimensions of applied behavior analysis: (a) its focus on the social validity of the behaviors on which the procedures and programs are applied; (b) the emphasis on behavior and its valid and reliable assessment; (c) technological descriptions of the procedures and programs that invite effective replication; (d) the experimental, analytic approach taken to the application of the procedures and programs; (e) the effectiveness of the procedures and programs in terms of socially valid changes in behavior; (f) the importance of establishing maintenance and generality across behaviors, settings, and time; and (g) the necessity for a conceptual system that integrates these dimensions with the behavioral nature of the applied behavioral procedures and programs. Second, we discussed the dissemination of behavioral applications and the need to develop quality control programs to achieve this end. And third, we concluded with some commentary on the necessity of examining the application of behavioral procedures and programs in larger social contexts.

In Chapter 3, just concluded, we have defined and introduced contemporary behaviorism in two ways. First we described its philosophical and historical developments from the era of classical Greek philosophy, through the emergence of modern philosophy, and into the rise of scientific psychology—drawing parallels and antiparallels between contemporary behaviorism and other views along the way. Second, we offered a conceptual system for the analysis of behavior, interrelating the roles played by the person, the environment, the historical context, and the current context.

In sum, we have introduced and defined the behavioral approaches to crime and delinquency, presented the basic dimensions of applied behavior analysis, and provided the historical, philosophical, and conceptual underpinnings of contemporary behaviorism. Our goal in doing so has been to provide the reader with some background for approaching the subsequent material in a conceptually systematic and integrative manner and in a manner that encourages enlightened support for, and constructive criticism of, the behavioral approaches to crime and delinquency.

ACKNOWLEDGMENTS

We would like to thank Lisa M. Johnson, Bryan D. Midgley, Susan M. Schneider, and James T. Todd for their helpful comments on an earlier draft of this chapter.

REFERENCES

Akers, R. L. (1973). *Deviant behavior: A social learning approach.* Belmont, CA: Wadsworth Publishing.

Anastasi, A., & Foley, J. P. (1948). A proposed reorientation in the heredity-environment controversy. *Psychological Review, 55,* 239–249.

Angell, J. R. (1904). *Psychology: An introductory study of the structure and function of humans conscious.* New York: Holt.

Arrington, R. L., & Deitz, S. M. (1986). A second call. *Behaviorism, 14,* 103–106.

Axelrod, S., & Apsche, J. (Eds.). (1983). *The effects of punishment on human behavior.* New York: Academic Press.

Ayllon, T., & Milan, M. A. (1979). *Correctional rehabilitation and management: A psychological approach.* New York: Wiley.

Baer, D. M. (1975). In the beginning there was the response. In E. Ramp & G. Semb (Eds.), *Behavior analysis: Areas of research and application* (pp. 16–30). Englewood Cliffs, NJ: Prentice-Hall.

Baer, D. M. (1981). The imposition of structure on behavior and the demolition of behavioral structures. In D. Bernstein & H. Howe (Eds.), *Nebraska Symposium on Motivation* (Vol. 29, pp. 217–254). Lincoln: University of Nebraska Press.

Baer, D. M., Wolf, M. M., & Risley, T. R. (1968). Some current dimensions of applied behavior analysis. *Journal of Applied Behavior Analysis, 1,* 91–97.

Balsam, P. D., & Tomie, A. (Eds.). (1985). *Context and learning.* Hillsdale, NJ: Erlbaum.

Bandura, A. (1969). *Principles of behavior modification.* New York: Holt, Rinehart & Winston.

Bandura, A. (1977). *Social learning theory.* Englewood Cliffs, NJ: Prentice-Hall.

Bechterev, V. (1913). *La psychologie objective.* Paris: Lebrairie Felix Alcan.

Bell, R. Q., & Harper, L. V. (Eds.). (1977). *Child effects on adults.* Hillsdale, NJ: Erlbaum.

Bernard, C. (1865). *An introduction to the study of experimental medicine.* New York: Dover Press.

Biglan, A. (1987). A behavior-analytic critique of Bandura's self-efficacy theory. *The Behavior Analyst, 10,* 1–15.

Bijou, S. W., & Baer, D. M. (1978). *Behavior analysis of child development.* Englewood Cliffs, NJ: Prentice-Hall.

Bishop, C. H., & Blanchard, E. B. (1971). *Behavior therapy: A guide to correctional administration and programming.* Athens, GA: Institute of Government, University of Georgia.

Boakes, R. (1984). *From Darwin to behaviorism.* Cambridge, England: Cambridge University Press.

Borgaonkar, D., & Shah, S. (1974). The XYY chromosome male-or syndrome. *Progress in Medical Genetics, 10,* 135–222.

Boring, E. G. (1950). *The history of experimental psychology.* Englewood Cliffs, NJ: Prentice-Hall.

Bowers, K. S. (1973). Situationism in psychology. *Psychological Review, 80,* 307–336.

Branch, M. N. (1977). On the role of "memory" in the analysis of behavior. *Journal of the Experimental Analysis of Behavior, 28,* 171–179.

Branch, M. N. (1987). Behavior analysis: A conceptual and empirical base for behavior therapy. *The Behavior Therapist, 10,* 79–84.

Braukmann, C. J., Kirigin, K. A., & Wolf, M. M. (1980). Group home treatment research: Social learning and social control perspectives. In T. Hirschi & M. Gottfredson (Eds.), *Understanding crime* (pp. 117–130). Beverly Hills: Sage.

Burgess, R. L., & Akers, R. L. (1966). A differential association-reinforcement theory of criminal behavior. *Social Problems, 14,* 128–147.

Carr, H. A. (1925). *Psychology: A study of mental activity.* New York: Longmans.

Catania, A. C. (1973). The psychologies of structure, function, and development. *American Psychologist, 28,* 434–443.

Catania, A. C. (1978). The psychology of learning: Some lessons from the Darwinian revolution. *Annals of the New York Academy of Sciences, 309,* 18–28.

Catania, A. C. (1984). *Learning.* Englewood Cliffs, NJ: Prentice-Hall.

Catania, A. C., & Brigham, T. A. (1978). *Handbook of applied behavior analysis: Social and instructional processes.* New York: Irvington.

Catania, A. C., Matthews, B. A., & Shimoff, E. (1982). Instructed versus shaped behavior: Interactions with nonverbal responding. *Journal of the Experimental Analysis of Behavior, 38,* 233–248.

Cohen, H. L., & Filipzak, J. (1971). *A new learning environment.* San Francisco: Jossey-Bass.

Commons, M. L., & Nevin, J. A. (Eds.). (1981). *Quantitative analyses of behavior: Discriminative properties of reinforcement schedules* (Vol. 1). Cambridge, MA: Ballinger.

Commons, M. L., Herrnstein, R. J., & Wagner, A. R. (Eds.). (1982a). *Quantitative analyses of behavior: Acquisition* (Vol. 3). Cambridge, MA: Ballinger.

Commons, M. L., Herrnstein, R. J., & Rachlin, H. (Eds.). (1982b). *Quantitative analyses of behavior: Matching and maximizing accounts* (Vol. 2). Cambridge, MA: Ballinger.

Commons, M. L., Herrnstein, R. J., & Wagner, A. R. (Eds.). (1985). *Quantitative analyses of behavior: Discrimination processes* (Vol. 4). Hillsdale, NJ: Erlbaum.

Commons, M. L., Kacelnik, A., & Shettleworth, S. J. (Eds.). (in press). *Quantitative analysis of behavior: Foraging* (Vol. 6). Hillsdale, NJ: Erlbaum.

Commons, M. L., Mazur, J. E., Nevin, J. A., & Rachlin, H. (Eds.). (1987). *Quantitative analyses of behavior: The effect of delay and of intervening events on reinforcement value* (Vol. 5). Hillsdale, NJ: Erlbaum.

Cooper, J. O., Heron, T. E., & Heward, W. L. (1987). *Applied behavior analysis.* Columbus, OH: Merrill.

Crozier, W. J., & Hoagland, H. (1934). The study of living organisms. In C. Murchison (Ed.). *A handbook of general experimental psychology.* Worcester, MA: Clark University Press.

Darwin, C. (1859). *On the origins of species by means of natural selection.* London: J. Murray.

Darwin, C. (1871). *The descent of man.* London: J. Murray.

Darwin, C. (1872). *The expression of emotions in man and animals.* London: J. Murray.

Day, W. F. (1969a). On certain similarities between the *Philosophical investigations* of Ludwig Wittgenstein and the operationism of B. F. Skinner. *Journal of the Experimental Analysis of Behavior, 12,* 489–506.

Day, W. F. (1969b). Radical behaviorism in reconciliation with phenomenology. *Journal of the Experimental Analysis of Behavior, 12,* 315–328.

Day, W. F. (1976a). Contemporary behaviorism and the concept of intention. In W. J. Arnold (Ed.), *Nebraska Symposium on Motivation, 1975* (Vol. 25, pp. 65–131). Lincoln: University of Nebraska Press.

Day, W. F. (1976b). Analyzing verbal behavior under the control of private events. *Behaviorism, 4,* 195–200.

Day, W. F. (1980). The historical antecedents of contemporary behaviorism. In R. W. Rieber & K. Salzinger (Eds.), *Psychology: Theoretical-historical perspectives* (pp. 203–262). New York: Academic Press.

Day, W. (1983). On the difference between radical and methodological behaviorism. *Behaviorism, 11*, 89–102.

Deguchi, H. (1984). Observational learning from a radical-behavioristic viewpoint. *The Behavior Analyst, 7*, 83–95.

Deitz, S. M., & Arrington, R. L. (1984). Wittgenstein's language games and the call to cognition. *Behaviorism, 12*, 7–14.

Dewey, J. (1896). The reflex arc concept in psychology. *Psychological Review, 3*, 357–370.

Dewey, J., & Bentley, A. F. (1949). *Knowing and the known.* Boston: Beacon Press.

Dollard, J., & Miller, N. E. (1950). *Personality and psychotherapy: An analysis in terms of learning.* New York: McGraw-Hill.

Ebbinghaus, H. (1908). *Abriss der psychologie.* Leipzig: Veit.

Epling, W. F., & Pierce, W. D. (1983). Applied behavior analysis: New directions from the laboratory. *The Behavior Analyst, 6*, 27–37.

Fantino, E., & Logan, C. A. (1979). *The experimental analysis of behavior: A biological perspective.* San Francisco: W. H. Freeman.

Fechner, G. F. (1966). *Elements of psychophysics* (H. Adler, Trans.). New York: Holt, Rinehart & Winston. (Original published in 1860)

Ferster, C. B. (1979). A laboratory model of psychotherapy: The boundary between clinical practice and experimental psychology. In P. Sjoden, S. Bates, & W. S. Dockens (Eds.). *Trends in behavior therapy* (pp. 23–38). New York: Academic Press.

Ferster, C. B., & Skinner, B. F. (1957). *Schedules of reinforcement.* Englewood Cliffs, NJ: Prentice-Hall.

Franks, C. M., Wilson, G. T., Kendall, P. C., & Brownell, K. D. (1984). *Annual review of behavior therapy: Theory and practice* (Vol. 10). New York: Guilford Press.

Gewritz, J. L. (1972). Some contextual determinants of stimulus potency. In R. D. Parke (Ed.), *Recent trends in social learning theory* (pp. 7–33). New York: Academic Press.

Giorgi, A. (1975). Convergences and divergences between phenomenological psychology and behaviorism: A beginning dialogue. *Behaviorism, 3*, 200–212.

Goldiamond, I. (1974). Toward a constructional approach to social problems: Ethical and constitutional issues raised by applied behavior analysis. *Behaviorism, 2*, 1–84.

Goldstein, A. P., & Glick, B. (1987). *Aggression replacement training: A comprehensive intervention for aggressive youth.* Champaign, IL: Research Press.

Goldstein, A. P., Carr, E. G., Davidson, W. S., & Wehr, P. (1981). *In response to aggression: Methods of control and pro-social alternatives.* New York: Pergamon.

Gollin, E. S. (Ed.). (1981). *Behavioral plasticity.* New York: Academic Press.

Gould, S. J. (1981). *The mismeasure of man.* New York: Norton.

Grunbaum, A. (1952). Causality and the science of human behavior. *American Scientist, 40*, 665–676.

Harries, K. D. (1980). *Crime and the environment.* Springfield, IL: Charles C Thomas.

Harshbarger, D., & Maley, R. F. (Eds.). (1974). *Behavior analysis and systems analysis: An intergrative approach to mental health programs.* Kalamazoo: Behaviordelia.

Harzem, P., & Zeiler, M. D. (Eds.). (1981). *Advances in analysis of behavior (Vol. 2). Predictability, correlation, and contiguity.* New York: Wiley.

Hayes, S. C. (1986). Behavioral philosophy in the late 1980s. *Theoretical and Philosophical Psychology, 6*, 39–43.

Hayes, S. C., & Brownstein, A. J. (1986). Mentalism, behavior-behavior relations, and a behavior-analytic view of the purposes of science. *The Behavior Analyst, 9*, 175–190.

Helmholtz, H. L. v. (1962). *Treatise on physiological optics.* New York: Dover. (Original published in 1857)

Hersen, M., Eisler, R. M., & Miller, P. M. (Eds.). (1982). *Progress in behavior modification* (Vol. 13). New York: Academic Press.

Higgins, S. T., & Morris, E. K. (1984). A review of the generality of free-operant avoidance conditioning to human behavior. *Psychological Bulletin, 96*, 247–272.

Hineline, P. N. (1980). The language of behavior analysis: Its community, its functions, and its limitations. *Behaviorism, 8*, 67–86.

Holland, J. G., & Skinner, B. F. (1961). *The analysis of behavior.* New York: McGraw-Hill.
Homans, G. C. (1969). The sociological relevance of behaviorism. In R. L. Burgess & D. Bushell
(Eds.), *Behavioral sociology* (pp. 1–24). New York: Columbia University Press.
Honig, W. K. (1966). *Operant behavior: Research and application.* Englewood Cliffs, NJ: Prentice-
Hall.
Honig, W. K., & Staddon, J. E. R. (1977). *Handbook of operant behavior.* Englewood Cliffs, NJ:
Prentice-Hall.
Hull, C. L. (1952). *A behavior system.* New York: Wiley.
James, W. (1890). *Principles of psychology.* New York: Holt.
James, W. (1907). *Pragmatism.* New York: New American Library.
Jeffery, C. R. (1965). Criminal behavior and learning theory. *The Journal of Criminal Law,
Criminology, and Police Science, 56,* 294–300.
Jeffery, C. R. (1971). *Crime prevention through environmental design.* Beverly Hills, CA: Sage.
Johnston, J. M., & Pennypacker, H. S. (1980). *Strategies and tactics of human behavioral research.*
Hillsdale, NJ: Erlbaum.
Kantor, J. R. (1924). *Principles of psychology* (Vol. 1). Chicago: Principia Press.
Kantor, J. R. (1926). *Principles of psychology* (Vol. 2). Chicago: Principia Press.
Kantor, J. R. (1945). *Psychology and logic* (Vol. 1). Chicago: Principia Press.
Kantor, J. R. (1947). *Problems in physiological psychology.* Chicago: Principia Press.
Kantor, J. R. (1950). *Psychology and logic* (Vol. 2). Chicago: Principia Press.
Kantor, J. R. (1953). *The logic of modern science.* Chicago: Principia Press.
Kantor, J. R. (1959). *Interbehavioral psychology.* Chicago: Principia Press.
Kantor, J. R. (1963). *The scientific evolution of psychology* (Vol. 1). Chicago: Principia Press.
Kantor, J. R. (1969). *The scientific evolution of psychology* (Vol. 2). Chicago: Principia Press.
Kantor, J. R. (1971). *The aim and progress of psychology and other sciences.* Chicago: Principia
Press.
Kantor, J. R. (1981). *Interbehavioral philosophy.* Chicago: Principia Press.
Kantor, J. R. (1982). *Cultural psychology.* Chicago: Principia Press.
Kantor, J. R. (1984). *Selected writings in philosophy, psychology, and other sciences.* Chicago:
Principia Press.
Kazdin, A. E. (1978). *History of behavior modification.* Baltimore: University Park Press.
Kazdin, A. E. (1984). *Behavior modification in applied settings* (3rd ed.). Homewood, IL: The
Dorsey Press.
Keller, F. S. (1969). *Learning: Reinforcement theory.* New York: Random House.
Keller, F. S. (1973). *The definition of psychology.* Englewood Cliffs, NJ: Prentice-Hall.
Krechevsky, I. (1939). Review of Skinner's *The behavior of organisms. Journal of Abnormal and
Social Psychology, 34,* 404–407.
Krumboltz, J. D., & Thoresen, C. E. (Eds.). (1969). *Behavioral counseling: Cases and techniques.*
New York: Holt, Rinehart & Winston.
Leitenberg, H. (Ed.). (1976). *Handbook of behavior modification and behavior therapy.* Englewood
Cliffs, NJ: Prentice-Hall.
Lewontin, R. C., Rose, S., & Kamin, L. J. (1984). *Not in our genes.* New York: Pantheon.
Loeb, J. (1900). *Comparative physiology of the brain and comparative psychology.* New York:
Putnam.
Loeb, J. (1916). *The organism as a whole, from a physiochemical viewpoint.* New York: Putnam.
Logue, A. W. (1979). Taste aversion and the generality of the laws of learning. *Psychological
Bulletin, 81,* 276–296.
Lowe, C. F. (1979). Determinants of human operant behavior. In M. D. Zeiler & P. Harzem (Eds.),
Reinforcement and the organization of behavior (pp. 159–192). New York: Wiley.
Lubinski, D., & Thompson, T. (1986). Functional units of human behavior and their integration: A
dispositional analysis. In T. Thompson & M. D. Zeiler (Eds.), *Analysis and integration of
behavioral units* (pp. 275–314). Hillsdale, NJ: Erlbaum.
Mach, E. (1960). *The science of mechanics* (T. J. McCormack, Trans.) LaSalle, IL: Open Court.
(Original work published in 1883)
Malcolm, N. (1977). *Memory and mind.* Ithaca, NY: Cornell University Press.

Marr, M. J. (1983). Memory: Models and metaphors. *The Psychological Record, 33,* 12–19.

Marr, M. J. (1985). Tis the gift to be simple: A retrospective appreciation of Mach's *The science of mechanics. Journal of the Experimental Analysis of Behavior, 41,* 129–138.

Martin, G., & Pear, J. (1983). *Behavior modification: What it is and how to do it.* Englewood Cliffs, NJ: Prentice-Hall.

Martin, R. (1975). *Legal challenges to behavior modification.* Champaign, IL: Research Press.

Matthews, B. A., Shimoff, E., Catania, A. C., & Sagvolden, T. (1977). Uninstructed human responding: Sensitivity to ratio and interval contingencies. *Journal of the Experimental Analysis of Behavior, 27,* 453–467.

Mayer, G. R., Butterworth, T., Nafpaktitis, M., & Sulzer-Azaroff, B. (1983). Preventing school vandalism and improving discipline: A three year study. *Journal of Applied Behavior Analysis, 16,* 355–369.

McDowell, J. J. (1982). The importance of Herrnstein's mathematical statement of the law of effect for behavior therapy. *American Psychologist, 37,* 771–779.

McKearney, J. W. (1977). Asking questions about behavior. *Perspectives in Biology and Medicine, 21,* 109–119.

Mead, G. H. (1934). *Mind, self, and society.* Chicago: University of Chicago Press.

Mednick, S., & Christiansen, K. O. (1977). *Biosocial basis of criminal behavior.* New York: Garden Press.

Meehl, P. E. (1986). Trait language and behavior. In T. Thompson & M. D. Zeiler (Eds.), *Analysis and integration of behavior units* (pp. 315–334). Hillsdale, NJ: Erlbaum.

Meichenbaum, D. M. (1977). *Cognitive behavior modification: An integrative approach.* New York: Plenum Press.

Meichenbaum, D. M., & Cameron, R. (1982). Cognitive-behavior therapy. In G. T. Wilson & C. M. Franks (Eds.), *Contemporary behavior therapy* (pp. 310–338). New York: Guilford Press.

Michael, J. (1974). Statistical inference for individual organism research: Mixed blessing or curse? *Journal of Applied Behavior Analysis, 7,* 647–653.

Michael, J. (1982). Distinguishing between discriminative and motivational functions of stimuli. *Journal of the Experimental Analysis of Behavior, 37,* 149–155.

Michael, J. L. (1985). Behavior analysis: A radical perspective. In B. L. Hammonds (Eds.), *Psychology and learning* (pp. 99–121). Washington, DC: American Psychological Association.

Millenson, J. R., & Leslie, J. C. (1979). *Principles of behavioral analysis.* New York: Macmillan.

Miller, N. E., & Dollard, J. (1941). *Social learning and imitation.* New Haven: Yale University Press.

Moore, J. (1975). On the principle of operationism in a science of behavior. *Behaviorism, 3,* 120–138.

Moore, J. (1980). On behaviorism and private events. *The Psychological Record, 30,* 459–475.

Moore, J. (1981). On mentalism, methodological behaviorism, and radical behaviorism. *Behaviorism, 9,* 55–77.

Moore, J. (1985). Some historical and conceptual relations among logical positivism, operationism, and behaviorism. *The Behavior Analyst, 8,* 53–63.

Morgan, C. L. (1894). *Introduction to comparative psychology.* London: W. Scott.

Morris, E. K. (1978). A brief review of legal deviance: References in behavior analysis and delinquency. In D. Marholin (Ed.), *Child behavior therapy* (pp. 214–238). New York: Gardner Press.

Morris, E. K. (1980). Applied behavior analysis for criminal justice practice: Some current dimensions. *Criminal Justice and Behavior, 7,* 131–145.

Morris, E. K. (1982). Some relationships between interbehavioral psychology and radical behaviorism. *Behaviorism, 10,* 187–216.

Morris, E. K. (1984). Interbehavioral psychology and radical behaviorism: Some similarities and differences. *The Behavior Analyst, 7,* 197–204.

Morris, E. K. (1985a). Wittgenstein's language games and the call to cognition: Comments on Deitz and Arrington (1984). *Behaviorism, 13,* 137–146.

Morris, E. K. (1985b). Public information, dissemination, and behavior analysis. *The Behavior Analyst, 8,* 95–110.

Morris, E. K. (1985c). The Molloy-Birnbrauer exchange: How many factors do a psychology make? *Behaviour Change, 3,* 1–14.

Morris, E. K., Higgins, S. T., & Bickel, W. K. (1982a). The influence of Kantor's interbehavioral psychology on behavior analysis. *The Behavior Analyst, 5,* 158–173.

Morris, E. K., Higgins, S. T., & Bickel, W. K. (1982b). Comments on cognitive science in the experimental analysis of behavior. *The Behavior Analyst, 5,* 109–125.

Morris, E. K., Higgins, S. T., & Bickel, W. K. (1983). Contributions of J. R. Kantor to contemporary behaviorism. In N. W. Smith, P. T. Mountjoy, & D. H. Ruben (Eds.), *Reassessment in psychology: The interbehavioral alternative* (pp. 51–89). Washington, DC: University Press of America.

Morris, E. K., Johnson, L. M., Powell, L. K., & Todd, J. T. (1987). Interbehavioral perspectives on legal deviance: Some considerations of context. In D. H. Ruben & D. J. Delprato (Eds.), *New ideas in therapy* (pp. 137–157). Westport, CT: Greenwood Press.

Morse, W. H., & Kelleher, R. T. (1977). Determinants of reinforcement and punishment. In W. K. Honig & J. E. R. Staddon (Eds.), *Handbook of operant behavior* (pp. 174–200). Englewood Cliffs, NJ: Prentice-Hall.

Newsom, C., Favell, J. E., & Rincover, A. (1983). Side effects of punishment. In S. Axelrod & J. Apsche (Eds.), *The effects of punishment on human behavior* (pp. 285–316). New York: Academic Press.

Nietzel, M. T. (1979). *Crime and its modification: A social learning perspective.* Elmsford, NY: Pergamon Press.

O'Donnell, J. M. (1985). *The origins of behaviorism: American psychology, 1870–1920.* New York: New York University Press.

Patterson, G. R. (1982). *Coercive family processes.* Champaign, IL: Research Press.

Pavlov, I. P. (1927). *Conditioned reflexes.* London: Oxford University Press.

Pepper, S. C. (1942). *World hypotheses.* Berkeley, CA: University of California Press.

Pierce, C. S. (1940). *Philosophical writings of Pierce* (J. Buchler, Ed.). New York: Dover.

Pierce, W. D., & Epling, W. F. (1983). Choice, matching, and human behavior: A review of the literature. *The Behavior Analyst, 6,* 57–76.

Polirstok, S. R., & Greer, P. D. (1977). Remediation of mutually aversive interactions between a problem student and four teachers by training the student in reinforcement techniques. *Journal of Applied Behavior Analysis, 10,* 707–716.

Reese, E. P. (1986). Learning about teaching from teaching about learning: Presenting behavior analysis in an introductory survey course. In W. P. Makosky (Ed.), *The Master Lecture Series* (Vol. 6, pp. 69–127). Washington, DC: American Psychological Association.

Reese, H. W. (1982). Behavior analysis and life-span developmental psychology. *Developmental Review, 2,* 150–161.

Reynolds, G. S. (1975). *A primer of operant conditioning.* Glenview, IL: Scott, Foresman.

Ribes-Inesta, E., & Bandura, A. (Eds.). (1976). *Analysis of delinquency and aggression.* Hillsdale, NJ: Erlbaum.

Ringen, J. (1976). Explanation, teleology, and operant behaviorism. *Philosophy of Science, 43,* 223–253.

Rogers-Warren, A., & Warren, S.F. (Eds.). (1977). *Ecological perspectives in behavior analysis.* Baltimore: University Park Press.

Romanes, J. (1882). *Animal intelligence.* London: Kegan Paul, Trench.

Rosenthal, T. L. (1982). Social learning theory. In G. T. Wilson & C. M. Franks (Eds.), *Contemporary behavior therapy: Conceptual and empirical foundations* (pp. 339–363). New York: Guilford Press.

Ruben, D. H., & Delprato, D. J. (Eds.). (1987). *New ideas in therapy.* Westport, CT: Greenwood Press.

Rucker, D. (1969). *The Chicago pragmatists.* Minneapolis: University of Minnesota Press.

Scheffler, I. (1974). *Four pragmatists: A critical introduction to Pierce, James, Mead, and Dewey.* London: Routledge & Kegan Paul.

Schlinger, H., & Blakely, E. (1987). *Function-altering effects of contingency-specifying stimuli. The Behavior Analyst, 10,* 41–45.

Schwartz, A., & Goldiamond, I. (1975). *Social casework: A behavioral approach*. New York: Columbia University Press.

Schwartz, B. (1974). On going back to nature [review of *Biological boundaries of learning*]. *Journal of the Experimental Analysis of Behavior, 21*, 183–198.

Schwitzgebel, R. K. (1964). *Streetcorner research: An experimental approach to the juvenile delinquent*. Cambridge, MA: Harvard University Press.

Sears, R. R., Maccoby, E. E., & Levin, H. (1957). *Patterns of child rearing*. Stanford, CA: Stanford University Press.

Seligman, M. E. P., & Hagar, J. L. (1972). *Biological boundaries of learning*. New York: Meredith.

Sidman, M. (1960). *Tactics of scientific research*. New York: Basic Books.

Sidman, M. (1986). Functional analysis of emergent verbal classes. In T. Thompson & M. D. Zeiler (Eds.), *Analysis and integration of behavioral units* (pp. 213–245). Hillsdale, NJ: Lawrence Erlbaum.

Skinner, B. F. (1935). The generic nature of the concepts of stimulus and response. *Journal of General Psychology, 12*, 40–65.

Skinner, B. F. (1938). *The behavior of organisms*. Englewood Cliffs, NJ: Prentice-Hall.

Skinner, B. F. (1945). The operational analysis of psychological terms. *Psychological Review, 52*, 270–277, 291–294.

Skinner, B. F. (1950). Are theories of learning necessary? *Psychological Review, 57*, 193–216.

Skinner, B. F. (1953). *Science and human behavior*. New York: Macmillan.

Skinner, B. F. (1956). A case history in scientific method. *American Psychologist, 11*, 221–233.

Skinner, B. F. (1957). *Verbal behavior*. Englewood Cliffs, NJ: Prentice-Hall.

Skinner, B. F. (1966a). What is the experimental analysis of behavior? *Journal of the Experimental Analysis of Behavior, 9*, 213–218.

Skinner, B. F. (1966b). The phylogeny and ontogeny of behavior. *Science, 153*, 1205–1213.

Skinner, B. F. (1969). *Contingencies of reinforcement*. Englewood Cliffs, NJ: Prentice-Hall.

Skinner, B. F. (1971). *Beyond freedom and dignity*. New York: Knopf.

Skinner, B. F. (1974). *About behaviorism*. New York: Knopf.

Skinner, B. F. (1975). The shaping of phylogentic behavior. *Journal of the Experimental Analysis of Behavior, 24*, 117–120.

Skinner, B. F. (1977). Herrnstein and the evolution of behaviorism. *American Psychologist, 32*, 1006–1012.

Skinner, B. F. (1981). Selection by consequences. *Science, 213*, 501–504.

Smith, L. D. (1986). *Behaviorism and logical positivism: A reassessment of the alliance*. Stanford, CA: Stanford University Press.

Smith, N. W., Mountjoy, P. T., & Ruben, D. H. (Eds.). (1983). *Reassessment in psychology: The interbehavioral alternative*. Washington, DC: University Press of America.

Stolz, S. B. (1978). *Ethical issues in behavior modification*. San Francisco: Jossey-Bass.

Stuart, R. B. (Ed.). (1981). *Violent behavior: Social learning approaches to prediction, management, and treatment*. New York: Brunner/Mazel.

Stumphauzer, J. S. (Ed.). (1973). *Behavior modification with delinquents*. Springfield, IL: Charles C Thomas.

Stumphauzer, J. S. (Ed.). (1979). *Progress in behavior modification with delinquents*. Springfield, IL: Charles C Thomas.

Stumphauzer, J. S. (1986). *Helping delinquents change: A treatment manual of social learning approaches*. New York: Haworth.

Tharp, R. G., & Wetzel, R. J. (1969). *Behavior modification in the natural environment*. New York: Academic Press.

Thompson, T. (1984). The examining magistrate for nature: A retrospective review of Claude Bernard's *An introduction to the study of experimental medicine*. *Journal of Experimental Analysis of Behavior, 41*, 211–216.

Thompson, T., & Zeiler, M. D. (Eds.). (1986). *Analysis and integration of behavioral units*. Hillsdale, NJ: Erlbaum.

Thorndike, E. L. (1911). *Animal intelligence*. New York: Macmillan.

Titchener, E. B. (1899). *An outline of psychology*. New York: Macmillan.

Todd, J. T., & Morris, E. K. (1983). Misconception and miseducation: Presentations of radical behaviorism in psychology textbooks. *The Behavior Analyst, 6,* 153–160.

Todd, J. T., & Morris, E. K. (1986). The early research of John B. Watson: Before the behavioral revolution. *The Behavior Analyst, 9,* 71–86.

Tolman, E. (1932). *Purposive behavior in animals and men.* New York: Century.

Turner, M. B. (1967). *Philosophy and the science of behavior.* New York: Appleton-Century-Crofts.

Verplanck, W. S. (1954). Burrhus F. Skinner. In W. K. Estes, S. Koch, K. MacCorquodale, P. E. Meehl, C. G. Mueller, W. N. Schoenfeld, & W. S. Verplanck (Eds.), *Modern learning theory* (pp. 267–316). New York: Appleton-Century-Crofts.

Wahler, R. G. (1980). The insular mother: Her problems in parent-child treatment. *Journal of Applied Behavior Analysis, 13,* 207–219.

Wahler, R. G., & Fox, J. J. (1981a). Response structure in deviant child-parent relationships: Implications for family therapy. In D. Bernstein & H. Howe (Eds.), *Nebraska Symposium on Motivation* (Vol. 29, pp. 1–46). Lincoln: University of Nebraska Press.

Wahler, R. G., & Fox, J. J. (1981b). Setting events in applied behavior analysis: Toward a conceptual and methodological expansion. *Journal of Applied Behavior Analysis, 14,* 322–338.

Wahler, R. G., & Graves, M. G. (1983). Setting events in social networks: Ally or enemy in child behavior therapy? *Behavior Therapy, 14,* 19–36.

Watson, J. B. (1913). Psychology as the behaviorist views it. *Psychological Review, 20,* 158–177.

Watson, J. B. (1919). *Psychology from the standpoint of a behaviorist.* Philadelphia: Lippincott.

Watson, J. B. (1924). *Behaviorism.* New York: W. W. Norton.

Whaley, D. L., & Malott, R. W. (1971). *Elementary principles of behavior.* Englewood Cliffs, NJ: Prentice-Hall.

Wilson, J. Q., & Herrnstein, R. J. (1985). *Crime and human nature.* New York: Simon & Schuster.

Wittgenstein, L. (1953). *Philosophical investigations* (G. E. M. Anscombe, Trans.). New York: Macmillan.

Wundt, W. (1910). *Principles of physiological psychology.* New York: Macmillan.

Yochelson, S., & Samenow, S. E. (1976). *The criminal personality. Volume I: A profile for change.* New York: Jason Aronson.

Zeiler, M. D. (1984). The sleeping giant: Reinforcement schedules. *Journal of the Experimental Analysis of Behavior, 42,* 482–493.

Zeiler, M. D., & Harzem, P. (Eds.). (1979). *Reinforcement and the organization of behavior* (Vol. 1). New York: Wiley.

Zeiler, M. D., & Harzem, P. (Eds.). (1983). *Advances in analysis of behavior (Vol. 3). Biological factors in learning.* New York: Wiley.

Zettle, R. D., & Hayes, S. C. (1982). Rule-governed behavior: A potential theoretical framework for cognitive-behavioral therapy. In P. C. Kendall (Ed.), *Advances in cognitive-behavioral research* (Vol. 1, pp. 73–118). New York: Academic Press.

Zuriff, G. E. (1985). *Behaviorism: A conceptual reconstruction.* New York: Columbia University Press.

II

BEHAVIORAL APPLICATIONS IN ADULT AND JUVENILE CORRECTIONS

4

Probation and Parole

MICHAEL T. NIETZEL AND MELISSA J. HIMELEIN

This chapter surveys the application of behavioral techniques to probationers and parolees. As we discuss later in the chapter, probation and parole officers face a set of demands that can be reconceptualized in behavioral terms. Principles of behavioral intervention and case management can then be derived that would be predicted to be effective change techniques for the probationers/ parolees. Polakow (1974), an early advocate of behavioral approaches to probation, has developed behavioral reconceptualizations of traditional probation activities such as record keeping, treatment plans, structures of contact with the probationer, accountability, and the use of incentives with probationers (see Nietzel, 1979, p. 191). The goals of these reconceptualizations have been to (1) reduce the use of aversive control with offenders, (2) tailor interventions to the individual needs of each client, (3) provide efficient, relatively easily learned techniques that can be applied in the natural environment, and (4) increase the chances that probation and parole will lead to the successful adjustment of the offender in the community.

Following a review of the history and special problems of probation and parole, we review behavioral interventions that have been used with probationers and parolees, paying special attention to the extent to which the previously mentioned four goals have been achieved. We conclude the chapter with (1) a discussion of the deficiencies in research methodology that plague the area and with (2) some recommendations for how a more solid link between behavior modification and probation/parole could be forged.

Probation and parole are the work horses of corrections, accounting for more than 75% of the offenders in this country's correctional systems (U.S. Department of Justice, 1982). Although probation and parole are examples of community-based corrections, they have many differences. Probation, which is about six times more frequent a disposition than parole, is administered by the courts when they *suspend* execution of a prison sentence and place the offender on probation for a specified period or when they *postpone* imposing the sentence contingent on the offender meeting the conditions of probation, at

Michael T. Nietzel and Melissa J. Himelein • Department of Psychology, University of Kentucky, Lexington, Kentucky 40506.

which time the sentence will be considered served. Probation is frequently given to juveniles, misdemeanants, and some adult first-time felons. More than one half of all criminal sentences in the United States involve probation (Carney, 1977).

Parole has been defined as "a form of conditional release of the prisoner from the correctional institution prior to the expiration of his sentence" (Tappan, 1960, p. 709). The restrictions imposed on parolees are aimed at two goals: (1) continued rehabilitation and readjustment of the offender and (2) continued protection of the public. Parole is an executive rather than a judicial responsibility and is usually administered by special parole boards, commissions, or agencies affiliated with correctional departments. The average prisoner in the typical state has approximately a 70% chance of being paroled (Cohen & Gobert, 1983).

Any correctional disposition is justified on its ability to meet four goals—incapacitation, retribution, deterrence, and rehabilitation. In the cases of probation and parole, the major rationale for their use has been rehabilitation, although neither one neglects the other objectives. Both practices are supported by the assumption that they will enhance the offender's chances of living lawfully, safely, and productively in the community.

Carney (1977) listed five justifications for using probation: (1) it maximizes the normalizing influences available in the community that are absent in most correctional institutions; (2) it minimizes the physical and psychological degradations that accompany imprisonment; (3) it attempts to "humanize" rehabilitation; (4) it is less expensive than institutional confinement; and (5) it is regarded as a more effective correctional procedure than incarceration. In a similar fashion, parole is tied to the principle that small, graduated adjustments are more easily accomplished than large, all-or-nothing ones. An additional, and often overlooked, function of probation and parole is that they regulate the size and nature of prison populations. Reductions in the use of either disposition would increase the need for prison construction and expansion, two very politically unpopular expenditures.

HISTORICAL PRECEDENTS

History of Probation

Although probation is often claimed as America's one unique contribution to correctional practice, it has at least four important predecessors in legal history.

Benefit of Clergy

Benefit of clergy involved the claim by the church that because clerics were subject to church law, their punishment, even for secular violations, should be left to the church rather than to the state. Newman (1968) claims the primary objective of this plea was avoidance of capital punishment and that many nonclerics tried to take advantage of it.

Judicial Reprieve

Judicial reprieve referred to the discretion of judges to temporarily suspend a sentence if they were dissatisfied with the verdict or when the convicted party applied for a pardon. This method was never intended to involve an indefinite suspension, as is the case with probation (Newman, 1968).

Recognizance and Bail

Recognizance developed in the fourteenth century as a preventive measure by which someone suspected of wrongdoing gave assurance to the state that subsequent offenses would not occur. This device was used both for suspected troublemakers and for those individuals actually arraigned in court for some criminal offense.

Bail originated in medieval England, where pretrial release of an accused was deemed necessary to eliminate prolonged periods of incarceration before trial. Sheriffs were allowed to relase a prisoner conditional upon his or her promise or a promise of a third party that the accused would appear for trial. From the outset, bail relationships in England were characterized by their personal nature. Social and geographical conditions in America necessitated a fortification of these methods because stable personal relationships were less frequent among recently formed settlements. As a result, the commercial bailbondsman appeared in America as a replacement for the third-party surety in England. The conditions of bail as practiced in ancient England closely approximated some of the conditions of our modern-day probation system.

Filing of Cases

The "filing" of a case involved the suspension of a sentence when the court felt that an immediate sentence was not required. Its implementation necessitated the consent of the defendant and whatever special conditions the court chose to impose.

The legal thread that tied these judicial devices together was the commonlaw tradition that courts could *temporarily* suspend sentences for specific purposes. The emergence of probation, however, assumed a judicial perogative to suspend a sentence *indefinitely* on the basis of several types of conditional criteria. This view was denied in the *Killits* decision,[1] in which the Supreme Court rejected the proposition "that those courts possessed the arbitrary discretion to permanently decline to enforce the law." In spite of the Supreme Court's objection to indefinite suspension, the flexibility provided by a system

---

[1]*Ex parte* United States, 242 U.S. 27-53 (1916).

of common law, and the general approval of the public enabled conditional (and indefinite) suspensions of sentence to continue.

The first statute legitimizing probation was passed in 1878 by Massachusetts, which had pioneered several forms of sentence suspension and had, as early as 1841, under the leadership of John Augustus, placed offenders on probationary status. An English attorney by the name of Matthew Davenport Hill also began his version of probation for youths in 1841. As early as 1681 in Albany, New York, a man who misbehaved toward his wife was ordered to be supervised by two local, "good" men who were to oversee his conduct toward his spouse. (Rubin, 1973).

All states now authorize probation. Probation was authorized at the federal level in 1925 when Congress passed the first federal probation law.

History of Parole

Maconochie and Crofton

Parole has several antecedents, beginning with England's seventeenth-century practice of *transportation* in which pardoned prisoners were shipped to the American colonies by private contractors paid by the government. Originally intended as a merciful alternative to the death penalty that retained social control and protection as priorities, transportation was first authorized by England's Vagrancy Act of 1597. By 1717, legislation had been passed that made it the standard penalty for certain crimes.

Transportation to America was terminated in part because slavery became a cheaper labor supply than indentured felons. England then began to send her convicts to Australia, although opposition to transportation was being voiced on several counts. These objections paralleled the criticisms one hears about parole as it is practiced today. Some critics objected to the lenience of transportation; others were concerned about its harshness and unfairness.

Captain Alexander Maconochie was a nineteenth-century English naval officer who was asked to write a report on the transportation issue in Australia. Although generally in favor or transportation, Maconochie wrote a report that was highly critical of the cruelty and deplorable conditions he found. Maconochie's reward for his report was to be appointed superintendent of the Norfolk Island Penal Colony. Convinced that Norfolk could be reformed and that prisoners could be taught to become responsible people, Maconochie developed a system that amounted to the first large-scale token economy in the history of rehabilitation. He favored a plan in which prisoners could earn better living conditions and an early release date contingent on "industry and good conduct." This idea took the form of a Marks System, a substitute for wages that allowed inmates to progress up a five-step ladder leading to unconditional freedom. The five phases were (1) rigid discipline and absolute confinement, (2) labor on work gangs, (3) limited freedom within prescribed areas, (4) conditional freedom, and (5) total freedom.

Maconochie's system also made use of the ticket-of-leave, a little-used procedure that actually predated Maconochie. The ticket-of-leave allowed prison officials to exempt a convict from a sentence on the condition that the convict was able to secure and maintain civil employment. After a number of years, a system was adopted by which a ticket-of-leave could be obtained only after a convict had served a certain set period of time. Conditional freedom (Step 4 in Maconochie's system) corresponded to the ticket-of-leave status.

Maconochie was fired after 4 years as Norfolk Island's superintendent, the end result of mounting criticisms that his reforms were insufficiently retributive. Cohen and Gobert (1983, p. 14) point out the irony that "while behavior modification and token economies are often characterized today as dehumanizing, Maconochie's programs were criticized for their leniency." Two other deficiencies of the Norfolk program contributed to its demise. First, it did not provide for supervision of released inmates, an omission that ignored the first rule of any correctional innovation—society must be protected. Second, it lacked an adequate labor market to absorb inmates after their release.

Both these problems were addressed by Sir Walter Crofton, a disciple of Maconochie and director of the Irish prison system. Crofton's program, termed the *intermediate system* (also known as the *Irish system*) consisted of three elements: (1) strict imprisonment, (2) intermediate imprisonment, and (3) ticket-of-leave. The first stage required very arduous, boring work by inmates who were kept in solitary confinement. During the second stage, prisoners were able to earn "marks" for a good employment record in public labor projects. After an inmate proved his reform during this stage and was offered employment outside the institution, he was promoted to the third, or ticket-of-leave, phase. Crofton developed a set of restrictive conditions that were in effect during this phase and that, if broken, could result in the reimprisonment of the violator.

Parole in the United States

In the United States, parole was patterned after Crofton's ideas and was first used in 1876 at the New York State Reformatory for Juveniles in Elmira under the direction of Superintendent Zebulon Brockway. Parole was quickly implemented by other states that already had adopted *good time* laws that permitted an early release from prison contingent on satisfactory behavior. The first federal parole law was passed in 1910. By 1945, all the states had parole systems, although the organization and administration of the systems varied considerably. In 1976, Congress passed the Parole Commission and Reorganization Act that formalized a more objective approach to release decisions, known as the "guidelines approach." Since the mid-1970s, broad-based objections to parole have led some states (e.g., Maine) to eliminate parole, whereas others (e.g., Illinois, Indiana, California) have curtailed it considerably. In 1981, a third of the states reported a declining use of parole; nationally, the number of parolees increased only 2% in 1981 (Cohen & Gobert, 1983).

The Indeterminate Sentence

The most important forerunner to parole, besides the programs of Maconochie and Crofton, was the indeterminate sentence (Cavender, 1982). The indeterminate sentence is one where the offender is committed to prison for an indefinite period of time. The precise time of release is determined by the amount of correctional progress shown by the prisoner. Intended to provide flexibility in determing the terms of incarceration, the indeterminate sentence consists of two basic elements: (a) discretion in the dispensation of punishment by judges and (b) delay in the final determination of length of confinement until a certain portion of the sentence has been served.

For many years, the indeterminate sentence has been thought to be an essential ingredient in parole. In fact, as we shall see, there is nothing incompatible with determinate sentences and parole in which certain reductions in sentence, specified to the offender in advance, are contingent on prescribed prison conduct.

Since the mid-1970s, discontent with indeterminate sentencing has grown, and many states have made efforts to shift sentencing systems toward what has been called fixed, determinate, or presumptive sentencing. The most common criticism of the indeterminate sentence is the well-documented finding of marked disparity among sentences imposed upon "similarly situated offenders" (e.g., Bagley, 1979; Carey, 1979; Griswold & Wiatrowski, 1983). In general, sentences are strongly related to the seriousness of the offense and the prior record of the offender (Gottfredson, 1979), but indeterminate sentencing allows for consideration of many other factors in the decision-making process.

A second objection to indeterminate sentencing comes from the widespread belief that prisoners cannot be rehabilitated (Griswold & Wiatrowski, 1983). Although the justification for the indeterminate sentence is its presumed value in treatment, it has not been demonstrated to have had a significant effect upon a released prisoner's reformation (see Martinson, 1974, for review). Manson (1977) argues that parole offers no more effective a weapon against recidivism than outright discharge, and he suggests that the prosocial activities in which inmates engage while in prison are merely for the benefit of parole review panels. According to Carey (1979), "The ideal of rehabilitation . . . is noble but unachievable in the overburdened American penal system" (p. 568).

Presumptive sentencing is supported by advocates of deterrence, retribution, or "just-deserts" models of penology. For example, von Hirsch (1976) construes punishment as the just consequence of illegal conduct: "Certain things are simply wrong and ought to be punished" (p. 39). Determinate sentencing mandates the setting of prison terms at the time of sentencing, solely on the basis of the blameworthiness of the criminal act. Such modifications can leave parole boards without a function, and in fact, the just-deserts model enthusiasts favor the curtailment or elimination of parole (von Hirsch & Hanrahan, 1979).

Although presumptive sentencing proponents contend that "flat time" would eliminate the problem of sentence disparity, most determinancy laws provide for a surprising amount of flexibility in sentencing. Judges are instructed to impose the normal term in an average case, but greater or lesser terms may be levied if the judge believes sufficiently aggravating or mitigating factors are present. For example, the penal code in Illinois lists 12 specific mitigating factors and 7 aggravating factors that magistrates may consider. Aggravating and mitigating circumstances are less clearly defined in some other states, and the resulting changes in sentences may be quite large. Such legislative schemes have been criticized by von Hirsch and Hanrahan (1981), who noted that "the leeway granted by these rules . . . leaves much room for unguided discretionary choices" (p. 300).

A second area of flexibility in determinate sentencing is release dates. Prisoners are able to secure early release through "good-time credits," a system in which inmates are rewarded for good behavior by sentence reductions of one third to one half the original term of imprisonment (von Hirsch & Hanrahan, 1981). Under determinate sentencing laws, the control of the duration of confinement has shifted from parole boards to prison authorities. One might argue that parole boards, which review a large number of cases across jurisdictions, could be more consistent in their decisions than would prison officials (Gottfredson, 1979).

Effectiveness and Current Status of Probation and Parole

Parole, and to a lesser extent, probation are being assailed from several directions as part of a more general attack on the criminal justice system. Several jurisdictions have passed statutes that either deny probation to certain types of offenders who once routinely received it or that reduce court discretion in assigning offenders to probation (Cohen & Gobert, 1983). Objections to parole have been even more vigorous and successful in limiting its use. At this time, no jurisdiction has eliminated probation, but the trend for parole is clearly toward greater curtailment or abolition.

Criticisms of probation and parole have been effective, in part, because they focus on real defects in both dispositions. A second reason for the dramatic impact of the objections is that they come from vastly different philosophical and political positions, resulting in a crisscross of criticism sure to ensnare almost any program. Conservatives object to the failure of rehabilitation represented by probation and parole; liberals complain about the unfairness involved in sentence disparities.

Probation

A general conclusion about the rehabilitative effects of probation is complicated by several factors. First, there are disagreements about which criteria should be used in measuring success. Programs that monitor arrests for new criminal offenses or base their recidivism figures on actual convictions will show lower recidivism rates than programs that combine rearrests with technical probation violations. Second, many programs do not consider differences in the seriousness of offenses for which probationees are arrested or convicted. A third problem concerns the tremendous differences in the scope of services subsumed under the rubric of probation. Some probation programs offer community-based educational, vocational, and counseling programs; others provide only the most limited levels of intervention aimed largely at the surveillance of probationers' activities.

Carney (1971) cites several studies that have claimed lower recidivism rates for probation than for imprisonment (Empey & Rabow, 1961; Irving & Sandhu, 1973; Rumney & Murphy, 1968; Sparks, 1971). Whether these differences are due to the special effects of probation or to the preselection of offenders less likely to recidivate under any conditions is not clear. Hartinger, Eldefonso, and Coffey (1973; cited in Abadinsky, 1977) report that approximately 75% of probation cases can be considered successful. Even with equivocal evidence about probation's differential effectiveness, the increased use of probation can usually be favored on economic grounds. It has been estimated that probation can be implemented at approximately 10% of the cost of imprisonment *without any reduced effectiveness,* rendering it a vary viable correctional alternative (Allen & Simonsen, 1975).

Parole

Many of the same problems that cloud evaluation of probation prevent an unambiguous assessment of the effects of parole. Definitions of recidivism vary greatly, as do the follow-up periods during which outcome data are collected. No uniform criteria are available upon which release decisions are made, thereby rendering any comparisons between different parole systems or between parole and continued incarceration a very hazardous venture. In an attempt to remedy these difficulties, a system of unified record keeping, the Uniform Parole Reports, was begun in 1974.

It has become common to accept pronouncements that no matter what correctional practice one implements, two thirds of the offenders will recidivate. The "two-thirds myth" is not well documented in the literature, and even those who have been very pessimistic in general about rehabilitative effects acknowledge that parolees have the lowest recidivism of all prison releases (Martinson & Wilks, 1977). In general, the success rate for parolees after 1 to 2 years of release is 60% to 70% (Glaser, 1969; U.S. Department of Justice, 1974). There is no adequate evidence that this success rate is produced by any specific element of parole such as supervision or case counseling (Carney, 1977). In fact, effects of parole cannot be attributed unambiguously to the parole process itself. As with probation, whatever outcomes are achieved may be due to the *selection* of offenders who would be more successful than their unselected cohorts under any regime, including serving out their prison sentences.

Criticisms of parole often center on parole boards who have the primary responsibility for making release decisions. Parole boards are forced to predict dangerousness, a task that professionals find excruciatingly difficult even under the best of conditions. Boards have been criticized for being too conservative, too liberal, arbitrary, subject to political patronage, unprofessional, and inefficient. The current trend in parole is to limit parole board discretion regarding prison release through statutes that (1) mandate sentence length, (2) eliminate categories of offenders from parole, and (3) specify objective guidelines in the granting of parole.

In the next two sections, we will review the literature on the use of behavioral approaches to probation and to parole. This material is organized according to intervention procedure. In the case of probation, following a summary of Tharp and Wetzel's very influential demonstration project in the late 1960s, we will discuss the use of contingency contracting, social skills training, covert sensitization, reframing and behaviorally based education, and system-level interventions. Fewer studies have examined behavioral approaches to parole. We organized this research into two categories of intervention: contingency contracting and job-finding skills.

BEHAVIORAL APPROACHES TO PROBATION AND PAROLE

Probation

If one were deliberately to design a system whose problems would beg for an answer based on behavioral technology, it is unlikely that the mix of problems presented by our probation system could be "improved" upon. Probation has very poorly operationalized goals that must be met with but few adequate resources. Although its personnel are poorly trained in behavioral science, they have been expected to master the social casework-medical model approach that has prevailed in the field since Gary Richmond's *Social Diagnosis* appeared in 1917 (Cohn, 1982). Their caseloads are unmanageably large; their clients are often indifferent if not hostile to the entire probation concept; and they face constant demands for accountability in controlling the behavior of their charges without knowledge of what techniques to use to accomplish that control.

Application of behavioral techniques to the multiple requirements facing probation was an innovation that began to occur in the 1960s. In 1965, R. B. Jamieson, a trial judge, wrote that

> the best thing judges could do would be to have trained psychologists devise and use suitable behavior therapy to extinguish the learned responses which lead probationers into crime. This would not involve psychoanalysis or any attempt to probe into the probationer's unconscious. It would not be based on Freudian principles. It would be based on principles which go back to Pavlov and have been further devel-

oped by J. B. Watson, C. L. Hull, B. F. Skinner and others. Behavior therapy of this type is less speculative, expensive and tedious and more exact and scientific than psychoanalytic therapy. Apparently it gets good results in the vast majority of cases, which psychoanalysis does not. (Jamieson, 1965, p. 7)

The seminal project in behavioral probation was the publication of Tharp and Wetzel's *Behavior Modification in the Natural Environment* (1969) in which the authors describe their triadic model of therapy for behaviorally disordered youths. Although this program did not focus on probationers *per se,* it included the type of "predelinquents" who are very frequently assigned to probation services. Unlike more dynamically oriented forms of therapy in which the professional interacts with the patient in a dyadic relationship, the triadic model incorporates an intermediate position that serves to bridge the therapist and patient roles. In Tharp and Wetzel's language, the "consultant" possesses the knowledge to effect change, the "mediator" possesses the necessary reinforcers, and the "target" possesses the problem. The rationale underlying the mediator's position is that the typical professional does not have access to requisite reinforcers; the mediator is selected because of his or her control over them. After receiving instruction in behavior analysis from the consultant, the mediator dispenses the reinforcers with the goal of modifying the target's maladaptive behavior.

Tharp and Wetzel applied their triadic model to a population of 77 school-, home-, and court-referred "predelinquent" children 6 to 16 years of age. Specific problem behaviors were identified for each subject, ranging in severity from refusal to do chores and defiance to truancy and stealing. All youths were considered to be academic underachievers with IQ scores of approximately 90 or better. Each subject was assigned to a consultant, or behavior analyst, who in conjunction with a supervising psychologist was responsible for the development of a treatment plan. Interventions were then implemented with the combined efforts of any potential mediating authorities, namely those persons occupying family, social, educational, or occupational roles in the youth's life.

Single-subject designs were used to evaluate the effectiveness of each youth's treatment. Outcome measures varied in specificity and reactivity, with input solicited from both mediators and consultants. An analysis of changes from the baseline rates of target behaviors, averaged across all subjects, revealed that nearly 90% of behaviors were reduced to one-half or less the baseline rate of occurrence after the intervention. Approximately 15% of the problem behaviors were completely eliminated. Because follow-up data proved difficult to collect, maintenance of these effects could not be adequately tested. Over 75% of target behaviors were described by parents as "improved" or "very improved," and some evidence for generalization of the effects was provided by the finding that parents also reported nonintervened problem behaviors as improved. Behavioral ratings of the effectiveness of the interventions in eliminating undesirable behaviors supported these results.

On the less positive side, a survey of police records indicated that 26 of the 77 subjects committed one or more offenses following the introduction of the treatment. The majority of these offenses however, occurred prior to termination, with only five subjects committing offenses during the 6-month follow-up period. Finally, a measure of school achievement failed to provide evidence for the triadic model's effectiveness, a result Tharp and Wetzel believed to be related more to the unreliability of grades as a criteria of academic performance than to a failing of the project.

Thorne, Tharp, and Wetzel (1967) demonstrated the applicability of the triadic model to work with youths already apprehended for criminal offenses. Using "subprofessional" agents to train probation officers in behavior modification techniques, thus teaching them to fulfill the role of mediator, the researchers provided descriptive evidence that powerful changes in the targets (delinquent youths) could take place. Because probation officers too often rely on aversive stimuli in their treatment of offenders, which tends to reduce misbehavior only temporarily, the use of schedules of positive reinforcement was emphasized. Rather than threatening a delinquent youth who skips school with incarceration (aversive intervention), a probation officer might attempt to construct an intervention whereby attendance in school was rewarded with extra privileges (positive reinforcement). The involvement of other mediators, such as parents or teachers, may become necessary so that the control over the target's reinforcers is expanded. In introducing the behavioral techniques to these significant others, the probation officer takes on the role of consultant. Ultimately, Thorne et al. envisioned juvenile probation officers as potential experts in behavior modification.

Five categories of behavioral techniques have been applied to probation. We will review each of these categories next.

Contingency Contracting

The most frequently applied technique in adult probation has been contingency contracting. The popularity of this approach is due in large measure to its required specification of achievable objectives and manipulatable consequences, two aspects of case management that have always frustrated probation officers.

One of the first comprehensive investigations of a behavioral approach to probation was a well-controlled study by Polakow and Doctor (1974; see also Doctor & Polakow, 1973). The subjects were 26 adults (15 females, 11 males) who had served an average of 12.5 months on probation prior to the study. They had been transferred to the program because previous probation officers, using traditional case management procedures, had found them too difficult to work with. Most of the crimes for which subjects had been convicted were drug related.

The probation period consisted of three graduated contingency phases. In Phase 1, the probationer earned a credit for weekly meetings with his or her probation officer. Accumulation of eight points allowed the participant to advance to Phase 2, where points were earned for attendance at a group meeting with other probationers. These group meetings were devoted to discussion of problems and support for self-correction of deviant behavior. Phase 2 lasted a minimum of 10 weeks. Phase 3 required participants to execute a written, individualized contract with their officer that specified new behaviors the probationers felt they needed to develop (e.g., obtaining employment and new social activities). In most instances, contracts were confined to the behavior that was considered to be the offender's most crucial deficit. Successfully completion of contracted behaviors resulted in predetermined reductions in the remaining probation time. Aversive control was minimized throughout the program. The only "punishment" was demotion to Phase 1 for violations of written probation conditions.

Participants had served an average of 12.5 months on traditional probation before beginning the contingency program. The authors compared participants' performance during the previous period of traditional probation to that achieved during the contingency management period. Program evaluation focused on four outcomes: number of probation violations, number of new arrests, proportion of probation time in which the participant was employed, and attendance at scheduled probation meetings. In comparison to the previous period of traditional probation, the contingency program was associated with significantly superior effectiveness on all four measures. The rearrest data were especially impressive. Although no systematic contingencies were applied to occurrence of illegal conduct, rearrests were one tenth as frequent under the contingency program as they were under the previous program. However, the absence of a no-treatment control or reversal phase in the design makes it impossible to rule out regression to the mean as an explanation for these results.

In a second phase of the research design, the results achieved during the contingency management program were contrasted with outcomes produced by an intensive supervision program in which the probation officer was responsible for a reduced caseload, thereby allowing more frequent contact with clients. The contingency management and intensive supervision caseloads were matched in size and amount of time spent with each probationer. The mean ages of the two caseloads were equivalent. Contingency management probation was more effective than intensive probation in decreasing the mean number of probation violations and new arrests and in increasing the number of months employed.

Contingency management probation has been applied to other drug-related offenses. Polakow (1975) treated a probated barbiturate addict with the simultaneous use of covert sensitization, behavioral rehearsal, and contingency contracting. The participant was a 24-year-old female who had been sentenced to 3 years of probation for a recent felony conviction involving the possession of dangerous drugs. The contract was similar to that of Polakow and Doctor (1973) in which successful completion of therapy assignments resulted in 1-week reductions in total probation time. Initially, the contract required performance of one nondrug activity per week. This criterion was increased gradually until, by the 35th week of treatment, the client was completing at least seven nondrug activities each week. Thirty weeks of covert sensitization produced a strong aversive reaction to imagined drug use and enabled the client to stop her barbiturate use. Behavioral rehearsal was used to strengthen the client's ability to deal more effectively with events that could be anxiety provoking for her. After 1 year of treatment, the client had been drug free for 3 months and was employed. At the end of 15 months, she had maintained these improvements and was dismissed from probation. Self-report and agency records indicated that the client remained drug free and continued to be employed 18 months after treatment termination.

Polakow and Doctor (1973) attempted to decrease a young married couple's use of barbiturates and marijuana. The participants were a 21-year-old man and his 23-year-old wife, both of whom had been sentenced to 3 years of probation for possession of marijuana. A contingency contract was negotiated between the therapist and the couple that specified that the couple must perform one non-drug-related social activity per week, completion of which would be reinforced by shortening their total probation time by a matching week. The wife agreed, further, to reinforce her husband's attempt to reduce drug use and gain employment. He in turn contracted to attempt to secure a job, which he accomplished successfully 2 weeks later. Over the 36 sessions of treatment, the number of required nondrug activities was increased gradually to seven per week. The couple also participated in group-based training in social skills and received instructions on how to negotiate their own marital contracts. Neither individual reported any drug use at a 1-year follow-up; the husband had retained his employment, and marital adjustment was satisfactory.

Behaviorally based probation has been successfully extended to other targets besides drug abuse. For example, Polakow and Peabody (1975) reported the treatment of a 30-year-old woman who had been placed on probation for child abuse involving her young son. Therapy was multifaceted and included (a) negotiation of a behavioral contract between the mother and son that set limits on the permissible behaviors for both parties (satisfactory performance of this contract resulted in a reduction of total probation time); (b) training to improve the mother's disciplinary control of her son's aggressive behavior; and (c) assertion training designed to develop a more effective interpersonal repertoire for the mother. An 18-month follow-up revealed sustained improvement for both mother and son. Detected child abuse was not reported in this interval.

Social Skills Training

The role of interpersonal skill deficits in the development of delinquency has received considerable attention in recent years. Spence (1982) has suggested that youths who are unable to obtain social, academic, and financial success due to poorly developed interpersonal skills are prone to inappropriate means of seeking these goals. It then follows that instruction of juvenile delinquents in appropriate social skills should be associated with a reduction in maladaptive behavior (Stumphauzer, 1986).

Although a number of investigations have attempted to assess the effect of social skills training on institutionalized offenders, few studies have focused on youths on probation and living at home. Alexander and Parsons (1973) investigated the effect of interpersonal skills training on the recidivism rates of juvenile offenders, a percentage of whom were on probation. Instruction in social skills was aimed at family patterns of communications; families were encouraged to divide communication more equally among family members, to request clarification more frequently, and to deliver positive feedback. These skills were learned via modeling, role-playing, and discussion techniques. As compared with groups of client-centered therapy, psychodynamic therapy, and no treatment, juveniles involved in social skills training demonstrated both improved family interaction patterns and lowered recidivism rates at 6- and 18-month follow-ups.

A somewhat different approach to skills training was undertaken by Hazel, Schumaker, Sherman, and Sheldon-Wildgen (1982) in their study of 13 youths on juvenile court probation. In contrast to the family instruction provided by Alexander and Parsons, Hazel *et al.* aimed their intervention strategy specifically at the juvenile offenders. Their program consisted of instruction in eight interpersonal skill areas including giving and accepting feedback, resisting peer pressure, negotiation, and problem solving. The training was designed to be as simple as possible, and it was run as a group program in an effort to make efficient use of the trainers' time. Though no control group was utilized, a multiple baseline design demonstrated substantial improvements in all skill areas. Youths involved in a "homenote" procedure that specified practice of the target skills at home made the most rapid progress. Posttraining ratings of satisfaction with the program by both the participants and their parole officers indicated a high degree of satisfaction, and the offenders also judged themselves to be more competent following training. Although recidivism rates were not collected in this study, the social skills intervention appeared to be successful in training the specific skills it addressed in a relatively short time period (20 hours).

Covert Sensitization

Maletzky (1980) compared the effectiveness of 24 weeks of covert sensitization ("assisted" by exposure to foul odors) in the treatment of four groups of sex offenders: (1) self-referred pedophiles, (2) court-referred pedophiles, (3) self-referred exhibitionists, and (4) court-referred exhibitionists. Of the entire court-referred sample ($n = 55$), 62% were referred as a condition of their probation, and 7% were referred as a requirement of their parole. Booster sessions were employed every 3 months for 3 years, and a large number of adjunctive techniques including homework, masturbatory reconditioning, environmental changes, and "thought changing" were employed. Outcome data (consisting of self-reports, plethysmograph records, peer reports, and legal records) collected up to 30 months posttreatment indicated that treatment was effective for all groups. Self-referred and court-referred participants did not differ in treatment responsiveness, an important result in light of the usual reservations about treatment effectiveness with nonvoluntary clients.

Reframing and Behaviorally Based Education

Kolko and Milan (1983) reported the successful use of "reframing" techniques and paradoxical instruction in the treatment of three delinquent youths who had not benefited from more traditional behavioral intervention.

Reframing refers to a tactic where the therapist explains some behavior in a manner that changes the meaning of that behavior for the client. In concert with a paradoxical instruction, reframing in this study consisted of "prescribing the symptom." For example, the youths were encouraged to maintain their truancy and misbehavior with comments such as the following:

> We don't want you to try things you might be too young and immature to handle. It seems it would be best for you if you didn't go to school until you grow through this childish stage; we don't want you to fight the urge to misbehave since you apparently aren't mature enough to handle it. (Kolko & Milan, 1983, p. 657)

Although paradoxical intention can be conceptualized in behavioral terms, its importance in this investigation was that it was used as an effective supplement to contingency contracting that by itself had not been an effective treatment for these youths. Although none of these youths (two males, one female) was on official probation, each had been referred by a juvenile court for treatment of a pattern of antisocial and school problems. Using a multiple baseline design across subjects, Kolko and Milan were able to demonstrate improvements in class attendance and academic grades associated with the use of paradoxical instruction. Contingency contracts were used to maintain those gains.

Brown (1980) compared the effectiveness of a 15-hour conventional education course with a 15-hour course in controlled drinking for a group of New Zealand drunken drivers placed on "periodic detention," a disposition quite similar to probation in this country. Participants ($n = 20$) in the controlled-drinking course received training in monitoring their blood alcohol levels through breathalyzer and videotape feedback and practiced controlled drinking in a simulated lab. Conventional education course subjects ($n = 20$) listened to lectures and films and then discussed topics pertaining to general effects of alcohol and drinking and driving. A control group ($n = 20$) reported as required to the Periodic Detention Center but received no educational program. Drivers in both treatment conditions showed significant improvements in psychological adjustment at a 12-month follow-up and in the incidence of drinking-and-driving episodes. Only those drivers who received the controlled-drinking course indicated a reduction in frequency of uncontrolled drinking.

System-Level Interventions

One interesting system-level approach to improving probation was California's probation subsidy program begun in 1966, which involves the application of contingency management to a large-scale social program. Probation subsidy is a system in which the state pays counties for each juvenile and adult offender placed on probation rather than incarcerated in a prison. It was founded on the simple, pragmatic principle that systems, like individuals, will produce outcomes that are reinforced.

Initially, the amount of payment in California's program was based on the product of the cost of institutional confinement times the amount by which a county reduced its commitments to the state's prisons. Pre-1966 commitment rates were used as the baseline. Although the program was originally viewed as a success and several other states followed California in introducing their own versions of subsidy, the more conservative political climate of the late 1970s resulted in the repeal of the original subsidy legislation and passage of a much more limited program that (1) exempted several categories of offenders from probation consideration, (2) based subsidies on counties *not increasing,* rather than decreasing, their prison commitment rates, and (3) computed a new base commitment rate derived from the average of 1973–1977 commitments per 100,000 population.

Probation subsidy reportedly saved California over 100 million dollars (Carney, 1977); however, it was not clear that it resulted in more effective rehabilitation of offenders or increased protection of the public. This latter problem ultimately led to a severe cutback of the subsidy system.

Parole

In comparison to probation, parole has used behavioral techniques less frequently. Elsewhere, we have speculated that the reason for this disparity may be due to the decreased enthusiasm for rehabilitation on the part of offenders who are completing the last portion of their correctional career as well as on the part of the parole officers who work with them (Nietzel, 1979). In addition, in comparison to probationers, parolees are likely to be older, have a longer criminal record, and have been convicted of more serious, violent offenses. These characteristics may militate against ambitious rehabilitative efforts. It is important to remember that probationers are often selected because they appear to be the best bets for community placement; parolees will typically not be such a select group of offenders.

Two categories of behavioral techniques have received the most attention in the parole literature: contingency contracting and training in job-finding skills.

Contingency Contracting

Boudin *et al.* (1974) reported an impressive community-based program for a large group of drug-dependent individuals, the majority of whom were opiate addicts. Ninety-one percent of the participants had been arrested on at least one occasion, and 76% had received at least one conviction for a criminal charge. Forty-two percent were nonvoluntary participants, having been required to take part in the program as a condition of their parole, probation, or work release. The report did not indicate what percentage of the nonvoluntary group were on parole, but 64% had served at least one prior prison sentence.

The program was based on an extension of the behavioral contracting approach that other research had indicated was effective with probated drug offenders. Four types of contracts were employed in the course of the treatment program. The first was a precontract agreement in which the participants made a material commitment to the project as a demonstration of their motivation. This commitment often took the form of depositing a sum of money or a highly valued personal item. Participants were also asked to undertake several responsibilities, including frequently contacting the project staff by phone and in person, writing daily diaries, seeking or continuing employment, and supplying several urine samples per week.

Following this baseline phase, a managerial contract was written that established an "individualized behavior program" in five areas: responsibilities, consequences, privileges, bonuses, and special considerations. Client responsibilities included such tasks as job procurement or job maintenance, attendance at all meetings with treatment staff, drug abstinence, self-monitoring of several dependent measures, making frequent phone contacts with the staff, daily preparation of a diary, and adherence to a urine-collection schedule. Participants also were required to establish a joint bank account with their contract manager. These bank accounts enabled participants to learn some basic budgeting skills, and they provided the treatment team with a mechanism for reinforcing adaptive behaviors.

Breaches of contracts resulted in specific penalities (usually a fine), whereas privileges and bonuses were earned by compliance with the conditions of the contracts. "Special considerations" involved changes in client status necessitated by such demands as parole conditions or leaves of absence. Krasnegor and Boudin (1973) also reported the adjunctive provision of aversive conditioning, behavioral rehearsal, and marital counseling as needed by certain individuals throughout the project.

Transitional contracts were introduced as a means of reducing project structure and increasing individual responsibility for those participants who demonstrated successful performance during the managerial contract phase. In the final stage of treatment, participants constructed personal contracts that established their individual long-term objectives and the behavioral means for attaining them.

The status of case outcomes was determined on the basis of four criteria: (1) work and school performance, (2) personal and social adjustment, (3) drug use, and (4) arrest and conviction history. Multiple sources of criteria evaluation were employed, including clinical observation, self-report, agency records, urinalyses, peer reports, and participant diaries. For a participant to be judged a positive case outcome, he or she had to demonstrate satisfactory performance in at least three of the four criteria areas. Any occurrence of extremely maladaptive adjustment (e.g., a felony arrest) precluded a judgment of positive case outcome.

Data were reported on 33 clients who had participated in the project for at least 15 days. Of these, 14 were current participants, whereas 19 had terminated treatment. Of the terminators, 6 were program graduates, all of whom were evidencing positive outcomes. Eleven of the terminators had stopped treatment against staff advice. Of these, 7 were meeting positive case criteria, 2 were classified as negative outcomes, and the status for the other 2 was unknown. Two participants terminated treatment for "other reasons"; both were classified as negative outcomes. The successful adjustment of the self-terminators was interesting, especially in light of the fact that some "occasional discreet use" of drugs was reported by this group, whereas drug use was very rare among program graduates. It is possible that this difference was an artifact of the drug preferences for the two groups. Program graduates were all primarily opiate users, whereas self-terminators tended to prefer barbiturates, a category of drugs that is both more easily obtained and less subject to severe social surveillance and sanction than the opiates. Whatever the explanation for this finding, the results do suggest that both abstinence and controlled drug use might be indicative of positive treament outcomes with different types of addicts. A follow-up of program graduates, ranging from 12 to 453 days, indicated maintenance of positive effects.

Two aspects of this program demand particular attention. First, the program demonstrated that a comprehensive, well-integrated treatment package could be applied to a large group of quite diverse drug abusers (some of whom were parolees) in a natural setting. Second, this is the only behaviorally oriented program of this type that has systematically prepared paraprofessional volunteers to implement the bulk of the intervention. The use of paraprofessionals in an ecologically representative treatment setting could increase the range of the addict population that perceives this program as viable. In fact, Boudin et al. (1974) reported that the percentage of younger and nonwhite participants has increased over the levels reflected by the initial program group.

Job-Finding Skills

Beginning with the pioneering work of Jones and Azrin (1973), behavior modifiers have developed programs designed to improve job-seeking and job-interviewing skills for the unemployed. Most programs are multicomponent efforts that include information sharing, modeling, video feedback, and behavior rehearsal often delivered in a group context. Job-interviewing skills programs have also been applied to offender populations. Most noteworthy of these projects is the work of Sharon Hall and her colleagues at the University of California at San Francisco. Hall, Loeb, Coyne, and Cooper (1981) randomly assigned 55 probationers and parolees to either an 11-hour behaviorally based job seekers' workshop or to a 3-hour information-only workshop. Participants were all heroin abusers.

The experimental workshop had three components: training for job interviews, instruction in completion of employment forms, and job search procedures. Training emphasized role playing, coaching appropriate verbal and nonverbal behaviors, practicing simulated job interviews, and videotaped feedback. Following training, participants were assessed at a simulated interview conducted by employees of a vocational rehabilitation service. Experimental participants were superior to controls, particularly on specific interview behaviors. Four-, 8-, and 12-week follow-ups were conducted on the percentage of participants who had a job, what salary they received, and how many job interviews they had attended. At the 12-week follow-up, 85.7% of the project participants versus 54% of the information-only controls had a full or part-time job, a difference that was statistically significant.

Results of this study were partially replicated by Hall, Loeb, LeVois, and Cooper (1981) with 60 methadone-maintenance clients, more than 40% of whom were on probation and parole. Again, at a 3-month follow-up, more treatment participants (52%) than controls (30%) had obtained employment. An additional and challenging finding of this study was that participants who had not been employed at all in the past 5 years did not find employment, regardless of treatment condition.

Behavioral enhancement of employment skills is not limited to drug offenders. Twentyman, Jensen, and Kloss (1978) reported that a mixed group of adult offenders receiving a behavioral training program were more effective on a mock job interview and tended to obtain employment more quickly than offenders given monetary incentives for attending interviews.

METHODOLOGICAL ISSUES

For those accustomed to the standards of research quality attained in areas such as evaluation of psychotherapy outcome or of interventions in classrooms, the body of research in behavioral probation and parole is quite disappointing. From the perspectives of internal and ecological validity, the research surveyed in this chapter is of marginal quality. Particular attention needs to be devoted to the following gaps in the available research.

Evaluation of Separate Treatment Components

Most behavioral approaches to probation and parole consist of a package of techniques applied as a whole to an individual offender or group of offenders. For example, Polakow and Doctor's (1974) program consisted of three graduated phases of contracting but did not evaluate the separate effects attributable to the separate phases. At this point, we have no basis for concluding that any particular behavioral package is superior to alternative packages, nor do we know which elements of a given package are the most potent ones. Research that "dismantles" interventions and then compares the effects of the various components would be an important contribution.

Development of Multimethod Outcome Measurement

Despite behavior modification's emphasis on overt behavior, many studies of parole and probation have emphasized self-report measures of outcome. An adequate battery of outcome data should include self-reports, reports by significant others, observation of specified target behaviors by trained assessors, and legal records. Maletzky's (1980) collection of self-reports, peer reports, physiological indexes, and legal records in his evaluation of sex offenders illustrates an ideal battery for outcome measurement.

Increased Attention to Generalization and Maintenance

Researchers in the area of probation and parole need to upgrade the status of their generalization and follow-up measures. Although most studies include a follow-up of some sort, it is often conducted at an interval of less than 1 year from program termination, and it often is limited to self-report data. Of course, the advantages of long-term assessment must be weighed against the practical disadvantages of subject attrition and greater expense, but most types of criminal conduct (particularly drug abuse that is overrepresented in this chapter's literature) will require relatively lengthy intervals for remission to be assessed adequately.

A related need is the comparative evaluation of alternative techniques designed to promote maintenance and generalization of effects. Is *in vivo* treatment preferable to the use of one or two "booster sessions" as a means of improving maintenance? Will generalization be best achieved by developing self-control skills or by decreasing the extent to which some behavior is under narrow stimulus control? These are questions that this literature has yet to address.

Expansion of Targets

The majority of behavioral probation and parole studies have dealt with persons charged with offenses related to substance abuse. In part, this situation is due to the greater willingness of the criminal justice system to use community-based programs for drug offenders as opposed to offenders charged with violent or major property crimes. The difference may also stem from the fact that the habitual quality of drug-related problems makes them more "treatable" from a psychobehavioral perspective than less regular episodes of violence or property offense. Regardless of the reason, exploration of whether a broader range of offenders can be effectively targeted by behavioral probation and parole is a critical research question.

FUTURE DEVELOPMENTS

The first published account of a behavioral training program for probation officers was by Deibert and Golden (1973). They did not, however, include an actual behavioral competence measure of program effects, a deficiency remedied by Burkhart, Behles, and Stumphauzer's (1976) evaluation of a 6-week workshop designed to teach basic principles and application of behavioral assessment/intervention to a group of nine officers from the Los Angeles County Probation Department. In comparison to officers who had been assigned randomly to a no-training control group, the behavioral trainees did not differ on paper-and-pencil measures of knowledge of or attitudes toward behavior modification. They were, however, significantly more skilled in conducting a behaviorally oriented interview, designing a behavioral analysis of the problem, and outlining a behaviorally based probation plan than their untrained peers. The authors concluded that the most valuable components of their training package were the modeled demonstrations of specific skills followed by supervised enactment of those behaviors by the trainees. Stumphauzer, Candelora, and Venema's (1976) 6-month follow-up of their nine trainees revealed that seven of the trainees were using behavioral techniques in their day-to-day work but that all the trainees reported the need for departmentalwide support if these changes were to be sustained. Of course, the behavior of probation and parole workers is controlled by the same variables and contingencies that control the behavior of the clients with whom they work. Their behavior will be maintained by its consequences, and if the consequences for practicing behaviorally based interventions are not positive, those interventions will soon be discontinued.

A major shortcoming of behavioral probation and parole has been the failure to train sufficient numbers of probation workers in behavior analysis and intervention. Our knowledge about the training of paraprofessionals is clearly adequate for the task (e.g., Bernstein, 1982), but in the past 15 years since Tharp and Wetzel introduced their triadic model, surprisingly little "giving away" of behavioral techniques to grass-roots workers has occurred. Despite the fact that probation and parole lack an effective technology, that the principles of behavior modification are relatively simple to learn, and that most research indicates positive outcomes with behavioral intervention for probationers and parolees, the field has not accepted the behavioral approach nearly as enthusiastically as one would have expected. What seems in many ways like the perfect marriage has not taken place. The two partners have remained separated for at least four pervasive reasons.

First, the unmanageable caseloads facing probation and parole officers permit very little time for innovative programming. Although behavior modification does emphasize time-limited treatments, we have probably underestimated how discouraging it is to face caseloads in excess of 100 offenders when the recommended load is around 35 offenders per officer. This overloading makes any planned intervention beyond routine surveillance very difficult and undoubtedly contributes to the emphasis on aversive control in probation and parole programs. The increased efficiency afforded by behavior modification techniques should be welcomed by correctional officals. In addition, although the research has shown that caseload size is not related to differential probation and parole outcomes (Lipton, Martinson, & Wilks, 1975), the lack of a relationship is probably explained by the absence of any potent behavior-change techniques regardless of caseload. It makes little difference how much time a parole worker has to spend with a client, if the worker has no effective techniques to use with him or her. Behavioral methods applied to small, intensive probation and parole caseloads may produce substantially larger effects than what has been reported to date.

Second, application of behavioral techniques to probation and parole is jeopardized by the hostility, mistrust, and misunderstanding directed at correctional behavior modification in the 1970s. Although most legal and ethical objections to behavior therapy focused on its application to confined prisoners, behavior modification was tarred with such a broad brush that the taint spread over almost any kind of intervention, even those not involving coercion. Fear of litigation and adverse publicity have probably discouraged many probation and parole agencies from developing more behaviorally oriented programs.

Third, public discontent with the goal of rehabilitation and the repeated examples of its failure that receive dramatic attention from the media have had a chilling effect on innovation throughout the correctional system, including probation and parole. One of the great ironies of current corrections is that the "lock-'em-up-longer" philosophy regarded as reactionary only 20 years ago is now considered to be the cutting-edge position in penology.

Fourth and finally, behavior modifiers themselves have not made the training of paraprofessionals a priority in either their research or their intervention programs. The reasons for this inertia are not difficult to understand. Training of paraprofessionals is not a glamorous activity; it is not the most intellectually or emotionally satisfying; it is not well remunerated; and it does not enjoy high status as a research topic. Add to this the discrepancies in values and training that mental health professionals and correctional officers bring to their interactions, and it is easy to see how the course of consultation may not run smoothly. In other words, the contingencies for collaboration are simply not there or are not as strong as the contingencies for avoidance.

Willie Sutton's justification for robbing banks was reputedly because "that's where the money is." Analogous logic should direct behavior modifiers toward probation and parole—that's where most of the offenders are. The need for an effective behavior change technology in probation and parole is complemented by the existence of just such a technology, but whether that technology is applied more systematically to the demands of probation and parole than it has in the past depends for the most part on whether mental health professionals and correctional personnel can work together (see Stumphauzer, 1986, for an example of this type of collaboration). They need to work together (1) to bring caseload levels down to realistic levels, thereby permitting individualized, contingency-based interventions; (2) to clarify the ethical and legal issues involved in different behavioral techniques and in community-based versus institutional programs; (3) to restore the public's commitment to rehabilitation as a goal to be balanced along with the other correctional goals of protection, punishment, and deterrence; and (4) to build contingencies that encourage professionals to train paraprofessionals in component behavior management skills and that encourage probation and parole workers to rely on those skills regularly.

REFERENCES

Abadinsky, H. (1977). *Probation and parole: Theory and practice.* Englewood Cliffs, NJ: Prentice-Hall.

Alexander, J. F., & Parsons, B. V. (1973). Short-term behavioral intervention with delinquent families: Impact on family process and recidivism. *Journal of Abnormal Psychology, 81,* 219–225.

Allen, H. E., & Simonsen, C. E. (1975). *Corrections in America: An introduction.* Beverly Hills: Glencoe Press.

Bagley, J. J. (1979). Why Illinois adopted determinate sentencing. *Judicature, 62,* 390–397.

Bernstein, G. S. (1982). Training behavior change agents: A conceptual review. *Behavior Therapy, 13,* 1–23.

Boudin, H., Valentine, V., Ingraham, R., Brantley, J., Ruiz, M., Smith, G., Catlin, R., & Regan, E. (1974). *Contingency contracting with drug addicts in the natural environment.* Unpublished manuscript, University of Florida.

Brown, R. A. (1980). Conventional education and controlled drinking education courses with convicted drunken drivers. *Behavior Therapy, 11,* 632–642.

Burkhart, B. R., Behles, M., & Stumphauzer, J. S. (1976). Training juvenile probation officers in behavior modification: Knowledge, attitude change, or behavioral competence. *Behavior Therapy, 7,* 47–53.

Carey, W. T. (1979). Determinate sentencing in California and Illinois: Its effect on sentence disparity and prisoner rehabilitation. *Washington University Law Quarterly, 1979,* 551–569.

Carney, L. P. (1977). *Probation and parole: Legal and social dimensions.* New York: McGraw-Hill.

Cavender, C. (1982). *Parole: A critical analysis.* Port Washington, NY: Kennikat Press.

Cohen, N. P., & Gobert, J. J. (1983). *The law of probation and parole.* New York: McGraw-Hill.

Cohn, A. W. (1982). Behavioral objectives in probation and parole: A new approach to staff accountability. *Federal Probation, 46,* 19–28.

Deibert, A. N., & Golden, F. (1973). Behavior modification workshop with juvenile offenders: Brief report. *Behavior Therapy, 4,* 586–588.

Doctor, R. M., & Polakow, R. L. (1973). A behavior modification program for adult probationers. *Proceedings of the 81st Annual Convention of the American Psychological Association* (pp. 941–942). Washington, DC: APA.

Empey, L. T., & Rabow, J. (1961). The Provo experiment in delinquency rehabilitation. *American Sociological Review, 26,* 679–695.

Glaser, D. (1969). *The effectiveness of a prison and parole system.* Indianapolis: Bobbs-Merrill.

Gottfredson, M. R. (1979). Parole guidelines and the reduction of sentencing disparity: A preliminary study. *Journal of Research in Crime and Delinquency, 16,* 218–231.

Griswold, D. B., & Wiatrowski, M. D. (1983). The emergence of determinate sentencing. *Federal Probation, 47,* 28–35.

Hall, S. M., Loeb, P., Coyne, K., & Cooper, J. (1981). Increasing employment in ex-heroin addicts I: Criminal justice sample. *Behavior Therapy, 12,* 443–452.

Hall, S. M., Loeb, P., LeVois, M., & Cooper, J. (1981). Increasing employment in ex-heroin addicts II: Methadone maintenance sample. *Behavior Therapy, 12,* 453–460.

Hartinger, W., Eldefonso, E., & Coffey, A. (1973). *Corrections: A component of the criminal justice system.* Pacific Palisades, CA: Goodyear Publishing.

Hazel, J. S., Schumaker, J. B., Sherman, J. A., & Sheldon-Wildgen, J. (1982). Group training for social skills. *Criminal Justice and Behavior, 9,* 35–53.

Irving, L. H., & Sandhu, H. S. (1973). *Offender typology and family interaction: An evaluation of probation success in Oklahoma.* Washington, DC: U.S. Government Printing Office.

Jamieson, R. B. (1965). Can conditioning principles be applied to probation? *Trial Judges Journal, 4,* 7–8.

Jones, R. J., & Azrin, N. H. (1973). An experimental application of a social reinforcement approach to the problem of job finding. *Journal of Applied Behavior Analysis, 6,* 345–353.

Kolko, D. J., & Milan, M. A. (1983). Reframing and paradoxical instruction to overcome "resistance" in the treatment of delinquent youths: A multiple baseline analysis. *Journal of Consulting and Clinical Psychology, 51,* 655–660.

Krasnegor, L., & Boudin, H. (1973). Behavior modification and drug addiction: The state of the art. *Proceedings of The 81st Annual Convention of the American Psychological Association* (pp. 913–914). Washington, DC: APA.

Lipton, D., Martinson, R., & Wilks, J. (1975). *The effectiveness of correctional treatment: A survey of treatment evaluation studies.* New York: Praeger Publishers.

Maletzky, B. M. (1980). Self-referred versus court-referred sexually deviant patients: Success with assisted covert sensitization. *Behavior Therapy, 11,* 306–314.

Manson, J. R. (1977). Determinate sentencing. *Crime and Delinquency, 23,* 204–207.

Martinson, R. (1974). What works? Questions and answers about prison reform. *Public Interest, 35,* 22–54.

Martinson, R., & Wilks, J. (1977). Save parole supervision. *Federal Probation, 41,* 23–26.

Newman, C. L. (Ed.). (1968). *Source book on probation, parole and pardons* (3rd ed.). Springfield, IL: Charles C Thomas.

Nietzel, M. T. (1979). *Crime and its modification: A social learning prospective.* New York: Pergamon Press.

Polakow, R. L. (1974). *Establishing behavior therapy in a public agency.* Paper presented at the annual meeting of The Association for the Advancement of Behavior Therapy, Chicago, IL.

Polakow, R. L. (1975). Covert sensitization treatment of a probationed barbiturate addict. *Journal of Behavior Therapy and Experimental Psychiatry, 6,* 53–54.

Polakow, R. L., & Doctor, R. M. (1973). Treatment of marijuana and barbiturate dependency by contingency contracting. *Journal of Behavior Therapy and Experimental Psychiatry, 4,* 375–377.

Polakow, R. L., & Doctor, R. M. (1974). A behavioral modification program for adult drug offenders. *Journal of Research in Crime and Delinquency, 11,* 63–69.

Polakow, R. L. & Peabody, D. (1975). Behavioral treatment of child abuse. *International Journal of Offender Therapy and Comparative Criminology, 19,* 100–103.

Rubin, S. (1973). *Law of criminal correction.* St. Paul, MN: West Publishing.

Rumney, J., & Murphy, J. P. (1968). *Probation and social adjustment.* New York: Greenwood Press.

Sparks, R. F. (1971). The effectiveness of probation. In L. Radzinowiez & M. E. Wolfgang (Eds.), *The criminal in confinement* (pp. 211–218). New York: Basic Books.

Spence, S. (1982). Social skills training with young offenders. In P. Feldman (Ed.), *Developments in the study of criminal behavior (Vol. 1): The prevention and control of offending* (pp. 107–134). New York: Wiley.

Stumphauzer, J. S. (1986). *Helping delinquents change: A treatment manual of social learning approaches.* New York: The Haworth Press.

Stumphauzer, J. S., Candelora, K., & Venema, H. B. (1976). A follow-up of probation officers trained in behavior modification. *Behavior Therapy, 7,* 713–715.

Tappan, P. (1960). *Crime, justice and correction.* New York: McGraw-Hill.

Tharp, R. G., & Wetzel, R. J. (1969). *Behavior modification in the natural environment.* New York: Academic Press.

Thorne, G. L., Tharp, R. G., & Wetzel, R. J. (1967). Behavior modification techniques: New tools for probation officers. *Federal Probation, 31,* 21–27.

Twentyman, C. T., Jensen, M., & Kloss, J. D. (1978). Social skills training for the complex offender: Employment seeking skills. *Journal of Clinical Psychology, 34,* 320–326.

U.S. Department of Justice (1974). *Success and failure of federal offenders released in 1970.* Washington, DC: U.S. Government Printing Office.

U.S. Department of Justice (1982). *Bureau of Justice Statistics: Bulletin, Probation and Parole 1981*. Washington, DC: U.S. Government Printing Office.

von Hirsch, A. (1976). *Doing justice*. NY: Hill & Wang.

von Hirsch, A., & Hanrahan, K. (1979). *The question of parole: Retention, reform, or abolition*. Cambridge, MA: Ballinger.

von Hirsch, A., & Hanrahan, K. (1981). Determinate penalty systems in America: An overview. *Crime and Delinquency, 27*, 289–316.

5

Behaviorally Based Group Homes for Juvenile Offenders

CURTIS J. BRAUKMANN AND MONTROSE M. WOLF

Perhaps the most systematic, and certainly the most long-lived and widely disseminated, application of the behavioral approach with juvenile offenders has been in the context of group homes. Research and development based on behavioral principles and procedures began at the University of Kansas in the late 1960s and continues to the present to establish and refine an effective, consumer-preferred, and replicable group home treatment model. Because that model—the Achievement Place or Teaching-Family model (Wolf, Phillips, & Fixsen, 1972)—has been the focal point of almost all of the behavioral research and development concerning group homes, this chapter will concentrate on that model. Following a summary of the results of evaluation research on the Teaching-Family approach, the chapter concludes with a discussion of how evaluation results have prompted major reconsideration of the original assumptions of the approach.

Whereas most of behavioral research with group homes has been conducted by the developers of the Teaching-Family model, a small body of research has been conducted by others, and this will be covered here as well. Some Teaching-Family-related research also has been conducted in the United Kingdom and The Netherlands as described by Yule and Brown in Chapter 14.

In order to place the behavioral approach to group home treatment of delinquents in proper perspective, we will start with a general background discussion about group homes for delinquents.

GROUP HOMES FOR DELINQUENTS

The placement of juvenile offenders in residential programs specifically established for that population dates from the first half of the nineteenth century (Empey, 1978). Such placement has often been in facilities isolated from the surrounding community by high walls, distance, or other physical

Curtis J. Braukmann and **Montrose M. Wolf** • Department of Human Development, University of Kansas, Lawrence, Kansas 66045.

barriers. One result of the relatively recent deinstitutionalization movement, however, has been an increase in the number of group homes for juvenile offenders (Keller & Alper, 1970; Vinter, Downs, & Hall, 1976).

〜 Group homes are small residential settings in which a group of 4 to 12 adolescents live with, and receive structure and guidance from, program staff (Gula, 1964; Vinter, 1976). Because these programs often are community-based, the participating youths frequently are concurrently enrolled in the local public schools, commonly return to their natural homes on some weekends, occasionally hold jobs in the community, and typically have some free time in the community. These programs are usually administered by private agencies funded, at least in part, on a purchase-of-service basis with public funds. Staffing can range from a conventional social work model involving hierarchical divisions of labor (e.g., director, shiftwork counselors, and non-professional houseparents) to an "ecological" model. In the latter model, unlike the former, the persons with moment-by-moment, direct-care responsibilities are considered professionals who have responsibility for treatment, community liaison, and child advocacy (Piper & Warner, 1980).

According to Piper and Warner (1980), the history of group home care for adolescent offenders began with a few programs developed in Chicago and New York in the 1910s. The number of group homes in this country did not increase significantly until after World War II, when interest was sparked by the European experience with group homes for orphaned and displaced children during and after the war (Hromadka, 1964). Wisconsin developed the first planned network of group homes for teenage offenders in the mid-1950s; Oregon, Minnesota, Washington, and Iowa followed suit in the 1960s (Piper & Warner, 1980). Perhaps the most publicized and scrutinized state-agency adoptions of group home programs have been in California, under the auspices of the California Youth Authority (Palmer, 1978), and in Massachusetts, where, in a 2-month period in 1972, Jerome Miller, then-director of youth services, released virtually the entire population of institutionalized juvenile offenders to less "secure" facilities, including group homes (Bakal, 1973; Ohlin, Coates, & Miller, 1974).

The first systematic research related to community-based group homes occurred in the Silverlake experiment in a middle-class Los Angeles neighborhood in 1964 (Empey & Lubeck, 1971). By that year, more than 300 group homes had been established in the United States (Gula, 1964); over 1,000 were said to be in existence by 1978 (Warner, 1978). This large increase in the number of group homes coincided with a considerable decrease in the number of institutionalized youths (Piper & Warner, 1980).

The growth of community-based group homes was in part a function of influences emanating from the national level. The President's Commission on Law Enforcement and the Administration of Justice (1967) severely criticized traditional institutional programs as being ineffective, inhumane, and expensive and advocated community-based alternatives. Furthermore, the National Advisory Commission on Criminal Justice Standards and Goals, which was funded by the Law Enforcement Assistance Administration (LEAA), recommended the development of more group homes. The LEAA, in turn, provided "seed money" for establishing many group homes during this period. Lerman (1982), reviewing LEAA data, found that 30,745 youths under 18 years of age were admitted to group homes/halfway houses in 1974. The growth of group homes leveled off during the early 1980s, and, with the cessation of federal funding for new community-based programs, group homes have continued to shift their funding base to state foster care and mental health programs (Piper & Warner, 1980).

In terms of social climate and extent of community linkages, group homes can vary across the institutionalization-normalization continuum, just as do other types of residential settings (Miller, Coates, & Ohlin, 1980). In general, however, group homes appear to be on the normalization end: A national survey of residents in group homes and traditional institutions found that group home clients rated their programs higher both in helpful client–staff relations and in preparation for returning to the community (Vinter, 1976).

Group homes appear not only to have more normalized social climates and community linkages than institutions, but they also appear to be more cost-effective. Vinter's (1976) national survey found that the per-offender year costs for group homes were less than half those for institutions, and Warner and Smith's national survey (cited in Piper & Warner, 1980) found per-youth group home costs to be less than two thirds those of traditional correctional institutions. In comparing group homes and institutions, though, one must note two things. First, cost comparisons may not reflect costs associated with staff training and auxiliary support services or services provided outside the group home at no direct cost to the group home (e.g., public education) (Whittaker, 1979). With regard to the latter costs, however, it should be noted that the per-youth costs to the public for educational, recreational, medical, and other services are undoubtedly higher in institutional programs because such programs must duplicate services already available to youths in the community. Second, youths in institutions, on average, are often found to have somewhat more serious histories of offending (Murray & Cox, 1979). Clearly, community tolerance and the limited control capabilities in group homes make these homes inappropriate for that portion of adjudicated youths who are dangerously aggressive (Piper & Warner, 1980). Nevertheless, group homes can successfully handle youths with serious offense histories (Murray & Cox, 1979; Vinter, 1976).

The behaviorally based Teaching-Family group home approach began in the late 1960s as the group home movement was beginning its rapid growth. Its development and its research base have been supported by a series of grants from the National Institute of Mental Health. As noted in Piper and Warner's (1980) review concerning group homes, the Teaching-Family model has assumed "nationwide stature as a distinctive approach to group home placement for problem youths" (p. 3). It has been observed to be unique in the applied behavioral and child care fields due to such factors as the explicitness with which its procedures are described, its data base, and its replicability (Liberman, 1980; Whittaker, 1979). With regard to replicability, James et al.

(1983) reported that there were more than 200 direct replication teaching-family homes in the United States and that the number was growing annually. It is to this behaviorally based approach that we now turn our attention for the remainder of the chapter.

TEACHING-FAMILY GROUP HOMES

Conceptualization Underlying the Treatment Model

The Teaching-Family approach rests on the view that an adolescent's behavior patterns, behavior discriminations, and skills are functions of past behavior–environment interactions (learning history), currently ongoing behavior–environment interactions, and genetic and organismic variables (Braukmann, Kirigin, & Wolf, 1980). In this conceptualization, inherited characteristics and environmental features in childhood—particularly parenting practices (e.g., relationship development, teaching, supervision, and discipline)—affect later developmental outcomes. In adolescence, earlier developed antisocial patterns tend to persevere (indeed, are self-perpetuating) and can be maintained and shaped further by ongoing behavior–environment interactions associated with continued inappropriate parenting, deviant peers, and school failure.

In this view, then, interventions with antisocial adolescents must attempt to alter ongoing behavior–environment interactions so as to differentially teach and support functional and prosocial skills and behavior discriminations. This is best accomplished in teaching-focused treatment environments that have a high "reinforcing value" for the youths involved, that is, that are associated with a wide variety of salient reinforcers (Braukmann et al., 1980). Youths are more likely to remain in such reinforcing environments, to be receptive to the teaching they provide, and to experience important personal consequences for behaving in ways approved or disapproved within them. The Teaching-Family group home approach emphasizes these intervention features, particularly the teaching and environmental support of social- and family-living skills. Armed with these skills, a youth may be more likely in young adulthood to become embedded in conventional networks of contingencies (cf. "communities of reinforcement," Baer & Wolf, 1970), such as stable and valued marriage and employment. These, in turn, can supply significant, differential reinforcement for prosocial behavior and may deter antisocial behavior by providing much to lose by such behavior.

Basic Organization and Staffing

Teaching-Family group homes are directed by married couples called "teaching parents," who live in a family-style home with an average of six young people who are between 12 and 17 years of age. These youths, who stay 6 to 12 months on average, typically have had repeated contact with the juvenile justice system prior to entering the group home. As will be described more fully in the course of this chapter, teaching parents receive ongoing instruction and supervision in the application of specific skill teaching, self-government, motivation, relationship development, and youth advocacy procedures. The role of teaching parent is a difficult and taxing one, and their average tenure is about 2 years, though this is considerably longer than has been found among direct-care workers in other group homes (Connis *et al.*, 1979). The couple usually has an assistant to help in the demanding, 24-hour-a-day job.

At the time of this writing, Teaching-Family group homes occurred with equal frequency in community-based and campus-based settings. Community-based homes are often large, renovated, older homes in residential neighborhoods. Campus-based homes are also large, family-style residences but are situated alongside other group homes on relatively large properties separate from residential neighborhoods. Often the campus-based programs are operated by agencies that have large private endowments. Although clusters of campus-based homes typically share administrators, each home is semi-autonomous and essentially responsible for its own day-to-day affairs, including treatment provision.

In addition to providing direct treatment for their youths and supervising daily household chores and school performance, teaching parents typically have important professional liaison responsibilities. In community-based settings, these include maintaining cooperative relations with local school personnel, court and welfare agency personnel, and the youths' birth or foster families, to which youths often go both after placement and for all or part of most weekends during placement. In campus-based programs, some of these liaison responsibilities may be handled by program staff other than the teaching parents. In both community- and campus-based contexts, teaching parents are supervised and advised in their efforts by training staff (often former teaching parents) from a local training site that has been approved by the National Teaching-Family Association. In many programs, the couples are also supervised by a local, nonprofit board of directors, and if the agency has multiple group homes, by an employee of the agency who has supervisory responsibility.

With this brief sketch of the organizational and staffing arrangements in Teaching-Family homes as background, we now turn to a description of the model's treatment and staff-training elements. Our exposition will follow a chronological, developmental path.

Treatment Procedures

The development of a set of explicit, replicable treatment procedures—as well as the examination and demonstration of their immediate effects—took place at the Achievement Place for Boys and Achievement Place for Girls group homes in Lawrence, Kansas. Early research examining the immediate effects of various treatment procedures on behavior of participating youths

used the reliable-observer measurement and within-subject design methodologies of "applied behavior analysis" (see Chapter 2, this volume).

It should be noted here that sometimes, for research purposes, the target
behaviors in the procedural studies reported in this chapter were selected
because of their ease of measurement, and sometimes multiple youths received quire similar interventions. Obviously, if one wants to demonstrate
that a given treatment procedure is effective, one needs to obtain reliable
measures and to vary only the procedure of interest, holding much else constant. It should not be inferred from such procedural research, then, that the
behaviors intervened on were the only or even the most important targets in
the individualized treatment plans for participating youths or that treatment
in Teaching-Family homes is unindividualized. In other words, it would be a
mistake to criticize the Teaching-Family approach as unindividualized on the
basis of published procedural reserach (cf. Braukmann, Kirigin, & Wolf,
1981).

It also bears mention that the procedural and outcome research we describe was conducted only under conditions of informed consent of participating youths and their parents or guardians. Furthermore, key features of much
of the research were youth involvement in the design of interventions and
youth input into determining the acceptability of the procedures and outcomes. Finally, we note that all the research described in this chapter has been
conducted within the context of community-based group homes.

Token Economy Motivation System

In undertaking to develop a group home, behavior-change program based
on learning theory, Elery and Elaine Phillips, the first teaching parents, and
their colleagues, Dean Fixsen and Montrose Wolf, took as a starting point the
development of a practical means of providing systematic, differential consequences for the behavior of participating youths. The usefulness of a token
economy approach to reinforcing behavior change had been previously demonstrated with a variety of populations, including preschool children (Staats,
Staats, Schultz, & Wolf, 1962), the developmentally disabled (Birnbrauer,
Wolf, Kidder, & Tague, 1965), adolescents in a remedial classroom (Wolf,
Giles, & Hall, 1968), as well as delinquents (Cohen, Filipczak, Bis, & Cohen,
1966).

At Achievement Place for Boys, a token economy motivation system was
developed in which "points" earned or lost as a function of appropriate or
inappropriate behavior were exchangeable for various "backup" reinforcers
(e.g., free time, extra TV, allowance) on a daily basis, and as the youth progressed, on a weekly basis. The economy was a flexible and positive one and
was used only until youths could maintain their appropriate behavior under
the more natural conditions of the "merit" and "homeward bound" systems.

Research on this token economy system showed that contingent token
consequences could both establish behaviors basic to participation in lawful,
productive, intra-, and extratreatment activities and eliminate behaviors likely to get the participants into further trouble. For instance, contingent point

consequences were shown to reduce participating youths' aggressive speech and to increase their rate of following instructions, saving money, maintaining their living areas, learning information, and doing homework (Phillips, 1968; Phillips, Phillips, Fixsen, & Wolf, 1971).

Research further showed that token economy consequences could be used effectively not only by the teaching parent couple but also by the participating youths (Bailey, Timbers, Phillips, & Wolf, 1971; Phillips, Phillips, Wolf, & Fixsen, 1973). In the Phillips *et al.* (1973) study, for example, the participating youths used the token system to affect each others' behavior. Of several "peer manager" systems tried, a reversal design revealed that the most effective and youth-preferred system involved a democratically elected peer manager (1) who had the authority both to give and take points from his confreres, depending on their performance on routine household tasks; and (2) who also earned or lost points from the teaching parents depending on how well the tasks had been accomplished.

In other studies, token consequences delivered at the Achievement Place home were shown to affect behavior outside the group home, both at the public schools (which the youths continued to attend) and in their natural homes (to which they returned most weekends). School and natural-home behavior was affected by "remote consequence procedures," that is, providing point consequences in the group home contingent upon teacher and parent reports on itemized checklists (Bailey, Wolf, & Phillips, 1970; Kirigin, Phillips, Fixsen, & Wolf, 1972; Turnbough, Brown, Fixsen, Phillips, & Wolf, 1973). For example, Bailey *et al.* (1970) studied the effects on classroom behavior of providing consequences in the group home for teacher checkmarks on a "daily report card" listing social and academic categories of classroom behaviors. Using a reversal design and in-classroom direct observation, the authors found that the introduction of the remote consequence procedure resulted in large, reliable improvements in classroom behavior.

Reinforcement Studies Not Done by the Developers of the Teaching-Family Approach. Liberman, Ferris, Salgado, and Salgado (1975) set up a group home in California based explicitly on the Teaching-Family approach and attempted to examine the replicability of findings by model developers (e.g., Phillips *et al.,* 1971) concerning the effectiveness of token reinforcement procedures. Using the measurement and single-subject design procedures of applied behavior analysis, Liberman *et al.* found that contingent consequences could effectively decrease participating youths' interruptions of conversations and increase both their promptness and the quality of their home maintenance behaviors but had no effect on their rate of saving money. The authors found that appropriate behaviors that had been increased through point consequences could be maintained not only through threats of consequences without delivery of those consequences but more importantly, through "warm encouragement and attention from the [teaching parents]" (p. 295). They speculated on the importance of social contingencies and the teaching parents' social interaction skills in affecting behavior change and maintenance. Research germane to this speculation is described later in this chapter.

In other systematic replications of the early behavior analytic research that had been conducted by developers of the Teaching-Family approach, Harris, Finfrock, Giles, Hart, and Tsosie (1975a) found that the remote consequence procedure (Bailey *et al.*, 1970) reduced the serious classroom misbehavior of youths in an Arizona-based behavioral group home. In a second study, Harris and his colleagues (1975b) found that the remote consequence procedure was effective in increasing the percentage of assignments completed at school from 40% to 75%. They also noted a correlated increase in the youths' school grades.

A final behavior-analytic study on group home reinforcement procedures conducted by other than the model developers was described by Wood and Flynn (1978) in their Florida-based project. This reversal-design study involved ongoing measurement of the personal room cleanliness maintained by six youths. The youths experienced conditions of baseline (no instructions or consequences related to room cleanliness), instructions without consequences, point consequences administered by the teaching parents, and point consequences self-administered by each youth. In the self-administered condition, the youths checked their rooms' cleanliness using a detailed checklist and received points depending both on the accuracy of their evaluation and the cleanliness of the rooms. Once the youths demonstrated accuracy, and at first only as long as they maintained accuracy, they were allowed to award points directly to themselves. The self-administered system was as effective as the teaching-parent-administered system and more effective in maintaining performance after contingencies were withdrawn.

Self-Government Systems

Following the development of the motivation system, research and development began on systems giving youths a share of the responsibility for program operation. As noted by Fixsen, Phillips, and Wolf (1973), many youths and adults in correctional settings develop an "informal type of self-government dependent upon group coercion and punishment that often is more severe than that allowed by formal rules" (p. 31). Much of this peer group influence is for antisocial behavior, and program staff often attempt to reduce or eliminate these informal self-government systems. Two types of self-government systems were developed and researched at Achievement Place, in part encouraged by other attempts to develop semi-self-government systems that encourage peer group influence for prosocial behavior (Empey, 1966; Makarenko, 1953).

We have already described the peer manager system that gives youths the responsibility for supervising and providing consequences for each other's routine program activities (Phillips, Phillips, Wolf, & Fixsen, 1973). The second semi-self-government system in the Teaching-Family approach is a group decision-making system centered on the "family conference," a daily meeting at which youths are instructed in rational problem-solving skills and are involved in making programmatic rules, determining rule violations, setting consequences, and planning treatment. Research has demonstrated the impor-

tant role of aspects of this semi-self-government system, including peer reporting and the youths' accepting of responsibility for their decisions (Fixsen *et al.*,
1973). Other research has shown the importance of significant participation in
family conference for the youths' satisfaction with treatment fairness, pleas-
antness, and educational value (Kifer, Ayala, Fixsen, Phillips, & Wolf, 1974).
Finally, research has also shown the effectiveness of procedures involved in
teaching important, socially validated, self-government skills to the youths
(Minkin *et al.*, 1981).

Teaching Procedures

The development of explicit teaching procedures for increasing the skills
of participating youths was given emphasis after initial failures to replicate
the successful program operated at Achievement Place by Elery and Elaine
Phillips. The failures dictated a closer look at the original program to see what
critical features were not being specified well and hence not being taught
adequately to those attempting replications. Intensive, informal, comparative
observations at both Achievement Place and inadequate replications led to
recognition of the significance of teaching functional social, academic, self-
care, and prevocational skills. In turn, this led to the identification of teaching
components such as providing each youth with (1) specific descriptions, clear
examples, and explicit demonstrations of desired and undesired behaviors; (2)
reasons for performing or avoiding behavior, especially reasons revealing the
concern and fairness of the teaching parents and pointing to the natural consequences of behavior; and (3) supervised opportunities to rehearse behavior and
to receive corrective feedback and positive consequences (see Braukmann,
Ramp, Tigner, & Wolf, 1984). This teaching technology was detailed and further developed; it was described in the evolving programmatic manual, *The
Teaching-Family Handbook* (Phillips, Phillips, Fixsen, & Wolf, 1972, 1974);
and was added to the emerging, practically oriented training program for
teaching parents (see later section on training).

Research was subsequently undertaken on the effects of the teaching
technology, using applied behavior-analytic designs and the direct observation
of behavior. A series of studies demonstrated the effects of behavioral teaching procedures on academic skills and vocational skills and on a variety of
social skills (e.g., negotiating, accepting criticism, conversing) judged to be
important in interactions with natural parents, group home teaching parents,
potential employers, policemen, adults in general, and peers (Ayala, Minkin,
Phillips, Fixsen, & Wolf, 1973; Braukmann, Maloney, Fixsen, Phillips, &
Wolf, 1974; Kifer, Lewis, Green, & Phillips, 1974; Kirigin, Phillips, Timbers,
Fixsen, & Wolf, 1977; Kuehn *et al.*, 1977; Maloney *et al.*, 1975; Maloney *et al.*
1976; Minkin *et al.*, 1976; Timbers, Timbers, Fixsen, Phillips, & Wolf, 1973;
Werner *et al.*, 1975).

In addition to individual analysis research designs and direct, reliable
observation of behaviors, many of these studies also involved social validity
procedures to determine the appropriateness of the goals, intervention pro-

cedures, and behavior changes (see Chapter 2 of this text for background on social validity procedures). Typical of these studies was Minkin *et al.* (1976), which sought to improve female group home participants' social interaction skills with adults. The assumption was that such skills would help the girls achieve increased acceptance by and opportunities with adult authorities in conventional settings, thereby perhaps both reducing their need to resort to illegal behavior and increasing the likelihood of their involvement in interpersonal contingency arrangements incompatible with illegal behavior. Such a focus on social skills is an example of an indirect intervention approach (see Chapter 2).

In order to determine what social interaction skills to teach the youths in the Minkin *et al.* study, normative data were collected. Five female college students and five female junior high students were videotaped while conversing with previously unknown adults. The conversational ability of each of these 10 students was then evaluated by a group of adult judges who viewed the tapes and rated each conversant. The average ratings by judges correlated highly ($r = .85$) with certain conversational behaviors measured reliably from the tapes. The procedure was replicated with a new group of students and a new group of raters. Equally high correlations between ratings and the identified conversational behaviors suggested that the identified behaviors were indeed important in conversations. Group home females' use of these behaviors was then assessed and, in multiple-baseline fashion, the youths were trained in the behaviors. The training increased the youths' use of the targeted behaviors in conversations with adults. Furthermore, independent adult raters rated the conversational performances of the youths considerably higher at posttreatment than at pretreatment.

Developing Mutually Reinforcing Relationships

In addition to developing and testing treatment procedures for teaching youths important skills, for motivating youths, and for providing them with involvement in decision making, other less easily researched procedures were developed, including procedures for establishing reinforcing relationships with the youths. A youth/teaching-parent relationship in which the teaching parents have a high "reinforcing value" (due to their mediation of positive consequences) was identified by program developers as an essential ingredient in making the overall treatment approach effective (Phillips *et al.*, 1974). Some empirical support for the suggestion that positive staff–youth relationships were important in producing desired treatment outcomes was provided by Solnick, Braukmann, Bedlington, Kirigin, and Wolf (1981). Direct observational measures were collected that were presumed to be indicative of the extent to which the youths found their teaching parents to be reinforcing, namely the youths' proximity to and talking to their teaching parents during unstructured periods in the group home. These measures were then correlated with the during-treatment delinquent behavior of participating youths, based on their self-reports. The measure of delinquency and reinforcing value were highly correlated inversely across eight group home programs: high levels of reinforcing value were related to low levels of delinquency. These results, which were replicated in a second set of eight homes (Solnick, Braukmann, Belden, Kirigin Ramp, & Wolf, 1981), are consistent with the contention that reinforcing relationships may play an important role in programs aimed at delinquency reduction and prevention (Braukmann, Kirigin, & Wolf, 1980).

Among the teaching-parent behaviors informally identified as enhancing interpersonal relationships were the positive teaching behaviors already discussed, including explanations and praise; individual, regular, and enjoyable time with each youth; consistent, repeated expressions of interest in, concern for, and appreciation of each youth; humor, encouragement, and enthusiasm; and offering and providing help to the youths in areas important to them (Bedlington, Kirigin, Wolf, Brown, & Tigner, 1979). Empirical support for the reinforcing properties of some of these and other behaviors was provided by Willner et al. (1977), which will be discussed in the next section.

Staff-Training and Quality-Control Procedures

By the early- to mid-1970s, the immediate effectiveness of the previously described and other treatment procedures had been convincingly demonstrated, and preliminary program evaluation outcome data suggested that the original group home was producing good behavioral and attitudinal changes (Eitzen, 1975; Kirigin et al., 1974; Phillips, Phillips, Fixsen, & Wolf, 1973). At that point, development began on a comprehensive technology for preparing new teaching-parents to replicate the program. The goal was not only to teach important treatment skills to trainees, but also to control the quality of attempted replication programs. Our training/quality-control strategies evolved as we observed our initial successes and failures and adjusted accordingly. The training/quality-control model that resulted was a yearlong, educational sequence involving two intensive, skill-focused workshops; ongoing in-service education of trainees by experienced trainers; and periodic professional and consumer evaluations. High professional and consumer evaluation ratings 1 year after the inception of training results in certification of the teaching parents, with subsequent annual evaluations determining whether recertification will occur. We researched various aspects of this training/quality-control model. Quasi-experimental research demonstrated the importance of the routine, consumer feedback evaluations both for quality control and for program survival (Braukmann et al., 1975).

Several within-subject and between-group design studies using direct behavioral observations of trainee performance, often in simulated situations, demonstrated the effectiveness of workshop training in teaching trainees the model's various socially validated and effective treatment components (Braukmann, Kirigin, Braukmann, Willner, & Wolf, 1983; Dancer et al., 1978; Kirigin et al., 1975; Maloney, Phillips, Fixsen, & Wolf, 1975; Willner et al.,

1977). In each case, the training procedures studied included oral and written instructions and behavior specifications; rationales for the learning and use of targeted teaching-parent skills; videotaped examples of teaching parents handling situations both appropriately and, for contrast and discussion, inappropriately; and opportunities for behavior rehearsals with detailed feedback. Among the most ambitious of these studies was that by Willner et al. (1977).

In the Willner et al. study (1977), the researchers sought to determine youth preferences for various teaching-parent interaction styles, to train teaching parents to use these preferred interaction skills, and to assess if youths enjoyed interactions more once the teaching parents were so trained. The study is presented here in some detail, because, as noted by Willner, Braukmann, Kirigin, and Wolf (1978), it demonstrates the critical role of youth input in the development of procedures and the role of research in tying treatment to training so as to improve the quality of both.

The study was initiated by asking 19 youths to (1) view a series of videotaped, simulated interactions between teaching parents and youths and (2) write down the specific teaching-parent behaviors that they liked or disliked. The resulting 790 comments were reliably sorted by independent observers into 29 behavioral categories. The youths were then asked to rate each of the categories according to how well they would like these social behaviors in their interactions with teaching parents. Most-liked categories included teaching parents speaking in a calm, pleasant tone of voice; offering to help the youth with a problem, activity, or task; joking and using humor with the youth; providing positive feedback (i.e., praise or recognition) for some accomplishment; being fair with and expressing concern for the youth; giving positive, tangible consequences (e.g., points) for a youth's efforts; giving informative explanations; using rationales for why a request was being made; using polite language; and being brief and concise. A number of these behaviors are among those described earlier that have been shown to be effective in changing youths' behavior. Furthermore, many of these behaviors are among those listed earlier as likely to foster mutually reinforcing relationships.

The second aspect of the study involved the training of teaching-parent couples in the use of these youth-preferred interaction behaviors. Using a multiple-baseline design across trainees, three married couples (i.e., six trainees) were trained at different points in time across a 5-month period during which we collected periodic assessments of each trainee's interaction behaviors with youths. Following training, consistent increases were seen in preferred interaction behaviors. The changes in behavior corresponded to increases in the youths' ratings of the trainees' videotaped interactions, suggesting that socially valid behaviors had indeed been selected and encouraged. Further evidence of the social validity of the behavior changes was obtained by comparing the trainees' pre- and posttraining behavior and their youth ratings with those of three successful teaching parents who were skillful and well-liked by their youths. Training brought the trainees' scores into the range of the successful teaching parents.

Dissemination and the National Association

With the development of fairly reliable and effective training procedures, we began disseminating the treatment model by training group home personnel from around Kansas, and soon thereafter, from other states as well. The strategy of training couples to run replication programs in Kansas worked well, but the strategy of training couples to run isolated programs in other states ultimately proved to be a less than optimal approach for various financial and logistical reasons. Fortunately, the training program was such that it, like the treatment program, was replicable; and individuals trained at our project in the treatment and training/quality-control methodologies began to accept positions in other studies where they could replicate our training/ quality-control efforts for homes in those states. This latter regional or clustered dissemination strategy has proven quite effective.

As noted earlier, there are now over 200 Teaching-Family group homes nationally. Most of the homes are for adolescents in trouble, but some are for retarded persons (Sherman, Sheldon, Morris, Strouse, & Reese, 1984) and for autistic and disturbed children (McClannahan, Krantz, McGee, & MacDuff, 1984).

Each home is associated with 1 of the more than 10 regional, certified training sites. Some are also associated with 1 of several "developing" sites that are working under the supervision of certified sites toward their own autonomous, certified status. Training site certification procedures parallel those for teaching parents and constitute a quality-control mechanism that is maintained by the National Teaching-Family Association, an organization begun for that purpose. The association establishes and enforces treatment, training, dissemination, and research standards with regard to the training sites and their individual homes.

Outcome Evaluations

Each of the several outcome evaluations of Teaching-Family programs have involved quasi-experimental designs (Cook & Campbell, 1979). Random assignment, especially to intrusive and long-term interventions, is usually not possible under field conditions because of political, ethical, and practical reasons.

A Preliminary Outcome Evaluation

Kirigin, Wolf, Braukmann, Fixsen, and Phillips (1979) reported a comparison between the first 18 male participants to attend the original Achievement Place group home and 19 youths who attended the primary Kansas institution for adolescent males. The institutionalized youths were selected post hoc by a probation officer as youths who would have been eligible for Achievement Place as an alternative to institutionalization. Because the two groups of youths differed with respect to age at admission to their programs, with the institutional group being older, comparisons were made after making age adjustments. Data on police and court contacts, posttreatment institutionalization, and school attendance suggested positive effects for the Teaching-Family youths, but the results were far from definitive, given potential group differences pretreatment, the small sample sizes, and the unestablished validity of the age-adjustement procedure. Further, the use of an institutional comparison group was problematic in the face of other evidence reported by Kirigin *et al.* (1979): Only about half of the 18 youths randomly selected to *not* enter the Achievement Place program were institutionalized within the following years. Accordingly, our subsequent Teaching-Family evaluation, which is presented next, employed, as a comparison group, youths placed in alternative group home programs.

A Kansas Evaluation Using Comparison Group Homes

Our dissemination of the Teaching-Family approach within Kansas permitted us to evaluate its effectiveness relative to other group home programs in the state (Kirigin, Braukmann, Atwater, & Wolf, 1982). This program evaluation included the original Achievement Place program, 12 group homes that were replications of Achievement Place, and 9 comparison group home programs. Altogether, 140 Teaching-Family youths and 52 comparison youths participated. Primary dependent measures were retrieved from court and police files and included number of alleged offenses, percentage of youths involved in those alleged offenses, and percentage of youths institutionalized. Other dependent measures were subjective ratings of consumer satisfaction with the treatment staff and the overall program. The latter ratings were obtained from such program consumers as the group home residents, their parents, local social and court agency personnel, and schoolteachers.

The results of the study showed significant differences during treatment, favoring the Teaching-Family programs on rate of alleged criminal offenses, percentage of youths involved in those offenses, and consumer ratings of the program. In the posttreatment year, however, none of the differences between the groups was significant on any of the outcome measures, with both groups' offense rates declining from pretreatment.

The history of evaluation of delinquency treatment has been one with few positive or differential results either during or following treatment. The posttreatment results of our comparison appeared to be generally consistent with this history, but the during-treatment results were not. Although the data were interpreted cautiously, given limitations in design and measurement, it appeared that the Teaching-Family programs provided a set of conditions that reduced delinquent behavior during treatment to a greater degree than did the comparison programs and did so in a manner that produced more positive ratings by the youth participants. The increased rates of offical delinquency seen during treatment in a majority of the comparison programs seemed to illustrate that placement in some group homes may exacerbate the problem it was intended to solve.

An Evaluation Conducted in North Carolina

Obviously, an evaluation conducted in Kansas does not address the effects of group homes using the Teaching-Family approach elsewhere. Robert Jones and Gary Timbers (1982) evaluated the effectiveness of Teaching-Family group homes associated with the first replication training site, located in North Carolina. Comparisons were based on preattrition samples of 137 youths referred to nine Teaching-Family homes and 80 youths who were referred to these nine homes but who, for reasons unrelated to their behavioral histories, received alternative treatment, ranging from probation to institutionalization. While the youths were in the program, differences were found favoring the Teaching-Family sample, mostly on school-related measures like attendance, grade point average, and general academic performance. In addition, some of the differences lasted beyond the period of group home stay. No differences were apparent, however, with regard to police and court contacts either during or after group home stay. This lack of difference was attributed by the authors as likely due to the generally low rates among both groups of such contacts, that is, a floor effect. Unfortunately, given the low rates of official contacts in the North Carolina site, self-report measures of delinquency were not collected (see Chapter 2 for some background on self-report measures), nor were there measures of changes in important nondelinquent behaviors other than those related to schools. The remaining evaluation studies have employed self-report measures to supplement official record data.

A National Evaluation

A nationally focused evaluation was conducted by Richard Jones and his colleagues beginning in 1975 (Jones, Weinrott, & Howard, 1981). It involved 51 programs in 10 states: 26 community-based homes (associated with three training sites) attempting the Teaching-Family model at the time the study began and 25 comparison facilities. Data on one or more outcome measures were collected on 354 Teaching-Family youths and 363 comparison youths. The Teaching-Family homes did significantly better on measures of consumer satisfaction and school performance during treatment and were less expensive to operate. The two samples were nearly equivalent, however, on during- and posttreatment measures of delinquency, institutionalization, self-esteem, and acquisition of adult roles.

Although the results of the Jones et al. (1981) study differed from the Kirigin et al. (1982) and the to be described Braukmann, Wolf, and Kirigin Ramp (1985) studies in not finding during-treatment differences on official measures of delinquency, it nevertheless was in concordance with these studies in finding a substantial pre- to during-treatment reduction for the Teaching-Family group in officially recorded nonstatus offenses (from 2.1 to 1.3 offenses per year). In fact, the primary difference among these studies was that Jones et al. (1981) also found a substantial pre- to during-treatment reduction for the comparison group (from 2.1 to 1.2 offenses per year).

The reason for the difference across studies in comparison-group performance may well be due to differences in the selection of comparison homes. With regard to the Jones *et al.* study:

> Altogether, approximately 60 comparison programs were asked to participate and cooperation from 31 (50% acceptance) was obtained. (Jones, 1976, p. 5)

If only half the approached homes agreed to participate, it is possible that the accepting programs were the better ones; hence they were more willing to be evaluated. In contrast, in both the Kirigin *et al.* (1982) and Braukmann, Wolf, and Kirigin Ramp (1985) studies, virtually all the approached potential-comparison homes agreed to participate in the research. (In all three studies, all approached Teaching-Family homes agreed to participate.) In the Braukmann, Wolf, and Kirigin Ramp (1985) study, which was most like the Jones *et al.* study in terms of data-collection demands on the participating homes, the high participation rate among approached comparison homes—which were selected for approach on the basis of careful matching to Teaching-Family homes with respect to the characteristics of youths served—was no doubt achieved because the homes were paid for their participation.

Thus, the positive features of the Jones *et al.* (1981) evaluation—large sample size, wide scope, and use of both official and self-report delinquency measures—must be weighed against possible selection bias. Another factor affecting the interpretation of this evaluation is that a sizable number of homes in the Teaching-Family sample did not receive satisfactorily frequent and complete training, consultation, and evaluation services by current standards. This was because the study was undertaken (1) before the advent of the National Teaching-Family Association (NaTFA) and its quality-control mechanisms (under NaTFA, one of the training sites involved in the study would not have been permitted to develop or continue in its inadequate form) and (2) before the current, regional-training-site approach to replication had completely replaced the strategy of training couples for isolated group homes spread across the country. Though some of the latter homes dropped the Teaching-Family approach during the course of the study because logistics precluded their receiving a satisfactory level of services, they continued to be considered Teaching-Family homes for research purposes.

Given the preceding considerations, it is difficult to reach firm conclusions from the national evaluation on the relative merits of the Teaching-Family approach, especially as it is now disseminated. Nevertheless, in the main, the results are fairly consistent with those of other evaluations. Although no other multisite evaluation has been undertaken, two additional studies of the approach in Kansas have been completed and are described next.

An Evaluation Concerning Effects of Drug Use and Abuse

Braukmann, Bedlington, Belden, Braukmann, Husted, Kirigin Ramp, and Wolf (1985) examined the effects of Teaching-Family and comparison group home programs in Kansas on participants' self-reported use and abuse of drugs and alcohol, and their performance of some prosocial behaviors. As noted in that publication, the research literature suggests that adolescents who are in residential programs due to their delinquent behavior are at high risk for drug and alcohol use and abuse, both in the short run and the long run. Braukmann *et al.* substantiated that drug use among youths assigned to group homes was fairly common. The results also indicated that youths ($n = 82$) in Teaching-Family homes had better during-treatment outcomes than youths ($n = 103$) in comparison group homes. Furthermore, a sample of Teaching-Family youths ($n = 28$) had better outcomes than a matched no-treatment comparison group of their friends ($n = 28$). In contrast, a sample of the youths ($n = 33$) in the comparison group homes did not differ on during-treatment measures from a matched no-treatment comparison group of their friends ($n = 33$). In the posttreatment year, however, no outcome difference was evident in any of the comparisons.

Regression analyses were conducted to attempt to account for variation in the during-treatment outcomes. Two process measures based on youth reports—the extent of teaching by group home staff and the extent of staff active disapproval of drug and alcohol use—appeared to underlie to some extent the better during-treatment outcomes in the Teaching-Family programs. The suggestion that teaching plays an important programmatic role was in keeping with both our basic assumptions and with previous data using direct observations of teaching behavior in group homes (Bedlington, Braukmann, Kirigin, & Wolf, 1979).

A Final Outcome Study

The largest and most comprehensive outcome study conducted in Kansas was described preliminarily in Braukmann, Wolf, and Kirigin Ramp (1985). Analyses involved 168 Teaching-Family youths (125 males and 43 females) and 205 youths (149 males and 56 females) in comparison group homes. Both pretreatment and during-treatment data existed for all youths, and posttreatment data existed for most of the youths. The groups were not different with regard to race or pretreatment school-related variables. Nor were they different on pretreatment measures of prior therapy, juvenile-justice-system involvement, noninstitutional out-of-home placement, and institutional placement. They were slightly different with respect to age, however: Teaching-Family participants were younger (15.2 years vs. 15.6 years) at program entry but not at program exit. Although the slight age difference pretreatment was judged inconsequential, all analyses were done twice, with and without age as a covariate.

In order to assess the seriousness of the youths' delinquent behavior, the 1-year pretreatment self-reported delinquency data were examined for the 373 youths on whom we had both pretreatment and during-treatment data. The Teaching-Family and comparison samples were highly similar pretreatment, with half of each sample falling into the "serious delinquent" category based on the typological criteria developed by Elliott and his colleagues in their National Youth Survey study. Elliott and Huizinga (1984) found that less than

5% of their national probability sample of adolescents (selected to be representative of the total 11- through 17-year-old population in the United States) met the criterion for classification as a serious delinquent, but this small portion accounted for 77% of all felony assaults, 79% of all felony thefts, 89% of all robberies, and 50% of all crimes reported.

The Teaching-Family and comparison groups were compared pre-, during, and posttreatment on eight self-reported delinquency scales derived from the National Youth Survey. Analyses of variance and covariance were done for combined male-and-female, male-only, and female-only samples. In almost every analysis, there were no differences pretreatment, significant differences during treatment favoring the Teaching-Family samples, and no differences posttreatment. Thus the findings based on self-reported delinquency of a recent Kansas sample were consistent with earlier findings based on the officially recorded delinquency of a different sample.

Analyses also were conducted using official police and court data. Again, during-treatment differences favoring the Teaching-Family sample were found, but neither pretreatment nor posttreatment differences were evident.

Teaching-Family and comparison groups were also compared on the Jesness Behavior Checklist that contains 14 staff-completed scales (e.g., Responsibility, Sociability, Social Control, Anger Control, Conformity, etc.) concerning youth behavior. The results suggested that, although there were no pretreatment differences between Teaching-Family and comparison groups, the Teaching-Family youths, especially males, were significantly better at program exit. Unlike the comparison youths, the Teaching-Family youths appeared to improve their behavior and skills during treatment. This finding is consistent with the delinquency differences reported before.

The Teaching-Family and comparison programs were also compared with regard to consumer satisfaction. For every consumer group (e.g., youths' parents, their teachers, placing-agency personnel, and the youths themselves), the ratings of Teaching-Family programs were significantly higher, replicating differences found in earlier studies.

Another set of comparisons between Teaching-Family and comparison youths concerns school-related performance. Generally speaking, the two groups of youths were not different pre-, during, or posttreatment on measures of self-reported grades or self-reported school attendance, with both groups performing better during- and posttreatment than at pretreatment.

A final outcome comparison concerned the circumstances under which youths exited their programs as reported by staff. Though, in the opinion of staff in both samples, many youths did not successfully complete their treatment before leaving, Teaching-Family youths were significantly more likely to be judged as completing treatment. Furthermore, Teaching-Family youths were more likely to leave under favorable circumstances and less likely to run away from their programs and not return.

To summarize this last in a series of evaluation studies, then, the data again appear to support a conclusion of an immediate and considerable impact on the behavior of participating youths. Again, however, differences favoring the Teaching-Family approach do not seem to survive the treatment period.

CONCLUSION

During the course of the research on the Teaching-Family group home approach, a highly specified and quality-controlled treatment model has been developed, disseminated, and evaluated. The evaluation research, with some exceptions, has suggested that the model was differentially effective during the treatment period, a rare finding in the long history of the evaluation of treatment programs for youths. Unfortunately, the research also has found that the differential during-treatment effect on delinquent behavior was not maintained after the youths left the group home programs.

Though the Teaching-Family and comparison groups did not differ post-treatment on most comparisons in the various outcome studies, the level of offending for both groups was considerably lower posttreatment than pretreatment. Similar pre-to posttreatment declines have been noted in other studies of residential treatment (e.g., Murray & Cox, 1979). A recent consideration of possible reasons for such declines among group home youths concluded that the decreases are probably at least partial functions of both intervention (i.e., treatment and "suppression" effects) as well as a selection-regression artifact (i.e., selecting youths for intervention on the basis of extreme behavior that subsequently regresses toward the mean) (Braukmann, Kirigin Ramp, & Wolf, 1986). Pre- to posttreatment decreases notwithstanding, it appears preliminarily that group home youths, on average, continue to offend posttreatment considerably above normative levels (Braukmann et al., 1986).

The lack of differential posttreatment effects in the studies reviewed and the continued above-normal illegal behavior posttreatment for many of the youths participating in Teaching-Family programs suggests that the Teaching-Family model in its current form does not seem to be a complete solution. Finding a more complete solution is important because group home youths, like adolescent offenders in general, appear to be at some risk for a variety of negative outcomes in adulthood beyond illegal behavior, including alcohol abuse, impoverishment, social isolation, hospitalization, overaggressiveness, chronic unemployment, desertion and nonsupport of families, and having children at risk of similarly poor outcomes (Wolf, Braukmann, & Kirigin Ramp, in press).

An original basic assumption was that Teaching-Family group home treatment would have a differential long-term impact that would carry over into youths' posttreatment environments. It was assumed that youths would learn important social, self-care, prevocational, family-living, and relationship skills that would help them to sustain their differential gains following treatment. Further, it was assumed that the youths' natural families could be helped to acquire more effective and positive parenting practices. Many of the youths, however, have had no parents with which to work, and available parents often have met Robin's (1966) definition of sociopathy. In fact, in our experience, the youths' parents often had problems as serious as the youths' and were as resistant to treatment.

Thus it now seems somewhat naive to have assumed that youths could maintain differential gains upon returning to families that were often uninterested in changing their inappropriate practices and may have been largely responsible for the youths' original problems (cf. Wilson & Herrnstein, 1985). Accordingly, the developers of the Teaching-Family model now assume that not only must many of the youths referred for treatment learn important skills, but they must also be provided with adequate families throughout the high-risk years of adolescence, so that they can make important, developmentally appropriate transitions into independent living, long-term intimate relationships, vocational or college education, and employment. Once these transitions have been completed, for example when most youths are in their mid-20s, these young adults' prosocial repertoires are more likely to be maintained by the ongoing reinforcement contingencies in the natural environment.

Group home youths need adequate families because adolescence is a period filled with many possibilities for mistakes, unrecognized options, and potentially tragic decisions. This is especially true for youths who, because of their histories of failed families, abuse and neglect, failure in school, and previous close association with deviant peer groups, are considerably more vulnerable than normal youths when guidance and support are absent. No one would recommend turning any youth out "into the street" at 15 or 16 years of age with no adequate family support. Yet this is what of necessity has happened with many Teaching-Family group home graduates.

Adequate families can serve as models for appropriate family behavior; provide shelter and financial support between jobs and schools, girl- /boyfriends, and marriages; and provide prosocial parental adult models who have significant reinforcement value and are a source of affection and attachment. Such families (1) can create a deterrence to deviance that rests on a youth's not wanting to risk the regard and affection of valued others by engaging in behavior disapproved of by them and (2) can reward the youth's appropriate behavior and achievements in education, family life, and employment both during adolescence and perhaps, as occurs in most adequate families, throughout the youth's life.

Unfortunately, many Teaching-Family group home youths do not currently have adequate families to provide these opportunities and conditions. This might be solved by adding a long-term special foster-care-program element to the Teaching-Family group home model (cf. Jones & Timbers, 1983; Meadowcroft, Hawkins, Trout, Grealish, & Stark, 1982). Given the seriousness of the problems of many group home youths, it may be that a special foster care program would not be appropriate as the sole treatment intervention. Once the youths' behaviors had been improved in the structured, intensive group home setting, however, transitions to special foster care settings could be accomplished without relinquishing the gains made in the group home. These transitions would be facilitated by opportunities while a youth is still in the group home for (1) the special foster care parents to work closely with the group home teaching parents and (2) "trial" weekend placements in special foster families in order to ensure that a good youth–foster-family match is achieved.

One direction for future application seems clear then because short-term "treatment" for long-term gain/rehabilitation may be an unrealistic goal in many cases. Indeed, the almost universal failure of all delinquency treatment attempts in the past suggests as much. Longer term participation in a program that can provide the elements of an "adequate family" into young adulthood may provide at least a partial solution. It may be possible to select, train, and monitor special foster parents in the same effective manner as teaching parents. This may provide youths with an adequate family that will, in the long term, break the cycle of deviance.

Appraisal of such procedures must await further research. As Maloney, Fixsen, and Phillips (1981) note, research is not merely an academic exercise or an advisable adjunct to service but an inseparable aspect of quality service. The development of the Teaching-Family model exemplifies how completely research can be part of behavioral interventions.

REFERENCES

Ayala, H. E., Minkin, N., Phillips, E. L., Fixsen, D. L., & Wolf, M. M. (1973, September). *Achievement Place: The training and analysis of vocational behavior.* Paper presented at the meeting of the American Psychological Association, Montreal.

Baer, D. M., & Wolf, M. M. (1970). Recent samples of behavior modification in preschool settings. In C. Neuringer & J. L. Michael (Eds.), *Behavior modification in clinical psychology* (pp. 10–25). New York: Appleton-Century-Crofts.

Bailey, J. S., Wolf, M. M., & Phillips, E. L. (1970). Home-based reinforcement and the modification of pre-delinquents' classroom behavior. *Journal of Applied Behavior Analysis, 3,* 223–233.

Bailey, J. S., Timbers, G. D., Phillips, E. L., & Wolf, M. M. (1971). Modification of articulation errors of pre-delinquents by their peers. *Journal of Applied Behavior Analysis, 5,* 19–30.

Bakal, Y. (Ed.). (1973). *Closing correctional institutions: New strategies for youth services.* Lexington, MA: Lexington Books.

Bedlington, M. M., Braukmann, C. J., Kirigin, K. A., & Wolf, M. M. (1979, December). *Treatment interactions, delinquency, and youth satisfaction.* Paper presented at the meeting of the Association for the Advancement of Behavior Therapy, San Francisco.

Bedlington, M. M., Kirigin, K. A., Wolf, M. M., Brown, W. G., & Tigner, D. M. (1979). Relationship development. In C. J. Braukmann & K. B. Maloney (Eds.), *Teaching-Parent training manual* (Vol. 1, pp. 73–96). Lawrence, KS: The University of Kansas Printing Service.

Birnbrauer, J., Wolf, M. M., Kidder, J., & Tague, C. (1965). Classroom behavior of retarded pupils with token reinforcement. *Journal of Experimental Child Psychology, 2,* 119–135.

Braukmann, C. J., Maloney, D. M., Fixsen, D. L., Phillips, E. L., & Wolf, M. M. (1974). An analysis of a selection interview training package for pre-delinquents at Achievement Place. *Criminal Justice and Behavior, 1,* 30–42.

Braukmann, C. J., Fixsen, D. L., Kirigin, K. A., Phillips, E. A., Phillips, E. L., & Wolf, M. M. (1975). Achievement Place: The training and certification of teaching-parents. In W. S. Wood (Ed.), *Issues in evaluating behavior modification* (pp. 131–152). Champaign, IL: Research Press.

Braukmann, C. J., Kirigin, K. A., & Wolf, M. M. (1980). Group homes treatment research: Social learning and social control perspectives. In T. Hirschi & M. Gottfredson (Eds.), *Understanding crime: Current theory and research* (pp. 117–130). Beverly Hills: Sage.

Braukmann, C. J., Kirigin, K. A., & Wolf, M. M. (1981). Behavioral treatment of juvenile delinquency. In S. W. Bijou & R. Ruiz (Eds.), *Behavior modification: Contributions to education* (pp. 211–231). Hillsdale, NJ: Lawrence Erlbaum Associates.

Braukmann, C. J., Ramp, K. K., Tigner, D. M., & Wolf, M. M. (1984). The Teaching-Family approach to training group-home parents: Training procedures, validation research, and outcome findings. In R. Dangel & R. Polster (Eds.), *Parent training: Foundations of research and practice* (pp. 144–161). New York: Guilford Press.

Braukmann, C. J., Bedlington, M. M., Belden, B. D., Braukmann, P. D., Husted, J. J., Kirigin Ramp, K., & Wolf, M. M. (1985). The effects of community-based group-home treatment programs for male juvenile offenders on the use and abuse of drugs and alcohol. *The American Journal of Drug and Alcohol Abuse, 11,* 249–278.

Braukmann, C. J., Wolf, M. M., & Kirigin Ramp, K. (1985). *Follow-up of group home youths into young adulthood* (Progress Rep., Grant MH20030). Lawrence, KS: The University of Kansas, Achievement Place Research Project.

Braukmann, C. J., Kirigin Ramp, K. & Wolf, M. M. (1986). *Follow-up of group home youths into young adulthood* (Competing Renewal Application, Grant MH20030). Lawrence, KS: The University of Kansas, Achievement Place Research Project.

Braukmann, P. D., Kirigin Ramp, K., Braukmann, C. J., Willner, A. G., & Wolf, M. M. (1983). Analysis and training of rationales for child care workers. *Children and Youth Services Review, 5,* 177–194.

Cohen, H. L., Filipczak, J. A., Bis, J. S., & Cohen, J. E. (1966). *Contingencies applicable to special education of delinquents.* Washington, DC: Department of Health, Education, and Welfare.

Connis, R. T., Braukmann, C. J., Kifer, R. E., Fixsen, D. L., Phillips, E. L., & Wolf, M. M. (1979). Work environment in relation to employee job satisfaction. *Child Care Quarterly, 8,* 126–142.

Cook. T. D., & Campbell, D. T. (1979). *Quasi-experimentation: Design and analysis issues for field settings.* Chicago: Rand McNally.

Dancer, D. D., Braukmann, C. J., Schumaker, J. S., Kirigin, K. A., Willner, A. G., & Wolf, M. M. (1978). The training and validation of behavior observation and specification skills. *Behavior Modification, 2,* 113–134.

Eitzen, D. S. (1975). The effects of behavior modification on the attitudes of delinquents. *Behavior Research and Therapy, 13,* 295–299.

Elliott, D. S., & Huizinga, D. (1984). The relationship between delinquent behavior and ADM problems. In *Proceedings of the ADAMHA/OJJDP Research Conference on Juvenile Offenders With Serious Drug, Alcohol, and Mental Health Problems.* Washington, DC: U.S. Government Printing Office.

Empey, L. T. (1966). *The Provo experiment: A brief review.* Los Angeles: University of Southern California, Youth Studies Center.

Empey, L. T. (1978). *American delinquency: Its meaning and construction.* Homewood, IL: Dorsey Press.

Empey, L. T., & Lubeck, S. G. (1971). *The Silverlake experiment: Evaluating community control of delinquency.* Lexington, MA: D. C. Heath.

Fixsen, D. L., Phillips, E. L., & Wolf, M. M. (1973). Experiments in self government with predelinquents. *Journal of Applied Behavior Analysis, 6,* 31–47.

Gula, M. (1964). Group homes—New and differentiated tools in child welfare, delinquency, and mental health. In Child Welfare League of America, *Group homes in perspective* (pp. 1–5). New York: CWLA.

Harris, V. W., Finfrock, S. R., Giles, D. K., Hart, B., & Tsosie, P. C. (1975a). *Improved classroom social behavior of delinquent American Indian youths using home-based consequences.* Unpublished manuscript, The Centers for Youth Development and Achievement, Tucson.

Harris, V. W., Finfrock, S. R., Giles, D. K., Hart, B., & Tsosie, P. C. (1975b). The effects of performance contingencies on the assignment completion behavior of severely delinquent youths. In E. Ramp & G. Semb (Eds.), *Behavior analysis: Areas of research and application* (pp. 309–316). Englewood Cliffs, NJ: Prentice-Hall.

Hromadka, V. G. (1964). European concept of child care and what we can learn from it. In Child Welfare League of America, *Group homes in perspective* (pp. 41–44). New York: CWLA.

James, I. L., Beier, C. H., Maloney, D. M., Thompson, L., Collins, L. B., & Collins, S. R. (1983). *1983 directory of the National Teaching-Family Association.* Boys Town NE: Father Flanagan's Boys' Home.

Jones, R. J., & Timbers, G. D. (1982). *Evaluation of group homes for delinquent youth* (Final Rep., Grant MH32854). Morganton, NC: BIABH Study Center.

Jones, R. J., & Timbers, G. D. (1983). *Professional parenting for juvenile offenders* (Final Rep., Grant MH15776). Morganton, NC: BIABH Study Center.

Jones, R. R. (1976, September). *Achievement Place: The independent evaluator's perspective.* Paper read at the meeting of the American Psychological Association, Washington, DC.

Jones, R. R., Weinrott, M. R., & Howard, J. R. (1981). *The national evaluation of the Teaching-Family model.* (Final Rep., Grants MH25631 & MH31018). Eugene, OR: Evaluation Research Group.

Keller, O. J., & Alper, B. S. (1970). *Halfway houses: Community centered correction and treatment.* Lexington, MA: Lexington Books.

Kifer, R. E., Ayala, H. E., Fixsen, D. L., Phillips, E. L., & Wolf, M. M. (1974, September). *The Teaching-Family model: An analysis of self-government systems.* Paper presented at the meeting of the American Psychological Association, New Orleans.

Kifer, R. E., Lewis, M. A., Green, D. R., & Phillips, E. L. (1974). Training pre-delinquent youths and their parents to negotiate conflict situations. *Journal of Applied Behavior Analysis, 7,* 357–364.

Kirigin, K. A., Phillips, E. L., Fixsen, D. L., & Wolf, M. M. (1972, September). *Modification of the homework behavior and academic performance of pre-delinquents with home-based reinforcement.* Paper presented at the meeting of the American Psychological Association, Honolulu.

Kirigin, K. A., Phillips, E. L., Fixsen, D. L., Atwater, J., Taubman, M. T., & Wolf, M. M. (1974). Achievement Place: Overall outcome measures and analysis. In *Achievement Place: Phase II final report.* Lawrence, KS: The University of Kansas, Achievement Place Research Project.

Kirigin, K. A., Ayala, H. E., Braukmann, C. J., Brown, W. G., Minkin, N., Fixsen, D. L., Phillips, E. L., & Wolf, M. M. (1975). Training teaching-parents: An evaluation and analysis of workshop training procedures. In E. A. Ramp & G. Semb (Eds.), *Behavior analysis: Areas of research and application* (pp. 161–174). Englewood Cliffs, NJ: Prentice-Hall.

Kirigin, K. A., Phillips, E. L., Timbers, G. D., Fixsen, D. L., & Wolf, M. M. (1977). Achievement Place: The modification of academic behavior problems of delinquent youths in a group home setting. In B. C. Etzel, J. M. LeBlanc, & D. M. Baer (Eds.), *New developments in behavioral research: Theory, method, and application* (pp. 473–487). Hillsdale, NJ: Lawrence Erlbaum Associates.

Kirigin, K. A., Wolf, M. M., Braukmann, C. J., Fixsen, D. L., & Phillips, E. L. (1979). Achievement Place: A preliminary outcome evaluation. In J. S. Stumphauzer (Ed.), *Progress in behavior therapy with delinquents* (pp. 118–145). Springfield, IL: Charles C Thomas.

Kirigin, K. A., Braukmann, C. J., Atwater, J., & Wolf, M. M. (1982). An evaluation of Achievement Place (Teaching-Family) group homes for juvenile offenders. *Journal of Applied Behavior Analysis, 15,* 1–16.

Kuehn, F. E., Kuehn, B. S., Minkin, N. L., Minkin, B. L., Barnard, J. D., Wolf, M. M., Phillips, E. L., & Fixsen, D. L. (1977). *Identifying, training, and validating preferred peer-supervision skills of delinquent youths.* Unpublished manuscript, The University of Kansas, Achievement Place Research Project, Lawrence, KS.

Lerman, P. (1982). *Deinstitutionalization and the welfare state.* New Brunswick, NJ: Rutgers University Press.

Liberman, R. P. (1980). Review of: Psychological treatment for chronic mental patients by Gordon L. Paul and Robert J. Lentz. *Journal of Applied Behavior Analysis, 13,* 367–371.

Liberman, R. P., Ferris, C., Salgado, P., & Salgado, J. (1975). Replication of the Achievement Place model in California. *Journal of Applied Behavior Analysis, 8,* 287–299.

Makarenko, A. S. (1953). *The road to life* (Vols. I, II, III). Moscow: Foreign Language Publishing House.

Maloney, D. M., Phillips, E. L., Fixsen, D. L., Wolf, & M. M. (1975). Training techniques for staff in group homes for juvenile offenders: An analysis. *Criminal Justice and Behavior, 2,* 195–216.

Maloney, D. M., Harper, T. M., Braukmann, C. J., Fixsen, D. L., Phillips, E. L., & Wolf, M. M. (1976). Teaching conversation-related skills to pre-delinquent girls. *Journal of Applied Behavior Analysis, 9,* 371.

Maloney, D. M., Fixsen, D. L., & Phillips, E. L. (1981). The Teaching-Family model: Research and dissemination in a service program. *Children and Youth Services Review, 3,* 343–355.

Maloney, K. B., Braukmann, C. J., Maloney, D. M., Braukmann, P. D., Ayala, H. E., Fixsen, D. L., Phillips, E. L., & Wolf, M. M. (1975, September). *Identification, measurement, and modification of adolescent social interaction skills.* Paper read at the meeting of the American Psychological Association, Chicago.

McClannahan, L. E., Krantz, P. J., McGee, G. G., & MacDuff, G. S. (1984). Teaching-Family model for autistic children. In W. P. Christian, G. T. Hannah, & T. J. Glahn (Eds.), *Programming effective human services* (pp. 383–406). New York: Plenum Press.

Meadowcroft, P., Hawkins, R. P., Trout, B. A., Grealish, E. M., & Stark, L. J. (1982, September). *Making foster-family-based treatment accountable: The issue of quality control.* Paper presented at the meeting of the American Psychological Association, Washington, DC.

Miller, A. D., Coates, R. B., & Ohlin, L. E. (1980). Evaluating correctional systems under normalcy and change. In M. W. Klein & K. S. Teilmann (Eds.), *Handbook of criminal justice evaluation* (pp. 593–610). Beverly Hills: Sage.

Minkin, N., Braukmann, C. J., Minkin, B. L., Timbers, G. D., Timbers, B. L., Fixsen, D. L., Phillips, E. L., & Wolf, M. M. (1976). The social validation and training of conversational skills. *Journal of Applied Behavior Analysis, 9,* 127–139.

Minkin, N., Minkin, B. L., Goldstein, R. S., Taylor, M., Braukmann, C. J., Kirigin, K. A., & Wolf, M. M. (1981). Analysis, validation, and training of peer-criticism skills with delinquent girls. In *Behavioral group therapy, 1981* (pp. 153–166). Champaign, IL: Research Press.

Murray, C. A., & Cox, L. A., Jr. (1979). *Beyond probation.* Beverly Hills: Sage.

Ohlin, L., Coates, R., & Miller, A. (1974). Radical correctional reform: A case study for the Massachusetts youth correctional system. *Harvard Educational Review, 44,* 74–111.

Palmer, T. (1978). *Correctional intervention and research.* Lexington, MA: Lexington Books.

Phillips, E. L. (1968). Achievement Place: Token reinforcement procedures in a home-style rehabilitation setting for pre-delinquent boys. *Journal of Applied Behavior Analysis, 1,* 213–223.

Phillips, E. L., Phillips, E. A., Fixsen, D. L., & Wolf, M. M. (1971). Achievement Place: The modification of the behaviors of pre-delinquent boys with a token economy. *Journal of Applied Behavior Analysis, 4,* 45–59.

Phillips, E. L., Phillips, E. A., Fixsen, D. L., & Wolf, M. M. (1972). *The Teaching-Family handbook.* Lawrence, KS: The University of Kansas Printing Service.

Phillips, E. L., Phillips, E. A., Fixsen, D. L., & Wolf, M. M. (1973, June). Behavior shaping works for delinquents. *Psychology Today,* pp. 74–79.

Phillips, E. L., Phillips, E. A., Wolf, M. M., & Fixsen, D. L. (1973). Achivement Place: Development of the elected manager system. *Journal of Applied Behavior Analysis, 6,* 541–561.

Phillips, E. L., Phillips, E. A., Fixsen, D. L., & Wolf, M. M. (1974). *The Teaching-Family handbook* (rev. ed.). Lawrence, KS: The University of Kansas Printing Service.

Piper, E., & Warner, J. R., Jr. (1980). Group homes for problem youth: Retrospect and prospects. *Child & Youth Services, 3*(3/4), 1–12.

President's Commission on Law Enforcement and Administration of Justice. (1967). *Juvenile delinquency and youth crime.* Washington, DC: U.S. Government Printing Office.

Robins, L. N. (1966). *Deviant children grown up.* Baltimore: Williams & Wilkins.

Sherman, J. A., Sheldon, J. B., Morris, K., Strouse, M., & Reese, R. M. (1984). A community-based residential program for mentally retarded adults: An adaptation of the Teaching-Family model. In S. C. Paine, G. T. Bellamy, & B. Wilcox (Eds.), *Human services that work: From innovation to standard practice* (pp. 167–179) Baltimore, MD: Paul H. Brookes.

Solnick, J. V., Braukmann, C. J., Bedlington, M. M., Kirigin, K. A., & Wolf, M. M. (1981). Parent-youth interaction and delinquency in group homes. *Journal of Abnormal Child Psychology, 9,* 107–119.

Solnick, J. V., Braukmann, C.J., Belden, B. D., Kirigin Ramp, K., & Wolf, M. M. (1981, September). *Group-home interactions and their relationship to drug use and delinquency.* Paper presented at the meeting of the American Psychological Association, Los Angeles.

Staats, A. W., Staats, C. K., Schutz, T. E., & Wolf, M. M. (1962). The conditioning of textual responses using "extrinsic" reinforcers. *Journal of the Experimental Analysis of Behavior, 5*, 33–40.

Timbers, G. D., Timbers, B. L., Fixsen, D. L., Phillips, E. L., & Wolf, M. M. (1973, September). *Achievement Place for pre-delinquent girls: Modification of inappropriate emotional behaviors with token reinforcement and instructional procedures.* Paper presented at the meeting of the American Psychological Association, Montreal.

Turnbough, P. D., Brown, W. G., Fixsen, D. L., Phillips, E. L., & Wolf, M. M. (1973, September). *Monitoring youths' and parents' behavior in the natural home.* Paper presented at the meeting of the American Psychological Association, Montreal.

Vinter, R. D. (Ed.), (1976). *Time out: A national study of juvenile correctional programs.* Ann Arbor: National Assessment of Juvenile Corrections, School of Social Work, The University of Michigan.

Vinter, R. D., Downs, G., & Hall, J. (1976) . *Juvenile corrections in the States: Residential programs and deinstitutionalization.* Ann Arbor: National Assessment of Juvenile Corrections, School of Social Work, The University of Michigan.

Warner, J. R., Jr. (1978). *One thousand group homes in the U.S.A.* (Document No. 45822). Rockville, MD: National Criminal Justice Reference Service.

Werner, J. S., Minkin, N., Minkin, B. L., Fixsen, D. L., Phillips, E. L., & Wolf, M. M. (1975). Intervention package: An analysis to prepare juvenile delinquents for encounters with police officers. *Criminal Justice and Behavior, 2,* 55–83.

Whittaker, J. K. (1979). *Caring for troubled children: Residential treatment in a community context.* San Francisco: Jossey-Bass.

Willner, A. G., Braukmann, C. J., Kirigin, K. A., Fixsen, D. L., Phillips, E. L., & Wolf, M. M. (1977). The training and validation of youth-preferred social behaviors of child-care personnel. *Journal of Applied Behavior Analysis, 10,* 219–230.

Willner, A. G., Braukmann, C. J., Kirigin, K. A., & Wolf, M. M. (1978). Achievement Place: A community treatment model for youths in trouble. In D. Marholin (Ed.), *Child behavior therapy* (pp. 239–273). New York: Gardner Press.

Wilson, J. Q. & Herrnstein, R. J. (1985). *Crime and human nature.* New York: Simon & Schuster.

Wolf, M. M., Giles, D. K., & Hall, R. V. (1968). Experiments with token reinforcement in a remedial classroom. *Behaviour Research and Therapy, 6,* 51–64.

Wolf, M. M., Phillips, E. L., & Fixsen, D. L. (1972). The Teaching-Family: A new model for the treatment of deviant child behavior in the community. In S. W. Bijou & E. L. Ribes-Inesta (Eds.), *Behavior modification: Issues and extensions* (pp. 51–62). New York: Academic Press.

Wolf, M. M., Braukmann, C. J., & Kirigin Ramp, K. (in press). Serious delinquent behavior may be part of a significantly handicapping condition: Cures and supportive environments. *Journal of Applied Behavior Analysis.*

Wood, R., & Flynn, J. M. (1978). A self-evaluation token system versus an external evaluation token system alone in a residential setting with predelinquent youth. *Journal of Applied Behavior Analysis, 11,* 503–512.

6

Basic Behavioral Procedures in Closed Institutions

MICHAEL A. MILAN

Continuing professional interest in the use of behavior change strategies with juvenile and adult offenders is amply documented by the literature reviews that have appeared during the past decade (Braukmann & Fixsen, 1975; Braukmann, Fixsen, Phillips, & Wolf, 1975; Burchard & Harig, 1976; Burchard & Lane, 1982; Davidson & Seidman, 1974; Geller, Johnson, Hemlin, & Kennedy, 1977; Johnson, 1977; Kennedy, 1976; Milan & Long, 1980; Milan & McKee, 1974; Musante, 1975; Nietzel, 1979; Sandford & Bateup, 1973; Stumphauzer, 1981). Most of these reviews have examined behavioral applications in both closed institutions and community-based settings. The reviewers have provided general descriptions of behavioral programs in the areas of crime and delinquency, the characteristics of the behaviors that have been targeted in those programs, and the legal and ethical issues inherent in providing services and conducting research in closed institutions.

This and the next chapter focus on the specific behavioral procedures that have been used in rehabilitation and management programs in closed institutions for juvenile delinquents and adult offenders. The present chapter reviews eight classes of procedures: (1) positive reinforcement, (2) negative reinforcement, (3) punishment, (4) time-out and response cost, (5) extinction, (6) differential reinforcement, (7) generalization training, and (8) social skills training. It also considers the selection of target behaviors in institutional programs and discusses the undesirable side effects that may accompany some behavioral procedures. The chapter following this one reviews the use of large-scale token economies in comprehensive rehabilitation and management programs. It also considers the legal, ethical, and professional issues surrounding the use of behavior procedures in closed institutions. Consequently, the full potential of the behavioral approach in rehabilitation and management pro-

Michael A. Milan • Department of Psychology, Georgia State University, Atlanta, Georgia 30303. Portions of this chapter were written while the author was Deputy Director for Programs, Florida Mental Health Institute, University of South Florida.

grams for institutionalized youthful and adult offenders can be assessed only after the material reviewed in both chapters has been considered.

The categorization of behavior change strategies in terms of discrete procedures is often problematic. First, most applied behavioral work involves combinations of several procedures. Accordingly, interventions will be categorized here in terms of the predominant procedure involved and/or the manner in which the authors of the reviewed studies have chosen to characterize their procedures. A second difficulty in categorizing intervention strategies involves making sometimes arbitrary distinctions between procedures. For instance, Michael (1975) has argued convincingly that conceptual distinctions between positive and negative reinforcement and between punishment and time-out are often meaningless.

Despite these difficulties, this chapter will continue the tradition of distinguishing between two classes of procedures that increase behavior—positive and negative reinforcement (Skinner, 1953)—and between two classes of procedures that suppress behavior—punishment and time-out or response cost. An additional distinction will be made in descriptions of research methodology between reversal and withdrawal experimental designs (Hersen & Barlow, 1976). Experimental designs in which contingencies are applied to one behavior and then to an incompatible other will be termed *reversal designs,* whereas experimental designs in which contingencies are introduced and then discontinued will be termed *withdrawal designs.*

ANALYSIS OF NATURALLY OCCURRING CONTINGENCIES

Before examining planned behavioral procedures, this chapter will place them in context by discussing the nature and impact of the unplanned contingencies they were designed to replace. Some of the earliest and perhaps most provocative work by behaviorists in correctional settings focused on the way social reinforcement and punishment, broadly defined, are provided naturally by staff and inmates following appropriate and inappropriate behaviors. This research undoubtedly grew out of the assumption that the inmate subculture is an important obstacle to effective rehabilitation and management programming in juvenile and adult institutions. Early investigators clearly saw the need to identify these interpersonal interaction patterns and to develop techniques and strategies that inmates and staff could employ to encourage appropriate or discourage inappropriate behavior.

Three studies with institutionalized delinquent females by Buehler, Patterson, and Furniss (1966) represent an early attempt to analyze naturally occurring patterns of social reinforcement and punishment. Interactions were described in terms of whether the content of youths' statements indicated acceptance of delinquent or of societal norms and whether peer responses to these prodelinquent or prosocial statements consisted of reinforcement or punishment. The first study revealed that the delinquents systematically reinforced the prodelinquent talk and punished the prosocial talk of their peers. The second study indicated that the peers used nonverbal more often than verbal communication in reinforcing and punishing behavior. The third study, a more fine-grained analysis, replicated the previous findings and also indicated that the staff was inconsistent in its responses to prodelinquent and prosocial talk, alternately rewarding and punishing inmates for the same class of verbal statements. The study also revealed that the amount of reinforcement and punishment provided by peers was considerably greater than that provided by staff.

More recent research has replicated some of these findings and called others into question. Sandford (1973) studied the control procedures used by staff in a New Zealand borstal (the equivalent of a boys training school). He found moderate to high agreement among staff concerning what constituted appropriate and inappropriate behavior, but, as in the Buehler *et al.* (1966) studies, inconsistency in responding to that behavior. Sanson-Fisher and Jenkins (1978) also found that the staff was inconsistent in responding to appropriate and inappropriate behavior in a maximum security institution for delinquent females. Contrary to the earlier work of Buehler *et al.* (1966), however, Sanson-Fisher and Jenkins's data indicated that, in the presence of staff, the inmates also were inconsistent in their responses. Moreover, Sanson-Fisher, Seymour, and Baer (1976) found that in the absence of staff, the delinquent females they studied were consistent but attended positively to prosocial behavior rather than either responding to it inconsistently (cf. Sanson-Fisher & Jenkins, 1978) or systematically reinforcing prodelinquent behavior (cf. Buehler *et al.*, 1966).

Comments

Clearly, additional research is required before any definitive statements can be made concerning inmate and staff responses to prodelinquent and prosocial behaviors or the effects of these on institutional life and community adjustment. It is certainly possible that reinforcement and punishment practices differ from context to context as suggested by the existing research. Moreover, the existing research has focused on delinquent females, leaving unexamined the social interaction patterns of delinquent males and adult offenders. Nonetheless, the available evidence suggests differential reinforcement and punishment of prodelinquent and prosocial behaviors and indicates that inmates are perhaps more systematic in the encouragement of prodelinquent behavior than are staffs in discouraging it. Sanson-Fisher and his colleagues have suggested ways in which staffs may be trained to increase appropriate social consequences and have shown how self-recording such behavior by inmates may be included in a token reinforcement program to achieve the same end (Sanson-Fisher *et al.*, 1976; Sanson-Fisher, Seymour, Montgomery, & Stokes, 1978; Seymour & Stokes, 1976).

POSITIVE REINFORCEMENT PROCEDURES

Positive reinforcement procedures are defined here as planned intervention strategies that employ the presentation or prolongation of a stimulus, event, or condition contingent upon an appropriate response in order to increase or maintain that and similar responses. *Response* is, of course, a shorthand term for an activity or class of activities. The stimuli, events, or conditions applicable in reinforcement procedures in closed institutions include words of approval, field trips, attending sporting events, edibles, reduced supervision, extra telephone or visiting privileges, and tokens.

With regard to the use of tokens, a distinction is made here between token reinforcement procedures and large-scale token economies. The simple token reinforcement procedures reviewed in this chapter involve a small number of inmates receiving tokens for one or two behaviors and exchanging them for a relatively small number of backup reinforcers. Also included here is the use of money as a token reinforcer that may be exchanged for items and commodities available within the institution. In contrast, token economies, which are described in the next chapter, are viewed as more complex contingency management systems that typically involve larger numbers of inmates, target behaviors, and backup reinforcers as well as include additional components to influence appropriate and inappropriate behavior.

One of the earliest examples of the planned use of positive reinforcement in a closed institution was provided by Tyler (1967). Tokens were awarded on a daily and weekly basis contingent upon teachers' estimates of the "effort" that a 16-year-old delinquent male youth was showing in the classroom. The tokens were exchanged for such backup reinforcers as the opportunity to wear personal clothes and to purchase items from the canteen. The results revealed a reliable but clinically insignificant improvement in grades over a 30-week period. The role that reinforcement played in the academic improvement was not demonstrated experimentally in this case study but probably accounted for the change.

In a another early example of positive reinforcement, Burchard (1967) examined the effect of token reinforcement on the appropriate classroom behavior of 12 anticosial retarded inmates. In a withdrawal design, tokens were awarded for in-seat behavior during the first condition, awarded noncontingently during the second condition and awarded contingently again during the third. As would be expected, the inmates were in their seats considerably more during the contingent condition.

Dominguez, Rveda, Makhlouf, and Rivera (1976) explored the influence of various environmental and reinforcement conditions on participation in social, educational, and vocational activities by imprisoned male offenders in Mexico. In their case study, materials for various forms of activities were made available during leisure hours. This produced no discernible increase in involvement in activities. When tokens that could be exchanged for field trips were awarded for participation in the activities, however, participation increased greatly (see Yule & Brown, chapter 14 of this volume, for further examples of international applications).

Building upon these basic demonstrations, several other studies have examined the effect of contingency management procedures on acquisition of academic behaviors. Bednar, Zelhart, Greathouse, and Weinberg (1970) compared traditional and token reinforcement procedures in a between-groups study with juvenile delinquents. During 18 consecutive weekly sessions of programmed reading instruction, one group worked on programmed reading material with no tangible reinforcement. The second group earned tokens that could be exchanged for money and that were contingent first on on-task behavior and then upon mastery of material. Individualized token bonuses were awarded contingently upon test scores that exceeded the previous week's average performance. The reinforcement group improved significantly more than the nonreinforcement group in reading and word comprehension on a standardized achievement test. A measure of the inmates' attitudes toward reading showed no significant difference between the two groups, but teacher ratings indicated that the students in the reinforcement group showed greater persistence, attention, liking of school, sociability, and cooperation.

The effects of positive reinforcement procedures on the behavior of adult male offenders in a maximum security correctional institution were studied systematically in a series of reports by McKee and his colleagues (Clements & McKee, 1968; McKee, 1971, 1974; McKee & Clements, 1971; McKee, Jenkins, & Milan, 1977; Yahres, 1973). Much of this work was conducted in a self-instructional school that blended contingency management and programmed instruction. McKee's approach to programmed academic (Yahres, 1973) and vocational (McKee, 1974) instruction begins with a specification of the strengths and weaknesses of each inmate's entering repertoire. Training objectives are then specified in behavioral terms; material is presented in a logical sequence of small modules; inmates respond actively at their own rate to the educational material; and immediate feedback is provided for correct and incorrect answers. McKee (1974) reported that with these procedures, 30% more inmates completed training than was anticipated, based on experience with traditional programs.

McKee (1974) also summarized several unpublished studies and reported that (1) the performance-contingent opportunity to select items from a "reinforcing event" menu resulted in a doubling of learning rate with no decline in test scores; (2) the self-recording of performance, supplemented with small monetary awards for sustained outstanding performance, resulted in a marked increase in academic progress and output; and (3) a change from contingent to noncontingent monetary consequences resulted in a substantial deterioration in test performance, thereby confirming the central role of contingency management procedures in his efforts. Similarly, McKee et al. (1977) found that inmates earning monetary reinforcement for academic progress had significantly higher learning rates than a comparable group without contingent reinforcement. An examination of the relationship between inmates entering reading level, entering overall grade level, and learning rate in the self-instructional school yielded only small and statistically insignificant correlations, thereby highlighting the importance of McKee's individualized diagnostic and prescriptive procedures.

Taken together, the results of McKee's work suggest that given a careful diagnostic and prescriptive process and age- and skill-appropriate material, inmates will generally progress at a faster rate when reinforcement is provided for progress and that this effect is independent of entering abilities. Moreover, these effects appear to hold up under a variety of contingency management formats. For example, Clements and McKee (1968) found that contingency contracts were of approximately equal effectiveness whether prescribed unilaterally by the teachers or negotiated with the inmates. Finally, accelerated rates of learning have been maintained through reinforcement for protracted periods of time (McKee, 1971), with inmates averaging gains of 1.4 grade levels on standardized achievement tests for 208 hours of study (McKee & Clements, 1971).

With the exception of the work of McKee and his colleagues, most studies on the effects of positive reinforcement in closed institutions have not focused directly on learning academic or vocational material. Meichenbaum, Bowers, and Ross (1968), for example, examined the effect of monetary reinforcement upon appropriate classroom behavior. The inmates in this study were 10 institutionalized delinquent females divided into two groups that attended morning or afternoon classes. In a multiple-baseline study across the two classes, appropriate behavior increased in each class when monetary reinforcement was available. A response cost procedure was then introduced wherein the inmates lost points contingent upon inappropriate classroom behavior. Performance was not clinically different in the response cost condition from that observed during reinforcement.

Stumphauzer (1970) examined the sensitivity of institutionalized youthful offenders to social reinforcement provided by a therapist. The focus of this study was the modification of preference for immediate gratification. The author asserted that the ability to wait for larger rewards, later in time, is an important product of the social development process. Further, in his view, juvenile delinquents and adult offenders reqresent a failure of this socialization. In the baseline phase of Stumphauzer's reversal study, four 19-year-old inmates showed a preference for immediate rather than delayed gratification as indexed by their choices in 25 hypothetical situations. Following baseline, the therapist then communicated social approval of choices reflecting either delayed or immediate gratification. Each type of choice increased when it was reinforced and decreased when its opposite was reinforced. Stumphauzer acknowledges that this study involves the same problems in interpretation present in all studies on the effects of verbal conditioning procedures, most notably the possibility that the inmates identified the contingencies and acted accordingly in response to the demand characteristics of the situation.

In a related study on the effects of modeling, Stumphauzer (1972) had prestigious inmates model delay-of-gratification choices and examined the effect on the subsequent choices of 18- to 26-year-old, newly admitted prisoners. The design involved randomly assigned treatment and control groups of 20 inmates each. To make the choices more realistic, inmates were actually granted one of their choices subsequent to testing. The inmates who observed prestigious models make delay-of-gratification choices were most likely to make similar choices at posttest and a 4-week follow-up. Moreover, the affect of modeling generalized to a delay-of-gratification choice not presented during the modeling procedure. Although delay of gratification was established, maintained, and generalized without extensive reinforcement in this study, Stumphauzer argued that establishing delay of gratification in a clincally meaningful sense would require repeated modeling by several models in diverse settings as well as the utilization of reinforcement procedures.

The final report to be reviewed in this section on positive reinforcement procedures made use of group rather than individual contingencies. Graubard (1968) explored the use of a group contract with emotionally disturbed delinquent youths in a residential treatment center. Inmates were first exposed to traditional teaching strategies involving no tangible reinforcers or group contingencies. During the second condition, the teacher negotiated with the inmates to establish individual goals as well as monetary and other reinforcers that the entire group would earn if everyone met their goals. The two conditions were then repeated. The results of this withdrawal design study revealed substantial decrements in antisocial behavior and substantial increments in academic performance when the group contingencies were in effect.

Comments

Although a group contingency is most probably an effective strategy for developing peer group pressure for appropriate behavior, such a procedure should be viewed as potentially hazardous when implemented without appropriate safeguards. Powerful group contingencies may encourage group members to use coercive and physically harmful sanctions with individuals who will not or cannot attain the requirements of the group contingency. Certainly, no responsible professional would advocate the planned use of group contingencies in settings in which each participant is not protected from the tyranny of the others and where a subculture of violence, such as is present in many closed institutions for juvenile and adult offenders, predisposes others to wield their tyranny in a most harsh and unforgiving manner. Future research in this area must therefore focus upon the development and assessment of procedures that will allow for the deployment of group contingencies in both an effective and humane manner.

In general, it is clear that positive reinforcement procedures have shown their rehabilitation and management potential in juvenile and adult institutions; however, much remains to be done. The activities that have been targeted for reinforcement have typically involved academic and vocational skills, appropriate behavior, and participation in a limited range of social activities. Unfortunately, as Emery and Marholin (1977) have observed, the relationship between some of these target behaviors and the criminal and delinquent activities in which the individuals have engaged in the community is difficult to see. Nonetheless, the teaching of academic and vocational skills in the correctional setting, although not sufficient, appears to be an important ingredient of rehabilitation programs, for it most probably increases the likelihood that inmates will find appropriate employment and earn an adequate wage after release from the institution. Yet the breadth and depth of additional target behaviors will have to be expanded dramatically in future efforts. Only then will it be appropriate to claim that behavioral efforts encompass the array of skills, competencies, and experiences necessary to increase significantly the likelihood of postrelease success.

NEGATIVE REINFORCEMENT PROCEDURES

Negative reinforcement procedures are defined here as planned intervention strategies that employ the termination or prevention of a stimulus, event, or condition contingent upon an appropriate response in order to increase or maintain that and similar responses. The process by which behavior is increased when it terminates aversive stimuli is also termed *escape conditioning,* whereas the process by which behavior is increased when it prevents aversive stimuli is also called *avoidance conditioning.* The stimuli, events, or conditions in negative reinforcement procedures in institutional settings may consist of such things as work assignments, classroom activities, and close supervision.

The difficulty in distinguishing between positive and negative reinforcement procedures (Michael, 1975) can be seen in the previously mentioned study by Clements and McKee (1968). In that study, when inmates completed academic assignments, they selected items from a reinforcing event menu. One item was the opportunity to leave the classroom and return to the living area within the prison. Psychologists may disagree about whether this is a positive or a negative reinforcement procedure, depending on whether they define the reinforcing event as gaining access to the prison living area or escaping from the classroom. Nevertheless, in most studies the categorization of a procedure as either positive or negative reinforcement is relatively clearcut, and it seems useful to discuss these studies as such in order to make clear the range of possible strategies.

Programs using negative reinforcement procedures are less numerous than those using positive reinforcement procedures, and most of these have been reported by Smith and his colleagues (Smith, Hart, & Milan, 1972; Smith, Milan, Wood & McKee, 1976). The negative reinforcement studies they report were conducted by correctional officers in a program to train them as behavioral technicians. The officers were instructed in basic social learning principles and in the role of objectivity, consistency, and reliability in behavior change procedures. The training program consisted of both classroom instruction and supervised practicum work. Pretest-posttest and between-group comparisons indicated that the training program resulted in improvements as measured by (1) the officers' performance on tests, (2) inmate evaluation of the officers' skills and personal characteristics, (3) direct observations of the officers' performance on the job, and (4) officers' completion of practicum exercises.

Many of the officers' practicum exercises met the technical definition of negative reinforcement, although they were described as "reward" programs by the inmates. One was carried out by a correctional officer in charge of the clothing room, who complained that a large number of the men under his supervision were reporting to work late each day. His use of threats, disciplinary reports, and similar practices had not corrected the situation. After collecting baseline data, he instituted a procedure wherein inmates arriving on time avoided a 2-hour shift after the evening meal. The correctional officer agreed that if all inmates arrived on time, either volunteers or supervisory personnel would work the evening shift. The procedure was effective. The percentage of inmates arriving on time for the morning shift increased from approximately 50% in baseline to approximately 85%.

This and the other negative reinforcement procedures devised by the correctional officers appeared both more reasonable and more humane than the common practice of writing disciplinary reports for poor performance and undesirable behavior. This is especially true when one recognizes that disciplinary reports often result in the eventual loss of good time (days, weeks, months, and years deducted from an inmate's sentence) and as a consequence extend the period of imprisonment. Disciplinary reports can also result in downgrading of job assignments, transfer to other institutions, or, perhaps, placement in segregation for a period of time. Moreover, the inmates characterized the negative reinforcement procedures as reward programs and came to view the officers who used the procedures as less punitive and more concerned with inmates.

The preceding comments should not be interpreted as an unqualified endorsement of the use of negative reinforcement procedures, for they apply only to those procedures that are construed as rewarding by inmates. Negative reinforcement procedures can also be deployed in a coercive manner likely to generate resistance, aggression, and other undesirable side effects. Milan and McKee (1974) have reported on an unplanned, naturally occurring "study" conducted within an adult maximum security institution that provides some evidence bearing on the effects and side effects of more coercive negative reinforcement procedures. These reseachers had the opportunity to monitor both janitorial tasks and acts of physical and verbal aggression before, during, and after a correctional officer conducted, on his own initiative, a harsh system of coercive supervision and disciplinary reports to ensure that inmates adequately performed their assigned tasks.

Inmate performance of the janitorial tasks was low before coercive supervision. During the period of coercive supervision, when inmates avoided disciplinary reports by doing their janitorial work, the performance of janitorial tasks increased, but only on days when the correctional officer was present. Following that period, the level of performance returned quickly to its original level. The incidence of aggression, which was low before the period of coercive supervision, increased during supervision and only gradually subsided after the termination of supervision. Indeed, the increase in verbal and physical aggression endured long after the termination of the negative reinforcement procedure. These data indicate that the coercive negative reinforcement procedure had no enduring effects upon the target behavior, did not generalize, and had side effects that outweighed its usefulness. Accordingly, positive reinforcement procedures and "rewarding" negative reinforcement procedures should be developed and deployed rather than relying on coercive negative reinforcement procedures.

Comments

Perhaps the most powerful "rewarding" negative reinforcement program that could be implemented in a closed institution would be one that led to the inmates' early release from the institution itself (Williams & Fish, 1972). Such "good time" programs are often said to represent correction's enlightened attempt to implement such a procedure. Most good time programs, however, are nothing more than a punitive subversion of that principle, for inmates are typically awarded automatically all good time when they enter the institution, and this is then taken away as inmates receive disciplinary reports or are penalized for other infractions (Smith, 1975).

The redesign of good time practices therefore appears to be a significant step toward developing more meaningful rehabilitation programs. Unqualified support of this course of action is fraught with danger, however. Given current correctional staffing patterns and expertise, a predictable outcome of such an effort would be a situation in which unreasonable contingencies were administered in a capricious manner, thereby subjecting inmates to more intolerable conditions than they now experience. At the same time, to tolerate the existing good time policies, which do little more than discourage inappropriate behavior and encourage passivity, is repugnant. Consequently, the cautious support of a small number of model programs under controlled conditions and supervised by qualified professionals seems the most appropriate course of action for behaviorists to adopt.

Clearly, changes in good time policies are long overdue. The behavioral psychologist has much to offer in the engineering of a more appropriate use of this potentially powerful reinforcer as well as in helping prescribe the way that it can be fairly and humanely employed both to achieve appropriate institutional goals and to encourage inmates to engage in rehabilitative activities. With appropriate safeguards and professional involvement, such efforts could well result in improvements in the quality of inmates' lives and perhaps in significant increases in the likelihood that they will succeed in our communities following their release.

PUNISHMENT PROCEDURES

Punishment procedures are defined here as planned intervention strategies in which the presentation or prolongation of a stimulus, event, or condition is made contingent upon an inappropriate response in order to suppress that and similar responses. The stimuli, events, or conditions presented or prolonged are typically described as undesirable or aversive by the person involved. In this sense, they are like those stimuli, events, or conditions escaped or avoided in negative reinforcement procedures.

One of the practicum exercises in the previously described correctional officer training program by Smith *et al.* (1976) exemplifies the planned use of a nonintrusive but effective punishment procedure. The correctional officer who served as kitchen steward was concerned with the frequent, unauthorized absences of several of his kitchen staff during the workday. During baseline, the steward recorded absences throughout the day, chastising those who had left when they returned, and encouraging them to change their ways under threat of disciplinary reports. During the punishment condition, inmates who left the work area were required to make up the time they missed at the end of the shift, thereby prolonging their stay in the kitchen. This resulted in a dramatic decrease in absences from more than one per day during baseline to only one in 9 days during the punishment condition.

Another example of a procedure meeting the technical definition of punishment has been provided by Levinson, Ingram, and Azcarate (1968), who were working with older delinquent youths institutionalized at the National Training School for Boys. The criterion for participation in the project was placement in segregation at least once per month for the preceding 3 months. Levinson *et al.* introduced the requirement that inmates attend 1.5 hours of group therapy per week until they accrued 3 successive months without additional placements in segregation. While in group therapy, the inmates were expected to explore the psychodynamic basis of their inappropriate behavior and the origins of those dynamics in their childhood family relations. Disciplinary reports dropped an average of 43% following the introduction of the group therapy requirement.

It is clear that Levinson *et al.* (1976) viewed the reduction of behavior that occasioned disciplinary reports to be a function of the aversive qualities of group therapy. They indicate that the inmates described group therapy as a waste of time; they were also repulsed by the content of the therapy sessions. Unfortunately, the nonexperimental case study design used by Levinson *et al.* prevents any firm conclusions concerning either the beneficial effects of required group therapy or the mechanism by which such an effect would occur. It is possible, for example, that regression toward the mean of the extreme rates of disciplinary actions that led to inclusion in the program, the psychodynamic content of therapy, or even the mere passage of time and everyday institutional experiences were responsible for the reduction in disciplinaries observed.

Comments

Although punishment procedures have been examined in detail in other applied settings (e.g., Bandura, 1969), this review indicates little study of them in closed institutions for juvenile and adult offenders. Nonetheless, the small amount of research that has been conducted suggests that procedures meeting the technical definition of punishment can serve as effective supplements to rehabilitation programs. None of the procedures reviewed used the type of intrusive, pain-inducing practices the lay public undoubtly associates with the term *punishment*. Instead, these effective punishment procedures employed the logical consequences of inappropriate behavior in a systematic manner. These procedures have been effective without subjecting inmates to undue hardship or discomfort and, because of their face validity, have apparently not generated the types of countercontrol that more intrusive procedures would appropriately occasion. These studies, then, provide a model for the generation of effective, acceptable, and humane procedures to discourage inappropriate behavior that may be employed to supplement positive reinforcement programs that foster incompatible appropriate behavior. Other issues to be considered in the use of such procedures are discussed at the close of the following section.

Time-Out and Response Cost Procedures

Time-out procedures are defined here as planned intervention strategies in which the termination or prevention of a stimulus, event, or condition is made contingent upon an inappropriate response in order to suppress that and similar responses. The stimuli, events, or conditions terminated or prevented in these "negative punishment procedures" (cf. Redd, Porterfield, & Anderson, 1979) are typically described as desirable or rewarding by the person involved. In this sense, they are like those stimuli, events, or conditions that are presented or prolonged in positive reinforcement procedures. Several variations of time-out will be discussed in this section: time-out, time-out from positive reinforcement, and response cost.

In the typical time-out procedure, the individual is either removed briefly from a setting in which social and nonsocial reinforcers are available freely, or the individual remains in a setting from which those reinforcers are removed briefly. A distinction must be made between time-out and administrative procedures such as detention, segregation, and punitive isolation. As will be discussed in this section, the duration of these latter practices, the manner in which they are administered, and their expected outcomes are markedly different from those of time-out.

A variation of the typical time-out procedure is called *time-out from positive reinforcement,* wherein an ongoing opportunity to earn positive reinforcers is suspended temporarily, contingent upon undesirable behavior. This variation is also termed *response-contingent extinction.* Response cost procedures can be considered a special form of time-out, for they also involve the response-contingent loss of reinforcers. In response cost, the individual is either required to relinquish tangible reinforcers, such as money or tokens in the form of a fine, contingent upon the undesirable response, or the effort required to earn reinforcement is increased. Consequently, response cost can be subdivided into two classes of consequences: "contingent reinforcement loss," involving the loss of conditioned reinforcers, such as tokens or money in a fine procedure, and "response requirement," wherein the amount of behavior or time required in earning reinforcers is increased (cf. Luce, Christian, Lipsker, & Hall, 1981).

Time-Out

Most studies examining the use of time-out in closed correctional institutions have been conducted with delinquent youths. Among the earliest of these studies is the work of Tyler and his colleagues (Burchard & Tyler, 1965; Tyler & Brown, 1967), conducted in a cottage of 20 youths and 6 staff members in a large training school. The antisocial behaviors targeted in these studies consisted of general rule violations and disruptive misbehavior. In the Burchard and Tyler (1965) study, the time-out procedure was explored in a single-inmate case study and consisted of placement in a $4' \times 8'$ time-out room in the corner of the cottage for a 15-minute period. The authors report a 63% drop in offenses. The Tyler and Brown (1967) study confirmed this effect. Here, the time-out procedure was examined in a withdrawal design involving 15 inmates, aged 13 to 15. The rate of misbehavior was low while time-out was in effect, increased dramatically during the period time-out was suspended, and then declined again to a low level when time-out was reinstated.

Tyler and Brown (1967) concluded that the use of swift, brief isolation can be an effective procedure for the control of misbehavior. They added that part of the effectiveness may be because the procedure is neither so severe that it encourages peer group support nor so demeaning that it produces resistance from the inmate. Moreover, the authors supplemented their procedure with reinforcement for appropriate behavior wherein inmates earned tokens for each hour that they were out of time-out.

Brown and Tyler (1968) extended the time-out procedure to the behavior of a 16-year-old who was emerging as the antisocial leader, or "Duke," of the delinquent group in a residential treatment program. The inmate was placed in 15-minute time-out contingent upon activities that contributed to his role as the Duke. Data consisted only of anecdotal observations. After the program had been in effect for 6 weeks, the cottage staff members reported a noticeable decrement in the inappropriate behavior of the youth. During the following month, various staff members made favorable comments in the daily log. These data suggest that the time-out procedure was effective in disrupting the evolving antisocial peer culture in the cottage, although the research design prevents a firm conclusion.

A final example of the use of a time-out procedure involves a 10-year-old boy with a 5-year history of compulsive stealing and a diagnosis of "mildly disturbed" who resided in a residential treatment center for disturbed children. In this case study, Wetzel (1966) targeted stealing incidents for the time-out procedure and used an overnight visit to the home of a favorite staff person, the institutional cook, as the reinforcing event to be prevented upon a reported incidence of stealing. The incidence of stealing gradually decreased over the 105-day treatment period. As the stealing declined, the youth established more acceptable peer relations, and the procedure was eventually terminated. As in all case studies, however, especially those that involve only anecdotal reports, the results must be viewed as only tentative.

These studies of time-out suggest that even in its briefest form, it can be an effective strategy for gaining control of aggressive and antisocial behaviors in institutions for delinquent youths. In addition, the use of brief time-out, if not abused, can be used to disrupt escalating behavioral chains and thereby prevent more serious problems. As is clear from these studies, however, when the procedures are terminated, at least after a short period of use, the suppressed behavior more often than not returns. Consequently, these procedures can only be advocated as ingredients in programs to control aggressive and antisocial behaviors that include procedures to teach skills and behaviors that are incompatible with these forms of maladjustment.

Response Cost

Turning to response cost, Burchard (1967) provides an example of how its use may contribute to the control of such antisocial behaviors as stealing, lying, cheating, and fighting. A response cost procedure was superimposed upon an ongoing seclusion policy for the control of antisocial behavior with a group of 12 mentally retarded adolescents and young adults in a residential program. In a withdrawal design, token deductions were first contingent, then noncontingent, and finally again contingent upon antisocial behavior. Results indicated lower amounts of antisocial behavior during response cost. This addition of response cost to the ongoing seclusion policy, however, was not completely effective in controlling the antisocial behavior. Obviously, these procedures are only a partial solution, and additional strategies to encourage appropriate behavior and to ensure maintenance and generalization beyond the treatment setting would be important components of a comprehensive treatment effort.

Little effort has been devoted to the comparison of the effectiveness of time-out and response cost. For this reason, a comparative study by Burchard and Barrera (1972) is especially deserving of note. They assigned 11 mentally retarded delinquent youths to four different groups in which time-out durations of 5 and 30 minutes and response cost magnitudes of 5 and 30 tokens were presented in counterbalanced sequences. The individual presentations of the four procedures followed a baseline condition in which the target behaviors, consisting of aggressive acts such as swearing, personal assaults, and destruction of property, were subjected to a combined 5-minute time-out and 5-token response cost procedure.

The results of the study indicated that the 5-token response cost was least effective, followed by the 5-minute time-out. Both were less effective than the time-out plus response cost baseline condition. The 30-minute time-out and 30-token response cost procedures were equally effective and produced considerably more suppression than the baseline condition. Burchard and Barrera noted that the effectiveness of time-out and response cost procedures undoubtedly depends upon the characteristics of the setting in which they are applied, including the quality of ongoing activities, the ease with which tokens are earned, and the number of tokens inmates may accumulate as "savings." They concluded that response cost appears preferable to time-out because it does not remove the inmate from either program activities or the opportunity to continue learning skills being taught in the rehabilitation setting.

Finally, Bassett and Blanchard (1977) have provided information concerning the seductively dangerous aspects of response cost procedures when they are effective. In their description of an unplanned, naturally occurring "study" in an adult correctional institution, they described the relationship between the presence and absence of close supervision of correctional staff by trained behaviorists and the staff's use of fines in a token economy. Participants were 11 college-educated staff members. They were responsible for 13 inmates and had received 24 hours of training in the operation of a token reinforcement program and the principles underlying its design and conduct.

During a 3-month baseline period, the correctional staff was supervised by professional behavior analysts who had participated in designing the program and in training the staff in its operation. A monthly average of 20 applications of the response cost procedure on five classes of behaviors occurred during that period. Professional supervision was then withdrawn and the correctional staff conducted the program autonomously for a period of 4 months, during which the number of applications of the response cost procedure increased to approximately 190 per month, with fines levied for 44 classes of behaviors. When this punitive trend was recognized, professional supervision was reestablished for an additional 4-month period, and the use of response cost declined to the baseline level.

A retrospective analysis indicated that, in the absence of professional supervision, the correctional staff added fines for the noncompletion of target behaviors whose completion earned token reinforcement, with some staff members fining inmates for behaviors that others ignored. When this practice failed to increase the number of tasks completed, the staff increased the magnitude of the fines. As would be expected, an analysis of the dropouts from the voluntary program during that time showed that the number of inmates disenrolling was between 7.8 and 11.2 times higher than during the periods of professional supervision.

Although the punitively oriented procedures that evolved in the Bassett and Blanchard (1977) study could easily be attributed to inadequate training and program design, a more likely explanation is that the naturally occurring contingencies in correctional institutions operate to separate correctional staff and inmates, pit them against each other, and induce those who control power to devise progressively more punitive strategies to suppress their opposition (Zimbardo, Haney, Banks, & Jaffy, 1975). Thus it appears that what can be abused will be abused if left unattended, and all programs, behavioral or not, should be subjected to professional supervision and peer review (Milan & McKee, 1976). Only by so doing will the profession ensure that effective programs are deployed and inmates are spared the potential abuse that such programs can produce.

Comments

Taken together, punishment, time-out, and response cost may be viewed as aversive control procedures and should be respected as such when their use is being considered. As early as midcentury, Skinner (1953) cautioned against the use of aversive control on the grounds that undesirable side effects would outweigh any positive effects. More recently, Balsam and Bondy (1983) have identified 10 classes of undesirable side effects that have been suggested in the behavioral literature, including emotionality, aggression, development of inflexible responses, and attempts to escape or avoid individuals or programs that employ aversive control. The prevalence of these undesirable effects, however, remains a matter of disagreement. For example, although Balsam and Bondy cite over 30 clinical articles that document the occurrence of these effects, Johnston (1985), in general accord with Axelrod and Apsche (1983), asserts that none of the undesirable side effects attributed to punishment is a general characteristic of the effects of "properly" administered punishment procedures.

The preceding comments should not be interpreted as justification for the use of aversive control in closed institutions for juvenile delinquents and adult felons. First, the "proper" administration of punishment may require procedures (e.g., Azrin & Holz, 1966) that cannot be approximated, much less realized, in most institutions. In addition, an easy acceptance of intrusive aversive control procedures may result in a climate that encourages their use as a first choice in lieu of less intrusive reinforcement procedures. And finally, the unnecessary use and reliance upon intrusive aversive control procedures and the undue hardship this can cause inmates, complemented by a democratic public's suspicious response to even the hint of the abusive use of such procedures, can bring discredit to the person, program, and profession that employs aversive control. Clearly, the use of such hazardous procedures should be weighed carefully. At the very least, intrusive aversive control procedures should not be applied capriciously for insignificant behaviors or without a complementary positive program. Intrusive procedures should be considered only when more positive and less intrusive procedures have been tried and have not succeeded. Finally, intrusive procedures should be consented to by inmates, subjected to peer review, and carried out in accord with accepted legal and ethical standards (e.g., Martin, 1975; Schwitzgebel, 1971).

EXTINCTION, DIFFERENTIAL REINFORCEMENT, AND GENERALIZATION TRAINING

The contributions of extinction, differential reinforcement, and generalization training to rehabilitation and management efforts in other treatment areas has been demonstrated clearly and repeatedly (e.g., Leitenberg, 1976). Little attention, however, has been directed to the study of these procedures in closed institutions for criminals and delinquents. This section will suggest ways in which they may be included in correctional programs as well as comment upon the unfortunate paucity of research on their use in closed institutions. Perhaps by so doing, research exploring the planned use of these procedures in the area of crime and delinquency will be spurred. As in previous sections, working definitions of the procedures and examples of their use will be provided.

Extinction

Most definitions of extinction are presented within the framework of the positive reinforcement procedure: when reinforcers no longer follow responses, as they do in the reinforcement procedure, decreases occur in the rate of those responses. *Extinction,* however, is more parsimoniously described as the breaking of an established response-consequence relationship. This latter definition of extinction applies to the breaking of the response-consequence relationships not only in positive and negative reinforcements but also in punishment and time-out as well. For these latter two procedures, the breaking of the response-consequence relationship would be expected to result in an increase in the previously punished or timed-out responses. Although the use of extinction alone to decrease undesirable behavior is well-documented in the behavioral literature (e.g., Martin & Pear, 1983), no studies in the areas of crime and delinquency have explored its utility independent of other procedures, such as differential reinforcement.

Differential Reinforcement

Differential reinforcement consists of the simultaneous deployment of both reinforcement and extinction procedures. Most typically, this involves reinforcement of appropriate behavior and the concurrent extinction of inappropriate behavior. Although no crime or delinquency studies have explored differential reinforcement as such, it was seen in Stumphauzer's (1970) previously described examination of the way in which social reinforcement can influence preference for immediate or delayed reinforcement. In that study, inmates were reinforced socially for choices reflecting immediate or delayed gratification in hypothetical situations. Implicit in that paradigm was a differential reinforcement procedure, for when social reinforcement was provided for delayed choices, immediate gratification choices were on extinction. Similarly, when reinforcement was provided for immediate choices, delayed reinforcement choices were on extinction.

Generalization Training

Generalization training typically involves the reinforcement of behavior in a variety of settings and situations in an effort to ensure that it will occur under nontraining conditions. The importance of including generalization training in correctional programs is highlighted by Horton's (1970) study of the degree to which appropriate and inappropriate behaviors generalized naturally from one setting to another. She examined the manner in which aggressive or nonaggressive behavior that was differentially reinforced by staff during leisure time activities in the classroom generalized to the living area. The study was conducted in an institution for adolescent males who had juvenile court records and diagnoses of adjustment reactions of childhood. In the reversal design employed, aggressive or nonaggressive behavior quickly came under the control of the differential reinforcement procedure in the classroom. Generalization to the living area, as assessed by measures of physical contact, was found for both aggressive and nonaggressive behaviors. The generalization measures, however, also indicated that the effect of reinforcing aggressive behavior was more powerful than the effect of reinforcing nonaggressive behavior. This study seems to capture the paradox of generalization. That is, the behavior that the behavior therapist wishes to discourage is often more potent and appears to generalize more easily than the behavior that the behavior therapist wishes to encourage.

Emshoff, Redd, and Davidson (1976) explored procedures that may be used to encourage generalization of appropriate behavior. Their study was conducted with disturbed and delinquent male adolescents who had histories of truancy, minor law violations, and psychiatric hospitalization. It involved a between-groups comparison of two forms of training of positive comments. Both groups participated in seven 30-minute training sessions conducted over a 2-week period. A standard training group received training and social and token reinforcement for prosocial talk from a single staff member in one setting. A generalization training group also received training and social and token reinforcements but by a variety of different staff members in several different settings. Measures taken before, during, and after training indicated that the generalization training group showed a significantly greater increase in prosocial statements during the generalization tests conducted with other staff in other settings during both training and follow-up periods.

A second study explored an alternative to traditional generalization training procedures. Snyder and White (1979), who were working in a residential training setting for behaviorally disturbed youths with records of truancy, aggression, theft, burglary, and drug abuse, hypothesized that failure of appropriate behavior to generalize from therapeutic settings was due, in part, to either the inmates' failure to develop instrumental private speech (self-instruction) for self-regulation or, alternatively, their development of private speech that interfered with attention to relevant environmental cues for appropriate behavior (for a more extended discussion, see Chapter 18, by Platt and Prout, this volume).

In a between-groups comparison incorporating random assignment procedures, Snyder and White (1979) trained a cognitive awareness group to recognize that their behaviors determined the reinforcers they earned and the penalties they experienced. A cognitive therapy group identified maladaptive self-statements and sought to replace them with adaptive ones. An assessment control group received no training. Pretreatment, posttreatment, and 6-week follow-up assessment showed that the cognitive therapy group achieved significantly greater increases in performance of daily living requirements and decreases in impulsive behaviors at the end of treatment. In addition, the effects seen at the end of treatment were either maintained or augmented at follow-up. A clear relationship existed between self-instructed behavior and the consequences experienced by the inmates. The effects of self-instruction training in the absence of this type of environmental support of instruction following are not clear, but behavior theory dictates that such support should be considered a necessary ingredient of effective programs and therefore planned for in similar intervention efforts.

Comments

The lack of research with institutionalized offenders focusing upon extinction, differential reinforcement, and generalization training is perhaps understandable, for most behaviorists working in the juvenile and adult justice systems have been more concerned with attacking critical behavioral problems and overcoming potentially dangerous behavior patterns than in the behavioral principles employed. Although extinction and differential reinforcement have been incorporated in many of the studies that have been previously discussed, there would seem to be value in studying these basic procedures more directly in an effort to elaborate their effectiveness and the conditions under which they should and should not be used.

Data bearing upon the side effects of extinction procedures would add to or confirm our knowledge of behavior at various stages of the extinction process. For example, the use of extinction procedures in juvenile and adult correctional institutions would probably result in an initial increase in problematic behavior as has been observed in other settings. Documentation of this and other expected effects of behavioral procedures would allow practitioners to make more informed decisions about the appropriateness of proposed programs, predict the time course of their effects, and encourage them to continue programs until changes are achieved.

Stokes and Baer (1977) have identified a range of strategies that may be

employed to achieve functional generalization. The generalization and maintenance of treatment effects is a continuing challenge to both behaviorists and
nonbehaviorists working in closed institutions as well as in other settings
throughout the juvenile and criminal justice continuum. Stokes and Baer's
exposition of how generalization may be achieved clearly indicates that behaviorists have begun the development of a technology that they may deploy,
when in a position to do so, to increase the likelihood that behavior changes
accomplished in one setting will generalize to other areas of the inmate's life.

SOCIAL SKILLS TRAINING

During recent years, many professionals working in juvenile and adult
correctional institutions have joined their colleagues in other settings (e.g.,
L'Abate & Milan, 1985) and have begun a systematic investigation of the use
of social skills training to remediate interpersonal problems. Although the
attention directed to social skills training is relatively new, this should not
lead to the conclusion that earlier efforts did not include skills training
efforts. Indeed, it is difficult to imagine a behavioral rehabilitation and management program that could be conducted without including formal or informal social skills training. A more likely interpretation is that the early programs, reflecting that zeitgeist, chose to focus on, analyze, and report other
aspects of these efforts. Similarly, the current interest in social skills training
reflects the current zeitgeist, and many of the programs in which social skills
research is conducted undoubtedly include other unanalyzed and unreported
components.

Social skills training incorporates many of the reinforcement procedures
described previously as well as many more that are beyond the scope of this
chapter (e.g., Bellack & Hersen, 1979; Eisler & Frederiksen, 1980). In general,
however, social skills training typically begins with an assessment of whether
the difficulties experienced by an individual involve a skills deficit, a motivational deficiency, and/or an emotional reaction that interferes with skills
performance. Skills training is called for when the first condition exists, with
other procedures employed instead of or in addition to skills training as the
assessment dictates (Milan & Kolko, 1985).

The first task in any skills training program is the identification of the
skills to be taught. Three general strategies have been utilized. The first has
been to rely on "clinical judgment." The second has been to review reports of
successful treatment programs and incorporate the skills common to some or
all. Both strategies risk including unimportant skills and overlooking important ones. The last and most preferable strategy has been to identify and
validate empirically the skills that distinguish criminal or delinquent populations from noncriminal or nondelinquent ones. An example of this strategy
has been provided by Freedman, Rosenthal, Donahoe, Schlundt, and McFall

(1978) in their analysis of deficits and competencies in delinquent and non-delinquent adolescent males.

Ten components of social skills training may be identified. First, the inmate is provided a rationale for training. Next, a representative problematic situation is described and then enacted by the inmate and trainer. Third, the enactment is critiqued, and the correct aspects of performance identified and reinforced. Next, the new and appropriate skills are demonstrated and coaching provided. Fifth, additional enactments and coaching sessions are conducted until mastery is achieved. Next, a second problematic situation is described and enacted. Seventh, the coaching and enactment process is repeated until mastery is again achieved. Following this, a series of additional problematic situations is described and mastered until the inmate regularly performs with mastery on the first trial. Ninth, the inmate is instructed and encouraged to practice the newly acquired skill in real-life situations. Finally, successful and unsuccessful real-life experiences are critiqued, and necessary refinements are made in the skills themselves or the situations in which they are employed until the performance is optimal. Reinforcement for appropriate behavior in both the therapeutic setting and the natural environment should be programmed and then attenuated to foster performance and generalization.

Several studies have explored the contribution of social skills training to rehabilitation and management efforts in closed institutions. Among the earliest of these was the work of Sarason (1968) in which inmates who were taught skills relevant to such diverse topics as finding a job and exhibiting self-control were compared with inmates who only role-played these topics. The institutionalized delinquent males in the taught group showed a greater willingness to acknowledge their deficiencies and less discrepancy between measures of present and idealized self than the matched controls who participated in the role-playing sessions.

In another early report, Kaufman and Wagner (1972) described the application of "barb technology" to the control of temper disorders in delinquent youths participating in residential and day treatment programs. The youths were taught appropriate ways of responding to "barbs" (confrontations likely to evoke emotional reactions). In general, the program consisted of skills training that incorporated (1) generating and shaping the necessary component behaviors to a high rate, (2) generalizing the behaviors to different situations, and (3) maintaining and stabilizing the behaviors. In a detailed case presentation, the authors described the application of the program to a 15-year-old male with a history of gang activity, hitting teachers and principals, gang fights, and thefts. Anecdotal reports suggested that anger control improved with the program and was maintained and then generalized to the community.

More recent work has examined the acquisition, generalization, and maintenance of specific skills. Spence and Marzillier (1979) taught basic social skills, such as appropriate eye contact, acknowledgments, and feedback responses, to five institutionalized delinquent males with problems ranging from aggression towards staff and peers to social isolation (for further discussion, see Chapter 14, by Yule and Brown, this volume). The effects of the training program were evaluated both by direct measures of the skills in a multiple-baseline design across inmates as well as by pretraining, posttraining, and follow-up staff rating and self-report questionnaires. The analysis of videotaped role plays demonstrated that the skills were acquired and retained at follow-up by all inmates. Staff ratings and self-report questionnaires indicated that improvements in behavior occurred outside the training setting for three of the participants. In another example, Shoemaker (1979) conducted group assertion training for institutionalized delinquent males. He suggested that as-yet-unanalyzed programmatic variables, such as the use of videotape and selection of trainers with "flair," are important factors influencing the effects of social skills training efforts. Similar social skills training programs have been developed and found effective with an adolescent male sex offender (McGurk & Newell, 1981) and adult male arsonists (Rice & Chaplin, 1979).

Ollendick and Hersen (1979) examined the effects of a general skills training program dealing with "how to get along with others" in a between-groups study with 27 institutionalized delinquent males. The inmates were assigned to three matched groups receiving (1) social skills training that focused on such things as good eye contact and requesting others to change their behavior, (2) discussions dealing with how to get along with others, or (3) a no-treatment control condition. The results indicated a trend for the social skills group to engage in less disruptive behavior after training than the two comparison groups. The social skills group significantly increased the number of token economy points earned for appropriate behavior relative to the two comparison groups. In addition, the social skills group showed a significantly greater internal locus of control and lower state anxiety on tests of those constructs after training.

Kolko, Dorsett, and Milan (1981) employed an even more extensive assessment regimen in the analysis of the effects of their anger control program for three institutionalized males with the diagnosis of adjustment reaction of adolescence. All three were enrolled in social skills training as a result to their ongoing displays of anger and aggressiveness, which included frequent temper tantruming. The skills, which were operationally defined and scored on 3-point scales, ranged from facial expressions to the content of verbal responses to provocations. In a multiple-baseline design across both skills and participants, empirically selected role-play scenarios were employed to validate the specific and generalized effects of training. In addition, *in vivo* probes were used to determine whether the changes in behavior achieved in training sessions were exhibited in other settings. Finally, the social validity of the program was assessed by staff ratings of general adjustment in group therapy sessions and in leisure time activities. In general, the results revealed that training was responsible for clinically significant increases in skill performance and generalization in the training setting, that the improvements were also exhibited in provocative situations outside of training, and that the changes were of sufficient magnitude to influence general adjustment ratings by staff unaware of the content and time of onset of the skills training program.

Comments

With the exception of the work of Rice and Chaplin (1979), all of the reported social skills training studies conducted in closed institutions have involved juvenile males. The skills that have been taught have not been identified empirically but have been based only on clinical judgment or reviews of previous skills training programs that themselves typically employed clinical judgment to identify and define social skills. In addition, assessment of the impact of training has been limited to effects during or immediately after training and, in some studies, at the end of a relatively brief follow-up period within the institution. The social skills training movement is just beginning to explore the broader issues involved in the rehabilitation and management of institutionalized juvenile and adult offenders. The studies that have been conducted suggest the potential of the approach. However, additional research remains to be conducted that employs behavior analytic procedures to identify the range of skills taught, that extends the approach to adult offenders, that explores how skills training may be integrated into other behavioral programs, that identifies long-term effects on community adjustment, and that validates procedures that may be deployed to maximize enduring effects.

DISCUSSION

It is time for our profession to renew its efforts to develop and validate effective and humane rehabilitation and management procedures in closed institutions and to extend those efforts both backward and forward along the correctional continuum so that adjustment, quality of life, and recidivism may be positively affected. When this occurs, those professionals who accept the challenge of continuing the exploration of behavioral procedures in closed institutions for juvenile and adult offenders will confront several related issues. Two of the most important involve a legal and ethical analysis of their goals and a functional analysis of whether the procedures they employ to achieve their goals generate undesirable side effects. Other issues will be discussed at the conclusion of the following chapter.

Selecting Goals for Institutional Programs

In 1972, Winett and Winkler charged that the goal of much classroom behavior modification up to that time had been to produce quiet, still, and docile students. O'Leary (1972) responded that Winett and Winkler misrepresented classroom behavior modification by failing to note that the goal of most programs was to remediate special problems so that academic progress would be more likely. Despite O'Leary's rejoinder, Winett and Winkler have sensitized the profession to this issue, and any classroom program with a primary objective of discouraging inappropriate behavior now deserves justification and monitoring beyond that normally expected of other programs.

The comments of Winett and Winkler (1972) also apply to work conducted in institutions for juvenile and adult offenders. As this review shows, although some studies focused on encouraging academic, vocational, and social skills, many others focused on such goals as the reduction of aggression, improvement of the hygienic conditions of the institution, and obedience to rules. O'Leary's (1972) response to Winett and Winkler is also true of these latter efforts because the goals of most were also to remediate special problems. Nonetheless, any procedure within an institution for juvenile or adult offenders with a primary objective of discouraging inappropriate behavior now requires justification and monitoring beyond that expected of other programs.

Although there has been considerable philosophical discussion of behaviors that *should not* be targeted in behavioral programs, little effort has been devoted to the empirical identification of behaviors that *should* be the target of behavioral procedures in closed institutions. Moreover, a cursory review of the general crime and delinquency literature reveals no definitive, empirically based specification of target behaviors. Consequently, behaviorists will have to conduct an empirical search for appropriate target behaviors. To be unbiased, that search will have to consider behaviors that contribute to the safe, hygienic, and humane operation of the institution as well as behaviors that contribute directly to the releasees' satisfying, productive, and lawful adjustment in the community.

Unfortunately, even a consideration of the possible targeting of behaviors that contribute to the safe, hygienic, and humane operation of institutions appears to risk alienating those who have adopted a fundamentalistlike interpretation of the position Winett and Winkler (1972) attempted to enunciate for our profession. Such professionals should consider, however, the careful empirical work of social scientists such as Crowther (1969) and Levin (1972) who have suggested that existing conditions of confinement cause real harm to inmates, add to the likelihood that they will commit additional crimes when they are released, and increase the severity of the crimes that are then committed. The regressive effects of imprisonment are undoubtly multidetermined, but the inconsistently applied, predominently coercive procedures that characterize contemporary institutional management practices are undoubtedly significant determining factors.

Professionals who may be alienated by a consideration of the possibility of targeting behaviors that contribute to the safe, hygienic, and humane operation of institutions should also consider the demands of the inmates of those institutions. In mid-1985, the electronic media provided continuing coverage of a prison riot in Alabama. The inmates delivered their list of concerns, and the media reported that among the major complaints was brutal and punitive treatment by guards. Although targeting behaviors that contribute to the improved operation of institutions will not remedy all ills of imprisonment, it may displace current and marginally effective coercive management practices with more positive ones. In so doing, these efforts may improve the psychological and physical quality of life of both the inmate and those responsible for their care.

Finally, only the most naively optimistic of professionals would argue that a rehabilitation program would succeed in an antirehabilitative management system. Much of the early behavioral work that contributed to the operation of institutions consisted of a prerehabilitative attack on an antirehabilitative system. That early work showed that positive reinforcement procedures were feasible and effective alternatives to the aversive control procedures they replaced and by so doing suggested how the infrastructure of institutions can be changed to create an environment for the development and operation of rehabilitation programs. Strategies professionals may employ to change the institutional milieu are discussed by Milan and Evans (1987). Those professionals who continue to be alienated by a consideration of the possibility of targeting behaviors that contribute to the safe, hygienic, and humane operation of institutions should reconsider the empirical support for their position, for the available evidence suggests it may well be counterproductive and inhumane not to do so.

Little research has been directed at the identification of critical target behaviors for rehabilitation programs once a prerehabilitative atmosphere has been created. Several federal court decisions have confirmed that institutionalized juvenile delinquents have a right to rehabilitation (e.g., *Morgan v. Sproat*, 432 F. Supp. 1130 S.D. Miss. 1977) (for a more extended discussion, see Chapter 21, by Sheldon, this volume). In addition, although most authorities (e.g., Rudousky, 1973) point out that no court decision that has been sustained on appeal has found that incarcerated adult felons have a right to education and training, the rhetoric of adult corrections and recent court decisions (e.g., *Pell v. Procunier*, 417 U.S. 817, 822, 1983) suggest that a time will come when such an argument is accepted. The appropriate content of such programs remains to be determined.

One potential source of empirical data concerning the important ingredients of institutional rehabilitation programs comes from correlational studies that have identified predictors of postrelease success, with success defined by such factors as recidivism and, if recidivism occurs, the severity of the offense committed. Some of that work, such as Kassenbaum, Ward, and Wilner's (1971) stepwise multiple linear regression analysis of the California Department of Corrections' Base Expectancy Score (BES) variables, focuses on the characteristics of offenders and of the offenses they have committed in the past. For example, Kassenbaum *et al.* reported that the five factors most predictive of postrelease success were that the offender (1) was older than typical when first arrested, (2) committed offenses other than burglary, (3) had no history of excessive use of alcohol, (4) had no history of excessive drug use, and (5) committed offenses other than theft. In a 36-month follow-up of 957 releasees from California prisons, Kassenbaum *et al.* reported a correlation of .62 between postrelease success and the 29 BES variables of which the previously cited five are representative.

Jenkins and his colleagues (Jenkins *et al.*, 1974) recognized that demographic information such as that generated by Kassenbaum *et al.* (1971) is of little value in the identification of target behaviors for institutional rehabilitation programs and sought instead to identify behavioral aspects of postrelease adjustment that were predictive of success. Factor analysis of data from a yearlong follow-up of 142 releasees from Alabama prisons revealed five factors that were correlated with postrelease success. The first and most powerful factor, which accounted for slightly more than 20% of the variance, involved employment adjustment and consisted of such variables as whether the releasees were working, the quality of their interaction with co-workers, and the size of the wage they were earning. The remaining four factors, which together accounted for approximately 20% more of the variance, involved (1) the manner in which the releasees dealt with interpersonal problems, (2) how they dealt with the routine demands of life, (3) whether they were apprehensive about rearrest and reimprisonment, and (4) the quality of their interactions with their family.

It appears that the procedures used to date that have focused on academic, vocational, and social skills in the hope of preparing inmates for employment have targeted the most important contributors to postrelease success. The efforts conducted to date, however, have not yet come to grips with the full range of factors that Jenkins *et al.* (1974) have suggested are necessary to maximize postrelease success. Moreover, our knowledge of the factors and related target behaviors must still be viewed as superficial and subject to the same errors in interpretation that endanger all attempts to deduce cause-and-effect relationships from correlational data. Renewed efforts in this area of behavioral assessment are certainly warranted.

Undesirable Side Effects of Behavioral Procedures

Another issue that will confront those who utilize and evaluate behavioral procedures in closed institutions involves the possibility that the behavioral procedures they employ will have undesirable side effects. The side effects of punishment and aversive control have been discussed previously. It has been argued that the possibility of encountering undesirable side effects in reinforcement programs also exists. Beginning in the early 1970s, social psychological research on "intrinsic motivation" (e.g., Deci, 1971; Kruglanski, Alan, & Lewis, 1972; Lepper, Greene, & Nesbett, 1973) has suggested that the implementation and subsequent termination of a reinforcement program may have the undesirable side effect of reducing performance to a level below that observed prior to the implementation of the program. Not until Levine and Fasnacht (1974) summarized the early work, however, and concluded that token rewards lead to token learning did behaviorists take serious note of the possible undesirable side effects of positive reinforcement procedures.

Accusations concerning the undesirable side effects of reinforcement procedures have not gone unchallenged. Among the first responses to criticisms of reinforcement programs were those of Bornstein and Hamilton (1975), Hoppe (1975), and Reiss and Sushinsky (1975). Bornstein and Hamilton noted that when deteriorations in performance below baseline levels occur following the termination of reinforcement procedures, these outcomes are typically reported in analog studies where baseline levels are high, whereas in the real world, a reinforcement program is typically implemented only when the baseline level is low. They also pointed out that contemporary behavior modifiers incorporate procedures in their programs to ensure continued high levels of performance as reinforcement is terminated.

Hoppe (1975) argued for a distinction between learning and performance and pointed out that reinforcement is more appropriately viewed as a factor affecting performance rather than learning as Levine and Fasnacht (1974) implied. Reiss and Sushinsky (1975) went on to question the validity of the theorizing about the causes of performance decrements to below baseline levels following the termination of reinforcement and questioned whether the findings of the social psychologists may be generalized to actual reinforcement programs because of the dissimilarity in the methods and procedures involved. They also pointed out that the behavior modification literature provides many examples that disconfirm the supposed undesirable side effect of reinforcement.

Ford and Foster (1976) provided a more detailed critique of the studies proporting to show performance decrements after reinforcement and concluded that the existing evidence was simply too inconclusive to recommend that extrinsic reward programs should be avoided. Levine and Fasnacht (1976) replied that these responses to their original statement (Levine & Fasnacht, 1974) had not persuaded them that extrinsic rewards do not undermine intrinsic interest in the rewarded behavior. They concluded by encouraging behaviorists to conduct a careful assessment to determine what is maintaining inappropriate behavior and to begin their intervention there rather than to merely superimpose an extrinsic reward program upon an existing set of contingencies that will again be prepotent when that reward program is withdrawn—not an unreasonable request.

Vasta (1981) has reviewed subsequent studies bearing on whether performance decrements to below baseline levels occur following the termination of reinforcement. Many of these studies attempted to overcome the analog nature of the early work by either creating more natural conditions or conducting research within the context of ongoing reinforcement programs. Vasta concludes that there is some truth to both sides of the argument summarized in the preceding paragraphs. He finds that the termination of reinforcement can indeed have the undesirable side effect Levine and Fasnacht (1974) attributed to it but that it is a far less common phenomenon than Levine and Fasnacht proclaimed it to be. Vasta also concludes that few social psychological theorists would predict the occurrence of performance decrements below baseline in all or even most reinforcement programs. The phenomenon itself is far from being understood. Although Vasta finds little cause for alarm, he does, however, recommend that professionals be sensitive to the possible occurrence of performance decrements below baseline so they may adjust their program to eliminate the phenomenon if these performance decrements should happen to appear.

Balsam and Bondy (1983) have suggested that reinforcement itself can have several undesirable side effects, including aggression, suppression of the target behavior, and inappropriate imitation of reinforcement procedures. Epstein (1985) has responded to this more recent critique of reinforcement procedures. He points out that critics have failed to distinguish between reinforcement, the schedule of reinforcement in effect (as in schedule-induced aggression), and other contingencies of reinforcement that are operative (as in the generalization of behavior from one setting to another). He concludes that reinforcement should not be considered suspect because poor contingencies may not produce desired effects. Instead, Epstein advocates a better understanding of the variables of which behavior is a function so that desirable effects may be better achieved and undesirable effects better prevented.

Balsam and Bondy (1985) add that many side effects of reinforcement are problems in response covariation wherein behavioral interventions affect the occurrence of nontargeted behaviors as well as targeted behaviors (e.g., Simon, Ayllon, & Milan, 1982). They conclude that the profession has not yet developed either an adequate conceptualization of the side effects of intervention procedures or an adequate understanding of the functional relationships between side effects, the properties of reinforcers, and the reinforcement or aversive control procedures in which they are used.

Although the preceding authors may not share the same views on the nature of the planned and unplanned effects of behavioral interventions, they do make it clear that the possibility of side effects warrants consideration when developing a program and designing an evaluation strategy so that they may be detected and corrected if they should occur. Moreover, they all agree that unplanned effects are deserving of more analytical efforts than have been devoted to them to date. Finally, critics of behaviorism may be expected to focus on the possibility of undesirable side effects of a reinforcement program in their arguments against the use of behavioral procedures. Consequently, professionals using behavioral strategies in applied settings in general, and in closed institutions for juvenile delinquents and adult felons in particular, should include the study of side effects in their plan, for they will undoubtedly have to deal with the issue of side effects whether or not such effects occur in their programs.

Acknowledgments

The author expresses his appreciation to Roy Sites and Betty Alfonso of the University of South Florida for assistance in reviewing the literature and typing and editing the original manuscript. The author also expresses his appreciation to Elaine Beal and Drue Rueger of Georgia State University for typing and editing revisions of the manuscript.

REFERENCES

Axelrod, S., & Apsche, J. (Eds.). (1983). *The effects of punishment on human behavior*. New York: Academic Press.

Azrin, N. H., & Holz, W. C. (1966). Punishment. In W. K. Honig (Ed.), *Operant behavior: Areas of research and application* (pp. 380–337). New York: Appleton-Century-Crofts.

Balsam, P. D., & Bondy, A. S. (1983). The negative side effects of reward. *Journal of Applied Behavior Analysis, 16*, 283–296.

Balsam, P. D., & Bondy, A. S. (1985). Reward induced response covariation: A side effect revisited. *Journal of Applied Behavior Analysis, 18*, 79–80.

Bandura, A. (1969). *Principles of behavior modification*. New York: Holt, Rinehart & Winston.

Bassett, J. E., & Blanchard, E. B. (1977). The effect of the absence of close supervision on the use of response cost in a prison token economy. *Journal of Applied Behavior Analysis, 10*, 375–379.

Bednar, R. L., Zelhart, P. F., Greathouse, L., & Weinberg, S. (1970). Operant conditioning priciples in the treatment of learning and behavior problems with delinquent boys. *Journal of Counseling Psychology, 17*, 402–407.

Bellack, A. S., & Hersen, M. (1979). *Research and practice in social skills training*. New York: Plenum Press.

Bornstein, P. H., & Hamilton, S. B. (1975). Token rewards and straw men. *American Psychologist, 30*, 780–781.

Braukmann, C. J., & Fixsen, D. L. (1975). Behavior modification with delinquents. In M. Hersen, R. M. Eisler, & P. M. Miller (Eds.). *Progress in behavior modification* (pp. 191–231). New York: Academic Press.

Braukmann, C. J., Fixsen, D. L., Phillips, E. L., & Wolf, M. M. (1975). Behavioral approaches to treatment in the crime and deliquency field. *Criminology, 13*, 299–331.

Brown, G. D., & Tyler, V. O. (1968). Time out from reinforcement: A technique for dethroning the "duke" of an institutionalized delinquent group. *Journal of Child Psychology and Psychiatry, 9*, 203–211.

Buehler, R. E., Patterson, G. R., & Furniss, J. M. (1966). The reinforcement of behavior in institutional settings. *Behaviour Research and Therapy, 4*, 157–467.

Burchard, J. D. (1967). Systematic socialization: A programmed environment for the habilitation of antisocial retardates. *Psychological Record, 17*, 461–476.

Burchard, J. D., & Barrera, F. (1972). An analysis of timeout and response cost in a programmed environment. *Journal of Applied Behavior Analysis 5*, 270–282.

Burchard, J. D., & Harig, P. T. (1976). Behavior modification and juvenile delinquency. In H. Leitenberg (Ed.), *Handbook of behavior modification and behavior therapy* (pp. 405–452). Englewood Cliffs, NJ: Prentice-Hall.

Burchard, J. D., & Lane, T. W. (1982). Crime and delinquency. In A. S. Bellack, M. Hersen, & A. E. Kazdin (Eds.), *International handbook of behavior modification and therapy* (pp. 613–652). New York: Plenum Press.

Burchard, J. D., & Tyler, V. O. (1965). The modification of delinquent behavior through operant conditioning. *Behaviour Research and Therapy, 2*, 245–250.

Clements, C. B., & McKee, J. M. (1968). Programmed instruction for institutionalized offenders: Contingency management and performance contracts. *Psychological Reports, 22*, 957–964.

Crowther, C. (1969). Crimes, penalties, and legislatures. *The Annals of the American Society of Political and Social Sciences, 38*, 147–158.

Davidson, W., & Seidman, E. (1974). Studies of behavior modification and juvenile delinquency: A review, methodological critique and social perspective. *Psychological Bulletin, 81*, 998–1011.

Deci, E. L. (1971). Effects of externally mediated rewards on intrinsic motivation. *Journal of Personality and Social Psychology, 18,* 105–115.

Dominguez, B., Rveda, M., Makhlouf, C., & Rivera, A. (1976). Analysis and control of activities in custodial human groups. In E. Ribes-Inesta & A. Bandura (Eds.), *Analysis of delinquency and aggression* (pp. 51–70). New York: Wiley.

Eisler, R. M., & Frederiksen, L. W. (1980). *Perfecting social skills: A guide to interpersonal behavior development.* New York: Plenum Press.

Emery, R. E., & Marholin, D. (1977). An applied behavior analysis of delinquency: The irrelevancy of relevant behavior. *American Psychologist, 32,* 860–873.

Emshoff, J. G., Redd, W. H., & Davidson, W. S. (1976). Generalization training and the transfer of prosocial behavior in delinquent adolescents. *Journal of Behaviour Therapy and Experimental Psychiatry, 7,* 141–144.

Epstein, R. (1985). The positive side effects of reinforcement: A commentary on Balsam and Bondy. *Journal of Applied Behavior Analysis, 18,* 73–78.

Ford, J. D., & Foster, S. L. (1976). Extrinsic incentives and token-based programs. *American Psychologist, 31,* 87–90.

Freedman, B., Rosenthal, L., Donahoe, C., Schlundt, D., & McFall, R. (1978). A social-behavioral analysis of skills deficits in delinquent and nondelinquent adolescent boys. *Journal of Consulting and Clinical Psychology, 46,* 1448–1462.

Geller, E. S., Johnson, D. F., Hemlin, P. H., & Kennedy, T. D. (1977). Behavior modification in a prison: Issues, problems, and compromises. *Criminal Justice and Behavior, 4,* 11–43.

Graubard, P. S. (1968). Use of indigenous groupings as the reinforcing agent in teaching disturbed delinquents to learn. In *Proceedings of the 6th Annual Convention* (pp. 613–614). New York: American Psychological Association.

Hersen, M., & Barlow, D. H. (1976). *Single case experimental designs: Strategies for studying behavioral change.* New York: Pergamon Press.

Hoppe, R. B. (1975). "Token" learning programs. *American Psychologist, 30,* 781–782.

Horton, L. E. (1970). Generalization of aggressive behavior in adolescent delinquent boys. *Journal of Applied Behavior Analysis, 3,* 205–211.

Jenkins, W. O., Witherspoon, A. D., DeVine, M. D., deValera, E. K., Muller, J. B., Barton, M. C., & McKee, J. M. (1974). *The post-prison analysis of criminal behavior and longtitudinal follow-up evaluation of institutional treatment.* Elmore, AL: Rehabilitation Research Foundation.

Johnson, V. S. (1977). Behavior modification in the correctional setting. *Criminal Justice and Behavior, 4,* 397–428.

Johnston, J. M. (1985). Controlling professional behavior [Review of *The effects of punishment on human behavior*]. *The Behavior Analyst, 8,* 111–119.

Kassenbaum, G., Ward, D., & Wilner, D. (1971). *Prison treatment and parole survival.* New York: Wiley.

Kaufman, L. M., & Wagner, B. R. (1972). Barb: A systematic treatment technology for temper control disorders. *Behavior Therapy, 3,* 84–90.

Kennedy, R. E. (1976). Behavior modification in prisons. In W. E. Craighead, A. E. Kazdin, & M. J. Mahoney (Eds.), *Behavior modification: Principles, issues, and applications* (pp. 321–340). Boston: Houghton Mifflin.

Kolko, D. H., Dorsett, P. G., & Milan, M. A. (1981). A total-assessment approach to the evaluation of social skills training: The effectiveness of an anger-control program for adolescent psychiatric patients. *Behavioral Assessment, 3,* 383–402.

Kruglanski, A. W., Alan S., & Lewis, T. (1972). Retrospective misattribution and task enjoyment. *Journal of Experimental Social Psychology, 8,* 493–501.

L'Abate, L., & Milan, M. A. (Eds.). (1985). *Handbook of social skills training and research.* New York: Wiley.

Leitenberg, H. (Ed.). (1976). *Handbook of behavior modification and behavior therapy.* Englewood Cliffs, NJ: Prentice-Hall.

Lepper, M. R., Greene, D., & Nesbett, R. E. (1973). Undermining children's intrinsic interest with extrinsic reward. *Journal of Personality and Social Psychology, 28,* 129–137.

Levin, M. A. (1972). Crime and punishment and social science. *The Public Interest, 27,* 96–103.

Levine, F. M., & Fasnacht, G. (1974). Token rewards may lead to token learning. *American Psychologist, 29,* 817–820.

Levine, F. M., & Fasnacht, G. (1976). Levine and Fasnacht reply. *American Psychologist, 31,* 90–92.

Levinson, R. B., Ingram, G. L., & Azcarate, E. (1968). "Aversive group therapy." Sometimes good medicine tastes bad. *Crime and Delinquency, 15,* 336–339.

Luce, S. C., Christian, W. P., Lipsker, L. E., & Hall, R. V. (1981). Response cost: A case for specificity. *The Behavioral Analyst, 4,* 75–80.

Martin, R. (1975). *Legal challanges to behavior modification.* Champaign, IL: Research Press.

Martin, G., & Pear, J. (1983). *Behavior modification: What it is and how to do it.* Englewood Cliffs, NJ: Prentice-Hall.

McGurk, B. J., & Newell, T. C. (1981). Social skills training with a sex offender. *The Psychological Record, 31,* 277–283.

McKee, J. M. (1971). Contingency management in a correctional institution. *Educational Technology, 11,* 51–54.

McKee, J. M. (1974). The use of contingency management to affect learning performance in adult institutionalized offenders. In R. Ulrich, T. Stachnik, & J. Mabry (Eds.), *Control of human behavior* (Vol. 3, pp. 177–186). Glenview, IL: Scott, Foresman.

McKee, J. M., & Clements, C. B. (1971). A behavioral approach to learning: The Draper model. In H. C. Rickard (Ed.), *Behavioral interventions in human problems* (pp. 201–222). New York: Pergamon Press.

McKee, J. M., Jenkins, W. O., & Milan, M. A. (1977). The effects of contingency management procedures on the rate of learning. *Quarterly Journal of Corrections, 1,* 42–44.

Meichenbaum, D., Bowers, K., & Ross, R. (1968). Modification of classroom behavior of institutionalized female adolescent offenders. *Behaviour Research and Therapy, 6,* 343–353.

Michael, J. (1975). Positive and negative reinforcement, a distinction that is no longer necessary; or a better way to talk about bad things. *Behaviorism, 3,* 33–44.

Milan, M. A., & Evans, J. H. (1987). Intervention with incarcerated offenders: A correctional community psychology perspective. In I. B. Weiner & A. K. Hess (Eds.), *Handbook of forensic psychology* (pp. 557–583). New York: Wiley.

Milan, M. A., & Kolko, D. J. (1985). Social skills training and complementary strategies in anger control and the treatment of aggressive behavior. In L. L'Abate & M. A. Milan (Eds.), *Handbook of social skills training and research* (pp. 101–135). New York: Wiley.

Milan, M. A., & Long, C. K. (1980). Crime and delinquency: The last frontier? In D. Glenwick & L. Jason (Eds.), *Behavioral community psychology: Progress and prospects* (pp. 194–230). New York: Praeger.

Milan, M. A., & McKee, J. M. (1974). Behavior modification: Principles and applications in corrections. In D. Glaser (Ed.), *Handbook of criminology* (pp. 745–775). Chicago: Rand McNally.

Milan, M. A., & McKee, J. M. (1976). The cellblock token economy: Token reinforcement procedures in a maximum security correctional institution for adult male felons. *Journal of Applied Behavior Analysis, 9,* 253–275.

Musante, G. J. (1975). Behavior modification in prisons and correctional facilities. In W. Doyle (Ed.), *Applied behavior modification* (pp. 109–129). St. Louis: C. Y. Mosby.

Nietzel, M. T. (1979). *Crime and its modification.* New York: Pergamon.

O'Leary, K. D. (1972). Behavior modification in the classroom: A rejoinder to Winett and Winkler. *Journal of Applied Behavior Analysis, 5,* 505–511.

Ollendick, T. H., & Hersen, M. (1979). Social skills training for juvenile delinquents. *Behaviour Research and Therapy, 17,* 547–554.

Redd, W. H., Porterfield, A. L., & Anderson, B. L. (1979). *Behavior modification: Behavioral approaches to human problems.* New York: Random House.

Reiss, S., & Sushinsky, L. W. (1975). Undermining extrinsic interest. *American Psychologist, 30,* 782–783.

Rice, M. E., & Chaplin, T. C. (1979). Social skills training for hospitalizd male arsonists. *Journal of Behavior Therapy and Experimental Psychiatry, 10,* 105–108.

Rudousky, D. (1973). *The rights of prisoners.* New York: Avon Books.

Sandford, D. A. (1973). Use of an operant model to analyze officer control procedures in a borstal. *Australia and New Zealand Journal of Criminology, 6,* 158–166.

Sandford, D. A., & Bateup, D. E. (1973). Learning how to behave: A review of the application of reinforcement to prison management. *Howard Journal of Penology and Crime Prevention, 13,* 278–184.

Sanson-Fisher, R., & Jenkins, H. J. (1978). Interaction patterns between inmates and staff in a maximum security institution for delinquents. *Behavior Therapy, 4,* 703–716.

Sanson-Fisher, R., Seymour, F., & Baer, D. (1976). Training paraprofessional staff to increase appropriate conversation by delinquents within a correctional institution. *Journal of Behaviour Therapy and Experimental Psychiatry, 7,* 243–247.

Sanson-Fisher, R., Seymour, F., Montgomery, W., & Stokes, T. (1978). Modifying delinquents' conversation using token reinforcement of self-recorded behavior. *Journal of Behaviour Therapy and Experimental Psychiatry, 9,* 163–168.

Sarason, I. G. (1968). Verbal learning, modeling, and juvenile delinquency. *American Psychologist, 23,* 254–266.

Schwitzgebel, R. K. (1971). *Development and legal regulation of coercive behavior modification techniques with offenders.* Washington, DC: U.S. Government Printing Office.

Seymour, F. W., & Stokes, T. F. (1976). Self-recording in training girls to increase work and evoke staff praise in an institution for offenders. *Journal of Applied Behavior Analysis, 9,* 41–54.

Simon, S. J., Ayllon, T. A., & Milan, M. A. (1982). Behavioral compensation: Contrast-like effects in the classroom. *Behavior Modification, 6,* 407–420.

Shoemaker, M. E. (1979). Group assertion training for institutionalized male delinquents. In J. S. Stumphauzer (Ed.), *Progress in behavior therapy with delinquents* (pp. 91–117). Springfield, IL: Charles C Thomas.

Skinner, B. F. (1953). *Science and human behavior.* New York: The Free Press.

Smith, R. R. (1975). A survey of good time policies and practices in American correctional agencies. *Journal of Criminal Justice, 3,* 237–242.

Smith, R. R., Hart, L. A., & Milan, M. A. (1972). Correctional officer training in behavior modification: An interim report. In *Proceedings of the 101st Annual Congress of Correction* (pp. 123–132). College Park, MD: American Correctional Association.

Smith, R. R., Milan, M. A., Wood, L. F., & McKee, M. A. (1976). The correctional officer as a behavior technician. *Criminal Justice and Behavior, 3,* 345–360.

Snyder, J. D., & White, M. H. (1979). The use of cognitive self-instruction in the treatment of behaviorally disturbed adolescents. *Behaviour Therapy, 10,* 227–235.

Spence, S. H., & Marzillier, J. S. (1979). Social skills training with adolescent male offenders: I. Short-term effects. *Behavior Research and Therapy, 17,* 7–16.

Stokes, T. F., & Baer, D. M. (1977). An implicit technology of generalization. *Journal of Applied Behavior Analysis, 10,* 349–367.

Stumphauzer, J. S. (1970). Modification of delay choices in institutionalized youthful offenders through social reinforcement. *Psychonomic Science, 18,* 222–223.

Stumphauzer, J. S. (1972). Increased delay of gratification in young prison inmates through initiation of high-delay peer models. *Journal of Personality and Social Psychology, 21,* 10–17.

Stumphauzer, J. S. (1981). Behavior modification with delinquents and criminals. In E. W. Craighead, A. E. Kazdin, & M. J. Mahoney (Eds.), *Behavior modification: Principles, issues, and application* (2nd ed., pp. 458–478). Boston: Houghton Mifflin.

Tyler, V. O. (1967). Application of operant token reinforcement to academic performance of an institutionalized delinquents. *Behaviour Research and Therapy, 5,* 1–9.

Tyler, V. O., & Brown, G. D. (1967). The use of swift, brief isolation as a group control device for institutionalized delinquents. *Behaviour Research and Therapy, 5,* 1–9.

Vasta, R. (1981). On token rewards and real dangers. *Behavior Modification, 5,* 129–140.

Wetzel, R. (1966). The use of behavioral techniques in a case of compulsive stealing. *Journal of Consulting Psychology, 30,* 367–374.

Williams, V. L., & Fish, M. (1972). The token economy in prison: Rehabilitation of motivation. *Journal of Correctional Education, 24,* 4–7.

Winett, R. A., & Winkler, R. C. (1972). Current behavior modification in the classroom: Be quiet, be still, be docile. *Journal of Applied Behavior Analysis, 5,* 499–504.

Yahres, H. (1973). The reeducation of criminals. In A. R. Roberts (Ed.), *Readings of prison education* (pp. 180–195). Springfield, IL: Charles C Thomas.

Zimbardo, P. G., Haney, D., Banks, W. C., & Jaffe, D. (1975). The psychology of imprisonment: Privation, power, pathology. In D. Rosenham & P. London (Eds.), *Theory and research in abnormal psychology* (pp. 270–287). New York: Holt, Rinehart & Winston.

7

Token Economy Programs in Closed Institutions

MICHAEL A. MILAN

The majority of the behavioral programs conducted in closed institutions for delinquent youth and adult offenders have involved the use of basic procedures to achieve circumscribed goals, as exemplified in the literature reviewed in the previous chapter. Because of the limited scope of those efforts, they cannot be considered true rehabilitation programs nor evaluated as such. Nevertheless, much of that work suggests ways in which rehabilitative goals may be achieved in more comprehensive programs. This chapter will review token economies (Ayllon & Azrin, 1968; Kazdin, 1977) that serve as models of how more comprehensive behavioral programs may be designed and operated within the institution to achieve meaningful rehabilitation and management goals while fostering a humane environment. The chapter will first describe token economies conducted in closed institutions for delinquent youths and adult offenders. It will then examine inmate reactions to token economy programs and the results of follow-up studies of the postrelease effects of such programs. The chapter will conclude with a consideration of barriers to the operation of behavioral programs and a discussion of the legal and professional acceptability of such programs.

The token economies that will be described are complex behavior rehabilitation and management systems involving many inmates. In each, a number of target behaviors are systematically related to a variety of backup reinforcers through a medium of exchange such as points, marks, or tokens. Quite often, the systems combine both positive reinforcement systems to encourage desirable behaviors and response cost contingencies to discourage undesirable behaviors. These elaborate programs go beyond the use of the basic token reinforcement and response cost procedures discussed in the previous chapter.

The use of token economy procedures in correctional institutions may date back to the work of Maconochie during the middle of the nineteenth century

---

Michael A. Milan • Department of Psychology, Georgia State University, Atlanta, Georgia 30303.

(Barry, 1958). His program, conducted on Norfolk Island off the coast of Australia, combined a point economy and a levels system (for a more extended discussion, see Chapter 4, by Nietzel and Himeline, this volume). It is reported that the recidivism rate for releasees from that program was as low as 2%, although the procedures used to assess the program were far from what are now considered acceptable. The goals of the token economies described in this chapter have been to target behaviors and arrange contingencies in a manner to foster offender rehabilitation and institution management. Although, in general, the range of target behaviors and continuity of services have not been sufficient to consider these token economies complete rehabilitative efforts, they do represent a significant movement in that direction and for this reason are deserving of careful consideration during the design of more comprehensive rehabilitation programs.

The identification and control of "naturally occurring" contingencies will undoubtedly be an ongoing concern in token economy efforts. Lachenmeyer (1969) commented on the importance of uncontrolled contingencies within the context of Burchard's (1967) token economy program, but the essence of his comments apply equally to all behavior modification efforts. Specifically, Lachenmayer described how countercontrolling social contingencies arranged by inmates, such as acting out when a response cost procedure is used, influence staff behavior (e.g., not subjecting those inmates to response cost procedures on subsequent occasions). Similarly, coercive procedures can result in the strengthening of the inmate counterculture because adherence to the counterculture is reinforced in that the mores of the counterculture allow inmates to engage in prohibited acts while avoiding negative sanctions (Milan & McKee, 1974). As Burchard (1969) has made clear, the problem of the control of social contingencies is a real one, and the challenge is to design behavioral programs that control these social contingencies, while overriding the harmful effects of contingencies that remain uncontrolled.

Token Economies with Juvenile Delinquents

Several large-scale token economies for institutionalized delinquents have been described in the literature, and their effects on the day-to-day activities of inmates have been validated in a systematic fashion. One of the earliest and most basic of these programs was reported by Tyler and Brown (1968), who examined the academic performance of delinquent males within a token economy. The study involved a between-groups comparison of the effects of contingent and noncontingent token reinforcement on mastery of the content of a daily television newscast. Nine inmates received tokens contingent upon their performance on tests of newscast content during the first phase of the study and then a noncontingent token "salary" during the second phase. A second group of six inmates experienced the two conditions in reverse order. Inmates exchanged their tokens for small snacks and the like. Although the difference between the two phases was not clinically significant (a mean of less than 1 question correct on 10-question multiple-choice tests), the difference was statistically significant and suggested the potential of token reinforcement procedures. This potential was confirmed in a later study with older offenders by Bassett, Blanchard, and Koshland (1975), who achieved more clinically significant improvements in news program attendance and in test performance using similar procedures.

Levinson and his colleagues (Ingram, Gerard, Quay, & Levinson, 1970; Karacki & Levinson, 1970) added an early endorsement of the potential of token economies. In a report of work conducted at the National Training School for Boys (NTSB), a federal institution for older, hard-core delinquent youths, Ingram *et al.* described a 7-day-a-week program operated during evening hours and weekends for youths diagnosed as psychopathic. The goals of the program were to increase positive behaviors and to control aggressive behaviors. Inmates earned points for appropriate behaviors and for winning in games and contests. A response cost procedure was applied to minor forms of inappropriate behavior, and a variable-length seclusion policy was used with more serious and aggressive forms of inappropriate behaviors. Here, the seclusion periods were typically in hours rather than in minutes, though the advantages, if any, of lengthy seclusion over brief time-out have yet to be demonstrated (see the previous chapter for discussions of response cost, time-out, and seclusion).

The primary dependent variables in the NTSB reseach consisted of time spent in programs, time away from programs, the occurrence of assaults, and whether an inmate's release from the institution was considered to be "positive" (i.e., parolled or remaining in the institution after completion of the program) or "negative" (i.e., disciplinary transfer or escape). Comparisons between the youths in the program and comparable inmates revealed that all differences favored the youths who were enrolled in the behavioral program, with many of the differences achieving statistical significance. The inability to assign inmates randomly to experimental and control groups, however, dictates that these findings be viewed with caution.

Kracki and Levison (1970) replicated the NTSB token economy at the Robert F. Kennedy (RFK) Youth Center with a range of inmates. Inmates were classified into five types and housed in separate cottages of up to 55 inmates each. Inmates received 6 hours of integrated educational and vocational training each weekday, with additional differential treatment as prescribed by the classification system. The token economy consisted of a basic point system and a bonus system and included activities that occurred in the inmates' cottages, in the school, and on work assignments.

As in the NTSB study, the goals of the RFK basic point system were to encourage appropriate behavior and discourage inappropriate behavior, with point earnings dependent upon performance ratings in three settings (cottage, shop, and classroom). The basic points, awarded at the end of each week, determined where in the RFK levels system the inmate would be placed during the following week. Higher point earnings led to placement at higher levels and access to more activities and privileges, including trips off grounds and discretion in dress. In the bonus point system, inmates earned points throughout each day for especially meritorious behavior. The bonus points could be used for the immediate purchase of such things as items from the commissary, day-to-day recreational activities, and rental of special rooms.

Although providing no data on program effectiveness, the RFK description is another example of early work suggesting the potential contribution of token reinforcement programs. A comparison of the effectiveness of the program's immediate and delayed reinforcement regimens would have provided information about the relative efficacy of immediate and delayed reinforcement in such settings and, perhaps, about the self-control skills that are necessary in delayed reinforcement situations.

An important consideration in the design of levels such as those in the RFK program is the manner in which the contingencies that govern promotion, maintenance, and demotion are implemented. Allison, Kendall, and Sloane (1979) have described one such arrangement in their juvenile hall program for delinquent youths. Inmates earned tokens contingent on fixed intervals of time without inappropriate behavior, a procedure termed a *DRO schedule of reinforcement* (differential reinforcement of other behavior). Inmates were required to earn 80% of the points available in order to advance from one level to another in a four-level system, and between 50% and 80% of the points available to maintain a given level. They were demoted a level when they failed to earn at least 50% of the points available.

In a case study, these requirements were applied initially to the total number of points that could be earned, independent of the area in which they were earned (school performance, observing general rules, dining hall conduct, grooming and dress, and room care). Average performance in the five areas was moderate to high but variable during the first condition. When promotion, maintenance, and demotion were contingent on meeting the percentage requirements within each of the areas of the program, high-level performance with reduced variability was achieved in each area, save the observing of general rules. This report, however, is only suggestive of the potential of these procedures for maintaining performance in a levels program, for the case study design prevents any firm conclusions.

Hobbs and Holt (1976) went beyond case study designs in their evaluation of a token economy in the cottages of a residential facility for delinquent male youths. Target behaviors included following rules in group games, completing assigned chores, avoiding assaultive behavior, and staying with the group while walking between buildings. Tokens, awarded at the end of the school period for classroom behaviors and before bedtime for the other target behaviors, could be used throughout the day to purchase such things as refreshments and cigarettes.

Following a baseline of routine institutional practices, the token economy was introduced in multiple-baseline fashion across three cottages of approximately 25 inmates each. A fourth cottage served as a control cottage wherein baseline conditions continued throughout the 14 months of the study. Clinically significant but uneven improvements in behavior were observed in each cottage as token economy was introduced. Hobbs and Holt reported that the costs of introducing the token economy were approximately $8 per inmate per month in 1975 dollars. Professional supervision of the token economy involved approximately 8 hours per week by an outside consultant, and each staff person devoted approximately 3 hours per week to additional activities involved in operating the token economy.

Hobbs and Holt (1976) also evaluated the effects of their program on completing academic work assignments, engaging in appropriate social interactions, being on task, and arriving in the classroom on time for 19 adolescent males. Tokens earned during class could be exchanged for the backup reinforcers on a weekly basis. In a withdrawal design study, the token economy was again found to have clinically significant but uneven effects on the various target behaviors. The multiple-baseline and withdrawal analyses by Hobbs and Holt's studies represent two of the more sophisticated early examinations of the use of token reinforcement procedures in a training school for delinquent youths. Greater specification of the target behaviors, however, would be warranted in future work, as would examination of how the delayed reinforcement procedures used could be supplemented to maximize performance and minimize variability of target behaviors.

Gambrill (1976) has described the effects of a token economy on the behavior of male juveniles in a detention hall that consisted of four units of approximately 30 inmates each. The target behaviors were maintenance tasks and activities incompatible with staff-identified inappropriate behavior during meals. Gambrill justified the selection of these targets on the basis that, if the program were effective, the staff would accept the expansion of the program to include more rehabilitative activities. The backup reinforcers were candy bars, coffee, recreational activities, and cosmetics. Following a 10-week staff training program, token programs were initiated in two units, whereas a third unit, which had an ineffective token program in operation, improved its programming. The fourth unit did not change its program and served as the control unit.

The first two units reduced the amount of dispensed "room time" (periods of time inmates were confined to their own rooms as a penalty for misbehavior) from 77 hours per week to 19 hours per week and from 58 hours per week to 38 hours per week, respectively. The third unit reduced the amount of room time dispensed from 21 hours per week to 12 hours per week. Room time dispensed in the control unit increased from 50 to 62 hours per week. In addition, the number of disciplinary reports in the first three units was reduced, while remaining stable in the control unit. These results suggest that positive behavioral procedures may be an alternative to presently used punitive procedures in short-term detention facilities. The indirect outcome measures (room time and disciplinary reports rather than actual misbehavior) and the policy of assigning inmates to units on the basis of age and "maturity" level, however, prevent any definitive conclusions concerning the procedures used.

In contrast to the work just described, Ross and McKay (1976) have described a token economy with delinquent females that did not have major positive effects and indeed may have resulted in a worsening of behavior. These findings are difficult to evaluate because the program and research design are only sketchily described. Nonetheless, the study is deserving of careful review for it suggests practices to be avoided or implemented with care. Ross and McKay began their token economy efforts with a pilot project in which inmates earned privileges for appropriate behavior. Initiation of the project was followed by a reduction in assaults, property damage, self-inflicted injuries, suicidal gestures, and absconding.

Based on the apparent success of the pilot project, a more "sophisticated" token economy program was implemented with 15 inmates in which privileges were earned for appropriate behaviors but only if inmates refrained from all inappropriate behaviors. The program yielded no differences in appropriate and inappropriate behaviors as measured by institutional incident reports relative to a control group matched on age, length of institutionalization, and IQ. Moreover, there was higher recidivism in the token economy group (53%) than the control group (33.3%). The program was then modified to permit inmates to earn privileges contingent upon appropriate behavior irrespective of inappropriate behavior, as in the pilot project. This was followed by an increase in negative incident reports, a decrease in positive incident reports, and an increase in the recidivism rate to 67%.

In their next effort to reverse an apparently deteriorating trend, Ross and McKay (1976) taught inmates principles of reinforcement and encouraged them to use the principles to modify the behavior of peers. No change in indicators of either institutional adjustment or recidivism followed the introduction of peer training. The token economy was then abandoned, and the training of inmates as the behavior therapists of their peers was emphasized. When an inmate entered the program, staff and more senior inmates used social reinforcement procedures to encourage and maintain appropriate behavior. As the inmate progressed, she was taught how to use social reinforcement procedures and encouraged to join staff and other inmates in the treatment of junior peers. This discontinuation of the token economy and reliance upon peer training and social reinforcement was followed by a decrease in inappropriate incident reports, an increase in appropriate incident reports, and a decrease in the 9-month recidivism rate to 7%.

Ross and McKay (1976, 1978) have offered several possible explanations for the apparent failure of their token economy and the success of the peer training program. They suggest that their token economy might have failed because the initial reliance on significant negative sanctions for inappropriate behavior established a climate of aggression, resistance, and countercontrol that was difficult to overcome. They also suggest that their emphasis on inappropriate behaviors may have sensitized staff to these acts and changed the manner in which the staff wrote incident reports and responded to the inmates. Finally, the authors suggest that their failure to include inmates in the design and refinement of the program may have been responsible for the aggression, resistance, and countercontrol observed.

Ross and McKay conclude that a behavior modification program in a closed institution cannot have beneficial effects on community adjustment on the grounds that posttreatment persistence of appropriate social behavior does not follow naturally from effective control over institutional behavior. Fodor (1972) adds that a rehabilitation program based on the male model of delinquency may be inappropriate for females. Other possible explanations for the failure of Ross and McKay's token economy—such as the contingencies involved in the earning and exchange of tokens or the manner and consistency with which staff implemented those contingencies—were not addressed in the reports and consequently cannot be estimated.

It is interesting to note that Ross and McKay (1978) posited that the peer training program succeeded because it (1) recognized the peer group as an important influence, (2) provided an effective means of inducing peer pressure toward prosocial behavior, (3) focused on strengths rather than weaknesses, (4) relabeled inmates as therapists rather than clients, (5) induced inmates to advocate a position they then adopted to reduce cognitive dissonance, and (6) was the inmates' program, not the administration's. These are most probably important elements of successful efforts and should be included in all behavioral programs. However, if Ross and McKay are advancing the position that these conditions produce "natural" posttreatment persistence of appropriate social behavior, caution is in order, for such has yet to be demonstrated, and as Stokes and Baer (1977) pointed out, the "train and hope" approach to generalization is the weakest of those that have been employed by behaviorists.

Two noteworthy large-scale and apparently successful token economies for delinquent youths were the Contingencies Applicable to Special Education (CASE) Project conducted by Cohen and his colleagues and the Karl Holton School for Boys token economy operated by Jesness and DeRisi (1973). Unfortunately, neither effort included systematic investigations of specific program components and motivational strategies, although some outcome data are provided. The CASE effort was divided into two parts, CASE I and CASE II, and has been described in a series of overlapping and sometimes redundant reports (Cohen, 1973; Cohen & Filipczak, 1971a,b; Cohen, Filipczak, & Bis, 1968, 1970; Cohen, Filipczak, Bis, Cohen & Larkin, 1968). The CASE projects were conducted in a federal training school for older delinquents and employed token economies wherein points were earned for academic activities—such as completing units of programmed instruction or passing examinations on segments of program material—and for engaging in personal hygiene and maintenance activities. The backup reinforcers consisted of such things as items purchased from the canteen, admission to recreational areas, use of offices for private study, and a private room. CASE I operated for only a portion of each weekday, whereas CASE II expanded to cover the total day, 7 days a week.

Inmates who participated in the CASE projects had been convicted of a variety of offenses, including homicide, rape, and armed robbery. They were typically school dropouts or school failures with a mean age of 16.7 years when they entered the program, an average IQ of 93.8, and an average grade level of

6.3 years. Outcome data revealed that for every 90 hours of educational work, the inmates increased an average of 1.89 academic months on the Stanford Achievement Test, 2.70 academic months on the Gates Reading Survey, and 12.09 IQ points as assessed by the Revised Beta (Cohen, 1973).

The Karl Holton token economy (Jesness & DeRisi, 1973) served youths similar to those in the CASE projects. The 390 inmates in this California Youth Authority program were between 15 and 21 years of age and lived in 50-bed living halls. The token economy consisted of two parallel systems similar to those described previously for the RFK Youth Center (Karacki & Levinson, 1970). Tokens consisted of Karl Holton dollars that could be exchanged for immediately available backup reinforcement and behavior change units that led to a recommendation for release. The tokens were available for three classes of activities, with routine hygiene and living hall maintenance activities earning 45% of the daily allotment of tokens, academic-related activities earning 28% of the allotment, and progress in the remediation of individual problems earning 27% of the allotment. Results of case studies of the effects of the introduction of Karl Holton dollars revealed a decrease in classroom misbehavior, as assessed indirectly by the number of points lost for inappropriate behavior in an ongoing response cost program and an increase in academic activities as measured by the number of contracts for the mastery of units of instruction that were completed by the inmates.

The final report to be noted in this section on institutional token economies for delinquent youths is Nay's (1974) comprehensive program for 115 female inmates and 87 staff members, which involved activities in cottages, classrooms, and vocational training shops. The target behaviors were based on a formal needs assessment. They included, for inmates, attending to academic tasks and decreasing aggressive behavior and, for staff, making direct requests and using social reinforcement. A token economy was designed in which inmates could earn points on a daily point card for appropriate behavior. A three-step procedure for the application of response cost to inappropriate behavior was also developed. This consisted of first giving a specific instruction, then giving a warning and second opportunity to follow the instruction if the initial instruction was not followed, and finally applying the response cost if the warning was not heeded. Both inmates and staff were trained in the operation of the token economy before it was implemented.

The case study evaluation of the program was based on interval recording of inmate and staff behavior during 8 weeks of baseline and 12 weeks of operation. Most inmate target behaviors improved, and half of the preimplementation to postimplementation differences were statistically significant. Staff changes in the appropriate direction were greater than those of the students. A supplementary evaluation of the token economy revealed that tardy slips decreased by 75%, broken windows decreased from 10 per month to 2 in 5 months, incidents of self-mutilation decreased from 5 per week to less than 1 per week, and stealing and escapes remained low, indicating no iatrogenic effects on these latter indexes of program acceptability.

Token Economies with Adult Offenders

Milan and his colleagues systematically explored the effects of token economies with an array of rehabilitation and management target behaviors in a maximum security correctional institution for adult male felons (Milan & McKee, 1976; Milan, Throckmorton, McKee, & Wood, 1979; Milan, Wood, & McKee, 1979). Milan and McKee (1976) have provided an initial description of the cellblock token economy that served as a basis for their rehabilitation and management efforts. A total of 56 inmates participated in that study, which was conducted on one cellblock of a maximum security state institution housing approximately 900 inmates. The inmates' average age was 23.6 years, and their average sentence length was 54.6 months. They had been convicted of a variety of crimes including grand larceny, burglary, robbery, murder, child molestation, and various drug-related charges. Their mean-tested grade level was 7.4 grades, and their mean IQ was 88.3.

The token economy operated 24 hours per day, 7 days per week on the cellblock. Activities occurring off the cellblock (typically consisting of job assignments or vocational training courses within the institution) were not targeted in this initial project but were included in subsequent efforts. Target behaviors included educational activities during evening and weekend times as well as personal hygiene and cellblock maintenance tasks. Backup reinforcers included activities available on the token economy cellblock, such as access to a television room, a pool room, and a comfortable lounge as well as the purchase of coffee, soft drinks, sandwiches, cigarettes, and the like in the token economy canteen.

The tokens consisted of points credited to inmate checking accounts as they were earned. When a target behavior was completed, it was immediately evaluated by a staff member, and the inmate was awarded points for his performance. Inmates had access to the backup reinforcers throughout the day and purchased the activities available on the cellblock or the items in the canteen by writing and exchanging checks. Accounts were balanced at the end of each day. Inmates with overdrawn accounts were assessed 10% interest per day on the overdrawn amount and were prohibited from purchasing additional backup reinforcers until their deficits were corrected. In addition, inmates with a regular pattern of overdrawn accounts were provided closer supervision and "money management" instruction to overcome the skill deficit represented by their overdrawing of accounts. All target behaviors were operationally defined, and inmates were provided instruction in the performance of each. The initial criteria for reinforcement allowed successive approximations of the target behaviors to ensure that inmates earned reinforcement as they mastered the skills required.

The first of the two sudies described by Milan and McKee (1976) focused on cellblock maintenance activities normally expected of individuals living in group settings. In an extended withdrawal design consisting of 13 experimental conditions spanning 420 days, the best efforts of a correctional officer to encourage inmates to perform these activities was compared to the effect of the noncontingent awarding of points, the contingent awarding of points, and an increase in the amount of points awarded. Results indicated that the correctional officer's efforts to encourage performance were no more effective than the routine conditions of baseline periods. Indeed, the data suggest that performance deteriorated in response to the correctional officer's increased efforts. However, the full array of aversive sanctions available in the correctional institution was not employed in this condition, for the correctional officer was denied the opportunity to use them. The noncontingent awarding of points was also no more effective than baseline conditions. The contingent awarding of points produced a clinically significant and enduring increase in the performance of the targeted behaviors. Continued monitoring of performance revealed a gradual and continuing improvement in performance and a reduction in variability over a year's time.

The second of Milan and McKee's (1976) two studies indicated that the introduction of the token economy did not impose deprivations upon the inmates, as indexed by their freedom to come and go from the token economy cellblock in order to participate in recreation and entertainment activities elsewhere in the prison. In addition, reinforcement for personal hygiene and cellblock maintenance activities did not produce discernible increases in the amount of time devoted to these activities, although the quality of each improved. Reinforcement for participation and performance in the educational program, however, did produce an increase in the amount of time spent in the classrooms on the cellblock.

Milan and McKee's (1976) behavioral analysis of the potential of token economies indicated that the immediate award of contingent points had a powerful impact on desirable behaviors and that these improvements could be accomplished without subjecting inmates to hardship or deprivation. Moreover, these improvements were attained without recourse to time-out or response cost procedures and did not generate the increases in aggressive and destructive behaviors that may be associated with the use of more punitively oriented inmate management practices. A small number of inmates, however, consistently abused the rules governing the operation of the token economy cellblock, and it appeared that supplementary procedures would be necessary to encourage these inmates to acquire and exhibit the skills necessary for full participation in the program. The solutions to these problems were examined in subsequent studies.

Milan, Throckmorton, McKee, and Wood (1979) used a withdrawal design to explore a procedure for encouraging adherence to the requirements of the cellblock token economy in the first of their two studies. They chose not to discourage rule violations through punishment but instead to achieve the same result through the reinforcement of its incompatible opposite—adherence to the rules of the token economy. The study focused on the inmates' use of a time clock to record the times at which they left and returned to the token economy cellblock. This record was used at the end of each day to determine the amount of time that the inmates spent away from the token economy cellblock and the amount of points they would be charged for their use of this backup reinforcer.

During baseline, unannounced attendance checks were conducted on the average of every 30 minutes. On the stated rationale that the inmates' failure to record their departure times was only an oversight for which they should not be penalized, the consequence of such behavior during baseline consisted only of adding to their total time off the cellblock the time between when they were last identified as being on the cellblock during a routine attendance check and the time at which they returned. Following baseline, a positive reinforcement condition was introduced wherein inmates earned a half hour of free time off the cellblock for each day they accumulated a violation-free record. It is appropriate to note that the backup reinforcer used here to encourage appropriate behavior was the same as that that was maintaining inappropriate behavior for any inmates who were indeed trying to "beat the system" by departing for short periods of time without recording their departure times. Rule violations decreased significantly from baseline during the positive reinforcement condition and then increased gradually during the return to baseline but did not return to the initial baseline level.

Although the failure of the behavior to reverse completely dictates that these results must be interpreted with caution, the sudden drop in rule violations that occurred when the positive reinforcement condition was implemented suggests the procedures were responsible for the change. The maintenance of appropriate behavior during the return to baseline suggests that attendance checks, conducted throughout the study on the average of every 30 minutes, were sufficient to maintain the appropriate behavior following the positive reinforcement program, even though they were inadequate to produce it. Although a search for and validation of procedures to produce enduring adherence to this rule without semihourly attendance checks would be interesting, the significance of the resulting findings might be questioned. If the effort resulted only in management procedures that did not generalize beyond the institution, the decision of what procedure to adopt would most probably be based on relative efficiency. If this behavior was an analog of a real-world problem, however, this target behavior might be used to examine and validate procedures applicable to behaviors of more general consequence. One such procedure might well be a straightforward increase in the amount of reinforcement for appropriate behavior.

Milan, Throckmorton, McKee, and Wood (1979) next explored the relationship between magnitude of token reinforcement and performance of target behaviors. The study focused on current events activities in the form of attendance at an evening television news program. During the 11 conditions of their parametric withdrawal-design study, the magnitude of token reinforcement for attendance at the news program was gradually increased and then decreased. Overall results showed that the average number of inmates attending the program was functionally related to the magnitude of reinforcement. An examination of individual performance records indicated, however, that some inmates began to attend the news program regularly when admission was free; others began when a small number of points was awarded; still others began when a larger number of points were awarded; and still others began when an even larger number of points were awarded. Some inmates, however, were unaffected irrespective of the magnitude of reinforcement. A strategy to motivate inmates who seemed insensitive to the magnitude of token reinforcement in token economies was explored in the following study.

The use of response chaining to maximize involvement when tokens alone produced less than optimal participation and progress was tested by Milan, Wood, and McKee (1979) using an extended withdrawal design. All inmates in the cellblock token economy were eligible to participate in a voluntary educational program that emphasized high-interest programmed material and individualized instruction. In the baseline condition, the importance of remedial education activities was emphasized, and inmates were encouraged to participate in the program during their leisure-time hours. Virtually no inmates participated. Next, the token economy was begun, and inmates earned tokens for completing and passing module tests. Participation in the educational program increased somewhat, but in general the inmates devoted little time to the educational program and mastered little material.

Finally, the chaining procedure was established in which achievement in the educational program was a prerequisite for access to selected backup reinforcers. Specifically, a "license," earned by achievement in the educational program, was required to purchase items from the cellblock canteen. Inmates who mastered material representing 10 hours of study time earned a license for the whole of the following week. Inmates mastering less material earned licenses for the portion of the week warranted by their effort and achievement in the educational program. The introduction of the licensing procedure resulted in marked increases in both participation in the educational program and the amount of material mastered. Virtually all the inmates in the token economy participated in the educational program during the licensing procedures, and virtually all who participated mastered material representing 10 hours of instruction.

The license procedure is an alternative to procedures that rely on the use of increased magnitudes of reinforcement for increased levels of appropriate behavior when those strategies risk the dilution of the token economy itself by the availability of "cheap money." Of course, if increased magnitudes of token reinforcement do not risk serious inflation, they may serve as powerful incentives. Kandel, Ayllon, and Roberts (1976) have provided an example of the effectiveness of such a strategy with institutionalized adult male offenders. Two inmates participated in their study, which was conducted during a daily 2-hour educational period using the same diagnostic and prescriptive regimen as that of Milan, Wood, and McKee (1979). Using a case study design, Ayllon and his colleagues first examined academic performance when the inmates earned a fixed amount of tokens for a fixed amount of work. During a second condition, the number of tokens that could be earned per unit of work increased exponentially as a function of the amount of work already completed. The levels of daily performance in math and English materials in the second condition were between 3.5 and 8.6 times higher than under the first.

The preceding two studies represent two markedly different approaches to fostering desirable behaviors in institutions for adult male offenders. Although these and similar efforts may be criticized on the grounds that token economies, like many public schools, fail to generate a continuing interest in and dedication to learning for its own sake in all inmates, this was not the goal of the token economies. Instead, the goal was to encourage inmates to acquire reading and writing skills that most would agree are both important contributors to successful adjustment and that do generalize from institution to community. That goal was achieved. There can be little doubt that as behavioral science and technology evolve, the loftier goals that may be proposed by critics of these initial efforts will also be achieved.

Several additional studies examining the effectiveness of token reinforcement procedures were conducted by Ayllon and his colleagues and have been reported by Ayllon, Milan, Roberts, and McKee (1979) in their collaborative description of the Motivating Offender Rehabilitation Environment (MORE) project and the cellblock token economy. Ayllon's MORE project was similar to Milan's cellblock token economy but also represents an extension of token reinforcement procedures to a vocational training setting.

Furthermore, the MORE project differed from the the cellblock token economy in that it used a credit card system to record earnings and expenditures rather than a checkbook banking system. It also involved all inmates in a small institution rather than inmates residing in one cellblock of a large institution. The approximately 200 male inmates in the MORE project were similar to those in the cellblock token economy. They ranged in age from 18 to 60 years; their crimes ranged from illegal possession of dangerous drugs to premeditated murder; and their lengths of sentence ranged from 1 year to life. The average prisoner was approximately 20 years old, had 1.5 years remaining to serve on his sentence, and had completed approximately 5 years of education but functioned at the second- to third-grade level.

In a series of case studies, the MORE project first sought to involve the inmates in academic and vocational training programs. An early study involved the development of a special activity area furnished with comfortable chairs, a game table, a record player, assorted records, and high-interest magazines not otherwise available in the institution. Inmates were given the opportunity to earn 15 minutes access to the activity area for every hour of classroom effort. Of the 175 inmates who could participate in the program, the incentive system increased average participation from 29 to 111 inmates per day. Once inmates began to participate in the education program, the MORE project explored the difference between "salary-based" and "performance-based" token reinforcement. Salary-based reinforcement consisted of points awarded for attendance, whereas performance-based reinforcement consisted of tokens awarded for achievement in the educational program. Nearly twice as much academic material was mastered in the same amount of time during the performance-based reinforcement procedure than during salary-based reinforcement.

Moving on to the vocational training area, the MORE project explored the effects of incentives on the mastery of instructional material dealing with both the theory underlying auto mechanics and the actual operation of various mechanical parts of the automobile. By alternately reinforcing inmates' mastery of theoretical and applied materials, Ayllon and his colleagues demonstrated that the inmates' efforts could be distributed among these two areas and maintained at high levels of performance. The MORE project continued its examination of the use of token reinforcement procedures in vocational settings by examining the use of these procedures to foster mastery of skills in a barbering program. The number of errors made by trainees during barbering tests under a no-reinforcement condition was compared to the number made under a "progressive" differential reinforcement of other behavior (DRO) schedule wherein progressively more error-free performances earned progressively larger amounts of token reinforcement. The number of errors made in the same amount of time during the progressive DRO reinforcement contingency was less than half the number made during the no-reinforcement contingency.

Finally, the MORE project examined the use of staff consultation to teach good work habits in job situations within the institution. The first objective of the consultative effort was to assist supervisors in developing criteria for excellent, good, satisfactory, and poor work performance. After these criteria were established, the consultative efforts progressed on to providing supervisors the skills needed to manage supervisees. The skills included such behavioral procedures as shaping behavior and providing specific, positive feedback for approximations of excellent behavior. Finally, work performance was also included within the token reinforcement program; the number of points earned was based upon the supervisors' ratings of each supervisee's work performance. The results of the programs, which were conducted with food service workers and janitors, showed that the percentage of excellent ratings earned increased significantly when shaping, positive feedback, and token reinforcement were implemented. Independent measures of on-task behavior confirmed these findings, with a significantly higher percentage of inmate workers rated as on task throughout the day during the consultation program than before it.

The potential contribution of token economy procedures to the rehabilitation of delinquent soldiers in a military setting has been explored by Colman and his colleagues in their work on a Walter Reed army hospital closed ward housing 18 servicemen with diagnoses of character and behavior disorders (Boren & Colman, 1970; Colman, 1970; Colman & Baker, 1969; Ellsworth & Colman, 1970). The servicemen participated in the program an average of 16 weeks. Half of the participants had civilian police records, a third were diagnosed as schizophrenic, and a quarter were diagnosed as neurotic. Soldiers with criminal charges pending against them and with alcohol problems, drug problems, or a history of sexual offenses were excluded from the program (Colman & Baker, 1969).

The Walter Reed program was divided into two levels or phases. Phase 1 involved a structured token economy similar to those described previously; it was in operation from approximately 7:45 in the morning to 4:30 in the afternoon. Inmates who performed well in Phase 1 were promoted to Phase 2, in which they assumed leadership roles and were excused from the token earning and exchange requirements of the token economy, thereby fostering generalization. The target behaviors involved various aspects of military life, including following the specifics of military routine and discipline. Educational offerings involved courses in a variety of practical skills, such as overcoming problems with authority and work projects in which the group worked as a team toward common goals. The backup reinforcers consisted of items from a canteen, opportunities to engage in such evening activities as watching television, 72-hour passes, and promotion to and continuance in Phase 2.

In his description of the general effects of the Walter Reed program, Colman (1970) stated that psychotic episodes and suicidal gestures, previously chronic hazards in the group, stopped completely. As a result of these changes, staff morale increased, personnel vountarily extended their tour of duty in the program, and others within the institution volunteered to serve on the unit despite the general aversion to treating character disorders. There was no evidence that the behaviorally programmed environment limited spontaneous meaningful relationships. Instead, relationships seemed to be fostered.

Boren and Colman (1970) examined the specific impact of the Walter Reed token economy in five studies. First, the effectiveness of the token economy was compared to the effectiveness of modeling in the performance of a routine military activity—a one-half mile run each morning. In general, the results indicated that modeling by an army officer had no effect on the percentage of soldiers participating in the run, but that increasing amounts of token reinforcement within the token economy resulted in increasing participation in the run, with between 30% and 60% of the soliders running on the average each day under the largest token reward condition.

The next two studies examined attendance at ward meetings. The first of these two studies explored the effects of the addition of a negative reinforcement procedure to positive reinforcement for attendance. Soldiers who attended ward meetings avoided a point fine. The addition of this procedure resulted in a dramatic decrease in attendance rather than the expected increase. Boren and Colman hypothesized that "rebellious" behavior increased because the soldiers saw the fine as the purchase price for nonattendance and extra time in bed. An alternative explanation would posit that this was another to-be-expected manifestation of a tendency to resist coercive control procedures.

The second of the two studies dealing with ward meetings explored an alternative strategy to increase attendance. In a procedure similar to the license employed by Milan, Wood, and McKee (1979), a response chaining procedure was introduced wherein the soldiers were required to attend meetings to be eligible to earn points for the rest of the day. The procedure resulted in a clinically significant increase in daily attendance. The fourth study examined the difference between group and individual contingencies in encouraging inmates to speak at group meetings. The individual reinforcement contingency was found to produce higher rates of public speaking than the group contingency. The last study examined the manner in which social praise or token reinforcement procedures influenced the kinds of problems the soldiers presented in group discussions. The results indicated that the content of discussions was influenced significantly more by token reinforcement procedures than by social praise.

Finally, Ellsworth and Colman (1970) extended the Walter Reed token economy to military work assignments. Six different motivational systems were examined. These varied along dimensions of leadership structure, decision making, token reinforcement, social reinforcement, and competition. It was concluded that a system that minimized punishment and maximized reinforcement, while giving members of the group carefully specified leadership roles and decision-making responsibilities in a graded fashion, proved to be the most effective, for it produced a balance of high levels of performance and low levels of resistance.

INMATE RECEPTIVITY TO TOKEN ECONOMIES

Several token economy programs in closed institutions have sought to determine their participants' receptivity to the procedures employed. Supplementary evaluations of Milan's cellblock token economy and Ayllon's MORE project have been reported by Ayllon et al. (1979). Perhaps the most telling indicator of the inmates' attitudes toward participation in token economies involves an incident that occurred between Milan's first and second cellblock token economy projects. During that interim period, most inmates left the cellblock through parole, expiration of sentence, or transfer to less secure (more desirable) institutional settings. A small number of inmates, however, continued to reside on the cellblock. Plans were made to move these inmates into the general population of the institution and to replace them with new participants. When the inmates were told that they were being transferred to other cellblocks within the institution, they refused to leave and instead began a sit-down strike of sorts, during which they demanded to see the institution's warden and classification officer to express their grievances. In short, when given the opportunity to vote with their feet on the relative desirability of behavior modification or routine correctional institution practices, they voted not to take a step and instead risked disciplinary procedures by refusing the orders of the correctional staff and demanding to see the senior officials of the institution. No disciplinary actions were taken, and the inmates were allowed to continue to reside on the token economy cellblock and participate in the second series of cellblock token economy studies.

The evaluation of attitudes toward Ayllon's MORE project was more formal, consisting of a 56-item survey concerning various aspects of prison life that was given to a random sample of 20% of the inmates. In general, over 80% of the inmates agreed that it was appropriate to make the backup reinforcers employed in the MORE project contingent upon desirable behavior and the mastery of skills. Only 25% of the inmates indicated that the use of reinforce-

ment procedures adversely affected respect for authority or the goals of rehabilitation. Over 90% of the inmates indicated that good time should also be a
backup reinforcer for appropriate behavior, with about half the inmates indicating that it should be withdrawn as punishment for inappropriate behavior.
It is interesting that over 90% of the inmates also indicated that alternatives
to punishment should be explored when an inmate continues to break rules. In
summary, the inmates were overwhelmingly in favor of the token economy
program and viewed the philosophy of making potential backup reinforcers
contingent upon both appropriate behavior and progress in rehabilitation programs as a preferred management strategy.

Two studies conducted in juvenile settings are in accord with these findings concerning the acceptability of behavioral programs to inmates. A comparison of perceptions of social climate by participants in token economy and
nontoken economy programs at a state training school suggests token economy
programs are also preferred by inmates of institutions for juveniles (Wilkinson & Reppucci, 1973). In that study, males between 12 and 16 years of age
were interviewed and administered the Moos's Social Climate Scale (SCS).
Results indicated that all seven of the SCS measures employed in the study
favored the token economy program, with five of the seven attaining statistical significance. Interview data suggested that inmates in the token economy
program also preferred the clear definitions of goals that are inherent in
behavioral efforts. Similar findings emerged when staff perceptions were
assessed.

Sandford (1973) has provided additional anecdotal evidence in accord with
the previous findings. He reports that the introduction of a token economy in a
New Zealand borstal resulted in a change in the emotional climate of the
institution. He observed that inmates no longer answered back to officers and
ceased exchanging derisive comments about officers. They also reminded each
other about or helped each other with appropriate behavior so all could earn
tokens. It is clear then that the use of carefully designed and operated token
economies as vehicles for humane management and rehabilitation programs
for juvenile and adult offenders in secure training schools and correctional
institutions appears acceptable to staff and inmate populations alike.

Outcome Studies

Of the five large-scale token economy efforts that have been described,
four examined long-term effects. The results of these follow-up studies are
mixed, for they suggest that the programs have had positive, long-term effects
but not as much or as enduring as many may have hoped. These mixed results
are provocative in that they also give rise to suggestions of what future efforts
should involve. These outcome studies must, however, be interpreted with
caution, for the constraints of real-world research typically prevented the
random assignment of inmates to experimental and control groups to best
control for threats to internal validity (Kazdin, 1980). Instead, comparisons

have typically been between naturally occurring groups of inmates "comparable" on such variables as type of offense, duration of imprisonment, age, and race.

Perhaps the most encouraging and experimentally pure outcome study was reported by Colman and Baker (1969) on the effectiveness of the Walter Reed program for delinquent soldiers. They reported a comparison between 46 soldiers participating in the program and another 48 soldiers who received either general psychiatric treatment or routine disciplinary action. The inmates were selected from soldiers admitted to Walter Reed General Hospital and diagnosed as exhibiting character and behavior disorders. Half the inmates were randomly assigned to the token economy program and the other half to traditional hospital treatment and disposition. Successful outcomes were defined as either completion of a tour of duty and honorable discharge or continuing satisfactory adjustment in a military unit. Failures were defined as less than honorable discharge, absence without leave, or presence in a military stockade at the time of follow-up. Of the soldiers who participated in the token economy, 69.5% were identified as successes; of the comparison group, only 28.3% were defined as successes.

The remaining three programs with a follow-up component employed quasi-experimental designs (Campbell & Stanley, 1963) involving similar, but naturally occurring, comparison groups. These three programs were the cellblock token economy study conducted by Milan and his colleagues, the CASE projects conducted by Cohen and his colleagues, and the Karl Holton token economy conducted by Jesness and his colleagues. The outcomes of the first two programs were remarkably similar. Jenkins et al. (1974) reported an 18-month postrelease follow-up of cellblock token economy inmates and other inmates who either received vocational training or participated in routine prison activities. During the early months of the follow-up period, the percentage of token economy releasees who were returned to prison for either parole violations or the commission of new crimes was markedly lower than for any of the comparison groups. By the end of the follow-up period, however, the rate of return for the token economy group, although still lowest, approximated those of the comparison groups. Nonetheless, the severity of the offenses for which the cellblock token economy inmates were returned to prison was markedly less than those of the comparison groups, with more of the token economy inmates returned for minor parole violations and fewer returned for serious crimes against persons.

As suggestive as these results are, they are most probably conservative estimates of the enduring effects of the cellblock token economy, for the comparisons suggesting minimal impact are flawed. For example, members of a comparison group that received vocational training offered by a state trade school were carefully screened and for that reason would be expected to show a lower base rate of recividism than the token economy group. Perhaps the most appropriate comparison group is the group that received vocational training in a federally funded manpower development and training project because the selection criteria for these inmates most closely approximated those for the inmates who participated in the token economy. Comparisons between these two groups showed a lower level of recidivism throughout the follow-up period and at 18 months for the token economy group, in addition to the previously described differences favoring the token economy in reasons for return to prison.

Although the preceding discussion suggests that the token economy group did tend to recidivate at a lower rate and for less serious offenses than did the more appropriate comparison group, the numbers involved in this comparison are small, with only 22 inmates contributing data to the token economy outcomes. Anything more than a tentative statement concerning the impact of the cellblock token economy would therefore be unwarranted. Moreover, Milan and his colleagues, cognizant of the necessity of transitional programs in generalization and maintenance efforts, never suggested that their limited institution-based endeavors would produce the community adjustment effects for which others may have unrealistically hoped.

Filipczak and Cohen (1972) have asserted that their 3-year follow-up indicated that Case II releasees had fewer violator warrants issued against them than other federal juvenile parole releasees. Filipczak and Cohen note, however, that trends in the violator warrant data indicate that Case II students would eventually recidivate near the national norm. Although these data are similar to those of the cellblock token economy study and suggest the Case II releasees committed fewer offenses and stayed out of trouble for a longer period of time than other federal juvenile releases, a small sample size and the difficulty in making comparisons between Case II and federal recidivism data indicate that these findings should be viewed as no less tentative than those for the cellblock token economy study.

Follow-up inmates from the Karl Holton School token economy involved a comparison of parole violation rates before and after implementation of the program as well as comparisons with a transactional analysis program for similar inmates conducted at the O. H. Close School and with two traditional programs that served inmates similar to those at the Holton and Close schools (Jesness, 1979). The numbers involved in these comparisons ranged from 398 to 842 inmates per comparison group. Jesness found no difference in parole violations between the Karl Holton token economy and O. H. Close transactional analysis programs at the end of the 12-month follow-up period. Parole violation for the two institutions, however, dropped from an average of 45.0% before the implementation of the programs to 32.6% after implementation. Moreover, data prorated by age to control for differences between institutions revealed parole violation rates of 42.5% and 42.8% for the other two schools in comparison to the Holton and Close combined prorated rate of 33.1%.

Comments

Taken together, these four follow-up studies suggest that some positive aftereffects of institutional token economy programs may indeed occur. It is not surprising that the most promising results were generated by a program in a military setting that returned soldiers to similar military service, suggesting that the more similar the rehabilitation setting is to the setting in which the releasees will find themselves, the more pronounced and enduring will be the effects. Viewed in this way, these outcome studies suggest it would be inappropriate to assert that improved programming in institutional settings, expanded to include a full array of target behaviors important for community adjustment, would in and of itself result in even lower levels of recidivism and more enduring effects in the community. Although such efforts are clearly called for, they most probably represent necessary but not sufficient ingredients of a successful rehabilitation program. Additional conditions necessary for postrelease success will undoubtedly involve the supplementary use of successive approximations of community life so that the skills taught in a prosthetic environment within an institution may be extended, added to, and fostered in community settings.

DISCUSSION

The work reviewed in this and the previous chapter makes it clear that behavioral approaches to rehabilitation and management have much to offer inmates and staff in closed institutions for juvenile delinquents and adult offenders. It is equally clear that the potential of behavioral approaches, elaborated clearly by Shah as early as 1966, is far from realized today. Juvenile deliquents and adult offenders who do not pose a threat to others should be diverted from institutions and provided services in the community to the greatest degree possible. For those who are institutionalized, rehabilitation will require continuity of programs so that (1) skills established in more restrictive settings can be maintained in the less restrictive settings, (2) skills appropriate to less restrictive settings are taught and practiced, and (3) provisions are made to maintain these skills as supervision is terminated. Consequently, to suggest that institutional programming alone will have large or enduring community effects is to argue in contradiction to an established body of literature bearing upon the generalization and maintenance of behavior change (e.g., Stokes & Baer, 1977).

The real potential of behaviorally based institutional programs for juvenile and adult offenders will not be tested until a continuum of care and training from prevention to postrelease follow-up is developed and behavioral strategies are deployed to ensure acquisition, generalization, and maintenance of productive behavior. Whether the real potential of behavioral appoaches to rehabilitation and management will be tested is unclear. As the reviews in this and the previous chapter reveal, the bulk of the behavioral research in institutional settings was conducted prior to 1980. More recent publications consist largely of review articles and a small number of social skills training efforts. It appears that those who conducted the early institutional programs have, for personal or professional reasons, moved on to other areas of endeavor, and others, with the exception of those interested in social skills training and research, have chosen not to continue this work. If the trend continues, this area will soon be in the unique position of having generated more reviews of programs than programs for review.

It would be easy to fault much of the research in this and the previous chapter on the grounds that it failed to meet contemporary standards concerning experimental design, reliability of measurement, stimulus generalization, response generalization, follow-up assessment of treatment effects, and the like. As behavioral technology advances, these early efforts in juvenile and adult correctional institutions will appear even more incomplete and unsophisticated. The absence of continuing progress in institutional settings is unfortunate, for it encourages many to compare programs of a decade or more ago to state-of-the-art standards for today. This would be analogous to concluding that behavioral approaches to mental health or education are incomplete and unsophisticated after reviewing nothing more current than such pioneering studies as Ayllon's (1963) report on the treatment of towel hoarding by a female psychiatric patient through the use of satiation and food reinforcement. Unfortunately, the dearth of more recent behavioral research in juvenile and adult correctional institutions dictates that work conducted a decade or more ago will be all that can be reviewed.

Despite the temptation to judge the appropriateness of applied behavior analysis in correctional institutions today in light of work that was done in the 1960s and early 1970s, practitioners have strongly endorsed the behavioral approach. Clingempeel, Mulvey, and Reppucci (1980) surveyed the 349 psychologists who indicated in the American Psychological Association's Manpower Survey that their primary employment setting was related to the criminal justice system. The objective of the survey was to determine working professionals' attitudes toward behavioral approaches to crime and delinquency. Of the 203 who responded, 70% provided services in correctional institutions. The results of the survey revealed that an overwhelming majority (75.8%) were in favor of the use of behavioral programs and procedures, whereas only a small minority (15%) were opposed. It is clear that early research has revealed the potential utility and effectiveness of behavioral programs in closed institutions and that those who work in such settings are in favor of their deployment.

Barriers to the Operation of Behavioral Programs

Several barriers to the operation of effective rehabilitation programs in closed institutions for juvenile delinquents and adults felons have been identified. One involves a conflict of theories and paradigms that is perhaps seen most clearly in the forensic area. With the notable exception of the work of Lawson, Greene, Richardson, McClure, and Padina (1971), behaviorists have had little success in designing comprehensive programs in settings for institutionalized mentally disordered and criminally insane offenders. Laws' (1974) critique of the system within which he worked suggests several reasons for this. The barriers he encountered included the conflicting views of psychopathology held by the behaviorally oriented staff operating his token economy and the psychodynamically oriented administrators who served as gatekeepers and who would not accept behavioral indexes of adjustment as signs of improvement warranting the inmates' release in lieu of the assessment and treatment of inferred intrapsychic processes. In addition, Laws points out that the inability to control admissions led to a heterogeneous population of inmates for whom it was difficult to program adequately with limited resources. Similarly, the inability to select staff or manage meaningful staff incentives made if difficult to ensure consistency in the operation of the token economy. Operating a program under such difficult circumstances could only have required a Herculean effort, and it is not surprising that when Laws recognized that his accomplishments in the face of such adversity would not lead to a change in climate sufficient to allow the token economy to succeed, he discontinued the program. Similar conflicts between custody and treatment, between psychology and criminology, and the like would be expected in other institutional settings.

Both Burchard (1973) and Ross and Price (1976) have described additional difficulties confronting behaviorists who operate programs in closed institutions. These range from confusion concerning what is and is not behavior modification, through the task of identifying and gaining control of meaningful reinforcers, to the previously discussed problems inherent in working in a closed institution while attempting to prepare inmates for life in an open society. Perhaps the most provoking analysis of barriers to the implementation of behavioral programs in closed institutions has been provided by Reppucci and Saunders (1974) who discuss eight problems they encountered while working with juvenile delinquents in a training school setting. Three of these, which Holt and Hobbs (1979) report were most serious in their work in a training school, involve the constraints placed on the program by the administration, the impact of political maneuvering and power struggles both within and beyond the institution, and the compromise of behavioral principles that are imposed by these factors. Additional problems cited by Reppucci and Saunders include the lack of resources necessary to develop an effective program, the difficulty involved in working through staff to influence inmate behavior, and the risk behaviorists run in generating resistance because they are seen by nonbehaviorists as being inflexible in their programming requirements.

Reppucci (1973) has suggested six general principles to be followed in the implementation of programs if the barriers to their operation are to be neutralized. These involve (1) enunciating a guiding philosophy that is understandable by and encouraging to staff and inmates, (2) developing an organizational structure that allows communication and accountability, (3) involving all relevant staff in the decision-making process, (4) utilizing employees in roles for which they are best suited, regardless of their credentials or job descriptions, (5) developing a return-to-the-community orientation and community involvement, and (6) maintaining a reasonable time perspective concerning the development and refinement of the program in the face of pressure to do too much too soon. In the final analysis, however, the judgment, ingenuity, and effort of the behaviorist proposing or operating the program will determine what compromises are acceptable and whether the program will succeed despite those compromises. Indeed, few of the programs described in this and the previous chapter would have been implemented if the founders had awaited an optimal or even amenable institutional environment.

Acceptability of Behavioral Programs

The final issue to be discussed involves the legal, ethical, and professional acceptability of behavioral programs in closed institutions for juvenile delinquents and adult offenders. Professionals considering devoting their efforts to rehabilitation programs in closed institutions should be aware that they will most probably encounter probing questions, if not hostile attacks, regarding the appropriateness of their work. Perhaps the most widely known legal challenge to a behavior modification program in a prison was the American Civil Liberties Union's National Prison Project suit on behalf of several inmates against the Federal Bureau of Prisons' Special Treatment and Rehabilitative Training (START) program in the Federal Medical Center for Prisoners at Springfield, Missouri (*Clonce v. Richardson*, No. 73 CV 373-S W.D. Mo. July 31, 1974). The mission of START was to accept aggressive and destructive inmates who posed a threat in the general population of Federal Bureau inmates and work with them so that they could return safely to the general prison population and participate in the rehabilitation programs offered there. The Federal Bureau discontinued START during litigation, and for that reason the court did not issue a final decision concerning the acceptability of the program.

This writer was called by the Federal Bureau as an expert witness early in the START suit. My testimony at an evidentiary hearing was that the National Prison Project suit was not without merit and that START violated a number of established behavioral principles such as the clear specification of target behaviors; the nonarbitrary evaluation of performance; the inclusion of meaningful short, intermediate, and long-term reinforcers; and the realistic balancing of what inmates and administration would provide and receive from each other throughout the program. The question, in my opinion, was not whether behavior modification programs should be operated in closed institutions but simply whether START was a good or bad program and whether it was helpful or harmful to inmates.

Several more recent behavior modification programs in closed institutions have also been challenged by the National Prison Project (e.g., *Canterino v. Wilson*, 546 F. Supp. 177 W.D. Ky. 1982). My interpretation of those court decisions is that the use of behavior modification has never been prohibited but that specific practices of specific programs, such as those present in START, have been found to be inappropriate and ordered discontinued or replaced with acceptable procedures. These results are certainly in the best interests of the inmates in these programs; and, lacking effective alternative strategies to correct abuses of inmates when they occur, the efforts of the

National Prison Project and similar public-interest groups should be encouraged by our community of professionals.

Behaviorists working in closed institutions for juvenile delinquents and adult offenders will also confront several ethical issues. The behavioral community appears to endorse the application of the general ethical standards of the profession of psychology in the regulation of its members (e.g., Stolz, 1977) rather than the construction of specific ethical principles for behaviorally oriented practitioners and the programs they operate. The paradoxical argument has been made, however, that these ethical principles require special consideration when applied to the work of behaviorists in the juvenile and criminal justice systems (Brown, Wienckowski, & Stolz, 1975). Those who hold this position would, for example, go beyond the informed consent procedure required in nonbehavioral correctional work (or behavioral noncorrectional practice) and ask the behaviorist to also determine whether the inmate is "truly" capable of giving informed consent. Behaviorists choosing to devote their efforts to inmates of closed institutions should be prepared to confront such dual standards and the professionals who would impose them.

Finally, behaviorists considering working with inmates in closed institutions for juvenile delinquents and adult offenders should contemplate their colleagues' reaction to behavioral work conducted in these settings. For example, in the American Psychological Association's report on the ethics of psychological intervention in the criminal justice system (Monahan, 1980), a prominent nonbehavioral psychologist asserted, without documentation, that it is not unusual for a mechanical or electrical apparatus to be a central element in behavior modification (pp. 75–76). Although the use of an electrical apparatus has been occasionally employed in the treatment of some specific sexual deviations, this approach is far from being the treatment of choice for even those problems (for an extended discussion, see Quinsey, Chaplin, Maguire, and Upfold, Chapter 13, this volume). An electrical or mechanical apparatus (excepting clocks and the like) was not employed in any of the studies reviewed within this and the previous chapter. Nonetheless, this distortion of the use of behavioral procedures in correctional settings appears to have the approval, if not the endorsement, of the American Psychological Association, for it was neither commented upon by the editor nor challenged elsewhere in the report.

Behaviorists have also questioned the programs that have been operated in closed institutions. Holland (1978), for example, has charged that behaviorists, although they should know better, have abandoned their behavioral orientation and view the solution of the problems of crime as the correction of personality flaws of the criminal—an interesting interpretation of the studies reviewed in this volume but at the least a forthright one. Other issues of professional acceptance may be less public. For example, an editorial consultant for a prominent journal of applied behavior analysis argued against the publication of a report by this writer that described research conducted in a closed institution for adult male inmates on the grounds that the participants were inherently incapable of giving informed consent and that "leaders" of the profession should therefore discourage such research. The associate editor concurred, ignoring the implications of this position for behavioral research in correctional settings as well as for research in noncorrectional settings, such as the schoolroom, where participants are perhaps even more incapable of giving the "truly" informed consent demanded.

The paucity of research conducted in the last decade suggests that the goal of the editorial consultant may have been achieved, and behaviorists, for whatever reasons, have retreated from closed institutions for juvenile delinquents and adult felons. This can only result in the prolongation of the conditions that exist in these institutions, thereby ensuring that Skinner's (1974) critique of those conditions will remain as true in the future as when written more than a decade ago:

> Whether we like it or not, the behavior of prisoners will continue to be modified by the world in which they live. Young offenders will learn new ways of breaking the law from their more experienced colleagues. Inmates will increase their contempt and disrespect for the enforcers of laws. . . . All this will continue unchecked if humane efforts to build more constructive environments are now frustrated.
>
> It is possible for prisoners to discover positive reasons for behaving well rather than the negative reasons now in force, to acquire some of the behaviors which will give them a chance to lead more successful lives in the world to which they will return, to discover that the educational establishment has been wrong in branding them as unteachable, and for the first time to enjoy some of achievement. But that can only be brought about through positive action. . . . Prisoners are being rewarded now, and their behavior is being systematically manipulated, and the result is Attica. It will continue to be Attica until the nature and the role of the prison environment are understood and changed. (p. 36)

At the conclusion of their general review of the behavioral literature on crime and delinquency published prior to 1980, Milan and Long (1980) characterized the field as behavioral psychology's last frontier. As other chapters in this volume reveal, slow progress is being made to push back that frontier, but work in closed institutions lags behind the work being done in noninstitutional settings. This is doubly unfortunate, for it appears that the iatrongenic effects of institutionalization are powerful, and they influence considerably more individuals than most informed members of the public suspect. Indeed, more juvenile and adult offenders are in detention facilities, training schools, and prisons each year than there are mentally ill and developmentally delayed persons in institutions (Milan & Long, 1980). Professionals who choose to devote their efforts to the rehabilitation of closed institutions and of the juvenile delinquents and adult offenders who reside within them will find they have embarked upon a challenging enterprise in an exciting world where they as individuals can have considerably greater positive impact then they could in most other areas of endeavor. Until that occurs, however, interventions in closed institutions for delinquent youths and adult offenders may well remain behavioral psychology's final frontier of application, research, and theory.

ACKNOWLEDGMENTS

The author expresses his appreciation to Elaine Beal, Tim Woltering, and Drue Rueger of Georgia State University for their assistance in typing and editing this manuscript.

REFERENCES

Allison, T. S., Kendall, S., & Sloane, D. (1979). New directions in a juvenile hall setting. In J. S. Stumphauzer (Ed.), *Progress in behavior therapy with delinquents* (pp. 73–90). Springfield, IL: Charles C Thomas.

Ayllon, T. (1963). Intensive treatment of psychotic behavior by stimulus satiation and food reinforcement. *Behaviour Research and Therapy, 1,* 53–61.

Ayllon, T., & Azrin, N. (1968). *The token economy: A motivational system for therapy and rehabilitation.* New York: Appleton-Century-Crofts.

Ayllon, T., & Milan, M. A., with the assistance of Roberts, M. D., & McKee, J. M. (1979). *Correctional rehabilitation and management: A psychological approach.* New York: Wiley.

Barry, J. V. (1958). *Alexander Maconochie of Norfolk Island.* Melbourne: Oxford University Press.

Bassett, J. E., Blanchard, E. B., & Koshland, E. (1975). Applied behavior analysis in a penal setting: Targeting "free world" behaviors. *Behavior Therapy, 6,* 639–648.

Boren, J. J., & Colman, A. D. (1970). Some experiments on reinforcement principles within a psychiatric ward for delinquent soldiers. *Journal of Applied Behavior Analysis, 3,* 29–37.

Brown, B. S., Wienckowski, L. A., & Stolz, S. B. (1975). *Behavior modification: Perspective on a current issue.* Washington, DC: U.S. Government Printing Office.

Burchard, J. D. (1967). Systematic socialization: A programmed environment for the habilitation of antisocial retardates. *The Psychological Record, 17,* 461–476.

Burchard, J. D. (1969). Residential behavior modification programs and the problem of uncontrolled contingencies: A reply to Lachenmeyer. *The Psychological Record, 19,* 259–261.

Burchard, J. D. (1973). Behavior modification with delinquents: Some unforeseen contingencies. In J. S. Stumphauzer (Ed.), *Behavior therapy with delinquents* (pp. 66–82). Springfield, IL: Charles C Thomas.

Campbell, D. T., & Stanley, J. C. (1963). *Experimental and quasi-experimental designs for research.* Chicago: Rand McNally.

Clingempeel, W. G., Mulvey, E., & Reppucci, N. D. (1980). A national study of ethical dilemmas of psychologists in the criminal justice system. In J. Monahan (Ed.), *Who is the client?* (pp. 126–152). Washington, DC: American Psychological Association.

Cohen, H. L. (1973). Motivationally-oriented designs for an ecology of learning. In A. R. Roberts (Ed.), *Readings in prison education* (pp. 142–154). Springfield, IL: Charles C Thomas.

Cohen, H. L., & Filipczak, J. A. (1971a). *A new learning environment.* San Francisco: Jossey-Bass.

Cohen, H. L., & Filipczak, J. A. (1971b). Programming educational behavior for institutionalized adolescents. In H. C. Rickard (Ed.), *Behavioral intervention in human problems* (pp. 179–200). New York: Pergamon Press.

Cohen, H. L., Filipczak, J. A., & Bis, J. S. (1968). CASE project: Contingencies applicable to special education. In J. Schlen (Ed.), *Research in psychotherapy* (pp. 34–41). Washington, DC: American Psychological Association.

Cohen, H. L., Filipczak, J. A., Bis, J. S., Cohen, J., & Larkin, P. (1968). Establishing motivationally-oriented educational environments for institutionalized adolescents. In J. Zubin & A. M. Freedman (Eds.), *The psychopathology of adolescence* (pp. 57–73). New York: Grune & Stratton.

Cohen, H. L., Filipczak, J. A., & Bis, J. S. (1970). A study of contingencies applicable to special education: CASE I. In R. E. Ulrich, T. Stachnik, & J. Mabry (Eds.), *Control of human behavior* (Vol. 2, pp. 51–69). Glenview, IL: Scott, Foresman.

Colman, A. D. (1970). Behavior therapy in a military setting. *Current Psychiatric Therapies, 10,* 171–178.

Colman, A. D., & Baker, S. L. (1969). Utilization of an operant conditioning model for the treatment of character and behavior disorders in a military setting. *American Journal of Psychiatry, 125,* 101–109.

Ellsworth, P. D., & Colman, A. D. (1970). The application of operant conditioning principles: Reinforcement systems to support work behavior. *American Journal of Occupational Therapy, 24,* 562–568.

Filipczak, J., & Cohen, H. L. (1972, September). *The CASE II continency management system and where it is going.* Paper presented at the meeting of the American Psychological Association, Honolulu.

Fodor, I. E. (1972). The use of behavior-modification techniques with female delinquents. *Child Welfare, 51,* 93–101.

Gambrill, E. D. (1976). The use of behavioral methods in a short-term detention setting. *Criminal Justice and Behavior, 3,* 53–66.

Hobbs, T. R., & Holt, M. M. (1976). The effects of token reinforcement on the behavior of delinquents in cottage settings. *Journal of Applied Behavior Analysis, 9,* 189–198.

Holland, J. G. (1978). Behaviorism: Part of the solution or part of the problem? *Journal of Applied Behavior Analysis, 11,* 163–174.

Holt, M. M., & Hobbs, T. R. (1979). Problems of behavioral interventions with delinquents in an institutional setting. In A. J. Finch & P. C. Kendall (Eds.), *Clinical treatment and research in child psychopathology* (pp. 323–347). New York: S. P. Medical and Scientific Books.

Ingram, G. L., Gerard, R. E., Quay, H. C., & Levinson, R. B. (1970). An experimental program for the psychopathic delinquent: Looking in the "correctional wastebasket." *Journal of Research in Crime and Delinquency, 7,* 24–30.

Jenkins, W. O., Witherspoon, A. D., Devine, M. D., deValera, E. K., Muller, J. B., Barton, M. C., & McKee, J. M. (1974). *The post-prison analysis of criminal behavior and longtitudinal follow-up evaluation of institutional treatment.* Elmore, AL: Rehabilitation Research Foundation.

Jesness, C. F. (1979). Theyouth center project: Transactional analysis and behavior modification programs for delinquents. In J. S. Stumphauzer (Ed.), *Progress in behavior therapy with delinquents* (pp. 56–72). Springfield, IL: Charles C Thomas.

Jesness, C. F., & DeRisi, W. M. (1973). Some variations in techniques of contingency management in a school for delinquents. In J. S. Stumphauzer (Ed.), *Behavior therapy with delinquents* (pp. 196–235). Springfield, IL: Charles C Thomas.

Kandel, H. K., Ayllon, T., & Roberts, M. D. (1976). Rapid educational rehabilitation for prison inmates. *Behaviour Research and Therapy, 14,* 323–331.

Karacki, L., & Levinson, R. B. (1970). A token economy in a correctional institution for youthful offenders. *The Howard Journal of Penology and Crime Prevention, 13,* 20–30.

Kazdin, A. E. (1977). *The token economy: A review and evaluation.* New York: Plenum Press.

Kazdin, A. E. (1980). *Research designs in clinical psychology.* New York: Harper & Row.

Lachenmeyer, C. W. (1969). Systematic socialization: Observations on a programmed environment for the habilitation of antisocial retardates. *The Psychological Record, 19,* 247–257.

Laws, D. R. (1974). The failure of a token economy. *Federal Probation, 38,* 33–38.

Lawson, R. B., Greene, R. T., Richardson, J. S., McClure, G. & Padina, R. J. (1971). Token economy program in a maximum security correctional hospital. *Journal of Nervous and Mental Disease, 152,* 199–205.

Milan, M. A., & Long, C. K. (1980). Crime and delinquency: The last frontier? In D. Glenwick & L. Jason (Eds.), *Behavioral community psychology: Progress and prospects* (pp. 194–230). New York: Praeger.

Milan, M. A., & McKee, J. M. (1974). Behavior modification: Principles and applications in corrections. In D. Glaser (Ed.), *Handbook of criminology* (pp. 745–775). Chicago: Rand McNally.

Milan, M. A., & McKee, J. M. (1976). The cellblock token economy: Token reinforcement procedures in a maximum security correctional institution for adult male felons. *Journal of Applied Behavior Analysis, 9,* 253–275.

Milan, M. A., Throckmorton, W. R., McKee, J. M., & Wood, L. F. (1979). Contingency management in a cellblock token economy: Reducing rule violations and maximizing the effects of token reinforcement. *Criminal Justice and Behavior, 6,* 307–325.

Milan, M. A., Wood, L. F., & McKee, J. M. (1979). Motivating academic achievement in a cellblock token economy: An elaboration of the Premack principle. *Offender Rehabilitation, 3,* 349–361.

Monahan, J. (Ed.). (1980). *Who is the client?* Washington, DC: American Psychological Association.

Nay, W. R. (1974). Comprehensive behavioral treatment in a training school for delinquents. In K. A. Calhoun, H. E. Adams, & K. M. Mitchell (Eds.), *Innovative treatment methods in psychopathology* (pp. 203–243). New York: Wiley.

Reppucci, N. D. (1973). Social psychology of institutional change: General principles for intervention. *American Journal of Community Psychology, 1,* 330–341.

Repucci, N. D., & Saunders, J. T. (1974). Social psychology of behavior modification: Problems of
implementation in natural settings. *American Psychologist, 29,* 649–660.

Ross, R. R., & McKay, H. B. (1976). A study of institutional treatment programs. *International
Journal of Offender Therapy and Comparative Criminology, 20,* 165–173.

Ross, R. R., & McKay, H. B. (1978). Behavioral approaches to treatment in corrections: Requiem
for a panacea. *Canadian Journal of Criminology and Corrections, 20,* 279–295.

Ross, R. R., & Price, M. J. (1976). Behavior modification in corrections: Autopsy before mortifica-
tion. *International Journal of Criminology and Penology, 4,* 305–315.

Sandford, D. A. (1973). An operant analysis of control procedures in a New Zealand borstal.
British Journal of Criminology, 13, 262–268.

Shah, S. A. (1966). Treatment of offenders: Some behavioral concepts, principles, and approaches.
Federal Probation, 30, 29–38.

Skinner, B. F. (1974, Feburary 26). To build constructive prison environments (letter to the
editor). *New York Times,* p. 36.

Stokes, T. F., & Baer, D. M. (1977). An implicit technology of generalization. *Journal of Applied
Behavior Analysis, 10,* 349–367.

Stolz, S. B. (1977). Why no guidelines for behavior modification? *Journal of Applied Behavior
Analysis, 10,* 541–547.

Tyler, V. O., & Brown, G. D. (1968). Token reinforcement of academic performance with institutionalized delinquent boys. *Journal of Educational Psychology, 59,* 164–168.

Wilkinson, L., & Reppucci, N. D. (1973). Perceptions of social climate among participants in token
economy and nontoken economy cottages in a juvenile correctional institution. *American
Journal of Community Psychology, 1,* 36–43.

III

PREVENTION AND INTERVENTION IN COMMUNITY SETTINGS

8

Law Enforcement and Crime Prevention

JOHN F. SCHNELLE, E. SCOTT GELLER, AND
MARK A. DAVIS

The primary mission of police departments as seen by both the public and police professionals is the management of crime. How to achieve crime prevention, however, is not agreed upon in professional police circles (Larson, 1972). Indeed, the absence of a validated crime prevention technology for police has been documented in numerous articles (e.g., Dixon, 1978; Pate, Bowers, & Park, 1976).

Crime prevention efforts within police departments traditionally have been concentrated in patrol programs that consume 70% to 90% of the typical departmental budget (Kalalik & Weldon, 1971). Such programs are thought to remove opportunities for crime and to increase the threat of apprehension (Larson, 1972). The effectiveness of patrol programs and of other police efforts at crime prevention have been examined in research studies. This chapter reviews such studies and provides examples of the application of behavior analysis technology to the development of crime prevention programs, including programs involving citizen participation (e.g., citizen patrol projects).

The first section of the chapter—"Police Crime Prevention and Behavior Analysis"—describes how behavioral methodology can be used by police departments to gather information on the efficiency of crime management procedures. The point is made that the development of useful information systems can lead to the development of a validated crime prevention technology. The second section of this chapter—"A Behavior Community Psychology Approach to Crime Prevention"—describes crime prevention programs that involve joint efforts between police departments and community groups. A behavior-analytic framework is used to classify and suggest prevention efforts involving citizen participation.

John F. Schnelle • Department of Psychology, Middle Tennessee State University, Murfreesboro, Tennessee 37132.   **E. Scott Geller** • Department of Psychology, Virginia Polytechnic Institute and State University, Blacksburg, Virginia 24061.   **Mark A. Davis** • Department of Psychology, Valdosta State College, Valdosta, Georgia 31698.

Police Crime Prevention and Behavior Analysis

Police departments have primarily concentrated their crime prevention efforts in two areas: patrol and criminal investigation. Patrol programs emphasize police visibility on the street. Criminal investigation divisions primarily investigate crimes after they occur and, based on information developed in the investigative process, attempt to solve crimes by apprehending criminals. The efficiency of both patrol and criminal investigation strategies, however, has been questioned in several experimental evaluations.

One major thesis here is that behavior analysis evaluation stategies can be applied to guide police departments in the development of more effective crime prevention programs. The behavior analysis model relies on continuous evaluation of programs as they are implemented (see Chapter 2). Evaluation strategies are incorporated in all program plans, and the evaluative information is used for continuous modification and refinement of the program. Because of the requirement for regular evaluation, the assessment strategies of behavior analysis have been designed so as to be relatively unobtrusive and inexpensive. Random assignment of subjects and control groups is seldom used. Instead, the collection of baseline data and the evaluation of treatments with individual analysis designs (e.g., reversal and multiple-baseline designs) are the stategies of preference. Illustrations of the behavior analysis approach to evaluating police patrol programs follow here. Patrol and criminal investigation programs are presented subsequently.

Police Patrol and Crime Prevention

A broad range of patrol strategies are typically employed by police departments, the more frequent of which are as follows. *Automobile patrol* involves a conspicuously marked vehicle operated by one or two uniformed officers with assigned responsibilities for a specific geographic zone. When the number of automobiles covering a zone is considerably higher than typical, saturation patrol strategies are said to be in effect. Another patrol strategy is *foot patrol*. This procedure usually involves uniformed officers walking in an assigned area and maintaining radio contact with other officers. *Helicopter or fixed-wing aircraft patrol* has been used primarily for traffic control and surveillance. Pilots of aircrafts generally maintain radio contact with other officers who are patrolling by automobile. *Directed patrol* uses crime data to direct patrol units to specific locations during time periods of predicted criminal activity. This latter strategy contrasts with "random patrol" procedures in which police officers simply maintain visibility in a general geographic zone.

Automobile Patrol

The first objective evaluation of an automotive patrol strategy took place in Kansas City, Missouri, in 1975 (Kelling, Pate, Diekmann, & Brown, 1975). The study evaluated the effects of both increasing and decreasing the number of marked cars that randomly patrolled specific areas. The Kansas City investigators defined random patrol as police time available for self-initiated patrol activities, a definition that did not assure that the patrolmen actually used the available time for self-initiated patrol purposes.

The Kansas City investigators increased time available for preventive patrol in five randomly chosen areas by doubling and tripling the number of patrol cars available for patrol (proactive zones). All patrol cars were withdrawn from a second group of five zones, with instructions to patrol on the border of those zones and to answer calls for service only within the zones (reactive zones). Finally, five zones were designated as control zones with the preexisting patrol level of one car per shift. It is surprising that the experimental manipulations, which were monitored for 1 year, did not produce significant differences between zones either on reports of crime or on survey measures of unreported crime.

These data attracted national publicity and criticism from several sources (Davis & Knowles, 1975). Questions were raised about the degree to which patrol was actually decreased in the reactive beats and increased in the proactive zones.

A second study, completed in Nashville, Tennessee, soon after the Kansas City study, also investigated the crime preventive impact of increasing patrol levels (Schnelle, Kirchner, Lawler, & McNees, 1975). The Schnelle *et al.* study differed from the Kansas City study in several ways. First, patrol staff was increased to a much higher extent. Thirty-five officers were assigned to three zones during periods when each zone was normally worked by two officers. This increased patrol lasted for 35 days. Second, the patrol focused on one specific crime—home burglaries. Third, unmarked patrol cars and plain-clothed personnel were used in the target zones. Finally, all police officers were given specific intelligence information concerning burglars who might be working in the area of coverage. The intervention was evaluated by collecting time-series data on crime rates before, during, and after the period of saturation patrol. The effects of the patrol were evaluated by contrasting crime rate levels during the intervention condition with levels during baseline and post-intervention phase. Despite an increase in the number of arrests for burglary-related charges within the target zone during the period of saturation patrol, no crime preventive effects could be documented. In particular, burglary rates within the area of saturation did not show a decrease from baseline to intervention.

A third experiment, also completed in Nashville, attempted to study further the "no crime-preventive effect" of the previous two studies. Two criticisms associated with prior studies were addressed. First, the previous patrol studies simply evaluated the effects of putting more police patrol cars into an area. No attempt had been made to assess the actual amount of preventive patrol that was conducted, even though the Kansas City experiment did involve observers riding with police. The second criticism was that the previous research did not provide evidence that the extra cars assigned to preventive patrol were actually free from such nonpatrol functions as answering calls for service or doing traffic work.

Schnelle, Kirchner, Casey, Uselton, and McNees (1977) addressed these criticisms. First, tachographs, which provide a continuous, time-based graphical readout of vehicle speed, distance traveled, engine operations, and use of emergency lights, were mounted on each of four marked patrol cars assigned to sautration patrol. Second, supervisors closely monitored each marked car on a daily basis to assure that it was staying in its assigned zone of coverage. Officers were given daily feedback on the total amount of vehicle movement and the amount of movement under 20 miles per hour. Sustained movement under 20 m.p.h. was thought by police to be an important component of preventive patrol.

Saturation patrol with four vehicles resulted in a 398% increase in total movement time in target zones compared to the typical one-car patrol. Moreover, a 3,000% increase occurred in moving time under 20 m.p.h. This, then, was the first documentation that police preventive patrol actually increased during saturation periods.

The four marked cars were simultaneously assigned 10-day periods during the day shift, first to Zone 1 and then to Zone 2. Despite the high increases in car movement, no significant decreases in levels of daytime reported crime or arrest rates were detected. The cars were next assigned to Zone 3 and Zone 4 during nighttime shifts for 10-day periods each. This assignment did produce a decrease in reported serious crime. Further reports, however, showed an immediate increase when the patrol cars were removed from the target zones.

The evaluation design employed in this study was a combination of multiple baseline and reversal designs. The effect of the car patrol in the saturated areas could be evaluated within each zone during baseline, intervention, and postintervention reversal periods. In addition, in both the day and nighttime evaluations, one zone was, in a period of saturation, whereas a second zone was still in a baseline period. Thus a multiple baseline comparison between saturation and nonsaturation control zones was possible. Because all zones were eventually treated, the design also permitted an analysis of how an intervention replicated across different zones.

Walking Patrol

Less experimental attention has been directed toward the walking patrol than car patrol, possibly because the former is less feasible for high-density, geographically small population areas. Furthermore, walking patrol is often conceptualized as producing more public-relations benefits through contact with the public.

Because the Nashville police department received money at different times to implement two walking patrols in two separate housing areas, the intervention effects were evaluated in a multiple-baseline fashion similar to that in the car saturation patrol described previously. Thus the evaluation was accomplished by using an evaluative design in keeping with the sequential approval of funds for the intervention.

The evaluation of the police walking patrol revealed that placing police on foot in a high-density area resulted in an increase in the report of crime primarily involving minor offenses. In other words, the increased accessibility of the police during walking patrol appeared to increase citizens reports of crimes that otherwise would have gone unreported (Schnelle, Kirchner, Lawler, & McNees, 1975).

Helicopter Patrol

Helicopter patrol is used by police departments primarily for traffic control and for "searches," as in the case of a lost child or escaped convict. Helicopters can also be used in a systematic patrol pattern to maximize police visibility. The obvious visibility benefits of helicopter patrol are that a helicopter (1) can cover a large amount of territory in a short time, (2) is unhampered by traffic flow and street geography, and (3), when flown low, is more noticeable to people on the ground than is an automobile. Perhaps because of these advantages, the two experimental evaluations of helicopter patrol described later have revealed some crime preventive effects. The helicopter patrol procedure was never designed to be applied in one area for a long time period primarily due to cost considerations; thus the best and least expensive design for evaluating the effects of helicopter patrol is the reversal design because periods of baseline, intervention, and postintervention are naturally available.

In the first study, helicopters were flown during daylight hours in a high-density population area. The helicopter patrol flew over an area of 5.7 square miles in an effort to maximize visibility. During two separate 12-day periods when the helicopter was flown, the number of home burglaries was significantly reduced below baseline periods (Schnelle et al., 1978). Home burglaries did not increase in areas adjacent to the saturation zone and nonburglary crime within the target zone did not change. An immediate increase in home burglaries, however, followed the removal of the helicopter patrol.

A second study by Kirchner et al. (1980) revealed a limitation of helicopter patrol beyond the temporary nature of its crime suppressant effects. In this study, helicopters patrolled both high- and low-density population areas in daylight hours. The low population suburban area was 9 to 12 times larger than the high-density urban area. Although burglary preventive effects were replicated in the high-density area, the helicopter patrol did not work well in the low-density area.

Directed Patrol

A good example of a directed patrol project using predictions about the location and timing of crime was reported by Schnelle et al. (1979). This study applied an alarm technology, in use at over 44 police departments, that provided an early warning to police when an armed robbery was in progress. Specifically, a small unobtrusive transmitter was placed in a cash drawer of participating businesses. Bait money was attached by a metal clip. When the money was removed, a recorded robbery message was transmitted to receivers both in a squad of four unmarked police cars and at police headquarters. Consistent with directed patrol principles, the alarms were placed in businesses where analysis predicted a high probability of armed robbery. The four unmarked cars assigned to the program worked in the immediate vicinity of the stores during time periods when armed robberies were most likely to occur.

The basic thrust of this "early warning" program obviously was to increase arrest rates within the target stores. This program, however, might also be considered to be crime preventive in several ways. First, the employees knew of the alarm and might have communicated this to customers. Second, the police answered several alarms to almost all target stores. These latter episodes should have increased police visibility in the target-store zones.

A total of five geographic areas in the city, with 20 to 40 stores each, were identified as "high risk" for armed robbery areas. Because a limited number of alarms and personnel to monitor the alarms were available, the intervention plan was, from the outset, to rotate the alarms throughout the zones. Thus multiple-baseline logic was applied to evaluate the armed robbery alarms.

Alarms were placed in 20 stores for an initial 6-month period. Previous to alarm placement, no "on-scene" armed robbery arrests occurred in the stores. During a 6-month test period, however, 60% of the robbery attempts resulted in on-scene arrests. This percentage of on-scene arrests decreased to zero when the alarms were removed. The entire experiment was replicated in 20 other target stores during a second 6-month period. Once again, the percentage of overall on-scene armed robbery arrests increased significantly when the alarms were in place.

It is surprising that rates of armed robbery attempts did not decrease either in the target stores or in the streets immediately surrounding the target stores. Robbery attempts stayed constant despite the extremely high probability of apprehension during that experimental period. Thus no crime preventive effects could be traced to the directed patrol program.

In summary, evidence shows a relationship between police visibility and crime reduction. The preceding studies of night car patrol and helicopter patrol provide evidence that police patrol can prevent crime. The studies showed, however, that (1) police visibility must be increased to extremely high levels before crime-preventive effects occur, (2) the effects on crime are temporary, and (3) the costs of maintaining sufficiently increased patrol visibility are prohibitive on a long-term basis. Thus the weight of the evidence suggests that police departments must look beyond traditional patrol efforts to prevent crime. One such new program direction has involved attempts to improve police criminal investigation and arrest efforts.

Police Investigation, Apprehension, and Prosecution

Criminal investigation divisions are second only to police patrol divisions in terms of budget and manpower. The obvious goal of police investigative efforts is to apprehend and prosecute crime offenders successfully. The implicit assumption is that crime will be reduced if police are efficient in the arrest and prosecution process.

Unfortunately, reports suggest that police are not particularly successful in arresting or prosecuting criminal offenders. For example, in Kansas City, over half of those arrested for serious crimes were not even indicted, and only one third of those indicted were found guilty or pleaded guilty (Pate *et al.*, 1976). Further data from Kansas City revealed that the police department averaged one felony conviction per 4,720 hours. Skogan and Antunes (1979) provided data from the Washington, DC, department, indicating that only 9% of commercial burglaries were cleared by arrests. The arrest and prosecution rates for home burglaries were even worse.

Greenwood, Chaiken, Petersillia, and Prusoff (1975) published an excellent overview of the criminal investigation process. The major findings were as follows. First, differences in investigative training, staff workload, and investigative procedures do not have significant effects on rates of arrest or crime clearance. Second, the methods by which police investigators are organized are not related to crime arrests and clearance rates. Third, more than one half of all serious reports of crime receive no more than superficial attention from investigators. Fourth, investigator time is largely confined to reviewing reports, documenting files, and attempting to interview victims of cases that will never be solved. Fifth, the single most important determinant of whether a case will be solved is whether the victim presents information to the responding patrol officer that identifies the prepetrator. Sixth, in relatively few departments do investigators consistently and thoroughly document the key facts necessary to assure that the prosecutor can obtain a conviction on the most serious charges. Finally, police failure to document case investigations thoroughly may contribute to case dismissal and a weakening of the prosecutor's plea bargaining position. Skogens and Antunes (1979) have also provided evidence suggesting that the manner in which police departments gather information, write reports, and organize cases for prosecution is inefficient.

A previous section of this chapter emphasized how evaluation technology could be used routinely by police departments to generate information on the crime preventive effects of patrol. The next section illustrates procedures to study and alter behaviors critical to investigation and information gathering, apprehension, and prosecution.

Police Report Writing

The first officer to gather information and investigate a crime scene is typically a patrol officer. This officer describes the crime and identifies and interviews witnesses. The information gathered in this initial report forms the basis of further investigation by detectives.

Greenwood *et al.* (1979) as well as Skogens and Antunes (1979) have reported that the information gathered in this initial report is the single most important factor in determining if the crime will be solved. They also reported that police do not complete the initial crime report efficiently, which has been confirmed informally in the Nashville police department by this chapter's first author.

A behavioral approach was taken to remediate inconsistent report writing in the Nashville department (Carr, Schnelle, Kirchner, Larson, & Risley, 1980). The first step was to identify the critical components of quality report writing. This was followed by frequent performance evaluation and immediate feedback designed to correct difficulties or strengthen satisfactory performance. The feedback was designed to be given not only to the officers who write reports but also to the supervisors ultimately responsible for the quality of the report writing reports.

The approach to report writing and supervision began with interviews of detectives and assistant district attorneys to identify components of reports considered critical to the follow-up of investigations and prosecution of suspects. From these interviews, checklists of important components were developed for general reports, crimes-against-person reports, and vehicle-related reports. The major items on the checklists concerned victim identification, crime classification, suspect description, witness statements, and an incident narrative.

The checklists were used in a report evaluation process in which officers submitted reports and work products to their patrol sergeant who in turn looked for information relevant to each item on the checklist. Items that were missing, incomplete, or illegible were marked incorrect; items that were present, complete, and legible were marked correct. The patrol sergeant then met with the reporting officers to inform them of the result. Sergeants were instructed to commend officers on reports that had all items correct and to also have the officers correct or rewrite reports containing incorrect items.

The Nashville police department is organized into three major shifts. The checklist-evaluation system was initiated in one shift after a 6-month baseline period designed to evaluate the normal quality of report writing. The intervention was applied to the second and third shifts after 8- and 10-month baseline periods, respectively. Thus, a multiple-baseline evaluation of the intervention was possible. Prior to the intervention, only 6% of all police reports contained fewer than two errors. Following the intervention, 88% of all reports contained two or fewer errors. The reduction in errors in each shift occurred when the intervention was applied to that shift.

Police Case Preparation and Prosecution

Police officers making arrests must prepare written arrest reports that describe the events leading to the arrest. The purpose of the reports is to document the key evidentiary facts, called "case elements," required by the state legal code for indictment and prosecution. The reports are the primary, and often the only, means of communication between the police and assistant district attorneys assigned to prosecute the cases. In many large departments, officers do not consistently and thoroughly document the case elements necessary to assure that the prosecutors can reasonably obtain convictions (Greenwood *et al.*, 1975). When police reports are incomplete, assistant district attorneys may be unable to prosecute cases unless they contact the arresting officers for more information or duplicate the investigatory efforts.

The strategy of improving case preparation performance by developing a checklist-evaluation system, as was done with police report writing, posed significant technical problems. First, more complex activity is required of a police officer in case preparation than in general report writing. Proof of key evidence and case elements often must be specified in narrative form and must be descriptive of the way in which the arrest occurred. Second, because proof of the key evidentiary facts can vary within any one class of arrests, and most certainly varies widely between arrest classes, evaluating quality of arrests is both time-consuming and difficult.

Instead of a training program, the department opted for development of a permanent procedural program for the preparation of police reports. The program that was developed can be called *prosthetic* (Lindsley, 1964) because it involved permanent arrangement of conditions to facilitate task performance by reducing response costs. Prosthetic programs can circumvent the complex social and motivational components necessary in training programs. For example, in other behavior-analytic research, establishment of permanent environmental procedures has promoted task performance in several settings (McClannahan & Risley, 1975; Twardosz, Cataldo, & Risley, 1974). In general, permanent procedural programs may be applicable when (1) training programs are impractical and expensive, (2) the number of people involved prohibits extensive individual contact, (3) targeted behaviors will always be performed in the designated setting, and (4) resources to maintain the program will be available.

At the Nashville police department, the selected environmental alteration was ongoing assistance by office personnel for officers preparing reports (Domash *et al.*, 1980). Officers reported to a special room at headquarters after making felony arrests. Staff members listened to officers dictate into tape recorders accounts of incidents that resulted in arrests. Next, staff members reviewed with the officers the case elements required for prosecution by the state legal codes. Staff members relieved officers of the tasks of typing reports, collecting related materials, and maintaining report files. Thus the major features of this program were (a) establishment of a central location for report preparation, (b) oral reviewing of cases with officers, (c) adding written summaries to reports of case elements, and (d) providing typing and paperwork services.

Before the case preparation room was established, officers described approximately 50% of all the case elements required for successful prosecution of arrest cases. After the intervention, officers documented 98% of the required case elements. District attorneys rated the arrest cases prepared in the case preparation room as superior to those prepared before the intervention.

Police Apprehension Programs

Given the data that arrests and case clearances are related to the quality of the initial investigation by patrol officers (Greenwood *et al.*, 1975), attempts to improve police arrest efficiency should logically be directed toward patrol officers who are first on the scene in most crimes. Improvement of police officers' ability to interview witnesses and generate suspect information should lead to improvements in arrest ratio efficiency.

Another program was designed in the Nashville police department to reinforce patrol officers' generation of sufficient and relevant criminal suspect information (Schnelle & Golden, 1982). Critical to this program was increasing patrol officers' participation throughout the process of information gathering, follow-up investigation, and criminal apprehension. Basically, if police officers gave sufficiently specific criminal suspect information to warrant a judgment by supervisors that the officers could successfully pursue a criminal investigation, the officers were given the opportunity to do so and to be free of other police duties.

The program involved police officers completing a form describing the problems they proposed to attack (e.g., home burglaries), the suspect information from which they would operate, and anticipated equipment and time needs. This form had to be signed by supervisors, who judged the potential value of the officer information and either approved or vetoed the project. Reasons for approval or disapproval were discussed in a committee meeting, and a progress report of the officers' investigation was monitored by the committee on a periodic basis. Patrol officers fulfilled normal work duties when not assigned to the specialized project.

This model has several critical aspects that differentiate it from the other police organizational procedures. First, the patrol officer was involved in the investigatory project from the beginning (i.e., suspect information generation) to the end (i.e., following up and developing the information into an arrest). Evidence from the behavioral management literature suggests that increasing employee involvement in the early stages of projects improves employee performance for a variety of reasons, not the least of which is improved employee morale and motivation (Lawler & Hackman, 1969; Porter, Lawler, & Hackman, 1975).

Second, only officers who took the time to submit a proposal for a project were given the opportunity for investigative work. Thus a strong selection factor was developed that assured that only the best and most highly motivated officers participated in the specialized investigation program, and supervisory problems in maintaining consistently high performance by officers were minimized.

Third, the generation of high-quality suspect information by officers was reinforced with the opportunity to develop that information into a criminal apprehension. This has an advantage over traditional police organization arrangements in which patrol officers supply the information to detectives but do not necessarily realize job advantages after that point.

Fourth, because the officers generating the information were given the flexibility to develop the case, the Nashville model increased the probability that the information would be applied to the best possible advantage. Logically, the officers supplying the information are in the best position to know the suspect, the areas in which the suspect operates, and informants who can supply useful information.

In six different patrol-initiated projects conducted in Nashville, the previously described model resulted in significant improvements in arrest rates for serious crimes and recovery of stolen property. The average arrest rate per 5-day block during the officer-initiated patrol was 1.36 compared to .13 during baseline periods.

Summary Concerning Investigation and Apprehension

Evidence for the crime preventive effects of improved police apprehension is less complete than that concerning the preventive effects of police patrol. Programs that have been developed to improve the efficiency of this system have produced some promising outcomes but have not been shown to be effective enough on a wide-scale or long-term basis. Nevertheless, a definite trend is developing in the police profession to emphasize criminal investigation, apprehension, and successful prosecution, rather than patrol visibility. In addition, the police have exhibited increased interest in the development of citizen crime prevention groups. This interest is reflected by the establishment of units in most major police departments with the mission of educating and organizing citizens in crime prevention efforts. The literature in this domain will be summarized next.

CITIZEN CRIME PREVENTION PROGRAMS

For more than a decade, the importance of involving citizens in anticrime efforts has been underscored by law enforcement agencies, criminal justice professionals, and researchers. Unfortunately, crime prevention programs designed to involve citizens have been plagued with difficulties in the areas of implementation and mobilization, program maintenance, and evaluation. The discussion that follows provides a brief overview of major citizen crime prevention (CCP) programs. These strategies are then recast into a behavioral perspective from which potential solutions to the problems encountered with CCP efforts are suggested. Although the framework employed is not new, several of the strategies advocated are untried, testifying to the need for additional research and experimentation.

Overview of Major CCP Programs

Citizen Crime Reporting Programs

Citizen crime reporting projects fall into two general classes: (a) direct facilitation and (b) education (Bickman et al., 1977). Direct facilitation includes programs designed to increase citizen surveillance and the reporting of crimes. For example, Whistle STOP promotes the use of special whistles to signal for help when a crime is observed in progress. Presumably, persons hearing the whistle will telephone police, thus increasing the probability of apprehension. Radio Watch programs need volunteers with access to citizen band radios and/or ham radios and the requisite skills for using them. Some programs have recruited taxi drivers to report suspicious activity or crimes in progress to a central dispatcher who in turn contacts the police. Again, increased surveillance and speedier reports are assumed to facilitate apprehension, which then presumably acts as a deterrent and thereby produces subsequent decreases in criminal activity. Finally, "blockwatchers" and "neighborhood watch programs" attempt to increase citizen crime reports through organized block associations in neighborhoods.

Educational programs have emphasized citizen *awareness* about public safety and crime reporting. This is accomplished through membership drives (i.e., recruitment and mobilization for neighborhood block clubs) and promotional meetings. Awareness interventions often involve one-time presentations by local law enforcement groups to various community and civic organizations or to neighborhood groups meeting in the home of interested citizens. Membership programs encourage local residents to join a crime prevention group with the goal of teaching members important surveillance skills, appropriate reporting procedures, and other crime prevention tactics.

The major findings and criticisms of citizen crime reporting programs have been delineated by Bickman *et al.* (1977). A drawback of the studies reported, however, was the decision *not* to evaluate the impact of citizen crime reporting activities on actual crime rates. Instead, the evaluation measures focused on program activities or measures of program output. The authors reasoned that the assumptions required to make causative statements about the relationship between increased reporting and crime reduction were difficult to defend. Similarly, past reviews of citizen crime prevention programs have characterized the "domino" linkage between program outputs and program impact as "slushy" at best (Taylor & Shumaker, 1982). In any case, data from the study by Bickman *et al.* were insufficient for an objective assessment of program impact. Hence, conclusions regarding the adequacy of citizen crime reporting projects have been quite subjective and open to question. Nonetheless, the Bickman group concluded that citizen crime reporting projects alone should not be expected to reduce crime relative to the societal factors typically associated with crime.

Internal evaluations based on such program outputs as number of reports, frequency of calls reporting "crimes in progress," and quality of reports were criticized by Bickman *et al.* for a variety of reasons. Most projects did not use adequate control groups, and feedback regarding the quality of reports was subject to contamination due to selective memory. Furthermore, it was impossible to rule out the possibility that the crime reporting purportedly associated with citizen crime prevention projects would have occurred anyway.

Two additional issues are problematic—program commitment and program maintenance. A valid measure of program commitment requires that a crime take place so that crime reporting behavior can be monitored; however, this does not address the degree of commitment among participants who never have the opportunity to witness crime. Furthermore, the participant commitment and interest so crucial to program maintenance may wane with actual reductions in crime and as a function of citizen migration in and out of project neighborhoods (Circel, McGillis, & Whitcomb, 1977).

Operation Identification Projects

Crime reporting by citizens is presumably most effective if it occurs while criminal acts are in progress. Often, however, crime reports occur after the fact, as in the case of individuals who return home to discover a burglary has taken place. "Operation identification" projects, a second major citizen crime prevention strategy, focus on the recovery of stolen property and a reduction in burglary rates. This strategy involves the marking of valuables and property with a unique, traceable number or name (Heller, Stengel, Gill, Kolde, & Schimerman, 1975). The assumption is that marking property (or posting warnings indicating the property is marked) makes merchandise less attractive to thieves and, therefore, acts as a deterrent.

A review of more than 75 operation identification projects by Heller *et al.* (1975) disclosed no evidence of an increase in apprehension/conviction rates or of subsequent reductions in burglary rates. In addition, recovery rates of stolen property were not significantly affected. Unfortunately, it is difficult to determine whether these failures were a function of faulty assumptions underlying the concept, lack of citizen participation, or faulty evaluation procedures. The majority of recruitment efforts managed to enroll only 10% or less of a community's residents. Moreover, evaluation results were often uninterpretable because operation identification activities have typically been but one component of a broader crime prevention package.

The apparent ineffectiveness of this strategy is not the only relevant criticism. Preparation of marking equipment and instructional materials combined with promotional and recruitment activities makes operation identification implementation and maintenance quite costly. Also, operation identification households are usually identified by a sticker or sign that is placed in a conspicuous location to indicate project participation. As such, it can be argued that even successful prevention may be merely a function of displacement. Specifically, burglary may be displaced to households or items outside the catchment area.

Security Surveys

Security surveys fall into the category of target-hardening approaches to crime prevention. The basic thrust of target hardening is the reduction of criminal opportunity. These surveys involve an on-site assessment of a physical facility and property in order to identify security risks and to provide instructions regarding potential countermeasures. These surveys, or crime prevention audits, are normally conducted by members of the police department or by trained volunteers. Presumably, participants who comply with survey recommendations for alleviating security weaknesses will reduce the likelihood of criminal victimization.

Again, the evaluation of residential security audits has been based primarily upon documented program activities rather than effects. A review of security survey projects by the International Training, Research, and Evaluation Council (1977) identified only a limited number of evaluations that addressed the impact of this technique on victimization rates. For the most part, methodologically sound research designs for assessing impact are not included in program implementation. Even if such designs were void, evaluation would be difficult due to low participation, which is typically less than 10% of the potential.

To date, the effectiveness of enrollment efforts has not been adequately examined, although door-to-door canvassing (a costly procedure) is superior to simple advertising for promoting audit requests. Moreover, the most cost-effective means for deploying personnel to conduct security audits has not been established. Finally, although participants need to be motivated to follow through with audit recommendations (e.g., obtain a dead bolt lock), research is also needed to assess compliance rates because so little data are available.

Citizen Patrol Projects

The major types of citizen patrols are building patrols and neighborhood patrols. Building patrols have emerged in public housing projects and typically entail surveillance activities by guards or residents on foot. The patrol area is restricted to a specific target building or complex. In contrast, because the target area generally involves an entire residential neighborhood or several city blocks, neighborhood patrols require more extensive coverage than building patrols. In most cases, automobiles are required for neighborhood surveillance.

A review of citizen patrol projects by Yin, Vogel, Chaiken, and Both (1977) identified a number of issues and problems, particularly with respect to neighborhood patrols. The life of most evaluated patrols averaged from 4 to 5½ years, with more than half of the patrols ceasing to function by 4 years. Successful patrols are characterized as having a good relationship with local police, thorough selection and training procedures, some form of affiliation with existing community organizations, and standard operating procedures. Neighborhood patrols, however, are limited by a lack of volunteers and, thus, their ability to provide adequate coverage. Furthermore, defining and assessing the occurrence of surveillance activity has proved to be a problem for evaluation.

To date, no evidence exists to suggest that citizen patrols promote vigilantism. In fact, participants are warned not to engage criminal suspects physically. However, one nationally known organization of unarmed citizens, called the Guardian Angels, eschews this passive approach in favor of actual apprehension, as provided by the constitutional right to make a citizen's arrest. Although its philosophy is controversial, this organization cites 383 citizen arrests in 4 years. Purportedly, the only casualty among the organization's 4,000 members occurred at the hands of a police officer (Sliwa, 1983).

In the next section of this chapter, we describe a technology for promoting better organization of citizen programs. The point is made that police departments have the mission, resources, and best-suited personnel to implement a technology that will improve citizen crime prevention programs.

Behavioral Community Psychology and Citizen Crime Prevention

With respect to citizen crime prevention activities, behavioral community psychology has been concerned with two different targets: (a) the criminal behavior that the programs attempt to prevent or mitigate and (b) the behavior of citizen crime prevention participants. As a general rule, behavioral community psychologists define the target behaviors that need to be changed specifically and objectively. Manipulation of environmental stimuli preceding and/or following the target behaviors can subsequently effect behavior change. It is this emphasis on specification and analysis that sets behavioral community psychology apart from other approaches to citizen crime prevention.

Previous studies of citizen participation in community crime prevention programs underscore an interest in the underlying motivational dynamics preceding involvement in crime prevention (Lavrakas & Herz, 1982). Although studies that address perceptions and attitudes of citizens have merit, strategies designed to influence crime prevention behaviors directly would seem to have more immediate practical significance for enhancing citizen crime prevention programs.

Behavioral community psychology and current thought in criminology appear to be quite compatible. Dixon (1978) asserted that the "contemporary" school of criminology holds that prevention, not rehabilitation, is the major concern of criminologists. This school of thought maintains that criminal behavior can be controlled through the direct alteration of the environment of potential victims, a rationale consistent with Clarke's (1980) argument for an emphasis on "situational crime prevention." Such an emphasis upon environmental determinants of criminal behavior is consonant with both applied behavior analysis and behavioral community psychology. As Dixon (1978) noted:

> The reason for this is that criminal opportunity is controllable to a large degree at its end point—within the victim's environment. Potential victims can reduce their vulnerability to criminal attack by taking proper security precautions. It is not necessary to identify the criminal, or take any action to directly affect his motivation or his access to skills and tools. What is necessary is that potential victims reduce criminal opportunity by understanding attack methods and taking precautions against them. (p. 1)

This is not to say that behavioral community psychology ignores the factors related to the so-called infrastructure of crime (e.g., unemployment, education, etc.); rather it endorses strategies and interventions that permit direct analysis of the problem whenever possible; albeit, some problems are not amenable to such direct attack.

Antecedent Strategies for Modifying Criminal Behavior

From the perspective of behavioral community psychology, most citizen crime prevention programs apply behavior change interventions that fall under the rubric of *antecedent approaches*. In general, antecedent strategies (also known as *prompting* and *response priming*) employ stimulus events that occur prior to a target behavior and are intended to decrease the probability of an undesirable target response (e.g., shoplifting) and/or increase the likelihood of a desirable target response (e.g., program participation). In contrast, consequent strategies involve manipulation of environmental stimuli that follow target responses with intent to increase or decrease response frequency. In the strictest sense, citizen crime prevention techniques seek not only to reduce criminal activity but attempt to prevent its occurrence. By definition, consequences are operative *after* an act has occurred; thus the preponderance of antecedent approaches is understandable. Note, however, that consequence strategies are particularly appropriate if they serve to increase the probability of "alternative" (desirable) responses, such as returning unpurchased merchandise instead of shoplifting.

Prompts (or antecedents) are classified according to various types of stimulus controls. For example, some prompts are specific in that they include instructions regarding the target behavior, whereas other prompts involve general appeals without specifying the target response. Prompts can also vary according to whether they specify a consequence that will follow a particular response. Finally, prompts can also serve as discriminative stimuli by announcing the availability of a particular consequence (see Geller, Winett, & Everett, 1982, Chapter 2, for further discussion of these different types of prompting strategies).

Table 1 illustrates some prompting strategies one might employ to prevent shoplifting. Note that some prompts (e.g., television camera) are nonverbal and actually operate as discriminative stimuli that influence the probability that the target behavior will or will not occur. Thus it is possible both to announce a consequence strategy and to signal consequence availability.

Some behavior change tactics depicted in Table 1 have been examined by researchers in the context of shoplifting (McNees, Egli, Marshall, Schnelle, & Risley, 1976) and newspaper theft from free-access racks (Geller, Koltuniak, & Shilling, 1984). In particular, McNees *et al.* (1976) found that identifying frequently stolen merchandise with obtrusive signs decreased shoplifting to near zero. Similarly, Geller *et al.* (1984) demonstrated the cost-effectiveness of antitheft messages in reducing the theft of newspapers from indoor and outdoor free-access racks. It is interesting that antitheft messages were equally effective for both a threat appeal (which emphasized detection and prosecution) and a personal appeal (which was designed to invoke empathy).

Other citizen crime prevention techniques can also be framed in terms of this antecedent matrix. For example, a citizen patrol project may be considered

**Table 1.   Categories of Prompting Strategies
as They Relate to Shoplifting Prevention**

		Announce consequence strategy	
		Yes	No
Announce availability of consequence	Yes	II "All packages are electronically monitored for the purpose of detecting and prosecuting shoplifters."	I One-way mirror Security guard Television camera
	No	III "Shoplifting is punishable by up to 5 years in prison and a $500 dollar fine."	IV General: "Shoplifting is a crime." Specific: "Pay for all merchandise."

Note. Adapted from *Preserving the Environment: New Strategies for Behavior Change* (p. 22) by E. S. Geller, R. A. Winett, and P. B. Everett, 1982, New York: Pergamon Press. Copyright 1982 by Pergamon Press.

as falling into Quadrant I because it does not announce a consequence strategy but does signal the availability of consequences (i.e., apprehension). Operation identification projects belong in Quadrant IV because they neither announce nor signal the availability of consequences. Security surveys are eligible for Quadrant IV when participants *comply* with any recommended countermeasures (e.g., dead bolt lock installation) and post the announcement that the countermeasures are in place. It should be noted that all of these antecedent strategies focus on promoting response avoidance rather than response occurrence.

Consequence Strategies for Modifying Criminal Behavior

Consequence strategies involve the manipulation of stimulus events following a target response in an effort to increase or decrease the behavior. These strategies also vary along two dimensions. First, these techniques can use positive or negative consequences. Second, the manipulation may involve the removal or application of stimuli. Again, a matrix composed of four quadrants emerges with a distinct strategy located in each quadrant (see Table 2).

An analysis of the criminal justice system according to this scheme is beyond the scope of this chapter; however, the extent to which citizen crime prevention programs contribute to the apprehension of persons engaged in criminal acts is relevant. Inasmuch as apprehension constitutes a negative consequence, then citizen crime-reporting projects are discernibly consequence oriented. Moreover, citizen crime patrols could be categorized in the same manner. Note that the emphasis is on decreasing (terminating) target behav-

**Table 2. Categories of Consequent Strategies
as They Relate to Shoplifting Prevention**

	Nature of consequence	
	Positive reinforcement	Positive punishment
Apply	One discount coupon for unpaid goods returned to the "displaced merchandise" bin adjacent to check out.	Record of a misdemeanor conviction listed on individual's permanent record
Action with consequence	Negative punishment	Negative reinforcement
Remove	11-month prison sentence for shoplifting camera equipment.	Avoid arrest and/or conviction by returning unpaid goods to the "displaced merchandise" bin adjacent to check out.

Note. Adapted from *Preserving the Environment: New Strategies for Behavior Change* (p. 22) by E. S. Geller, R. A. Winett, and P. B. Everett, 1982, New York: Pergamon Press. Copyright 1982 by Pergamon Press.

ior. Hence, only two of the four quadrants have been applied with regularity in citizen crime prevention (namely punishment). Again, the nature of crime prevention stresses the reduction and prevention of criminal acts, while largely ignoring the role of alternative, desirable behavior.

The sections to follow are directed toward fostering behaviors that will facilitate citizen crime prevention programs. Once again, the reader is referred to Tables 1 and 2 for the framework of the approaches described. The reader should also be aware that many of the strategies advocated are untried, testifying to the need for innovative experimentation.

Facilitating Citizen Crime Prevention with Antecedents: Mobilization and Recruitment

The probability of a successful intervention is increased when specific observable behaviors can be targeted and reliably measured. Essentially, citizen involvement is the goal of recruitment and mobilization efforts during the early stages of citizen crime prevention activities. One could argue that the act of joining a group or organization is readily observable and amenable to measurement. As such, the target behavior requiring intervention is citizen participation.

For the most part, the strategies used to draw people into crime prevention groups have focused on prompting strategies such as media advertising, public service announcements, and distribution of crime prevention literature. The most successful method has been the more costly, personalized door-to-door canvassing.

A careful analysis of these common strategies could maximize their utility. For example, the efficacy of prompting strategies has been shown to have a limited impact in facilitating behaviors to protect the environment (Geller,

Winnett, & Everett, 1982). As Geller, Winett, and Everett (1982) noted, however, the success of prompting strategies is more likely when they (1) specify the behavior desired, (2) are administered in close proximity to an opportunity to emit the target behavior, (3) request behavior that is relatively convenient, and (4) are delivered in polite, nondemanding language. Consequently, a systematic investigation of these factors in current citizen crime prevention prompting strategies might enhance methods for attracting potential program participants.

Door-to-door recruitment, though generally regarded as effective, has also been costly (Heller *et al.*, 1975). Another antecedent strategy that may be more cost-effective could incorporate modeling strategies (Bandura, 1969). For instance, television presentations depicting a model citizen would portray the positive (or aversive) consequences associated with joining (or not joining) a crime prevention group. Currently, a television spot entitled "Take a Bite Out of Crime" presents a model who experiences negative and positive consequences before and after organizing a community crime prevention group. Unfortunately, data are not available on the impact of this advertisement as a modeling strategy.

Ostrom (1978) maintained that, with respect to citizen involvement, "solidary" incentives (e.g., opportunities to socialize) are superior to "material" incentives. This is consistent with Taylor and Shumaker's (1982) contention that persons who choose to join may do so for the purpose of affiliation. As such, modeling strategies used to promote crime prevention might use social reinforcement contingencies as another component of recruitment efforts.

Block associations have used the house-party concept, block parties, and other recreational activities to promote interest in citizen crime prevention programs (Washnis, 1976). Furthermore, intact community organizations offer significant possibilities for citizen crime prevention promotion and, what is more important, extant memberships permit the use of antecedent strategies for increasing recruitment behavior. For instance, large-scale efforts to promote seat-belt usage in community and industrial settings have incorporated a number of procedures, including (a) incentive fliers and merchant-donated prizes (Geller, Johnson, & Pelton, 1982; Geller, Paterson, & Talbott, 1982); (b) employee raffles (Geller, 1982); and (c) bingo games (Geller, Johnson, & Pelton, 1982; Johnson & Geller, 1984). Similar methods could be employed as a way to increase recruitment activity among organizational members.

Training citizens in surveillance skills, security survey procedures, or target-hardening techniques is an important part of any effective citizen crime prevention program. Even with creative incentive tactics, citizens will not engage in crime prevention behaviors if these behaviors have not been learned. Educational strategies include both one-time presentations and ongoing information programs in which participants are provided with crime prevention techniques. A prominent behavioral technique, programmed instruction, could be adapted as a strategy to teach important crime prevention practices and train volunteers to conduct security surveys and dissemination tactics. Similarly, Winett *et al.* (1982), who have been investigating the value of media presentations on energy conservation behavior, suggest that such presentations can have substantial large-scale impact beyond that produced by simple group discussions and other instructional techniques.

Large-scale applications would be a prerequisite for media strategies to be cost-effective; however, some potential problems must be addressed prior to widespread use of the media for crime prevention purposes (Sacco & Silverman, 1982). For instance, media-depicted crime prevention could lead to citizen isolation and withdrawal if it heightens the fear of potential victims. Nonetheless, crime prevention through mass media has clear potential for introducing citizen crime prevention techniques to a large portion of the population.

In commenting on the lack of maintenance of viable block clubs, Washnis (1976) cited the need for formal training of leaders. The importance of leadership in successful crime prevention programs has been emphasized by a number of sources (Roehl, Berger, & Cook, 1982; Taylor & Shumaker, 1982; Washnis, 1976). Roehl et al. suggested that organization and communication skills are common characteristics of successful project leaders. One may ask, "Can these skills be trained?" Behavior practitioners have designed a number of instructional training programs with the goal of reducing dependence on professional change agents. For example, the training of teachers (Copeland & Hall, 1976) and parents (Graziano, 1977) as behavior managers has reduced the time and expense required for maintaining behavior change programs in the school and home. With respect to citizen crime prevention efforts, Fawcett, Miller, and Braukmann (1977) have described an effective package for training community canvassing behaviors. By identifying skills that constitute effective leadership and adapting the techniques cited before, practioners could foster the development of a behavioral training technology for community leadership in crime prevention.

Training technology might also be applied to specific types of criminal acts. For example, the crime of rape has been the focus of numerous research efforts. One concern has been to identify those behaviors likely to promote protection from an attack or prevent an attack altogether (Bart, 1980). Some researchers have attempted to package and disseminate rape prevention "techniques" to the general public (Storaska, 1975). The development of tactics to ward off sexual assault is certainly a worthy area for applied research because considerable controversy still exists regarding the effectiveness of these strategies across situations (Estrella & Forst, 1981).

Common "bunko" operations or "scams" and confidence games might be combated by teaching citizens the tactics used in credit card fraud and theft, passing bad checks, and bank/insurance schemes. A prime target for such instructional packages is the elderly (Cook, Skogan, Cook, & Antunes, 1978). Moreover, Powell (1981) noted that the worst problem for elderly citizens is "fear" of victimization that frequently leads to withdrawal and isolation resembling a self-imposed house arrest. Training and education packages for this group could have added value if they identify and foster alternative behaviors incompatible with social isolation, namely organizing, joining, and attending citizen crime prevention meetings.

With enrollment and mobilization activities underway, a shift in goals and behavior targets is often warranted (Taylor & Shumaker, 1982). At this point, one can make an important distinction between *involvement*—the number of residents enrolled or reached, and *participation*. The latter refers to behaviors contributing directly to actual crime prevention objectives.

Consider the fact that block clubs typically require participant willingness to exchange information about personal schedules and habits, to watch others' homes, and to report suspicious activities to police. This commitment by residents has been difficult both to promote and measure (Bickman *et al.*, 1977). A partial solution to this problem is the use of pledge card commitment programs. For example, Geller (1982) described a successful safety-belt incentive program that provided opportunities for signing and turning in a "seatbelt pledge card." Signing the pledge provided a chance to win a weekly lottery, and it also represented a public commitment to "buckle up" (see also Streff & Geller, 1986). Similar designed programs might be useful for increasing citizen crime prevention program commitment and the likelihood that participants would actively engage in CCP activities.

Facilitating Citizen Crime Prevention with Response Consequences

Maximum feasible participation is a catch phrase associated with the war on poverty programs of the 1960s. Gluck (1978) wrote that the phrase has never been adequately operationalized. A behavioral approach, however, requires precisely defined, attainable goals for recruitment (e.g., identifying the percentage of residents needed for organizing activities). This is consonant with Dixon's (1978) recommendation that practitioners establish a workable model of citizen crime prevention participation. With targeted participation rates in place, both verbal and written feedback mechanisms can be employed to demonstrate the status of recruiting efforts and the adequacy of neighborhood coverage. The positive impact of response feedback on performance is a consistent finding in the psychologial literature (Annett, 1969).

A contributing factor to the maintenance problem in citizen crime prevention programs was suggested by the National Advisory Commission on Criminal Justice Standards and Goals (1974):

> Many anticrime organizations are born as the result of local crises, and become crises-dependent for their continued existence. If subsequent crises do not materialize the organization loses motivation and momentum. (p. 18)

Several studies relevant to program maintenance suggest a number of strategies for sustaining citizen crime prevention programs. For example, Miller and Miller (1970) demonstrated that practical forms of incentives, namely donated items such as clothing and household goods, increased the attendance of welfare recipients at self-help community organization meetings. Other applications of behavioral community psychology have used reward procedures to increase attendance and participation of elderly citizens in senior center programs (Bunck & Iwata, 1978) and participation of neighborhood service center staff in a helping skills program (Stokes, Mathews, & Fawcett, 1978). These procedures could be criticized as somewhat "contrived"; however, they represent means by which programs of value can be maintained.

Actual surveillance behavior is virtually impossible to observe or monitor, except when the observation of a crime or suspicious activity is verbally reported to police. A partial solution to this problem would be the use of self-monitoring or surveillance logs by participants. Self-monitoring was sufficient to maintain the daily recording of residential electricity meters and subsequent energy savings (Winett, Neale, & Grier, 1979). A checklist could be used for daily, weekly, or monthly recording of surveillance activities and checked by block leaders or program managers on an intermittent basis. Incentive programs could be instituted to reinforce the self-monitored surveillance manifested by these data. Obviously, this strategy would not be practical on a continuous basis but could be useful as an occasional prompting strategy for increasing and maintaining surveillance tactics (or at least the reporting of surveillance).

SUMMARY

Many efforts have been made to involve citizen volunteer groups in crime prevention programs. The procedures applied have not been well defined, and the outcomes of such programs are ambiguous. Furthermore, the role of police departments in the development of citizen programs are not well specified. A conceptual framework that assists in the planning of future citizen crime prevention programs has been outlined in the latter half of this chapter. In addition, a behavior change technology to facilitate the organization of effective crime prevention has been described.

In the light of the limitations of traditional patrol and apprehension programs, as described in the first half of this chapter, police and others are seeking nontraditional methods to prevent crime. It seems clear that police departments, which already dedicate personnel to public relations and crime prevention, are in the best position to implement the technical principles described in this chapter. The use of a community behavior change technology to organize citizen groups would be a significant departure from normal police procedures. Likewise, the use that has been made of behavioral technology in the Nashville Police Department to attempt to improve police patrol, investigation, apprehension, and prosecution efforts represents a significant departure from normal police procedures. Nevertheless, such departures seem justified by the limitations of traditional police crime prevention efforts.

REFERENCES

Annett, J. (1969). *Feedback and human behavior: The effects of knowledge of results, incentives and reinforcement on learning and performance.* Baltimore: Penguin Books.

Bandura, A. (1969). *Principles of behavior modification.* New York: Holt, Rineheart & Winston.

Bart, P. (1980). *Avoiding rape: A study of victims and avoiders* (Final Report). Washington, DC: National Institute of Mental Health.

Bickman, L., Lavrakas, P. J., Green, S. K., North-Walker, N. Edwards, J., Borkowski, S., Shane-Dubow, S., & Wuerth J. (1977) *Citizen crime reporting projects* (National Evaluation Program Phase I Summary Report). Washington, DC: U.S. Government Printing Office.

Bunck, T. J., & Iwata, B. A. (1978). Increasing senior citizen participation in a community-based nutrituous meals program. *Journal of Applied Behavior Analysis, 11,* 75–86.

Carr, A. E., Schnelle, J. F., Kirchner, R. E., Larson, L. E. & Risley, T. R. (1980). Effective police field supervision: A report writing program evaluation program. *Journal of Police Science and Administration, 8,* 212–222.

Clarke, R. V. G. (1980). Situational crime prevention: Theory and practice. *British Journal of Criminology, 20,* 136–147.

Cook, F. L., Skogan, W. G., Cook, T. D., & Antunes, G. E. (1978). Criminal victimization of the elderly: The physical and economic consequences. *The Gerontologist, 18,* 338–349.

Copeland, R., & Hall, V. (1976). Behavior modification in the classroom. In M. Hersen, R. M. Eisler, & P. M. Miller (Eds.), *Progress in behavior modification* (Vol. 3, pp. 45–78). New York: Academic Press.

Davis, E. M., & Knowles, L. (1975). A critique of the report: An evaluation of the Kansas City preventive patrol experiment. *Police Chief, 6,* 123–128.

Dixon, R. W. (1978). *Practice of crime prevention: Understanding crime prevention* (Vol. 1). Louisville: National Crime Prevention Institute.

Domash, M. A., Schnelle, J. F., Stromatt, E. L., Stromatt, A. F., Larson, L. D., Kirchner, R. E., & Risley, T. R. (1980). Police and prosecution systems: An evaluation of a police criminal case preparation program. *Journal of Applied Analysis, 13,* 397–406.

Estrella, M. M., & Forst, M. L. (1981). *Family guide to crime prevention.* New York: Beaufort Books.

Fawcett, S. B., Miller, L. K., & Braukmann, C. J. (1977). An evaluation of a training package for community canvassing behaviors. *Journal of Applied Behavior Analysis, 10,* 31–47.

Geller, E. S. (1982). *Corporate incentives for promoting safety belt use: Rationale, guidelines and examples.* Washington, DC: U.S. Department of Transportation.

Geller, E. S., Johnson, R. P., & Pelton, S. L. (1982). Community-based interventions for encouraging safety belt use. *American Journal of Community Psychology, 10,* 183–195.

Geller, E. S., Paterson, L., & Talbott, E. (1982). A behavioral analysis of incentive prompts for motivating seat belt use. *Journal of Applied Behavior Analysis, 15,* 403–415.

Geller, E. S., Winett, R. A., & Everett, P. B. (1982). *Preserving the environment: New strategies for behavior change.* New York: Pergamon Press.

Geller, E. S., Koltuniak, T. A., & Shilling, J. S. (1984). Response avoidance prompting: A cost-effective strategy for theft deterrence. *Behavioral Counseling and Community Interventions, 3,* 28–42.

Gluck, P. R. (1978). Citizen participation in urban services—Administration of a community-based crime prevention program. *Journal of Voluntary Action Research, 7,* 33–44.

Graziano, A. M. (1977). Parents as behavior therapists. In M. Hersen, R. M. Eisler & P. M. Miller (Eds.), *Progress in behavior modification* (Vol. 4, pp. 251–298). New York: Academic Press.

Greenwood, P. W., Chaiken, J. M., Petersilia, J., & Prusoff, L. (1975). *The criminal investigation process, Volume III: Observations and analysis.* Santa Monica, CA: The RAND Corporation.

Heller, N. B., Stenzel, W. W., Gill, A. D., Kolde, R. A., & Schimerman, S. R. (1975). *Operation identification Projects: Assessment of effectiveness* (National Evaluation Program Phase I Summary Report). Washington, DC: U.S. Government Printing Office.

International Training, Research, and Evaluation Council. (1977). *Crime prevention security surveys* (National Evaluation Program Phase I Summary Report). Washington, DC: U.S. Government Printing Office.

Johnson, R. P., & Geller, E. S. (1984). Contingent versus noncontingent rewards for promoting seat belt usage. *Journal of Community Psychology, 12,* 113–122.

Kakalik, J. S., & Weldon, S. (1971). *Aids to decision making in police patrol.* A report prepared for the Department of Housing and Urban Development. Santa Monica, CA: RAND Corporation.

Kelling, G. L., Pate, T., Diekmann, D., & Brown, C. E. (1975). *The Kansas City preventive patrol experiment: A technical report.* Washington, DC: Police Foundation.

Kirchner, R. E., Schnelle, J. F., Domash, M., Larson, L., Carr, A., & McNees, M. P. (1980). The applicability of a helicopter patrol procedure to diverse areas: A cost-benefit evaluation. *Journal of Applied Behavior Analysis, 13,* 143–148.

Larson, R. C. (1972). *Urban police patrol analysis.* Cambridge: M.I.T. Press.

Lavrakas, P. J., & Herz, E. J. (1982). Citizen participation in neighborhood crime prevention. *Criminology, 20,* 479–498.

Lawler, E. E., & Hackman, J. R. (1969). Impact of employee participation in the development of pay incentive plans: A field experiment. *Journal of Applied Psychology, 53,* 467–471.

Lindsley, O. (1964). Direct measurement and prosthesis of retarded behavior. *Journal of Education, 147,* 62–81.

McClannahan, L. E., & Risley, T. R. (1975). Design of living environments for nursing home residents. *Journal of Applied Behavior Analysis, 8,* 261–268.

McNees, M. P., Egli, D. S., Marshall, R. S., Schnelle, J. F., & Risley, T. R. (1976). Shoplifting prevention: Providing information through signs. *Journal of Applied Behavior Analysis, 9,* 399–405.

Miller, L. K., & Miller, L. (1970). Reinforcing self-help group activities of welfare recipients. *Journal of Applied Behavior Analysis, 3,* 57–64.

National Advisory Commission on Criminal Justice Standards and Goals. (1974). *A call for citizen action: Crime prevention and the citizen.* Washington, DC: U.S. Government Printing Office.

Ostrom, E. (1978). Citizen participation in policing: What do we know? *Journal of Voluntary Action Research, 7,* 102–108.

Pate, T., Bowers, R. A., & Parks, R. (1976). *Three approaches to criminal apprehension in Kansas City: An evaluation report.* Washington, DC: Police Foundation.

Porter, L. W., Lawler, E. E., & Hackman, J. R. (1975). *Behavior in organizations.* New York: McGraw-Hill.

Roehl, J. A., Berger, K., & Cook, R. F. (1982). *National evaluation of the urban crime prevention program* (Interim Report). Washington, DC: Institute for Social Analysis.

Sacco, V. F., & Silverman, R. A. (1982). Crime prevention through mass media: Prospects and problems. *Journal of Criminal Justice, 10,* 257–269.

Schnelle, J. F., & Golden, S. (1982). *Participatory management in police work.* Unpublished manuscript, Middle Tennessee State University.

Schnelle, J. F., Kirchner, R. E., Lawler, J. R., & McNees, M. P. (1975). Social evaluation research: The evaluation of two police patrol strategies. *Journal of Applied Behavior Analysis, 8,* 232–240.

Schnelle, J. F., Kirchner, R. E., Casey, J. D., Uselton, P. H., & McNees, M. P. (1977). Patrol evaluation research: A multiple-baseline analysis of saturation police patrolling during day and night hours. *Journal of Applied Behavior Analysis, 10,* 33–40.

Schnelle, J. F., Kirchner, R. E., Macrae, J. W., McNees, M. P., Eck, R. H., Sondgrass, S., Casey, J. D., & Uselton, P. H. (1978). Police evaluation research: An experimental and cost-benefit analysis of a helicopter patrol in high crime area. *Journal of Applied Behavior Analysis, 11,* 11–21.

Schnelle, J. F., Kirchner, R. E., Galbaugh, F., Domash, M., Carr, A., & Larson, L. (1979). Program evaluation research: An experimental cost-effectiveness analysis of an area robbery intervention program. *Journal of Applied Behavior Analysis, 12,* 615–623.

Skogan, W. G., & Antunes, G. E. (1979). Information apprehension and deterrence: Exploring the limits of police productivity. *Journal of Criminal Justice, 7,* 217, 241.

Sliwa, L. (1983). Urban crime and citizen action. *Community Action, 1,* 17–20.

Streff, F., & Geller, E. S. (1986). Strategies for motivating safety belt use: The application of applied behavior analysis. *Health Education Research, 1,* 47–59.

Stokes, T. F., Mathews, R. M., & Fawcett, S. B. (1978). Promoting participation in a community-based educational program. *Journal of Personalized Instruction, 3,* 29–31.

Storaska, F. (1975). *How to say no to a rapist and survive.* New York: Random House.

Taylor, R. B., & Shumaker, S. A. (1982). *Community crime prevention in review: Problems, progress, and evaluations.* Baltimore, MD: Center for Metropolitan Planning and Research, John Hopkins University.

Twardosz, S., Cataldo, M. F., & Risley, T. R. (1974). An open environment design for infant and toddler day care. *Journal of Applied Behavior Analysis, 4,* 529–546.

Washnis, G. J. (1976). *Citizen involvement in crime prevention.* Lexington, MA: Lexington Books.

Winett, R. A., Neale, M. S., & Grier, H. C. (1979). The effects of self-monitoring and feedback on residential electricity consumption. *Journal of Applied Behavior Analysis, 12,* 173–184.

Winett, R. A., Hatcher, J. W., Fort, T. R., Leckliter I. N., Love, J. Q., Riley, A. W., & Fishback, J. F. (1982). The effects of videotape modeling and daily feedback on residential electricity conservation, home temperature and humidity, perceived comfort, and clothing worn: Winter and Summer. *Journal of Applied Behavior Analysis, 12,* 381–402.

Yin, R. K. Vogel, M. E., Chaiken, J. M., & Both, D. R. (1977). *Citizen patrol projects* (National Evaluation Program, Phase I Summary Report). Washington, DC: U.S. Government Printing Office.

9

Diversion and Neighborhood Delinquency Programs in Open Settings
A Social Network Interpretation

CLIFFORD R. O'DONNELL, MICHAEL J. MANOS, AND
MEDA CHESNEY-LIND

The purpose of this chapter is to examine and interpret the results of diversion and neighborhood delinquency programs, both of which contain some similarities and differences. In a general sense, both are designed to divert youths from delinquency and, given that their intent is the same, the division into the two categories is somewhat arbitrary. For historical reasons, however, *diversion* refers to alternatives for those youths who would otherwise be processed in a court of law and, in some cases, be placed in a correctional institution. In contrast, *neighborhood programs* are designed for those youths considered at higher risk for delinquency than other youths, rather than as alternatives for court processing. Though some neighborhood programs accept court referrals, these programs are not under the jurisdiction of the court and accept referrals from other sources. Participation in neighborhood programs is voluntary.

Both diversion and neighborhood programs developed within a social service tradition. These programs attempt to reduce delinquency by providing youths with counseling, health care, foster placement, employment opportunities, and recreational, social, and academic activities in various combinations. In general, more of these services are provided in the neighborhood programs because their purpose is to meet the needs of youth to the extent that program resources allow. The implicit assumption is that delinquency is, at least in part, a result of the lack of these resources. In contrast, the primary purpose of diversion programs is to serve as an alternative to court processing.

Behavioral neighborhood delinquency programs (e.g., Schwitzgebel & Kolb, 1964; Tharp & Wetzel, 1969) developed within this social service tradi-

Clifford R. O'Donnell • Department of Psychology and Youth Development and Research Center, University of Hawaii at Manoa, Honolulu, Hawaii 96822. **Michael J. Manos** • Youth Development and Research Center, University of Hawaii at Manoa, Honolulu, Hawaii 96822. **Meda Chesney-Lind** • Youth Development and Research Center and Women's Studies Program, University of Hawaii at Manoa, Honolulu, Hawaii 96822.

tion, were based on the development of behavioral principles, and were influenced by behavioral applications in other areas such as education. The behaviorists contributed to this tradition, conceptually, by showing how delinquent behavior might be learned; technically, by implementing behavior change techniques; and methodologically, by placing a greater emphasis on specificity of measurement, research design, and program evaluation. The behavioral and nonbehavioral neighborhood programs, however, share common goals, activities, and services, and, as presented later, consistent results. For these reasons, behavioral and nonbehavioral programs are integrated where appropriate in this review.

Following the presentations of diversion and neighborhood programs, a social network interpretation of these program results is offered. The implications of the interpretation for these programs and the development of future alternatives are discussed.

DIVERSION

The concept of diversion began with the establishment of the juvenile court at the turn of this century (Levine & Levine, 1970). The purpose of the juvenile court was to divert delinquent youth from the processing of the adult court system and thereby provide for protection and assistance in a paternal manner. By the 1920s, the assistance was typically individual casework and institutional care (Levine & Levine, 1970). Over the years, the juvenile court system came to be increasingly criticized for its failure to provide constitutional rights, its ineffectiveness in reducing delinquency, and its inappropriate responsiveness to socioeconomic status and community pressure (Blakely & Davidson, 1981).

Ironically, it became necessary to divert youth from the juvenile court. This need became apparent with two events: the Supreme Court decision in *Gault* (1967), which specified the constitutional rights of juveniles, and the recommendation of the President's Commission on Law Enforcement and the Administration of Justice (1967) that alternatives to the juvenile court be developed. The recognized need for diversion culminated in the passage of the landmark Juvenile Justice and Delinquency Prevention Act of 1974 that encouraged both the diversion of youth offenders from court processing and the deinstitutionalization of status offenders. This act also funded the implementation and evaluation of community-based alternatives. In most cases, these alternatives involved counseling, sometimes with family members, and release. Foster care or residential placement was typically available when necessary. Both the diversion of status offenders from institutions, commonly referred to as *deinstitutionalization,* and the diversion of youth offenders from court processing are considered later.

Overall, deinstitutionalization programs have demonstrated little effect on offense rates, typically measured by official statistics such as arrests and court contacts (Klein, 1979; Kobrin & Klein, 1982). For example, when institutionalization was compared to a deinstitutionalization program that provided crisis intervention, brief counseling, and temporary placement if necessary, no differences in delinquent offenses and only a modest reduction in status offenses emerged (Spergel, Reamer, & Lynch, 1981). Klein (1979) reviewed six programs and reported that the results were positive for only one and equivocal for five. In addition, in each of the eight sites of the National Evaluation of the Deinstitutionalization of Status Offender Programs (Kobrin & Klein, 1982), little difference in recidivism occurred between program groups and those who left the institutions before the programs began. The positive side to these results is that deinstitutionalization does not seem to increase offense rates. Indeed, in a study of juvenile crime, rates did not increase following the closing of juvenile correctional institutions in Massachusetts (Coates, Miller, & Ohlin, 1978). Therefore, as Kobrin and Klein (1982) concluded, the absence of an effect of deinstitutionalization on recidivism does not support reinstitutionalization because the same results were achieved with deinstitutionalization as with incarceration but at a lower cost.

Klein (1979) also reviewed 13 programs of diversion from court processing and reported that the results were positive for 3, negative for 2, and equivocal for 8. Since that review, a variation in the counseling of referred juveniles has developed in which they are confronted with the possible consequences of delinquent behavior. The original program of this type, the Juvenile Awareness Project at Rahway State Prison in New Jersey, received widespread attention through the award-winning film, *Scared Straight*. The Rahway plan was simple and dramatic. Referred youth were taken in groups into a maximum security prison for a grueling 2-hour session with inmates. Claims made in the film that the program was 90% successful encouraged some 38 states to explore and, in many cases, to institute similar programs. Evaluations of these programs using matched control groups, however, indicated higher arrest rates among boys who participated in the program (Buckner & Chesney-Lind, 1983; Finckenauer, 1979).

It has been suggested that this dearth of positive results may be due to the poor implementation of diversion programs (Klein, 1979). These programs did not divert and, by selecting clients who would not otherwise enter the criminal justice system, they actually "widened the net." For example, in one study, counsel-and-release treatment did not decrease referrals to the juvenile court and reduced delinquency only among those who were not likely to be referred to the juvenile court anyway (Lipsey, Cordray, & Berger, 1981). The failure to divert and the extension of contact to additional youngsters is undesirable for two reasons. First, it contradicts the purpose of the program to divert and, by doing so, does not permit an evaluation of the effectiveness of diversion. Second, there is some evidence, presented later, to suggest that contact with the criminal justice system is associated with a higher rate of offenses.

By their very nature, diversion programs involve some contact with the criminal justice system. Even counsel-and-release treatment requires contact to arrange counseling and process the release. More extensive programs maintain contact when the programs are administered by the police or court. In these cases, the youths have been diverted from the more traditional punitive processing but not from the criminal justice system. Worst of all, contact is extended to others when programs accept referrals of juveniles who would not otherwise enter the system.

The effect of contact with the criminal justice system can be assessed by comparisons between groups with different degrees of contact. In one study, youths on probation who were not contacted by a probation officer had fewer and less serious subsequent offenses than did those who were contacted (McEachern, Taylor, Newman, & Ashford, 1968). Although the youths were not randomly assigned, this result could not be explained by prior offense history because those who did not receive probation services had a worse record. In addition, Klein (1979, p. 192; Lincoln, Teilman, Klein, & Labin, 1977) was able to assign juveniles randomly to conditions of release, referral to a community-based diversion program, or to regular court processing. Although self-report data indicated no differences in delinquent activity, official recidivism over 27 months was lowest for those who were released and highest for those processed by the court. This suggests that those who have the most contact with the court may be more likely to be arrested independent of delinquent behavior.

Three studies have included a comparison with those who have had no contact with the criminal justice system. Ageton and Elliott (1974) examined self-reports from over 2,300 students in each of their 4 years in high school. They found that among those who reported engaging in delinquent acts, the scores on the Socialization scale of the California Psychological Inventory of those who were apprehended by the police changed in a more asocial direction than those who were not apprehended. In a more direct evaluation, Gold and Williams (1969) matched youths who had been arrested for delinquent behavior with those who had self-reported an undetected offense at about the same time. Although the small sample ($N=20$) precluded a firm conclusion, in well over half of the comparisons, youths who were caught went on to commit more offenses than their unapprehended counterparts. Finally, Farrington (1977) compared 14-year-old boys with similar self-reported delinquency and found a subsequent increase in delinquency for those who were convicted of a crime by the age of 18 and a decrease in delinquency for those who did not appear in court. Although each of these studies requires some qualification and additional evidence, a clear direction is apparent: the less contact with the criminal justice system, including its diversion programs, the better.

The juvenile court was established to divert youths from adult courts, and diversion programs were developed to divert youths from the juvenile court. But, before we discuss diverting youths from diversion programs, we should consider the results of programs not under the jurisdiction of the criminal justice system. For if these latter programs are not more effective, then something other than just diversion is needed. In this section, we examine neighborhood intervention and discuss the findings with those of diversion programs.

NEIGHBORHOOD INTERVENTION

Neighborhood intervention comes in many forms. The general term is used here to indicate nonresidential delinquency projects that are not based exclusively on the family, school, or court. The two forms reviewed next are (1) those in which various activities are made available in high-delinquency areas and (2) those in which services are offered to high-risk youths referred by police, courts, schools, parents, and social agencies. All provide many more forms of intervention than counseling and residential placement.

Activities in High-Delinquency Areas

The rationale for developing programs in high-delinquency areas is that delinquency can be reduced by offering group activities as alternatives to delinquent behavior. Some programs have offered payment for interviews and tests (Schwitzgebel & Kolb, 1964), recreation (e.g., Burchard, Harig, Miller, & Amour, 1976; Pierce & Risley, 1974), academic training (e.g., O'Donnell & Stanley, 1973), or all three (e.g., O'Donnell, Chambers, & Ling, 1973). In a past innovation, Stumphauzer, Veloz, and Aiken (1981) examined the activities of nondelinquents who resided in a high-delinquency area and used this information to develop alternatives to gang activities (e.g., escort services for the elderly and the cleanup of high-crime properties). Although studies in these areas have presented successful in-program evaluations, none offered adequate comparisons on delinquency. Indeed, because of self-selection factors, comparisons are difficult to make when youths voluntarily make differential use of facilities.

This problem of self-selection occurs less frequently in projects where social workers form relationships with juvenile gangs and organize activities. In the Midcity project (Miller, 1962), intensive contact was established with seven different gangs totaling 205 members. Social workers spent an average of about 20 hours a week with their groups over a 10- to 34-month period. They organized club meetings, athletics, dances, and fund-raising dinners, provided counseling, referred some youths for therapy, and served as intermediaries with agencies. Despite these efforts, no significant pre-post differences in delinquency data were reported by the detached workers in official statistics or in age-adjusted frequency of court appearances. Nor did any differences occur in analyses with five comparison gangs.

In the Group Guidance Project (Klein, 1971), similar activities were implemented with four gangs with a total membership of about 800. An analysis of age-adjusted offense frequencies obtained from probation records over 8 years revealed a clear association between the project and an increase in delinquency among the gang members. Further analysis showed that the project was associated with this increase in delinquency because the program activities increased the size and cohesiveness of the gangs. In effect, fringe members became more involved with the core gang members because of participation in the activities offered by the project. Also, the increase in offenses was among those ordinarily committed with others and not in those typically committed alone. As a result of these findings, Klein altered his strategy. Instead of offering services to gang members that increased their contact with each other, a new program was designed to reduce gang activities and membership.

This program, called the Ladino Hills Project (Klein, 1971), focused on employment as an alternative to gang activity and gang cohesiveness. Cohesiveness was measured by the direct observation of gang members on the street during regular driving patrols. A comparison of 49 boys with periods of both employment and unemployment showed that they were less likely to be observed on the street on working days. In addition, their probation records revealed that their offenses occurred more frequently during their periods of unemployment. For the gang as a whole, cohesiveness decreased by up to 40% and the total number of offenses by 35%. The number of offenses per member did not change, but the reduction in the size of the gang reduced the total number of offenses. Because members were not followed up after they left the gang, it is not known how many continued delinquent activities on their own. Given that youths left gang membership and that the data from the two projects supported a strong relationship between delinquent and gang activities, it is reasonable to assume that their participation in delinquent activities was reduced. Nevertheless, documentation of the magnitude of the change would have been useful in assessing the effectiveness of this form of intervention.

Services to Referred Youths

A tradition of obtaining referrals from the police, schools, parents, and social agencies and providing multiple services began with the well-known Cambridge-Somerville Youth Study in 1935 (McCord, 1978). In this tradition, access to these services is through a trained worker assigned to each youngster. Two of these projects offered comprehensive services such as family assistance, academic tutoring, medical and psychiatric attention, group sessions with peers and parents, summer camps, and recreation. In the first project, the Cambridge-Somerville Youth Study, boys between 5 and 13 years of age were visited by a counselor an average of twice a month for about 5 years (McCord, 1978). In the other project, the Seattle Atlantic Street Center Experiment (Berleman, Seaberg, & Steinburn, 1972), seventh-grade boys aged 12 to 14 were contacted by a male social worker an average of 171 times per year for 1 to 2 years. In both of these studies, youths were carefully matched and randomly assigned to treatment and control groups. The results were strikingly the same: although the programs were highly rated by the participants, objective measures indicated that few differences emerged, and those that did favored the control groups. These measures included an 18-month follow-up of police contacts and school discipline in the Seattle study and a remarkable 30-

year follow-up of criminal behavior, death, disease, occupational status, and job satisfaction in the Cambridge-Somerville study (McCord, 1978).

Behaviorists entered this tradition with the classic work of Tharp and Wetzel (1969). The services were less comprehensive than previous programs that offered services to referred youths but were specifically designed to improve the referred behavior. These interventions were based on a triadic model in which a small number of professional consultants supervised a larger number of indigenous nonprofessionals, who intervened with a larger number of youths (Tharp & Wetzel, 1969). Individual intervention plans based on contingency contracting were developed. Overall, the targeted behaviors improved (Fo & O'Donnell, 1974; Tharp & Wetzel, 1969).

In two studies, the effects of this type of behavioral program on delinquent offenses were assessed in comparisons with youths randomly assigned to control groups. In the first study, comparisons over 3 years with 335 project and 218 control youngsters showed lower arrest rates for youths in the program who had been arrested for a major offense in the prior year but higher arrest rates for those without such an arrest (O'Donnell, Lydgate, & Fo, 1979). It appeared that the program was helpful for more serious offenders and harmful for those with minor or no recent arrests, perhaps because of contact between these two groups within the program. In the other study, less serious offenders were specifically excluded, and opportunities for contact among the participants were minimized (Davidson et al., 1977; E. Seidman, 1984, personal communication). In a 2-year follow-up, self-reports indicated no differences with the control group, but some success was indicated in that official police and court contact data favored the program youth.

Finally, some programs have offered primarily employment-related activities to older youth. As was the case with street gangs, these studies also have demonstrated some success. Mills and Walter (1977) trained court-referred youth with felony convictions in basic job skills and their employers in the use of reinforcement. Behavior contracts were developed between the employers and the delinquents. A comparison group was formed of those for whom a job was not available within 1 week of referral. One year after the initial interview, 91% of the participants and only 30% of those in the comparison group were arrest-free. Although random assignment was not possible in this study, it was achieved in two other studies. In the first, Quay and Love (1977) evaluated the Juvenile Services Program that provided employment and academic and counseling services. Their data indicated the program was effective with some participants, mostly those with status rather than criminal offenses and for those not referred by the juvenile court. In the second, Shore and Massimo (1979) presented a 15-year follow-up on 19 boys who had a history of school and antisocial problems. Ten had participated in their vocationally oriented counseling, evaluation, and placement program, and 9 were in the control group. Among the 10 in the program, 7 had successful employment histories and 7 were arrest-free, compared to 4 and 1, respectively, of the 9 control males. Although the numbers are small, the findings provide some support for an employment-oriented approach. These results are discussed within the context of the pattern of findings from the diversion and neighborhood intervention programs that follows.

A SOCIAL NETWORK INTERPRETATION

A social network interpretation of the results of diversion and neighborhood programs is presented first and is followed by a social network interpretation of the association between delinquency and contact with delinquent peers.

Results of Diversion and Neighborhood Programs

A number of possible conclusions can be drawn from this overview of diversion and neighborhood programs. One is to advocate a policy of no intervention for status offenders and the least possible contact with the criminal justice system for minor offenders. The results of the diversion programs support this conclusion, which has indeed been suggested before (Schur, 1973). In addition, the data support employment-based intervention with older youth and a consideration of other alternatives for younger children. Burchard and Lane (1982) came to this conclusion in their excellent review of behavioral programs in crime and delinquency. Their careful analysis supported a greater emphasis on family interventions for younger adolescents.

Although not in disagreement with these conclusions, we suggest that a key link through these studies is the social network of youth. The findings of the diversion studies suggest that contact with the criminal justice system is an important variable. Such contact affects the social network of youth by increasing interactions with people in official positions within the criminal justice system. Some of these people can directly influence the likelihood of arrest. For example, probation officers may become aware of probation violations in the course of their contact with the youths; moreover, police officers' perception as well as prior knowledge of the juvenile may influence their decisions to arrest (Chambliss, 1973; Piliavin & Briar, 1964). This social network effect may help to explain the higher official recidivism rates of those processed in court even when their self-reports show no differences in delinquency from those who were not processed in court (Farrington, 1977; Klein, 1979, p. 192). In addition, relationships with delinquent peers would be expected to increase with the amount of contact with the criminal justice system.

Many studies have demonstrated the importance of peer relationships in delinquency (e.g., Belson, 1975; Voss, 1969). The results indicate that, aside from previous delinquent behavior, the strongest prediction of delinquency is association with delinquent peers (Hawkins & Lishner, 1987). The strength of this association was illustrated in a study of delinquency among high-school students (Ageton & Elliott, 1974). A self-report measure was used to assess the students' delinquency level. In addition, the self-reported delinquency level of each participant's peers was derived from the list of students named by the student as those with whom there was the most contact. The summary of these data presented in Table 1 show that as the delinquency level of the student rises, the percentage of peers with a high delinquency level increases markedly.

The social network of youth is also affected by the group nature of many of the activities of the neighborhood intervention programs. The group sessions, summer camps, and recreational activities provided by the multiservice programs of the Cambridge-Somerville Youth Study (McCord, 1978) and the Seattle Atlantic Street Center Experiment (Berleman et al., 1972) offered numerous opportunities for the development of peer contact and friendship relationships. The procedures of the Buddy System (Fo & O'Donnell, 1974; O'Donnell et al., 1979) ensured these relationships because three youngsters from the same neighborhood were assigned to each "buddy," who often interacted with them as a group, and programwide social activities included all of the youngsters in the program. These opportunities for contact among participants with and without criminal records were thought responsible for the reverse effects on arrest rates, which increased for those without a record of a major offense in the prior year and decreased for those with such a record. If this type of network effect occurred in the Cambridge-Somerville and Seattle Atlantic programs, it certainly would have mitigated against any beneficial

Table 1.   The Self-Reported Delinquency
Level of High-School Students
and Their Peers[a]

Delinquency level			
Student	Peers	N	%
Low	Low	449	53
	Moderate	144	17
	High	253	30
	Total	846	100
Moderate	Low	273	44
	Moderate	112	18
	High	232	38
	Total	617	100
High	Low	129	26
	Moderate	76	16
	High	285	58
	Total	490	100
	Grand total	1,953	

[a]Computed from the combined numbers of those with and without police contact presented in "The Effects of Legal Processing on Delinquent Orientations" by S. S. Ageton and D. S. Elliott, 1974, Social Problems, 22, Table 2.

aspects of the programs. The Buddy System appears to have been harmful to those with no or minor delinquency records and to have helped the more serious offenders by providing opportunities for friendships with those who were less delinquent.

This network interpretation is supported by comparison with the procedures and results of a similar program (Davidson et al., 1977). The Davidson program specifically excluded less serious offenders and minimized the opportunities for contact among the participants. This program was the only one of four similar programs (which includes Cambridge-Somerville, Seattle Atlantic, and the Buddy System) in which offenders were not likely to have contact with each other and the only one in which police and court data showed lower delinquency rates for the program group.

Additional support comes from an analysis of the Hawaii version of the Scared Straight program (Buckner & Chesney-Lind, 1983), which showed that the higher arrest rates among boys who participated in the session with prisoners was largely due to those who were members of other ongoing delinquency prevention programs. Specifically, no increase in arrests occurred among those who simply came to the session as part of a school activity. This result led to the conclusion that the negative effect was

> probably a product of some members of the treatment group's concurrent involvement in long-term delinquency prevention programs, rather than the simple result of exposure to the prisoner-run program itself. (p. 227)

In other words, the higher frequency of arrest occurred among those whose contact with delinquent peers was ensured by their participation in these other programs.

Klein's work with street gangs has provided what may be the most direct evidence for a network interpretation. In the Group Guidance Project, he found that the increase in the offenses of gang members was among those offenses ordinarily committed with others and not in those typically committed alone. The project was associated with this increase because the program activities increased the size and cohesiveness of the gangs. In effect, fringe members became more involved with core gang members because of participation in the activities offered by the project. In response to these results, the Ladino Hills project was designed to reduce gang cohesiveness by offering alternatives to group activity, such as employment efforts, instead of programs that brought members together. This strategy was successful in both decreasing cohesiveness and reducing the total number of offenses (Klein, 1971).

The Ladino Hills Project may be the only one in which the program was purposely designed to disrupt the delinquency network. Some of the activities of other programs, however, are also likely to affect peer contacts, and hence have positive effects. The results of Klein's study, for example, suggest that successful employment can reduce contact with delinquent friends, and thereby indicates that at least some of the success of employment-oriented programs (Mills & Walter, 1977; Quay & Love, 1977; Shore & Massimo, 1979) may be due to a network effect. Studies in which changes in peer contacts were examined also support this interpretation. For example, in one study, delinquency was associated with friendships made in high school among lower-achieving students; when some of these students dropped out of high school, peer contact and delinquency was reduced (Elliott & Voss, 1974). In another study of a comparison of those who stopped and those who continued to engage in delinquent acts, those who stopped had terminated contact with delinquent peers (Knight & West, 1975).

This social network interpretation of the results of the diversion and neighborhood intervention programs suggests that a major factor in the effectiveness of these programs is their effect on relationships, especially peer relationships. This is particularly important during follow-up, when the maintenance of program effects is assessed. Regardless of the nature of the intervention program, if contact with peers who are engaged in delinquent activities is increased, the effect of the intervention on delinquency will be diminished. In the case of status and less serious offenders, it is likely that delinquency will be increased. Despite the recognition of the importance of contact with delinquent peers, such contact is rarely considered in the design of intervention programs or in the assessment of their effects. The mistake made in the design of many of our programs is that they facilitate contacts among participants rather than with prosocial peers. Obviously, delinquency is not prevented by introducing youngsters to delinquents. What is needed are more interventions that specifically alter the social networks of youths to reduce contact with delinquent peers and increase prosocial relationships. Although the association between delinquency and contact with delinquent peers may be subject to several interpretations, interventions that alter youth networks are needed regardless of the cause of the association. The existence of the association in itself suggests that our efforts should be directed toward reducing contact among higher risk youths, rather than offering activities that facilitate their contact with each other. For diversion programs, this interpretation suggests that the objective include diversion of delinquent youths from contact with each other.

Association between Delinquency and Contact with Delinquent Peers

A social network interpretation of the association between delinquency and contact with delinquent peers may also be useful to help redesign our programs to reduce contact among delinquent youths. In this interpretation of how this association might occur, relationships among youths at higher risk for delinquency develop on the same basis as other relationships—propinquity and similarities are important. Many youths of about the same age, living in the same neighborhood, attending the same school, sharing common interests, and facing similar problems are likely to have contact with each other in the course of everyday activities. Those who, for example, face similar difficulties such as academic failure, abusive parents, or multiproblem families are also at higher risk for delinquency (Chesney-Lind, 1987; Rutter & Giller, 1984).

Continued academic failure among some adolescents can increase truancy, and chronic family problems can decrease the time spent at home as well as decrease the parental supervision of friends and activities. Therefore, some of these higher risk youths are likely to develop relationships with each other not only because of their similarities but also because they have more leisure time for peer activities due to their reduced involvement in school or family. Others may come together because of common interests in quasi-legal or illegal activities, such as drug use. And of course, the opportunities for these relationships to develop and be maintained are increased when group activities are provided by programs for youths referred because of their higher risk for delinquency.

Although the emphasis of this illustration is on the development of peer relationships, it is worth noting that these events affect other relationships as well. In effect, the social networks of the youths are altered to increase some peer relationships, at the expense of time spent in other activities. Relationships with those involved in these other activities are likely to be weakened by this change. The process that increases contact with delinquent peers may thereby reduce contact with prosocial peers or family members as well.

Social networks are used here to refer to the contacts among people, but these contacts occur in the course of activities. Therefore network changes are associated by their nature with changes in activities. The relationship is reciprocal—changes in activities increase the likelihood of changes in social contacts and vice versa (O'Donnell & Tharp, 1982). The greater the change in one, the more likely the change in the other. When networks are altered, the changes in activities occur in the direction consistent with the network changes. In one study, for example, randomly assigned high-ability college students performed better academically when they were placed in residence halls with other high-ability students (De Coster, 1966). In another study, Brown (1968) assigned science majors to floors in a residence hall dominated by humanity majors and humanity majors to floors dominated by science majors. More of those whose majors were in the minority changed their majors to those of the majority or became less certain of their choice. That delinquents also change their activities in the direction of their network was indicated in a study of the effect of marriage on the criminal records of males under the age of 21. Although their premarital delinquent records were matched, the criminal records of men after marriage were much worse for those who married women with a criminal record (Knight, Osborn, & West, 1977). Presumably, the network change of their marriages increased their criminal activities or, at least, altered their activities so as to make these husbands more likely to be arrested.

Activity changes can increase the chances of arrest of youths who have greater contact with delinquent peers in several ways. First, because such contact is likely to be at the expense of contact with school, family, or prosocial peers, more activities are likely to be peer-controlled or lacking adult involvement. Several findings link peer-controlled activities, especially those that include some delinquent peers, to delinquency. In their study of juvenile social networks, Schwendinger and Schwendinger (1982) found the least amount of delinquency in networks controlled by adults, and Wilson (1980) reported ineffective parental supervision as the variable most associated with delinquent activities. People who participate more in group activities report a greater sense of obligation and responsibility to others in the group (O'Donnell, 1980). Therefore, some youths may be more likely to engage in illegal activity because of the commitment to peers that they developed by their participation in peer-controlled activities. Others may have merely been present when one of their peers committed an illegal act. Of course, participation in these activities also provides opportunities for delinquent behavior to be learned through modeling, reinforcement, and exposure to new information and values. All of these possibilities would increase the chances of arrest of youths who have greater contact with delinquent peers. The frequency with which these or other possibilities actually result in delinquent behavior is not known. Longitudinal, naturalistic studies of peer-group activities are needed to address this important question.

This social network interpretation places delinquency within a matrix of transactions among behaviors, individuals, relationships, and activities. Therefore interventions that alter the social networks of youths are not likely to occur in programs that focus primarily on individual behaviors, for even when these behaviors change within the program, network relationships may remain the same. What is needed is a shift in emphasis from individual to network change. The implications of such a shift on delinquency programs are discussed in the following section.

IMPLICATIONS

A greater emphasis on network change will have little affect on the activities of some programs. The activities of these programs already promote network change and should be expanded. For example, successful employment programs typically have the natural consequence of reducing time in peer settings. In the Ladino Hills project (Klein, 1971), peer contacts, gang cohesiveness, and the total number of offenses were thereby reduced. Methods have been developed for the employment of young-adult offenders (Crozat & Kloss, 1979); work–study programs could be used with high-school students (Epstein, 1973). In addition to teaching useful skills, these programs may reduce the peer contact among lower-achieving students that has been associated with delinquency (Elliott & Voss, 1974).

It is possible that other programs could also be beneficial if their procedures were altered to discourage the development of a delinquent network. For example, multiple-service programs (such as Cambridge-Somerville, Seattle Atlantic, and the Buddy System) could minimize contacts among participants by providing services individually rather than in groups. The success of the one program that did so (i.e., Davidson et al., 1977) suggests that this can be a viable strategy. It may also be worthwhile to reexamine other types of programs that to date appear to have had no affect on delinquency. One such type of program is social skills training (Spence & Marzillier, 1981). Social skills training may be effective if the procedures did not permit contact among peers at higher risk for delinquency and if efforts were made to promote the new skills in the development of prosocial relationships and activities. An assessment of the activities of nondelinquent peers would be useful to determine the skills needed to promote these prosocial relationships.

In all projects, the assessment of the social networks of the participants would be informative for evaluation and program development. Minimally, such assessment is necessary to check for the existence of a delinquent network effect. The most important implication, however, will require more extensive program change. What has been suggested is that the effectiveness of delinquency programs has been impaired by the general lack of consideration of the context of delinquent behaviors within settings and social networks. The consideration of settings and social networks will require a systems approach. The relevance of a systems approach to delinquency is illustrated in the two examples that follow.

The first example of a systems approach is based on the concept of settings (O'Donnell, 1984). In this example, settings are locations in which organized activities occur. Settings provide participants with roles for the activities and access to the available resources. These roles and the use of the resources influence participation in the setting and affect the behavioral development and social networks of the participants. Roles are composed of specific behaviors. Participation is influenced by the demand for these behaviors relative to their supply within the setting. When demand is high relative to available supply, participation is encouraged, and the standard for acceptable performance is lowered. These conditions favor those with less competence in the desired behaviors and encourage their involvement in the setting. In contrast, the opposite occurs when supply exceeds demand. In these situations, standards rise and those with relatively lower competence are discouraged from participation and are more likely to withdraw.

Participation in the activities of a setting provides access to its resources; not only the physical resources but the social resources as well. People are sources of support, information, labor, specific skills, and access to other settings. Social interaction can provide many opportunities for behavior development as reinforcement, modeling, stress reduction, and exposure to new information and values occur in the course of setting activities. In this manner, the behavior development and social networks of the participants are affected by the activities of each of the settings in which they participate.

Within this systems approach, delinquent behavior is a function of the setting in which it occurs, and variations in the rates of delinquent behaviors among individuals are a function of the settings in which they currently participate, their degree of participation in each, and the behaviors and social network that they developed in previous settings. Their degree of participation in peer-controlled settings may be particularly important. Adolescents commonly participate in some peer-controlled settings that allow new roles to be attempted and permit transitional behaviors, including sexual activity, experimental drug use, and minor criminal acts. For most, these experiences are a temporary part of growing up. For others, however, participation in adult-controlled settings is limited because the available supply exceeds the demand for their behaviors and has raised the standards for acceptable performance. Their withdrawal is thereby encouraged. These individuals are likely to become more involved in peer-controlled settings and to thereby increase the probability of their participation in delinquent activities (O'Donnell, 1984; Schwendinger & Schwendinger, 1982). This analysis suggests the importance of assessing the types of settings as well as the social networks of juveniles participating in delinquency programs.

The second example is centered on the family—an ecological model based on earlier work by Bronfenbrenner (1979) and Belsky (1980). In their presentation of this system, Belsky and Vondra (1987) analyzed child maltreatment as a function of the interrelationship of the developmental history of the parents, child characteristics, the marital relationship, cultural values of child-rearing practices, and extrafamilial factors, such as a restricted social network, social isolation, and unemployment. Any one of these factors can have both direct and indirect effects on the others. For example, unemployment may directly reduce the resources available to a child and indirectly change a parent–child relationship by affecting the marital relationship. In general, their review of the literature indicated the marital relationship as the most important support system for parent–child relations, followed by the family social network.

Of specific importance to delinquency, their review also supported the link between interspousal hostility and the aggressive, antisocial behavior of adolescent sons, and aggression as a "primary pattern of response to abuse," especially in older children. Chesney-Lind (1987) has suggested that physical and sexual abuse in the home may be a particularly important influence on the rate of female offenses. She noted that a study of females in detention in Washington found that upward of 40% were victims of abuse and 17% were incest victims (National Institute of Mental Health, 1977) and that of the females surveyed in the Wisconsin juvenile justice system, 79% reported bodily injury from physical abuse, 50% sexual assault, and 32% sexual abuse by family members or family friends (Youth Policy and Law Center, 1982). Those who run away from these problem homes before becoming adults are more likely to become involved in vice and criminal activities and to be arrested (Wilson, 1980).

If some delinquency is a function of the misfunctioning of the family system, then policies that reduce this misfunctioning might also reduce delinquency, even though the delinquent behavior was not directly targeted. Consistent with their ecological model, Belsky and Vondra (1987) focused on services to support the family system and prevent some of the problems that occur within it, especially child maltreatment. They offered examples of services for family development. Suggested were formal training for parenthood in school and childhood classes, family planning services for teenagers, support services for parents through health, day-care, and workplace personnel, and a community service network designed for early intervention. In each, the use of geographic and setting propinquity was encouraged to extend the social networks of the participants.

Both of these examples represent larger systems in which delinquency may be considered. The eventual success of doing so shall be determined by the effectiveness of the interventions derived from them.

Summary

Diversion programs are intended to divert youth from the juvenile court system and typically offer counseling and release or residential placement when necessary. Findings to date show little or no effect. These programs have been criticized for poor implementation, widening the net by extending contact to youth who would not otherwise enter the system, and maintaining too much contact with participants. The failure of these programs to divert, the findings that juvenile crime rates do not increase when youths are released from correctional institutions, and studies indicating that youth offenders who are not apprehended are less likely to commit additional offenses than those who are caught, all support a policy that the less contact with the criminal justice system the better. Neighborhood delinquency programs offer activities in high-delinquency areas or to referred high-risk youths. Overall, the results of these programs have been mixed, with some success demonstrated for employment-related activities.

A key link between these findings is the role played by the social network of youth. In this interpretation, the major factor in the effectiveness of interventions was the effect on relationships, especially with peers. This suggests a shift in emphasis from individual to network change. The implications are that the activities of some programs already promote network change and should be expanded, that in others the procedures may have to be altered so as to discourage the development of delinquent networks, and that a systems approach is needed to consider delinquent behaviors within settings and networks.

References

Ageton, S. S., & Elliott, D. S. (1974). The effects of legal processing on delinquent orientations. *Social Problems, 22,* 87–100.

Belsky, J. (1980). Child maltreatment: An ecological integration. *American Psychologist, 35,* 320–335.

Belsky, J., & Vondra, J. (1987). Child maltreatment: Prevalence, consequences, causes and intervention. In D. Crowell, I. Evans, & C. R. O'Donnell (Eds.), *Childhood aggression and violence: Sources of influence, prevention, and control* (pp. 159–206). New York: Plenum Press.

Belson, W. (1975). *Juvenile theft: The causal factors.* New York: Harper & Row.

Berleman, W. C., Seaberg, J. R., & Steinburn, T. W. (1972). The delinquency prevention experiment of the Seattle Atlantic Street Center: A final evaluation. *Social Service Review, 46,* 323–346.

Blakely, C., & Davidson, W. S. (1981). Prevention of aggression. In A. P. Goldstein, E. G. Carr, W. S. Davidson, & P. Wehr (Eds.), *In response to aggression: Methods of control and prosocial alternatives* (pp. 319–345). New York: Pergamon.

Bronfenbrenner, V. (1979). *The ecology of human development: Experiments by nature and design.* Cambridge: Harvard University Press.

Brown, R. (1968). Manipulation of the environmental press in a college residence hall. *Personnel and Guidance Journal, 46,* 555–560.

Buckner, J. C., & Chesney-Lind, M. (1983). Dramatic cures for juvenile crime: An evaluation of a prisoner-run delinquency prevention program. *Criminal Justice and Behavior, 10,* 227–247.

Burchard, J. D., & Lane, T. W. (1982). Crime and delinquency. In A. S. Bellack, M. Hersen, & A. E. Kazdin (Eds.), *International handbook of behavior modification and therapy* (pp. 613–652). New York: Plenum Press.

Burchard, J. D., Harig, P. T., Miller, R. B., & Amour, J. (1976). New strategies in community-based intervention. In E. Ribes-Inesta & A. Bandura (Eds.), *Analysis of delinquency and aggression* (pp. 95–122). Hillsdale, NJ: Lawrence Earlbaum.

Chambliss, W. (1973). The saints and the roughnecks. *Society, 11,* 24–31.

Chesney-Lind, M. (1987). Girls and violence: An exploration of the gender gap in serious delinquent behavior. In D. Crowell, I. Evans, & C. R. O'Donnell (Eds.), *Childhood aggression and violence: Sources of influence, prevention, and control* (pp. 207–229). New York: Plenum Press.

Coates, R. B., Miller, A. D., & Ohlin, L. E. (1978). *Diversity in a youth correctional system: Handling delinquents in Massachusetts.* Cambridge: Ballinger.

Crozat, P., & Kloss, J. D. (1979). Intensive community treatment: An approach to facilitating the employment of offenders. *Criminal Justice and Behavior, 6,* 133–144.

Davidson, W. S., Seidman, E., Rappaport, J., Berck, P. L., Rapp, N. A., Rhodes, W., & Herring, J. (1977). Diversion program for juvenile offenders. *Social Work Research and Abstracts, 13,* 40–49.

De Coster, D. (1966). Housing assignments for high ability students. *Journal of College Student Personnel, 7,* 10–22.

Elliott, D. S., & Voss, H. L. (1974). *Delinquency and dropout.* Lexington, MA: D. C. Heath.

Epstein, Y. M. (1973). Work-study programs: Do they work? *American Journal of Community Psychology, 1,* 159–172.

Farrington, D. P. (1977). The effects of public labelling. *British Journal of Criminology, 17,* 112–125.

Finckenauer, J. O. (1979). Scared crooked. *Psychology Today, 13,* 6–11.

Fo, W. S. O., & O'Donnell, C. R. (1974). The buddy system: Relationship and contingency conditions in a community intervention program for youth with nonprofessionals as behavior change agents. *Journal of Consulting and Clinical Psychology, 42,* 163–169.

Gault, Application of. 387 U.S. 1, 85, 87 S.Ct. 1428, 1458 (1967).

Gold, M., & Williams, J. R. (1969). National study of the aftermath of apprehension. *Prospectus, 3,* 3–12.

Hawkins, J. D., & Lishner, D. (1987). Social development and the prevention of antisocial behavior among low achievers. In D. Crowell, I. Evans, & C. R. O'Donnell (Eds.), *Childhood aggression and violence: Sources of influence, prevention, and control* (pp. 263–282). New York: Plenum Press.

Klein, M. W. (1971). *Street gangs and street workers.* Englewood Cliffs, NJ: Prentice-Hall.

Klein, M. W. (1979). Deinstitutionalization and diversion of juvenile offenders: A litany of impediments. In N. Morris & M. Tonry (Eds.), *Crime and justice: An annual review of research: Vol. 1* (pp. 145–200). Chicago: University of Chicago Press.

Knight, B. J., & West, D. J. (1975). Temporary and continuing delinquency. *British Journal of Criminology, 15,* 43–50.

Knight, B. J., Osborn, S. J., & West, D. J. (1977). Early marriage and criminal tendency in males. *British Journal of Criminology, 17,* 348–360.

Kobrin, S., & Klein, M. W. (1982). *National evaluation of the deinstitutionalization of status offender programs: Executive summary.* Washington, DC: U.S. Department of Justice.

Levine, M., & Levine, A. (1970). *A social history of the helping services: Clinic, court, school and community.* New York: Appleton-Century-Crofts.

Lincoln, S. B., Teilmann, K., Klein, M., & Labin, S. (1977). *Recidivism rates of diverted juvenile offenders.* Paper presented at the meeting of the National Conference on Criminal Justice Evaluation. Washington, DC.

Lipsey, M. W., Cordray, D. S., & Berger, D. E. (1981). Evaluation of a juvenile diversion program: Using multiple lines of evidence. *Evaluation Review, 5,* 283–306.

McCord, J. (1978). A thirty-year follow-up of treatment effects. *American Psychologist, 33,* 284–289.

McEachern, A. W., Taylor, E. M., Newman, J. R., & Ashford, A. E. (1968). The juvenile probation system: Simulation for research and decision-making. *American Behavioral Scientist, 11,* 1–45.

Miller, W. B. (1962). The impact of a 'total-community' delinquency control project. *Social Problems, 10,* 168–191.

Mills, C. M., & Walter, T. L. (1977). A behavioral employment interpretation program for reducing juvenile delinquency. *Behavior Therapy, 8,* 270–272.

National Institute of Mental Health (1977). *Study of females in detention, King County, Washington.* Washington, DC: U.S. Government Printing Office.

O'Donnell, C. R. (1980). Environmental design and the prevention of psychological problems. In M. P. Feldman & J. F. Orford (Eds.), *The social psychology of psychological problems* (pp. 279–309). New York: Wiley.

O'Donnell, C. R. (1984). Behavioral community psychology and the natural environment. In C. R. Franks & C. Diament (Eds.), *New developments in practical behavior therapy: From research to clinical application* (pp. 495–524). New York: Haworth Press.

O'Donnell, C. R., & Stanley, K. (1973). Paying students for academic performance: A demonstration project. *Journal of Community Psychology, 1,* 215–216.

O'Donnell, C. R., & Tharp, R. G. (1982). Community intervention and the use of multi-disciplinary knowledge. In A. S. Bellack, M. Hersen, & A. E. Kazdin (Eds.), *International handbook of behavior modification and therapy* (pp. 291–313). New York: Plenum Press.

O'Donnell, C. R., Chambers, E., & Ling, K. (1973). Athletics as reinforcement in a community program for academic achievement. *Journal of Community Psychology, 1,* 212–214.

O'Donnell, C. R., Lydgate, T., & Fo, W. S. O. (1979). The buddy system: Review and follow-up. *Child and Family Behavior Therapy, 1,* 161–169.

Pierce, C. H., & Risley, T. R. (1974). Recreation as a reinforcer: Increasing membership and decreasing disruptions in an urban recreation center. *Journal of Applied Behavior Analysis, 7,* 403–411.

Piliavin, I., & Briar, S. (1964). Police encounters with juveniles. *American Journal of Sociology, 70,* 206–214.

President's Commission on Law Enforcement and the Administration of Justice (1967). *Task force report: Juvenile delinquency and youth crime.* Washington, DC: U.S. Government Printing Office.

Quay, H. C., & Love, C. T. (1977). The effect of a juvenile diversion program on rearrests. *Criminal Justice and Behavior, 4,* 377–396.

Rutter, M., & Giller, H. (1984). *Juvenile delinquency: Trends and perspectives.* New York: Guilford Press.

Schur, E. (1973). *Radical non-intervention.* Englewood Cliffs, NJ: Prentice-Hall.

Schwendinger, H., & Schwendinger, J. (1982). The paradigmatic crisis in delinquency theory. *Crime and Social Justice, 17,* 70–78.

Schwitzgebel, R., & Kolb, D. A. (1964). Inducing behavior change in adolescent delinquents. *Behaviour Research and Therapy, 1,* 297–304.

Shore, M. F., & Massimo, J. L. (1979). Fifteen years after treatment: A follow-up study of comprehensive vocationally-oriented psychotherapy. *American Journal of Orthopsychiatry, 49,* 240–245.

Spence, S., & Marzillier, J. S. (1981). Social skills training with adolescent male offenders—II. Short-term, long-term and generalized effects. *Behaviour Research and Therapy, 19,* 349–368.

Spergel, I. A., Reamer, F. G., & Lynch, J. P. (1981). Deinstitutionalization of status offenders:

Individual outcome and system effects. *Journal of Research in Crime and Delinquency, 18,* 4–33.

Stumphauzer, J. S., Veloz, E. V., & Aiken, T. W. (1981). Violence by street gangs: East side story? In R. B. Stuart (Ed.), *Violent behavior: Social learning approaches to prediction, management and treatment* (pp. 68–82). New York: Brunner/Mazel.

Tharp, R. G., & Wetzel, R. J. (1969). *Behavior modification in the natural environment.* New York: Academic Press.

Voss, H. L. (1969). Differential association and containment theory: A theoretical convergence. *Social Forces, 47,* 381–391.

Wilson, H. (1980). Parental supervision: A neglected aspect of delinquency. *British Journal of Criminology, 20,* 203–235.

Youth Policy and Law Center. (1982). *Wisconsin female juvenile offender study project.* Madison, WI: Author.

10

Family-Based Interventions for Crime and Delinquency

TERU L. MORTON AND LINDA S. EWALD

Historically, the family has been the target for early detection, treatment, and prevention of delinquency and crime. Values, standards for behavior, and skills of social influence and achievement are learned in the family, and evidence is now mounting that criminal/delinquent behavior has partial roots there (Coull, Geismar, & Waff, 1982; Druckman, 1979; Emshoff & Blakely, 1983; Fischer, 1983; Parsons & Alexander, 1973; Rutter & Giller, 1984; Stuart, 1971).

Family-based interventions in the area of criminal behavior have focused on juvenile delinquency and on crimes occurring within the family (e.g., child and spouse abuse, incest, and child neglect). Growing awareness about family-based crimes and sensitivity to the psychological damages they produce has resulted in recent increases in both reporting and treatment efforts. Behavioral treatments within the family whether for delinquency or for abuse and neglect, may target just the offender or the entire family. Furthermore, the treatment alternatives can range from focused approaches to alleviate a specific problem to broad-band approaches to alleviate a wide range of simultaneously impinging problems.

Family-based intervention represents an "ecological" approach when the entire family context as well as the extrafamilial context is considered in assessment and intervention. An ecological approach assumes that all aspects of an individual's life must be considered in understanding and dealing with his or her situation. By way of example, Belsky (1980) has provided an ecological framework for understanding child abuse when he described it as a multifaceted problem influenced by four levels of forces: ontogenic development (the role of the individual), the microsystem (the role of the family), the exosystem (the role of the community), and the macrosystem (the role of culture or society). In a parallel fashion, an ecological framework would appear to be useful for understanding the etiology of delinquency and other family-based crimes.

Teru L. Morton • Vanderbilt Institute of Public Policy Studies, Vanderbilt University, Nashville, Tennessee 37203.   Linda S. Ewald • Department of Psychology, University of Hawaii at Manoa, Honolulu, Hawaii 96822.

This chapter begins with a descriptive overview of the family system. A cursory attempt is made to demonstrate the interconnected nature of family relationships and behavioral patternings. Findings that suggest intergenerational transfer of family characteristics and deviancies are presented. Next, the case is made for conceptualizing the entire family system as the context for treating certain forms of crime and delinquency. Discussion then turns to intervention and prevention efforts targeting juvenile delinquency within the family context. Following this, crimes that occur within the family are discussed, with the focus, in turn, on spouse abuse, child abuse, child neglect, and sexual abuse. Recent developments in ecological approaches to a wide range of family problems are next reviewed. The final section summarizes the nature of treatment and prevention research to this time, highlights some of the philosophical and methodological problems in the area, and suggests directions for further theoretical, empirical, and clinical efforts.

DESCRIPTIVE OVERVIEW OF THE FAMILY SYSTEM

Family members, roles, and behaviors are interdependent, and the family environment consists of many behavioral contingencies linking specific behaviors of its members. When one family member acts, another often reacts, and this intertwining and interdependence exist in the past, the present, and the future. Researchers of family violence have provided relatively recent evidence that dysfunctional conflict-resolution attempts may run in families, spreading laterally and intergenerationally. Thus child abusers were often abused themselves as children (Conger, Burgess, & Barrett, 1979; Gil, 1970; Justice & Justice, 1979; Kempe, Silverman, Steele, Droegmueller, & Silver, 1962; Steele, 1976; Webster-Stratton, 1985), spouse abusers had spouse-abusing parents (Kalmuss, 1984; Pagelow, 1981; Walker, 1984), and families characterized by spouse abuse are also likely to be characterized by child abuse (Steinmetz, 1977a,b; Straus, 1980; Straus, Gelles, & Steinmetz, 1980; Walker, 1979, 1984). In addition, a history of having experienced abuse and/or neglect as a child is associated with later delinquent and criminal behavior (McCord, 1983; Steele, 1976).

The dysfunctional family system, unable to solve its inevitable problems and interpersonal conflicts effectively, is likely to become increasingly dysfunctional. For example, the family characterized by coercive behavior can experience the escalating reciprocity of coercion. Families with ineffective communication—defensiveness, rigidity, attributions of malevolence, and competitive, retaliatory interaction modes—are not effective at problem solving, and as problems accumulate, the family increasingly approximates the multiproblem, highly stressed, and dysfunctional family so familiar to workers in the areas of delinquency and family violence.

The role of coercion in many dysfunctional families was probably best presented by Patterson (1982) in his *Coercive Family Process*, which summarized the many studies that he and his colleagues had conducted with aggression-prone and dysfunctioning families. Coercion is the use of aversive means to influence another person. In turn, the recipient of coercion has a strong tendency to reciprocate, and the reciprocal coercion overall may escalate in intensity (Burgess & Richardson, 1984; Morton, 1986). Patterson (1982) has demonstrated that coercion can "contage" throughout the family and become the dominant means of attempting conflict resolution. Such dysfunctional family process has been linked with delinquency (Lysaght & Burchard, 1975; Rutter & Giller, 1984; Wodarski & Ammons, 1981) and with violence and other problems (Burgess, Anderson, Schellenbach, & Conger, 1981; Burgess & Richardson, 1984; Lorber, Felton, & Reid, 1984; Reid, Taplin, & Lorber, 1981).

Multiproblem, crisis-ridden homes are often handicapped by poverty and low education (Dumas & Wahler, 1983; Gil, 1970; Straus et al., 1980). In addition, family members may have little positive and supportive community contact. Wahler and his colleagues have described a subset of mothers referred to child guidance clinics for their overly aggressive children as "insular" (Wahler, 1980a,b; Wahler & Afton, 1980; Wahler & Dumas, 1984; Wahler & Fox, 1980; Wahler, Leske, & Rogers, 1979). Curiously, these stressed mothers describe their few contacts with such extrafamilial people as kinfolk and community agency helpers as coercive, and these mothers are more coercive with their unruly child on days when they have had such contacts. Wahler suggests that insular mothers perceive unsolicited and well-intentioned community outreaches as "manding," threatening, unfriendly, and intrusive.

In their work with families of aggressive children, Patterson, Reid, Jones, and Conger (1975) have described mothers who have disturbances in behavior (coercive), affect (dysphoric), and perceptual systems (attributions of blame and malevolent intent) similar to those described by Wahler and his colleagues as well as to the battered women described by Walker (1981, 1984). Insularity may be a feature of the role strain in the mother, who is centrally placed in coercion dynamics, receiving and often giving an inordinate amount of coercion in her attempts to manage an out-of-control family (Morton, 1986).

The child's contribution to the occurrence of violence within the family has been noted by a number of investigators. Comparisons between abused children and normal controls indicate that the former exhibit higher rates of aversive and aggressive behavior (Bousha & Twentyman, 1984; George & Main, 1979; Hoffman-Plotkin & Twentyman, 1984; Reid et al., 1981; Reidy, 1977). Abused children also have more behavioral problems and are less socially competent (Wolfe & Mosk, 1983). Lorber et al. (1984) have hypothesized that the coercive process between parent and child reinforces and perpetuates the child's aversive behavior, even though it may lead to a physically violent response by the parent.

Several researchers have pointed to the influence of children's behavior upon their parents (Bell & Harper, 1977; Emery, Binkoff, Houts, & Carr, 1983; Houts, Shutty, & Emery, 1985). The abused child may play a role in eliciting abuse from the parent, either through physical characteristics of the child, such as prematurity or mental retardation or through aversive behavior. The negative attributes of the child may cause the parent's abusive behavior or may be the result of the abuse.

Family collusion, where families resist agency intervention into their albeit dysfunctional patterns, has been observed by many writers. Family systems theory would explain this in terms of a kind of equilibrium mainte- nance, a collective effort to maintain family boundaries under new threat from the outside. Collusion is a clear problem in incestuous families but has also been observed in abusive and delinquent families as well. Many tech- niques of behavior change accordingly require initial clinical consideration of developing adequate rapport and preparing the family members to receive treatment (Gambrill, 1983; Patterson, 1982).

Much of the work on dysfunctional families has thus suggested the need for multifocus prevention and early detection and treatment (McAuley & McAuley, 1977). It is presumed, but not always well supported empirically, that assisting a family member in child management, marital conflict resolu- tion, or self-control will have a positive impact on other family members and familial relationships. It is also increasingly presumed that positively influ- encing one generation will affect future generations, perhaps breaking the cycle of dysfunction. Obviously, long-term follow-up data on all family mem- bers are of critical importance in testing these assumptions (Blythe, 1983; Gambrill, 1983; Graziano & Mooney, 1984; Isaacs, 1982; Plotkin, Azar, Twen- tyman, & Perri, 1981; Smith, 1984). Presumptions about the development of family dysfunction, and the success of treatments to alter such development, will be most satisfactorily tested in multilevel longitudinal follow-up studies.

JUVENILE DELINQUENCY: INTERVENTION AND PREVENTION

Juvenile delinquency is a serious problem that apparently is increasing in this country. For example, Graziano and Mooney (1984) have reported that arrests for young people have more than doubled in the last decade; in addi- tion, more crimes are committed by children under 15 than by adults over 21. In discussing juvenile delinquency, one should not conceive of it as a unitary syndrome. Delinquency includes the "hard crimes" that also would be criminal if committed by an adult as well as the "soft delinquencies" (e.g., running away, truancy, etc.) that are violations for children but not for adults. Some of the more common delinquent behaviors for which behavioral treatments have been applied effectively in family-based contexts are fire setting, stealing, drug abuse, and running away.

As suggested earlier, the family is implicated in descriptions of causality and treatment of delinquency. Delinquent families have multiple problems in most cases, including communication difficulties, coercive influence modes, delinquency in other siblings, and criminal histories in the parents. Usually the delinquent also has school problems, social skill deficits, and other related problems. For purposes of this review, we will discuss behaviorally based interventions in delinquent families distinguishing between focused and broad-band approaches.

Focused Approaches to Treatment of Specific Problems

Fire Setting

Most of the small amount of research on fire setting by juveniles have used single-case studies, in part because fire setting is such an infrequent behavior that reliable baseline comparisons are lacking (Graziano & Mooney, 1984). Due to its dangerousness, fire setting needs to be resolved as quickly as possible and applied behavior analysis techniques are good for this. A small number of focused studies have been conducted treating the child in the family, using a behavior therapy approach (Holland, 1969; Kolko, 1983; Stawar, 1976; Welsh, 1971).

Stealing

Stealing is thought to be difficult to treat because it is surreptitious and immediately reinforcing, moreover, when there is punishment, it is often delayed (Henderson, 1981; Stumphauzer, 1976). Very few studies have been reported utilizing family members in the treatment of theft. Stumphauzer (1976) used a treatment approach combining self-control techniques, a family contract, and bibliotherapy to treat a 12-year-old girl with a 5-year history of frequent stealing. The self-control techniques, based on Meichenbaum and Goodman (1971) and Kanfer and Karoly (1972), involved self-reinforcement of appropriate behavior incompatible with stealing, for example, the self-statement, "I did very well, I did not steal." In addition, the girl kept track of her own stealing, recording it on a graph.

The family contracting, based on Stuart (1971), involved attention to non-stealing rather than to stealing. The girl was rewarded with praise, money, special activities, and favorite meals for not stealing. The bibliotherapy involved giving the father books on behavioral parenting techniques to use in setting up behavioral programs for the other children. Family sessions were conducted in which plans for the girl's increased social interaction and independence were discussed and implemented. The girl's stealing apparently had stopped by the sixth week of treatment and had not recurred by the 18-month follow-up. Family functioning apparently had improved greatly, as well.

Henderson (1981) has described a behavioral technique designed to treat juvenile stealing, referred to as individualized combined treatment (ICT). The juvenile involved must "want" to stop stealing and must have an adult willing to help. The intervention attempts to help the juvenile gain self-control through the use of biofeedback, relaxation training, and cognitive control (e.g., self-talk, see Meichenbaum & Goodman, 1971). In addition, control over the external environment is facilitated by the juvenile's use of a diary to record incidents of nonstealing and by parental monitoring and reinforcement of nonstealing. Ten children between 8 and 15 years of age who had been stealing for at least 6 months were treated. A follow-up revealed that 2 of the 10 youths had reoffended within 2½ to 5 years. In a further follow-up study, Henderson (1983) compared the 10 clients to 17 others treated by a variety of other methods, such as counseling or punishment. During the follow-up period, the

ICT children spent more time without stealing. The study has a number of weaknesses, including the lack of random assignment to groups and the fact that the author treated all of the ICT cases and did the follow-ups himself (Henderson, 1983).

Drug Abuse

Cassady (cited in Schaefer, Briesmeister, & Fitton, 1984) hypothesized that the use of physical and social punishment by parents leads to an attempt by their children to avoid the situation through drug use. Treatment was aimed at increasing the use of positive reinforcement through use of a family contract and training the parents to use behavioral techniques. Eight court-referred adolescents and their parents participated in the study. Types of reinforcers and punishers already in use were first determined, along with the target behaviors the parents desired to increase or decrease. In addition, a hierarchical listing of known reinforcers for the adolescents and also of the types of disciplines leading to rebellious behaviors were generated. Based on this information, a contract was drawn up in each family between the parents and child, with a counselor mediating. Each behavior to be changed by either the parent or child was paired with a contingency. Parents kept a checklist to monitor the occurrence of targeted behaviors. Treatment averaged 8½ months, during which time weekly family sessions were held with the counselor, weekly parent group meetings took place, and counselors maintained phone contact with families. Five of the eight families successfully completed the program, with no recurrence of drug abuse reported at 3-, 6-, and 9-month follow-ups.

Frederiksen, Jenkins, and Carr (1976) used contingency contracting with a 17-year-old poly-drug-abusing male and his family. Rather than addressing the drug-abusing behavior itself, however, the therapist focused on improving family interactions and increasing alternative, prosocial behaviors incompatible with drug usage, such as attendance at vocational school, proper car usage, and curfew compliance. Following contract negotiation sessions, all three family members reported increased satisfaction with the family relationship. Actual implementation of the contract resulted in a further increase in satisfaction. Chemical analysis of urine samples taken at irregular intervals during the treatment phase and a follow-up period of 1 year revealed a marked decrease in drug usage.

Running Away

Findings on families with runaways indicate that the parents tend to be inconsistent in their management of the child's behavior and unrealistic in their expectations for the child. A pattern of coercive interaction characterizes family members, with much negativity and little positive interchange (Wodarski & Ammons, 1981). Wodarski and Ammons described a multifaceted behavioral treatment program for runaways and their families that was presented as a training package for juvenile justice workers. The treatment consisted of these programs: (1) a child management program to train parents in the use of effective behavioral techniques, (2) a family enrichment program to increase communication and problem-solving skills among family members, and (3) a social enrichment program to improve the child's interpersonal skills. Positive reinforcement, modeling, and contingency contracts were utilized throughout the group-format treatment procedure. No data on effectiveness were presented, however.

Broad-Band Approaches Targeting the Delinquent's Family

These family interventions focus on changing the whole family system so that it no longer fosters or permits delinquent behavior. Such change efforts typically stress positive, clear, and consistent parental discipline; improved communication and better ways to make change agreements; or the use of contracts for behavior change within the family. The two primary sets of behavioral techniques used here are parent training and contracting.

Parent Training

Parent training involves teaching parents to be change agents for problematic child behaviors. Originally developed for parents of younger, difficult children, such training programs usually provide basic information about child developmental processes and assist the parent(s) in identifying desired and undesired behaviors. Parents are usually taught to praise more, criticize less, and be more attentive and consistent in their parenting. Such parent-training packages, often combined with self-control skill training, have been used effectively for a wide range of child and delinquent problems (Alvord, 1971; Conger, Lahey, & Smith, 1981; Crozier & Katz, 1979; Denicola & Sandler, 1980; Egan, 1983; Jeffrey, 1976; Jensen, 1975; McPherson, McDonald, & Ryer, 1983; Patterson, 1976; Polakow & Peabody, 1975; Sandler, VanDercar, & Milhoan, 1978; Wolfe & Manion, 1984). Parent training improves the supervisory capacity of the parents, helping them to attend to more specific behaviors and to respond contingently and more effectively to them. This is important because parental supervision has been shown to be inversely related to delinquency (Fischer, 1983), such that there is a sevenfold greater rate of delinquency in families with lax supervision than in families with strict supervision (Wilson, 1980).

Csapo and Friesen (1979) used such training effectively with parents of "hard core delinquents"—out-of-control, aggressive juveniles who were former school dropouts and persistent offenders, constantly in trouble with the law, and likely to be transferred to adult court. Group training for these parents consisted of viewing a film to acquaint the parents with learning theory principles in parenting. Treated families had no court involvements during the study, lowered rates of teenagers' deviant behaviors according to observational and parental report data, and increased parental knowledge of behavior management procedures. These changes were significantly greater than those of an untreated control group. This study was significant because the degree of delinquency was considerable, and numerous behaviors were assessed from several vantage points. Nevertheless, long-term follow-up recidivism rates were not reported, a serious consideration because they would be expected to be high.

Contracting

Contracting is perhaps the best known component of family-based behavioral treatments for juvenile delinquency. Popularized by the seminal work of Richard Stuart (Stuart, 1971; Stuart & Lott, 1972), contracts schedule the exchange of positive reinforcers among two or more persons. Rutherford (1975) gives examples of behavioral contracts with delinquent adolescents in four different settings, showing how these formal written documents specify privileges and responsibilities of the parties involved. He points out the necessity of the adolescent's participation in developing the contract. Note that this arrangement differs from the parent-training model, which does not require the child's agreement.

Behavioral contracting is used extensively by the multicomponent Youth Services Program (YSP) of the Dallas police department (Douds, Engelsgjerd, & Collingwood, 1977), a program designed to reduce recidivism rates by diverting juvenile offenders from the traditional criminal justice system. According to these authors, contracting provides immediate help at intake in reinstating parental control and authority. Another therapeutic aspect is the change in emphases from negative controls to the use of rewards. Furthermore, parents report improvements at follow-up in the youths' home-rule following, communication with parents, school attendance of studying, and involvement in organized activities. Because YSP has multiple components, including general skills training of parent and youth, the single effects of contracting cannot be extracted.

Contracting has been used effectively for school-referred predelinquents, where contracts were drawn up between both the youth and the teacher and the youth and the parent (Stuart, Jayaratne, & Tripodi, 1976). In this study, where contracting was the sole intervention, the experimental group showed more improvement than the untreated control, though the differences were only minor. This is to be expected because multicomponent treatments are likely to be considerably more powerful in changing recalcitrant delinquent/predelinquent behaviors.

It is interesting that Stuart and Lott (1972) analyzed the characteristics of behavioral contracts in a multicomponent treatment for 79 predelinquent/delinquent youths and their families and found that (1) contracts were related more to therapist than client features and (2) contract characteristics were unrelated to treatment outcome. It appeared that the determinant of treatment outcome was not contracting *per se* but such other factors as the process of negotiating the contract or the facilitation of communication. Thus

Stuart himself urges the supplementing of contracting with other interventions (Stuart *et al.,* 1976) and draws attention to the therapist's clinical skills in structuring a climate of compromise (Stuart & Lott, 1972).

Lysaght and Burchard (1975) argued that contracting in delinquent families should be supplemented with intervention in "styles of interaction" to ensure greater effectiveness. These researchers suggest that such interaction changes might properly be attempted prior to, or concurrently with, the use of contracting because interaction is required to develop and monitor contracts and to provide consequences. Again, ensuring that the conditions are optimal for a contracted behavior exchange may require clinical skills and a battery of interventions.

An alternative to behavioral contracting is the use of the therapist or change agent as a mediator or arbitrator of specific conflicts. Kifer, Lewis, Green, and Phillips (1974) trained three parent–youth pairs in negotiation behaviors. Behavioral rehearsal and social reinforcement were used in simulation sessions directed by the trainers. The predelinquent youths and their parents were successfully trained to negotiate agreements in conflict situations, and these skills generalized to actual conflicts in the home. It is clear that the ability to negotiate settlements to conflicts improves family functioning in the home of a delinquent or predelinquent. Negotiation or communication skills training, though different from contracting, has a similar long-term goal of improved cooperation and conflict resolution.

Sometimes parents will not agree to participate in treatment when they see their child as the problem, or they may be uncooperative or untrainable. This was the situation in a case study reported by Fedoravicius (1973). Here a 16-year-old boy whose stealing, lying, arguing, disobeying, and truancy at home and at school were extremely disruptive was brought in for treatment by his parents. When attempts to retrain the parents to more appropriately reinforce their son's behavior failed, the son was trained. In a 12-week intervention, the boy was taught operant principles, instructed to ignore and remain silent when lectured or criticized, and to prompt positive parental behavior (ask for assistance) when a reinforcement occasion was needed. During the course of treatment, the stealing and lying apparently stopped, and the parents reported increasing congeniality and cooperation. Although academic difficulties continued, the relationship between parents and son had improved markedly and remained positive 9 months after termination. Although the dynamics of the change cannot be known with certainty from a case study such as this, this report suggests an interesting way to affect conflictual and nonproductive parent–child interactions and exemplifies the reciprocal conditioning between parents and children noted by others (e.g., Osofsky, 1971).

The most impressive results reported to date for family treatment of court-referred juvenile delinquents are those of Alexander and his colleagues at the University of Utah (Alexander & Barton, 1976, 1980; Alexander, Barton, Schiavo, & Parsons, 1976; Alexander & Parsons, 1973; Klein, Alexander, & Parsons, 1977; Parsons & Alexander, 1973). Originally termed *systems-*

behavioral family therapy, this group later relabeled the approach *functional family therapy* (Barton & Alexander, 1981). Amalgamating constructs and techniques derived from both family systems and social learning theory, this treatment is focused on the family interaction system and on the functions of delinquency and delinquency-related behaviors in maintaining family equilibrium. Alexander *et al.* pursue a "therapy first, education second" strategy, in which techniques to reduce family resistance and collusion are employed before teaching contracting, parent training, or communication/negotiation/conflict resolution skills. Cognitive reframing, or relabeling, is used to change attributions of intent or malevolence; paradoxical directives are also used to reduce the felt coerciveness of court-ordered treatment. The therapist works in a variety of ways to stage a cooperative context for the discussion of difficult issues and for the rehearsal of family problem-solving efforts. Finally, the therapist endeavors to undermine the family's definition of the problem (delinquency) and replace it with a definition that removes blame and defensiveness and is accepted by the family. Once adequate rapport has been defined and the family system has been "primed," concepts of reinforcement and contingency contracting that emphasize equivalence of rights and responsibilities for all family members are introduced. Treatment is tailored to the family and may involve parent training, communication training, anger control instruction, and the like as necessary.

Alexander and his colleagues (1976) randomly assigned 86 families to either the "behaviorally oriented, short-term family systems" experimental treatment or to one of three comparison conditions: no-treatment controls, a client-centered family approach, and an eclectic-dynamic approach. They then employed a multilevel evaluation model for assessing the effect of their family systems intervention on delinquency. Consistent with the view that the family system is the locus of socialization for its members and therefore the appropriate target for intervention in delinquency cases, the evaluation strategy assessed outcome in terms of primary, secondary, and tertiary prevention of delinquency. The behavioral-systems treatment proved superior to the client-centered and no-treatment groups in improving family interaction and conflict resolution measures (equality of speech, silence, and frequency and duration of positive interruptions). This was construed as superior tertiary delinquency prevention.

Superiority to all three comparison treatments was shown on the secondary prevention level, when racidivism rates of the originally identified delinquents at 6 to 18 months follow-up proved to be statistically lower—less than half the rates in the other conditions. Finally, primary prevention outcome was defined as reduction in the delinquency rate of *siblings* of the initially referred delinquents. Here, too, the behaviorally oriented family systems approach proved quite superior to all the other treatment conditions, reducing sibling recidivism 250% compared to the other conditions at follow-ups conducted 2½ to 3½ years after treatment termination. The clear value of this research is the demonstration that a behavioral treatment applied within the family system may not only change family interaction patterns but may effectively alter delinquency not only in the presenting delinquent but also in other members of the system.

The pioneering work of Alexander and his colleagues represents the most apparently successful and best-documented approach to the treatment and prevention of juvenile delinquency within the family. The importance of employing relevant outcome measures and hard data on not only improvement in family functioning but also on *recidivism* cannot be overstated. Relatively few treatment studies have incorporated recidivism data with follow-up periods of adequate length.

Weathers and Liberman (1975) reported a three-session behavioral treatment for 28 "recidivistic" delinquent adolescents and their parents, using contingency contracting supplemented by communication skills training and videotape feedback. All but 6 of these families dropped out of treatment, and contracting was found to have at best a slight effect in reducing the verbal abusiveness of adolescents toward their parents. These researchers concluded that serious, "recidivism-prone" delinquency is not amenable to treatment by contingency contracting alone.

In closing this discussion on behavioral family-based treatments of delinquency, it might be wise to refer to previous reviews of behavioral treatments of delinquency. Davidson and Seidman (1974), reviewing studies published between 1960 and mid-1973 that dealt with applications of behavior modification techniques to delinquents, reported positive outcomes across a range of settings. None of the measured outcomes, however, were changes in delinquent behaviors—rather they were changes in other behaviors such as academic and social skills. In a later review, Emery and Marholin (1977) supported this contention, noting that only 3.7% of target behaviors were delinquent behaviors *per se,* leaving the distressing question of the relationship between targeted behaviors and future delinquency. Furthermore, few of the studies reviewed employed a true functional analysis of the delinquent behavior. In reviewing 40 projects designed to prevent delinquency, Lundman and Scarpitti (1978) noted similar problems—few of the studies targeted actual delinquent behaviors, many did not evaluate whether delinquency rates had actually been reduced, and most were uncontrolled and utilized subjective evaluations of effectiveness.

A more recent review of behavioral treatments for delinquency by Graziano and Mooney (1984) concludes that although behavioral programming within the natural environment of the family system appears to be the most promising treatment strategy, we must continue to improve upon measures of delinquency, recidivism, and other, related, behaviors. Finally, in another review, Ulrici (1983) observed that behavioral interventions without family participation did not significantly reduce recidivism, that overall aspects of the family needed to be addressed if recidivism was to be affected by a treatment, and that family systems approaches were equally effective with or without behavioral components. All reviewers have consistently cried out for more well-controlled, relevant data as well as for much needed follow-up data. All have pushed for a prevention focus and for examination of cost-effectiveness of available treatments for delinquency.

CRIMES OF ABUSE AND NEGLECT WITHIN THE FAMILY

In this decade the veil of privacy surrounding the family has been challenged, and the wrongful acts of family members toward one another have been acknowledged (Friedman, Sandler, Hernandez, & Wolfe, 1982; Gambrill, 1983). Concern with domestic violence and parental neglect has stemmed from their wrongfulness and illegality and from the view that these conditions may foster later patterns of criminal, antisocial behavior. The greatest concern has been with child abuse due to the defenseless position of the abused and to the court's role as *parens ex patrius,* or guardian protector of children when their parents or other caretakers are negligent or harmful. More recent concern has focused on spouse abuse. Here, feminists and social welfare programs organizing emergency shelter homes have pointed to the greater vulnerability and social disadvantage of women, the spouse typically most abused (Walker, 1981). Sexual abuse of children within the family context and child neglect have also received increasing attention. As with delinquency, abusiveness within the family appears to worsen over time (Kelly, 1983), and efforts to break the cycle have been seen as prevention of later, more severe abuse. Spouse abuse, child abuse, child neglect, and sexual abuse of children will be taken up in turn.

Spouse Abuse

Astonishingly high rates of conjugal abuse have been reported recently, producing strong political reactions. In introducing her Family Violence and Treatment Act in 1978, Representative Mikulski noted that one fourth of all murders in this country occur within the family, and half of these are spousal killings; moreover, each year, 16% of American couples report an abusive episode, and 10% report an extreme level of physical abuse ("Family Violence," 1978). Estimates of interspousal violence are 50% to 60% in the general population (Straus, 1980), with 3.3 million wives and more than one-quarter million husbands in this country subjected to severe beatings from their spouses (Steinmetz, 1977a). Such marital violence is distributed across all social classes. Violent spouses may be exemplary citizens in all other respects (Steinmetz, 1978) or violent in several realms outside of the marriage—80% of Walker's (1984) male batterers were also involved in such activities as child and parent abuse, incest, pet harming, object destruction, and violence toward other people.

The dynamics of spouse abuse have been conceptualized at the structural/sociological level and at the individual/relational level (Bagarozzi & Giddings, 1983). Structural/sociological approaches point out that cultural norms that maintain and organize the family unit may also legitimate and facilitate interspousal violence (Bagarozzi & Giddings, 1983; Hotaling & Straus, 1980; Walker, 1984). Intervention from this perspective requires changing the societal factors thought to foster and maintain domestic violence—defining physical force as unacceptable in family relationships, eliminating sexism, limiting media violence, and reducing government programs that encourage mobility thereby jeopardizing the extended family, and the like (Straus, 1980).

The clinical treatments for spousal abuse assume more of the individual/relational perspective. Treatment of the couple is probably best elaborated by Margolin's (1979) model of conjoint marital therapy designed to enhance anger management and reduce spouse abuse. This social learning model targets the reciprocity of coercion and escalation of violence thought to underlie marital conflict (Gottman, Markman, & Notarius, 1977; Margolin, 1977). Therapy thus focuses on helping a couple (1) avoid or dissipate the escalation of conflict and (2) set the occasion for their desired relationship changes through a constructive problem-solving approach. The treatment program includes seven components for the therapist to follow:

1. Identifying the cues that contribute to angry exchanges so they can be used as discriminative cues for coping responses antagonistic to anger; diaries and role-played simulations are methods of cue identification
2. Establishing ground rules (e.g., the unacceptability of abusiveness) and consequences for rule violation (e.g., separation)
3. Developing a plan of action to interrupt the conflict pattern; this requires early disengagement that does not provoke escalating anger, and includes neutrally toned observations ("I'm getting angry"), avoidance of being drawn into the argument, and leaving
4. Eliminating provocation (e.g., the provocative remarks, the dirty dishes in the sink, and the apologetic manner that enrages)
5. Modifying faulty thinking regarding relationship functioning (e.g., "You won't love me if I disagree with you" or "You'll get the best of me if I don't fight back")
6. Developing problem-solving skills such as defining a problem nonvindictively and in a neutrally descriptive manner, communicating attentiveness and understanding to the other, brainstorming specific suggestions for solutions and formalizing the change agreement; Jacobson and Margolin (1979) have described problem-solving training in considerable detail
7. Improving the general tone of the relationship by increasing the number of mutually pleasurable activities

This comprehensive, behaviorally based marital skills training program rests on a number of treatment strategies proven successful with conflicted but not severely abusive couples (Jacobson, 1981; Jacobson & Margolin, 1979). Although Margolin (1979) supplies an exemplary case study, definitive research demonstrating the effectiveness of this training with more violent or uncooperative and collusive couples is still needed.

Where physical abuse is severe or where couples seem resistant to change, additional steps may be necessary before such a structured skills training approach is likely to succeed. Therapists might temporarily accept a spouse's or couple's implicit theories of anger, personality, or marriage to establish empathic rapport, even if these are incongruent with the theoretical framework underlying treatment. In addition, therapists may also supplement couple treatment with treatment for alcoholism, support groups for battered wives, and/or rational emotive therapy groups for battering men (Bagarozzi & Giddings, 1983).

Where separation or divorce may be the appropriate course of action or where one partner will not participate in therapy, treatments may be employed in individual or group rather than couple therapy contexts. Treatments for anger control (Beck, 1980; Beck, Rush, Shaw, & Emery, 1979; Bedrosian, 1982; Ellis, 1976; Novaco, 1978) also increase self-control by requiring that the client pinpoint the onset of feeling angry, delay impulsive responding, identify irrational beliefs about oneself or one's spouse that "drive" the anger, substitute more realistic, tolerant beliefs, and dissipate anger in an alternative manner (e.g., relaxation, thought stopping, acting lovingly followed by self-reward). Stress management and communication training are frequently included in such broad-band treatments.

Recent findings suggest the intergenerational transmission of spousal aggression (Kalmuss, 1984). Thus treatments are focused on children of conflicted parents to decrease future spousal violence in those children. An interesting program of this type is the Child and Family Services of Knox County, Tennessee (Gentry & Eaddy, 1980). Their family systems approach, Treatment of Children in Spouse Abusive Families Project, addresses the entire family system to reduce the parents' spouse abuse (secondary prevention) and to reduce the probability of intergenerational transfer of spouse abuse (primary prevention).

These workers advocate immediate protection for victims and their children at a shelter facility but are at the same time concerned about the effect of permanent separation on the children. They note that separation can promote confusion, guilt, and traumatic loss—not necessarily teaching that violence is detrimental to personal relationships. Therapeutic services in this program include modeling of appropriate touching and affection, teaching parents nonviolent child management techniques, and providing instruction about behaviors appropriate to children of different ages. Family nights are held, during which the whole family interacts together in a structured positive activity. This program differs from the typical shelter program in the depth and length of treatment programming, the inclusion of the abuser in treatment, and the preventive efforts directed at children.

Child Abuse

Perhaps no topic related to family living has received more attention in recent times than that of child abuse. Although estimates of incidence vary widely, a figure of 250,000 cases per year is conservative, given the probable underreporting of cases. The number of reported child abuse cases has increased substantially in recent years (Barahal, Waterman, & Martin, 1981; Smith, 1984), although this may be explained in part by heightened awareness and willingness to report in conjunction with mandatory reporting laws. As attention has turned to the high costs to both society and family members associated with removal of the child from the home and placement in foster care (Kent, 1976), there has been a corresponding interest in treatments that both eliminate the abuse and keep the family system intact.

Definitions of abuse have troubled this area. All involve the infliction of pain or injury upon the child, some involve the concept of "intentionality" or rely on "community censure." Intention to hurt, of course, requires a judgment that may contain a bias; reference to community norms recognizes variation in behavioral patterns and standards across communities and cultural subgroups (e.g., Dubanoski, 1982; Dubanoski, Evans, & Higuchi, 1978; Morton, 1986).

Irrespective of definitional nuance, certain statements can nonetheless be made about child abuse. Most instances, it appears, are the result of parents' attempts to discipline their children (Gil, 1970). Where parents are not effective in such disciplining, the child will become increasingly less manageable and provocative from the parent's point of view, and an angry, impulsive, stress-founded view of the child can prompt increased possibilities of hurtful parental actions (Burgess & Richardson, 1984; Lorber et al., 1984; Reid et al., 1981). Malevolent views of the child as purposefully "naughty" or "spiteful" have also been shown to be related to abusive disciplining on the part of the parent (Larrance & Twentyman, 1983).

It is not unexpected, then, to find that parent effectiveness training consisting of training in effective child management is a treatment of choice (Blythe, 1983; Gambrill, 1983). This form of training is generic and was described in detail in an earlier section. In review, the strategy involves training the parent to (1) pinpoint the child's appropriate and inappropriate behaviors, (2) provide consistent consequences for those behaviors, (3) monitor behavioral changes, (4) shape more complex behavioral clusters through successive approximation, and (5) use effective communication and (to the degree that the child is old enough) behavioral contracting (Kelly, 1983). This training has already been found to be effective with other populations (e.g., Patterson & Fleischman, 1979).

Arguments for the use of parent effectiveness training derive from findings that abusive parents show inconsistent discipline techniques (Elmer, 1967; Smith & Hanson, 1975; Young, 1964), have difficulties maintaining limits with their children (Reid et al., 1981), are more negative and less interactive with their children (Bousha & Twentyman, 1984; Conger & Lahey, 1982), and generally less responsive to, and stimulating of, their infants (Dietrich, Starr, & Kaplan, 1980).

Often such parent training is provided in a preassembled package. Packages may vary according to (a) whether bibliotherapy is employed and, if so, what materials are read; (b) whether training occurs in an individual or group context; (c) the nature of modeling, rehearsal trials, and corrective/instructive feedback employed (Mastria, Mastria, & Harkins, 1979); (d) whether parents are given special incentives for attendance, compliance, or successful behavior change, such as money, a movie or restaurant pass, or—the most typical— reduction in a court-ordered probationary period (Ambrose, Hazzard, & Haworth, 1980); and (e) whether an office-based training experience is followed by a home-based training model (Wolfe, Sandler, & Kaufman, 1981).

For the most part, parent effectiveness training has been found to improve child management skills and to reduce child abuse incidents (Blythe, 1983), but these studies are generally short term, for example, 12 months (see Wolfe & Sandler, 1981; Wolfe et al., 1981; Wolfe et al., 1982). Although adequate parent behavior change and sometimes child change are typically reported, most reports describe multimodal treatment programs where the addition of other procedures makes it impossible to tease out the contribution of parent training alone (Gambrill, 1983). Although long-term follow-up research is clearly desired here, Blythe (1983) is among several who have argued that before applied researchers dismantle their programs and test specific treatment programs, they should first aim for more precision and specificity in describing the treatment(s) they deliver.

Based on findings concerning abusive parents, a number of current approaches to treating child abuse have therefore concentrated on addressing the parent's emotional responses and reactions. Abusive parents, compared to controls, have been shown to have different stress responses. They are more hyperresponsive to stimuli and more irritated by aversive stimuli, (Bauer, 1982) and they show more heightened arousal patterns in general (Disbrow, Doerr, & Caulfield, 1977), and, more specifically, to crying and smiling in children (Frodi & Lamb, 1980) and to stressful parent–child situations (Wolfe, Fairbank, Kelly, & Bradlyn, 1983); they are also more impulsive (Rohrbeck & Twentyman, 1983). Correspondingly, they view problematic parent–child situations as more aversive (Plotkin & Twentyman, 1983), report higher levels of stress (Mash, Johnston, & Kovitz, 1983; Rosenberg & Reppucci, 1983), and report themselves less able to cope with stress (Gaines, Sandgrund, Green, & Power, 1978).

Given the disproportionate number of abused children who are young and developmentally delayed (Hoffman-Plotkin & Twentyman, 1981; Johnson & Morse, 1968), the likelihood of irritable, angry, stress-founded impulses in abusive parents is high indeed. Vasta (1982) has suggested that abuse may occur within the context of physical punishment when heightened arousal and impulsivity interact with a coercive system of family functioning, as described earlier in the chapter.

Efforts at addressing abusive parents' emotional responses have focused on anger control training (e.g., Nomellini & Katz, 1983). They may be taught incompatible behaviors, such as systematic muscular relaxation, deep breathing, counting to 10, or "doing something else." They are taught to anticipate escalating feelings of irritation or to identify situations that provoke mounting anger and to substitute more appropriate behaviors such as thought stopping or reframing the situation. Thus the focus of such treatment is on self-management rather than child management. Gilbert (1976) has provided a helpful description of *in vivo* desensitization for a mother afraid to interact with her child for fear of harming her.

The majority of such treatment programs combine self- or anger-control training with child-management training (Barth, Blythe, Schinke, & Schilling, 1983; Conger *et al.*, 1981; Crozier & Katz, 1979; Denicola & Sandler, 1980; Egan, 1983; Kelly, 1983; Koverola, Elliot-Faust, & Wolfe, 1984; Smith & Rachman, 1984). Behavioral techniques have also been employed in treating the abusive parent's tension headaches (Campbell, O'Brien, Bickett, & Lutzker, 1983) or depression (DeBortali-Tregerthan, 1979; Smith & Rachman, 1984). The development of coping skills and stress management techniques has been shown to increase success in treating the abusive parent. In conjunction with a treatment focused on increasing the amount of positive time spent with the child (Reavley & Gilbert, 1979), such efforts to improve the parent–child interaction in child abuse families show some promise.

An interesting research line in this area has focused on the cognitive and attributional components of the abusive parent's relationship to his or her child. The most thematic work in this regard is the model of child abuse developed by Twentyman and his colleagues (Azar, Fantuzzo, & Twentyman, 1984; Morton, Twentyman, & Azar, 1986; Twentyman, Rohrbeck, & Amish, 1984). This model proposes a four-stage sequence of deficits and dysfunctions in child abuse. First, in Stage 1, the parent has either unrealistically low expectations about child development, which could lead to lack of age-appropriate stimulation and subsequent cognitive/emotional delay in a young child, or unusually high expectations of the child, which could lead to abuse-prone frustration because of perceived underperformance by an able child (Azar, Robinson, Hekimian, & Twentyman, 1984; Twentyman & Plotkin, 1982). In Stage 2, the child behaves in a way that is inconsistent with parental expectations. It appears from the work to date that abused children are indeed "difficult" (Gambrill, 1983), being both more aggressive and noncompliant and more passive and nonverbally aggressive than other children (Bousha & Twentyman, 1984; Hoffman-Plotkin & Twentyman, 1984). In Stage 3, the parent makes an idiosyncratic interpretation of the child's behavior, such as an attribution of the child's malevolent intent or basic punishment-deserving character (Larrance & Twentyman, 1983; Plotkin & Twentyman, 1983). Finally, in Stage 4, the parent aggresses on the child, resulting in abuse.

This model has been helpful in identifying where and when additional reattribution therapy or "reframing" techniques should be employed for child abuse families. Numerous studies have shown that abusive parents do, in fact, have unrealistic expectations for their children (Blumberg, 1974; Elmer, 1967; Steele, 1976; Young, 1964). Current parent-training or multimodal child abuse intervention efforts frequently incorporate some education about developmental milestones for children. Where children fail to comply because they do not comprehend the instruction or have not yet acquired the behavior requested and then receive punishment because they are viewed as disrespectful, stubborn, or mean, the necessary skill building is impeded, and a "self-fulfilling prophecy" of a provocative, difficult, abuse-driven child is likely.

Reattribution techniques have been found applicable in such instances, helping the parent accept a different explanation for the child's behavior (Morton et al., 1986; Twentyman et al., 1984). This is often tantamount to getting the parent to see the situation from the child's point of view. Thus the infant's crying is labeled as a normal and healthy hunger cue. The toddler drawing on the wall is seen as a creative explorer. The young child's continued crying in the newly implemented "time-out" condition is seen as a predictable and normal "extinction burst." And the growing conditioned tension experienced by the parent around the difficult child is reframed as a physical discomfort that can be addressed with a variety of self-management techniques.

As is the case in other families described so far, child abuse families also suffer from deficient social skills and the correspondent social isolation and lack of social support systems (Bakan, 1971; Bennie & Sclar, 1969; Giovanni & Billingsley, 1970; Kempe, 1973; Light, 1973; Polansky, Chalmers, Butterweise, & Williams, 1979; Young, 1964). Stress, in combination with lack of social support system, accounted for 36% of the variance in child abuse rates in one sample (Barbarino, 1976). Because social supports act as a buffer for stress and an aid in emotional mastery (Barrera, Sandler, & Ramsay, 1981; Caplan, 1974; Cassel, 1974; Eaton, 1978; Hirsch, 1980; Masten & Garmezy, 1985; Murphy & Moriarty, 1976; Norbeck, Lindsey, & Carrieri, 1981; Sandler, 1980; Sarason, Levine, Basham, & Sarason, 1983; Schaefer, Coyne, & Lazarus, 1981; Werner & Smith, 1982), multimodal treatments may well contain social skills training and attempts to encourage and increase social support systems. In addition, marital discord and abuse are so often found in these families that marital therapies, such as those already described in the spouse abuse discussion (Azrin, Naster, & Jones, 1973; Bagarozzi & Giddings, 1983; Margolin, 1979), are frequently added (Conger et al., 1981; Kelly, 1983). These components are most likely to be found in long-term, broad-band prevention programs, which will be discussed in the final section of this chapter.

Although attention toward child abuse has focused mostly on the abusive parent, the clear possibility exists of intervening directly with the child, who is likely to demonstrate developmental delays in language, social, cognitive, and/or emotional spheres. Several researchers have suggested working with the child, either to reduce behaviors that are aversive to the parent and increase reinforcing behaviors (Azar, Fantuzzo, & Twentyman, 1984; Dubanoski et al., 1978), or to train the child to modify the parents' maladaptive behavior (Emery et al., 1983; Houts et al., 1985). Frazier and Levine (1983) have provided an interesting description of a case study in which both classical and operant conditioning were used to change an abused child's behavior so that it was less offensive to the mother. Although the tactic of direct intervention with the child appears promising, such an approach has not yet been demonstrated to reduce child abuse in well-specified studies with appropriate design features. The treatment techniques commonly used for abused children include residential family therapy, crisis nurseries, and child psychotherapy

(Martin, 1976). Again, the nature and effect of these types of child approaches have not been fully examined in a behaviorally specific manner.

In summary, the behavioral approach to treating child abuse within the family context is recent but quite promising. Most of the primary and collateral techniques employed such as child management training and anger control training have been adopted from earlier work with other populations. In addition, "cognitive-behavioral" perspectives draw attention to distortions in the meaning of the abused child's behavior and suggest promising applications of "reframing" and "relabeling" strategies. To date, however, well-controlled treatment studies demonstrating long-term elimination of child abuse using these latter methods are nonexistent. The major reviewers of the field (e.g., Blythe, 1983; Gambrill, 1983; Isaacs, 1982; Plotkin *et al.*, 1981; Smith, 1984) are in agreement that we need better descriptions of the client populations and referral sources, clearer specification of the treatment(s) employed, and more, as well as more reliable, outcome measures. Because of the high-risk nature of the problem, treatment ethics may prevail over design elegance in research in the near future.

Neglect

Child neglect is a problem that often takes a backseat to child abuse. Nevertheless, more neglect cases are reported to social service departments each year than abuse cases (Gambrill, 1983). Forms of neglect may include lack of cleanliness, inattention to medical problems, poor supervision, and inadequate provision of food. Some researchers stress the importance of considering neglectful parents as a group separate from abusive parents, with characteristics of their own (Azar, Robinson, Hekimian, & Twentyman, 1984; Larrance & Twentyman, 1983; Plotkin *et al.*, 1981).

Two studies have presented treatment strategies for specific aspects of child neglect. Both studies are a part of Project 12-Ways, a program that is discussed more fully later in the chapter. Rosenfeld-Schlichter, Sarber, Bueno, Greene, and Lutzker (1983) reported treating a family in which severe child neglect was occurring, by focusing on improvement in personal cleanliness. The family consisted of a mother and four children, the youngest two of whom were reported by their teachers to be foul smelling, unwashed, and dressed in dirty clothes. Because the mother had been noncompliant with agency intervention in the past, treatment included involving a 13-year-old son in improving the cleanliness of the two younger children. The boy received an allowance contingent upon ensuring that the children bathed and were judged clean by their teachers. Two other components of the treatment package involved having a homemaker assist the mother in washing the family's clothes each week and having weekly unscheduled home visits by counselors during the children's bath time. During the period of intervention, the children's personal cleanliness improved considerably, as rated by their teachers. In addition, teachers reported increased interaction with other children in their classes. Through the use of various combinations of allowance for the 13-year-old, visits by the counselor, and laundry service, it was found that the laundry service was a necessary component of the treatment—without it cleanliness ratings decreased.

In a single-case experimental study, Sarber, Halasz, Messmer, Bickett, and Lutzker (1983) trained a mentally retarded, illiterate mother of a 4-year-old to plan nutritious meals and shop for groceries. The child had been placed in foster care due to neglect by the mother, especially in the area of nutrition. The woman was first taught to identify food groups, using modeling and contingent reinforcement. She was then taught to plan nutritious meals using a menu chart and color-coded cards containing pictures of food items, to devise a grocery list of needed foods, and to do her grocery shopping using a binder containing the picture cards of the foods needed. Results of the intervention showed that the woman was able to plan and shop for nutritious meals following training. The skills were maintained and generalized to a new store, and the child was subsequently returned home. These two studies indicate that specific behavioral interventions may be useful in improving neglectful situations.

Sexual Abuse of Children

Incest is becoming more and more recognized as an area of concern. Meiselman (1978) noted that one or two cases of incest per million people are reported each year but that a more accurate estimate would be that 1 or 2 people out of 100 have experienced an incestuous act. James (1977) puts the figure at 4 people out of 100. As attitudes about sexuality, abortion, and the like become increasingly relaxed, the incidence of incest may be on the rise (Kempe & Kempe, 1984). A number of strategies for the treatment of incestuous families have been described, but very few are behavioral in nature.

Justice and Justice (1979) described the use of contracts and group therapy to treat sexual abuse. They initially see the entire family together to assess how the family members interact. Thereafter, the parents alone are in group therapy with other couples. The authors discussed six common problem areas in incestuous families, along with strategies for intervention. For each problem area, the husband and wife contract to make specific changes. Symbiosis, involving parent–child role reversal is commonly considered to be the most crucial problem area. In therapy, parents are taught to seek nurturing in a more healthy way. A second problem area is the marital relationship. Partners are taught to increase their positive interaction and decrease negative communication. Other problem areas include a poor sexual relationship, lack of socialization, stress, and alcoholism. For each of these areas, a contract is formed, specifying agreed-upon behaviors by the couple. Couples contract to have sex with each other, and they increase their socialization with other couples, practice relaxation exercises to reduce stress levels, and attempt to stop drinking (attending Alcoholics Anonymous if necessary) if alcoholism is a problem.

An alternative to a focus on the couple is treatment for the child. Becker,

Skinner, and Abel (1982) have reported a case study in which the mother of a 4-year-old incest victim served as both data collector and therapist. The child was sexually molested by her father during a visitation session. The parents, who were separated, were in the process of obtaining a divorce. Following the incestuous incident, the child had lost a considerable amount of weight by refusing to eat her meals, was depressed and anxious, engaged in self-injurious behaviors, and experienced phobic reactions.

During a 1-week baseline period, data were collected by the mother on the child's weight and number of meals eaten, phobic and self-injurious behaviors, and verbalizations about the father. The child's affect was rated on a happiness scale. Treatment consisted of a token reinforcement system administered by the mother in which the child received money for completed meals. The mother was instructed to ignore phobic and self-injurious behaviors and to listen to and comfort the child when she talked about the molestation but not to initiate the topic. The mother continued to collect data during the 4 months of treatment and 2 months of follow-up. Results suggested that the program was successful in increasing the number of meals the child ate and thus her weight and in decreasing her self-injurious and phobic behaviors. In addition, the child's general affect improved. The study, though without controls, suggests the efficacy of using parents as behavioral therapists with child sexual assault victims and identifies an area for further research.

ECOLOGICAL OR INTEGRATIVE/COMBINED APPROACHES

It is becoming more and more clear that a family-based intervention program must be tailored to the specific case. Assessment should involve a detailed analysis of the full range of family problems, resources, and coping strategies (Azar, Fantuzzo, & Twentyman, 1984; Belsky, 1980; Dubanoski *et al.*, 1978). Moreover, treatment strategies involving multifaceted approaches may be more useful than the narrow approaches that have characterized the field in the past (Lutzker, 1984; Lutzker, McGinsey, McRae, & Campbell, 1983).

One program that may serve as an exemplar is Project 12-Ways in Illinois, which employs an ecobehavioral approach to the treatment and prevention of child abuse and neglect (Lutzker, 1984; Lutzker, Frame, & Rice, 1982). By ecobehavioral, it is meant that child abuse and neglect must be considered within the environment in which it occurs. Child maltreatment is conceptualized as a multifaceted problem requiring a comprehensive, multifaceted intervention that fully considers the broad environment in which the problem occurs (Lutzker, Wesch, & Rice, 1984). Project 12-Ways attempts to affect as many of the factors contributing to the occurrence of child abuse and neglect as possible by careful assessment and provision of a broad range of services. Clients generally receive only one or two services at a time, and treatments are usually provided in the home to facilitate generalization and to avoid the problem of no-shows for clinic appointments (Lutzker, 1984).

Parent–child training, based on the paradigm of Peed, Roberts, and Forehand (1977), is the most frequently used treatment component, with over 90% of families receiving it (Lutzker *et al.*, 1984). Other services offered include home safety training, marital counseling, job finding, money management, self-control, and stress reduction training, leisure time counseling, health maintenance, nutrition, personal cleanliness, toilet training, shoe tying, communication skills, alcoholism treatment referral, and service to unwed mothers (Lutzker, 1984; Lutzker *et al.*, 1984; Rosenfield-Schlichter *et al.*, 1983). Campbell *et al.* (1983) used parent training, stress reduction for migraine headaches, and marital counseling to treat a 12-Ways family in which the mother expressed a desire to kill her daughter. Improvement in all three targeted areas was maintained at 1-year follow-up. Tertinger, Greene, and Lutzker (1984) have described a home safety program to educate parents about home hazards and child-proofing methods and to provide them with feedback on the number and locations of dangerous conditions in the home. They reported a consistent reduction in the number of hazardous items in the homes following implementation of the education-feedback package for six 12-Ways families. Initial evaluation of program services are promising (Lutzker, 1984; Lutzker *et al.*, 1984), but further research is needed to determine whether the effectiveness of an ecobehavioral approach is greater than that of other, more narrow approaches to child abuse and neglect.

Project 12-Ways is an exemplar for a broad-based, multifaceted treatment and prevention program for child abuse and neglect. Such integrative/combined approaches can be found in other areas as well. Emshoff and Blakely (1983), in describing a mixture of advocacy and a behavioral contracting approach for a delinquent youth population, have argued the value of an ecological framework that captures performance criteria from the police, courts, and school systems. The Hartwig Project (Rose, Sundel, Delange, Corwin, & Palumbo, 1970) is another example of a basically ecobehavioral approach to juvenile offenders in an open community setting.

The ecological treatment programs described so far in the literature are, in general, probably still not sufficiently expansive nor pervasive. In addition, in our "broader-is-better" zeal, we are humbled by some earlier lessons of such enrichment programs. McCord (1978) has reported on a long-term (20-year) follow-up of delinquent males treated in just such an integrative approach. Davidson and Wolfred (1977) have also conducted a follow-up of a behavior modification program for delinquents that had been highly successful in achieving within-program targeted behaviors. In both studies, treated individuals, compared to nontreated controls, were found to be worse off upon follow-up, having had more juvenile justice contacts and having been more likely to be placed in institutions. These studies suggest the importance of attending not only to the immediately targeted behavior change but also to other broader, more global outcomes and measures—particularly the criterion-related behaviors, such as rates of abuse and incarceration.

In summary, the research on family-based interventions for crime and delinquency is grounds for reasonable optimism—on balance. Since changing the behavior of one family member has a "ripple effect" on the behaviors of other family members and on family interaction patterns generally, many treatment and prevention possibilities exist for such families. The trend toward multifaceted programs directed at the family unit, as seen in the integrative/ecobehavioral approaches, appears quite promising in this regard. Future efforts in this direction will be substantially assisted by basic research yielding useful and socially valuable predictors of delinquency and family crime and by research that maps the relationships between family members' behaviors—both within and between individuals—across a longer time span. The extension of appropriate change measures to other family members may improve evaluation of long-term intervention and prevention effectiveness, as exemplified by the reduced recidivism rates of the siblings of delinquents treated in the family context (Alexander & Parsons, 1973). Extending treatment to other family members, training them to modify one anothers' behaviors (e.g., Azar, Fantuzzo, & Twentyman, 1984; Dubanoski et al., 1978; Emery et al., 1983; Federovicius, 1973) is another viable and promising avenue for future treatment and outcome research.

Several issues surface in considering use of ecobehavioral and broad-band treatment or prevention strategies with whole families. One issue concerns ethical considerations when prevention efforts target high-risk families or individuals, particularly when the long-term hazards of such a label and intervention are not fully known. The possibility that targeting high-risk groups for such efforts might operate as a self-fulfilling prophecy, provoking the very behaviors the program was designed to eliminate and violating human rights as well (e.g., Lundman & Scarpitti, 1978); this must be investigated systematically.

Another issue concerns the effects of court-mandating treatment for individuals and families. Wolfe, Aragona, Kaufman, and Sandler (1980) found that this increased by fivefold the likelihood of a family's completion of their treatment program. Given that many of these families are resistant to entering treatment and present serious retention problems, with key family members often frequently absent from treatment sessions, this finding is significant. Others have stressed the use of incentives for treatment that are specifically tailored for each family (e.g., Gambrill, 1983). More research on the long-term effectiveness of various methods of "entering a family system" and adequately motivating a family to continue to remain in treatment is needed. This issue of volitional participation is relevant to all court-ordered treatments but is particularly salient when treatment is extensive—requiring participation by more than the offending individual or where one or more of the mandated treatment components is not obviously and directly related to the illegal criterion behavior.

Where multicomponent, broad-based family intervention is employed or where there is court involvement, the treatment may well involve a growing number of agencies. Although not always considered part of treatment per se, interagency collaboration becomes another of the therapist's functions, with multiple agency involvement possibly either interfering with or facilitating clients' progress. The number and nature of agencies involved, the manner of their involvement, and the amount of interagency collaboration and cooperation should probably be described in detail in reports of treatment efforts. In addition, to the degree that multiple agency involvement is part of the clients' experience, this area of social service delivery becomes a suitable area of inquiry.

In cases where delinquency or destructive family interaction is pronounced, court or other agency involvement is typical, especially with respect to whether or not the offender or victim should be removed from the home. In many places, this decision is determined by law and public policies. Such determination has considerable import for prognoses for different intervention and prevention attempts. Removal from the family of an abused child or a juvenile delinquent raises questions concerning that child's long-term adjustment in the alternative care or rehabilitation system as well as the welfare of the remaining children in the home, if they and their parents do not receive services. A court-ordered separation of abusive parents from their children will have impact on numerous adjustment indexes for all family members involved. Nonetheless, children do have a right to court protection and, where prognosis is poor and potential risks are high, separation of family members would appear to be the humane intervention. The knotty issue of whether to work with the family or to move toward separation has obvious policy and practice relevance. It also represents an area of policy still is great need of an adequate data base and an area deserving of systematic and objective inquiry.

The needs in this area of treatment and prevention for broad assessment (across multiple family members and target and nontarget behaviors) for multicomponent and multitarget treatments specifically tailored to the family (i.e., ecological approaches) and for gradual lessening of concern for long-term maintenance of gain have been discussed. The ecological approach is a promising one but requires careful assessment and functional analysis of the problem(s), greater attention to the effectiveness of individual treatment components, and long-term assessment of criterion and associated behaviors. Taken as a whole, the literature highlights the promise of family-based interventions not only to treat the specific presenting problem of delinquency or abuse and neglect but also to furnish the family with new skills in living to ensure maintenance of this change and prevention of later problems. Realization of this promise, however, will require further efforts to develop adequate prediction, viable means of entering the family system, demonstration of cost-effective outcomes, and data-guided public policies concerning when and how best to help families help themselves.

REFERENCES

Alexander, J. F., & Barton, C. (1976). Behavioral systems therapy for families. In D. H. Olson (Ed.), *Treating relationships* (pp. 167–188). Lake Mills, IA: Graphic Publishing.
Alexander, J. F., & Barton, C. (1980). Intervention with delinquents and their families: Clinical,

methodological, and conceptual issues. In J. P. Vincent (Ed.), *Advances in family intervention assessment and therapy* Greenwich, CT: JAI Press.

Alexander, J. F., & Parsons, B. V. (1973). Short term behavioral intervention with delinquent families: Impact on family process and recidivism. *Journal of Abnormal Psychology, 81,* 219–225.

Alexander, J. F., Barton, C., Schiavo, R. S., & Parsons, B. V. (1976). Systems-behavioral intervention with families of delinquents: Therapist characteristics, family behavior, and outcome. *Journal of Consulting and Clinical Psychology, 44,* 656–664.

Alvord, J. R. (1971). The home token economy: A motivational system for the home. *Corrective Psychiatry and Journal of Social Therapy, 17,* 6–13.

Ambrose, S., Hazzard, A., & Haworth, J. (1980). Cognitive-behavioral parenting groups for abusive parents. *Child Abuse and Neglect, 4,* 119–125.

Azar, S. T., Fantuzzo, J. W., & Twentyman, C. T. (1984). An applied behavioral approach to child maltreatment: Back to basics. *Advances in Behaviour Research and Therapy, 6,* 3–11.

Azar, S. T., Robinson, D. R., Hekimian, E., & Twentyman, C. T. (1984). Unrealistic expectations and problem-solving ability in maltreating and comparison mothers. *Journal of Consulting and Clinical Psychology, 52,* 687–691.

Azrin, H. N., Naster, B. J., & Jones, R. (1973). Reciprocity counseling: A rapid learning-based procedure for marital counseling. *Behaviour Research and Therapy, 11,* 365–383.

Bagarozzi, D. A., & Giddings, C. W. (1983). Conjugal violence: A critical review of current research and clinical practices. *American Journal of Family Therapy, 11,* 3–15.

Bakan, D. (1971). *Slaughter of the innocents.* San Francisco: Jossey-Bass.

Barahal, R. M., Waterman, J., & Martin, H. P. (1981). The social cognitive development of abused children. *Journal of Consulting and Clinical Psychology, 49* (4), 508–511.

Barrera, M., Sandler, I. N., & Ramsay, T. B. (1981). Preliminary development of a scale of social support: Studies on college students. *American Journal of Community Psychology, 9,* 435–447.

Barth, R. P., Blythe, B. J., Schinke, S. P., & Schilling, R. F. (1983). Self-control training with maltreating parents. *Child Welfare, 62,* 313–324.

Barton, C., & Alexander, J. F. (1981). Functional family therapy. In A. S. Gurman & D. P. Kniskern (Eds.), *Handbook of family therapy* (pp. 403–443). New York: Brunner/Mazel.

Bauer, W. D. (1982). *Abusing, neglectful, and comparison mothers' responses to child and non-child stressors.* Unpublished master's thesis, University of Rochester.

Beck, A. T. (1980, December). *Cognitive aspects of marital conflict.* Paper presented at the Annual Convention of the Association for the Advancement of Behavior Therapy, New York.

Beck, A. T., Rush, A. J., Shaw, B. F., & Emery, G. (1979). *Cognitive therapy of depression.* New York: Guilford Press.

Becker, J. V., Skinner, L. J., & Abel, G. G. (1982). Treatment of a four-year-old victim of incest. *American Journal of Family Therapy, 10,* 41–46.

Bedrosian, R. C. (1982). Using cognitive and systems intervention in the treatment of marital violence. In J. C. Hansen & L. R. Barnhill (Eds.), *Clinical approaches to family violence* (pp., 117–138). Rockville, MD: Aspen Systems Corporation.

Bell, R. Q., & Harper, L. V. (1977). *Child effects on adults.* Hillsdale, NJ: Lawrence Erlbaum Associates.

Belsky, J. (1980). Child maltreatment: An ecological integration. *American Psychologist, 35,* 321–335.

Bennie, E., & Sclar, A. (1969). The battered child syndrome. *American Journal of Psychiatry, 125,* 975–979.

Blumberg, M. L. (1974). Psychopathology of the abusing parent. *American Journal of Psychotherapy, 28,* 21–29.

Blythe, B. J. (1983). A critique of outcome evaluation in child abuse treatment. *Child Welfare, 62,* 325–335.

Bousha, D. M., & Twentyman, C. T. (1984). Mother-child interactional style in abuse, neglect, and control groups: Naturalistic observations in the home. *Journal of Abnormal Psychology, 93,* 106–114.

Burgess, R. L., & Richardson, R. A. (1984). Coercive interpersonal contingencies as a determinant of child maltreatment: Implications for treatment and prevention. In R. S. Dangel & R. A. Polster (Eds.), *Parent training: Foundations of research and practice* (pp. 239–259). New York: Guilford Press.

Burgess, R. L., Anderson, E. A., Schellenbach, C. J., & Conger, R. D. (1981). A social interactional approach to the study of abusive families. In J. P. Vincent (Ed.), *Advances in family intervention, assessment and theory: An annual compilation of research* (Vol. 2). Greenwich, CT: JAI Press.

Campbell, R. V., O'Brien, S., Bickett, A. D., & Lutzker, J. R. (1983). In-home parent training, treatment of migraine headaches, and marital counseling as an ecobehavioral approach to prevent child abuse. *Journal of Behavior Therapy and Experimental Psychiatry, 14,* 147–154.

Caplan, G. (1974). *Support systems and community mental health: Lectures on concept development.* New York: Behavioral Publications.

Cassel, J. (1974). Psychosocial processes and "stress": Theoretical formulations. *International Journal of Health Services, 6,* 471–482.

Conger, R. D., & Lahey, B. B. (1982). Behavioral intervention for child abuse. *The Behavior Therapist, 5,* 49–53.

Conger, R. D., Burgess, R. L., & Barrett, C. (1979). Child abuse related to life change and perceptions of illness: Some preliminary findings. *The Family Coordinator, 28,* 73–78.

Conger, R. D., Lahey, B. B., & Smith, S. S. (1981, July). *An intervention program for child abuse: Modifying maternal depression and behavior.* Paper presented at the Family Violence Research Conference, University of New Hampshire, Durham.

Coull, V. C., Geismar, L. L., & Waff, A. (1982). The role of the family in the resocialization of juvenile offenders. *Journal of Comparative Studies, 13,* 63–75.

Crozier, J., & Katz, R. C. (1979). Social learning treatment of child abuse. *Journal of Behavior Therapy and Psychiatry, 10,* 213–220.

Csapo, M., & Friesen, J. (1979). Training parents of hard core delinquents as behaviour managers of their children. *Canadian Counsellor, 13,* 68–74.

Davidson, W. S., & Seidman, E. (1974). Studies of behavior modification and juvenile delinquency: A review, methodological critique, and social perspective. *Psychological Bulletin, 81,* 998–1011.

Davidson, W. S., & Wolfred, T. R. (1977). Evaluation of a community-based behavior modification program for prevention of delinquency. *Community Mental Health Journal, 13,* 296–306.

DeBortali-Tregerthan, G. J. (1979). Behavioral treatment of child abuse: A case report. *Child Behavior Therapy, 1,* 287–294.

Denicola, J., & Sandler, J. (1980). Training abusive parents in child management and self-control skills. *Behavior Therapy, 11,* 263–270.

Dietrich, K. N., Starr, R. H., Jr., & Kaplan, M. G. (1980). Maternal stimulation and care of abused infants. In T. M. Field, S. Goldberg, D. Stern, & A. M. Sostek (Eds.), *High-risk infants and children: Adult and peer interactions.* New York: Academic Press.

Disbrow, M. A., Doerr, H., & Caulfield, C. (1977). Measuring the components of parents' potential for child abuse and neglect. *Child Abuse and Neglect, 1,* 279–296.

Douds, A. F., Engelsgjerd, M., & Collingwood, T. R. (1977). Behavior contracting with youthful offenders and their parents. *Child Welfare, 56,* 409–417.

Druckman, J. M. (1979). A family-oriented policy and treatment program for female juvenile status offenders. *Journal of Marriage and the Family, 41,* 627–636.

Dubanoski, R. A. (1982). Child maltreatment in European- and Hawaiian-Americans. *Child Abuse and Neglect, 5,* 457–465.

Dubanoski, R. A., Evans, I. M., & Higuchi, A. A. (1978). Analysis and treatment of child abuse: A set of behavioral propositions. *Child Abuse and Neglect, 2,* 153–172.

Dumas, J. E., & Wahler, R. G. (1983). Predictors of treatment outcome in parent training: Mother insularity and socioeconomic disadvantage. *Behavioral Assessment, 5,* 301–313.

Eaton, W. W. (1978). Life events, social supports, and psychiatric symptoms: A reanalysis of the New Haven data. *Journal of Health and Social Behavior, 19,* 157–165.

Egan, K. J. (1983). Stress management and child management with abusive parents. *Journal of Clinical Child Psychology, 3,* 292–299.

Ellis, A. (1976). Techniques of handling anger in marriage. *Journal of Marriage and Family Counseling, 2,* 305–315.

Elmer, E. (1967). *Children in jeopardy: A study of abused minors and their families.* Pittsburgh: University of Pittsburgh Press.

Emery, R. E., & Marholin, D. (1977). An applied behavior analysis of delinquency: The irrelevancy of relevant behavior. *American Psychologist, 32,* 860–873.

Emery, R. E., Binkoff, J. A., Houts, A. C., & Carr, E. G. (1983). Children as independent variables: Some clinical implications of child-effects. *Behavior Therapy, 14,* 398–412.

Emshoff, J. G., & Blakely, C. H. (1983). The diversion of delinquent youth: Family-focused intervention. *Children and Youth Services Review, 5,* 343–356.

Family Violence. (1978, March). *California State Psychologist, 30,* 33.

Fedoravicius, A. S. (1973). The patient as shaper of required parental behavior: A case study. *Journal of Behavior Therapy and Experimental Psychiatry, 4,* 395–396.

Fischer, D. G. (1983). Parental supervision and delinquency. *Perceptual and Motor Skills, 56,* 635–640.

Frazier, D., & Levine, E. (1983). Reattachment therapy: Intervention with the very young physically abused child. *Psychotherapy: Theory, Research and Practice, 20,* 90–100.

Frederiksen, L. W., Jenkins, J. O., & Carr, C. R. (1976). Indirect modification of adolescent drug abuse using contingency contracting. *Journal of Behavior Therapy and Experimental Psychiatry, 7,* 377–378.

Friedman, R. M., Sandler, J., Hernandez, M., & Wolfe, D. A. (1982). Child abuse. In E. J. Mash & L. G. Terdal (Eds.), *Behavioral assessment of childhood disorders* (pp. 221–255). New York: Guilford Press.

Frodi, A. M., & Lamb, M. E. (1980). Child abusers' responses to infant smiles and cries. *Child Development, 51,* 238–241.

Gaines, R., Sandgrund, A., Green, A. H., & Power, E. (1978). Etiological factors in child maltreatment: A multivariate study of abusing, neglecting, and normal mothers. *Journal of Abnormal Psychology, 87,* (5), 531–540.

Gambrill, E. D. (1983). Behavioral intervention with child abuse and neglect. In M. Hersen, R. M. Eisler, & P. M. Miller (Eds.), *Progress in behavior modification* (Vol. 15, pp. 1–56). New York: Academic Press.

Garbarino, J. (1976). A preliminary study of some ecological correlates of child abuse: The impact of socioeconomic stress on mothers. *Child Development, 47,* 178–185.

Gentry, C. E., & Eaddy, V. B. (1980). Treatment of children in spouse abusive families. *Victimology: An International Journal, 5,* 240–250.

George, C., & Main, M. (1979). Social interactions of young abused children: Approach, avoidance, and aggression. *Child Development, 50,* 306–318.

Gil, D. G. (1970). *Violence against children: Physical child abuse in the United States.* Cambridge: Harvard University Press.

Gilbert, M. T. (1976). Behavioural approach to the treatment of child abuse. *Nursing Times, 72,* 140–143.

Giovanni, J., & Billingsley, A. (1970). Child neglect among the poor: A study of parental adequacy in families of three ethnic groups. *Child Welfare, 49,* 196.

Gottman, J. M., Markman, H., & Notarius, C. (1977). The topography of marital conflict: A sequential analysis of verbal and nonverbal behavior. *Journal of Marriage and the Family, 39,* 461–477.

Graziano, A. M., & Mooney, K. C. (1984). *Children and behavior therapy.* New York: Aldine.

Henderson, J. Q. (1981). A behavioral approach to stealing: A proposal for treatment based on ten cases. *Journal of Behavior Therapy and Experimental Psychiatry, 12,* 231–236.

Henderson, J. Q. (1983). Follow-up of stealing behavior in 27 youths after a variety of treatment programs. *Journal of Behavior Therapy and Experimental Psychiatry, 14,* 331–337.

Hirsch, B. J. (1980). Natural support systems and coping with major life changes. *American Journal of Community Psychology, 8,* 159–172.

Hoffman-Plotkin, D., & Twentyman, C. T. (1981, April). *Cognitive and behavioral characteristics of abused and neglected children.* Paper presented at the Third International Congress on Child Abuse and Neglect, Amsterdam.

Hoffman-Plotkin, D., & Twentyman, C. T. (1984). A multimodal assessment of behavioral and cognitive deficits in abused and neglected preschoolers. *Child Development, 55,* 794–802.

Holland, C. J. (1969). Elimination by the parents of fire-setting behaviour in a 7-yr-old boy. *Behaviour Research and Therapy, 7,* 135–137.

Hotaling, G. T., & Straus, M. A. (1980). Culture, social organization, and irony in the study of family violence. In M. A. Straus & G. T. Hotaling (Eds.), *The social causes of husband-wife violence.* Minneapolis: University of Minnesota.

Houts, A. C., Shutty, M. S., Jr., & Emery, R. E. (1985). The impact of children on adults. In B. B. Lahey & A. E. Kazdin (Eds.), *Advances in clinical child psychology* (Vol. 8, pp. 267–307). New York: Plenum Press.

Isaacs, C. D. (1982). Treatment of child abuse: A review of the behavioral interventions. *Journal of Applied Behavior Analysis, 15,* 273–294.

Jacobson, N. S. (1981). Behavioral marital therapy. In A. S. Gurman & D. P. Kniskern (Eds.), *Handbook of family therapy.* New York: Brunner/Mazel.

Jacobson, N. S., & Margolin, G. (1979). *Marital therapy: Strategies based on social learning and behavior exchange principles.* New York: Brunner/Mazel.

James, K. (1977). Incest: The teenager's perspective. *Psychotherapy: Theory, Research, and Practice, 14,* 146–155.

Jeffrey, M. (1976). Practical ways to change parent-child interaction in families of children at risk. In R. E. Helfer & C. H. Kempe (Eds.), *Child abuse and neglect. The family and the community.* Cambridge: Ballinger.

Jensen, R. E. (1975, September). *A behavior modification program to remediate child abuse.* Paper presented at the Annual Convention of the American Psychological Association, Chicago.

Johnson, B., & Morse, H. A. (1968). Injured children and their parents. *Children, 15,* 147–152.

Justice, B., & Justice, R. (1979). *The broken taboo: Sex in the family.* New York: Human Sciences Press.

Kalmuss, D. (1984). The intergenerational transmission of marital aggression. *Journal of Marriage and the Family, 46,* 11–19.

Kanfer, F. H., & Karoly, P. (1972). Self-control: A behavioristic excursion into the lion's den. *Behavior Therapy, 3,* 398–416.

Kelly, J. A. (1983). *Treating child-abusive families: Intervention based on skills-training principles.* New York: Plenum Press.

Kempe, C. (1973). A practical approach to the protection of the abused child and rehabilitation of the abusing parent. *Pediatrics, 57,* 804.

Kempe, C. H., Silverman, F., Steele, B., Droegmueller, W., & Silver, H. (1962). The battered child syndrome. *Journal of the American Medical Association, 181,* 17–24.

Kempe, R. S., & Kempe, C. H. (1984). *The common secret: Sexual abuse of children and adolescents.* New York: W. H. Freeman & Co.

Kent, J. T. (1976). A follow-up study of abused children. *Journal of Pediatric Psychology, 1,* 25–31.

Kifer, R. E., Lewis, M. A., Green, D. R., & Phillips, E. L. (1974). Training predelinquent youths and their parents to negotiate conflict situations. *Journal of Applied Behavior Analysis, 7,* 357–364.

Klein, N. C., Alexander, J. F., & Parsons, B. V. (1977). Impact of family systems intervention on recidivism and sibling delinquency: A model of primary prevention and program evaluation. *Journal of Consulting and Clinical Psychology, 45,* 469–474.

Kolko, D. J. (1983). Multicomponent parental treatment of firesetting in a six year old boy. *Journal of Behavior Therapy and Experimental Psychiatry, 14,* 349–353.

Koverola, C., Elliot-Faust, D., & Wolfe, D. A. (1984). Clinical issues in the behavioral treatment of a child abusive mother experiencing multiple life stresses. *Journal of Clinical Child Psychology, 13,* 187–191.

Larrance, D. T., & Twentyman, C. T. (1983). Maternal attributions and child abuse. *Journal of Abnormal Psychology, 92,* 449–457.

Light, R. (1973). Abused and neglected children in America: A study of alternative policies. *Harvard Educational Review, 43,* 556–598.

Lorber, R., Felton, D. K., & Reid, J. B. (1984). A social learning approach to the reduction of coercive processes in child abusive families: A molecular analysis. *Advances in Behaviour Research and Therapy, 6,* 29–45.

Lundman, R. J., & Scarpitti, F. R. (1978). Delinquency prevention: Recommendations for future projects. *Crime and Delinquency, 24,* 207–220.

Lutzker, J. R. (1984). Project 12-Ways: Treating child abuse and neglect from an ecobehavioral perspective. In R. F. Dangel & R. A. Polster (Eds.), *Parent training: Foundations of research and practice* (pp. 260–297). New York: Guilford Press.

Lutzker, J. R., Frame, R. E., & Rice, J. M. (1982). Project 12-Ways: An ecobehavioral approach to the treatment and prevention of child abuse and neglect. *Education and Treatment of Children, 5,* 141–155.

Lutzker, J. R., McGinsey, J. F., McRae, S., & Campbell, R. V. (1983). Behavioral parent training: There's so much more to do. *The Behavior Therapist, 6,* 110–112.

Lutzker, J. R., Wesch, D., & Rice, J. M. (1984). A review of Project 12-Ways: An ecobehavioral approach to the treatment and prevention of child abuse and neglect. *Advances in Behaviour Research and Therapy, 6,* 63–73.

Lysaght, T. V., & Burchard, J. D. (1975). The analysis and modification of a deviant parent-youth communication pattern. *Journal of Behavior Therapy and Experimental Psychiatry, 6,* 339–342.

Margolin, G. (1977, December). *A sequential analysis of dyadic communication.* Paper presented at the Annual Convention of the Association for the Advancement of Behavior Therapy, Atlanta.

Margolin, G. (1979). Conjoint marital therapy to enhance anger management and reduce spouse abuse. *American Journal of Family Therapy, 7,* 13–24.

Martin, H. P. (1976). *The abused child: A multidisciplinary approach to developmental issues and treatment.* Cambridge: Ballinger.

Mash, E. J., Johnston, C., & Kovitz, K. (1983). A comparison of the mother-child interactions of physically abused and non-abused children during play and task situations. *Journal of Clinical Child Psychology, 12,* 337–346.

Masten, A. S., & Garmezy, N. (1985). Risk, vulnerability, and protective factors in developmental psychopathology. In B. B. Lahey & A. E. Kazdin (Eds.), *Advances in clinical child psychology* (Vol. 8, pp. 1–52). New York: Plenum Press.

Mastria, E. O., Mastria, M. A., & Harkins, J. C. (1979). Treatment of child abuse by behavioral intervention: A case report. *Child Welfare, 58,* 253–261.

McAuley, R., & McAuley, P. (1977). *Child behavior problems: An empirical approach to management.* New York: Free Press.

McCord, J. A. (1978). Thirty-year follow-up of treatment effects. *American Psychologist, 33,* 284–289.

McCord, J. (1983). A forty year perspective on effects of child abuse and neglect. *Child Abuse and Neglect, 7,* 265–270.

McPherson, J. J., McDonald, L. E., & Ryer, C. W. (1983). Intensive counseling with families of juvenile offenders. *Juvenile and Family Court Journal, 34,* 27–33.

Meichenbaum, D., & Goodman, J. (1971). Training impulsive children to talk to themselves: A means of developing self-control. *Journal of Abnormal Psychology, 77,* 115–126.

Meiselman, K. (1978). *Incest: A psychological study of causes and effects with treatment recommendations.* San Francisco: Jossey-Bass.

Morton, T. (1986). Childhood aggression in the context of family interaction. In D. H. Crowwell, I. M. Evans, & C. O. O'Donnell (Eds.), *Childhood aggression and violence: Sources of influence, prevention, and control.* New York: Plenum Press.

Morton, T. L., Twentyman, C. T., & Azar, S. T. (1986). Cognitive-behavioral assessment and treatment of child abuse. In N. B. Epstein, S. Schlesinger, & W. Dryden (Eds.), *Cognitive-behavioral therapy with Families.* New York: Brunner/Mazel.

Murphy, L. B., & Moriarty, A. E. (1976). *Vulnerability, coping, and growth from infancy to adolescence.* New Haven: Yale University Press.

Nomellini, S., & Katz, R. C. (1983). Effects of anger control training on abusive parents. *Cognitive Therapy and Research, 7,*57–68.

Norbeck, J. S., Lindsey, A. M., & Carrieri, V. L. (1981). The development of an instrument to measure social support. *Nursing Research, 30,* 264–269.

Novaco, R. W. (1978). Anger and coping with stress: Cognitive behavioral interventions. In J. P. Foreyt & D. P. Rathjen (Eds.), *Cognitive behavior therapy: Research and application* (pp. 135–173). New York: Plenum Press.

Osofsky, J. (1971). Children's influences upon parental behavior: An attempt to define the relationship with the use of laboratory tasks. *Genetic Psychology Monographs, 83,* 147–169.

Pagelow, M. (1981). Factors affecting women's decisions to leave violent relationships. *Journal of Family Issues, 2,* 391–414.

Parsons, B. V., Jr., & Alexander, J. F. (1973). Short-term family intervention: A therapy outcome study. *Journal of Consulting and Clinical Psychology, 41,* 195–201.

Patterson, G. R. (1976). The aggressive child: Victim and architect of a coercive system. In L. A. Hamerlynck, L. C. Handy, & E. J. Mash (Eds.), *Behavior modification and families: Theory and research* (Vol. 1). New York: Brunner/Mazel.

Patterson, G. R. (1982). *Coercive family process.* Eugene, OR: Castalia.

Patterson, G. R., & Fleischman, M. J. (1979). Maintenance of treatment effects: Some considerations concerning family systems and follow-up data. *Behavior Therapy, 10,* 168–185.

Patterson, G. R., Reid, J. B., Jones, R. R., & Conger, R. E. (1975). *A social learning approach to family intervention, Vol. 1: Families with aggressive children.* Eugene, OR: Castalia.

Peed, S., Roberts, M., & Forehand, R. (1977). Evaluation of the effectiveness of a standardized parent-training program in altering the interaction of mothers and their noncompliant children. *Behavior Modification, 1,* 323–350.

Plotkin, R. C., & Twentyman, C. T. (1983). *Cognitive mediation of disciplinary situations in mothers who maltreat their children.* Unpublished doctoral dissertation, University of Rochester.

Plotkin, R. C., Azar, S., Twentyman, C. T., & Perri, M. G. (1981). A critical evaluation of the research methodology employed in the investigation of causative factors of child abuse and neglect. *Child Abuse and Neglect, 5,* 449–455.

Polakow, R. L., & Peabody, D. L. (1975). Behavioral treatment of child abuse. *International Journal of Offender Therapy and Comprehensive Criminology, 19,* 100–103.

Polansky, N., Chalmers, M., Butterweise, R., & Williams, P. (1979). Isolation of the neglectful family. *American Journal of Orthopsychiatry, 49,* 149–152.

Reavley, W., & Gilbert, M. T. (1979). The analysis and treatment of child abuse by behavioural psychotherapy. *Child Abuse and Neglect, 3,* 509–514.

Reid, J. B., Taplin, P. S., & Lorber, R. (1981). A social interactional approach to the treatment of abusive families. In R. B. Stuart (Ed.), *Violent behavior: Social learning approaches to prediction, management and treatment* (pp. 83–101). New York: Brunner/Mazel.

Reidy, T. J. (1977). The aggressive characteristics of abused and neglected children. *Journal of Clinical Psychology, 33,* 1140–1145.

Rohrbeck, C. A., & Twentyman, C. T. (1983). *A multimodal assessment of impulsiveness in abusing, neglecting, and non-maltreating mothers and their preschool children.* Unpublished doctoral dissertation, University of Rochester.

Rose, S. D., Sundel, M. M., Delange, J., Corwin, L., & Palumbo, A. (1970). The Hartwig project: A behavioral approach to the treatment of juvenile offenders. In R. Ulrich, R. Stachnik, & J. Mabry (Eds.), *Control of human behavior: From cure to prevention* (Vol. 2, pp. 220–230). Glenville, IL: Scott, Foresman.

Rosenberg, M. S., & Reppucci, N. D. (1983). Abusive mothers: Perceptions of their own and their children's behavior. *Journal of Consulting and Clinical Psychology, 51,* 574–582.

Rosenfield-Schlichter, M. D., Sarber, R. E., Bueno, G., Greene, B. F., & Lutzker, J. R. (1983). Maintaining accountability for an ecobehavioral treatment of one aspect of child neglect: Personal cleanliness. *Education and Treatment of Children, 6,* 153–164.

Rutherford, R. B., Jr., (1975). Establishing behavioral contracts with delinquent adolescents. *Federal Probation, 39,* 28–32.

Rutter, M., & Giller, H. (1984). *Juvenile delinquency: Trends and perspectives.* New York: Guilford Press.

Sandler, I. N. (1980). Social support resources, stress, and maladjustment of poor children. *American Journal of Community Psychology, 8,* 41–52.

Sandler, J., VanDercar, C., & Milhoan, M. (1978). Training child abusers in the use of positive reinforcement techniques. *Behavior Research and Therapy, 16,* 169–175.

Sarason, I. G., Levine, H. M., Basham, R. B., & Sarason, B. R. (1983). Assessing social support: The Social Support Questionnaire. *Journal of Personality and Social Psychology, 44,* 127–139.

Sarber, R. E., Halasz, M. M., Messmer, M. C., Bickett, A. D., & Lutzker, J. R. (1983). Teaching menu planning and grocery shopping skills to a mentally retarded mother. *Mental Retardation, 21,* 101–106.

Schaefer, C., Coyne, J. C., & Lazarus, R. S. (1981). The health-related functions of social support. *Journal of Behavioral Medicine, 4,* 381–406.

Schaefer, C. E., Briesmeister, J. M., & Fitton, M. E. (1984). *Family therapy techniques for problem behaviors of children and teenagers.* San Francisco: Jossey-Bass.

Smith, J. E. (1984). Non-accidental injury to children—I. A review of behavioural interventions. *Behaviour Research and Therapy, 22,* 331–347.

Smith, J. E., & Rachman, S. J. (1984). Non-accidental injury to children—II. A controlled evaluation of a behavioural management programme. *Behaviour Research and Therapy, 22,* 349–366.

Smith, S. M., & Hanson, R. (1975). Interpersonal relationships and child-caring practices in 214 parents of battered children. *British Journal of Psychiatry, 127,* 515–525.

Stawar, T. L. (1976). Fable mod: Operantly structured fantasies as an adjunct in the modification of fire-setting behavior. *Journal of Behavior Therapy and Experimental Psychiatry, 7,* 285–287.

Steele, B. F. (1976). Violence within the family. In R. E. Helfer & C. H. Kempe (Eds.), *Child abuse and neglect: The family and the community* (pp. 3–23). Cambridge, MA: Ballinger.

Steinmetz, S. K. (1977a). *The cycle of violence: Assertive, aggressive, and abusive family interaction.* New York: Praeger.

Steinmetz, S. K. (1977b). The use of force for resolving family conflict: The training ground for abuse. *The Family Coordinator, 26,* 19–26.

Steinmetz, S. K. (1978). Violence between family members. *Marriage & Family Review, 1,* 1–16.

Straus, M. A. (1980). Wife beating: How common and why? In M. A. Straus & G. T. Hotaling (Eds.), *The social causes of husband-wife violence.* Minneapolis: University of Minnesota Press.

Straus, M. A., Gelles, R. J., & Steinmetz, S. K. (1980). *Behind closed doors: Violence in the American family.* Garden City, NY: Anchor/Doubleday.

Stuart, R. B. (1971). Behavioral contracting within the families of delinquents. *Journal of Behavior Therapy and Experimental Psychiatry, 2,* 1–11.

Stuart, R. B., & Lott, L. A., Jr. (1972). Behavioral contracting with delinquents: A cautionary note. *Journal of Behavior Therapy and Experimental Psychiatry, 3,* 161–169.

Stuart, R. B., Jayaratne, S., & Tripodi, T. (1976). Changing adolescent deviant behaviour through reprogramming the behaviour of parents and teachers: An experimental evaluation. *Canadian Journal of Behavioural Science, 8,* 132–144.

Stumphauzer, J. S. (1976). Elimination of stealing by self-reinforcement of alternative behavior and family contracting. *Journal of Behavior Therapy and Experimental Psychiatry, 7,* 265–268.

Tertinger, D. A., Greene, B. F., & Lutzker, J. R. (1984). Home Safety: Development and validation of one component of an ecobehavioral treatment program for abused and neglected children. *Journal of Applied Behavior Analysis, 17,* 159–174.

Twentyman, C. T., & Plotkin, R. C. (1982). Unrealistic expectations of parents who maltreat their children: An educational deficit that pertains to child development. *Journal of Clinical Psychology, 38,* 497–503.

Twentyman, C. T., Rohrbeck, C. A., & Amish, P. L. (1984). A cognitive-behavioral approach to child abuse: Implications for treatment. In S. Saunders, A. M. Anderson, C. A. Hart, & G. M.

Rubenstein (Eds.), *Violent individuals and families: A handbook for practitioners* (pp. 87–111). Springfield, IL: Charles C Thomas.

Ulrici, D. K. (1983). The effects of behavioral and family interventions on juvenile recidivism. *Family Therapy, 10,* 25–36.

Vasta, R. (1982). Physical child abuse: A dual-component analysis. *Developmental Review, 2,* 125–149.

Wahler, R. G. (1980a). The insular mother: Her problems in parent-child treatment. *Journal of Applied Behavior Analysis, 13,* 207–219.

Wahler, R. G. (1980b). The multiply entrapped parent: Obstacles to change in parent-child problems. In J. P. Vincent (Ed.), *Advances in family intervention, assessment and theory* (Vol. 1). Greenwich, CT: JAI Press.

Wahler, R. G., & Afton, A. D. (1980). Attentional processes in insular and noninsular mothers: Some differences in their summary reports about child problem behaviors. *Child Behavior Therapy, 2,* 25–41.

Wahler, R. G., & Dumas, J. E. (1984). Changing the observational coding styles of insular and noninsular mothers: A step toward maintenance of parent training effects. In R. F. Dangel & R. A. Polster (Eds.), *Parent training: Foundations of research and practice* (pp. 379–416). New York: Guilford Press.

Wahler, R. G., & Fox, J. J. (1980). Solitary toy play and time out: A family treatment package for children with aggressive and oppositional behavior. *Journal of Applied Behavior Analysis, 13,* 23–39.

Wahler, R. G., Leske, G., & Rogers, E. S. (1979). The insular family: A deviance support system for oppositional children. In L. A. Hamerlynck (Ed.), *Behavioral systems for the developmentally disabled, Vol. 1. School and family environments* (pp. 102–127). New York: Brunner/Mazel.

Walker, L. E. (1979). *The battered woman.* New York: Harper & Row.

Walker, L. E. (1981). A feminist perspective on domestic violence. In R. B. Stuart (Ed.), *Violent behavior: Social learning approaches to prediction, management, and treatment.* New York: Brunner/Mazel.

Walker, L. E. (1984). *The battered woman syndrome.* New York: Springer.

Weathers, L., & Liberman, R. P. (1975). Contingency contracting with families of delinquent adolescents. *Behavior Therapy, 6,* 356–366.

Webster-Stratton, C. (1985). Comparison of abusive and nonabusive families with conduct-disordered children. *American Journal of Orthopsychiatry, 55,* 59–69.

Welsh, R. S. (1971). The use of stimulus satiation in the elimination of juvenile fire-setting behavior. In A. M. Graziano (Ed.), *Behavior therapy with children* (pp. 283–289). Chicago: Aldine-Atherton.

Werner, E., & Smith, R. (1982). *Vulnerable but invincible: A longitudinal study of resilient children and youth.* New York: McGraw-Hill.

Wilson, H. (1980). Parental supervision: A neglected aspect of delinquency. *British Journal of Criminology, 20,* 203–235.

Wodarski, J. S., & Ammons, P. W. (1981). Comprehensive treatment of runaway children and their parents. *Family Therapy, 8,* 229–240.

Wolfe, D. A., & Manion, I. G. (1984). Impediments to child abuse prevention: Issues and directions. *Advances in Behavior Research and Therapy, 6,* 47–62.

Wolfe, D. A., & Mosk, M. D. (1983). Behavioral comparisons of children from abusive and distressed families. *Journal of Consulting and Clinical Psychology, 51,* 702–708.

Wolfe, D. A., & Sandler, J. (1981). Training abusive parents in effective child management. *Behavior Modification, 5,* 320–335.

Wolfe, D. A., Aragona, M. A., Kaufman, K., & Sandler, J. (1980). The importance of adjudication in the treatment of child abusers: Some preliminary findings. *Child Abuse and Neglect, 4,* 127–135.

Wolfe, D. A., Sandler, J., & Kaufman, K. (1981). A competency based training program for child abusers. *Journal of Consulting and Clinical Psychology, 49,* 633–640.

Wolfe, D. A., St. Lawrence, J., Graves, K., Brehoney, K., Bradlyn, D., & Kelly, J. A. (1982).

Intensive behavioral parent training for a child abusive parent. *Behavior Therapy. 13,* 438–451.

Wolfe, D. A., Fairbank, J. A., Kelly, J. A., & Bradlyn, A. S. (1983). Child abusive parents' physiological responses to stressful and non-stressful behavior in children. *Behavioral Assessment, 4,* 363–371.

Young, L. (1964). *Wednesday's children: A study of child neglect and abuse.* New York: McGraw-Hill.

11

School Programs for Delinquency Prevention and Intervention

THEODORE W. LANE AND JANICE MURAKAMI

Early theorizing on delinquency and deviancy, starting in the 1930s, produced a voluminous body of theoretical perspectives. These perspectives were attempts to explain the etiology of delinquency and deviancy in terms of such factors as personality, family and genetic predispositional factors, and sociological conditions. They had in common the aim to propose a superordinate theory: an accounting of the spectrum of delinquent behavior by reference to a unitary underlying cause. Social learning theorists, making their contribution to the explanation of delinquency within the last 20 years, have proposed a somewhat different position, namely that delinquent and deviant behavior is multiply determined, a view that has now been widely accepted (Feldman, 1977; Hirschi & Selvin, 1967; Johnson, 1979).

Learning theories, the underpinnings of behavioral analysis, attempt to articulate the relationship between behavior and environment. Learning theorists have postulated that delinquent behaviors, like many other classes of behaviors, are the result of socialization processes operating in various social environments. Behavior–environment contingencies within diverse social environments affect the acquisition, performance, maintenance, and generalization of behaviors. Thus delinquency and deviant behaviors are, in part, a function of the environment (Braukmann, Fixsen, Phillips, & Wolf, 1975).

Applied behavior analysts attempt to use the principles of learning theory, and the procedures based thereon, to address problems of social significance. This approach attempts applications that are of immediate, practical relevance to prevention, intervention, and policymaking. In their early applications, applied behavior analysts (or behavior therapists or behavior modifiers) intervened successfully with a wide variety of identifiable, specific clinical problems (Kanfer & Goldstein, 1975; Leitenberg, 1976). As their confidence in the robustness of their procedures increased, behavior analysts pro-

---

Theodore W. Lane • Cumberland County Mental Health Center, Children and Youth Program, Fayetteville, North Carolina 28301.   **Janice Murakami** • Department of Psychology, University of Vermont, Burlington, Vermont 05405.

gressed to broader and more complex social issues such as crime and delinquency.

As social scientists converged on multifactorial explanations of delinquency and the need to address the problem from a larger sociological and
ecological perspective, policymakers were also looking at the social conditions
associated with delinquency. The school setting, a primary social environment
for adolescents, became one focus for intervention. The President's Task Force
on Juvenile Delinquency and Youth Crime (Schafer & Polk, 1967) strongly
called attention to the school setting as an important social environment in
need of reform for the prevention and remediation of delinquency. These same
sentiments were echoed by policymakers of the National Advisory Commission on Criminal Justice Standards and Goals (Task Force for Community
Crime Prevention, 1973).

THE RELATIONSHIP BETWEEN SCHOOL AND DELINQUENCY

Evidence has accumulated that school can contribute to deviant and disruptive behaviors or promote law-abiding, appropriate behaviors (Zimring &
Hawkins, 1968). For example, a body of research suggests that a person's
experience of general school failure is an important determinant in both initiation and perpetuation of delinquent or deviant behavior (Polk, 1975). Nevertheless, the specific contributions of school to delinquency have not received
enough research attention. The Oregon School, as it has come to be known, has
generated the largest coordinated body of research studies in this area (Kelly,
1980). In general, the thrust of the Oregon research has been on aspects of
schools' organizational structures and operating processes that may initiate
and perpetuate deviant and delinquent activities. Kelly (1980) summarized
findings on the relationship between delinquency and some school factors,
including formal student stratification systems (e.g., ability grouping and
tracking), counselor and teacher selection processes, and the school's operating
ideology (see also Rutter & Giller, 1984; Safer, 1982a). That school and school-
related factors are important contributors to delinquency initiation and perpetuation is unequivocal. Yet, precisely which school factors and processes
make this contribution and how they interact with extraschool factors is not
well understood because of the neglect in this area of research.

The prevalent assumptions are that educational attainment can help prevent a criminal career by providing the means for adolescents to obtain socially approved success and rewards and that consistent school attendance can
decrease the availability of illegitimate opportunities. Unfortunately, though,
one of the educational system's most conspicuous failures is its inability to
retain students. About 30% of pupils drop out of school (Ahlstrom & Havighurst, 1971) and do so around age 16, the prevailing upper age limit for
compulsory attendance (National Center for Educational Statistics, 1983).
Dropping out has long been viewed as a youth's response to chronic school
failure and frustration. Hirshoren, Schultz, Manton, and Henderson (1970)

have suggested, however, that a sizable number of "dropouts" have been "pushed out" by the school because of its reciprocal experience of failure and frustration.

Like dropping out, delinquency has been viewed as youth reaction to experiences of school failure and frustration (Koval & Polk, 1967; Kvarceus, 1945). Elliott and Voss (1974) have suggested that both dropping out and delinquency are responses to school failure. Moreover, their research indicates that adjudication for delinquency is associated with increased probability of subsequent dropout, which in turn, interestingly enough, leads to a reduction in delinquency, perhaps due to the removal of the aversive experiences of school failure and frustration (see also Leblanc, Biron, & Provonost, 1979; Mukherjee, 1971). These studies assessed only short-term effects of school dropout, however, because all were completed by the time the subjects were 19 years old.

The long-term effects of dropping out of school on subsequent criminal behavior were investigated by Polk et al. (1981). Higher rates of criminality were demonstrated for dropouts in their early 20s, as compared to same-age graduates. Similar long-term effects were reported by Bachman and O'Malley (1978) and by Hathaway, Reynolds, and Monachesi (1969). Finally, both the short- and long-term effects of dropout on subsequent criminal behavior, controlling for relevant postschool experiences, were reexamined by Thornberry, Moore, and Christenson (1985). Their results clearly indicate that dropping out of school is significantly and positively associated with later criminal behavior. Unlike earlier investigations, however, these results were evident at both short- and long-term assessment periods. Thus delinquent behavior increased during the year following school departure, and dropout status was also positively related to criminal behavior during young adulthood.

If successful participation in school is an important mitigating factor against dropout and delinquency, it is imperative that schools provide adequate special education services and programs to meet the multiple needs of their difficult pupil population. More systematic research on the structures and processes of schools will be needed to help design innovative programs that maximize success and minimize failure. As the amelioration of negative school experiences is accomplished, the number of delinquents "manufactured" by the schools may be reduced (Kelly, 1978).

HISTORY OF SPECIAL EDUCATION SERVICES

Laws mandating compulsory school attendance until a certain age were adopted by every state between 1852 and 1918 (Achenbach, 1975). Subsequent to these legal mandates, schools began to identify many children as failing to conform to the school norms and standards for social and academic performances. Because these children were required to attend school, despite their failings, the need for special instruction was recognized. In practice, the goal of specialized education was to provide for the instructional needs of these exceptional children, while minimizing the interference with and disruption of the regular students' education.

Historically, special education services were uniformly provided for all exceptional children, with little attempt to make subgroup discriminations with regard to age or categorical needs. Students with learning deficits were lumped together in one setting with conduct-disordered, emotionally disturbed, and physically and mentally handicapped students. Legal, educational, and clinical paradigms have since evolved so that discriminations among these exceptional students can be more carefully made. For example, in the early 1960s, separate special education classes for the emotionally disturbed (ED) and the learning deficient or disabled (LD) were instituted. These discriminations, however, have fallen short for those students whose primary problem is conduct disorder.

In the final version of Public Law 94-142 (Education for All Handicapped Children), a separate special education category for the conduct-disordered is conspicuously missing. If the student who displays serious misconduct also demonstrates a chronic emotional disturbance or specific learning disability, then these latter conditions become the critical criteria for access to special education services. The primary reason for referral to LD and ED classes, however, is often the student's misconduct. Safer (1982b) has argued that the exclusion of behavior disorder as a formal special education category makes little sense because this group tends to have the least successful secondary school outcome. (For a review of other issues and problems concerning special education services for the behaviorally disordered, see Safer, 1982b,c.)

In an effort to evaluate systematically the consequences of the PL 94-142 legislation for behaviorally disordered adolescents, Hirshoren and Heller (1979) conducted a survey to identify the state of the art in public school programming. Their findings suggest that the mandate has served as an impetus for more conscientious provision of special education services at the secondary-school level. Program alternatives remain limited for behaviorally disordered adolescents, but identification, eligibility, and placement procedures have improved.

Special Education at the Secondary-School Level

Typically, special education services for secondary-school students have lagged behind such services for younger pupils. The prevalent assumption seems to be that the younger the age, the greater the immediate benefits that will accrue. It has been estimated that more than three quarters of the youth receiving special education services are of elementary-school age (Dunn, 1973). In 1972, Bullock and Brown, who conducted a local survey of 126 public and private schools in Florida, reported that only 15% of the special programs were serving adolescents. In 1964, Morse, Cutler, and Fink reported that 32% of the public schools that offered special programs for behaviorally disordered children did so at the junior high-school level, compared to 11% at the senior high-school level. Despite disproportionate special-education attention aimed at younger age grades, the research to date does not clearly demonstrate that early intervention ensures improved achievement or adjustment later on (Palmer & Anderson, 1979). In fact, school misconduct becomes most serious at the junior high and secondary-school levels, regardless of the timing of the intervention (Marrone & Anderson, 1970; Safer, 1982c).

Morse *et al.* (1964) summarized the predicament faced by secondary schools:

> By the time disturbed children reach high school age, they are much more difficult to handle, their pathology is likely to be deeply ingrained, and their antisocial behavior as often as not has taken them out of school into the hands of a secondary social agency. Their less bright prognosis, and the limited efficacy of educationally oriented remediation makes the schools less willing to undertake special programs of this sort for them. (p. 21)

Traditional School Approaches for Behaviorally Disordered Youth

Traditionally, the school's response to the behaviorally disordered or delinquent youth has been exclusion. This approach at present takes such forms as expulsion from school, suspension, "allowing" students to drop out, and exclusion from the normal classroom. The major arguments, both overt and covert, for the "benign" acceptance of early dropouts include budgetary and human-effort savings from not having to design, operate, and justify special programs. The popular rationale is that special programs have not clearly demonstrated success in attracting youths and producing lasting positive gains. Counterarguments are based mainly on the putative relationship between length of stay in school and increased chances for better-paying adult jobs. For a fuller discussion of these issues, see Safer (1982c).

As Morse *et al.* (1964) suggested, when behaviorally disordered or delinquent adolescents have received educational services, it was usually provided in separate social agency settings. These settings include correctional or detentional institutions, residential group homes, or special schools in removed sites. The advantages and disadvantages of such exclusionary practices have been well debated but with little resolution (Budnick & Andreacchi, 1967; Krohn, 1964). The debates, however, have at least served to highlight caveats about the practice of educational segregation. Major pragmatic concerns about educational segregation include inadequate quality control, negative, iatrogenic effects of stigmatization, and difficulty returning students to the mainstream.

In addition to exclusionary practices, traditional within-school efforts with this population include reduced school time and/or a vocationally oriented component embedded within the educational program. A split school day of academic and actual work experience and academic instruction through the use of vocational materials are typical examples. Discussion of the contrasts between traditional and "newer" educational approaches for the behaviorally disordered population has been provided by Kauffman and Nelson (1977). Generally, the more innovative approaches have been extensions of the traditional approaches, with the addition of program evaluation components. Applied behavior analysts have been primarily responsible for the design of innovative programs with evaluation components and for the introduction of new therapeutic teaching interventions.

Early Behavioral Interventions in the School Setting

The use of behavioral techniques within the school setting has emerged slowly over the past 20 years (Jenson, 1978). Early work was directed toward modifying the behaviors of preschool or elementary-school-age pupils (Becker, Madsen, Arnold, & Thomas, 1967; Patterson, 1965; Zimmerman & Zimmerman, 1962). Some of the earliest behavioral research with high-school students was conducted by Hall, Panyan, Rabon, and Broden (1968) and by McAllister, Stachowiak, Baer, and Conderman (1969). Initially, the research was conducted in normal classroom settings with students who demonstrated disruptive classroom behaviors or other behaviors that interfered with the students' learning. For reviews of remedial teaching procedures with disruptive students, see Ayllon and Rosenbaum (1977), Ruggles and LeBlanc (1982), and Swift and Spivack (1974).

Behavioral Interventions for School-Related Problems of Delinquents

Behavioral interventions with delinquents grew out of research with regular secondary-school adolescents. Behavioral procedures first found effective with mainstreamed students were then applied to the problem behaviors of more difficult, unmotivated students. The Tyler (1967) and Tyler and Brown (1968) studies exemplify the effective use of token economy programs for modifying academic and classroom attending behaviors of institutionalized delinquents. Application of contingent token reinforcement techniques for successfully modifying the classroom behavior and academic performance of institutionalized delinquents has also been reported by Cohen (1968) and Meichenbaum, Bowers, and Ross (1968). Contingency contracting was another behavioral procedure implemented on an individual basis with truants (MacDonald, Gallimore, & MacDonald, 1970) and other students in the public school system exhibiting problems of school nonattendance, hyperaggression, stealing, and poor achievement motivation (Cantrell, Cantrell, Huddleston, & Woolridge, 1969). Group-oriented contingencies were also shown to be as effective as individualized procedures in modifying school-related behavior of delinquents (Alexander, Corbett, & Smigel, 1976). Classroom applications of group-oriented contingencies have been reviewed in detail by Litow and Pumroy (1975).

The application of behavioral principles on a program level easily followed from the success of group-level procedures. Token economy programs, found to be robust in more restrictive settings (Bednar, Zelhart, Greathouse, & Weinberg, 1970; Tyler & Brown, 1968), were redesigned for special classroom settings (Broden, Dunlap, & Clark, 1970; Miran, Lehrer, Koehler, & Miran,

1974; Santogrossi, O'Leary, Romanczyk, & Kaufman, 1973). Another program-level use of behavioral principles was introduced by Tharp and Wetzel (1969), who developed a consultation program for behaviorally maladjusted students in the schools, using teachers, in part, as mediators between the behavioral specialist and the targeted individual. A similar consultation model was successfully implemented on a home-based as opposed to a school-based level (Patterson, 1974). Supervising adults, trained in the youths' homes, were able to help alter the youths' deviant school behaviors. Finally, to advance the use of behavioral interventions on a broader, ecological level, Gottfredson (1983) advocated and proposed a model of organizational change for school-based prevention of delinquency.

CURRENT BEHAVIORAL SCHOOL-RELATED TRENDS WITH DELINQUENTS

Overall, a number of trends have emerged that have influenced the behavioral delinquency literature as well as the positions schools have taken toward the remediation of delinquency. First, the need to continue to intervene on an individual basis as well as on social conditions that promote and maintain delinquency has received growing recognition. Given this, school and school-based programs have become a focus for the prevention of and intervention in delinquency (Wenk, 1974). Second, natural-community alternatives to restrictive correctional settings have been strongly emphasized for delinquents (Stumphauzer, 1979). The therapeutic and ethical rationales for natural-environment service delivery have been presented cogently by Morris (1978). The deinstitutionalization movement has provided increased impetus for schools to take greater responsibility in providing school-based programs and to rely less on alternative school programs outside of the educational system (Filipczak & Wodarski, 1979). Third, greater use of significant people in the youths' natural environment has been made in the remediation of delinquency (Stumphauzer, 1973). Teachers, parents, and other supervising adults have become active participants in the youths' treatments. Fourth, and finally, as skill training has become the primary model of intervention with delinquents, the range of target behaviors focused on in school programs has broadened. Thus social/interpersonal behaviors that interfere with the process of learning have been addressed in school programs, along with the traditional academic and vocational skills.

To date, efficacy studies on special education programs for the prevention or remediation of delinquency are sparse and are too weak methodologically to provide a clear direction for program design. Furthermore, not enough consensus exists among concerned parties—including special educators, community leaders, legislators, and researchers—regarding the goals of special education for the behaviorally disordered and delinquent population. The remainder of this chapter will focus on a critical analysis of (1) what is currently being done from a behavioral point of view (beginning with a description of that point of view), (2) the effectiveness of this work, and (3) its future directions, including relevant special issues and problems.

DELINQUENCY: A BEHAVIORAL PERSPECTIVE

As presented in Part I of this volume, within a learning theory framework, an individual's behavior results from the interaction between the individual's own response tendencies and the physical and social environments. Thus interventions can be directed at both the individual's specific behaviors and at the setting in which the behaviors occur, whether that setting is the immediate environment (e.g., classroom, seating arrangement) or larger institutional and societal conditions. Morris and Braukmann (this volume) argue that both the delinquent's behavior and the larger social, economic, and legal contexts need to be taken into account to effectively reduce delinquency. Limiting one's perspective to either one or the other would be incomplete.

Delinquency-prone youngsters can be seen as lacking appropriate skills that would enable them to obtain sanctioned rewards and to abandon illegitimate sources of gratification. The trend in the applied behavioral analysis of delinquency is away from controlling or eliminating unwanted, antisocial behaviors and toward teaching prosocial behaviors. This trend is due, in part, to the fact that delinquent behavior, *per se,* does not lend easily to punishment because it is of such low frequency and occurs under covert stimulus conditions, which make it a difficult target (Emery & Marholin, 1977). Also, punishment does not provide youths alternative ways of obtaining rewards. Expanding youths' behavioral repertoires to include adaptive skills could potentially increase their chances of surviving successfully in the community, while at the same time providing youths with behaviors that may be incompatible with delinquency (Baer, 1975). On a cautionary note, the presumed relationship between the acquisition of prosocial, delinquent incompatible behaviors and a reduction in delinquency still needs empirical demonstration (Emery & Marholin, 1977). Finally, the use of procedures to establish adaptive, alternative skills has been proposed as a step toward not only intervening on current delinquency but also preventing further delinquent and criminal behavior.

Less research has been conducted with interventions directed at the environmental, as opposed to the individual, level. The focus, however, has been toward introducing environmental contingencies that have the effect of increasing an individual's repertoire of prosocial skills to secure sanctioned rewards and minimizing the contingencies that may be maintaining or setting the occasion for delinquent-type behaviors.

SCHOOL-BASED DELINQUENCY PREVENTION/INTERVENTION PROGRAMS

Numerous studies have demonstrated the efficacy of behavioral procedures for reducing disruptive classroom behavior and promoting academic performance (e.g., Barrish, Saunders, & Wolf, 1969; Broden *et al.*, 1970; Harris, Finfrock, Giles, Hart, & Tsosie, 1975; Maloney & Hopkins, 1973; McAllister *et al.*, 1969; Schumaker, Hovell, & Sherman, 1977; for reviews, see Ayllon & Rosenbaum, 1977; Ruggles & LeBlanc, 1982). Nevertheless, evaluations of the impact of these procedures in the reduction or prevention of delinquency have been minimal. Only four series of studies have been performed that attempt to assess the impact of school-based behavioral programs on rates of delinquent behavior (Bry & George, 1980; Filipczak, Friedman, & Reese, 1979; Heaton, Safer, Allen, Spinnato, & Prumo, 1976; Stuart, Tripodi, Jayaratne, & Camburn, 1976).

Generally, these latter school-based behavioral programs have shared the following characteristics: (a) services are provided primarily at the junior high-school level; (b) student participants are selected for the programs because of serious school discipline problems; (c) the majority of student participants have *not* been adjudicated delinquent prior to program participation; (d) behavioral intervention procedures are utilized to enhance school attendance and academic achievement and decrease negative in-school behavior; (e) at least part of the participant's school day is spent in the mainstream (i.e., regular classrooms); and (f) a behavioral family-intervention component is included in the program.

Stemmers Run Junior High

Safer, Heaton, and their colleagues have reported the results of a contingency management program established in a junior high school for seventh-, eighth-, and ninth-grade students (Heaton & Safer, 1982; Heaton *et al.*, 1976; Safer, Heaton, & Parker, 1981). The assistant principal selected students for the program on the basis of multiple suspensions and numerous office referrals for misconduct during the previous year. Students participated in the program for an average of 1½ years. For the purpose of program evaluation, these students were compared with similar students from two other junior high schools. Random assignment was not achieved.

Students in the treatment group participated in a special class program in the morning that included individualized academic instruction in English, social studies, math, and science. During these morning sessions, the students received points for appropriate academic and social behaviors. Academic and behavioral goals were derived from weekly contracts negotiated by the individual students and their teacher for that subject. The points earned during the morning session were exchangeable for various reinforcers during the afternoon session: access to the "reinforcement room" (containing games such as pool, table tennis, cards, and checkers, in addition to soft drinks and candy); participation in a weekly auction for materials donated by local businesses (e.g., movie and dance tickets); admission to special classes held in the school during the afternoon such as art, music, gym, and shop; and early dismissal from school with parental consent. Students received a "disturbing and disruptive behavior slip" when they engaged in serious misconduct in the school. If two slips were received during one class period, the student was dismissed from the program, sent home, and required to participate in a parent conference before reentry into school.

In addition to the previously mentioned components, meetings were held periodically with the parents in order to provide feedback on student performance in school and to develop home-based reinforcement systems to support appropriate school behaviors and academic performance. Home reinforcers for school performance were negotiated in a family conference and were formalized in a behavioral contract signed by all parties. Students were returned to their regular classrooms gradually through the use of a transition program. The transition program involved a series of phases designed to achieve generalization, including self-evaluation, less frequent feedback, use of nonprogram teachers in the program classroom, introduction of group instruction, attendance in regular classrooms, and gradual fading of in-school reinforcers.

Control-group students remained in their regular school classes, and all customary mental health services remained available to them. For a more detailed description of the program and its various components, refer to Heaton, Safer, and Allen (1982).

As reported by Safer *et al.* (1981), annual outcome measures for each of the five program years (1973–1979) included academic performance (Wide Range Achievement Test scores, student grades), school misconduct (school behavioral suspensions, days out of school for disciplinary reasons, disciplinary withdrawals or expulsions), and absenteeism. Additionally, a 4-year follow-up evaluation of the first two program years included the following measures: absence rates, suspension rates, office referrals for misconduct, classroom conduct ratings, grades, and educational longevity (number of days attending high school, graduation rate, frequency of withdrawal prior to graduation).

Annual outcomes reported by Safer *et al.* include the following. First, program participants engaged in significantly less school misconduct than control students across all three school misconduct measures in every program year. Second, across the five program years, at least 80% of the program participants received passing grades compared to an average of 48% for the control group students. In terms of the Wide Range Achievement Test (WRAT), positive pre- to posttest change scores were significantly greater for the program participants during two of the five program years. No significant differences on the WRAT were demonstrated between groups following the first, fourth, or fifth program years. And third, in general, no differences were demonstrated between groups in yearly absence rates.

Four-year follow-up outcomes reported by Safer *et al.* include the following. First, 80% of the program participants entered senior high school, whereas only 49% of the control students did so. Second, of the students who entered senior high school, no difference between groups was demonstrated in the number of days attended. Third, 27% of the first-year program participants graduated from high school, whereas only 10% of the control students graduated. This difference, however, is not statistically significant. Comparison of high-school graduation rates between program participants and control students who actually entered senior high school was not reported. And fourth, first offense rates and recidivism data were collected from 1977 to 1980 to determine the impact of the program on delinquent behavior (Safer, Heaton, & Parker, 1982, Note G). Although the program did not decrease recidivism, it did in general decrease first offenses for the first two of the three years. Nonetheless, the total difference for first offense rates between the program participants and control students was not significant.

Given the poor performance of these student participants upon entrance into senior high school, Trice, Parker, and Safer (1982) implemented and compared two behavioral senior high-school interventions for disruptive students. The authors compared the school performance of three groups of disruptive students: (1) those entering high school during a 2-year period, 1975 to 1977, when no special program was available; (2) those receiving a self-contained program in the 10th grade (1977/1978); and (3) those with access to a resource program in the 10th grade (1978/1979). Disruptive students in each of these groups were similar in age at entry, sex composition, 9th-grade attendance and suspension rates, and 9th-grade standardized achievement test scores.

Students in the self-contained program received academic instruction in their major subject areas by one teacher and an aide. Part-time consultation was provided by a bachelor's-level behavioral consultant and a PhD psychologist. Intervention procedures used in this program were similar to procedures used in the behavioral junior high-school program described earlier, including daily progress reports sent to parents and the awarding of points for academic performance exchangeable for weekly reinforcers. In addition, all students were paid for vocational instruction received during the afternoon in an off-site workshop. In contrast, students participating in the resource program were enrolled in regular sections from the start of the school year but were referred to the resource program for academic difficulty or persistent behavior problems. The resource program was staffed by a teacher/counselor and two aides who provided tutoring, individual instruction, counseling, and in-school detention services. In addition, about half of these students participated in a modified vocational program. Access to paid work experience was contingent on receiving positive daily reports from the major subject area teachers. If positive daily reports were not received, students remained in the resource program for detention. These students could earn early dismissal from detention by completing academic tasks.

Students in the three different groups (i.e., no special program, self-contained program, and resource program) were compared on the following variables: 10th-grade attendance, suspension rate, final GPA, and pre- to posttest changes in standardized achievement test scores. In addition, measures included the number of students completing the 10th grade, number of students reenrolling the following year, and the number of students enrolled 2 years later. Students participating in the resource program performed better than students in the other two groups across all measures. In general, students participating in the self-contained program were associated with more negative outcomes than students participating in no special program.

These studies by Safer and his colleagues suggest, first, that behavioral intervention during junior high school increases the number of students who subsequently enter senior high school and, second, that without further programming in the high-school setting, these students perform poorly and drop out of high school before graduation. If, however, additional intervention services are provided upon entrance into high school, these negative outcomes may be diminished. Finally, a resource program providing a variety of academic and behavioral interventions (e.g., teacher consultation, individualized instruction, contingent work experience, and dropout prevention) within the least restrictive environment appears to be the treatment of choice in this regard.

Preparation through Responsive Educational Programs

Filipczak and his colleagues have described the implementation and evaluation of Preparation through Responsive Educational Programs (PREP; Filipczak, Friedman, & Reese, 1979), a federally funded program that served a rural, a suburban, and an urban junior high school over a 5-year period. Approximately 600 troubled students within the Maryland public school system were served by the program during the time of the evaluation. Students were eligible for the program on the basis of academic and social problems including failing grades, disciplinary referrals, absenteeism, tardiness, suspensions, poor performance on standardized tests, and contacts with the police or other agencies that serve troubled youth. Enrollment in PREP was for a 1- to 2-year period during the seventh-, eighth-, or ninth-grade school years. Participation in the program was on a voluntary basis.

Students received 2 hours of individualized and small-group instruction in reading, English, and mathematics. Social skills training to facilitate immediate and generalizable social skills for in- and out-of-school problems was presented in small and large groups for 45 minutes each day. In addition, students were enrolled in four other classes within the regular school program. Positive reinforcers were delivered contingent on academic performance and appropriate social behavior. Behavioral contracts were negotiated concerning performance in non-PREP classes. Reinforcers included praise, performance ratings, grades, and tangible or activity rewards such as leisure-time soda breaks, movies, field trips, and game time. Training was provided for families in order to promote increased parental involvement in the development and implementation of home behavior management programs and to promote participation in school activities. For a more detailed description of the program operations, see Filipczak, Friedman, and Reese (1979).

Evaluation of PREP has been reported in numerous articles and includes short- and long-term results (Filipczak, Archer, & Friedman, 1980; Filipczak, Archer, Neale, & Winett, 1979; Filipczak & Friedman, 1978; Filipczak, Friedman, & Reese, 1979; Filipczak & Wodarski, 1982; Friedman, Filipczak, & Fiordaliso, 1977; Reese & Filipczak, 1980; Wodarski & Filipczak, 1982; for a more detailed review, see Burchard & Lane, 1982). Short-term outcome was assessed via standardized test scores, grades in both PREP and non-PREP classes, negative in-school behavior, and attendance.

Short-term outcome results are summarized as follows. First, PREP students performed moderately better than controls on standardized achievement tests. These results were more evident during certain years of the program than in others and varied across school settings (Filipczak, Friedman, & Reese, 1979). Second, PREP students demonstrated greater improvement in class grades than controls during the program year compared to the prior year. These results, however, were not found consistently across program years or school settings (Friedman et al., 1977; Reese & Filipczak, 1980). Third, PREP students demonstrated significantly greater school attendance than comparison groups in the majority of sites and years. Specific behavioral programming was necessary to obtain these results (Filipczak, Friedman, & Reese, 1979; Filipczak et al., 1980). And fourth, the PREP program did not systematically effect change in student in-school negative behavior (i.e., suspensions, disciplinary referrals, teacher ratings) relative to comparison groups (Filipczak et al., 1980).

A follow-up of 1 and 4 years for the first-year participants in the PREP program at the suburban junior high school was reported by Wodarski and colleagues (Wodarski & Filipczak, 1982; Wodarski, Filipczak, McCombs, Koustenis, & Rusilko, 1979). The 60 students who participated in this yearlong program were matched and randomly assigned to the total PREP program or a no-treatment control group. Each group included 30% females, and 30% nonwhites. Because this was the most successful year in PREP's history on the basis of direct outcome measures, the probability of finding significant and positive long-term effects is arguably greater for this year than for any other.

At the 1-year follow-up, PREP students demonstrated fewer suspensions, fewer disciplinary referrals, greater school attendance, and greater overall grade point averages for English and math classes than the controls. No statistical analyses were reported.

The 4-year follow-up was reported for 40 of the original sample of 60 students (21 PREP, 19 controls). At this time, 21 students were juniors, and 19 were seniors; their mean age was 17.8 years. Baseline measures suggested that the follow-up sample was comparable to the original sample. Comparisons were made with t tests on 119 self-report variables from among four general domains: access to socially acceptable roles, involvement in reinforcing relationships, incentives for prosocial behavior, and juvenile problem behavior. No significant between-group differences were demonstrated beyond chance expectations among the items directly related to the program evaluation.

Although the PREP program was able to demonstrate some positive short-term outcomes, positive long-term outcomes were not evident. These results support the findings of Safer and his colleagues that gains achieved during junior high-school intervention are lost upon entrance into high school without additional high-school intervention.

Family and School Consultation Project

Stuart and his associates have reported a number of studies involving behavioral contracts with predelinquent youth in school settings (Stuart, Jayaratne, & Tripodi, 1976; Stuart & Tripodi, 1973; Stuart, Tripodi, Jayaratne, & Camburn, 1976). Stuart and Tripodi (1973) compared the outcomes for three behavioral treatment groups differing in their prescribed length of treatment—15 days, 45 days, or 90 days—and a *post hoc* untreated control group consisting of subjects whose parents declined an initial interview with the project staff. All the research participants were junior high-school students referred for severe social disruption in school, and 16% demonstrated preintervention court contacts. Treatment included the development of behavioral contracts followed by the initiation of procedures for modifying communication, facilitating adherence to contracts, and coordinating the school-related efforts of parents and teachers.

The results indicated no differences between the three treatment groups, suggesting that the length of treatment was not related to outcome. Although significant differences were found in favor of treated students relative to control students for attendance and grades in school, no differences were found between groups in tardiness or court contacts. The composition of the control group, however, was influenced by severe selection biases (i.e., treatment refusers who were undoubtedly tougher cases). Thus the positive outcomes reported before need to be interpreted with caution, whereas the negative outcomes are particularly disappointing.

Subsequently, Stuart and his associates provided behavioral intervention for 87 predelinquents in the Family and School Consultation Project, a federally funded program (Stuart, Jayaratne, & Tripodi, 1976; Stuart, Tripodi, Jayaratne, & Camburn, 1976). The students were referred by school personnel from grades 6 through 10. Across both studies, 56% of the students were from one-parent households, 49% of the students' families had incomes less than $9,000/year in 1973, and approximately 61% of the families included four or more children. The students generally had no previous court contacts. Intervention consisted of about 15 hours devoted entirely to the use of behavioral contracting. Contracts were established between the student and the teacher as well as between the student and the family. The contracts specified privileges that could be earned by meeting specific responsibilities. Bonuses were provided for unusually positive achievements, and sanctions were applied for lapses in contract compliance. Initially, family contracts involved home-based consequences for school behavior, whereas subsequent targets involved home behavior.

Students in the program were compared with randomly assigned control students on various parent and teacher-report measures as well as on grades, attendance, and subsequent court contacts. Across the studies, 9 out of the 18 measures of parent and teacher ratings were statistically significant, all favoring the treatment group. No differences, however, were found in grades, attendance, or court contacts. These latter data on the most important outcomes suggest that the intervention program was largely unsuccessful.

Preventive Intervention

Bry and her associates have reported the development and evaluation of a behavioral early intervention program for junior high-school students with school adjustment problems (Bien & Bry, 1980; Bry, 1982; Bry & George, 1979, 1980). In the initial study, Bien and Bry (1980) evaluated the relative effectiveness of four school-based programs of varying intensities, including a no-program condition, in preventing further problems from developing among the participants. Students were selected for the program on the basis of exhibiting two of the following three characteristics: low academic motivation, family problems, and disciplinary referrals to the vice principal's office. Out of a class of 555, 40 seventh-grade students met the criteria for program participation. These students were matched in blocks of four and randomly assigned to one of four conditions: (a) no program—no special services other than services typically available within the school; (b) teacher conference program; (c) teacher conference and group meeting program; or (d) teacher conference, group meetings, and parent contact program.

The teacher conference program consisted of biweekly individual teacher conferences. These conferences were held with every teacher who had a student assigned to this condition and involved approximately 45 minutes each week. Program staff asked teachers about student goals and progress and told teachers that these students could do better in school.

The teacher conference and group-meeting program involved additional twice-weekly group meetings for the student participants. Half the students met in the morning and half in the afternoon. The program staff utilized behavioral group methods developed by Rose (1972). Discussion focused around student performance in school during the week and involved approximately 2 hours each week. Students earned points during the meetings for following group rules, coming to school and being on time, lack of discipline referrals, and achieving teacher-set goals. Points were accumulated during the year toward an extra school trip.

The final condition included not only teacher conferences and group meetings but also two parent conferences during the year and periodic parent contact via phone, letter, or home visits. During the parent conferences, the program was explained, and plans were made for ongoing contact. Frequency of parent contact during the year varied according to student performance, ranging from twice a week to once a month. These contacts were used to praise parents for their efforts in helping their children. This intervention involved approximately 2½ hours per week. For a more detailed description of program operations, refer to Bry and George (1979).

Outcome measures included grades, attendance and promptness, discipline referrals, disruptive classroom behavior, and teacher ratings of severity of school problems. Change scores were calculated for each subject on each of the five outcome variables. Premeasures consisted of sixth-grade performance or performance during the first quarter of the seventh grade. Postmeasures consisted of performance during the last three quarters of the seventh grade, final grades, or ratings made during the last month of the seventh grade. The results indicated that program intensity had a significant effect on grades and observed classroom behavior in the morning programs but not in the afternoon programs. Only the most intense condition, which included parent contact, had a greater effect than no program at all (Bien & Bry, 1980).

Bry and George (1979, 1980) evaluated the full treatment program (i.e., teacher conferences, small group meetings, and parent contact) in two outcome studies. In each study, 40 students meeting the program criteria used in the Bien and Bry (1980) study were paired and randomly assigned to the intervention program or a no-treatment control group. Students participated in the intervention program for 2 years during the seventh and eighth grades. Results indicated that the intervention prevented deteriorations in school grades and attendance. No group differences in tardiness or disciplinary actions were demonstrated (Bry & George, 1979, 1980).

Bry (1982) has reported the 1- and 5-year follow-up evaluations of the early intervention program. For a year subsequent to the 2-year treatment program, booster sessions were offered every other week for intervention students. These sessions followed the same format as the original program. One-year posttreatment follow-up results were as follows. First, intervention students engaged in significantly fewer serious school problems than the control students. Serious school problems included: five or more school suspensions, denied promotion, more than 50 days absence from school, or more than 20 days being late to school. Second, significantly more intervention students (80%) than control students (55%) obtained at least one job by the time of the follow-up interview. Third, no between-group differences were demonstrated for drug or alcohol abuse on the basis of student self-report data. And fourth, whereas 11 intervention students reported a sum of 19 instances of criminal behavior (defined as vandalism, car theft, grand theft, and robbery), 18 control students reported 45 instances. This difference approached statistical significance.

Bry (1982) also presented 5-year follow-up data, which assessed the impact of the program on delinquent behavior. The average age of the 30 intervention and 30 control students included in the follow-up was 19.5 years. The chief probation officer of the county probation department provided the author with the number of students with court files from each group and the number of students from each group with drug-related arrests. According to Bry, only serious or chronic offenses are recorded in these files. Significantly fewer intervention students (10%) had county court files than control students (30%). No between-group differences were demonstrated in drug-related arrests.

Environmental Intervention

As stated earlier in this chapter, little research attention has been directed at the environmental, as opposed to the individual, level. One such behavioral intervention program, however, has been reported by Mayer, Butterworth, Nafpaktitis, and Sulzer-Azaroff (1983). These investigators implemented a training and consultation package designed to increase the reinforcing ambience of the school and assessed its impact on vandalism and student disruption. Over a 3-year period, teams of school personnel from 18 elementary and junior high-schools attended training workshops in behavioral strategies for reducing vandalism and disruption by students in school. In addition, these teams met regularly at their respective schools to plan and implement programs on a schoolwide basis.

The intervention program was evaluated using a multiple-baseline design in which treatment was delivered following either 4 or 13 months of baseline. Outcome results indicate, first, that rates of praise delivered by teachers in project schools increased significantly, whether the teachers were directly involved in the project or not. Second, rates of off-task behavior by students decreased significantly following treatment. Third, and finally, vandalism costs decreased significantly more in treatment than control schools, with an average reduction of 78.5%. Thus reduction of delinquent behavior as measured by school vandalism was demonstrated. Although other within-school and out-of-school delinquent behavior was not assessed, these results are encouraging and suggest that environmental interventions should be investigated further using the principles and procedures of applied behavior analysis.

Summary

The four individual-level school-based behavioral programs (i.e., Stemmers Run, PREP, Family and School Consultation, and Preventive Intervention) had the following goals or objectives in common: (1) promotion of academic performance, (2) reduction of in-school negative behavior, (3) promotion of academic longevity, and (4) prevention of delinquent behavior on the part of the student participants. In relation to these goals, the results taken as a whole seem to suggest the following. First, these programs are able to effect positive short-term changes in academic performance. The students, however, need to participate in the program for more than 1 year in order for these results to be realized. Second, the evidence is unclear regarding the impact of these programs on negative in-school behavior. Only one of the four programs reported positive short-term effects in this regard (Safer et al., 1981). These results are clearly troublesome, given the body of literature supporting the efficacy of behavioral procedures in the reduction of disruptive school behavior (Ayllon & Rosenbaum, 1977). Third, no evidence exists that these changes in academic performance and negative in-school behavior are maintained for more than 1-year posttreatment. Fourth, these programs appear to enhance student entry into high school. Without special programming in the high-school setting, however, program participants perform poorly and do not graduate in greater numbers than nonparticipants. Fifth, little indication exists that these programs reduce the likelihood of subsequent delinquent behavior on the part of student participants. Only one of the programs reported findings suggesting such an effect (Bry, 1982). This could be a function of programmatic differences or differences among student participants across programs.

In terms of programmatic differences, booster sessions were provided for a year subsequent to the 2-year treatment program in Bry (1982). These sessions may have contributed positively to students' high-school adjustment that, in turn, may have contributed to a reduction in delinquent behavior.

Finally, behavioral school-focused environmental interventions can contribute to delinquency prevention/reduction efforts. Mayer *et al.* (1983) demonstrated a reduction in school-related delinquency (i.e., vandalism) as a function of such an intervention.

CONCLUSIONS

Outcomes generally have been disappointing across the full range of efforts aimed at delinquency prevention and reduction. These results may be partially attributable to failure to positively affect academic longevity (Thornberry *et al.*, 1985). If this is the case, providing high-school intervention in addition to junior high-school intervention may enhance academic longevity that, in turn, may reduce the probability of delinquent behavior. Limited support for this hypothesis has been provided by Trice, Parker, and Safer (1982) and Bry (1982). Further evaluative outcome studies, however, are essential to clearly demonstrate such relationships.

Berrueta-Clement, Schweinhart, Barnett, and Weikart (1987) reported long-term outcomes of the Perry Preschool Project that provide indirect support for the preceeding hypothesis. Compared to matched, randomly assigned comparison subjects not receiving preschool intervention, subjects who participated in the Perry Preschool Project for 1 or 2 years demonstrated significantly lower rates of delinquent and criminal behavior in adolescence and early adulthood. In addition, participants demonstrated higher rates of employment and postsecondary education and training and lower rates of welfare dependence and teenage pregnancies and births. The authors present an empirically based causal model suggesting that at least part of the reason for these long-term outcomes is the enhancement of academic success through secondary school. Specifically, preschool education and initial IQ determine IQ at entrance into school, which, in turn, is related to average achievement and to years in special education. Success in these areas determine educational attainment through age 19, which causes a reduction in official delinquency (Berrueta-Clement *et al.*, 1987).

These findings lend support to the hypothesis that school success reduces the probability of delinquent behavior. These data also suggest that preventive intervention should begin prior to entrance into elementary school rather than waiting until junior high or high school to implement treatment.

In the absence of preschool intervention, however, or in cases where problems occur subsequent to preschool, intervention is nonetheless indicated. Studies reviewed in this chapter suggest that behavioral interventions implemented during junior high school can effect positive change in academic performance and enhance student entrance into high school. Component analyses are lacking, but it appears that positive reinforcement of academic performance and parent participation are important contributors to these outcomes. There is also some indication that positive outcomes can be achieved when students are in the mainstream for the majority of their school day (Bry & George, 1979, 1980).

The data indicate that additional intervention is necessary to maintain gains achieved during junior high school and to prevent school dropout. If provided in the high-school setting, intervention should allow students to remain in the mainstream to the extent possible, and self-contained classroom intervention should be avoided (Trice et al., 1982). Further investigation is necessary to identify effective behavioral treatment procedures and to determine whether or not these high-school interventions will enhance academic longevity and/or reduce delinquent and criminal behavior.

Finally, behavioral school-focused environmental interventions can contribute to delinquency prevention/reduction efforts (Mayer et al., 1983). Further development and evaluation of these intervention models are clearly indicated.

REFERENCES

Achenbach, T. (1975). The historical context of treatment for delinquent and maladjusted children: Past, present, and future. Behavior Disorders, 1, 3–14.

Ahlstrom, W., & Havighurst, R. (1971). 400 losers: Delinquent boys in high school. San Francisco: Jossey-Bass.

Alexander, R. N., Corbett, T. F., & Smigel, J. (1976). The effects of individual and group consequences on school attendance and curfew violations with predelinquent adolescents. Journal of Applied Behavior Analysis, 9, 221–226.

Ayllon, T., & Rosenbaum, M. (1977). The behavioral treatment of disruption and hyperactivity in school settings. In B. Lahey & A. Kazdin (Eds.), Advances in clinical child psychology (pp. 85–118). New York: Plenum Press.

Bachman, J., & O'Malley, P. (1978). Youth in transition: Adolescence to adulthood (Vol. 6). Ann Arbor: University of Michigan Press.

Baer, D. (1975). In the beginning, there was a response. In E. Ramp & G. Semb (Eds.), Behavior analysis: Areas of research and application (pp. 16–30). Englewood Cliffs, NJ: Prentice-Hall.

Barrish, H. H., Saunders, M., & Wolf, M. (1969). Good behavior game: Effects of individual contingencies for group consequences on disruptive behavior in a classroom. Journal of Applied Behavior Analysis, 2, 119–124.

Becker, W., Madsen, C., Arnold, C., & Thomas, D. (1967). The contingent use of teacher attention and praise in reducing classroom behavior problems. Journal of Special Education, 1, 287–307.

Bednar, R. L., Zelhart, P. F., Greathouse, L., & Weinberg, S. (1970). Operant conditioning principles in the treatment of learning and behavior problems with delinquent boys. Journal of Counseling Psychology, 17, 492–497.

Berrueta-Clement, J., Schweinhart, L., Barnett, W., & Weikart, D. (1987). The effects of early educational intervention on crime and delinquency in adolescence and early adulthood. In J. D. Burchard & S. N. Burchard (Eds.), The prevention of delinquency (pp. 220–240). Beverly Hills: Sage.

Bien, N. Z., & Bry, B. H. (1980). An experimentally designed comparison of four intensities of school-based prevention programs for adolescents with adjustment problems. Journal of Community Psychology, 8, 110–116.

Braukmann, C., Fixsen, D., Phillips, E., & Wolf, M. (1975). Behavioral approaches to treatment in the crime and delinquency field. *Criminology, 13,* 299–331.

Broden, M., Dunlap, A., & Clark, R. (1970). Effects of teacher attention and a token reinforcement system in a junior high school special education class. *Exceptional Children, 36,* 341–349.

Bry, B. H. (1982). Reducing the incidence of adolescent problems through preventive intervention: One- and five-year follow-up. *American Journal of Community Psychology, 10,* 265–276.

Bry, B. H., & George, F. E. (1979). Evaluating and improving prevention programs: A strategy from drug abuse. *Evaluation and Program Planning, 2,* 127–136.

Bry, B. H., & George, F. E. (1980). The preventive effects of early intervention on the attendance and grades of urban adolescents. *Professional Psychology, 11,* 252–260.

Budnick, A., & Andreacchi, J. (1967). Day school for disturbed boys. In P. H. Berdowitz & D. P. Rothman (Eds.), *Public school education for dusturbed children in New York City* (pp. 57–77). Springfield, IL: Charles C Thomas.

Bullock, L., & Brown, R. (1972). *Educational provisions for emotionally disturbed children: A status report.* Gainesville: University of Florida, Florida Educational Research Development Commission.

Burchard, J. D., & Lane, T. W. (1982). Crime and delinquency. In A. S. Bellack, M. Hersen, & A. E. Kazdin (Eds.), *International handbook of behavior modification and therapy* (pp. 613–652). New York: Plenum Press.

Cantrell, R., Cantrell, M., Huddleston, C., & Woolridge, R. (1969). Contingency contracting with school problems. *Journal of Applied Behavior Analysis, 2,* 215–220.

Cohen, H. (1968). Educational therapy: The design of learning environments. In J. M. Shlien (Ed.), *Research in psychotherapy* (Vol. 3, pp. 21–53). Washington, DC: American Psychological Association.

Dunn, L. (1973). An overview. In L. Dunn (Ed.), *Exceptional children in the schools: Special education in transition* (2nd ed., pp. 3–63). New York: Holt, Rinehart and Winston.

Elliott, D., & Voss, H. (1974). *Delinquency and dropout.* Lexington, MA: Lexington Books.

Emery, R., & Marholin, D. (1977). An applied behavior analysis of delinquency: The irrelevancy of relevant behavior. *American Psychologist, 32,* 860–873.

Feldman, M. P. (1977). *Criminal behavior: A psychological analysis.* London: Wiley.

Filipczak, J., & Friedman, R. M. (1978). Some controls on applied research in a public secondary school: Project PREP. In A. C. Catania & T. A. Brigham (Eds.), *Handbook of applied behavior analysis: Social and instructional processes* (pp. 564–583). New York: Irvington Publishers.

Filipczak, J., & Wodarski, J. S. (1979). Behavioral intervention in public schools: Implementing and evaluating a model. *Corrective and Social Psychiatry and Journal of Behavior Technology, Methods and Therapy, 25,* 104–116.

Filipczak, J., & Wodarski, J. S. (1982). Behavioral interventions in public schools: I. Short-term results. In D. J. Safer (Ed.), *School programs for disruptive adolescents* (pp. 195–199). Baltimore: University Park Press.

Filipczak, J., Archer, M. B., Neale, M. S., & Winett, R. A. (1979). Issues in multivariate assessment of a large-scale behavioral program. *Journal of Applied Behavior Analysis, 12,* 593–613.

Filipczak, J., Friedman, R. M., & Reese, S. C. (1979). PREP: Educational programming to prevent juvenile problems. In J. S. Stumphauzer (Ed.), *Progress in behavior therapy with delinquents* (pp. 236–258). Springfield, IL: Charles C Thomas.

Filipczak, J., Archer, M. B., & Friedman, R. M. (1980). In-school social skills training: Use with disruptive adolescents. *Behavior Modification, 4,* 243–264.

Friedman, R. M., Filipczak, J., & Fiordaliso, R. (1977). Within-school generalization of the Preparation through Responsive Educational Programs (PREP) academic project. *Behavior Therapy, 8,* 986–995.

Gottfredson, G. (1983). Schooling and delinquency prevention: Some practical ideas for educators, parents, program developers, and researchers. *Journal of Child Care, 1,* 51–64.

Hall, R., Panyan, M., Rabon, D., & Broden, M. (1968). Instructing beginning teachers in reinforcement procedures which improve classroom control. *Journal of Applied Behavior Analysis, 1,* 315–322.

Harris, V. W., Finfrock, S. R., Giles, D. K., Hart, B. M., & Tsosie, P. C. (1975). The effects of performance contingencies on the assignment completion behavior of severely delinquent youth. In E. A. Ramp & G. Semb (Eds.), *Behavior analysis: Areas of research and application* (pp. 309–316). Englewood Cliffs, NJ: Prentice-Hall.

Hathaway, S., Reynolds, P., & Monachesi, E. (1969). Follow-up of the later careers and lives of 1,000 boys who dropped out of high school. *Journal of Consulting and Clinical Psychology, 33*, 370–380.

Heaton, R. C., & Safer, D. J. (1982). Secondary school outcome following a junior high school behavioral program. *Behavior Therapy, 13*, 226–231.

Heaton, R. C., Safer, D. J., Allen, R. P., Spinnato, N. C., & Prumo, F. M. (1976). A motivational environment for behaviorally deviant junior high school students. *Journal of Abnormal Child Psychology, 4*, 263–275.

Heaton, R. C., Safer, D. J., & Allen, R. P. (1982). A contingency management program for disruptive junior high school students: I. A detailed description. In D. J. Safer (Ed.), *School programs for disruptive adolescents* (pp. 217–239). Baltimore: University Park Press.

Hirschi, T., & Selvin, H. (1967). *Delinquency research: An appraisal of analytic methods.* New York: Free Press.

Hirshoren, A., & Heller, G. (1979). Programs for adolescents with behavior disorders: The state of the art. *The Journal of Special Education, 13*, 275–281.

Hirshoren, A., Schultz, E., Manton, A., & Henderson, R. (1970). A survey of public school special education programs for emotionally disturbed children. *Special Education Monograph.* Urbana-Champaign, IL: University of Illinois Department of Special Education.

Jenson, W. (1978). Behavior modification in secondary schools: A review. *Journal of Research and Development in Education, 11*, 53–63.

Johnson, R. E. (1979). *Juvenile delinquency and its origins.* Cambridge, England: Cambridge University Press.

Kanfer, F., & Goldstein, A. (1975). *Helping people change.* New York: Pergamon Press.

Kauffman, J., & Nelson, M. (1977). Educational programming for secondary school age delinquent and maladjusted pupils. *Behavioral Disorders, 2*, 29–37.

Kelly, D. (1978). *How schools manufacture "misfits".* Rowland Heights, CA: Newcal Publications.

Kelly, D. (1980). The educational experience and evolving delinquent careers: A neglected institutional link. In D. Shichor & D. Kelly (Eds.), *Critical issues in juvenile delinquency* (pp. 99–114). Lexington, MA: Lexington Books.

Koval, J., & Polk, K. (1967). Problem youth in a small city. In M. Klein (Ed.), *Juvenile gangs in context* (pp. 123–138). Englewood Cliffs, NJ: Prentice-Hall.

Krohn, H. (1964). The role of special education in the rehabilitation of emotionally disturbed children. In P. Knoblock (Ed.), *Educational programming for disturbed children: A decade ahead* (pp. 58–70). Syracuse: Syracuse University Press.

Kvarceus, W. (1945). Delinquency: A by-product of the schools? *School and Society, 59*, 350–351.

Leblanc, M., Biron, L., & Provonost, L. (1979). *Psycho-social development and delinquency evolution.* Unpublished manuscript, University of Montreal.

Leitenberg, H. (1976). *Handbook of behavior modification and behavior therapy.* Englewood Cliffs, NJ: Prentice-Hall.

Litow, L., & Pumroy, D. (1975). A brief review of classroom group-oriented contingencies. *Journal of Applied Behavior Analysis, 8*, 341–347.

MacDonald, W. S., Gallimore, R., & MacDonald, G. (1970). Contingency counseling by school personnel: An economic model of intervention. *Journal of Applied Behavior Analysis, 3*, 175–182.

Maloney, K. B., & Hopkins, B. L. (1973). The modification of sentence structure and its relationship to subjective judgements of creativity in writing. *Journal of Applied Behavior Analysis, 6*, 425–433.

Marrone, R., & Anderson, N. (1970). Innovative public school programming for emotionally disturbed children. *Journal of Orthopsychiatry, 40*, 694–701.

Mayer, G. R., Butterworth, T., Nafpaktitis, M., & Sulzer-Azaroff, B. (1983). Preventing school vandalism and improving discipline: A three-year study. *Journal of Applied Behavior Analysis, 16*, 355–369.

McAllister, L., Stachowiak, J., Baer, D., & Conderman, L. (1969). The application of operant conditioning techniques in a secondary school classroom. *Journal of Applied Behavior Analysis, 2,* 277–285.

Meichenbaum, D., Bowers, K., & Ross, R. (1968). Modification of classroom behavior of institutionalized female adolescent offenders. *Behaviour Research and Therapy, 6,* 343–353.

Miran, M., Lehrer, P., Koehler, R., & Miran, E. (1974). What happens when deviant behavior begins to change? The relevance of a social systems approach to behavior problems with adolescence. *Journal of Community Psychology, 2,* 370–375.

Morris, E. (1978). A brief review of legal deviance. In D. Marholin (Ed.), *Child behavior therapy* (pp. 214–238). New York: Gardner Press.

Morse, W., Cutler, R., & Fink, A. (1964). *Public school classes for the emotionally handicapped: A research analysis.* Washington, DC: Council for Exceptional Children.

Mukherjee, S. (1971). *A typological study of school status and delinquency.* Unpublished doctoral dissertation, University of Pennsylvania, Philadelphia.

National Center for Education Statistics. (1983). *Digest for education statistics 1983–1984.* Washington, DC: U.S. Government Printing Office.

Palmer, F., & Anderson, L. (1979). Long term gains from early interventions: Findings from longitudinal studies. In E. Zigler & J. Valentine (Eds.), *Project Head Start: A legacy of the war on poverty* (pp. 433–466). New York: Free Press.

Patterson, G. (1965). An application of conditioning techniques to the control of a hyperactive child. In L. Ullmann & L. Krasner (Eds.), *Case studies in behavior modification* (pp. 370–375). New York: Holt, Rinehart & Winston.

Patterson, G. (1974). Interventions for boys with conduct problems: Multiple settings, treatments and criteria. *Journal of Consulting and Clinical Psychology, 42,* 471–481.

Polk, K. (1975). Schools and the delinquency experience. *Criminal Justice and Behavior, 2,* 315–338.

Polk, K., Adler, C., Bazemore, G., Blake, G., Cordray, S., Coventry, G., Galvin, J., & Temple, M. (1981). Becoming adult: An analysis of maturational development from age 16 to 30 of a cohort of young men. *Final report of the Marion County Youth Study.* Eugene: University of Oregon.

Reese, S. C., & Filipczak, J. (1980). Assessment of skill generalization: Measurement across setting, behavior, and time in an educational setting. *Behavior Modification, 4,* 209–224.

Rose, S. D. (1972). *Treating children in groups: A behavioral approach.* San Francisco: Jossey-Bass.

Ruggles, T., & LeBlanc, J. (1982). Behavior analysis procedures in classroom teaching. In A. Bellack, M. Hersen, & A. Kazdin (Eds.), *International handbook of behavior modification and therapy* (pp. 959–996). New York: Plenum Press.

Rutter, M., & Giller, H. (1984). *Juvenile delinquency.* New York: Guilford Press.

Safer, D. J. (1982a). Some factors influencing school misconduct. In D. J. Safer (Ed.), *School programs for disruptive adolescents* (pp. 5–20). Baltimore: University Park Press.

Safer, D. J. (1982b). Special education and programs for behavior problem youth. In D. J. Safer (Ed.), *School programs for disruptive adolescents* (pp. 111–132). Baltimore: University Park Press.

Safer, D. J. (1982c). Dimensions and issues of school programs for disruptive youth. In D. J. Safer (Ed.), *School programs for disruptive adolescents* (pp. 67–90). Baltimore: University Park Press.

Safer, D. J., Heaton, R. C., & Parker, F. C. (1981). A behavioral program for disruptive junior high school students: Results and follow-up. *Journal of Abnormal Child Psychology, 9,* 483–494.

Safer, D. J., Heaton, R. C., & Parker, F. C. (1982). A contingency management program for disruptive junior high school students: II. Results and follow-up. In D. J. Safer (Ed.), *School programs for disruptive adolescents* (pp. 241–253). Baltimore: University Park Press.

Santogrossi, D., O'Leary, K. D., Romanczyk, G., & Kaufman, K. (1973). Self-regulation by adolescents in a psychiatric hospital school token system. *Journal of Applied Behavior Analysis, 6,* 277–287.

Schafer, W., & Polk, K. (1967). Delinquency and the schools. In *The President's Commission on*

Law Enforcement and Administration of Justice Task Force report: Juvenile delinquency and youth crime (pp. 222–277). Washington, DC: U.S. Government Printing Office.

Schumaker, J. B., Hovell, M. F., & Sherman, J. A. (1977). An analysis of daily report cards and parent-managed privileges in the improvement of adolescents' classroom performance. Journal of Applied Behavior Analysis, 10, 449–464.

Stuart, R. B., & Tripodi, T. (1973). Experimental evaluation of three time-constrained behavioral treatments for predelinquents and delinquents. In R. D. Rubin, J. P. Brady, & J. D. Henderson (Eds.), Advances in behavior therapy (Vol. 4, pp. 1–12). New York: Academic Press.

Stuart, R. B., Jayaratne, S., & Tripodi, T. (1976). Changing adolescent deviant behavior through reprogramming the behavior of parents and teachers: An experimental evaluation. Canadian Journal of Behavioral Science, 8, 132–144.

Stuart, R. B., Tripodi, T., Jayaratne, S., & Camburn, D. (1976). An experiment in social engineering in serving the families of predelinquents. Journal of Abnormal Child Psychology, 4, 243–261.

Stumphauzer, J. (Ed.). (1973). Behavior therapy with delinquents. Springfield, IL: Charles C Thomas.

Stumphauzer, J. (Ed.). (1979). Progress in behavior therapy with delinquents. Springfield, IL: Charles C Thomas.

Swift, M., & Spivack, G. (1974). Therapeutic teaching: A review of teaching methods for behaviorally troubled children. Journal of Special Education, Monograph 4, 259–289.

Task Force for Community Crime Prevention. (1973). Programs for education. In National Advisory Commission on Criminal Justice Standards and Goals, Community crime prevention (pp. 140–173). Washington, DC: U.S. Government Printing Office.

Tharp, R. G., & Wetzel, R. J. (1969). Behavior modification in the natural environment. New York: Academic Press.

Thornberry, T., Moore, M., & Christenson, R. (1985). The effect of dropping out of high school on subsequent criminal behavior. Criminology, 23, 3–18.

Trice, A. D., Parker, F. C., & Safer, D. J. (1982). A comparison of senior high school interventions for disruptive students. In D. J. Safer (Ed.), School programs for disruptive adolescents (pp. 333–340). Baltimore: University Park Press.

Tyler, V. (1967). Application of operant token reinforcement of academic performance with institutionalized delinquent boys. Psychological Reports, 21, 249–260.

Tyler, V., & Brown, G. (1968). Token reinforcement of academic performance with institutionalized delinquent boys. Journal of Educational Psychology, 59, 164–168.

Wenk, E. (1974). Schools and delinquency prevention. Crime and Delinquency Literature, 6, 236–258.

Wodarski, J. S., & Filipczak, J. (1982). Behavioral intervention in public schools: II. Long-term follow-up. In D. J. Safer (Ed.), School programs for disruptive adolescents (pp. 201–214). Baltimore: University Park Press.

Wodarski, J. S., Filipczak, J., McCombs, D., Koustenis, G., & Rusilko, S. (1979). Follow-up on behavioral intervention with troublesome adolescents. Journal of Behavior Therapy and Experimental Psychiatry, 10, 181–188.

Zimmerman, E., & Zimmerman, J. (1962). The alteration of behavior in a classroom situation. Journal of Experimental Analysis of Behavior, 5, 59–60.

Zimring, F., & Hawkins, G. (1968). Deterrence and marginal groups. Journal of Research in Crime and Delinquency, 5, 100–114.

IV

SPECIAL TOPICS IN INTERVENTION AND EVALUATION

12

Criminal Justice Interventions with Drug and Alcohol Abusers

The Role of Compulsory Treatment

MAXINE L. STITZER AND MARY E. McCAUL

This chapter examines the relationship between substance abuse and crime within a behavioral framework and considers various intervention strategies that can be implemented through the criminal justice system with substance abusers who become involved with that system. The broad intervention strategies covered are supply restriction, incarceration, community supervision, and compulsory treatment. These approaches, designed to reduce criminal activity and substance use, are all consistent with behavioral principles of response suppression. Other behavioral principles that involve strengthening of alternative prosocial behaviors have not generally been applied with substance abusers by the criminal justice system. From a behavioral viewpoint, the interventions employed by the criminal justice system have usually involved avoidance paradigms in which incarceration or other legal sanctions would be imposed as a consequence of inappropriate behavior. Avoidance contingencies have been applied directly by the criminal justice system in community supervision programs designed to suppress drug abuse in the community. These contingencies have also been used to promote participation of criminally involved substance abusers in drug and alcoholism treatment programs.

The chapter is divided into three major sections. The first characterizes substance abuse as a behavioral disorder and describes the associations between substance abuse and crime; the second reviews criminal justice interventions with drug and alcohol abusers, with particular emphasis on the evaluation of compulsory treatment approaches, and the third summarizes the variables that appear to influence treatment outcomes for substance abusers. Discussing drug and alcohol abuse within a single chapter provides an opportunity to point out similarities as well as differences in their relationships to

Maxine L. Stitzer and **Mary E. McCaul** • Departments of Psychiatry and Behavioral Sciences, Johns Hopkins University School of Medicine/Key Medical Center, Baltimore, Maryland 22124.

crime and in the criminal justice intervention strategies that have been used with abusers.

SUBSTANCE ABUSE AND CRIME

Both substance abuse and crime can be conceptualized within a behavioral framework that relies on objective definitions of behavioral disorders and that emphasizes the determinants and controlling variables of disorders. This section will present a behavioral overview of drug and alcohol abuse and then describe the types of substance abuse—crime relationships that are characteristic for drug and alcohol abuse.

Behavioral Overview of Drug and Alcohol Abuse

Substance abuse can be conceptualized as an operant behavior (self-administration of a substance) maintained by its reinforcing consequences (e.g., pharmacological drug effects) and influenced in predictable ways by other environmental variables. Support for a behavioral model comes primarily from the striking cross-species similarities between animal and human self-administration. A past review by Griffiths, Bigelow, and Henningfield (1980) presents evidence for similarities in (1) the types of drugs that are self-administered by human and nonhuman species, (2) the patterns of drug intake, and (3) the environmental and pharmacological factors that influence rates and patterns of self-administration. These striking cross-species similarities suggest that the excessive self-administration of certain substances is a biologically normal event, whose etiology and maintenance depend more upon the potent reinforcing properties of drugs and less on unique characteristics of the individual than has been previously recognized.

The fact that drugs can act as powerful reinforcers to maintain behavior implies that every human has the potential to become a substance abuser. This clearly does not happen. Rather, large individual differences are seen in the amount, type, and pattern of drug use. The factors that determine whether a particular individual will become an abuser are as yet poorly understood, although they certainly include such things as availability of abusable substances and the behavior (verbal and otherwise) of friends and family with regard to substance use. What does seem clear from observation of individuals entering treatment for drug and alcohol abuse is that the drug reinforcer has by that time become a predominant influence in their lives as evidenced by an overriding concern with acquisition and effects of the substance as well as repeated episodes of self-administration. Other material and social reinforcers that maintain considerable amounts of behavior in nonabusers may still have reinforcing efficacy for substance abusers, but the potency of these nondrug reinforcers appears to be less than that of the drug reinforcer as judged by the behavioral time allocation and choice behavior of abusers. Perhaps the most important difference between abusers and nonabusers is the extent to which drug reinforcers have attained preeminence in their lives and control over their behavior.

Substance Abuse and Crime Associations

One potential association between crime and substance abuse is that crime can function as a response maintained by the acquisition of drug reinforcers. This is the relationship typically used to explain the high crime rates among narcotic drug abusers, although drug purchases from crime-generated income are not restricted to "hard" drugs; alcohol purchases may also contribute to the need for crime-generated income among individuals lacking in legitimate income sources (Strug et al., 1984). A strong relationship between illicit narcotic drug use and criminal behavior, especially property crimes, has been clearly established through survey research (Ball, Shaffer, & Nurco, 1983; McGlothlin, Anglin, & Wilson, 1978; Shaffer, Nurco, & Kinlock, 1984). For example, Ball et al. (1983) interviewed 354 Baltimore narcotic addicts about their lifetime criminal activities and drug use. These subjects described a total of 774,777 crime days (days on which at least one crime was committed) during 1,223,930 days at large in the community; overall 63% of their days at large or about 230 days of a year were spent engaging in one or more crimes. Drug dealing and theft accounted for the majority of crimes reported (27% and 38%, respectively), whereas illegal gambling, con games, violence, and assorted other crimes comprised the remainder. Interview data such as these undoubtedly provide a more realistic picture of the criminal activity of drug abusers than do arrest and incarceration data because only a very low percentage of crimes result in arrest (estimated at less than 1% for crimes overall). The sheer quantity of criminal activity reported by drug abusers is impressive.

One of the strongest relationships that has emerged from the survey studies of crime among long-term drug abusers is that the amount of crime committed is clearly associated with current addiction status. Thus, in the survey studies by Ball and co-workers, 88% of the crime reported occurred during periods of active addiction. Similar data are reported by McGlothlin et al. (1978) who also showed a quantitative relationship between reported amounts of drug use and crime. The largest increment in criminal activity, however, was associated with daily narcotics use; crime levels associated with less than daily use were similar to those seen during periods of nonaddiction. This relationship suggests that reductions in drug-related crime might be effectively achieved by reducing incidence of drug use alone and particularly by eliminating daily drug use.

A second potential relationship between drugs and crime involves drug-facilitated aggression and drug-produced performance impairment. This is the relationship typically used to explain the association between alcohol use and crime. Thus excessive users of alcohol tend to perform illegal and criminal acts while they are intoxicated, rather than as a prerequisite to becoming intoxicated. Specifically, alcohol abusers can become involved with the criminal justice system by driving while intoxicated, by being drunk and/or disorderly in public, and by committing a violent, assaultive, or other type of crime while intoxicated. Although alcohol's disinhibiting and performance-impairing effects may contribute to criminal behavior, such behavior is clearly not an inevitable consequence of drinking; many people are able to drink alcohol without getting into assaultive confrontations or automobile accidents. Instead, complex dose, tolerance, situational, and individual history variables may interact to determine the behavior of an intoxicated individual. Reduction or elimination of alcohol use should be an effective control strategy for those who do engage in dangerous or criminal acts while intoxicated.

CRIMINAL JUSTICE INTERVENTIONS

A behavioral model suggests that several strategies that have been used by the criminal justice system may be expected to reduce drug and alcohol self-administration by abusers. These include interventions that increase the cost or effort required to obtain drugs (supply restriction), that prevent or reduce the drug-taking response (incarceration), and that alter the environmental consequences of drug use versus abstinence (community supervision programs). The criminal justice system has also used compulsory participation in drug and alcohol abuse treatment programs as an alternative to legal sanctions in an attempt to influence substance-abuse-related crime indirectly. In the following sections, the efficacy of these approaches will be reviewed and evaluated.

Supply Restriction

Law enforcement agencies expend considerable efforts to prevent the entry of illegal drugs into the country. Making drugs illegal and restricting their availability have the desirable effect of suppressing the overall prevalence of drug self-administration. The legal and widely available intoxicant, alcohol, is much more frequently abused than is any controlled drug. For instance, a recent psychiatric epidemiology study found that about 2% of the U.S. urban population could be classified as abusers of any drug including marihuana (2.5%–3% of males were so classified), whereas about 5% of the overall urban population and 8% to 10% of males were classified as alcohol-dependent or alcohol abusers by psychiatric diagnostic criteria (Myers et al., 1984). Restriction of alcohol availability could no doubt lower abuse rates, although this strategy is not available to the criminal justice system. Changes in the legal drinking age, for example, and legislation requiring bartenders to stop serving clearly intoxicated patrons are supply-restriction strategies that reduce consumption in specific drinker groups, whereas cost manipulations such as increased taxation are effective modulators of liquor purchases and overall alcoholism rates (Lau, 1975; Popham, Schmidt, & de Lint, 1975; Seeley, 1960).

Although reducing the overall prevalence of use, supply restriction also escalates drug cost, which has the less desirable effect of increasing the amount of money and effort needed to obtain drugs. This relationship is particularly important in the case of illicit narcotics abuse, where increased cost may be reflected in higher rates of criminal behavior associated with obtaining money for drug purchases. The criminogenic effect of high illicit opiate drug cost has recently been partially offset by providing legally available alternatives to illicit drugs in the form of methadone maintenance treatment. Because alcohol is still relatively inexpensive, most abusers do not need to engage in crime in order to obtain their drug of choice.

Incarceration

Removal of the drug- or alcohol-abusing criminal from society eliminates (or dramatically suppresses) substance use temporarily while the abuser is under close institutional monitoring and may suppress future drug use and/or criminal behavior to the extent that imprisonment acts as a punisher. The effects of incarceration on subsequent substance use and crime have been evaluated only for narcotics abusers. Alcohol problems among criminal offenders are not reliably identified, nor have alcoholic criminal offenders been followed up systematically.

Imprisonment might be an effective intervention strategy if the punishment and enforced abstinence aspects of the event reliably led to subsequent abstinence in the community. Longitudinal studies of drug abusers suggest, however, that relapse rather than abstinence is the more common sequela to incarceration. In a well-known and carefully conducted longitudinal study, Vaillant (1966) followed 100 New York narcotic abusers who were first-time admissions to the Lexington Public Health Service Hospital in 1952. Self-reported outcome status was corroborated by community sources including parole officers, relatives, friends, and institutional records. During the 12-year follow-up period, this group of 100 subjects was institutionalized 625 times either in prisons (92% of the sample) or in hospitals where they went voluntarily to detoxify from narcotics. When institutionalization consisted of short-term voluntary hospitalization or prison sentences of less than 9 months duration, only 5% of the episodes were followed by 1 year or more of drug abstinence. Prison sentences of 9 or more months without subsequent parole supervision resulted in long-term abstinence episodes on about 15% of occasions. In contrast, long prison sentences (9 or more months) that were followed by at least 1 year of parole supervision resulted in abstinence on 67% of occasions for the few subjects ($N = 30$) exposed to this set of conditions, even though 80% of these same 30 subjects had previously relapsed after short imprisonment or hospitalization. Vaillant's data suggest, then, that neither response suppression nor punishment aspects of incarceration are sufficient to eliminate drug use and crime; recidivism and relapse are the rule rather than the exception following periods of incarceration. The study does suggest, however, a potential benefit from long-term community supervision following periods of incarceration.

COMMUNITY SUPERVISION

The criminal justice system, through its parole and probation services, has another potentially effective mechanism for influencing the behavior of substance abusers who have already committed crimes. Parole and probation officers can monitor substance abusers and can impose contingencies that may shape behavior. Specifically, return to prison has typically been used as an eventual consequence of poor parole or probation performance, whereas continued freedom in the community is the positive outcome for socially acceptable behavior. As with incarceration, evaluation of community supervision approaches has been conducted with drug abusers but not with alcoholics. Although Vaillant's data suggest that incarceration has little impact on the long-term outcomes of drug abusers, the punishing effects of imprisonment might be strengthened if return to incarcerated status were made directly contingent upon relapse to drug use. Two contemporary studies that evaluated community supervision programs incorporating this contingency, however, have shown only modest benefits from such an approach.

McCabe, Kurland, and Sullivan (1975) described an intensive outpatient urinalysis monitoring program conducted with 371 recently paroled male narcotics abusers in Baltimore. Subjects reported to a clinic for daily urinalysis and weekly group psychotherapy sessions throughout their parole that lasted a median of 17 months. An opiate-positive urine test resulted in confrontation by the program staff (presumably an aversive event), and relapse to heavy narcotics use set the occasion for temporary hospitalization or reincarceration. Only 6% of program enrollees were able to complete their parole period totally abstinent; an additional 10% completed the program with low levels of drug use and no reinstitutionalization. The rest either absconded from the program (26%) or returned to prison as a result of drug use (58%). These results are similar to those reported by Vaillant for unsupervised drug abusers following their release from the Lexington hospital. From a practical standpoint, the program clearly was not very effective in preventing relapse. It is likely that failure was related to a lack of immediacy and consistency in imposing contingencies in a situation where each parole agent was typically responsible for a caseload of 80 to 100 individuals.

The California Civil Addict Program (CAP) provided another contemporary opportunity to evaluate the efficacy of close community supervision with relapse-contingent return to incarcerated status as a strategy for altering the behavior of drug abusers (McGlothlin, Anglin, & Wilson, 1977). In this case, some beneficial effects were demonstrated. The CAP program, as initiated in 1961, provided for a 7-year involuntary commitment that could be ordered by the courts in lieu of criminal proceedings for persons convicted of a crime who were also judged to be narcotics-addicted. During the first stage of commitment, the abuser was incarcerated for 6 or more months at an inpatient rehabilitation center where group therapy, schooling, and vocational training were provided. Upon release to outpatient status, the abuser was placed under relatively strict parole supervision (agent case loads averaged about 32 parolees) that included regular urinalysis monitoring. During the early phases of the program, detection of regular drug use or other serious parole violations resulted in return to the inpatient rehabilitation center, although a several-month delay between the start of daily drug use and return to the inpatient unit was apparently not uncommon (Anglin, McGlothlin, & Speckart, 1981). Persons who went 3 years without detected regular drug use and were otherwise free of serious parole violations were eligible for early discharge from the program.

For the evaluation of this program, a treatment sample ($N = 289$) was selected from 1964 civil commitment admissions, whereas controls were a closely matched group ($N = 292$) of narcotics abusers who had been committed during the early years of the program but who were subsequently discharged by writ during their first inpatient stay because of procedural errors made by the courts. The evaluation is based on self-report data from lengthy in-person interviews conducted in 1974 to 1975 by trained staff. Subjects were asked to provide detailed quantitative information about their legal status, narcotic and nonnarcotic drug use, income sources, and criminal activities for each successive period of nonincarcerated time between onset of regular narcotic use and the interview. Scheduled interviews were completed with 88% of the living subjects.

Outcome data generally showed a significant advantage for the supervised group during nonincarcerated time. For example, as shown in Figure 1, the legally supervised group during the commitment period reported a lower percentage of nonincarcerated time engaging in daily narcotic drugs use than did the control group, especially during the early years of commitment. When data from the commitment period were analyzed as an average percentage of nonincarcerated time per subject spent using narcotics drugs, the commitment group was significantly lower than the control group (31% and 48% of nonincarcerated time, respectively). The treated group also reported significantly more employment and less criminal activity than the control group during the commitment phase. The average percentage of time incarcerated during the 7-year commitment period, however, was similar for the two groups (about 50%), although the treatment group tended to have more short periods of incarceration in the program's inpatient unit, whereas the control group tended to have fewer but longer periods of incarceration in prison. Positive effects of the commitment program, although still apparent as trends, were no longer statistically significant after the 7-year commitment period. By the time of the interview, the groups did not differ on urinalysis or self-report rates of recent opiate use; approximately 45% of both groups were using narcotics regularly (reported use in the past 4 weeks plus denials with positive urine) at the time of the interview.

Results of the CAP evaluation suggest that prolonged and intensive community supervision that includes contingent return to inpatient status based on opiate-positive urine tests might suppress drug use and criminal activity during the time abusers are enrolled in the program, although such a program clearly does not prevent relapse. Caution must be used in interpreting these

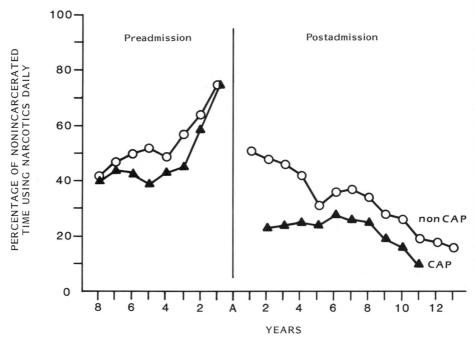

Figure 1. Percentage of nonincarcerated time during which subjects reported using narcotics daily is shown for 8 pre- and 13 postadmission years. The vertical line at A denotes admission to the California Civil Addict Program (CAP). The CAP group ($N = 289$) was committed to the program for 7 years; the non-CAP group ($N = 292$) was discharged from the program by writ shortly after admission due to procedural errors. From "A Follow-up of Admissions to the California Civil Addict Program" by W. H. McGlothlin, M. D. Anglin, and B. D. Wilson, 1977, *American Journal of Drug and Alcohol Abuse, 4*. Reprinted by permission.

results, however, primarily because retrospective self-reports of study participants over a considerable time span were used to assess outcomes; such data are clearly subject to distortion by subjects who knew that they had or had not received a special treatment intervention. Also the daily narcotic use measure reported ignores a considerable amount of regular use that is occurring with somewhat lesser frequency; analysis of the data that took a broader range of drug use into account might have altered the outcome picture.

As with any multicomponent intervention, it is impossible to tell from the CAP evaluation report what role, if any, was played by relapse-contingent incarceration in producing the modest benefits observed for the program. Although placing legal contingencies on return to drug use may appear to be a good idea, this consequence will always be considerably delayed beyond the time of first relapse to use, even under the best of circumstances. Studies that varied the immediacy of legal consequences for drug relapse would be very useful. Not only would such studies evaluate the importance of this variable, but they might also stimulate the development of methods to circumvent the traditionally cumbersome implementation procedures for incarceration.

Further improvement in the effectiveness of community supervision approaches could possibly be achieved through more intensive and systematic applications of behavioral management principles during parole and probation. The use of a single dramatic event, which is imposed only after undesirable behavior has escalated beyond an acceptable level, is not an optimal behavior-management strategy. It would be better to have smaller consequences that could be implemented immediately following instances of particular target behaviors. For example, changes in the length or intensity of parole and probation supervision could be used in a contingent fashion to promote improvements in drug use and other target behaviors.

Polakow and Doctor (1973, 1974) used reduction of probationary sentences as a reinforcer in individualized contingency-contracting procedures to promote improved prosocial behaviors among probationers with a variety of drug-related offenses (see also Chapter 4, by Nietzel and Himelein, this volume). Subjects had been transferred to the experimental program after parole officers encountered difficulty in controlling their behavior. During the first 18 weeks of the contracting program, subjects received credits for attending weekly meetings, at first individually with the probation officer and then in group meetings with other probationers. After demonstrating adequate performance in this phase, an individualized contract was drawn up that specified reductions in probation time that could be earned for achieving specific prosocial behavioral goals such as obtaining and holding a job. Violation of probation conditions resulted in demotion to the first program level (weekly meetings with the probation officer), but otherwise no coercion or punishment was used. The experimental program was compared with an intensive supervision condition in which contacts occurred 1 to 4 times monthly and caseloads were about 50 per probation worker. Results from both a within- and a between-subject analysis with the same group of subjects were reported. The contingency contracting program resulted in better attendance at scheduled meetings, fewer probation violations, fewer arrests, and more employment than did the control condition. Thus results of the contingency-management program appeared promising.

Compulsory Drug Abuse Treatment

A community supervision program such as the California Civil Addict Program is, in essence, an obligatory treatment program managed by the Department of Corrections. As an alternative to operating their own treatment program, the criminal justice system could require that identified drug abusers and alcoholics enroll in ongoing treatment programs run by other specialized agencies. The behavioral contingency (avoiding legal sanctions) is then placed on treatment participation rather than directly on drug use or criminal behavior. This approach makes the assumption that reductions in substance use achieved through treatment will be accompanied by reductions in substance-abuse-related crimes.

Two treatment modalities are available for drug abusers: methadone maintenance and drug-free therapeutic communities, both of which have been shown effective in reducing illicit drug use and associated criminal behaviors in evaluations conducted with self-selected patient samples (see later discussion). The choice of treatment assignment depends on two primary factors: (1) what drugs are being abused—methadone maintenance is appropriate only for opiate abusers, whereas drug-free treatment would be appropriate for abusers of both opiate and nonopiate drugs, and (2) the goals of treatment—methadone maintenance involves continued dependence upon a prescribed narcotic drug, whereas therapeutic communities generally emphasize total abstinence from drugs as the treatment goal.

Methadone Maintenance

Methadone is an orally effective, long-acting opiate drug that is used as a pharmacological substitute for short-acting illicit opiate drugs such as heroin. During treatment, patients ingest a daily dose, usually under nursing supervision at a clinic dispensary, that maintains a stable level of opiate tolerance and dependence. Methadone clinics generally treat about 150 to 250 patients at any one time. In addition to dispensing methadone, these treatment clinics provide counseling services in which cooperation with clinic requirements, elimination of illicit drug use, and participation in legitimate employment or other productive activities is emphasized.

There is no standard policy that dictates the duration of methadone maintenance treatment. One recent follow-up study of 821 methadone maintenance patients found an average treatment duration of 190 days with 47% in treatment over 300 days (Simpson, Savage, & Lloyd, 1979). As far as the goals of treatment are concerned, two opposing philosophies can be discerned in individual clinic policies. Some clinics advocate time-limited maintenance and an eventual drug-free treatment goal, whereas other clinics advocate indefinite high-dose maintenance with social and personal stability as treatment goals (Hargreaves, 1983). The high relapse rate that is seen following treatment termination, even among otherwise well-adjusted patients (e.g., Senay, Dorus, Goldberg, & Thornton, 1977), suggests that long-term maintenance may be the better justified treatment goal for many opiate abusers.

Methadone is a medical rather than a behavioral treatment modality. However, by eliminating the need for daily illicit drug acquisition and ingestion, methadone treatment sets the occasion for other non-drug-related behaviors to emerge or to increase in frequency. Further, some of methadone's pharmacological effects, particularly its satiating and reinforcing effects, can be conceptualized within a behavioral framework.

During satiation, an organism is provided with liberal amounts of the reinforcer for which it has been working. In the case of a heroin abuser, liberal amounts of heroin would be supplied, thus eliminating the effectiveness of additional drug. Because most opiate drugs share pharmacological cross-tolerance, however, satiation can be achieved with any one of several opiate compounds. Methadone has been chosen from among the available drugs for use in the treatment of opiate dependence because of its oral efficacy and relatively long duration of action. Providing the abuser with daily methadone is analogous to feeding an experimental subject before offering food as a reinforcer; the reinforcing potency of the food would be diminished, although possibly not eliminated. Similarly, physiological, subjective, and reinforcing effects of short-acting opiate drugs are diminished during methadone treatment (Jones & Prada, 1975; McCaul, Stitzer, Bigelow, & Liebson, 1983). Satiation is in part responsible for the reduced illicit drug use seen during methadone treatment.

The daily methadone dose also produces mild opiatelike physiological and subjective effects that are detectable by patients (McCaul, Bigelow, Stitzer, & Liebson, 1982) and that make the drug itself reinforcing for opiate abusers. These reinforcing opiate drug effects probably account for the relative popularity of this treatment modality among opiate abusers and the relatively good treatment retention that this modality enjoys (Bale et al., 1980; Newman & Whitehill, 1979).

The efficacy of methadone maintenance treatment has been reasonably well documented. Striking improvements have been observed on measures of opiate drug use and criminal behavior in studies that compared pre- to post-treatment status of self-selected treatment patients (Anglin et al., 1981; Bale et al., 1980; McLellan, Luborsky, O'Brien, Woody, & Druley, 1982; Sells & Simpson, 1980; Simpson et al., 1979). Of course, pre- to posttreatment assessments in self-selected clients cannot provide convincing evidence for a causal relationship between treatment and any improved outcomes observed. More convincing evidence comes from outcome assessment studies conducted in situations where methadone treatment was withdrawn for experimental reasons (Newman & Whitehill, 1979) or due to clinic closures (McGlothlin & Anglin, 1981).

Newman and Whitehill, for example, initially stabilized 100 Hong Kong opiate addicts on 60 mg/day of methadone and then randomly assigned them under blind conditions to continuing methadone maintenance treatment or to gradual (1 mg/day for 60 days) methadone withdrawal followed by placebo maintenance. Subjects were informed of the two possible study conditions to which they might be assigned but were given no information about their actual assignment or dose during the program. Maintenance subjects showed much better treatment outcomes than did subjects for whom active treatment was withdrawn. The most prevalent cause of treatment failure was relapse to illicit opiate drug use (defined as six consecutive opiate-positive urine tests). Sixty-two percent of treatment-withdrawal subjects as compared with 10% of maintenance subjects met this relapse criteria during the 3-year evaluation. In addition, 30% of withdrawal subjects, as compared with 6% of maintenance subjects, dropped out of treatment for unknown reasons during the 3-year evaluation and were counted as treatment failures. Thus, only 16% of the methadone maintenance patients were treatment failures (relapse or dropout), whereas this was true for 92% of treatment-withdrawal patients.

The evaluation studies described here have provided fairly convincing evidence for beneficial effects of methadone maintenance during episodes of

treatment participation. It is clear, however, that methadone treatment does
not totally eliminate drug use and crime, either during treatment or over the
long term. In one posttreatment outcome assessment (Sells & Simpson, 1980),
for example, only 26% of methadone maintenance patients were classified as
opiate-abstinent (based on self-report) during the 3-year posttreatment evaluation period, whereas an additional 27% had moderately good outcomes (no
criminality but some drug use and/or being back in active treatment).

Compulsory Methadone Maintenance Treatment

Given that methadone maintenance reduces both drug use and drug-related crime during treatment, the use of legal contingencies during parole and
probation to achieve and maintain treatment participation for criminally involved narcotics abusers would appear logical. Little evidence exists, however,
that legal status is related either to treatment entry or to treatment outcome
for methadone maintenance patients (Anglin et al., 1981; Harford, Ungerer, &
Kinsella, 1976). For example, a study by Anglin et al. (1981) showed that
concurrent parole supervision added little to the therapeutic benefits of methadone maintenance. This study compared treatment outcomes of a patient
sample (N = 136) first admitted to methadone maintenance while on parole
status under the California Civil Addict Program with that for a matched
sample of first methadone admissions (N = 136) not in the CAP program. The
CAP patients were under the long-term (7-year) commitments with intensive
low case load parole contact and the regular urinalysis monitoring described
earlier. The stipulation that patients be returned to inpatient status following
evidence of excessive drug use, however, was considerably relaxed in California by the time these subjects were in treatment. Considerable overlap in legal
status actually existed for the samples—45% of the nonparole group was on
probation at methadone entry, and 29% were on probation with urine monitoring. Outcome data were obtained in an intensive interview, as previously
described, in which subjects reported their drug use, treatment status, income
sources, and criminal activity for successive episodes of nonincarcerated time
from the onset of addiction to the time of the interview in 1978 to 1979, an
average of 6.6 years after admission to the methadone program; interviews
were completed with 90% of living subjects.

During the 6 years following initial methadone treatment admission, the
CAP parole group reported spending somewhat more time enrolled in methadone treatment and somewhat less time using narcotics daily than did the
nonparole group. Data for self-reported daily narcotics use is shown in Figure
2. These differences between the parole and nonparole groups, however, were
small and not statistically significant. In contrast, entry into methadone
maintenance treatment had a profound impact on both drug use (Fig. 2) and
criminal behavior for both groups. This study supported previous findings
about the efficacy of methadone maintenance treatment but showed that continuing outpatient parole supervision as practiced by the CAP after 1970 (with
less stringent contingencies for return to inpatient status after relapse) added

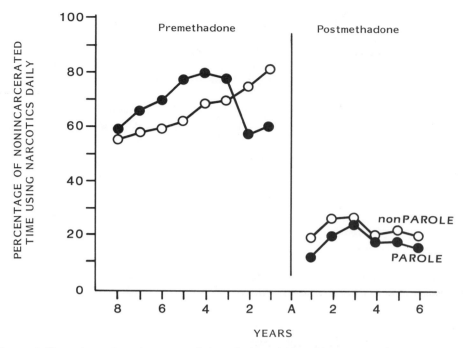

Figure 2. Percentage of nonincarcerated time during which subjects reported using narcotics daily is shown for 8 pre- and 6 postadmission years. The vertical line at A denotes admission to methadone maintenance treatment. The parole group ($N = 136$) entered treatment for the first time while on parole status under the California Civil Addict Program; the nonparole group ($N = 136$) were first treatment admissions not on the Civil Addict Program. From "The Effect of Parole on Methadone Patient Behavior" by M. D. Anglin, W. H. McGlothlin, and G. Speckart, 1981, *American Journal of Drug and Alcohol Abuse, 8.* Reprinted by permission.

little to the therapeutic benefit of methadone treatment. Overlap in the legal supervision status of the groups, however, may have reduced the sensitivity of the comparison.

Therapeutic Communities

Residence in a drug-free therapeutic community (TC) constitutes the second major treatment modality for drug abusers. These inpatient facilities typically have 15 to 35 drug abusers in residence on the program at any given time. Total abstinence is generally the treatment goal, but nonopiate drugs may be prescribed in some programs. The type of therapy offered and the demands placed on residents for conformity and behavior change varies considerably across programs; therapeutic communities are best known for Synanon-type confrontational therapy that is expected to promote change through self-examination. From a behavioral perspective, therapeutic community treatment prevents drug acquisition and self-administration by removing drug availability and promotes appropriate social and verbal behaviors. This is accomplished in a highly structured environment that in most programs includes graded levels of social status, privileges, and responsibilities. New enrollees enter at the lowest level and progress upward as they acquire and practice the appropriate behavioral skills. Prompting, modeling, behavioral rehearsal, and intense social reinforcement and social punishment by both staff and other patients are used to promote behavior change. Length of stay in a therapeutic community is generally expected to be 6 months to 2 years, with residents gradually moving into the natural community as they acquire interpersonal skills and obtain stable employment.

Among patients who self-select their treatment modality, therapeutic communities produce posttreatment outcomes at least as good as those seen with methadone maintenance (Bale *et al.*, 1980; Sells & Simpson, 1980). Further, patients who remain in treatment for at least 2 to 3 months (again, a self-selected group) generally show better long-term outcomes than do methadone maintenance patients, especially drug-free outcomes. The efficacy of therapeutic community treatment has not been demonstrated to date in a study that randomly assigns subjects to treatment. It is clear, however, that efficacy of the therapeutic community treatment modality is limited by its low acceptability. A study by Bale *et al.* (1980) clearly demonstrated that methadone maintenance retains patients in treatment much better than do therapeutic communities. The therapeutic communities studied, designed for 6-month enrollments, lost half their patients in less than 2 months. About 80% of methadone patients remained in treatment at 6 months after admission, whereas less than 2% of the therapeutic community patients remained in treatment this long. Legal contingencies may be able to overcome patient acceptability to some extent, thus exposing criminally involved drug abusers to the potential benefits of long-term therapeutic community treatment. Of course, empirical data are needed to determine whether therapeutic community treatment is equally beneficial for compulsory and voluntary patients.

Compulsory Therapeutic Community Treatment

Several studies suggest that patients with criminal justice involvement remain in therapeutic community treatment longer than do volunteers, although data are mixed on whether this translates into better treatment outcomes (Collins & Allison, 1983; Copemann & Shaw, 1976; Harford *et al.*, 1976). Copemann and Shaw (1976), for example, compared 21 narcotic abusers who had entered a residential therapeutic community under legal pressure, to 27 abusers with similar characteristics but who had entered treatment under voluntary status. The legally coerced group remained in treatment twice as long as the voluntary group (110 vs. 51 days) and had better scores on a posttreatment composite outcome measure. In a statistical analysis of data from a representative national sample of drug abuse treatment participants, Collins and Allison (1983) also showed that criminal justice referrals had longer treatment durations in both residential and outpatient drug-free programs than did voluntary patients. Controlling for covariates known to influence retention such as age, sex, drug use severity, and depression (but not criminal history), these investigators found that criminal justice referrals stayed in treatment about 52 days longer than other voluntary patients. In this study, all groups showed similar improvement on outcome measures during the first 6 months of treatment. In contrast, Harford et al. (1976) found no difference in retention or outcome for legally involved and free patients among 404 first-treatment admissions to drug abuse programs in New Haven. The few available studies suggest that legal pressure might be an effective method for maintaining residential treatment participation among opiate abusers, but there are presently no good data to support the therapeutic value of this treatment approach.

Community Supervision versus Compulsory Treatment

Two intervention approaches have been discussed in this section—(1) direct community supervision by criminal justice personnel and (2) methadone maintenance treatment—both of which appear to reduce drug use and crime among treated narcotics abusers. Comparison of Figures 1 and 2 suggests that intensive community supervision with relapse-contingent return to incarceration (Fig. 1) and methadone maintenance treatment either with or without additional criminal justice supervision (Fig. 2) produce similar reductions in self-reported levels of daily narcotic use during nonincarcerated time. Methadone's beneficial effects, however, were achieved with less incarceration time; methadone maintenance patients spent about 18% of their time in prison (Anglin et al., 1981) as compared with about 50% incarceration time for community supervision clients (McGlothlin et al., 1977). Thus methadone maintenance would appear to be a more generally effective and efficient approach to drug abuse treatment than is intensive community supervision. What is not clear, though, is whether criminal justice contingencies could be used either to increase treatment enrollment or to improve outcomes over those obtained with voluntary treatment. As currently practiced, parole and probation supervision does not appear to have much of an impact on treatment outcome for drug abusers. Unfortunately, it is difficult to identify the reasons for this because available treatment evaluation reports fail to describe either the content of legal contingencies employed with drug abusers or the consistency with which any stated contingencies are enforced. Studies in which drug-abusing parolees and/or probationers were randomly assigned to receive or not receive clearly specified legal consequences based on treatment participation would be useful for assessing the potential role of the criminal justice system in the treatment of criminally involved drug abusers.

Compulsory Alcoholism Treatment

Alcoholics generally become involved with the criminal justice system when they are arrested for driving under the influence (DUI), for violence or assaultiveness while intoxicated, or for public drunkenness and disorderly conduct. In the case of violent, assaultive, and property crimes, where the offender may or may not be intoxicated, the criminal justice system has generally lacked resources for screening the total volume of offenders in order to identify cases where alcoholism is a contributing factor. Thus legal sanctions have generally been applied to these offenders, with few cases considered for treatment referral as a way to address an underlying problem. In contrast, for DUI and public drunkenness cases, where intoxication is necessary for the offense to occur and where an assumption of underlying alcoholism is probable, decriminalized approaches, including treatment referral, have been increasingly adopted by the courts.

Alcoholism Treatment

The treatment programs to which alcoholics may be referred are quite diverse in terms of the duration, setting, cost, and format of treatment. Both inpatient and outpatient components may be offered as well as a variety of individual and group-counseling services. In spite of the apparent diversity of treatment programs, all tend to share a basic treatment approach that consists, first, of attempts to persuade the patient that he or she has a drinking problem; second, to persuade the patient that the solution to this problem is to give up drinking alcohol entirely; and third, to help patients cope with the changes in their activities and relationships that result when drinking is eliminated. Development of satisfying interpersonal relationships between patients and staff is probably critical for the success of these persuasive efforts and allows for the use of positive social reinforcement to promote and maintain therapeutic changes. Participation in Alcoholics Anonymous self-help groups is always encouraged as a component of treatment, and disulfiram (Antabuse) is generally available as an adjunct to counseling treatment for those who will agree to take it. Disulfiram is a drug that produces no effects on its own but that, by interfering with alcohol metabolism, results in an unpleasant reaction after alcohol ingestion, which includes flushing, sweating, palpitations, and nausea. The reaction is sufficiently aversive that patients typically do not drink while they are taking disulfiram. Acceptability of disulfiram treatment is generally low, however, and compliance with prescribed disulfiram regimens is poor. Other than general social reinforcement for sobriety, explicit behavioral management techniques are rarely if ever incorporated into typical alcoholism treatment programs.

Many evaluations of alcoholism treatment efficacy have been conducted with noncriminal populations. Few conclusions can be drawn, however, concerning the efficacy of these programs because of inadequate study designs. A given treatment episode, however, results in long-term abstinence in relatively few individuals. For example, long-term follow-up of 548 male patients who had attended several randomly selected typical treatment programs (Polich, Armor, & Braiker, 1981) found that only 9% achieved stable abstinence of 4 years' duration following a given treatment episode, although a larger percentage (26%) had accumulated at least 2 years of abstinence (in episodes of 3 months or longer) during the 4-year posttreatment period. Short-term (1- or 2-year) posttreatment abstinence rates of 10% to 20% have also typically been reported in other treatment evaluation studies (Fitzgerald, Pasewark, & Clark, 1971; Fuller & Roth, 1979; Gerard & Saenger, 1966). Although total abstinence is generally the goal of alcoholism treatment, a small subgroup (perhaps 10 to 15%) of less impaired alcoholics may drink moderately without resumption of associated alcoholism problems (Polich *et al.*, 1981; Vaillant & Milofsky, 1982). The remaining 60% to 80% of treatment participants generally continue to drink, at least sporadically, and to experience alcohol-related problems after treatment, although their clinical picture may be much improved over what it was at treatment entry. In the absence of controlled random-assignment studies, the role that treatment participation plays in achieving observed posttreatment improvements is difficult to evaluate, especially because it is known that a significant proportion (e.g., 20% to 25%) of people identified as alcoholics at one point in time will be abstinent or much improved at later assessment time points (Polich *et al.*, 1981; Smart, 1975; Vaillant & Milofsky, 1982).

Effects on Retention

Although the long-term efficacy of alcoholism treatment appears to be limited, in general patients probably do control their drinking successfully during treatment participation, whereas relapse is associated with treatment noncompliance and dropout. Thus legal contingencies might improve outcomes by promoting a higher prevalence or maintaining a longer duration of active treatment participation. Of course, the efficacy of such an approach would have to be empirically tested. Small-scale studies have shown that legal contingencies can effectively promote participation in alcoholism treatment. Rosenberg and Liftik (1976), for example, studied socially stable (i.e., employed and living with their families) Boston drunk drivers who were placed on 12-month probation and permitted to keep their licenses provided they participated in treatment. Compulsory patients ($N = 49$) attended treatment sessions an average of 16.4 times during the 6-month evaluation compared to 6.3 times for a group of voluntary patients ($N = 58$) matched on social stability factors. Dropout rates during weeks 1 to 4 were 19% for the compulsory and 62% for the voluntary patient groups, whereas by the end of 19 weeks, 59% of the compulsory patients were still enrolled in the clinic compared with 5% of the voluntary patients. This study illustrates the poor retention that is often seen in alcoholism treatment and demonstrates that legal contingencies can be an effective way to keep alcoholics in treatment. Because of the high dropout rate among the controls, no evaluation of treatment outcome was possible.

In another small sample ($N = 19$) study with alcoholic, violent offenders, regular treatment attendance (but not abstinence) was a parole requirement for experimental subjects, whereas voluntary subjects were required only to keep their first appointment at the clinic, though urged to continue attending

(Gallant, Faulkner, Stoy, Bishop, & Langdon, 1968). Strong legal contingencies were operating because parole violators were returned to the courts to complete lengthy prison sentences. All but one of the compulsory subjects attended treatment regularly for 6 months or more, whereas only a single voluntary patient did so. Dramatic between-group differences in 1-year outcomes were also noted. Seven of the 10 compulsory subjects were abstinent (by treatment clinic report) and working during the parole year, whereas all of the voluntary subjects were either back in prison (56%), at large with a parole violation (22%), or drinking in the community (22%). These studies have shown that legal contingencies can be used to achieve good alcoholism treatment program attendance. Whether the duration of treatment participation is positively related to long-term outcomes for compulsory patients is a question that must be answered by research conducted specifically with criminally involved populations. The effect of compulsory treatment attendance on drinking and crime outcomes will be assessed in the following sections for those subgroups—drinking drivers and public drunkenness offenders—where a number of evaluations have been conducted.

Treatment Efficacy in Driving under the Influence (DUI) Offenders

The treatment alternative for drunk driving offenders is especially appealing to the criminal justice system because contested sentences and processing of DUI cases are reduced. Alcoholism treatment would appear to be an appropriate intervention for most drinking drivers; studies suggest that about half of those arrested for DUI can be classified as alcoholic or problem drinkers (Fine, Scoles, & Mulligan, 1975; Nichols, Weinstein, Ellingstad, & Struckman-Johnson, 1978; Swenson & Clay, 1980).

The Alcohol Safety Action Project (ASAP), a federally sponsored program that operated between 1970 and 1977, promoted treatment referral for drunk drivers and evaluation of the efficacy of this approach. The primary outcome measure in these evaluation studies was DUI recidivism or rearrest rate; treatment effects on drinking behavior were not typically measured. DUI recidivism is a gross measure that can only remotely reflect the incidence of drunk driving and that can be influenced by many nontreatment factors including driving exposure, local detection and arrest rates, and local court practices in charging and convicting. Such recidivism is, however, the most reliable measure available for assessing the impact of various interventions on highway safety.

ASAP data derived from about 200,000 court-mandated referrals to treatment programs or alcohol safety schools (Nichols et al., 1978) suggest that alcohol treatment programs were generally ineffective in reducing subsequent DUI recidivism rates for problem drinkers. Cumulative rearrest rates for both treated and untreated subjects were about 15% to 20% at 18 months following treatment entry and nearly 40% by 36 months. Neither the characteristics of the drivers nor of the treatment programs to which they were referred is well described in ASAP evaluation summaries. Analysis by treatment types did suggest, however, that subjects who attended programs with small-group, personalized, interactive formats had better outcomes than those attending larger, briefer, or more impersonal programs. It should be noted that educational classes or alcohol safety schools for drinking drivers are different from treatment programs because they focus only on specific issues related to drunk driving and alcohol-induced performance impairment rather than on drinking as a pervasive life problem. These schools might be expected to have a smaller impact on drinking and alcohol-related problems than more traditional treatment programs.

The best study available concerning effects of compulsory treatment on DUI recidivism used a randomly assigned untreated control group, lengthy participation in state-of-the-art treatment interventions, and strong motivation for treatment participation—contingent deferral of legal sanctions (Reis, 1982). The study evaluated recidivism outcomes for about 1,000 Sacramento DUI arrestees with a single prior conviction after random assignment to one of four conditions: (1) no-treatment control, (2) brief (15 minutes) biweekly personal interview, (3) group therapy sessions (weekly for 4 months, then biweekly for 8 months; 15 clients per group), and (4) group therapy sessions with three-times-weekly disulfiram ingestion required during the first 6 treatment months. During the treatment year, prosecution on the DUI charge was deferred. As shown in Figure 3, all the treatment groups (including the biweekly brief contact) had lower DUI recidivism rates than did the no-treatment control group. By the end of the first year following random assignment, 13% of the treated groups and 22% of the control group had been rearrested. Although the treated groups performed significantly better than the control group, treatment clearly did not prevent recidivism. Further, although a significant treatment effect was demonstrated, the social impact of these treatment effects must be questioned because of their small magnitude and their lack of persistence after treatment.

The finding that 15-minute biweekly interviews focused on drinking and life problems produced outcomes similar to those from elaborate 32-hour group counseling treatment programs is consistent with other evidence that participation in alcoholism treatment *per se* may be as important as the specific type of treatment offered (Edwards *et al.*, 1977; Emrick, 1975; Polich *et al.*, 1981). The fact that disulfiram was not more efficacious than counseling treatment alone in improving recidivism is due in part to the high rates of noncompliance observed in the disulfiram group. Only 47.5% of chemotherapy subjects completed their assigned treatment (as measured by clinic records). In contrast, about 70% of subjects assigned to other groups completed their counseling attendance requirements. Thus, even the threat of legal sanctions did not completely overcome resistance to disulfiram treatment. This treatment did, however, produce the largest reductions in drinking, as measured by post-treatment self-reports.

The Reis (1982) study showed that alcoholism treatment can improve DUI recidivism outcomes over the short term when administered in place of immediate prosecution on drunk driving charges. The relative effectiveness of treat-

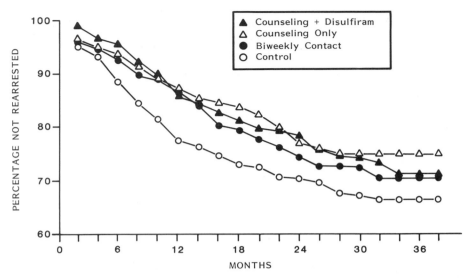

Figure 3. Cumulative percentage of subjects not rearrested for DUI is shown over a 36-month posttreatment admission period. Subjects were randomly assigned to one of four treatment conditions following their second DUI arrest: counseling and disulfiram ($N = 217$), counseling only ($N = 219$), biweekly contact ($N = 326$), or no-treatment control ($N = 341$). From *The Traffic Safety Effectiveness of Educational Counseling Programs for Multiple Offense Drunk Drivers* by R. E. Reis, 1982, Washington, DC: Department of Transportation, National Highway Traffic Safety Administration.

ment, however, is likely to diminish as the severity and immediacy of legal sanctions increases for comparison subjects. Some uncontrolled studies have suggested that legal sanctions that include license actions may reduce DUI recidivism more effectively than deferred prosecution combined with educational class attendance (Hagen, 1977; Popkin, Li, Lacey, Stewart, & Waller, 1983; Salzberg & Klingberg, 1983). Popkin *et al.*, for example, compared DUI recidivism rates for 33,835 North Carolina first offenders who received limited driving privileges while attending a 10-hour educational class (typically held over a period of 4 weeks) with 16,429 drunk drivers who, for unspecified reasons, were not referred to the educational class but were given the usual legal sanctions, which were likely to include license suspension or 12-month limited privileges. After controlling for age, race, and blood alcohol levels at the time of arrest, the study found that recidivism rates were consistently higher for the educational class subjects than for the legal sanction subjects and that this was true across several time frames both during the license suspension period, when driving exposure was reduced, and afterward.

The available data appear to show that drinking drivers can be effectively channeled into treatment programs by the courts and that better treatment participation can be obtained for compulsory than for voluntary treatment patients. Data are mixed, however, as to whether this translates into better treatment outcomes. Thus, although court-referred drunk drivers have become an integral part of alcoholism treatment program enrollments, at present little evidence exists to support the efficacy of compulsory treatment for this group.

Treatment Efficacy in Public Drunkenness Offenders

Public drunkenness arrests are largely confined to homeless alcoholics who typically have not acted violently or broken any other laws. The objective of these arrests is not punishment, deterrence, or rehabilitation but rather control of an unpleasant situation and provision of short-term shelter and protection for the derelict alcoholic. Public drunkenness arrests tend to be chronic. The same individual may be rearrested scores of times during the year. Questions have been raised as to whether directing police department and court resources to this disadvantaged group of individuals with chronic social and medical problems is appropriate or cost-effective. As a result, both attitudes and laws have moved toward "decriminalization" of public drunkenness. Police now frequently deliver homeless alcoholics to detoxification units rather than to jails. The treatment community also questions its involvement with this group, and as a result, the treatment services offered are frequently perfunctory. As with other subgroups of alcoholics, treatment effects are frequently not demonstrated in controlled studies. For example, a study by Ditman, Crawford, Forgy, Moskowitz, and Macandrew (1967) found no differences in recidivism among groups of chronic drunkenness offenders randomly assigned to clinic treatment, Alcoholics Anonymous treatment, or no-treatment conditions. Of the 241 men studied, 65% to 70% were rearrested during the follow-up period (1 year minimum), and most of those rearrested continued to have multiple offenses.

Compulsory disulfiram treatment might be appropriate for public drunkenness offenders, in view of the chronic nature of their drinking problems, although medical complications might preclude treatment for a segment of this population. A few studies have suggested that appropriate contingencies may be able to overcome to some extent the poor compliance that may be expected with this modality. In one study by Haynes (1973), arrested public drunkenness offenders could choose between a 90-day jail sentence or 1-year probation with twice-weekly supervised disulfiram ingestion. During the first program year, 138 alcoholics elected to take disulfiram, where only 3 chose the jail sentence. Forty-seven percent were still receiving disulfiram at the end of one year, while the rest had absconded from the program (25%), left town with permission (10%), or were in jail (12%). Average arrest rates for subjects remaining in town (program successes plus in jail) were 3.8 arrests for the year preceding disulfiram treatment and 0.3 arrests during the year of treatment. This uncontrolled study suggested that deferral of a relatively severe legal sanction might be an effective way to promote disulfiram treatment participation. Another descriptive study by Brewer and Smith (1983) examined outcomes for 18 chronic offenders, most of whom also had histories of arrest for theft or violence. Most of the subjects agreed to begin taking disulfiram prior to their court date and were subsequently mandated to compulsory treatment during probation. Overall, 5 (28%) refused treatment, 2 (11%) were arrested while in treatment, and 11 (61%) took disulfiram and were successful for at least 12 weeks, with an average abstinence duration of 30 weeks for the entire group.

Less promising results were reported by Gallant et al. (1968) who randomly assigned 84 chronic drunkenness offenders to one of four treatment conditions during probation: (1) group therapy at an alcoholism clinic for 6 months, (2) group therapy and disulfiram treatment for 6 months, (3) disulfiram only for 6 months, and (4) routine sentencing with no compulsory treatment. Treatment dropout rate was high, and average arrest rates were unchanged during the treatment period; only 7 of the original subjects were judged to be successes at the end of 6 months. The authors noted that many of the subjects were in such poor physical and mental conditions that the likelihood of regular attendance at a treatment clinic was minimal. A potentially more important factor was that jail sentences scheduled as a consequence of treatment noncompliance were not reliably imposed. A subsequent study by this group (Gallant et al., 1973) showed similar negative results even when compulsory inpatient treatment (4-week minimum) was included as one of the treatment assignments. Only 17 of 210 original subjects were available for evaluation at 1-year follow-up, of whom 13 (6% of the original group) were judged to be successes. We are not told in this study whether or not legal contingencies were consistently imposed.

Legal sanctions are not the only consequences that can be used in contingent arrangements to promote improved outcomes in chronic drunkenness offenders. Miller (1975) developed and evaluated a contingency management intervention that operated through the cooperation of community agencies and that did not require involvement of the criminal justice system. Twenty chronic drunkenness offenders were selected from the jail population in Jackson, Mississippi. Ten were randomly assigned to the control condition and received routine services from helping agencies in the city. For the experimental group, special arrangements were made with the Salvation Army residential mission and with the Manpower temporary employment agency that stipulated that their services would be available to experimental subjects during the study period only if the subjects maintained sobriety. If either agency personnel or research staff observed a subject to be grossly intoxicated, however, services would be suspended for 5 days. Research staff defined sobriety as a blood-alcohol concentration below .01-mg percentage with readings obtained during randomly scheduled community contacts about once every 5 days. Subjects in the behavioral intervention group were arrested on average 1.7 times during the 2 months before the program and 0.3 times during the 2 months of the program; the control group maintained approximately the same number of arrests pre- (1.4) as postintervention (1.3). Experimental subjects also increased the amount of time spent working from an average of 3.2 hours per week perintervention to an average of 12 hours per week postintervention; control subjects decreased their average weekly hours of work from 4.4 to 3.2

hours. This study showed that a significant impact on drinking and arrest rates could be obtained by arranging for potent and relevant reinforcers in the community to be delivered contingent upon sobriety and withdrawn upon evidence of excessive drinking. Another convincing demonstration of the effectiveness of a community reinforcement intervention for promoting sobriety among chronic alcoholics has been provided by Hunt and Azrin (1973). Such community-based contingency programs might be considered by the criminal justice system as an addition or alternative to compulsory treatment approaches with public drunkenness offenders.

Factors Influencing Treatment Outcomes

The quantity and quality of available research is generally insufficient to make confident statements about the efficacy of a compulsory treatment approach with substance abusers. In the case of drug abuse, relatively effective treatment modalities are available, but legal contingencies have not been adequately evaluated for their ability to increase treatment enrollment and retention. In the case of alcoholism, legal contingencies have been used effectively to promote treatment participation, especially among DUI and public drunkenness offenders, but the limited ability of available treatments to influence drinking behavior may hinder the overall effectiveness of a compulsory treatment approach. It is clear that more development and evaluation is needed to improve both criminal justice contingencies and substance abuse treatments. In this section, four factors will be discussed that are likely to influence treatment outcomes of compulsory patients and that must be considered if optimal strategies are to be developed for criminally involved substance abusers. These factors are (1) treatment efficacy, (2) client characteristics, (3) contingencies maintaining treatment participation, and (4) concurrent legal sanctions.

Treatment Efficacy

If substance abusers always eliminated their self-administration behaviors during and after treatment episodes, then the portion of crime related to substance abuse could be reliably eliminated by requiring all criminally involved substance abusers to participate in treatment. The efficacy of a compulsory treatment approach is limited, however, by the ability of currently available treatments to impose control over substance self-administration behaviors. As discussed previously, drugs and alcohol are potent reinforcers that tend to gain control over large portions of abusers' behavior; these strongly maintained drug-reinforced behaviors are not easy to eliminate. Thus single-treatment episodes infrequently result in permanent abstinence from the abused substance, although some currently available treatments (e.g., methadone and disulfiram maintenance) can have important benefits, especially during the time of treatment participation.

Substance abuse treatment programs have largely relied on medical interventions (e.g., methadone and disulfiram maintenance) and persuasive interpersonal interactions to alter patient behavior. The efficacy of these treatments might be improved by implementing behaviorally based contingency management interventions focusing on a broad range of social adjustment areas including employment, family and social relations as well as drug and alcohol use (Caddy & Block, 1983; Hunt & Azrin, 1973; Grabowski, Stitzer, & Henningfield, 1984). One hindrance to behavioral treatment approaches, however, is the limited control that treatment clinics have over relevant reinforcers and punishers in the lives of their patients. Contingencies that involved criminal justice consequences could be effective elements in the treatment of criminally involved substance abusers provided that these consequences could be easily and flexibly implemented in response to the occurrence (or nonoccurrence) of target behaviors.

Treatment efficacy might also be improved by changing the entire substance abuse treatment delivery system. For example, Thompson, Koerner and Grabowski (1984) have proposed an innovative treatment delivery system for narcotics abusers based on behavioral principles in which a full range of medical, educational, vocational, psychological, and social services would be supplied to individual abusers as needed via a brokerage system. Brokers would set treatment goals, arrange for delivery of specific treatment and social services, and monitor progress and dispense privileges (including money) to clients contingent upon evidence of therapeutic progress. Community service providers would be reinforced for successful client outcomes by the continued patronage of brokers seeking effective services for their clients.

Continued evaluation of both new and existing treatments is critical for determining the utility of compulsory treatment approaches. For example, treatment evaluation studies consistently show that substance abuse treatment dropout rates tend to be high but that treatment outcomes are positively related to the duration of treatment participation. Because data showing a positive relationship between treatment duration and outcome are obtained almost exclusively from voluntary patients, these data cannot distinguish between the effects of differential patient motivation and the effects of long-term sobriety monitoring and other beneficial therapeutic processes. Studies that examined the relationship between treatment duration and outcome for compulsory patients assigned to different treatment durations would be important for deciding between these two interpretations. If longer treatment durations do lead to better outcomes, this would provide a firm rationale for compulsory treatment approaches.

Client Characteristics

Treatment evaluation studies make it clear that pretreatment social stability factors are important predictors of treatment outcome. Socially stable clients with intact jobs and families have a much better treatment prognosis than do socially disadvantaged clients. This suggests that clients with different social stability levels may require different types or amounts of treatments and also suggests that improving social stability factors in poorly functioning clients might lead to better outcomes. Although extensive criminal background is usually associated with less time in treatment and poorer performance during treatment in methadone maintenance programs (McLellan, 1983), pretreatment criminality does not necessarily exclude a good treatment outcome for drug abusers. For example, McLellan, Ball, Rosen, and O'Brien (1981) found comparable amounts of improvement among methadone maintenance patients whose pretreatment income was derived largely from illegal activities or from legitimate employment. Comparable data are not available for criminally involved alcoholics, although the study by Gallant *et al.* (1968) suggests that alcoholic criminal offenders can respond favorably to treatment.

Eventually, it may be possible to select optimally effective treatment types or treatment components on the basis of pretreatment client characteristics. McLellan and co-workers have recently begun to identify problem-profile factors that can predict differential treatment outcomes (McLellan, Childress, Griffith, & Woody, 1984; McLellan, Luborsky, Woody, O'Brien, & Druley, 1983; McLellan, Woody, Luborsky, O'Brien, & Druley, 1983). For example, McLellan *et al.* (1984) found that drug abusers with high levels of psychiatric disability (as measured by the Addiction Severity Index) had better outcomes when enrolled in methadone maintenance than in therapeutic community treatment. Another example comes from Reis's (1982) study of DUI second offenders. Subjects with low educational levels (high school or less) did equally well in brief biweekly contact and group therapy conditions, whereas subjects with higher educational levels did poorly in the biweekly contact condition. More research of this type should be conducted so that the criminal justice system can utilize findings in making optimally effective treatment referrals.

Contingencies Maintaining Participation

Most substance abuse treatment participants are subject to some sort of pressure from family, friends, or employers that contributes to the decision to enter treatment. Legal pressure is therefore just one of many possible sources of contingencies maintaining treatment participation. The effectiveness of legal contingencies will in general depend upon their strength and immediacy. Possibly the most potent way to motivate treatment participation is with contingent deferral of legal sanctions. Indeed, the number of substance abusers who enter treatment will likely depend upon the degree of aversiveness of deferred legal sanctions (e.g., length of jail sentence, amount of fine). Studies in which substance abusers were randomly assigned to receive different legal sanctions that could be deferred by treatment participation would be highly instructive. Such research, however, would probably not be tolerated in practice. An alternative, though less desirable, strategy might be to compare treatment-entry data from different jurisdictions or judges who typically impose greater or lesser sanctions for comparable offenses.

Parole and probation services provide the mechanism for monitoring substance abusers while they are in treatment and for implementing contingencies designed to maintain treatment participation. The efficacy of legal contingencies for maintaining treatment participation will probably depend upon how consistently and immediately sanctions can be imposed as a consequence of treatment dropout or failure. For this purpose, a prison sentence, which might be most effective in a deferral arrangement for motivating initial treatment entry, might be relatively ineffective for motivating continued participation because the courts are unlikely to send substance abusers into the overcrowded prisons for relatively minor noncriminal violations. Further, the use of a single highly aversive consequence, which is usually not imposed until undesirable behavior has escalated beyond tolerable limits, is not as effective for behavioral control as the use of smaller consequences that can be implemented immediately upon detection of single instances of undesirable behavior. Fines could be used in this manner, as could driving license actions for DUI offenders, but only if court procedures allowed for immediate and consistent implementation of contingencies. Contingencies could also be set up that utilize changes in the duration and intensity of criminal justice monitoring. For example, clients who remained in treatment and performed well could have their probation or parole sentences gradually reduced, whereas treatment termination would result in lengthening the sentence and an abrupt return to an intensive supervision program that would include urinalysis and/or breathalyzer monitoring. In this way, the treatment and criminal justice systems might be able to implement cooperatively the contingencies that would optimally motivate treatment retention and desirable behavior change in criminally involved substance abusers.

Concurrent Legal Sanctions

Although treatment may produce demonstrable improvements in criminal behavior of substance abusers, legal sanctions may also be effective in this regard. Issues that have received little or no research attention are the relative benefits (both short and long term) of legal sanctions versus treatment and the interactions between legal sanctions and treatment. For example, in most of the DUI studies described, legal sanctions were deferred for the no-treatment control group, which subsequently may have performed more poorly than the treated groups. Performance of the control group, however, might improve as legal sanctions became more severe and more immediate. Thus, similar short-term outcomes might be achieved via different mechanisms. A critical consideration, though, would be whether treatment and legal sanctions had different effects on long-term outcomes. Treatment is an appealing alternative to legal sanctions precisely because it is expected to have both a longer term benefit and to influence a broader range of outcome variables. For drug abusers, who may have habituated to criminal justice sanctions, compulsory treatment offers a potentially effective alternative. More studies are needed for all types of legally involved alcoholics, however, that examine the interaction between legal sanctions and treatment in order to develop optimal intervention strategies.

SUMMARY AND CONCLUSIONS

This chapter has examined the relationship between substance abuse and crime within a behavioral framework and considered various intervention strategies including incarceration, community supervision, and compulsory treatment that can be implemented with criminally involved substance abusers. A punishment approach to crime reduction among substance abusers seems unlikely to succeed primarily because of the low detection rate of criminal behavior among drug abusers (e.g., theft) and alcoholics (e.g., drunk driving). Furthermore, incarceration by itself does not appear to have any effect on the future likelihood of returning to substance abuse and related crime. Because reductions in drug and alcohol use are generally accompanied by reduced criminal activities, however, indirect approaches to crime reduction including compulsory treatment make sense when dealing with criminally involved substance abusers.

Intensive community supervision programs (such as the California Civil Addict Program) that include substance use monitoring and relapse-based legal consequences may reduce substance use while the program is in effect but cannot prevent relapse. Although better community monitoring programs might be designed, compulsory treatment provides an appealing alternative to the criminal justice system for handling substance abusers because potentially effective community monitoring functions can be carried out by these specialized treatment agencies rather than by the criminal justice system itself and because a wider range of treatment services can be offered that may positively influence long-term outcomes. The available treatment evaluation studies with drug and alcohol abusers, however, have been generally disappointing as far as demonstrating the efficacy of a compulsory treatment approach is concerned. Two reasons have been suggested to account for this state of affairs. First, criminal justice contingencies may not be optimal for promoting and maintaining treatment participation. Second, available treatments may not be optimal for controlling substance abuse and promoting rehabilitation.

Although a behavioral perspective has been employed in discussing substance abuse and related crime, review of the treatment evaluation literature suggests that neither the criminal justice system nor the treatment programs to which substance abusers are referred have adopted potentially effective behavioral contingency management techniques for influencing their charges. In the case of criminally involved drug abusers, for example, there do not currently appear to be any systematic criminal justice contingencies operating related to the initiation, duration, or success of treatment participation. Nor has there been any attempt to incorporate legal consequences (e.g., changes in parole/probation requirements) into treatment interventions for drug and alcohol abusers. The use of relevant legal consequences to promote treatment retention and continued abstinence could be an effective approach to the treatment of criminally involved substance abusers. It is clear, however, that both flexibility in the range of consequences available for contingency management and a high degree of cooperation between treatment and criminal justice programs would be needed to incorporate legal consequences into treatment and develop optimally effective interventions. High-quality studies that include objective measures of substance use will be needed to evaluate the efficacy of any innovative programs and establish the utility of behaviorally based compulsory treatment programs.

Certainly no evidence has come to light suggesting that compulsory treatment is harmful to substance abusers. To this extent, current criminal justice practices appear justified. Neither, however, would current referral and treatment practices appear to promote optimal outcomes. Hopefully, analytic exercises such as those contained in this chapter will help to promote the development and evaluation of innovative behaviorally based procedures for managing difficult groups of criminally involved substance abusers.

REFERENCES

Anglin, M. D., McGlothlin, W. H., & Speckart, G. (1981). The effect of parole on methadone patient behavior. *American Journal of Drug and Alcohol Abuse, 8*, 153–170.

Bale, R. N., Van Stone, W. W., Kuldau, J. M., Engelsing, T. M. J., Elashoff, R. M., & Zarcone, V. P. (1980). Therapeutic communities vs. methadone maintenance. *Archives of General Psychiatry, 37*, 179–193.

Ball, J. C., Shaffer, J. W., & Nurco, D. N. (1983). The day-to-day criminality of heroin addicts in Baltimore—A study in the continuity of offense rates. *Drug and Alcohol Dependence, 12*, 119–142.

Brewer, C., & Smith, J. (1983). Probation linked supervised disulfiram in the treatment of habitual drunken offenders: Results of a pilot study. *British Medical Journal, 287*, 1282–1283.

Caddy, G. R., & Block, T. (1983). Behavioral treatment of methods for alcoholism. In M. Galanter (Ed.), *Recent developments in alcoholism* (pp. 139–165). New York: Plenum Press.

Collins, J. J., & Allison, M. (1983). Legal coercion and retention in drug abuse treatment. *Hospital and Community Psychiatry, 34*, 1145–1149.

Copemann, C. D., & Shaw, P. L. (1976). Effects of contingent management of addicts expecting commitment to a community based treatment program. *British Journal of Addiction, 71*, 187–191.

Ditman, K. S., Crawford, G. G., Forgy, E. W., Moskowitz, H., & Macandrew, C. (1967). A controlled experiment on the use of court probation for drunk arrests. *American Journal of Psychiatry, 124*, 64–67.

Edwards, G., Orford, J., Egert, S., Guthrie, S., Hawker, A., Hensman, C., Mitcheson, M., Oppenheimer, E., & Taylor, C. (1977). Alcoholism: A controlled trial of "treatment" and "advice." *Journal of Studies on Alcohol, 38*, 1004–1030.

Emrick, C. D. (1975). A review of psychologically oriented treatment of alcoholism. II. *Journal of Studies on Alcohol, 36*, 88–108.

Fine, E. W., Scoles, P., & Mulligan, M. (1975). Under the influence: Characteristics and drinking practices of persons arrested the first time for drunk driving, with treatment implications. *Public Health Reports, 90*, 424–429.

Fitzgerald, B. J., Pasewark, R. A., & Clark, R. (1971). Four-year follow-up of alcoholics at a rural state hospital. *Quarterly Journal of Studies on Alcohol, 32*, 636–642.

Fuller, R. K., & Roth, H. P. (1979). Disulfiram for the treatment of alcoholism. *Annals of Internal Medicine, 90,* 901–904.

Gallant, D. M., Bishop, M. P., Faulkner, M. A., Simpson, L., Cooper, A., Lathrop, D., Brisolara, A. M., & Bossetta, J. R. (1968). A comparative evaluation of compulsory (group therapy and/or Antabuse) and voluntary treatment of the chronic alcoholic municipal court offender. *Psychosomatics, 9,* 306–310.

Gallant, D. M., Faulkner, M., Stoy, B., Bishop, M. P., & Langdon, D. (1968). Enforced clinic treatment of paroled criminal alcoholics. *Quarterly Journal of Studies on Alcohol, 29,* 77–83.

Gallant, D. M., Bishop, M. P., Mouledoux, A., Faulkner, M. A., Brisolara, A., & Swanson, W. A. (1973). The revolving-door alcoholic. *Archives of General Psychiatry, 28,* 633–635.

Gerard, D. L., & Saenger, G. (1966). *Out-patient treatment of alcoholism.* Toronto: University of Toronto Press.

Grabowski, J., Stitzer, M. L., & Henningfield, J. E. (Eds.). (1984). Behavioral intervention techniques in drug abuse treatment. *NIDA Research Monograph 46, DHHS Publication No. ADM 84-1282.* Washington, DC: U.S. Government Printing Office.

Griffiths, R. R., Bigelow, G. E., & Henningfield, J. E. (1980). Similarities in animal and human drug-taking behavior. In N. K. Mello (Ed.), *Advances in substance abuse: Behavioral and biological research* (pp. 1–90). Greenwich, CT: JAI Press.

Hagen, R. E. (1977). *Effectiveness of license suspension or revocation for drivers convicted of multiple driving-under-the-influence offenses.* State of California. CAL-DMVRSS-77-59.

Harford, R. J., Ungerer, J. C., & Kinsella, J. K. (1976). Effects of legal pressure on prognosis for treatment of drug dependence. *American Journal of Psychiatry, 133,* 1399–1404.

Hargreaves, W. A. (1983). Methadone dose and duration for maintenance treatment. In J. R. Cooper, F. Altman, B. S. Brown, & D. Czechowicz (Eds.) *Research on the treatment of narcotic addiction. State of the art* (pp. 19–79). *NIDA Treatment Research Monograph Series, DHHS Publication No. ADM 83-1281.* Washington, DC: U.S. Government Printing Office.

Haynes, S. N. (1973). Contingency management in a municipally-administered Antabuse program for alcoholics. *Journal of Behavior Therapy and Experimental Psychiatry, 4,* 31–32.

Hunt, G. M., & Azrin, N. H. (1973). A community-reinforcement approach to alcoholism. *Behaviour Research and Therapy, 11,* 91–104.

Jones, B. E., & Prada, J. A. (1975). Drug-seeking behavior during methadone maintenance. *Psychopharmacologia, 41,* 7–10.

Lau, H. (1975). Cost of alcoholic beverages as a determinant of alcohol consumption. In R. J. Gibbins, Y. Israel, H. Kalant, R. E. Popham, W. Schmidt, & R. G. Smart (Eds.), *Research advances in alcohol and drug problems* (pp. 211–245). New York: Wiley.

McCabe, O. L., Kurland, A. A., & Sullivan, D. (1975). Paroled narcotic addicts in a verified abstinence program: Results of a five-year study. *International Journal of the Addictions, 10,* 211–228.

McCaul, M. E., Bigelow, G. E., Stitzer, M. L., & Liebson, I. (1982). Short-term effecLs of oral methadone in methadone maintenance subjects. *Clinical Pharmacology and Therapeutics, 31,* 753–761.

McCaul, M. E., Stitzer, M. L., Bigelow, G., & Liebson, I. A. (1983). Intravenous hydromorphone: Effects in opiate-free and methadone maintenance subjects. In L. S. Harris (Ed.), *Problems of drug dependence 1982* (pp. 238–244). *NIDA Research Monograph No. 43, DHHS Publication No. ADM 83-1264.* Washington, DC: U.S. Government Printing Office.

McGlothlin, W. H., & Anglin, M. D. (1981). Shutting off methadone. *Archives of General Psychiatry, 38,* 885–892.

McGlothlin, W. H., Anglin, M. D., & Wilson, B. D. (1977). A follow-up of admissions to the California Civil Addict Program. *American Journal of Drug and Alcohol Abuse, 4,* 179–199.

McGlothlin, W. H., Anglin, M. D., & Wilson, B. D. (1978). Narcotic addiction and crime. *Criminology, 16,* 293–315.

McLellan, A. T. (1983). Patient characteristics associated with outcome. In J. R. Cooper, F. Altman, B. S. Brown, & D. Czechowicz (Eds.), *Research on the treatment of narcotic addiction. State of the art* (pp. 500–529). *NIDA Treatment Research Monograph Series, DHHS Publication No. ADM 83-1281.* Washington, DC: U.S. Government Printing Office.

McLellan, A. T., Ball, J. C., Rosen, L., & O'Brien, C. P. (1981). Pretreatment source of income and response to methadone maintenance: A follow-up study. *American Journal of Psychiatry, 138,* 785–789.

McLellan, A. T., Luborsky, L., O'Brien, C. P., Woody, G. E., & Druley, K. A. (1982). Is treatment for substance abuse effective? *Journal of the American Medical Association, 247,* 1423–1428.

McLellan, A. T., Luborsky, L., Woody, G. E., O'Brien, C. P., & Druley, K. A. (1983). Predicting response to alcohol and drug abuse treatments. *Archives of General Psychiatry, 40,* 620–625.

McLellan, A. T., Woody, G. E., Luborsky, L., O'Brien, C. P., & Druley, K. A. (1983). Increased effectiveness of substance abuse treatment: A prospective study of patient-treatment "matching." *Journal of Nervous and Mental Disease, 171,* 597–605.

McLellan, A. T., Childress, A. R., Griffith, J., & Woody, G. E. (1984). The psychiatrically severe drug abuse patient: Methadone maintenance or therapeutic community? *American Journal of Drug and Alcohol Abuse, 10,* 77–95.

Miller, P. M. (1975). A behavioral intervention program for chronic public drunkenness offenders. *Archives of General Psychiatry, 32,* 915–917.

Myers, J. K., Weissman, M. M., Tischler, G. L., Holzer, C. E., Leaf, P. J., Orvaschel, H., Anthony, J. C., Boyd, J., Burke, J. D., Kramer, M., & Stoltzman, R. (1984). Six-month prevalence of psychiatric disorders in three communities. *Archives of General Psychiatry, 41,* 959–965.

Newman, R. G., & Whitehill, W. B. (1979). Double-blind comparison of methadone and placebo maintenance treatments of narcotic addicts in Hong Kong. *Lancet, 8141,* 485–488.

Nichols, J. L., Weinstein, E. B., Ellingstad, V. S., & Struckman-Johnson, D. L. (1978). The specific deterrent effect of ASAP education and rehabilitation programs. *Journal of Safety Research, 10,* 177–187.

Polakow, R. L., & Doctor, R. M. (1973). Treatment of marijuana and barbiturate dependence by contingency contracting. *Journal of Behavior Therapy and Experimental Psychiatry, 4,* 375–377.

Polakow, R. L., & Doctor, R. M. (1974). A behavioral modification program for adult drug offenders. *Journal of Research in Crime and Delinquency, 11,* 63–69.

Polich, J. M., Armor, D. J., & Braiker, H. B. (1981). *The course of alcoholism: Four years after treatment.* New York: Wiley.

Popham, R. E., Schmidt, W., & de Lint, J. (1975). The prevention of alcoholism: Epidemiological studies of the effects of government control measures. *British Journal of Addicton, 70,* 125–144.

Popkin, C. L., Li, L. K., Lacey, J. H., Stewart, J. R., & Waller, P. F. (1983). *An initial evaluation of the North Carolina alcohol and drug education traffic schools.* Chapel Hill: University of North Carolina Highway Safety Research Center.

Reis, R. E. (1982). *The traffic safety effectiveness of educational counseling programs for multiple offense drunk drivers.* Washington, DC: Department of Transportation, National Highway Traffic Safety Administration.

Rosenberg, C. M., & Liftik, J. (1976). Use of coercion in the outpatient treatment of alcoholism. *Journal of Studies on Alcohol, 37,* 58–65.

Salzberg, P. M., & Klingberg, C. L. (1983). The effectiveness of deferred prosecution for driving while intoxicated. *Journal of Studies on Alcohol, 44,* 299–306.

Seeley, J. R. (1960). Death by liver cirrhosis and the price of beverage alcohol. *Canadian Medical Association Journal, 83,* 1361–1366.

Sells, S. B., & Simpson, D. D. (1980). A case for drug abuse treatment effectiveness based on the DARP research program. *British Journal of Addictions, 75,* 117–132.

Senay, E. C., Dorus, W., Goldberg, F., & Thornton, W. (1977). Withdrawal from methadone maintenance. *Archives of General Psychiatry, 34,* 361–367.

Shaffer, J. W., Nurco, D. N., & Kinlock, T. W. (1984). A new classification of narcotic addicts based on type and extent of criminal activity. *Comprehensive Psychiatry, 25,* 315–328.

Simpson, D. D., Savage, L. J., & Lloyd, M. R. (1979). Follow-up evaluation of treatment of drug abuse during 1969 to 1972. *Archives of General Psychiatry, 36,* 772–780.

Smart, R. (1975). Spontaneous recovery in alcoholics: A review and analysis of the available research. *Drug and Alcohol Dependence, 1,* 277–285.

Strug, D., Wish, E., Johnson, B., Anderson, K., Miller, T., & Sears, A. (1984). *The role of alcohol in the crimes of active heroin users*. Washington DC: U.S. Department of Justice.

Swenson, P. R., & Clay, T. R. (1980). Effects of short-term rehabilitation on alcohol consumption and drinking-related behaviors: An eight-month follow-up study of drunken drivers. *International Journal of the Addictions, 15*, 821–838.

Thompson, T., Koerner, J., & Grabowski, J. (1984). Brokerage model rehabilitation system for opiate dependence: A behavioral analysis. In J. Grabowski, M. L. Stitzer, & J. E. Henningfield (Eds.) *Behavioral intervention techniques in drug abuse treatment* (pp. 131–146). *NIDA Research Monograph No. 46, DHHS Publication No. ADM 84-1282*. Washington, DC: U.S. Government Printing Office.

Vaillant, G. E. (1966). A twelve-year follow-up of New York narcotic addicts: I. The relation of treatment to outcome. *American Journal of Psychiatry, 122*, 727–737.

Vaillant, G. E., & Milofsky, E. S. (1982). Natural history of male alcoholism. *Archives of General Psychiatry, 39*, 127–133.

13

The Behavioral Treatment of Rapists and Child Molesters

VERNON L. QUINSEY, TERRY C. CHAPLIN, ANNE MAGUIRE, AND DOUGLAS UPFOLD

Crimes of sexual aggression, such as child molestation and rape, are common in Western societies. Although exact figures are difficult to obtain because of vagaries in victim-reporting practices and differences in legal definitions over regions, serious acts of sexual aggression are almost exclusively committed by males and constitute a serious social problem. A sizable minority of sexually aggressive men commit sexual crimes at high frequencies over long periods of time (Abel, Becker, & Skinner, 1985; Groth, Longo, & McFadin, 1982). These individuals, who are the primary focus of the present chapter, are infrequently arrested by the police or, if apprehended and incarcerated, often reoffend upon release (Abel *et al.*, 1985).

Clinicians and behavioral scientists have sought to develop methods that will modify the sexually aggressive behaviors of these men. Because of the seriousness and frequency of their crimes, each cessation of offending by a sexually aggressive person is important. Despite the importance of developing effective interventions for these offenders, however, not much evaluative research on interventions has been conducted. Most of the methodologically acceptable literature is recent, and the field is a long way from having definitive evaluations of any treatment methods. This chapter provides an introduction to the behavioral treatment of sex offenders through the description of a particular program.

Traditionally, sex offenders have been treated using psychotherapeutic methods, most frequently group psychotherapy. These psychotherapeutic methods have diverse rationales, but many appear to rest on the assumption that sex offenders have character traits that must be altered. Unfortunately, the search for unique character traits among sex offenders has not yet proved successful (e.g., Quinsey, 1977, 1984, 1986; Quinsey, Arnold, & Pruesse, 1980),

Vernon L. Quinsey, Terry C. Chaplin, Anne Maguire, and Douglas Upfold • Research Department, Mental Health Centre, Penetanguishene, Ontario, Canada L0K 1P0. This work was supported in part by a series of grants from the Ontario Mental Health Foundation.

and no trait theory has been able to explain the different sorts of sexual misbehaviors that offenders consistently exhibit.

More direct measurement of phenomena that are known or thought to be related to the behaviors of interest has proved useful, however. For example, sexual arousal, as measured by penile expansion to slides or stories, has been shown to be under stimulus control (Quinsey, Chaplin, & Upfold, 1984; Quinsey, Steinman, Bergersen, & Holmes, 1975). The stimuli that occasion sexual arousal among sex offenders are related to their offense histories, so that sex offenders can be differentiated both from nonsex offenders and sex offenders with different offense histories by measurements of their sexual arousal to a variety of stimuli.

The findings of individual differences in sexual arousal patterns, together with advances in other areas of the behavioral literature, have led to a new rationale for the treatment of sex offenders and a new treatment methodology. Briefly, sexual behaviors may be conceptualized as behaviors like any others. In this view, undesirable sexual behaviors are assumed to be the result of skill deficits and/or inappropriate behaviors acquired at an earlier time, in particular, the acquisition of inappropriate or "deviant" masturbatory fantasies. The task of treatment, therefore, is to provide the offender with the requisite skills and techniques for the self-management of his future sexual behavior. Broadly speaking, these assumptions are those of the social competence model (Rice & Quinsey, 1980).

In a social competence model, sexual behavior is considered to be learned behavior, involving the acquisition of the specific behaviors involved in sexual activity, the association of particular stimuli and fantasies with sexual arousal, and the acquisition of attitudes toward various sexual activities and sexual partners. In all likelihood, the same processes underlying the acquisition of acceptable sexual behaviors underlie the acquisition of inappropriate or aggressive sexual behaviors. Although the evidence supports the assumption that sexual behaviors are learned, the precise mechanisms are, at present, unclear. In addition, certain associations (such as an association of aggression with sexual arousal or an association of female characteristics or youthful appearance with sexual arousal) may be particularly easy to learn because of the historical influence of evolutionary selection pressures on reproductive behavior (Quinsey, 1984). The belief that sexual behavior is learned encourages the development of behavioral procedures in the treatment of persons who exhibit inappropriate sexual behaviors. As an aside, though, behavioral methods of treatment might be efficacious even if the behaviors were not learned or, conversely, nonbehavioral methods might be appropriate with behaviors that are learned.

The program to be described in this chapter was developed using an explicit logic. First, measures were sought that either had a prima facie theoretical relationship to sexual offending or differentiated identifiable subgroups of sex offenders from other offenders and from persons who had not committed an offense of any kind. After such measures were identified, interventions were designed that would change offenders so that they had posttreatment scores on these measures similar to those of nonoffenders or that would produce changes expected to be related to lower recidivism. The final task was to determine whether these measures were related to recidivism and whether changes on these measures were related to lower recidivism rates.

THE SETTING

Traditionally, treatment programs for serious sex offenders have been housed in correctional institutions or mental health facilities for forensic psychiatric patients. These typically all-male, secure institutions are still the most common sites for sex offender treatment programs. Some of these institutions have different kinds of offenders, and others specialize in the housing and treatment of sex offenders alone. These institutions must not only provide custodial care and treatment but also make decisions about whether or when these men should be released. These decisions are related to complex issues of law and social policy. More recently, a number of programs have been implemented in the community; some of these programs treat persons under a variety of legal mandates, whereas others treat only voluntary clients who are under no legal coercion (e.g. Abel *et al.*, 1985).

The setting of any program provides a set of opportunities and constraints that structures the form the program can take (Quinsey, 1981). This section of the chapter describes the institution in which the treatment program highlighted in this chapter—the "Oak Ridge" Sex Offender Program—is housed.

Oak Ridge is a 300-bed, all-male, maximum security hospital in Penetanguishene, Ontario. It is operated by the Provincial Ministry of Health but is built in the style of an old prison. Patients enter Oak Ridge in several distinct legal categories: (a) persons under warrants of remand who are referred by the courts for a pretrial or presentence psychiatric assessment, (b) persons under warrants of the lieutenant governor who are referred by the courts after having been found not guilty by reason of insanity or, more rarely, unfit for trial, and (c) involuntarily certified patients who are referred from federal or provincial correctional institutions as mentally ill or from regional psychiatric or mental retardation facilities as severe management problems.

Oak Ridge is a second-stage institution that accepts and refers patients primarily to and from other institutions, and very seldom to or from the community. The patient population is very heterogeneous in its characteristics, including length of stay. Adequate staffing has always been a problem, and there are few professional staff, as is characteristic of such institutions. Although the program characteristics of Oak Ridge are complex, the programs themselves tend to be designed for all patients on a given ward, and include work placement, patient-run milieu therapy, or token economy programs. Phenothiazines and other medications are commonly used. A more detailed description of various aspects of Oak Ridge has been presented elsewhere (Quinsey, 1981).

HISTORICAL DEVELOPMENT

Although current behavioral programs for sex offenders are usually conceptualized in terms of social learning theory (e.g., Bandura, 1969), they are the historical result of early treatment efforts in the behavior therapy tradition (e.g., Wolpe, 1958), most particularly assertion training and studies on aversion therapy with homosexuals (e.g., Feldman, 1966). To a large extent, current behavioral programs for sex offenders represent the behavior therapy approach, together with Freund's (1981) psychophysiological method of measuring male sexual preference. An overview of the history of behavior therapy and early work with sex offenders has been provided by Yates (1970).

At the time the Oak Ridge sex offender program was started, in 1972, the literature on the assessment and treatment of rapists and child molesters was very limited. As time went on, however, more information became available from the literature and from our own studies that encouraged the modification of our treatment procedures. Reviews of the literature can be found in Abel, Blanchard, and Becker (1978), Kelly (1982), Langevin (1983), Laws and Osborn (1983), Quinsey (1973, 1977, 1983, 1984, 1986), and Quinsey and Marshall (1983).

We started measuring child molesters' sexual-age preferences using a technique pioneered by Freund (for a review, see Freund, 1981) and attempted to modify these preferences with classical conditioning techniques (Quinsey, Bergersen, & Steinman, 1976). We subsequently added sex education, heterosocial skill training (Whitman & Quinsey, 1981), and training in self-management techniques (Pithers, Marques, Gibat, & Marlatt, 1983). In addition, Abel and his colleagues (Abel, Blanchard, Barlow, & Guild, 1977) developed a technique to assess sexual arousal to sexual themes (e.g., force, bondage, etc.) that allowed us to include rapists in our treatment and assessment efforts. Finally, we have added treatment techniques such as signaled punishment (Quinsey, Chaplin, & Carrigan, 1980), satiation (Marshall, 1979), and olfactory aversion (Maletzky, 1980) in a continuing attempt to improve our ability to modify inappropriate sexual arousal. These procedures are described in more detail later.

This program, then, has evolved from the simple use of classical conditioning to modify child molesters' inappropriate sexual-age preferences to a multifaceted program of skill acquisition and self-control. Similar changes have occurred in other behavioral sex offender programs. These changes, we believe, have led to a much stronger treatment intervention. At the same time, however, the changes have made the overall program difficult to evaluate. Fortunately, the recent literature does contain some evidence that behavioral treatment packages of the kind described in this chapter are efficacious. Davidson (in preparation), for instance, has followed up sex offender inmates who had received behavioral treatment (sex education, social skills, and aversion therapy) and compared them with a cohort of similar inmates who were released before the availability of the behavioral program. Child molester inmates who had received treatment were convicted significantly less frequently for new sex offenses than child molesters who had not received the program; unfortunately, no differences were found between treated and untreated rapists. Kelly (1982) has reviewed 32 behavioral studies that used a variety of treatment techniques in the treatment of child molesters and concluded that behavioral techniques do lower sexual recidivism rates; fewer data, however, are available on the behavioral treatment of rapists (Quinsey, 1984).

At present, the sex offender program at Oak Ridge has five components: (1) laboratory assessment of sexual arousal, (2) problem identification, (3) heterosocial skill training, (4) sex education, and (5) modification of inappropriate sexual preferences. These components are described individually next.

THE PROGRAM

Laboratory Assessment of Sexual Arousal

The assessment of sexual arousal, although not yet entirely standardized, is performed in a similar manner by a variety of laboratories. Laws and Osborn (1983) have presented a very detailed outline of how such laboratories operate.

Each sex offender who is referred to the Oak Ridge Sex Offender Program for treatment is first assessed in the sexual behavior laboratory. The laboratory is equipped with a sound attenuating and electrically shielded patient's chamber, a rearview projection screen, and apparatus for automatically scheduling slides and audiotaped material and for monitoring penile circumference and skin conductance. Penile circumference is monitored on a Beckman Dynograph at two levels of magnification and on a digital voltmeter.

Depending on the nature of the patient's offense history, he receives a slide test of sexual-age preference or an audiotaped test designed to measure his arousal to rape stimuli. Because the two methods of assessment are similar, the visual assessment method is described here in detail, and the methods for the auditory stimulus assessment are described more briefly later.

During assessment sessions, patients are seated in a reclining chair. Penile circumference is measured by means of a mercury-in-rubber strain gauge placed around the shaft of the patient's penis. The gauge is connected to a Parks Electronic Model 270 Plethysmograph. A desk top is placed across the arms of the chair to prevent the patient from seeing or manipulating his penis.

The patient is instructed to relax, remain as still as possible, keep his eyes on the translucent screen, and try to imagine the person represented in each slide as a potential sex partner. A standard array of slides is then presented to the patient. This array consists of two slides of each of the following categories: adult females, adult males, pubescent females, pubescent males, child females between the ages of 6 and 11, child males between 6 and 11 years of age, child females under the age of 5, male children under the age of 5, explicit heterosexual activity, and landscapes. Each slide is presented for a period of 30 seconds. Penile circumference is recorded from 2 seconds following slide presentation until 30 seconds after the slide offset. The interslide interval is 30 seconds, although this is extended if the response does not return to baseline (the starting position). The patient's sexual arousal pattern is determined by the relative levels of response to each of the 10 slide categories.

In the auditory assessment, stimuli are presented via an intercom. On our standard tape, these stimuli consist of 18 audiotaped scenarios describing various interactions with an adult female, read in a male voice in the first person. Five of these scenarios describe consenting heterosexual interaction, five describe nonconsenting heterosexual interaction (rape), five describe nonsexual violence, and three describe sexually neutral interactions. The patient is instructed to try to imagine that he is the person speaking on the tape. Maximum penile circumference within the interval from 2 to 180 seconds after stimulus onset is recorded. A 30-second interval precedes the next stimulus, during which responses are not scored.

We have conducted a lengthy series of studies designed to validate various aspects of our measurement of sexual arousal. In our first study (Quinsey *et al.*, 1975), we found that penile responses to slides of persons varying in age and gender discriminate child molesters from normals (community volunteers and nonsex offender patients), whereas verbal reports do not. Penile responses also relate closely to the child molesters' histories of victim choice. Child molesters showed more sexual arousal to slides of children who were the same ages and genders as their victims than did others. Incest offenders exhibit less inappropriate age preference than other child molesters (Quinsey, Chaplin, & Carrigan, 1979).

Rapists exhibit relatively more sexual arousal to audiotaped descriptions of brutal rapes than to consenting sex stories in comparison to normal subjects (Quinsey, Chaplin, & Varney, 1981). Some rapists show sexual arousal to descriptions of nonsexual violence as well, and the amount of this arousal is related to whether they have in the past physically injured their victims (Quinsey & Chaplin, 1982). Normal subjects show less arousal when the victim does not consent and very little when the victim is described as suffering. Rapists' arousal, however, is not affected by victim consent or suffering (Quinsey & Chaplin, 1984). Rapists are best differentiated from nonsex offenders on the basis of their sexual arousal when the rape stories are cruel and short.

Although penile response measurement is far superior to verbal report, sexual arousal measures can be faked by some persons and must always be interpreted with caution (Quinsey & Bergersen, 1976; Quinsey & Carrigan, 1978). Although faking is frequently not a problem in initial testing (Quinsey *et al.*, 1975), it becomes more of a difficulty in treatment. In treatment, this problem can be addressed, if not solved, by attempting to ensure that the results of psychophysiological assessment do not determine whether the offender is kept within the institution, which is sometimes difficult, and in presenting the treatment issue to the patient as not involving a "cure" but as learning to control inappropriate arousal. From a research or evaluative perspective, the issue of faking is bypassed by relating sexual arousal measures directly to recidivism.

Problem Identification

Within many institutions for the treatment of offenders, serious problems exist in the rational selection of suitable targets for intervention and in the assignment of offenders to various treatment programs. The emphasis in assessment is often on diagnosis and various legal issues rather than on the identification of offender problems that might be amenable to modification and much less on collaboration with the offender in the design of an individualized program that can address these problems. Quinsey and Maguire (1983) have found that, although experienced forensic clinicians agreed on psychiatric diagnosis and on whether an offender would benefit from phenothiazines, they exhibited little agreement as to the appropriateness of other behavioral and nonbehavioral methods of intervention. In addition, there was little agreement as to how much these various treatments (or any treatment) might benefit a given offender. Given this lack of consensus, it is not surprising that the offenders themselves are often skeptical and frequently resistive when offered the opportunity to participate in treatment programs of various kinds.

The purpose of the problem identification program is for therapists and patients to reach the same view of what treatment is appropriate and relevant before treatment proceeds. Therapeutic compliance and active patient commitment are seen to follow from a "theory" of sexual offending that is shared by the offender and the therapist.

The program is run in a group format with four to seven patients and two staff members. Patients are selected who have one or more offenses involving child molestation or rape, have sufficient verbal ability to participate in the group, and are at least potentially interested in treatment. The goal of the program is to produce a written theoretical account of each patient's sexual offense pattern to which all group members subscribe.

The first meeting begins with an elementary exposition by one of the therapists on the scientific method. Specificity of explanation is stressed with a variety of examples. Consistency between the evidence and the phenomena to be explained is advanced as the criterion for acceptance of a theory. An illustration of this issue is provided later. The accepted theories are, of course, acknowledged not to be absolutely true but are the best that can be developed given the state of our knowledge.

The second group meeting is concerned with a general discussion of why a man might rape a woman and later why a man might molest a child. Typically, group members advance explanations couched in dynamic terms that they have learned in group psychotherapy or idiosyncratic justifications for their behavior.

At the third meeting, a therapist hands out a sheet containing a "personality profile" of each patient that is asserted to be a provisional explanation of the patient's offense history. Each profile is typed with the patient's name at the top and the therapist's signature at the bottom. Actually, the profiles are identical and are taken from Ulrich, Stachnik, and Stainton (1963). The profiles contain assertions that are true of everyone or so vague as to be meaningless. The therapist asks for written feedback on the accuracy and adequacy of his preliminary effort. The purpose of this procedure is to vividly demonstrate the type of explanations that are not desirable and to indicate how one can check on the validity of explanations of behavior. Patients are typically enthusiastic in their acceptance of the profile's validity. After a very careful description of how the profiles were obtained, however, patients often see the nature of their task more clearly, particularly the need for specificity, and they become more skeptical of glib and vague explanations.

In the remaining sessions, each patient in turn presents an oral autobiography. Each autobiography takes from 2 to 6 hours. Notes are maintained and checked informally against the patient's history (e.g., relatives' accounts, police reports, etc.). At the conclusion of the history, a brainstorming session is held. The hypotheses that emerge from this session are systematically checked against the autobiography and eliminated where inconsistent with the autobiographical material. Sometimes, other information such as laboratory tests of sexual preferences are included as data. The therapist, working backward from the offenses, produces a theory of proximal factors (circumstances immediately surrounding the offenses) and distal or predisposing factors, which are more remote in time. This theory is presented to the group and the final revision (as amended by group discussion) accepted by the group. A copy of the theory is given to the patient, and one is put on his clinical file.

Theory construction is a difficult task. Where possible, the scheme put forward by Pithers et al. (1983) is used to organize the material. An example may clarify these points. A patient in one of the groups had committed a series of rape murders. During the time in which the murders were committed, the patient was very depressed about his wife openly having an affair with another man. The patient naturally enough attributed these murders to his depression. Through the autobiographical material, however, we could demonstrate that the "depression," perhaps more properly labeled as *anger,* was only one of the proximal causes and that the explanation was much more complex and involved factors that had occurred much earlier in time. The patient, had in fact, attempted to rape a woman many years before his marriage. This occurrence led to questions about sadistic sexual fantasies that the patient acknowledged and that were confirmed by psychophysiological assessment. The final list of relevant problems included assertion deficits, sadistic fantasies, and a number of other difficulties.

The procedures described here appear to resemble those used in any treatment program and, in particular, those used in psychodynamic programs. There is an important difference, however. Specifically, the explanations themselves are pitched at a low level of inference and are very data-oriented. The amount of objective detail used to support the explanations is sufficient to convince most of the patients of the explanations' validity without difficulty, particularly because the data and often the theories are supplied primarily by the patients themselves.

Patients are usually pleased with the results of the program initially but later begin asking what the theory means with respect to their treatment. At that point, the therapist is in a position to inform the patient what can and cannot be addressed with existing programs. On occasion, an individual program has to be developed, or the patient may have to be referred elsewhere within the institution for programs (such as those for alcohol abuse) in addition to, or instead of, the sex offender programs. Because of the detailed knowledge of the sex offense pattern that the therapist has acquired, a program of self-management can often be advanced and elaborated upon in subsequent treatment.

The problem identification program is the newest module in our treatment program, and, as yet, no evaluative data are available.

Heterosocial Skills Training

It is widely believed that many sex offenders are socially incompetent in a variety of areas (Marshall & Barbaree, 1984). Thus, in addition to attempting to suppress inappropriate behavior, both behavioral and nonbehavioral treatment programs frequently incorporate methods to improve various aspects of sex offenders' social abilities. At Oak Ridge, the heterosocial skills program is designed to improve the social skills of rapists and child molesters and to reduce their heterosocial anxiety. The rationale for this approach is that offenders must be able to obtain sexual gratification in an appropriate manner in order for appropriate behaviors to be reinforced. The naturally occurring rewards in appropriate sexual interactions are probably critical in reducing recidivism. Heterosocial skill deficits, however, need not have played an etiological role, although they may have, particularly in combination with other factors. This point is important because of Stermac and Quinsey's (1986) finding that rapists show the same level of social skills in interacting with females as with males and are not differentiable from other patients who are not sex offenders. Both groups of patients were, however, less skilled than nonpatient, low socioeconomic status controls.

Patients are assessed before and after treatment using the same measures. Because not all sex offenders have social skills problems, the assessment is used to determine which sex offenders should be offered this treatment. The treatment itself is behavioral in nature and involves modeling, coaching, videotape feedback, and extensive rehearsal in a group context; more detail is provided later.

Assessment

Likely candidates are interviewed at some length regarding their dating history before formal assessment. The nature of the assessment and treatment program is explained in detail at this initial interview. The formal assessment begins with a 10-minute conversation with a female who is unknown to the patient. This conversation is videotaped. The patient is instructed to converse on any topic except the assessment itself. He is asked to behave as if the woman were a potential date but is not required to ask her for a date. The female is instructed to converse in a friendly but passive manner and not to initiate conversation. She is instructed to interrupt silences of 5 to 10 seconds with an innocuous comment (e.g., "Nice weather we are having"). The patient and female confederate subsequently fill out questionnaires that measure their perceptions of the conversation.

Two trained females later independently rate a videotape of the conversation according to patient anxiety, social skill level, and a variety of other measures. We have obtained good interrater reliabilities on these measures (Stermac & Quinsey, 1986; Whitman & Quinsey, 1981).

The second phase of the assessment involves the Heterosocial Adequacy Test (Perri, Richards, & Goodrich, 1978). This measure has been shown to have high internal consistency, interrater reliability, ability to discriminate known groups, and sensible correlations with other measures (e.g., high correlations with subjects' self-ratings of heterosocial skill and low correlations with the Taylor Manifest Anxiety Scale). Our version of the Heterosocial Adequacy Test has been adapted for our population and consists of 20 audiotaped heterosocial situations. The situations involve interactions that are highly likely to occur, are of moderate difficulty, and prompt a wide range of responses. The patient is asked to respond as he would if the situations were actually occurring. The patient's verbal response (or indication of a nonverbal response) is recorded on a second tape recorder. These responses are evaluated on dimensions of social skillfulness by two independent raters following the methods of Perri *et al* (1978).

Finally, the patient completes four questionnaires: the Social Avoidance and Distress Scale, the Fear of Negative Evaluation Scale (both developed by Watson & Friend, 1969), the Assertiveness Questionnaire (Callner & Ross, 1976), and a dating history questionnaire that provides information on the frequency, duration, and perceived success of past relationships. The psychometric characteristics of these questionnaires are acceptable and are given in the original references.

The assessment determines the extent to which the patient has difficulty in heterosexual interactions. For patients who exhibit substantial heterosocial skill deficits, the assessment data provide a pretreatment baseline with which to compare subsequent performance, together with a specification of which areas require improvement.

Treatment

A male and a female therapist together with four to six patients constitute a group. The first session is devoted to introductions and establishing rapport. Group members state their objectives. The confidentiality of material discussed in the group is stressed. The remaining sessions focus on learning specific skills, following a curriculum that has been adapted from McGovern *et al.* (1975).

The first topic concerns asking a female for directions in an appropriate manner. This skill is intentionally simple and nonthreatening and is used to habituate patients to videotaping and receiving videotaped and verbal feedback on their performance. It provides an experience of initial success. Each of the skills is introduced and taught in the same manner. The therapists first describe the technique and model the appropriate behaviors. Then each of the patients, in turn, role-plays the situation with the female. A videotape of the performance is then discussed. Feedback always starts with praise and ends with constructive criticism. Specific behaviors, such as posture, eye contact, spacing, clarity of speech, voice volume, and speech content are addressed.

The next few sessions are spent teaching the importance of listening in becoming a good conversationalist. A listening game is employed to demonstrate listening skills. Listening is a major focus of all the sessions that follow and is, therefore, discussed in great detail. Concentrating on listening also serves as a distraction from becoming anxious or concerned with how to respond when the other person is finished speaking. Patients are encouraged to use open (e.g., "What do you think about X?") as opposed to closed questions (e.g., "Do you like X?"). The emphasis is on asking questions that allow the partner to give an extended rather than a "yes" or "no" response. The patient is then expected to listen to the response so that he can ask another related open question. Other techniques that are taught include: (a) paraphrasing (a technique used to rephrase the statement the other person has just made in order to demonstrate that one is listening), (b) perception checking (a technique used for clarifying the other person's feelings on the topic being discussed), (c) elaboration (a technique used to express an opinion or experience similar to the one being discussed by the other person), (d) association (a technique used to switch topics in a conversation to a related topic), and (e) answer-ask (a technique used to encourage the other person to express feelings by offering one's own first). Everyone is expected to learn each new technique before progressing to the next technique. Each practice conversation in which the patient engages is expected to include the newest technique learned and, as applicable, any techniques learned earlier. By using this style of teaching, the length of each conversation increases in preparation for the topic of informal dating.

"Informal dating" is introduced next because it is very similar to the longer conversations the patient has been practicing. An informal date is described as a date that occurs on the spur of the moment. For example, the patient encounters a woman he knows and with whom he has had a conversation in the past and asks her to join him for lunch or a beer. Such a date does not involve preparation and, therefore, prevents unnecessary preparatory anxiety. In a role-playing format, the patient is expected to engage in a short conversation with the woman and then ask her to join him for a beer. He constructs the scene for this encounter in accordance with his life-style. For example, if he often shops in a mall, then this is where the scene is set. The conversation they engage in while having a beer is exactly as it would be in the longer conversations that have been practiced. It is stressed at this point that beginning a heterosexual relationship is very similar to starting any friendship and can, therefore, be expected to develop slowly. The second and third dates are very similar to the first but can involve a more formal meeting (e.g., going out for dinner).

The other topics in the social skills program include phoning to ask for a date, introducing a woman to friends or family, complimenting a woman, and dealing with annoyance and rejection. At the completion of this 60-hour program, the patient completes the assessment procedure described earlier for a second time in order to measure his improvement.

Evaluation

Whitman and Quinsey (1981) have shown that blind ratings of sex offenders' heterosocial skills increase significantly from pre- to posttreatment. A sex education control condition that involved a similar amount of group time and interaction with a female therapist did not affect social skills ratings.

Sex Education Program

The rationale for sex education is much the same as for heterosocial skill training. In order for sex offenders to develop appropriate sexual relationships, they must have an understanding of appropriate sexual behavior and community values. Many sex offenders lack sexual knowledge and maintain beliefs that appear likely to encourage further sex offending (Abel *et al.*, 1985; Quinsey, 1977, 1984; 1986).

Assessment

Patients are assessed at the beginning and end of treatment on a variety of paper-and-pencil measures. The Sex Education Quiz examines the objective knowledge covered by the course curriculum. The quiz is divided into a section that requires patients to match biological labels with corresponding anatomical structures in diagrams of male and female reproductive systems, a section that contains multiple-choice items, and a section that requires patients to supply appropriate terms in paragraphs describing ovulation, sperm production, and pregnancy. A brief version of this quiz has been developed for patients with more limited academic skills.

The Cognition Survey (Chaplin & Quinsey, 1984) was taken from various sources in the literature; some of it was adapted from work done by Abel and Marshall and their colleagues. The survey consists of a set of statements relating to specific sexual beliefs and is organized into three categories of 36 items each. Patients indicate the extent of their agreement with each item. The child molestation category items involve beliefs that may serve to maintain sexual behaviors with children (e.g., "A child who doesn't physically resist an adult's sexual advances wants to have sex with the adult"). The rape category is similar (e.g., "Many women fantasize about rape and privately hope it happens to them"). The general category relates to commonly held beliefs about sexuality (e.g., "Athletes make better lovers than nonathletic people").

Further questionnaires measure attitudes toward rape (Feild, 1978), attitudes toward women (Spence, Helmreich, & Stapp, 1973), social self-esteem (Lawson, Marshall, & McGrath, 1979), social anxiety (Record, 1977), and sex roles (Bem, 1974).

Treatment

The sex education program is divided into an objective knowledge section and a subjective or value-related section. The order of presentation, depth, and relative focus of the sections are tailored to the needs of each particular group of patients. Instruction is done in a group format with a male and a female therapist and a group of four to six patients.

Each therapist takes responsibility for presenting specific lecture material. Lecture topics for the objective portion include history of sexuality, male sexuality, male sexual response, female sexuality, female sexual response, sexual intercourse, masturbation, conception, pregnancy, childbirth, birth control, sex-related diseases, sexual dysfunctions, and sexual variations and deviations. Value-related topics include relationships and marriage, sexual behavior, norms and parameters, sexual attitudes, sex and the law, sex and morals, and stages of moral development.

After each lecture, a question period is followed by a discussion of related issues. Whenever possible, audiovisual aides are used to present or clarify the material. Periodic quizzes are given to help assess progress.

An effort is made to relate the material to the offenders' own lives. Often, discussions deal with aspects of institutional life, such as lack of privacy, lack of access to females, and the stigma attached to "being a sex offender." A sense of group cohesion is developed, particularly in the early sessions, by the use of awareness exercises. For example, dilemmas involving competing values are presented to the group in a concrete situation. Members are then asked to choose how they would respond to the situation and present a justification for their choice.

Although the intent of the course is essentially instructional, some time is spent addressing group process issues and dealing with interpersonal issues among group members and, occasionally, helping with current problems the patients may be having on the wards.

Evaluation

Large increases in factual knowledge, as reflected by paper-and-pencil tests, are associated with participation in this program (Whitman & Quinsey, 1981). Evaluations of any shifts in attitudes that may be produced by the course have yet to be conducted.

Modification of Inappropriate Arousal

Because of the relationship of inappropriate sexual arousal patterns to sexual offending (Marshall & Barbaree, 1984; Quinsey, 1984, 1986), nearly all behavioral programs contain an element that is directed to the modification of deviant arousal. At Oak Ridge, several forms of behaviorally oriented laboratory treatment procedures are offered in order to modify sexual arousal patterns, as manifested by changes in penile circumference to various stimuli. Basically, the aim is to lower patients' penile arousal to inappropriate stimuli. This section outlines the criteria patients must meet in order to be accepted into a treatment program, briefly describes several of the treatment procedures, and outlines the evaluation of progress throughout treatment.

A patient must meet several criteria in order to be considered for the laboratory treatment procedures. First, the patient must display an inappropriate sexual arousal pattern on one of our standard assessments; that is, the patient must show relatively high sexual arousal to sexually inappropriate stimuli as compared with appropriate stimuli. The two basic assessments (visual assessment for age preference and auditory assessment for activity preference) were described earlier. An assessment must have occurred within the 6 months immediately preceding treatment, or the patient is reassessed. Second, the patient must understand and admit that he has a problem with his sexual arousal. Third, he must understand the nature of the therapy. Finally, the patient must be cooperative and consent to the treatment procedures. Patients are informed that treatment is voluntary and that they are free to withdraw from the program at any time, for whatever reason, without penalty.

Methods

Four basic treatment procedures are used: biofeedback, signaled punishment, olfactory aversion, and masturbatory satiation. All treatment occurs in the sexual behavior laboratory described previously.

Biofeedback is used with either auditory or visual stimuli (Quinsey, Chaplin, & Carrigan, 1980). It involves the illumination of lights inside the chamber that informs the patient of the state of his arousal. In this procedure, a patient either views slides or listens to audiotapes while his penile circumference is monitored. Plethysmograph output is sent to a Schmitt Trigger (an analog-to-digital converter) that illuminates lights when a certain preselected criterion is surpassed. The criterion is set by the therapist and is approximately half of the maximum response exhibited during the preceding session. Stimuli are constructed individually for each patient.

In the case of visual stimuli, several sets of slides are generated from our pool. Each set consists of 10 slides of adult females, and 10 slides representing each of the patient's deviant categories as determined by the assessment. Audiostimuli consist of six scenarios describing consenting heterosexual activity and six scenarios describing nonconsenting heterosexual activity (rape). Scenarios are either chosen from the pool of previously recorded tapes or are generated by the therapist with the aid of the patient to reflect the relevant inappropriate fantasies.

In a treatment session, a patient views slides and/or listens to tapes while his penile circumference is being monitored. If penile circumference surpasses the preset criterion during presentation of an appropriate stimulus, a blue light is illuminated. Alternatively, if the criterion is exceeded during presentation of a deviant stimulus, a red light is presented. A patient would normally participate in a series of biofeedback sessions involving a different set of stimuli, presented in a different random order each day.

Signaled punishment uses the same stimuli and the red and blue lights as described above (Quinsey & Marshall, 1983; Quinsey, Chaplin, & Carrigan, 1980). A mildly painful (but harmless) electric shock, however, is associated with arousal to inappropriate stimuli. During the recording interval for a deviant stimulus, a brief shock is delivered via a probability generator at the end of 40% of the 5-second intervals in which the patient was above criterion (i.e., the red light was on). These shocks are delivered via an arm band that is attached to the upper part of the patient's left arm. Shock intensity is determined by the patient before each session.

Olfactory aversion is similar to signaled punishment but, rather than using a shock, an aversive odor is associated with arousal to deviant stimuli (Laws, Meyer, & Holmen, 1978; Maletzky, 1980). We have experimented with several noxious odors including those obtained from rotting meat, valeric acid, and ammonia. During a session, the patient is instructed that when the red light is illuminated, indicating that his penile circumference has surpassed the preset criterion during the presentation of an inappropriate stimulus, he is to inhale deeply from a squeeze bottle containing the odoriferous substance. The therapist can monitor the patient's behavior via a one-way mirror to ensure compliance with the instructions.

Masturbatory satiation is the final method of modifying sexual arousal that is used in our laboratory (Marshall, 1979). Unlike the preceding treatments, penile circumference is not monitored throughout this procedure. A patient is taken into the assessment chamber and is seated on the reclining chair. The therapist sits outside the chamber where he can see the patient through the one-way mirror and hear him via the intercom. The patient is instructed to masturbate while verbalizing a consenting (and age-appropriate) heterosexual fantasy until ejaculation. At this point the patient continues to masturbate but now verbalizes his deviant fantasies. The patient masturbates and fantasizes throughout a long series of hour-long sessions. The goal of treatment is to satiate the patient with his inappropriate fantasies through their extensive rehearsal in a state of low sexual arousal (Marshall, 1979).

Evaluation of Progress

Each patient participates in a pretreatment assessment. In the case of an auditory session, the standard tape described before is used in the pretreatment assessment. In the case of visual sessions, a pretreatment set of slides (known as the individual diagnostic sequence) is constructed for a patient's particular deviant interest group. This set consists of 5 slides of adult females,

5 of sexually neutral scenes, and 10 slides selected from the patient's deviant category(ies).

A patient's course of treatment is determined by his progress throughout sessions. Normally, a patient would begin with a preintervention assessment followed by five sessions of biofeedback. A postintervention readministration of the original assessment would then follow. The assessments, though, do not use the slides or audiotaped scenarios used in treatment, thus making the tests a conservative estimate of the generality of treatment effects. If significant improvement has been made from the biofeedback sessions, treatment could end here. Otherwise, the patient would enter the signaled punishment phase of treatment. Normally, this would consist of 10 sessions, followed by another assessment. If progress were slow but there appeared to be some trend and the patient were willing, another 10 sessions and assessments would follow. The criterion for considering preferences to be changed is a statistically significant shift. Considering the number of test stimuli and the single-subject design, this is a very conservative criterion.

If significant changes were not achieved or if for some reason the patient were unwilling to receive the shocks, olfactory aversion would be employed. This would occur in blocks of 5 or 10 sessions, depending on the patient's apparent progress, with each block being followed by an assessment. Masturbatory satiation would be used only in those instances where significant changes could not be brought about with the previously mentioned programs and would be employed only in cases where the patient was sufficiently verbal and had well-formed deviant fantasies.

Evaluation

Quinsey, Chaplin, and Carrigan (1980) found that signaled punishment significantly decreased sexual arousal to children in 10 out of 14 child molesters treated with this technique. Signaled punishment was more effective than a biofeedback alone or a classical conditioning aversion technique. Physiological posttreatment measures of sexual preference for child as opposed to adult stimuli have been found to be significantly (although weakly) related to sexual recidivism over a follow-up period averaging 29 months (Quinsey, Chaplin, & Carrigan, 1980). Over longer periods (averaging 34 months), however, only pretreatment measures of relative sexual age preference were related to recidivism. These results suggest that treatment effects do not last indefinitely and, therefore, support Maletzky's (1980) strategy of employing quarterly "booster" sessions; child molesters treated in Maletzky's program have been found to have very low recidivism rates.

PROBLEMS

One of the difficulties in treating institutionalized men in any setting is that the results of treatment and/or assessment occasionally have a bearing on release decisions. Because of this, some patients decide on their own or, more frequently, are advised by their lawyers not to participate. This situation arises because patients or their lawyers sometimes believe that laboratory evidence of inappropriate sexual arousal would result in longer confinements for their clients. This is particularly true of patients who have previously asserted that they are "cured." Another difficulty relates to the length of time some patients are kept in the institution. Some patients, for example, sex murderers, are kept for many years. Although we attempt to treat sex offenders at the time when they have some chance for release, the indeterminate nature of their committals makes this a difficult issue. One must avoid the situation where a patient is not considered for release because he has not been treated and is not treated because he is not considered releasable.

A number of problems in program implementation are associated with the types of patients whom we see. Most are very low in socioeconomic status and, although we attempt not to impose our values, this leads to concerns about the content of the material taught in the heterosocial skills and sex education programs, as the therapists (and literature) are middle class. A large minority of our patients are retarded, and some are low-functioning psychotics. These patients have difficulties in attending to the material and in retaining it. In our group programs, we form homogeneous groups based on verbal ability in order to be able to perform the repetition that is necessary for those who need it.

All of the difficulties associated with treatment in a maximum security institution affect the sex offender program; these problems include conflicts between security and treatment, difficulties in attracting and keeping treatment staff, few female staff, and the like. A more important problem, however, is the lack of aftercare. Patients released from Oak Ridge are scattered among institutions of disparate kinds located across all of Ontario. Developing a systematic and consistent program of clinical follow-through under these circumstances is simply impossible at present.

Turning to the issue of program evaluation, the sort of evaluations that are and are not feasible should be clear, given the nature of the present program. Pre- and posttreatment change studies are relatively easy to do, as are assessment validation studies that depend on the differentiation of known groups. Follow-up studies are difficult but can be done so that changes in theoretically relevant variables associated with treatment can be related to subsequent recidivism. What is even more difficult is a follow-up comparison of randomly selected treated and untreated sex offenders. Although we assess more persons than we treat, the treated and untreated groups are not comparable. Persons who are treated by us must first be accepted by the institution, which means that they are "sicker," have more offenses, and are often less intelligent than the majority who are refused admission. They then must be accepted by us for treatment, which means that they have the types of problems we treat—inappropriate sexual arousal, poor social skills, and inadequate sexual knowledge. Most of the offenders who are accepted by the institution exhibit the sorts of difficulties that we treat. Our treatment cases, unlike our assessment cases, are a highly selected and unusual group of sex offenders.

CONCLUSIONS

Our experience, as well as others' (e.g., Kelly, 1982; Laws & Osborne, 1983; Marshall & Barbaree, 1984), has shown that a behaviorally oriented treatment program for sex offenders can be maintained within a maximum security institution. The Oak Ridge program results in improvement among theoretically relevant measures, such as sexual knowledge, heterosocial skills, and sexual arousal patterns. The program appears to lead to lessened recidivism in the short term.

In the future, more sophisticated follow-up studies are required. Although we and others have shown that short-term change in various target behaviors can be produced with behavioral programs, the relative contributions of the various treatment modalities to long-term outcome are unknown. Several research strategies are required to provide the answers to this and related questions: the comparison of comparable treated and untreated cases; the multivariate prediction of outcome from multiple measures of therapeutic change; and between-groups comparisons of different treatment interventions.

ACKNOWLEDGMENTS

We wish to thank Grant Harris and Marnie Rice for their reviews of an earlier version of this chapter.

REFERENCES

Abel, G. G., Becker, J. V., & Skinner, L. J. (1985). Behavioral Approaches to treatment of the violent offender. In L. H. Roth (Ed.), *Clinical treatment of the violent person* (pp. 100–123). (Crime and Delinquency Issues: A monograph series). Washington, DC: National Institute of Mental Health.

Abel, G. G., Blanchard, E. B., Barlow, D. H., & Guild, D. (1977). The components of rapists' sexual arousal. *Archives of General Psychiatry, 34,* 895–903.

Abel, G. G., Blanchard, E. B., & Becker, J. V. (1978). An integrated treatment program for rapists. In R. T. Rada (Ed.), *Clinical aspects of the rapist* (pp. 161–214). New York: Grune & Stratton.

Bem, S. L. (1974). The measurement of psychological androgyny. *Journal of Consulting and Clinical Psychology, 42,* 155–162.

Callner, D. A., & Ross, S. M. (1976). The reliability and validity of three measures of assertion in a drug addict population. *Behavior Therapy, 17,* 659–667.

Chaplin, T. C., & Quinsey, V. L. (1984). *Cognition Survey.* Unpublished questionnaire. Mental Health Centre, Penetanguishene, Ontario.

Davidson, P. R. (in preparation). *Behavioral treatment for incarcerated sex offenders.* Psychology Department, Queen's University, Kingston, Ontario.

Feild, H. S. (1978). Attitudes toward rape: A comparative analysis of police, rapists, crisis counselors, and citizens. *Journal of Personality and Social Psychology, 36,* 156–179.

Feldman, M. P. (1966). Aversion therapy for sexual deviations: A critical review. *Psychological Bulletin, 65,* 65–79.

Freund, K. (1981). Assessment of pedophilia. In M. Cook & K. Howell (Eds.), *Adult sexual interest in children* (pp. 139–179). London: Academic Press.

Groth, A. N., Longo, R. E., & McFadin, J. B. (1982). Undetected recidivism among rapists and child molesters. *Crime and Delinquency, 28,* 450–458.

Kelly, R. J. (1982). Behavioral reorientation of pedophiliacs: Can it be done? *Clinical Psychology Review, 2,* 387–408.

Langevin, R. (1983). *Sexual strands: Understanding and treating sexual anomalies in men.* Hillsdale, NJ: Lawrence Erlbaum.

Laws, D. R., & Osborn, C. A. (1983). How to build and operate a behavioral laboratory to evaluate and treat sexual deviance. In J. G. Greer & I. R. Stuart (Eds.), *The sexual aggressor: Current perspectives on treatment* (pp. 293–335). Toronto: Van Nostrand Reinhold.

Laws, D. R., Meyer, J., & Holmen, M. L. (1978). Reduction of sadistic arousal by olfactory aversion: A case study. *Behaviour Research and Therapy, 16,* 281–285.

Lawson, J. S., Marshall, W. L., & McGrath, P. (1979). The Social Self-Esteem Inventory. *Educational and Psychological Measurement, 39,* 308–311.

Maletzky, B. M. (1980). Self-referred vs. court-referred sexually deviant patients: Success with assisted covert sensitization. *Behavior Therapy, 11,* 306–314.

Marshall, W. L. (1979). Satiation therapy: A procedure for reducing deviant sexual arousal. *Journal of Applied Behavior Analysis, 12,* 10–22.

Marshall, W. L., & Barbaree, H. E. (1984). A behavioral view of rape. *International Journal of Law and Psychiatry, 7,* 51–77.

McGovern, K. B., Arkowitz, H., & Gilmore, S. K. (1975). Evaluation of social skill training programs for college dating inhibitions. *Journal of Counseling Psychology, 22,* 505–512.

Perri, M. G., Richards, C. S., & Goodrich, J. D. (1978). Heterosocial Adequacy Test (HAT): A behavioral role-playing test for the assessment of heterosocial skills in male college students. *Journal Supplement Abstract Service Catalog of Selected Documents in Psychology, 8,* 16 (ms.1650).

Pithers, W. D., Marques, J. K., Gibat, C. C., & Marlatt, G. A. (1983). Relapse prevention with sexual aggressives: A self-control model of treatment and maintenance of change. In J. G. Greer & I. R. Stuart (Eds.), *The sexual aggressor: Current perspectives on treatment* (pp. 214–239). Toronto: Van Nostrand Reinhold.

Quinsey, V. L. (1973). Methodological issues in evaluating the effectiveness of aversion therapies for institutionalized child molesters. *Canadian Psychologist, 14,* 350–361.

Quinsey, V. L. (1977). The assessment and treatment of child molesters: A review. *Canadian Psychological Review, 18,* 204–220.

Quinsey, V. L. (1981). The long term management of the mentally disordered offender. In S. J. Hucker, C. D. Webster, & M. Ben-Aron (Eds.), *Mental disorder and criminal responsibility* (pp. 137–155). Toronto: Butterworths.

Quinsey, V. L. (1983). Prediction of recidivism and the evaluation of treatment programs for sex offenders. In S. Simon-Jones & A. A. Keltner (Eds.), *Sexual aggression and the law* (pp. 27–40). Burnaby, British Columbia: Criminology Research Centre, Simon Fraser University.

Quinsey, V. L. (1984). Sexual aggression: Studies of offenders against women. In D. Weisstub (Ed.), *Law and mental health: International perspectives* (Vol. 1, pp. 84–121). New York: Pergamon.

Quinsey, V. L. (1986). Men who have sex with children. In D. Weisstubb (Ed.), *Law and mental health: International perspectives* (Vol. 2, pp. 140–172). New York: Pergamon.

Quinsey, V. L., & Bergersen, S. G. (1976). Instructional control of penile circumference. *Behavior Therapy, 7,* 489–493.

Quinsey, V. L., & Carrigan, W. F. (1978). Penile responses to visual stimuli: Instructional control with and without auditory sexual fantasy correlates. *Criminal Justice and Behavior, 5,* 333–342.

Quinsey, V. L., & Chaplin, T. C. (1982). Penile responses to nonsexual violence among rapists. *Criminal Justice and Behavior, 9,* 312–324.

Quinsey, V. L., & Chaplin, T. C. (1984). Stimulus control of rapists' and non-sex offenders' sexual arousal. *Behavioral Assessment, 6,* 169–176.

Quinsey, V. L., & Maguire, A. M. (1983). Offenders remanded for a psychiatric examination: Perceived treatability and disposition. *International Journal of Law and Psychiatry, 6,* 193–205.

Quinsey, V. L., & Marshall, W. L. (1983). Procedures for reducing inappropriate sexual arousal: An evaluation review. In J. G. Greer & I. R. Stuart (Eds.), *The sexual aggressor: Current perspectives on treatment* (pp. 267–289). New York: Van Nostrand Reinhold.

Quinsey, V. L., Steinman, C. M., Bergersen, S. G., & Holmes, T. F. (1975). Penile circumference, skin conductance, and ranking responses of child molesters and "normals" to sexual and nonsexual visual stimuli. *Behavior Therapy, 6,* 213–219.

Quinsey, V. L., Bergersen, S. G., & Steinman, C. M. (1976). Changes in physiological and verbal responses of child molesters during aversion therapy. *Canadian Journal of Behavioural Science, 8,* 202–212.

Quinsey, V. L., Chaplin, T. C., & Carrigan, W. F. (1979). Sexual preferences among incestuous and non-incestuous child molesters. *Behavior Therapy, 10,* 562–565.

Quinsey, V. L., Arnold, L. S., & Pruesse, M. G. (1980). MMPI profiles of men referred for pre-trial psychiatric assessment as a function of offense type. *Journal of Clinical Psychology, 36,* 410–417.

Quinsey, V. L., Chaplin, T. C., & Carrigan, W. F. (1980). Biofeedback and signaled punishment in the modification of inappropriate sexual age preferences. *Behavior Therapy, 11,* 567–576.

Quinsey, V. L., Chaplin, T. C., & Varney, G. (1981). A comparison of rapists' and non-sex offenders' sexual preferences for mutually consenting sex, rape, and physical abuse of women. *Behavioral Assessment, 3,* 127–135.

Quinsey, V. L., Chaplin, T. C., & Upfold, D. (1984). Sexual arousal to nonsexual violence and sadomasochistic themes among rapists and non-sex offenders. *Journal of Consulting and Clinical Psychology, 52,* 651–657.

Record, S. A. (1977). *Personality, sexual attitudes and behavior of sex offenders.* Unpublished PhD dissertation, Queen's University, Kingston, Ontario.

Rice, M. E., & Quinsey, V. L. (1980). Assessment and training of social competence in dangerous psychiatric patients. *International Journal of Law and Psychiatry, 3,* 371–390.

Spence, J. T., Helmreich, R., & Stapp, J. (1973). A short version of the Attitudes Towards Women Scale (ATW). *Bulletin of the Psychonomic Society, 48,* 587–589.

Stermac, L. E., & Quinsey, V. L. (1986). The social competence of incarcerated sexual assaulters. *Behavioral Assessment, 8,* 171–185.

Ulrich, R. E., Stachnik, T. J., & Stainton, N. R. (1963). Student acceptance of generalized personality descriptions. *Psychological Reports, 12,* 831–834.

Watson, D., & Friend, R. (1969). Measurement of social-evaluative anxiety. *Journal of Consulting and Clinical Psychology, 33,* 448–457.

Whitman, W. P., & Quinsey, V. L. (1981). Heterosocial skill training for institutionalized rapists and child molesters. *Canadian Journal of Behavioral Science, 13,* 105–114.

Wolpe, J. (1958). *Psychotherapy by reciprocal inhibition.* Stanford: Stanford University Press.

Yates, A. J. (1970). *Behavior therapy.* Toronto: Wiley.

14

Some Behavioral Applications with Juvenile Offenders outside North America

WILLIAM YULE AND BARRIE J. BROWN

In spite of the widespread interest in applying behavioral approaches with juvenile delinquents in the United Kingdom and Europe (Brown, 1977a, 1979), few published evaluations, or even descriptions, of such applications are available. Thus the present chapter surveys the known published work on behavioral applications to delinquency outside North America and attempts to account for the sparsity of such applications. Although the chapter focuses mostly on work in the United Kingdom, this reflects the relative strength there of behavioral applications with young offenders, rather than any characteristic bias on the part of the authors. The review excludes work with adult criminals.

The paucity of applications outside North America does not reflect any disagreement between North American and other criminologists as to either the failure of traditional institutional approaches to deal with delinquency or, indeed, the inadequate view of criminality presented by the psychiatric model. As far as the latter is concerned, Taylor, Walton, and Young (1973) launched an early attack in the United Kingdom on psychiatric approaches to understanding delinquency and criminality. They criticized these approaches for not taking sufficient account of the problematic nature of definitions of delinquency, for ignoring the stigmatizing effects of the criminal justice process on the offender, and for failing to account for the fact that, far from being a preserve of a pathological minority, some degree of delinquency is a commonplace and temporary condition of the majority.

Criticisms of traditional institutional programs were given support by the Home Office Research Unit in its "Kingswood" study (Cornish & Clarke, 1975). The study was a comparison between a "therapeutic community" and more traditional incarceration in which the youths were not asked to participate in managing their own programs. The two groups were formed by random allocation of 173 teenage delinquents at a residential welfare institution for

William Yule • Department of Psychology, Institute of Psychiatry, University of London, London, England SE5 8AF.   Barrie J. Brown • Bloomsbury Health Authority, 4 St. Pancras Way, London, England NW1 0PE.

delinquents, known at the time as an "approved" school. The results showed that reconviction rates were around 70% within 2 years for both programs. This finding was consistent with the generally negative picture emerging at this time of the potential of institutions that are rooted in a child welfare tradition and separated from the community to prevent further criminality (Clarke & Martin, 1971). Indeed, it appeared that such institutions even afforded opportunities for the learning of additional delinquent responses (Dunlop, 1974; Sinclair & Clarke, 1973).

The dearth of behavioral applications outside North America, then, is not due to a belief that traditional institutional approaches work. Rather, one factor is the social and political environment in many countries worldwide. Progressive legislative changes have occurred rapidly in most developed countries in the world in the last 30 years and, broadly speaking, along a similar course (Tutt, 1982). The emphasis prior to the 1960s was on the provision of "welfare" for delinquents, with models of practice aimed at providing care, control, and treatment (Tutt, 1974). In recent years, this cluster of aims has been questioned in research such as the Kingswood study, with both a consequentially rapid decline in the use of welfare (treatment) programs in residential settings and a significant shift toward an emphasis on justice-oriented policies (e.g., punishment) for juvenile offending. One result of this shift has been a rapid increase in the use of custody for delinquents. In the United Kingdom, for example, Tutt (1982) showed that the number of 14- to 17-year-olds sent to detention centers and borstals (custodial penal settings for youths) increased from 2,408 in 1968, to 4,377 in 1973, and to 7,297 in 1978. At the same time, the welfare sector of provision in most countries has taken up enthusiastically the decarceration strategy pioneered by Miller in Massachussets (Miller, Ohlin, & Coates, 1977).

It is in the context of such legislative changes and professional and service developments worldwide that, in spite of widespread interest in behavioral applications to juvenile delinquency, these applications have not been implemented widely nor subjected extensively to careful evaluation. The following review reflects an exhaustive search of the literature in the English language and a selective search of the German, Dutch, and French literature. We begin with applications in the United Kingdom, where most of the relevant efforts have taken place.

Applications of the Behavioral Model in the United Kingdom

Gilbey House

Gilbey House, a 15-bed unit in a school for delinquent boys situated within the conurbation of Birmingham, England, was, until January 1977, an "intensive care" unit for youths for whom a period of residential care and education was felt to be necessary (Brown, 1977b). In an attempt to both reduce the length of time spent by each boy in Gilbey and to increase the probability that he would benefit from the experience following his discharge, Gilbey House was transformed into a program based upon behavioral principles.

The boys were able to earn tokens by achieving personal and behavioral targets that were based on a baseline analysis of assets and deficits exhibited by each boy before admission. Tokens could be exchanged for a wide range of backup reinforcers, including extra home leave, sweets, toys, cigarettes, games, puzzles, and modeling kits. Once the youths were accustomed to earning tokens, the difficulty levels of individual targets were raised; these were reviewed at 3-week intervals. The boys carried a token card around with them listing individual target behaviors, and they earned tokens when a target was achieved. The tokens consisted of small ink-stained motifs that were different for each member of staff. At the end of each day, the boys cashed their tokens into a bank and either spent or saved them for a future purchase of privileges. As the program developed during the first 6 months, a series of levels of functioning was identified through which boys passed as their behavioral repertoire increased.

A system of punishment was employed to reduce undesirable behaviors. If a boy broke one of the basic house rules in the unit (e.g., smoking illicitly or causing damage), he was given a card with a fixed penalty written on it. For example, the punishment card for smoking illicitly was 50 tokens. The boy had to earn 50 tokens (using the same targets as on his normal token card) before he could reenter the main program. Until the 50 tokens were earned, he was unable to accumulate any further tokens to place into his bank, nor could he consume any backup reinforcers.

Evaluation of the first 23 boys in the Gilbey program suggested that the original aim of rapid and extensive expansion of the boys' skill repertoires was, broadly speaking, achieved (Brown et al., 1978). Whether or not these boys would have fared as well or better in an alternative residential setting remains unanswered because controlled allocation of clients was not possible.

Several views emerged from this early application of behavioral methods with delinquents. For instance, although the child-care workers had grasped the principles of a behavioral approach to child care, serious shortcomings occurred in support for care staff. Analysis of staff–child interaction suggested that monitoring the program and giving detailed regular feedback at a very detailed level were essential parts of the overall approach (Brown & Christie, 1981). To provide continuous monitoring, it was necessary to make available both staff time and expertise in observational techniques and research design. A critical issue linked to the problem of evaluation was the attitude of those running the program toward having their performance constantly and critically examined. In Gilbey, although criticism was an apparently extremely painful experience for the care workers, it seemed much more acceptable if staff members working in the unit were themselves involved in examining their own as well as colleagues' performance.

Unit 1, Orchard Lodge

A second attempt to develop a comprehensive behavioral program in care settings with young offenders in the United Kingdom was begun at Orchard Lodge in 1983. Orchard Lodge is a regional resource center that provides remand, assessment, and treatment facilities for courts and social services in part of southeastern London; it caters to adolescent boys aged 14 to 18 years. From the outset, the program has aimed to return as many offenders as possible to their own community. Within Orchard Lodge, Unit 1 was established as an intensive alternative to long-term residential care elsewhere in the welfare/justice systems in the United Kingdom (Brown, 1984). The model for this program was the Teaching-Family (Achievement Place) approach first developed in Kansas (Braukmann & Fixsen, 1975; see Braukmann & Wolf, Chapter 5, this volume) but with some significant omissions and modifications.

Staffing in Unit 1 had to be adapted to the conditions of service laid down by employers and unions in the United Kingdom. The two original Achievement Place programs in Kansas and many of their later derivatives are directed by two teaching parents (a married couple) who are the major staff resource of the unit, often with the assistance of a full- or part-time alternate or helper. In Unit 1, the use of aspects of the Teaching-Family model required the services of a team of child care staff who can assist the senior teaching parents in operating the program while they are on holiday or take a day off.

In Unit 1, the teaching parents, like their counterparts in the United States, adopt an individual approach. The specific behavioral goals for the young people are based on behaviors that members of their families, schools, and community, along with the young people themselves and their teaching parents, decide are priorities. The program is, in this way, uniquely suited to changing the relevant, individual behaviors of delinquent, disturbed, or disadvantaged young people.

One major feature incorporated into Unit 1 from the Teaching-Family model is its community-based orientation. The program serves young people from the neighborhood in which the program is located. There are three other child care houses nearby, together with a special school, sports hall, and administrative facilities. Obvious differences, however, exist between Unit 1's location and staffing and the typical Teaching-Family group homes. Unit 1 is a large family home divided into two separate family groups, one or the other of which provides the primary focus of the behavioral program for each young person. The staff team in each group comprises one group leader teacher parent and five care workers. Each care worker undertakes the role of keyworker for one or two clients in the family group as well as an overall responsibility from time to time for the programs of the rest of the family group.

Evaluation of the Unit 1 program has focused on within-program process and on a preliminary analysis of outcomes for the first eight youths discharged and followed up for 1 year. All eight of the followed-up youths had been referred to the program from institutional care settings and were deemed suitable for placement only in long-term institutional care by virtue of the severity and frequency of their previous offending. The oldest youth was 17 years old and the youngest 13 years old at the time of admission, with an average age of 14.5 years. All the youths came from families living within 5 miles of Unit 1, but only two of the youths had intact, two-parent families.

After discharge, five of the youths were placed either at home or in an alternative community-based setting and remained in those placements for the full year of the follow-up. The remaining three were returned to long-term institutional or custodial care. The five successful youths avoided further offending, both while in the program and throughout the 1-year follow-up period. In contrast, the unsuccessful group committed five offenses during the program (involving two youths) and two more during the follow-up (by one youth). Although comparison with other programs must be made with caution because of the small number of youths involved and the inability to place youths in Unit 1 randomly, these results provide some cause for optimism because other evaluations of custodial and residential institutional care have shown much less positive outcomes (Cornish & Clarke, 1975; Tutt, 1982).

Training in Teaching Interactions

Another feature of the Unit 1 program has been the availability of postgraduate research students to carry out a series of small-scale studies of the process of establishing and maintaining the program. Limited space permits only a brief description of two of this series: an evaluation of a training course for care workers in the use of teaching interaction skills and an analysis of the antecedents of successful and unsuccessful compliance bidding by teachers working with Unit 1 youths. The study of teaching interactions was initiated because of the importance of good social reinforcement in achieving generalization of newly acquired skills outside the training environment (Kirigin, Wolf, Braukmann, Fixsen, & Phillips, 1979). Teaching interactions were specified according to detailed teaching methods that have been shown to enhance acquisition and generalization of social and other skills. Examples of these methods are the use of praise, giving feedback, defining the task, and so on.

Before the basic training in behavioral skills was begun at Unit 1, Carr (1982) attempted to develop an *in vivo* measure of the teaching-interaction skills used by care workers, noting the lack of published assessment of such skills with respect to the original Achievement Place homes. She succeeded in piloting a reliable and cross-situationally stable measure of teaching-interaction elements used by care workers. The measure involved a structured observational schedule in the treatment setting itself. The study also developed a role-play test of the use of teaching interaction elements during the training session. Results from a study of the first training course for Unit 1 staff showed that the role-play scores increased significantly for all components of the teaching interaction; however, the *in vivo* measure suggested that trained staff improved their performance in naturalistic interaction only in the area of rationale giving. A new basic skills training course is now underway at Unit

1, and the Carr *in vivo* measure will be incorporated into the evaluation of the course.

Compliance Bidding

In response to requests for assistance from teachers, a study was carried out that aimed at isolating teacher behaviors associated with disruption and noncompliance in the classrooms in which Unit 1 youths were placed. Abbott (1984) piloted an *in vivo* measure of interactions in which compliance was requested. Teachers were found to use a narrow range of methods in asking youths to carry out a task. Some teachers made frequent demands, others very infrequent ones. Some made requests irrespective of whether the youth was looking toward them, and some followed up a demand with prompts and reminders, whereas others did not intrude. Significant associations were found between these three aspects of teacher behavior and levels of compliance. Compliance was increased when the teacher used infrequent demands, waited for the pupil to orient to the teacher, and did not then intrude into the compliance response. Results from this study are now being incorporated into training programs for teaching parents working at Unit 1.

Other Institutional Programs in the United Kingdom

The Gilbey and Unit 1 programs represent the most extensive attempts to introduce behavioral methods of working with young people in institutions in the United Kingdom. Other limited applications have also been attempted, such as that at Aycliffe School, a residential center for young offenders located in the countryside near to the Tyneside conurbation in the northeastern section of England. After a brief period of training on token economies for a small team of care workers, Franklin House, a house for eight adolescent boys with long histories of offending, was opened at Aycliffe School (McCafferey, 1977). A token currency (actually, a large supply of Australian half-penny coins) was introduced. Maintenance and personal targets were established for the eight boys, and a recording system was put into operation. Social reinforcement, teaching-interaction skills, and self-government skills were not incorporated into this program.

The program at Aycliffe (McCafferey, 1977) has been further developed as a comprehensive behavioral regime for young offenders by means of "sequential treatment" (Hoghughi, 1979). This means that the youths are graduated through a series of houses, each offering a higher degree of self-government within a token economy motivation system. The treatment involves enhanced use of social reinforcement by peers to maintain control. Other than a description of the systems employed in the sequence of programs, no other process or comparative evaluation data have yet been published.

A second program focusing on behavioral methods was established at a correction center for young offenders in the United Kingdom (Cullen & Seddon, 1980). Twelve adolescent offenders (aged 16 to 21 years) with a variety of behavioral disturbances participated in a points incentive scheme for 6 months. Results showed within-subject decreases in frequency of offending within the center and increases in social interaction skills. Staff training, consistency, and administration of the program presented major problems. It was not possible to allocate clients randomly to treatment and control groups, and no attempts were made to follow up the youths after discharge.

A third behavioral program in an institutional setting offering welfare to young offenders has been developed at Glenthorne, a government-run, secure treatment unit for 60 male and female youths who are dangerous and persistent delinquents (Reid, 1982). The program has specialized in the analysis of problems that appear in applying behavioral methods with young offenders in institutions. Staff working at Glenthorne have published a series of small-scale descriptive studies on these problems as well as on the establishment of a variety of monitoring processes. These studies include an analysis of staff consistency in punishing disruptive and inappropriate behavior (Tobin, 1979). Experience at Glenthorne in the use of response-cost techniques had suggested that staff consistency in pinpointing disruptive behavior was low. Although independent direct observation was employed, the focus of the study remained on behaviors that were defined as inappropriate or disruptive by the institution. The study did not seek to establish what happens when attempts are made to employ teaching interactions with disruptive behaviors, nor did it examine the effects of directed teaching on self-control and self-government skills that would be useful to the clients either in Glenthorne or when they returned to the community.

Another series of studies of punishment at Glenthorne (Stallard, 1980) was unable to demonstrate any significant difference between (a) a fixed interval time-out, (b) a response-cost program involving reduced access to backup privileges and increased token earning requirements, and (c) physical time-out with release contingent on appropriate behavior. Nevertheless, the team at Glenthorne preferred to use physical time-out only, apparently because the response-cost program led to confrontations (Reid, 1982). No corroborative evidence has been published to support preferability of time-out and, significantly, no analysis has been made of the way the Glenthorne response-cost program was actually used. There has been no attempt, either, to develop those aspects of the system's response to problem behavior that focus on teaching interactions or corrective teaching.

The nature of the problem facing the clinical directors at Glenthorne is similar to that described by Miller et al. (1977) in the Massachusetts institutions and that facing Phillips (1978) in the development of Boys Town in Omaha. How can conflicting objectives be met, such as the promotion of skills development, self-control, and self-determination by the client, on the one hand, and institutional safety and control, on the other? The Glenthorne team has elected to examine this question directly rather than close the institution (which it cannot do) or fundamentally reorganize it. Current research is attempting to identify what resources are necessary for maintaining the individualized treatment perspective. The first publication to emerge from this research suggests that (a) contractual agreements between managers and care staff focusing on positive interactions with the clients, (b) practical skills training for staff, and (c) staff–staff support meetings together produced an increase in positive treatment methods as measured by direct observation and survey techniques (Fletcher, 1981). The contribution of individual elements of this program was not discussed, but the direction and results of the research are encouraging indeed.

Applications in the Community in the United Kingdom

Only two community-based projects employing an approach broadly based on the behavioral model have been established in the United Kingdom. Birmingham Action for Youths (BAY) is a nonresidential center in an inner-city neighborhood that offers an alternative education and activity program for young people who would otherwise be placed into long-term residential care due to extensive delinquent activity (McGivern, 1980). Youths entering the program undergo a brief assessment of assets and deficits in educational, work, social, and self-management areas. Contracts are drawn up by the youth and a care worker that pinpoint personal targets in each area. The youths then enter an individual program, in which points are used to motivate the acquisition and practice of target skills. A second stage of the program, the teaching of work skills, was also established in the BAY program, with the goal of enabling the skills acquired at the center to generalize into the workplace (Preston, 1982).

Preston (1982) examined the effects of the program on (a) 26 youths, 16 to 17 years of age, who participated in only the first stage of the program, and (b) a subsequently selected sample of 24 youths admitted to both stages; self-selection did not determine participation in the second stage. Results indicated that both groups had similar rates of employment at discharge (65%). After 3 months, however, only 23% of the youths without the work training offered in the second stage were still employed, compared with 63% of those with that training. Unfortunately, later follow-up showed no significant difference between the two groups, with more than 50% of the total sample unemployed. There was also no significant difference between the groups in convictions at 6 months (21% vs. 23%); more than 10% had been sentenced to a term of imprisonment. These latter figures, however, may be evidence of a better response to community care than would have occurred with institutional care because Tutt (1982) and several others have widely reported reconviction rates of 73% for detention center youths 2 years after discharge, and 83% for borstal youths. Caution must be sounded, however, in spite of the optimism of Preston (1982) because her follow-up data refer only to 6 months postdischarge. Moreover, at the time the research was under way, unemployment among teenagers was at a much lower level in urban areas of the United Kingdom than in late 1984. Finally, comparison with the Tutt (1982) data necessarily assumes the youths in the two studies were indeed alike on such factors as seriousness of delinquency.

The BAY program evaluation failed to carry out any detailed process analysis of the effectiveness of specific components of the program offered to the youths; and, as in the case of all other evaluations reviewed here, major difficulties were evident in attempting to carry out process and comparative research while providing innovative practice. There was, for example, no opportunity for random allocation of youths to the program or to comparable alternative resources in the welfare/custody systems. One striking shortcoming of the program was that, in spite of the fact that BAY purported to offer a community alternative to custodial or residential intervention, what went on in a youth's home was both ignored by and divorced from the program offered in the center.

A similar failure to analyze process, network, and comparative effects is evident in the Shape program (Ostapuik, 1982). Shape offers an experimental behavioral program for young offenders aged 16 to 24 years referred by the probation or social services in an urban area. The program has attempted to provide progressive rehabilitation through phased living accommodations, work experience and work skills training, and social or survival skills training. For the majority of youths, returning to their own family has been impossible; they all have demonstrated a wide range of self-care, social, and work skills deficits. It is in these three areas of behavior change that Shape has attempted to teach new skills through placement in a hostel and the use of self-government, skills-training programs, and behavioral contracting. Independent living accommodation is offered when progress is made in the three skills areas.

Ostapuik (1982) has reported that the method by which clients were admitted to the project was via the probation services, but more than 50% of referrals felt to be acceptable by the project team did not subsequently arrive. Unfortunately, he fails to provide details of specific causes of attrition in the takeup of places except to say that "some of the clients were discouraged from joining the program due to poor physical conditions obtaining at the time" (Ostapuik, 1982, p. 153). It remains possible that a self-selection process operated for this program with the effect that only the most motivated clients from the pool of referred cases actually arrived. Evaluation of the project consisted of a description of the outcomes of 36 clients, which was the total client population during a 24-month period in 1977 to 1979. Only 14 of these had been followed up for 18 months, whereas 12 had been discharged from the project for 6 months or less. Reoffending was the only measure used to measure success, and on this criterion, 22% had failed within 18 months or less.

Social Skills Training with Delinquents in the United Kingdom

In the United Kingdom, social skills training has been greatly influenced by Argyle's (1969) analysis of the components of social interaction skills (Spence, 1979). For example, Spence (1981) studied videotapes of 70 young male offenders during a standardized 5-minute interview with a previously unknown adult—a situation analogous to the youth going for a job interview.

Thirteen behaviors, such as eye contact, verbal initiation, and speech dys-fluency, were rated, some of which were found to relate significantly to the overall impression made by the youth during the interview. Spence concluded that the study provides some social validation data for the behaviors that should be trained in programs with delinquent youths.

Spence and Marzillier (1979) used a multiple-baseline design with five adolescent male offenders to investigate the effects of a sophisticated social skills training program. They demonstrated that, in the short term, the inter-vention effectively increased eye contact and decreased irritating fiddling but with marked individual differences in other microlevel social skills. In a larger study, Spence and Marzillier (1981) reported on longer-term effects of social skills training with 32 adolescent male offenders who were compared with 20 adolescents in an attention placebo group and 24 in a no-treatment control group. The adolescents received twelve 1-hour treatment sessions spaced over 6 weeks. The single-subject design showed that the findings of the earlier study were replicated insofar as there were improvements in certain basic social skills. Indeed, these improvements remained at a 3-month follow-up point. The data obtained via staff in the living units, however, did not reflect these gains. Boys who received social skills training self-reported more criminal acts at a 6-month follow-up but had been convicted of fewer offenses during that period than boys in the other two groups.

Although it is tempting to conclude that social skills training had helped the boys to be more frank in their disclosures to researchers while being able to avoid detection, the situation is clearly more complex. Spence and Marzillier (1981) and Hollin and Henderson (1984) noted that gains made in the experi-mental situation either did not generalize to the natural environment or were not noticed by the adults making more global ratings. In any case, reconviction rates are notoriously difficult to interpret (Braukmann & Fixsen, 1975). Hol-lin and Henderson (1981, 1984) also failed to find differences in reconviction rates at 1-year follow-up when comparing seven (six reconvicted) adolescents who received social skills training and seven (four reconvicted) who had no treatment.

It is worth stressing that in these few studies, the therapy was given while the adolescents were institutionalized. Despite attempts to plan for the gener-alization of the newly trained skills, the effects of training are difficult to isolate from a background of other, massive changes in the boys' environment at the time.

OTHER EUROPEAN PROGRAMS

At the time of writing, we know of three projects in Europe that have attempted to set up replication of all or part of the Teaching-Family model. These were in Germany, the Netherlands, and Belgium and are discussed next. There are indications that behavioral programs with delinquents are being contemplated or implemented in parts of Italy, Norway, Portugal, Denmark, France, and Bavaria, but to date we know of no published descriptions or results.

Bonner and his colleagues were financed by the German government to develop an Achievement Place home in Marburg, West Germany (Bonner *et al.*, 1980). They consulted with colleagues in the United States and spent nearly 3 years in training staff and writing a German version of the Achievement Place manual (Bonner *et al.*, 1980). Considerable alteration had to be made to accommodate cultural differences. In particular, the German approach emphasized cognitive concepts and components more than operant ones. Unfortunately, just as the team was ready to work with the first youths, the program fell victim to the economic recession and was closed down.

Experiences in the Netherlands have been somewhat more positive. In the early 1970s, psychologists from the Paedologisch Institute in Amsterdam had success in using behavioral methods with 19 adolescent offenders. The youths were offered skills-training and problem-solving techniques on an out-patient basis using a broadly based social learning theory approach (Bartels, 1981; Slot & Bartels, 1983). Encouraged by their success and with the support of the Dutch Ministry of Justice, Bartels and Slot set up the first full-scale replication of Achievement Place in Europe in 1980. A second group home, or Kursushuis, as they are termed, has now opened, and a third will open shortly. Each Kursushuis works with six youths and is staffed by two teaching parents and one assistant, each of whom (officially) works 40 hours per week.

Bartels and Slot have had success in recreating the atmosphere and the Teaching-Family interactions in the Kursushuis. Both the present authors have visited Achievement Place homes in Kansas and now in the Netherlands, and the similarity is remarkable. The first Kursushuis is situated in a small town some 20 kilometers from Amsterdam. During their time at the Kursushuis, all boys attend school or work regularly. The programs seem somewhat more individualized than those initially present in the Kansas prototype, but otherwise the treatment package is similar. Strong emphasis is placed on using teaching interactions to teach skills of everyday living, on using a token economy to motivate the youths, and on using self-government, which has a long history in youth treatment in Holland.

As with the original model, the teaching parents were trained by psychologists who continue to act as consultants to the program while also evaluating it. Slot (1984) has presented preliminary data on the first 12 boys to enter and leave the program. Using a number of measures that had previously been validated by the researchers, these 12 were compared with boys who had been sent to a semiclosed institution for similar offenses. The data showed that boys entering the Kursushuis were similar to those sent to the state institution; hence the model was definitely dealing with youths who had serious delinquency records. The results on the six boys who had been discharged for at least 6 months showed that they spent less time (a mean of 12.5 months, with a standard deviation of 2.4 months) in the Kursushuis than the comparison boys did in the institution (a mean of 14.8 months, with a standard deviation of 9.9 months). Both the boys themselves and the social workers responsible for them were very positive about all aspects of the treatment program, even though the token economy is often seen as somewhat strict by Dutch standards of child care practice. Six months after discharge, five of the six boys still showed considerable improvements on a variety of behavioral measures. The one who did not show improvement on the scales was the only one to be given a custodial sentence during this period. No comparable data are available for the institutionalized boys. Slot (1984) emphasizes that these results are quite preliminary but encouraging. He and Bartels have shown that the Teaching-Family model can be adapted to a very different culture despite initial administration difficulties. We will return to these difficulties later.

Van Oost (1984) has described a residential facility in Belgium for 15 adolescent girls, aged 14 to 20 years. It is staffed by social workers and psychologists and has a predominantly social learning theory and family therapy orientation. Girls are referred to this center, called the Ferry, by juvenile courts or local protection committees. The main educational goal of the Ferry is one of social competence in such areas as self-management, adequate school behavior, and interpersonal and community skills. Many of the teaching components of the Achievement Place model are incorporated explicitly in the work at the Ferry—skills training, problem solving, group meeting—but the early stages of the points system was judged to be inappropriate for the client group. Contact between the girls and their families is encouraged.

During the first 4 years of the Ferry's operation, 40 girls were admitted. Their average age was 16 years, 6 months (range 14 years, 4 months, to 20 years, 6 months) and they stayed an average of 1 year, 2 months. Of the 28 who had left at the time of Van Oost's (1984) report, 20 returned to the community—6 to their family home, 9 to married or living-together situations, and 5 to living on their own. Eight were discharged to institutions—3 to psychiatric clinics, 4 to centers, and 1 to jail. Given the delinquent nature of the girl's behavior prior to admission, these preliminary results appear somewhat encouraging, but in the absence of both more detailed follow-up data on the quality of their adjustment and data on comparison groups, one must be cautious in interpreting the results.

INITIATIVES WORLDWIDE

Although we are aware of interest in applying the Achievement Place and other behavioral models to the treatment of delinquent behavior in a variety of other countries in South America and Europe, we have not located many published studies other than the following from New Zealand and Australia. We have, therefore, no way of knowing how representative these are, and so they are presented for information purposes only.

Sandford (1973) carried out a study in a small, open borstal (correctional school for adjudicated delinquents) for 50 boys in New Zealand. An observational analysis of the interaction between the boys and the officers revealed that officers spent 78% of their time not interacting with the boys. The introduction of contingent reinforcement to improve picking up clothes in the shower and changing areas was very successful when points could be exchanged for attending a film. The author noted that the introduction of this minimal program improved the emotional climate of the unit and resulted in more cooperative behavior between boys and officers.

The remaining three examples all came from the Nyandi Treatment and Research Centre for Adolescents in Perth, Western Australia. The Nyandi Centre is for delinquent adolescent girls aged 14 to 18 years. A basic, staff-directed, token economy operated in the facility. Seymour and Stokes (1976) reported a study with four girls in the maximum security unit who had not responded to the basic program. The girls were expected to participate daily in four training areas: classroom, office, workshop, and kitchen. It was decided to introduce a self-recording system using a multiple-baseline design. Self-recording by the girls, with tokens administered by the staff, was successful with three of the girls in increasing the nmber of training experiences and the amount of praise evoked from the staff.

Jodrell and Sanson-Fisher (1976) demonstrated with five girls in the same center that tangible rewards were more effective than social reinforcers in teaching them social skills, compliance, and social greetings. In a further study, Sanson-Fisher and Seymour (1976) worked with six girls and trained the staff to alter delinquency-oriented conversations. They were successful in increasing the number of prosocial comments when staff were present, but the gains did not generalize when staff were absent.

GENERAL DISCUSSION

Producing the preceding survey has been both exciting and depressing. It has been exciting insofar as we have identified a small number of instances in which a range of behavioral methods, including those of the Teaching-Family approach, have been applied with some success outside North America. It has been depressing in that, so far as compared with the volume of high-quality studies in the United States, so little published work originates elsewhere. In the main, with notable exceptions in the Netherlands and some in Britain, most studies have been descriptive and speculative rather than data-based. Why should this be so? To answer, we need to consider the social, legal, and cultural constraints on workers in other countries.

It must be remembered that each country develops its own legal framework for dealing with offenders. Most European countries have well-developed judicial, welfare, and educational systems that, in the main, are more likely to be organized centrally than is the case in the United States. It is very difficult to introduce change to such an existing system.

For example, in Britain, the responsibility for working with delinquent youths lies mainly with social service departments. With the increasing professionalization of both residential child care staff and of field social workers, there are very clear national agreements on employment and conditions of work. When residential staff can only work a 35- to 38-hour week, this constraint directly conflicts with the concept of their acting as teaching parents along the lines developed in Kansas. As noted before, considerable compromises have had to be made both in Holland and in Britain to allow that approach to develop. The Dutch solution has been to set up the homes in collaboration with voluntary charitable bodies but with considerable backing from the central government. The German experience illustrates how sole reliance on the central government means that changes in policy can have disastrous consequences.

Both at Orchard Lodge and at Nyandi, considerable progress has been made in introducing behavioral treatments not only within institutions but also within the maximum security units within the centers. Clearly, helping adolescents change their behavior with respect to the normal community is difficult when the youths are incarcerated in a maximum security unit, but in both the Orchard Lodge and Nyandi centers it has been demonstrated that the quality of the children's lives during incarceration can be improved by the use of behavioral methods. Moreover, behavioral methods have demonstrated the feasibility and value of undertaking single-case studies to examine aspects of the treatment programs operating in a wide variety of settings.

We have identified differences in the statutory provision of services as one barrier to innovation, but this is not a sufficient explanation for the restricted adoption of behavioral approaches, including the Teaching-Family approach, outside the United States. World economic recession is undoubtedly a contributing cause, but above all, it seems to us that there is a major need for more training opportunities at all levels—for administrators, psychologists, social workers, and care staff. Although it is possible to learn *about* behavioral approaches such as the Teaching-Family model from publications and short visits, until there are more facilities for intensive and continuing training, the spread of behavioral approaches internationally will continue to depend on the isolated initiatives of a few individuals. In Europe, we hope to collaborate under the umbrella of the Commissioners of the European Community and so, hopefully, a decade from now we can write more of data-based achievements than promises. Behavioral work like that begun in the United States has had a beneficial impact on international thinking about the treatment of delinquent adolescents, but thinking has still to be translated into effective action.

REFERENCES

Abbott, K. (1984). *The antecedents of compliance and noncompliance in the classroom.* Unpublished master's thesis, Institute of Psychiatry, University of London.

Argyle, M. (1969). *Social interaction.* London: Methuen.

Bartels, A. A. J. (1981). *Juvenile delinquency and social skills: Behavioral training, individual and large scale applications.* Unpublished manuscript, Paedologisch Institute, Department Ambulatorium, Amsterdam.

Bonner, D. H., Distel, A., Dorfler, C. H., Fruhauf, T., Jaroszek, S., Jager, R., Knabe, C., Muschik, A., Rehbein, K., & Schulz, H. J. (1980). *Lernwohngruppen-Programm handbuch.* Marburg/Lahn: Philipps-Universitat.

Braukmann, C. J., & Fixsen, D. L. (1975). Behavior modification with delinquents. In M. Hersen, R. M. Eisler, & P. M. Miller (Eds.), *Progress in behavior modification* (Vol. 1, pp. 191–231). New York: Academic Press.

Brown, B. J. (1977a). Experienze di Token Economy Nella Riabiliasione Della Delinquenza Minorile. *Programmazione Psicologica, 3–4,* 69–77.

Brown, B. J. (1977b). Gilbey House: A token economy management scheme in a residential school for boys in trouble. *British Association for Behavioural Psychotherapy Bulletin, 5,* 79–89.

Brown, B. J. (1979). A behavioural approach to adolescents in trouble. *Journal of Adolescence, 2,* 77–87.

Brown, B. J. (1984, September). *An application of social learning theory to a residential setting for young offenders.* Paper presented to the 14th Congress of the European Association for Behavior Therapy, Brussels.

Brown, B. J., & Christie, M. M. (1981). *Social learning practice in residential child care.* Oxford, England: Pergamon.

Brown, B. J., Beddow, J., Merker, A., Spence, S., Leheay, C., & Christie, M. (1978). *The Gilbey token economy management system for delinquent boys in residential care: A review of the first year.* Unpublished internal review document. Tennal School, Birmingham, England.

Carr, S. J. (1982). *Some aspects of the use of "teaching interactions" in a residential setting for young male offenders.* Unpublished master's thesis. Institute of Psychiatry, University of London.

Clarke, R. V. G., & Martin, D. N. (1971). *Absconding from approved schools.* London: Her Majesty's Stationery Office.

Cornish, D. B., & Clarke, R. V. G. (1975). *Residential treatment and its effects on delinquency* (Research Study No. 32). London: Home Office.

Cullen, J. E., & Seddon, J. W. (1980). *The application of a behavioural regime to disturbed young offenders* (DPS Report Series 1, No. 15). Feltham, Middlesex, England: Directorate of Psychological Services, Home Office.

Dunlop, A. B. (1974). *The approved school experience.* H. O. R. S. No. 25. London: Her Majesty's Stationery Office.

Fletcher, D. S. (1981). *The generation and maintenance of staff treatment effort in an institution for severely disturbed adolescents.* Unpublished manuscript, Glenthorne Youth Treatment Centre, Birmingham, England.

Hoghughi, M. S. (1979). The Aycliffe token economy. *British Journal of Criminology, 19,* 384–399.

Hollin, C. R., & Henderson, M. (1981). The effects of social skills training on incarcerated delinquent adolescents. *International Journal of Behavioural Social Work Abstracts, 1,* 145–185.

Hollin, C. R., & Henderson, M. (1984). Social skills training in the young offender: False expectations and the "failure of treatment." *Behavioural Psychotherapy, 12,* 331–334.

Jodrell, R. D., & Sanson-Fisher, R. W. (1976). Basic concepts of behaviour therapy: An experiment involving disturbed adolescent girls. *Australian Occupational Therapy Journal, 23,* 101–108.

Kirigin, K. A., Wolf, M. M., Braukmann, C. J., Fixsen, D. L., & Phillips, E. L. (1979). Achievement Place: A preliminary outcome evaluation. In J. S. Stumphauzer (Ed.), *Progress in behavior therapy with delinquents* (pp. 118–145). Springfield, IL: Charles C Thomas.

McCafferey, A. J. (1977). *The token economy in Franklin House.* Unpublished manuscript, Aycliffe School, Aycliffe, County Durham, England.

McGivern, M. A. (1980). *Intermediate Treatment—the development and assessment of an approach to community care.* Paper read at the 1980 World Congress on Behavior Therapy, Jerusalem.

Miller, A. D., Ohlin, L. E., & Coates, R. B. (1977). *A theory of social reform: Correctional change processes in two states.* Cambridge, MA: Ballinger.

Ostapuik, E. B. (1982). Strategies for community intervention in offender rehabilitation: An overview. In M. P. Feldman (Ed.), *Developments in the study of criminal behaviour* (Vol. 1, pp. 135–166). Chichester, England: Wiley.

Phillips, E. L. (1978). *Progress report: A 1977 evaluation of the Boys Town Youth Care Department programs* (Monograph Series). Omaha, NE: Boys Town Community-Based Programs.

Preston, M. A. (1982). Intermediate treatment: A new approach to community care. In M. P. Feldman (Ed.), *Developments in the study of criminal behaviour* (Vol. 1, pp. 167–190). Chichester, England: Wiley.

Reid, I. (1982). Development and maintenance of a behavioural regime in a secure treatment setting. In M. P. Feldman (Ed.), *Development in the study of criminal behaviour* (Vol. 1, pp. 79–106). Chichester, England: Wiley.

Sandford, D. A. (1973). An operant analysis of control procedures in a New Zealand borstal. *British Journal of Criminology, 13,* 262–268.

Sanson-Fisher, R. W., & Seymour, F. W. (1976). Training institutionalized staff to alter delinquent conversation. *Journal of Behaviour Therapy and Experimental Psychiatry, 7,* 243–247.

Seymour, F. W., & Stokes, T. F. (1976). Self-recording in training girls to increase work and evoke staff praise in an institution for offenders. *Journal of Applied Behavior Analysis, 9,* 41–54.

Sinclair, I. A. C., & Clarke, R. V. G. (1973). Acting out and its significance for the residential treatment of delinquents. *Journal of Child Psychology and Psychiatry, 14,* 283–291.

Slot, W. (1984, September). *Achievement Place in the Netherlands: First results.* Paper presented to the 14th Congress of the European Association for Behaviour Therapy, Brussels.

Slot, W., & Bartels, A. A. J. (1983). Outpatient social skills training for youth in trouble: Theoretical background, practice and outcome. In W. Everaerd, C. B. Hindley, A. Bot, & J. J. Van Der Werff (Eds.), *Development in adolescence,* (pp. 176–191). The Hague: Martinus Nighoff Publishers.

Spence, S. H. (1979). Social skills training with adolescent offenders: A review. *Behavioural Psychotherapy, 7,* 49–56.

Spence, S. H. (1981). Validation of social skills of adolescent males in an interview conversation with a previously unknown adult. *Journal of Applied Behavior Analysis, 14,* 159–168.

Spence, S. H., & Marzillier, J. S. (1979). Social skill training with adolescent male offenders: I. Short-term effects. *Behaviour Research and Therapy, 17,* 7–16.

Spence, S. H., & Marzillier, J. S. (1981). Social skills training with adolescent male offenders: II. Short-term, long-term, and generalization effects. *Behaviour Research and Therapy, 19,* 349–368.

Stallard, P. N. (1980). *An experiment to investigate the effects of three types of time out procedures on the frequency, place, and type of inappropriate behaviour displayed by a group of delinquent adolescents.* Unpublished master's thesis, University of Birmingham, England.

Taylor, L., Walton, P., & Young, J. (1973). *The new criminology: For a social theory of deviance.* London: Routledge & Kegan Paul.

Tobin, M. R. (1979). *The sequence and distribution of disruptive/inappropriate behaviour in a group of behaviourally disordered adolescents.* Unpublished master's thesis, University of Birmingham, Birminghan, England.

Tutt, N. (1974). *Care or custody.* London: Longman.

Tutt, N. (1982). An overview of intervention with young offenders: The political and legal contexts. In M. P. Feldman (Ed.), *Developments in the study of criminal behaviour* (Vol. 1, pp. 1–26). Chichester, England: Wiley.

Van Oost, P. (1984, September). *Modification of delinquent behaviour in female adolescents and their families: A residential approach.* Paper presented to the 14th Congress of the European Association for Behaviour Therapy, Brussels.

15

Behavioral Approaches with Juvenile Offenders

A Meta-Analysis of Long-Term Treatment Efficacy

RAND GOTTSHALK, WILLIAM S. DAVIDSON II,
JEFFREY MAYER, AND LEAH K. GENSHEIMER

> Time marched on and eventually modern humans—homo sa-
> piens sapiens—emerged, creatures who, to an extraterrestrial
> observer, must seem to be more than a little perverse. Unlike
> no other animal, we wage war on each other. We knowingly
> exploit limited resources in our environment and seem to
> expect that our profligacy can go on forever. And we choose to
> ignore deep chasms of injustice, consciously inflicted both
> between nations and within nations. In a sense it is humans
> who rule the world: our extraordinary creative intelligence
> gives the potential to do more or less anything we want. But,
> an extraterrestrial observer may wonder, isn't the ruler just a
> little bit crazy?
>
> —Leakey & Lewin, 1977, p. 10

Recent times have seen intense concern expressed over the prevalence of crime. In annual surveys conducted from 1972 through 1982, U.S. citizens were asked, "Is there more crime in this area than there was a year ago, or less?" Each year save one, the most common response was "more crime," indicating the belief that crime has been an ever-increasing phenomenon in this society (Gallup, 1982). A 1980 survey indicated that at least 70% of the respondents reported taking at least one set of precautionary measures when going out of their residence (Research and Forecasts, Inc., 1980). Consistently, crime and lawlessness have been mentioned in surveys as one of the three most important social issues of our times (Roper Organization, 1982).

Officially reported index crimes increased more than 30% over the last decade. During this interval, all arrests increased 31%, whereas arrests for violent crimes increased 37% (FBI, 1981). A similar picture emerges from

Rand Gottshalk, William S. Davidson II, and Jeffrey Mayer • Department of Psychology, Michigan State University, East Lansing, Michigan 48824.   Leah K. Gensheimer • Department of Psychology, Arizona State University, Tempe, Arizona 85281.

victimization surveys. From 1973 to 1979, victimization surveys indicated that crimes of violence (exemplified by rape and assault) increased significantly. Further, these surveys indicated that household larceny increased a full 25% (National Institute of Justice, 1982).

Although survey results and official records suffer from methodological difficulties that make direct interpretation a tricky undertaking (Kushler & Davidson, 1981), a strong case can be made that crime remains at the forefront of the American scene both in public perception and actual fact. This chapter focuses on the portion of this problem that involves juvenile offenders. This subpopulation of offenders was selected for four reasons. First, in order to conduct a scientific review of the literature relevant to behavioral approaches to violence and aggression, an identifiable group had to be selected. Because the field of aggression and antisocial behavior is replete with definitional issues, it was felt best to select a specifiable subpopulation to investigate. Juvenile delinquents represent a distinguishable subgroup that can be identified reliably in the research literature. Second, crimes committed by juveniles represent a substantial and identifiable proportion of the violence and antisocial behavior reported in America. Over one fifth of all arrests, 19% of arrests for violent crimes, and 36% of arrests for index crimes are attributable to juveniles (FBI, 1980). Third, juveniles represent a group that has received considerable attention from behavior analysts. Identifiable programs of intervention are available, and a substantial research literature exists assessing the current efficacy of the procedures. Finally, youthful antisocial behavior has been related to antisocial behavior in adulthood (e.g., Faretra, 1981; Robins, 1966) but is more amenable to intervention. Hence, the possibility for prevention of violence and antisocial behavior would appear to be maximized by focusing on youth.

This chapter provides a meta-analysis of the research literature on behavioral interventions with juvenile offenders as representative of the efficacy of behavioral interventions with violent and aggressive behavior. Prior to proceeding with the actual meta-analysis, behavioral approaches to the problems of youthful violent and antisocial behavior are placed in their historical and theoretical contexts. Next, the specifics of the meta-analytic methodology are described; these methods draw heavily on the work of Hunter, Schmidt, and Jackson (1982) and Glass, McGaw, and Smith (1981). Following this, a description of the results of the meta-analysis is presented. Finally, implications are drawn for behavioral interventions in the area of violence and antisocial behavior.

HISTORICAL CONTEXT

The advent of official "juvenile delinquency" dates to the end of the 1800s. Prior to the initiation of the juvenile court in the state of Illinois in 1899, delinquent youth were handled either by the adult criminal justice system or through more informal means in houses of refuge (Krisberg & Austin, 1978). A separate system for handling juvenile offenders was established for the dual purposes of protecting youths from the inhumane treatment conditions prevalent in adult correctional institutions and protecting society from the ineffective interventions provided by refuge homes. The juvenile justice system was to act as a concerned parent and serve a corrective function (Mennel, 1972; Schultz, 1973).

Having been created with all the fervor of a progressive social movement at the turn of the century, the handling of juvenile offenders proceeded with little controversy or attention until the middle 1960s. As part of the general dissatisfaction expressed with social institutions during that decade, traditional interventions with juveniles came under attack on three fronts: research reports and reviews, Supreme Court decisions, and criticisms of intervention assumptions (Blakely & Davidson, 1982).

First, a series of systematic investigations and reviews appeared that criticized the effectiveness of treatment approaches to juvenile delinquents (Grey & Dermody, 1982; Levitt, 1971). The book *Children in Trouble* by Pulitzer-prize-winning author Howard James appeared in 1969, maligning the inhumane conditions in institutions for the detention and treatment of juvenile offenders.

Second, the juvenile justice system was criticized for failing to follow through on its "deal" with juvenile offenders under the *parens patriae* doctrine. Given both the inhumane conditions and ineffective treatments that juveniles were subjected to, the U.S. Supreme Court held in the case of Gault (*In re* Gault, 1967) that procedural informality was no longer justified. In its majority opinion, the Supreme Court stated that regardless of the good intentions of procedural informality and parentlike treatment, the juvenile was getting the worst of both worlds. Given the inhumane and ineffective conditions present in many juvenile treatment facilities, procedural informality could not be justified.

Finally, treatment techniques were based on the assumption that the causes of juvenile delinquency were best understood by studying the individual characteristics of convicted offenders. Given the assumption that delinquency was operationally defined as an official crime, research indicated that juvenile delinquency was a phenomenon prevalent primarily among deviant lower-class youth. Several self-report studies of youth involvement in illegal behaviors, however, indicated that such behaviors were widespread. These findings raised the possibility that unlawful acts were unrelated to social standing (Erickson, 1973; Williams & Gold, 1972). Thus it was argued that the study of apprehended or institutionalized youth yielded more information about the decision-making processes of juvenile justice system officials than it did about the causes of antisocial behavior.

As can be seen from this discussion, theory and intervention in the area of juvenile delinquency have often been in a state of turmoil. In order to understand adequately the context into which behavioral interventions were initially applied, the theoretical context must be further elaborated. For purposes of organization, the next section has been divided in to brief discussions of micro- and macrolevel variables.

THEORETICAL CONTEXT

Microlevel Variables

A major influence on traditional interventions with delinquents has been a focus on individual differences. Individuals who possessed certain physiological or psychological characteristics were thought to be more likely to display antisocial behavior. Within the area of juvenile delinquency, this group-differences paradigm was used by the Glueck and Glueck (1951). Their classic study compared 500 institutionalized delinquent subjects with 500 noninstitutionalized "normal" youth. Comparisons were made on over 400 individual characteristics including a variety of personal, physical, and social variables that produced a large number of statistically significant differences. Other group comparison studies consistently reported differences between delinquents and nondelinquents (Andrew, 1981; Waldo & Dinitz, 1967). Similar comparisons have been made in terms of socialization (Smith & Ausnew, 1974), moral development (Prentice, 1972), family communication patterns (Alexander & Parsons, 1973), learning disabilities (Broder, Dunivant, Smith, & Sutton, 1981), social skills (Gaffney & McFall, 1981), interpersonal contingencies (Stuart, 1971), intelligence (Mednick & Christiansen, 1977), and problem-solving skills (Spivack & Shure, 1982). In each instance, juvenile delinquents were shown to be less well off than their nondelinquent counterparts.

Macrolevel Variables

Other prominent theories used to explain delinquency and guide intervention efforts have focused on macroenvironmental variables. The general position has been that the source of delinquent behavior is found in the social structural environment. Cultures, social structures, social opportunities, and social institutions have all been cited as causally related to delinquency.

For instance, the observation that some societies are remarkably lacking in evidence of aggression led to propositions that cultural factors are the source of antisocial behavior. For example, Viniaminov reported no cases of murder in the over 20 years he spent living among the Aleutian people (Pelto & Pelto, 1976). In other cases, the social conflict inherent in complex materialistic societies is thought to foster crime (Cloward & Ohlin, 1960; Merton, 1957). Complex capitalistic societies have provided equal access to the materialistic goals of society but have allowed differential access to opportunities of goal attainment based on social position. One specific social institution often linked to macrovariable explanations of delinquency is the school. Underachievement, misconduct, and dropping out have been thought to result from factors prevalent in the school–student interaction rather than from individual differences in delinquent and nondelinquent youth. The student experiences frustration and isolation in an environment that stresses competition and success. This unfortunate situation has been alleged to produce delinquency (Elliott, Ageton, & Canter, 1979; Elliott & Voss, 1974; Polk & Schafer, 1972).

A third position suggests that delinquency can only be understood in the context of both the behavior of individuals and the societal response to that behavior. Often termed *social labeling theory*, such interactionist positions have argued that society defines deviance. In essence, this position has stated that environmental labeling in response to a perceived deviant act makes "deviants" deviant (Becker, 1963). Deviance, and hence delinquency, is created by certain people's reaction to an act (Glaser, 1975; Matza, 1969).

THE ADVENT OF BEHAVIORAL APPROACHES TO JUVENILE DELINQUENCY

The use of behavioral approaches with juvenile delinquency was related to the theoretical and historical context just described. The general dissatisfaction with the power of individual-differences explanations of delinquency and the apparent ineffectiveness of the resulting traditional modes of treatment and punishment opened the door for new alternatives to be considered. Further, the more environmentally oriented propositions of differential opportunity, differential association, and social conflict theories, as well as social labeling theory, were somewhat consistent with behavioral explanations. Nothing was inherently deviant in a given act; hence deviant actions might be thought of as behaviors alterable through learning principles.

Early writings in the field tended to emphasize the compatibility of the general principles and strategies of behavior modification with the needs of the legal system. Behavioral approaches required specification of behavior changes in clear language. This enhanced the appeal of behavioral procedures for the legal system. The emphasis on specifiable behavioral acts, overt as opposed to unobservable events, and on the importance of behavioral consequences involved terms and concepts familiar to the juvenile justice system (Steketee, 1973). Although not always meaning the same thing, behaviorists and judges shared a language in ways that other treatment modalities did not. The behavioral procedures for juvenile delinquents emphasized the importance of parents, on-line staff, caseworkers, teachers, and other "nonprofessionals" in the natural environment. The field of treatment for juvenile offenders had always been faced with the unavailability of expensive professionals. In fact, working with juvenile offenders was often considered to be the bottom of the status hierarchy of human service professionals (Saul & Davidson, 1982). The suggestion that many years of graduate- or doctoral-level education were unnecessary before interventions could be attempted allowed behaviorists somewhat easy access to juvenile delinquents (Tharp & Wetzel, 1969).

A core tenet of the behavioral approach was that in order for change to be successful and durable, the intervention had to include procedures to increase desired or socially appropriate behaviors. In contrast, most traditional interventions had focused only on removing undesirable performances. Cohen's influential work at the National Training School for Boys (Cohen, 1968) outlined a series of principles that illustrate this basic premise of the approach:

> Learning, putting in new successful behaviors, not unlearning, is the program for successful rehabilitation. The unlearning part is done by the individual differentiating his own behaviors by the newly learned set of values which are imprintable and discoverable through the educational process. (p. 1)

Finally, behaviorists became involved in interventions with juvenile delinquents by default. Positions in juvenile justice were not popular with human service professionals. Psychologists, in particular, had not been very active in interventions with juvenile delinquents, due in part to the extent to which traditional theoretical formulations saw adolescent antisocial behavior as relatively intractable. Further, available empirical evidence suggested that juvenile delinquents did not appear to be positively affected by traditional psychotherapy (e.g., Grey & Dermody, 1972; Levitt, 1971). Hence, when the general behavioral movement was gaining momentum in the mid-1960s, behaviorists were willing to provide an alternative to traditional intervention approaches.

STATUS OF BEHAVIORAL APPROACHES: THE NEED FOR A META-ANALYSIS

During the last half of the 1960s and the early part of the 1970s, behavioral approaches were used with delinquent youth in institutional settings (e.g., Cohen, 1968), community residential settings (e.g., Phillips, 1968), and within the youth's natural family (e.g., Stuart, 1971). By the mid-1970s, reviews of the efficacy of behavioral approaches with juvenile delinquents began to appear. Two edited volumes devoted entirely to behavioral approaches to juvenile delinquents were published (Stumphauzer, 1971, 1978). Both presented examples of strikingly positive results. Scientific reviews of the research literature were also generally positive but consistently pointed out the need for increased methodological adequacy (Davidson & Seidman, 1974; Emery & Marholin, 1977). Most of these early reviews, and the research they covered, focused on the extent to which behavioral principles had been adequately demonstrated with juvenile delinquents. For example, these reviews examined the extent to which principles of reinforcement, situational specificity of behavior, and generalization training had been demonstrated with juvenile delinquent populations. The time has now come to take these issues one step further and ask to what extent the research to date has provided evidence of the efficacy of behavioral procedures in producing desired long-term outcomes. The move to examine long-term outcomes involves a move from what others have labeled *process* questions to *outcome* questions (Davidson, Redner, & Saul, 1983; Paul, 1969).

This chapter addresses this question using the methods of meta-analysis proposed by Hunter *et al.* (1982) and Glass *et al.* (1981). The methods of meta-analysis were developed in response to the perceived need to bring specificity, standardization, and replicability to the process of literature reviews. In the past, reviewers have summarized a body of research literature by either over-all impression or vote counting. Reviews were often concluded by statements such as "of the blank studies reviewed, blank percent demonstrated the hypothesized relationship." In the raging debates that often followed such reviews, particularly in such areas as the efficacy of psychotherapy, disagreements have often arisen over the method of the review. More specifically, arguments have arisen over the replicability of the inclusion/exclusion criteria for various studies (Smith, Glass, & Miller, 1980).

A further issue applicable to research reviews addressed by the method of meta-analysis focuses on the conversion of results from different studies into a common metric. Previous reviews have suffered from the lack of replicability of procedures due to differences in outcome variables, research designs, and statistical standards. This can result in different conclusions from separate reviews of the same literature. Further, once outcome variables have been converted to a standard metric, an examination of the relationship, if any, between outcomes and other study characteristics becomes possible. This allows the reviewer to address a series of interesting questions about the efficacy of behavioral approaches to juvenile delinquents in general, about the size of the observed effects across studies, and about any particular characteristics of the interventions that appear to lead to more positive or more negative outcomes.

A basic assumption of this chapter is that the most important question that now needs to be addressed is the general efficacy of behavioral approaches to juvenile delinquents compared to no-treatment or treatment/usual controls. To the extent that other specific interventions are included in treatment/usual groups, this review will address the efficacy of behavioral approaches relative to other treatments. The specific method of meta-analysis employed rests on the assumption that the aggregation of results across studies can provide stronger conclusions than are possible with any individual study. By compensating for methodological flaws inherent in any particular study, aggregation of results across studies should allow identification of consistent effects. If a number of studies, all with different methodological flaws come to the same conclusion, then the confidence that can be placed in that conclusion is increased. Because this review examines the methodological characteristics of the published research, we can see the extent to which the literature taken as a whole addresses particular methodological issues.

Highlights of the Review

Domains Covered

This review and meta-analysis cover the published literature on behavioral interventions with delinquent youth from 1967 through 1983. Several other definitional issues further specify the basis of the meta-analysis. First, only outcome studies were included. To be included, a study had to assess dependent variables that showed generalization from the intervention across time, behavior, or setting. Research that only reported results on behaviors within the treatment setting were excluded as being process studies. The decision rule used in selecting studies was that some follow-up assessment outside the treatment had to be performed in order for the study to be included. Only studies that investigated officially delinquent youth were included. This criterion demanded that the subjects be youth who were referred by juvenile/family court officials or the police for official delinquency. Studies involving "troubled youth, maladjusted youth, antisocial youth, underachieving children, and adjustment reactions of adolescents" were excluded. Including such work would have broadened the review to include a population that was overly heterogeneous. This decision rule was particularly critical because delinquency is viewed as a sample of violent and antisocial behavior within the context of this review. Further, only studies that specifically described the use of behavioral procedures were included, for instance, those studies reporting the systematic application of behavioral procedures such as contingency management, positive reinforcement, token economies, behavioral contracts, or modeling.

This meta-analysis was based on studies collected from a computer-based search of the *Psychological Abstracts*. The literature search was based on the following key words: *juvenile delinquents, treatment, intervention,* and *outcome studies*. This computer search produced abstracts for 643 studies. These abstracts were then read by the authors and nonoutcome studies of interventions with juveniles excluded. Of the 643 studies, 163 appeared to be outcome studies with juvenile delinquents. The 163 studies were then read for potential coding and inclusion in the review. Of the 163 studies, 91 were actually codable for the meta-analysis. This set of 91 studies included all types of interventions, 25 of which were of behavioral. These 25 studies are listed in Table 1. The procedures specified for calculating effect size (Glass *et al.*, 1981; Hunter *et al.*, 1982) require that all designs be reduced to comparisons between two groups or two time periods. Hence, more complex designs, such as contingency management versus modeling versus a control, had to be coded multiple times (e.g., the contingency management group versus the control, and then the modeling group versus the control). For the present meta-analysis, this occurred three times, resulting in 30 distinct "studies" being coded.

Coding Methods for the Meta-Analysis

The 30 studies were divided among the four authors and coded according to procedures described later. Coding was done onto separate sheets prior to

Table 1. Studies Used in the Meta-Analysis

Alexander, R. N., Corbett, T. F., & Smigel, J. (1976). The effects of individual and group consequences on school attendance and curfew violations with predelinquent adolescents. *Journal of Applied Behavior Analysis, 9,* 221–226.

Alexander, J. F., & Parsons, B. V. (1973). Short term behavioral intervention with delinquent families. *Journal of Abnormal Psychology, 81,* 219–225.

Davidson, W. S., & Robinson, M. R. (1975). Community psychology and behavior modification. *Corrective and Social Psychiatry, 21,* 1–12.

Davidson, W. S., & Wolfred, T. R. (1977). Evaluation of a community-based behavior modification program for prevention of delinquency: The failure of success. *Community Mental Health Journal, 13,* 296–306.

Eitzen, D. S. (1976). The self-concept of delinquents in a behavior modification treatment program. *Journal of Social Psychology, 90,* 203–206.

Emshoff, J. G., Redd, W. H., & Davidson, W. S. (1976). Generalization training and the transfer of prosocial behavior in delinquent adolescents. *Behavior Therapy and Experimental Psychiatry, 7,* 141–144.

Hendrix, C. E., & Heckel, R. V. (1982). The effects of a behavioral approach on modifying social behavior in incarcerated male delinquents. *Journal of Clinical Psychology, 36,* 77–79.

Hobbs, T. R., & Holt, M. M. (1976). The effects of token reinforcement on the behavior of delinquents in cottage settings. *Journal of Applied Behavior Analysis, 9,* 189–198.

Holt, M. M., & Hobbs, T. R. (1979). The effects of token reinforcement, feedback, and response cost on standardized test performance. *Behavior Research and Therapy, 17,* 81–83.

Jesness, C. (1975). Comparative effectiveness of behavior modification and transactional analysis programs for delinquents. *Journal of Consulting and Clinical Psychology, 43,* 758–779.

Kirigin, K. A., Braukmann, C. J., Atwater, J. D., & Wolf, M. M. (1982). An evaluation of teaching-family group homes for juvenile offenders. *Journal of Applied Behavior Analysis, 15,* 1–16.

Klein, N., Alexander, J., & Parsons, B. (1977). Impact of family systems intervention on recidivism and sibling delinquency: A model of primary prevention and program evaluation. *Journal of Consulting and Clinical Psychology, 45,* 469–474.

O'Donnell, C. R., & DeLeon, J. L. (1973). A contingency program for academic achievement in a correctional setting: Gains and time in school. *Journal of Community Psychology, 1,* 285–287.

Ollendick, T. H., & Hersen, M. (1979). Social skills training for juvenile delinquents. *Behavior Research and Therapy, 17,* 547–554.

Parsons, B. V., & Alexander, J. F. (1973). Short-term family intervention. *Journal of Consulting and Clinical Psychology, 41,* 195–201.

Reid, J. B., & Patterson, G. R. (1976). The modification of aggression and stealing behavior of boys in the home setting. In E. Ribes-Inesta & A. Bandura (Eds.), *Analysis of delinquency and aggression.* Hillsdale, NJ: Erlbaum.

Ross, R. R., & McKay, H. B. (1976). A study of institutional treatment programs. *International Journal of Offender Therapy and Comparative Criminology, 20,* 165–173.

Sarason, I. G. (1976). A modeling and informational approach to delinquency. In E. Ribes-Inesta & A. Bandura (Eds.), *Analysis of delinquency and aggression.* Hillsdale, NJ: Erlbaum.

Sarason, I., & Ganzer, V. (1973). Modeling and group discussion in the rehabilitation of juvenile delinquents. *Journal of Counseling Psychology, 20,* 442–449.

Sloane, H. N., & Ralph, J. L. (1973). A behavior modification program in Nevada. *International Journal of Offender Therapy and Comparative Criminology, 17,* 290–296.

Spence, S. H., & Marzillier, J. S. (1979). Social skills training with adolescent male offenders II. Short term, long term and generalized effects. *Behavior Research and Therapy, 19,* 348–368.

Stuart, R. B. (1971). Behavioral contracting within the families of delinquents. *Journal of Behavior Therapy and Experimental Psychiatry, 2,* 1–11.

Weathers, L., & Liberman, R. P. (1975). Contingency contracting with families of delinquent adolescents. *Behavior Therapy, 6,* 356–366.

(continued)

Table 1. *(Continued)*

Weinrott, M. R., Jones, R. R., & Howard, J. R. (1982). Cost effectiveness of teaching family programs for delinquents. *Evaluation Review, 6,* 173–201.
Werner, J. S., Minkin, N., Minkin, B. L., Fixsen, D. L., Phillips, E. L., & Wolf, M. M. (1975). Intervention package: An analysis to prepare juvenile delinquents for encounters with police officers. *Criminal Justice and Behavior, 2,* 55–85.

computer entry. The methods specified by Glass *et al.* (1981) and Hunter *et al.* (1982) were followed. Overall, the goal of coding was to capture important characteristics of the study and to reduce study findings to a standard metric for outcome results. The procedures followed involved independent coding of the methodological characteristics of each study, a rating of the effect demonstrated in the study, and a calculation of the effect size according to the formula presented by Hunter *et al.* (1982). One tenth of the studies were rated independently by two raters to examine interrater reliability. The overall percentage agreement for study characteristics, rated effects, and calculated effects size was 86%.

Study Characteristics

Table 2 presents a summary of the study characteristics that were coded. These variables represented a coding of the characteristics of the subjects, the location of the intervention in the juvenile justice system, the components of the intervention, the characteristics of the investigator, and the characteristics of the methodology. Coding of such variables allowed a description of the literature on which assessment of outcome effect size was based. It also allowed an examination of the relationship of some study characteristics and effect size.

Effect-Size Calculations

At the heart of the meta-analytic method is the calculation of effect size. This meta-analysis involved five potential effect-size indexes for each of several different types of outcome variables. First, an overall effectiveness rating was assigned to each study. Second, a general rating was assigned to each study on the basis of the overall conclusion drawn by the author of each article or chapter. Third, a specific rating of effectiveness was assigned to each dependent variable within each study. This third rating was done on the basis of the conclusion drawn in the research article or chapter concerning effects on the specific dependent variable in question. These first three indexes of effectiveness were done on a 3-point scale of positive effect, no effect, and negative effect. These three methods represent different versions of what others have called the ballot box or voting methods of literature review. They represent the types of summary ratings that previous reviews of the efficacy of behavioral procedures have employed. Fourth, standardized effect scores were calculated

Table 2.   Study Characteristics

Subject dimensions

1. Adjudicated (yes/no)
2. Percentage male
3. Average age

Relationship to juvenile justice system

1. Intervention inside system (yes/no)
2. Intervention included diversion (yes/no)

Intervention components

1. Setting: whether the intervention took place in an institution, community residential program, or community/nonresidential setting
2. Duration: the average length of the intervention in weeks
3. Intensity: the average number of hours of intervention

Characteristics of investigator

1. Discipline of authors
2. Intervener had influence over treatment process: coded none, to some extent, to a great extent
3. Investigator had influence over treatment process: coded none, to some extent, to a great extent

Methodological characteristics

1. Implementation measurement—assessment of intervention integrity
2. Evidence of unplanned variability in intervention: evidence of lack of compliance or other problems in treatment integrity
3. Multiple-baseline used (yes/no)
4. Reversal conditions used (yes/no)
5. Data collectors blind to experimental conditions/hypotheses (yes/no)
6. Description of control group: no-treatment, treatment as usual, subjects as own control (pre/post designs), or no-control group
7. Assignment of subjects to treatment: random, matching, or non-random
8. Assignment of interveners to participants: random, matching, or nonrandom

for reported pre- to postchanges for each dependent variable within each study. Pre-post effect sizes were calculated by subtracting the postmean from the premean and dividing by the pre-standard deviation. Glass *et al.* (1981) argue that the pre-effect or control group standard deviation is the least biased estimate of the true standard deviation because it has not been affected by the intervention. Fifth, experimental versus control group effect sizes were calculated for each dependent variable within each study. The experimental/control effect sizes were calculated by subtracting the experimental group postmean from the control group postmean and dividing by the control group standard deviation. Both of the pre-versus-post and experimental-versus-control effect sizes produced an index in standard deviation units.

Table 3 summarizes the variables that were coded for each dependent variable within each study. For each type of dependent variable, multiple

Table 3.   Calculation of Effect Size

For each of the following types of dependent variables, ratings were made for each study when sufficient data were present

1. Recidivism: arrests, court charges, or other indicants of official involvement in the juvenile justice system for illegal behavior. Up to three recidivism outcomes were coded per study

2. Self-report delinquency: self-reports of illegal acts

3. Program behavior: assessments of within-program behavior such as subsequent diagnoses, rates of release, violations of probation, rates of rule compliance, etc. Up to two program behavior outcomes were coded per study

4. Vocational behavior: assessment of job or employment-related performance

5. Academic behavior: assessments of academic performance such as achievement tests, grades, etc. Up to two academic behavior outcomes were coded per study

6. Other social behavior: assessments of other interpersonal performances (e.g., conversations in a group setting). Up to two social behavior outcomes were coded per study

7. School/work attendance: assessments of attendance in school or a job. Up to two attendance outcomes were coded per study

8. Self-concept: assessments of self-esteem and self-concept

9. Other attitudinal: assessments of other attitudes

10. Other cognitive: assessments of other cognitive variables

11. Ratings of global adjustment: ratings or reports of nonspecific adjustment not covered under preceding variables categories

Variables coded for each dependent variable

1. Method of data collection: behavioral observation, archival, self-report, paper-and-pencil, interview, rating by others

2. Reliability assessment: type of reliability reported, if any

3. Reliability of assessment

4. Research design for specific dependent variable

5. Length of follow-up period in weeks

6. Number of subjects for pre/post comparison

7. Significance level of pre/post comparison

8. Effect size for pre/post comparison

9. Effectiveness rating of pre/post change for specific dependent variable

10. Number of experimental subjects for experimental/control comparison

11. Number of control subjects for experimental/control comparison

12. Significance level for experimental/control comparison

13. Effect size for pre/post comparison

14. Effectiveness rating of pre/post change for specific dependent variable

measures were present in some studies. For example, recidivism could be measured by police arrests, complaints to the juvenile court, and institutionalization. Where data were presented for multiple variables within type, each one was coded separately. The types of dependent variables coded and the maximum number of variables per type coded for any single study were recidivism (maximum of three per study), self-report delinquency (maximum of one per study), program behaviors (maximum of two per study), vocational behavior (maximum of one per study), academic performance (maximum of two per study), social behavior (maximum of two per study), school or work attendance (maximum of two per study), attitudinal variables (maximum of two per study), self-esteem (maximum of one per study), global ratings of adjustment (maximum of one per study), and other cognitive/attitudinal variables (maximum of one per study). Two other coding rules were important. Studies that reported no statistical information (e.g., case studies) were included in the "ballot box" ratings. Some of the single-subject or multiple-baseline designs reported no statistics that allowed for calculation of effect sizes. In cases where graphs of specific behavioral outcomes were included, effect sizes were calculated for pre-post differences by treating baseline and reversal intervals as predata and treatment and follow-up intervals as postdata. This procedure called for the coder to extrapolate from the graph the actual rate of a given performance at each observation interval. It was necessary to collapse post- and follow-up data due to the small number of studies that included both, precluding treating them as separate variables. The number of observations was used as being analogous to the number of subjects in effect-size calculations.

RESULTS OF THE META-ANALYSIS

Descriptive Findings

Table 4 describes the characteristics of the studies and interventions included in the meta-analysis. The table has been divided into sections describing investigators, subjects, relationship to the juvenile justice system, components of the intervention, and characteristics of the methodology.

Study Characteristics. Although the search of the literature went back to 1967, the first outcome study did not appear until 1971. The largest number of studies published in any one year was eight in 1976. The fact that no studies published in 1983 were included in the review is reflective of time lag in the *Psychological Abstracts* system.

Investigator Characteristics. Eighteen (60%) of the articles were written by psychologists with the remainder being spread equally across the other social scientists. No other discipline was represented by more than two articles. As can be seen from Table 4, the service deliverers had some or much influence over the setting in which the intervention took place in all of the studies, indicating that the behavioral literature is characterized by interven-

Table 4. Description of Studies

Study characteristics

Publication date

1971—1		1977—2	
1972—0		1978—0	
1973—6		1979—4	
1974—0		1980—0	
1975—4		1981—2	
1976—8		1982—3	

Investigator characteristics

1. Percentage of authors who are psychologists	60%
2. Service deliverer influence	
Great extent of influence	63%
Some influence	37%
No influence	0%
3. Experimenter influence	
Great extent of influence	56%
Some influence	33%
No influence	11%

Subject dimensions

1. Average percentage male	78%
2. Average age	15.7
3. Studies with adjudicated youth	83%

Relationship to juvenile justice system

1. Intervention within the system	79%
2. Intervention included diversion	4%

Intervention components

1. Setting	
Institutional	43%
Community residential	33%
Community nonresidential	24%
2. Average duration	
Mean number of weeks	18.1
Median number of weeks	8.0
3. Average intensity	
Mean number of hours	51.2
Median number of hours	16.0
4. Use of token economy	57%
5. Use of behavioral contracting	50%
6. Use of positive reinforcement	80%
7. Use of modeling/role playing	50%

Methodological characteristics

1. Studies measuring implementation	37%
2. Evidence of unplanned treatment variation	17%
3. Studies including reversal	10%
4. Studies including multiple baseline	30%
5. Studies including "blind" data collection	27%
6. Control-group type	
No treatment	27%
Treatment/usual	40%
Other	33%
7. Studies including random assignment to treatment	40%
8. Studies including random assignment to intervener	3%

tions using change agents who were central to the setting rather than bringing in outside consultants to carry out the intervention. Further, in 89% of the studies, the researcher was judged to have played a role in designing and implementing the intervention under investigation. This also represented a substantial rate of investigators having influence over treatment. This finding can be viewed from two vantage points. On the one hand, many program evaluation experts have argued for the importance of independence between the program staff and evaluators (e.g., Rossi, Freeman, & Wright, 1982). On the other hand, arguments have been made that investigators can have confidence in the integrity and fidelity of the treatment only through intensive involvement in the interventions (Fairweather & Tornatzky, 1977). Therefore, it is noteworthy that virtually all of the studies reviewed involved some input by investigators into treatment.

Subject Dimensions. It is also important to note the type of youth involved in these studies. Several variables indicated that this literature reflects interventions undertaken with adjudicated delinquents in residential placement. For example, 83% are with formally adjudicated delinquent youths, 79% took place within settings run by the juvenile justice system, and 76% were in residential settings. On average, these 30 studies involved a subject population consisting of 78% males. This figure is compatible with national proportions of males in officially delinquent populations. The subjects were on average roughly 15½ years of age. Only one study involved diversion from the system.

Intervention Components. The data on the intensity of the interventions were somewhat skewed. The mean duration of interventions was about 18 weeks. This number, however, is an overestimate of the typical intervention due to a positively skewed distribution. A somewhat better estimate of the length of interventions represented among these 30 studies is the median length of intervention of 8 weeks. Similarly, the mean number of hours of intervention was just over 51 hours. When the median is examined, a more typical intervention involved 16 hours of treatment. Eighty percent of the studies used positive reinforcement procedures in one form or another. Roughly 50% of the studies used token economies, behavioral contracting, and/or modeling/role playing. It should be noted that any given study could have used any or all of these interventions.

Overall, then, the behavioral interventions that are the topic of this meta-analysis can be described as involving an adjudicated male delinquent population in residential placement. The investigators tended to have at least some control over the interventions. The interventions were relatively short term and involved 16 hours of treatment on average. This intervention profile matches that discussed by previous reviews of this literature over the last decade (e.g., Davidson & Seidman, 1974; Emery & Marholin, 1977; Nietzel, Winett, McDonald, & Davidson, 1977).

Methodological Characteristics. Although nearly 40% of the studies reported monitoring the implementation of the intervention, only 17% of them reported any evidence of unplanned variation in the treatment. This is particularly troublesome with a population of adolescent delinquents. How differential dropout and lack of participation in the treatment, for example, are handled is essentially unknown. Such issues as the strength and integrity of the intervention make interpretation of outcomes extremely difficult.

This literature also has major problems with respect to research methodology. Only a minority of studies included adequate reversals, multiple baselines, or randomly assigned control groups. The proportions of studies including these methodological safeguards were nearly identical to those reported by Davidson and Seidman (1974) a decade ago. Almost 30% of the studies, however, did include data collectors blind to experimental conditions; this was a dramatic improvement over such rates noted in previous reviews. Because this set of studies was preselected to be those focusing on outcome issues, a particularly unfortunate observation was that only 40% involved experimental and control group comparisons with random assignment to treatment groups, a procedure critical for examination of efficacy (Campbell & Stanley, 1966; Davidson *et al.*, 1983; Gold, 1974; Paul, 1969). Finally, the role of change-agent characteristics continued to be totally overlooked by this literature. The relationship of change-agent characteristics to treatment efficacy was not examined, and only one study attempted to control for potential confounds of change-agent characteristics through random assignment.

Effectiveness Results

Table 5 shows the "ballot box" effectiveness ratings for various dependent variables. Our ratings and the authors' ratings were extremely consistent, providing another indicant of interrater agreement. In the vast majority of cases, the intervention demonstrated positive effects. This observation was true for recidivism as well as a variety of types of variables coded. When multiple variables were within type, the rated effects were averaged as part of the coding process. The number of instances of ratable results other than recidivism or social behavior was small, but is reported in Table 5 to provide the reader a sense of the type of outcome variables employed in this literature. The low number of entries in Table 5 indicates the infrequency of using multiple outcomes within any given study. In summary, the data indicate that when the study author's conclusion and our ratings of effectiveness are examined, behavioral procedures are judged to have positive effects on juvenile delinquency. The conclusions from Table 5 are very similar to previous reviews that have appeared over the last decade.

A different story emerges when one considers quantitative effect sizes according to the methods specified by Hunter *et al.* (1982) and Glass *et al.* (1981). Table 6 shows the quantitative effect sizes for the overall set of studies and for each of several types of dependent variables. Each column deserves some explanation.

The mean effect size (Column A) is the effect size in each study added together and divided by the number of studies having a calculable effect size for the variable in question. The last four columns use the methods of Hunter *et al.* (1982) to correct for sampling error in the effect-size estimates. An effect size based on a large number of subjects should be more accurate than one

Table 5. Summary of "Ballot Box" Effectiveness Data

Variable	Positive effect	No effect	Negative effect
Overall ratings of effectiveness			
Our rating	22(73%)	6(20%)	2(7%)
Author's rating	24(80%)	5(17%)	1(3%)
Recidivism			
Pre/post vote	2(67%)	0	1(33%)
E/c vote[a]	8(54%)	5(33%)	2(13%)
Self-report delinquency			
Pre/post vote	Insufficient numbers ($N = 1$)		
E/c vote	Insufficient numbers ($N = 1$)		
Program behavior			
Pre/post vote	Insufficient numbers ($N = 1$)		
E/c vote	4(100%)	0	0
Academic performance			
Pre/post vote	2(67%)	0	1(33%)
E/c vote	Insufficient numbers ($N = 2$)		
Social behavior			
Pre/post vote	8(89%)	1(11%)	0
E/c vote	8(89%)	0	1(11%)
Attendance			
Pre/post vote	2(67%)	0	1(33%)
E/c vote	Insufficient numbers ($N = 1$)		
Attitude measures			
Pre/post vote	Insufficient numbers ($N = 0$)		
E/c vote	Insufficient numbers ($N = 1$)		
Self-esteem			
Pre/post vote	Insufficient numbers ($N = 1$)		
E/c vote	Insufficient numbers ($N = 0$)		
Global adjustment			
Pre/post vote	Insufficient numbers ($N = 0$)		
E/c vote	1(25%)	3(75%)	0
Cognitive measures			
Pre/post vote	Insufficient numbers ($N = 2$)		
E/c vote	Insufficient numbers ($N = 2$)		
Calculated overall effectiveness vote			
Pre/post vote	14(82%)	2(12%)	1(6%)
E/c vote	18(85%)	1(5%)	2(10%)

[a]Experimental/control vote.

based on a small number of subjects. Therefore, effect sizes are weighted by sample size, and a mean (Column B) and variance (Column C) were obtained. This variance was corrected for sampling error by subtracting the amount of variance due to sampling error from the amount of variance obtained. According to rules of thumb discussed by Hunter *et al.* (1982), if 75% of the obtained variance is due to statistical artifacts (of which sampling error is one), then all variance is considered to be artifactual.

Table 6 indicates that both the average and weighted effect sizes are positive for those variables with a sufficient number of studies to make calculations worthwhile. This is consistent with the results of the analysis of the effectiveness ratings based on both our conclusions and those drawn by the authors of the studies. The corrected variances of the effect sizes, however, were quite substantial in most cases. These corrected variances approach the mean effect size. These calculations could not be corrected with estimates of the reliability of measures used in the reviewed studies because reliability data were reported very infrequently. For only one variable, pre-post social behavior, was most of the variance due to sampling error.

A parsimonious way to summarize the meta-analysis is to look at the confidence intervals surrounding the corrected effect sizes, which is statistically equivalent to examining whether the difference between means is significant or to determining whether an observed correlation coefficient is significantly different from zero. In the present meta-analysis of 30 studies, the power of such tests is enhanced because the total number of subjects across studies is taken into account. In all cases but two, the confidence interval includes zero and ranges into negative values. Hence, we are unable to reject the alternative hypothesis of no effect. This is true in all cases except experimental control comparisons on program behaviors and pre-post comparisons of social behavior. The effect size for the overall variable set and effect sizes for recidivism, the only two variables available for substantial numbers of studies, both included negative values within their confidence interval ranges. Relationships between calculated effect size and effectiveness ratings were examined. The correlations were consistently significant and positive, indicating a relationship between rated effectiveness and calculated effect size.

In summary, the conclusions that can be drawn from the ballot box and meta-analysis procedure are dramatically different. The ballot box method leads to the conclusion that behavioral interventions produce positive effects with delinquent populations. But, because the confidence intervals surrounding the calculated effect sizes consistently include zero, the statistical methods of calculating effect sizes do not support such a conclusion of positive effects.

DISCUSSION

The two types of methods of reviewing the outcome literature of the efficacy of behavioral methods with juvenile offenders produced contrary findings. Considering rated effectiveness, both the study authors' conclusions and

Table 6. Calculated Effect Size[a]

Variable	A	B	C	D	E	F
Recidivism						
Pre/post	3	.60	.65	—	—	—
E/c	14	.25	.13	.13	4%	−.057–.82
Self-report delinquency						
Pre/post	0	—	—	—	—	—
E/c	1	.27	—	—	—	—
Program behavior						
Pre/post	2	.87	1.52	—	—	—
E/c	5	.57	.54	.07	14%	.04–1.04
Academic performance						
Pre/post	2	.07	.17	—	—	—
E/c	2	.26	.29	—	—	—
Social behavior						
Pre/post	5	.92	.71	.01	78%	.53–.90
E/c	7	.29	.24	.24	7%	−.77–1.26
Attendance						
Pre/post	1	−.01	—	—	—	—
E/c	1	−.52	—	—	—	—
Attitude measures						
Pre/post	0	—	—	—	—	—
E/c	2	.46	.28	—	—	—
Self-esteem						
Pre/post	1	.92	—	—	—	—
E/c	0	—	—	—	—	—
Global adjustment						
Pre/post	0	—	—	—	—	—
E/c	3	.07	.02	—	—	—
Cognitive measures						
Pre/post	1	.51	—	—	—	—
E/c	1	.91	—	—	—	—
Calculated overall effectiveness						
Pre/post	12	.74	.65	.71	2%	−1.00–2.30
E/c	19	.46	.25	.17	2%	−0.55–1.06

[a]Column A = number of studies reporting the dependent variable;   Column B = the mean effect size;   Column C = the weighted mean effect size;   Column D = the corrected variance of the effect size;   Column E = % of observed variance due to sampling error; and Column F = 95% confidence interval for effect size.

our general and specific ratings, behavioral interventions produced uniformly positive effects, with a high degree of correspondence between our ratings and the conclusions reached by the studies' authors. Vote counting and ballot box methods of outcome studies produced the same conclusions as similar reviews that have focused more broadly on behavioral interventions with delinquents (e.g., Davidson & Seidman, 1974; Emery & Marholin, 1977; Nietzel *et al.*, 1977).

For the quantitative effect sizes, the mean effective sizes were uniformly positive. When the statistical magnitude of the effects was considered, however, the hypothesis that no effects were observed could not be rejected; the confidence interval surrounding all effect-size means included zero. Variables such as recidivism, traditionally viewed as a critical outcome variable, did not appear to be consistently positively related to behavioral interventions. In addition, when all studies were combined across all types of outcomes, which included a large number of subjects across studies, still no significant effects were obtained. This examination of the statistical significance of the effect in standard score units leads to the conclusion that no substantial outcome evidence exists for the efficacy of behavioral techniques in affecting violence and antisocial behavior as represented by juvenile offenders.

The inconsistency of the conclusions provided by these two methods of review is certainly reason for pause. Why should these two methods of review produce such different conclusions? The "ballot box" method indicates consistently positive effects, whereas the calculated effectiveness method indicates that the effects observed are not significantly different from zero. First, the calculated effect-size methodology provides a distinct standard against which to judge effectiveness. This criterion demands that sufficient data be reported to allow effect-size calculation, but effect size could only be calculated for 19 of the studies. Although a significant correlation existed between calculated effect size and rated effectiveness ($p < .01$ in all cases), the 19 studies for which effect size is calculable are rated effective 60% of the time compared to a 80% rate among those studies for which an effect cannot be calculated. This suggests that the samples of studies to which the two methods of summarizing effects can be applied were different. Specifically, case studies and studies that incompletely report results are more likely to be judged as indicating positive effects. In other words, studies where effect size could be calculated appeared to be carried out in a more rigorous fashion.

Second, the procedures employed in calculating effect size often require estimation of effect size when partial data are reported. These procedures may be statistically conservative, resulting in the underestimation of true effect size. This effect, however, should be offset by the increased power gained by summarizing effects across studies and the resulting large number of studies.

Third, the methods of calculated effect may provide a more accurate metric against which to assess observed effects. Given the bias in publication policy toward positive and significant effects, calculated effect size provides a statistically sound metric with which to summarize reported effects.

The body of literature reviewed continues to suffer from a number of methodological flaws that have been pointed out over the last decade (Blakely & Davidson, 1984; Davidson & Seidman, 1974; Emery & Marholin, 1977). Whether these methodological shortcomings increase Type I or Type II errors in this body of literature is difficult to discern. For example, better controlled studies have a greater chance of detecting intervention effects. Yet artifactual effects (e.g., biased data collectors and nonequivalent control groups) would be expected to disappear with proper methodological controls. Unfortunately, the effects of such methodological shortcomings will be entangled in the overall assessment of effects until more consistent quality research is available.

One shortcoming in this literature that the meta-analysis has highlighted is the minimal amount of data reported in the published literature. The major methodological characteristics were extremely difficult to discern for many studies. For example, such basic dimensions as intervention length and intensity were uncodable 20% and 57% of the time, respectively. In addition, the lack of consistent reporting of critical methodological information and results produced missing data in this review. As alluded to before, the missing data had the effect of making examination of interrelationships between methodological characteristics and effect sizes virtually impossible. Even more critical were the difficulties experienced in obtaining sufficient information to make effect-size calculations. The practice of reporting only significance levels without reporting means and variances is problematic, especially when examining nonsignificant findings that are frequently reported without statistical documentation, potentially biasing meta-analyses in prointervention directions.

This review has also raised conceptual issues relevant to standard views of behavioral interventions and the applied analysis of behavior. The core issue is the appropriateness of examining the effectiveness of behavioral procedures using outcomes from follow-up time periods and/or settings. From a strict functional analysis point of view, behavior is a function of its environmental antecedents and consequences. If intervention takes place in settings different from those in which outcomes will be assessed, the generalization of behavior change is what is being examined, not the effectiveness of the intervention procedures directly. As argued in the introduction of this chapter, previous literature reviews have adequately addressed the issue of behavioral interventions directly affecting a variety of performances with delinquent youth. The relevant question for public policy must now turn to the long-term effects of these procedures. If we fail to find positive effects, behavioral interventions may well be ineffective with delinquents. From a behavioral perspective, however, such a conclusion may say as much about the settings and their relevance to the follow-up environment in which our interventions take place.

The extent to which juvenile delinquents accurately represent a broader concern with issues of violence and aggression raises an additional concern. In many instances, the real focus of interventions aimed at reducing violence and aggression is on rather infrequent events. Reducing officially recorded arrests, events that occur at most a few times a year, is an extremely difficult standard for any intervention procedure. Further work clearly needs to be done examining the relationship between the more intermediate outcomes of behavioral interventions and more global outcomes such as recidivism.

This review has pointed to a number of needed future directions. The two methods of summarizing existing studies provide different conclusions, thus raising questions about the efficacy of behavioral procedures in the area of violence and aggression when long-term effects are examined. Most notably, the review indicates the need for more outcome studies conducted with more methodological rigor. This review has also highlighted the need to examine the efficacy of behavioral procedures in other than residential settings. Better quality research carried out in settings closer to the follow-up environment should allow more definitive conclusions about the long-term impact.

REFERENCES

Alderman, J. D., Cranney, L. A., & Begans, P. (1981). *ABC News-Washington Post Poll, Survey No. 0029*. New York: ABC News.

Alexander, J. F., & Parsons, B. V. (1973). Short-term behavioral intervention with delinquent families: Impact on family process and recidivism. *Journal of Abnormal Psychology, 81,* 219–225.

Andrew, J. M. (1981). Delinquency: Correlating variables. *Journal of Child Clinical Psychology, 10,* 136–140.

Becker, H. S. (1963). *The outsiders*. Glencoe, IL: The Free Press.

Blakely, C., & Davidson, W. S. (1984). Behavioral approaches to delinquency: A review. In P. Karoly (Ed.), *Adolescent behavior disorders* (pp. 241–284). New York: Pergamon.

Broder, P. K., Dunivant, N., Smith, E. C., & Sutton, L. P. (1981). Further observations on the link between learning disabilities and juvenile delinquency. *Journal of Educational Psychology, 73,* 838–850.

Campbell, D., & Stanley, J. (1966). *Experimental and quasi-experimental designs for research*. Chicago: Rand McNally.

Cloward, R., & Ohlin, L. (1960). *Delinquency and opportunity*. Glencoe, IL: The Free Press.

Cohen, H. L. (1968). Educational therapy: The design of learning environments. *Research in Psychotherapy, 3,* 21–58.

Davidson, W. S., & Seidman, E. (1974). Studies of behavior modification and juvenile delinquency. *Psychological Bulletin, 81,* 998–1011.

Davidson, W. S., Redner, R., & Saul, J. A. (1983). Research modes in social and community change. In E. Seidman (ed.), *Social intervention*. Beverly Hills: Sage.

Elliott, D. S., & Voss, H. L. (1974). *Delinquency and dropout*. Lexington, MA: Lexington Press.

Elliott, D. S., Ageton, S. S., & Canter, R. J. (1979). An integrated theoretical perspective on delinquent behavior. *Journal of Research in Crime and Delinquency, 16,* 3–27.

Emery, R. E., & Marholin, D. (1977). An applied behavior analysis of delinquency. *American Psychologist, 32,* 860–871.

Erickson, M. L. (1973). Group violations, socioeconomic status, and official delinquency. *Social Forces, 52,* 41–52.

Fairweather, G. W., & Tornatzky, L. G. (1977). *Experimental methods for social policy research*. New York: Pergamon Press.

Faretra, G. (1981). A profile of aggression from adolescence to adulthood. *American Journal of Orthopsychiatry, 51,* 439–453.

FBI. (1980). *Uniform crime report*. Washington, DC: U.S. Government Printing Office.

FBI. (1981). *Uniform crime report*. Washington, DC: U.S. Government Printing Office.

Gaffney, L. R., & McFall, R. M. (1981). A comparison of the social skills in delinquent and nondelinquent adolescent girls using behavioral role-playing inventory. *Journal of Consulting and Clinical Psychology, 49,* 959–967.

Gallup, G. H. (1981). *The Gallup Poll*. Princeton, NJ: The Gallup Poll.

In re Gault, 387, U.S. 1 (1967).

Glaser, D. (1975). *Strategic criminal justice planning*. Washington, DC: U.S. Government Printing Office.

Glass, G. V., McGraw, G., & Smith, M. L. (1981). *Meta-analysis in social research*. Beverly Hills: Sage.

Glueck, S., & Glueck, E. (1951). *Unraveling juvenile delinquency*. Cambridge, MA: Harvard University Press.

Gold, M. A. (1974). A time for skepticism. *Crime and Delinquency, 20,* 20–24.

Grey, A. L., & Dermody, H. E. (1972). Reports of casework failure. *Social Casework, 16,* 207–212.

Hunter, J., Schmidt, F., & Jackson, G. (1982). *Cumulating research findings across studies*. Beverly Hills: Sage.

James, H. (1969). *Children in trouble*. New York: Christian Science Monitor.

Krisberg, B., & Austin, J. (1978). *The children of Ishmael*. Palo Alto, CA: Mayfield Press.

Kushler, M., & Davidson, W. S. (1981). Community and organizational level change. In A. P. Goldstein, E. G. Carr, W. S. Davidson, & P. Wehr (Eds.), *In response to aggression* (pp. 346–401). New York: Pergamon.

Leakey, R. E., & Lewin, R. (1977). *Origins*. New York: Dutton, 1977.

Levitt, E. L. (1971). Research on psychotherapy with children. In A. Bergin & S. L. Garfield (Eds.), *Handbook of psychotherapy and behavior change*. New York: Wiley.

Matza, D. (1969. *Becoming deviant*. Englewood Cliffs, NJ: Prentice-Hall.

Mednick, S., & Christiansen, K. O. (1977). *Biosocial basis of criminal behavior*. New York: Garden Press.

Mennel, R. M. (1972). Origins of the juvenile court. *Crime and Delinquency, 18,* 68–78.

Merton, R. K. (1957). *Social theory and social structure*. New York: The Free Press.

National Institute of Justice. (1982). *Criminal victimization in the United States*. Washington, DC: U.S. Government Printing Office.

Nietzel, M. T., Winett, R. A., McDonald, M. L., & Davidson, W. S. (1977). *Behavioral approaches to community psychology*. New York: Pergamon Press.

Paul, G. L. (1969). Behavior modification research: Design and tactics. In J. Frank (Ed.), *Behavior therapy: Appraisal and status*. New York: McGraw-Hill.

Pelto, G. H., & Pelto, P. J. (1976). *The human adventure*. New York: Macmillan.

Phillips, E. L. (1968). Achievement Place: Token reinforcement procedures in a homestyle rehabilitation for "predelinquent" boys. *Journal of Applied Behavior Analysis, 1,* 213–223.

Polk, K., & Schafer, W. K. (1972). *Schools and delinquency*. Englewood Cliffs, NJ: Prentice-Hall.

Prentice, N. M. (1972). The influence of live and symbolic modeling on promoting moral judgements of adolescent delinquents. *Journal of Abnormal Psychology, 80,* 157–161.

Research and Forecasts, Inc. (1980). *The Figgle Report on fear of crime: America Afraid*. Willoughby, OH: Figgle International.

Robins, L. N. (1966). *Deviant children grown up*. Baltimore: Williams and Wilkins.

Roper Organization. (1982). *Opinion roundup, Public Opinion 5*.

Rossi, P., Freeman, H., & Wright, S. (1982). *Evaluation: A systematic approach*. Beverly Hills: Sage.

Ryan, W. (1976). *Blaming the victim*. New York: Vintage.

Saul, J., & Davidson, W. (1982). Child advocacy in the juvenile court: A clash of paradigms. In G. Melton (Ed.), *Child advocacy* (pp. 29–42). Beverly Hills: Sage.

Schultz, J. L. (1973). The cycle of juvenile court history. *Crime and Delinquency, 19,* 457–476.

Smith, M. L., Glass, G. V., & Miller, T. I. (1980). *The benefits of psychotherapy*. Baltimore: Johns Hopkins University Press.

Smith, P. M., & Ausnew, H. R. (1974). Socialization as related to delinquency classification. *Psychological Reports, 34,* 677–678.

Spivack, G., & Shure, M. B. (1982). The cognition of social adjustment. In B. B. Lahey & A. E. Kazdin (Eds.), *Advances in child clinical psychology*. New York: Plenum Press.

Steketee, J. P. (1973, September). *Community and behavioral approaches to delinquency: The court's perspective*. Paper presented at the American Psychological Association Convention, Montreal, Canada.

Stuart, R. B. (1971). Behavioral contracting within the families of delinquents. *Journal of Behavior Therapy and Experimental Psychiatry, 2,* 1–11.

Stumphauzer, J. (1971). *Behavior therapy with delinquents*. Springfield, IL: Charles C Thomas.

Stumphauzer, J. (1978). *Progress in behavior therapy with delinquents.* Springfield, IL: Charles C Thomas.

Tharp, R., & Wetzel, R. (1969). *Behavior modification in the natural environment.* New York: Academic Press.

Waldo, G. P., & Dinitz, S. (1967). Personality attributes of the criminal: An analysis of research studies 1950–1965. *Journal of Research in Crime and Delinquency, 4,* 185–202.

Williams, J. R., & Gold, M. (1972). From delinquent behavior to official delinquency. *Social Problems, 20,* 209–229.

16

Program Evaluation in Crime and Delinquency

ROBERT J. JONES

Societies whose posture toward criminal or deviant behavior is essentially retributive need not concern themselves with the assessment of the methods they apply to those accused of such behaviors. Such societies do not expect the convicted offender to "get better," though they may hope or presume that one effect of the retribution (e.g., incarceration, loss of the offending bodily part) might be to limit the future occurrence of the behavior in question. The retribution serves as its own end.

Only when a society aspires to do more for its offending members than simply incarcerate or otherwise punish them does the issue of assessment or evaluation present itself. That our society does so aspire is reflected most directly in the word it has adopted, conventionally, to convey its intentions vis-à-vis criminally adjudicated adults and delinquent youth. That word, of course, is *corrections*. The term tends, curiously, to anticipate the effects of the procedures that it collectively denotes. Perhaps more legitimately and certainly more importantly, it implies that our society's responses to criminality or delinquency are aimed at producing a result, an effect, a change—a correction. The unspoken unanimity surrounding that global aim does not, however, extend to the methods recommended for accomplishing it—for effecting the desired change. Like the skinning of the proverbial cat, many more than one approach has been tried, and many more still proposed.

Because we aspire to "correct" offensiveness, because we are inclined to entertain and encourage a variety of tacks toward that end, and because we have good reasons to care about the effects of those differing approaches (namely the number of people and tax dollars involved in our molar correctional effort), we are powerfully inclined to pose questions about the relative merits of the alternative strategies adopted. What works? What works best? How much does it cost? Can we do better? Enter the need for correctional program evaluation.

Program evaluation in the correctional sciences refers, broadly, to the

Robert J. Jones • Appalachian State University, BIABH Study Center, 204 Avery Avenue, Morganton, North Carolina 28655.

process by which questions concerning the *value* or efficacy of correctional programs are answered. The primary purpose of this chapter is to identify and discuss the important considerations and choices made before and during the course of program evaluations that influence the veracity and, thus, the utility of the answers produced by them. A second objective will be to point out and illustrate the special perspective that the field of applied behavior analysis has brought to the understanding of criminal and deviant behavior, the possible methods for the remedy of such behavior, and the strategies and techniques by which those methods might best be assessed.

No attempt will be made to review the outcomes of extant evaluations—several such reviews, many of them fairly recent and quite comprehensive (e.g., Davidson & Seidman, 1974; Lipton, Martinson, & Wilks, 1975; Romig, 1978), are available in the current correctional literature. Specific studies from that literature will, however, be used to illustrate those factors that have tended, historically, to distinguish correctional evaluations whose results have found their way into social policy and practice from others whose conclusions have enjoyed less impact, or at least less import, within the correctional community. In addition, both hypothetical and real examples from the behavioral literature will be included to illustrate the various ways applied behavior analysis has, and can, influence the construction of correctional program evaluations.

THE LANGUAGE AND CONVENTIONS OF PROGRAM EVALUATION

It may be useful to begin the enterprise with a brief discussion of some of the definitions, concepts, and conventions that have come to characterize the practice of evaluation in the field of corrections. The range of activities that can be legitimately captured under the rubric of *program evaluation* is broad indeed (see discussion by Jones, in preparation). At one extreme are vigorously constructed, methodologically sophisticated, often independently mounted (and typically expensive) efforts to compare systematically the relative merits and weaknesses of two or more approaches with a common correctional population. Such evaluations conventionally enjoy the special status of evaluation *research* (McSweeny, Fremouw, & Hawkins, 1982; Struening & Guttentag, 1975). At the other extreme are the myriad "in-house" assessments undertaken by individual correctional programs or agencies, often on shoestring budgets, in a nominal effort to determine whether basic goals within the program are being met. The present discussion will concern itself mainly with evaluation efforts toward the former end of the continuum, though it is worth noting that modest but carefully planned in-house evaluations can produce more useful results than much more ambitious but conceptually or methodologically flawed independent evaluations.

A useful distinction among the different kinds and levels of program evaluations has been forwarded by Scriven (1972) and now enjoys broad currency in the general evaluation literature (e.g., Fitz-Gibbon & Morris, 1978;

Hawkins & Meadowcroft, 1983; McSweeny *et al.*, 1982). Scriven suggests the descriptor *formative* be applied to evaluations of ongoing programs in which the primary purpose of the evaluation is to provide data that can be used to guide continuing adjustments and refinements in the program. By contrast, the notion of the "summative" evaluation is typically reserved for more ambitious and more costly, one-time evaluations intended to produce a final summary statement concerning the effects of a specific, usually demonstration-level, project or program. In general, but not exclusively, this chapter will be concerned with issues surrounding evaluations of the summative variety.

A final distinction, also noted by Scriven (1972) and others, may prove useful here. It concerns the differences of purpose between *comparative* and *descriptive* evaluations and relates to the kinds of questions a particular evaluation seeks to address. Formative, in-house evaluations usually involve data of a noncomparative sort—data that can be used to answer absolute or descriptive questions such as, "How many clients were served during the last fiscal year and at what cost per client?" Conversely, summative evaluations are most often concerned with questions of a qualitative nature, questions incorporating such phrases as *how well, how expensive, how better or worse, how much better*. Qualitative questions such as these invariably imply a comparison: "better than what?" or "less expensive compared with what?" Comparative evaluations are more inclined than descriptive evaluations to seek data and conclusions that may be brought to bear on social policy decision making and that extend beyond the immediate needs or domain of the specific programs included in the evaluations. The evaluation considerations of interest here are those most commonly associated with comparative assessments.

To review, *program evaluation* as used here will refer to the process, including all of the choices and considerations that constitute it, of answering questions about the efficacy of specific approaches or treatments in the correctional arena. What efficacy means is determined by the questions to be answered by a specific evaluation effort. Questions concerning program or treatment costs, impact, and durability are, among others, questions of efficacy. Questions that raise the issue of relativity (e.g., *relative* program costs, impact, etc.) are associated with the subgroup of summative evaluations called *comparative evaluations*.

Some Persisting Misconceptions

Among the various questionable presumptions, flawed truisms, and misconceptions within the correctional evaluation field are at least three worthy of note here. The first of these has been alluded to already and is more characteristic of the consumers of correctional evaluation results than of those who produce those results. It is the subtle tendency to assume, prima facie, an inherent correspondence between the scope, sophistication, and cost of an evaluation and the value of its findings (i.e., bigger is necessarily better). This inclination is interestingly illustrated in what has come to be called the "nothing works" hypothesis.

On the one hand, comprehensive reviews of correctional evaluations—including some of the largest, most ambitious, and methodologically sophisticated studies attempted over two decades—have found those evaluations wanting in terms of their collective ability to produce systematic and definitive direction for the field and have led to the "nothing works" position (Lipton *et al.*, 1975; Martinson, 1974). Critics of this position, conversely, have argued against the pessimism of this posture essentially on grounds that its proponents' conclusions have fallen victim to "the dangers of overemphasis on design, data analysis, and outcome measures to the exclusion of other criteria of adequacy" (Quay, 1977, p. 342; see also critique by Palmer, 1975). The point is that clean and comparatively simple evaluations addressed to purposely delimited questions can produce results whose value may be obscured by their modest scope.

A second presumption bordering on misconception—and one that is also more prevalent among evaluation consumers than evaluators—is that the worth or value of evaluations that produce negative results is somehow inherently diminished by the direction of the findings. In point of fact, program evaluations that can correctly and definitively identify even promising correctional interventions as marginally practical or inefficacious may be of equal utility, from a social policy standpoint, with comparably definitive studies *recommending* a tenable treatment alternative. A now classic example of the former is, of course, the Cambridge-Sommerville Youth Study (McCord, 1978; Powers & Witmer, 1951). Definitively derived negative results are unquestionably more useful than murky or indefinitive assessments, whatever the purported direction of their findings.

A final incorrect presumption, this one seemingly as prevalent among evaluators themselves as well as the consumers of their efforts, is that program evaluation research, the variables that affect its utility, and the considerations that should precede its implementation are somehow different in kind from other types of research or experimentation. Although perhaps more a curiosity than a problem, correctional program evaluators—especially first-timers—tend to assume that they are operating under a different set of rules than they might be if they were conducting an experimental comparison of two teaching techniques or of several potentially effective medications for hypertension or of schedule effects with Holtzman rats. In actuality, the experimenters in all of these examples (including the correctional program evaluator) are operating in the same empiricodeductive vat. The rules and accepted conventions governing their choice of methods are the same and the potential threats to the validity of their efforts nearly identical. As Glaser (1977) has observed, "The differences between useful evaluative studies and good basic research are not very great" (p. 173).

Comparative program evaluations, correctional or otherwise, are experiments. They differ from other kinds of experiments—and the differences can be pronounced—not in terms of the sampling or methodological concerns that must be observed but rather in terms of the complexity of the context or environment in which the experiment/evaluation is conducted and the ease of establishing control over the many factors always lurking to compromise the utility of the enterprise. All of the recommendations about experiments set down by Campbell and Stanley (1963) 20 years ago still obtain, and they apply as well to program evaluations as to other forms of scientific experimentation.

Applied Behavior Analysis and Correctional Program Evaluation

With these concepts, distinctions, and modest cautions in mind, let us turn to the place of applied behavior analysis within the correctional evaluation arena. Applied behavior analysis is, at once, a philosophy about why people do what they do, a system of logical inquiry, and a technology of behavior change. The general principles that have come to define applied behavior analysis as a subscience of psychology and as a legitimate extension of the experimental analysis of behavior began to be articulated during the 1960s (e.g., see Baer, Wolf, & Risley, 1968). This formulation was prompted by the curiously abrupt recognition among various operant learning theorists of the day that what they were observing and recording in their animal laboratories could be applied, virtually intact, to the solution of human problems. Among the more compelling potential applications were the problems of antisocial and deviant behaviors, delinquency, and criminality. This marked the beginning of an alliance.

The subsequent relationship between applied behavior analysis and the correctional sciences has been a close and productive one. Behaviorally based interventions have found their way into virtually all of the arms, agencies, and institutions of the American criminal justice system (see discussions by Braukmann, Fixsen, Phillips, & Wolf, 1975; Burchard & Harig, 1976; Davidson & Seidman, 1974; Milan & McKee, 1974). The broader premises and dimensions of behavior analysis have been specifically related to their application in criminal justice practice (Morris, 1980).

The influences of applied behavior analysis on *evaluation practices* in the correctional field have been more subtle than the behavioral contributions to correctional intervention *per se,* however. This is because both fields have, historically and independently, embraced the basic notion of evaluation and have borrowed from the same science in devising their respective research and evaluation strategies. The question of "who learned what from whom?" sometimes arises, and the answer, not uncommonly, is that the knowledge (or technique or posture) arose from a third source, namely sound scientific practice.

Applied behavior analysis has, nevertheless, left its distinctive mark, however subtly, on the philosophy and conduct of program evaluation in correctional settings. That mark is simply more apparent at some levels of program evaluation process than at others. The fundamental concept of *functional behavior analysis* has not only suggested worthy correctional interventions but can be usefully brought to bear on the important theoretical issues that must be considered in the initial conception of correctional evaluations. *Social validation,* another uniquely behavioral concept, can strengthen evaluations at the levels of design and measurement as well as conception and can profoundly influence the real social impact of correctional evaluation results. The abiding concern with causality, and the *reversal designs* forwarded by behavior analysis to search it out, have useful implications for correctional evaluations at the levels of conception, methodology, and analysis. Correctional evaluation methods have also been broadly influenced by the behavior-analytic preoccupation with *observable behavior* as the focal datum of interest and with its objective and reliable assessment.

These and other contributions of applied behavior analysis will be highlighted in the ensuing review of the choices, decisions, and considerations that confront all correctional program evaluators and that, collectively, influence the credibility and utility of the product of their work. In the interest of convenience, the discussion will be organized chronologically around the decision or choice points in the approximate order they are encountered in the process of conceiving, preparing for, implementing, and disseminating the results of typically mounted evaluations. It should be borne in mind that the decisions to be described are never equally spaced in time—they tend, in fact, to cluster toward the front end of the total evaluation period—and that the decisions made at the earlier choice points often dictate or seriously limit the options and choices available at later stages of the enterprise.

Choice Points in Correctional Program Evaluation

The impetus to mount summative or comparative evaluations of correctional treatments usually, though not invariably, occurs in the context of the development of a new or novel treatment approach. Similarly, formative evaluations of long-standing programs are either ongoing or are initiated when new questions are raised concerning their costs, effectiveness, and the like. The point of *program conception,* thus, marks the first opportunity for relevant decision making that can influence the value of a subsequent evaluation of the proposed program. As will be seen directly, the degree to which the concept or formulation of a new intervention follows logically from a tenable theoretical model of criminality or delinquency will have a powerful bearing on the utility of the results of an evaluation of that intervention.

The second important choice point in formulating a program evaluation occurs when a commitment to evaluate has been arrived at. Apart from issues of evaluation funding, the most important decisions that arise at this point concern *who will devise and conduct the evaluation* and *what questions are to be addressed* by it.

These decisions set the stage for an array of critical choices typically subsumed under the heading of *evaluation methodology*. Methodological considerations most notably center on the formulation of an overall evaluation design and include the somewhat separate, often difficult, but equally important choices about dependent measures. As Jones (1982) has pointed out regarding delinquency follow-up evaluations, the core decisions in this latter connection are what to measure, when to measure, and how to measure.

The actual *implementation* of the evaluation proceeds from these three categories of choices and activities. Although implementation represents the most time-consuming part of the evaluation process, it is, ideally, not a time for critical decision making. That is, if the previous choices have been made judiciously and preparations for the evaluation laid out carefully, the period of evaluation implementation, *per se,* will be occupied primarily with data collection. Most decisions at this level of the process should be concerned with procedural adjustments relating to unanticipated events or problems. Major alterations in evaluation methods at this stage can be expected, with great certainty, to play havoc with the last category of evaluation activities (i.e., data analysis and interpretation).

This final, interpretive aspect of the process involves the analysis and summarization of data produced by the evaluation in preparation for the *dissemination* of those *results and the conclusions* surrounding them. The complex task of data analysis has been widely addressed elsewhere and is beyond the scope of this chapter. Brief attention will, however, be given to the importance of dissemination of evaluation conclusions and how that dissemination bears on the generality and replication of correctional interventions.

Let us now explore the issues and considerations at these various choice points—and the implications of the specific decisions arrived at—in greater detail.

Conception of the Intervention Program

The initial conception of a correctional intervention, strictly speaking, precedes any formalized consideration of its evaluation. New ideas about altering the deviant proclivities of criminals and delinquent youth arise out of the day-to-day experiences of practitioners in correctional settings, from the data-based theorizing of scholars in the social sciences, and from the distress of administrators and social policymakers wanting more for their correctional dollar. It is nevertheless true that the manner in which new interventions are conceived and developed may profoundly affect the usefulness of evaluating such interventions at all and, thus, their ultimate social impact.

The Relevance of Theory

The most common criticism leveled at the progenitors of correctional interventions (and subsequently at those who attempt to evaluate them) is the persistent failure to relate such interventions to existing causal theories of delinquent and criminal behaviors (e.g., Elliott, 1980a; Glaser, 1977, 1980). Jones (1982) has observed, for whatever comfort it may afford, that this absence of a theoretical base for interventions and evaluations of them likely extends beyond corrections to the other social and health sciences as well. In any case, the problem is pervasive and warrants attention here.

Correctional interventions that are arbitrary, esoteric, or lodged largely in convention are vulnerable, from both practical and scientific standpoints. They are vulnerable practically because even otherwise valid evaluations suggesting their effectiveness will not be able to explain convincingly why they work. They are vulnerable scientifically because they are unlikely to be replicated or widely adopted in the absence of such causal explanation. In other words, correctional evaluations ought to attempt to determine both whether and why interventions of interest work; if the latter of these two issues is ignored, the generalizability or external validity (Campbell & Stanley, 1963; Mahoney, 1978) of the findings will be seriously impaired (see discussion by Glaser, 1980).

Beyond the important issue of generality of results, other problems are associated with the evaluation of interventions that lack clear theoretical underpinnings. Not the least obvious of these is that theory-based interventions, although they can offer no guarantees, are more likely to produce predictable results than are arbitrary or convention-based treatments. This is particularly true, of course, if the underlying theory is comprehensive and embodies current data and debate.

Another difficulty with atheoretical intervention evaluations, one of several articulated by Elliott (1980a), is that the interpretation of their outcomes is rendered unnecessarily problematic. This weakness involves the distinction between "process" and "impact" evaluation. These concepts will be central to a subsequent discussion about the formulation of evaluation questions; thus it may be helpful to introduce them here. Impact evaluations are intended to determine if and how much the intervention "package" affected or impacted the dependent variable(s) of interest, typically—in corrections—some measure of the subjects' during- or posttreatment rate of repeating delinquent or criminal acts. By contrast, the purpose of a process evaluation is to determine whether and how well the specific, intermediate objectives of the intervention were accomplished. (The notion of process evaluation is the newer, and likely less familiar, of the two concepts and tends to assume a grounding in theory of the intervention being evaluated). In defense of theory-based interventions, in general, and process evaluations in particular, Elliott (1980a) argues that "it is essential in any evaluation to determine that the immediate program objectives were, in fact, achieved" (p. 242).

To illustrate, consider a hypothetical impact evaluation of the Teaching-Family model (TFM) (Phillips, Phillips, Fixsen, & Wolf, 1971; Wolf, Phillips, & Fixsen, 1972) of delinquency intervention mounted without benefit of a process evaluation component. The model represents a treatment package offered in the context of group home care and is, in fact, derived from a behavioral theory. The theory postulates that improved performance in school, among other things, should produce a decrease in the likelihood of delinquent activities. Furthermore, the treatment package constituting the model does incorporate specific elements (e.g., a school-note reporting system by which the school behavior and performance of clients is communicated to treatment providers on a daily basis so that differential consequences can be arranged for both poor and improved academic performance) designed to facilitate overall school performance. Now let us attempt to interpret possible impact outcomes, in the absence of a specific process evaluation of the effects of the school-related components of the treatment package. For simplicity's sake, we will assume that all other elements of the treatment program are demonstrated to have no impact on the dependent measure and that everything hinges on the impact of the school-related component.

The first possibility is that the level of delinquent activity among treatment youth is unaffected by the intervention. Can we conclude that the school-related component of the TFM is flawed and failed to produce the expected academic gains? No, because we neglected to measure that aspect of the *process.* Can we conclude that the underlying theory is deficient in relating academic progress to diminished deviancy? No again, and for the same reason. The interpretation is equally compromised if we hypothesize positive effects on the dependent measure of delinquent activity.

If, however, our evaluation had incorporated an intermediate (process) assessment of school performance in addition to the formal impact measure (delinquent activity rate) of focal interest, the same results—positive or negative—would produce comparatively clear, and likely useful, interpretations. If, for instance, delinquency rates persisted in the face of substantially improved school performance, we could make a defensible case for program success and at least partial failure of the underlying theory. If, conversely, the program did impact delinquency rates but without benefit of measurable improvement in school performance, we would be forced to acknowledge program failure and would remain unenlightened as to the viability of the school performance/delinquency connection forwarded by the underlying learning theory. Better grades *and* reduced delinquency would, of course, indicate the tenability of both the program and the theory from which it emanated. The incorporation of process considerations deriving from theory-founded impact evaluations can, unquestionably, improve the general usefulness of the latter.

An additional point, also suggested by Elliott (1980a), is that theory-independent interventions may, in fact, encourage "a general resistance to evaluation on the part of program personnel and a failure to utilize evaluation findings in the ongoing operation of the program" (p. 244). Elliott's point is that program staff, despite their often abiding indifference to theory *per se,* do discriminate between evaluations that might lead to constructive changes in the way things are done and those that are poorly conceived (i.e., atheoretical) and thus unlikely to result in significant adjustments in either their activities or the effects thereof.

The Functional Analysis of Behavior. Unfortunately, the practitioners of applied behavior analysis cannot be exempted from related criticism. The elegant and succinctly put directive that dominated this subscience in its early years has tended, more recently, to have gotten lost in the shuffle. That directive was, of course, to analyze problem behaviors functionally and to derive corrective strategies from such functional analyses (Holland & Skinner, 1961; Skinner, 1953). That advice is tantamount to the suggestion that behaviorists not lose sight of their theory. I have personally noted a tendency, of late, among students of behavior management to construct clinical interventions that ignore the contingencies of reinforcement surrounding the undesirable behavior and how that behavior functions to serve the client in the presence of those contingencies. A review of learning-based delinquency interventions suffering this same shortcoming has been offered by Emery and Marholin (1977).

The beauty of a functional analysis of deviant (or other) behavior is that it simultaneously identifies the causal or controlling links between the behavior and its environmental influences, suggests the direction of an appropriate intervention, and provides the basis for theory construction surrounding the problem. These things, in turn, can direct the conceptual phase of both process and impact evaluations of the intervention program.

A Persisting Problem. In the face of the number and compelling nature of reasons for planning correctional interventions around strong theoretical explanations of deviant behavior, one might well ask why theory-derived interventions remain the exception rather than the rule. The question is not easy to answer—simple laziness or pedestrianism on the part of correctional practitioners, perhaps, or a curious disinclination to foray into the more ethereal (theoretical) regions of their craft. If this is so, then the theoriticians must assume at least part of the blame; first, for failing to cast their revelations in terms that are meaningful and relevant to the practitioners; second, for sometimes keeping their distance from the workaday world of correctional practice. This is speculation, of course. In deference to correctional practitioners, I would prefer to think that the difficulty may relate more to a well-intentioned impatience to get to the thing at hand (i.e., the correctional application) than to any endemic aversion to things theoretical. Correctional practitioners are problem solvers and are sometimes more inclined, like a roofer with a rainstorm coming, to reach for the tool closest at hand than to climb down the ladder for the correct one. Alternately, as has been suggested by Elliott (1980a), conventional strategies and methods in the correctional field may have become as institutionalized as the buildings that house some of them. That is, they may be "employed because they have become proper and accepted things to do for youth in trouble, because they are relatively easy to implement, and because people are trained to provide this service or treatment" (p. 238).

A Theory "Sampler" for Evaluators

Certainly, in any case, the difficulty does not stem from any dearth of thoughtful theoretical rationales to which correctional planners might anchor their interventions. Although it is beyond the purview of this chapter to elucidate the theoretical constructions that have been forwarded to account for delinquent and criminal behaviors, several warrant at least passing attention here. The three sociological theories that have enjoyed the most durable currency and interest in this century are control theory (see historical discussion by Empey, 1978) with its relatively recent emphasis on the importance of the social bond (Hirschi, 1969); strain theory postulated by Cloward and Ohlin

(1960) upon which control theorists have attempted to improve; and social learning theory as advanced, generally, by Bandura (1969) that attempts to account specifically for deviant versus conforming behavior by invoking the concept of net, differential social reinforcement (Akers, 1977). (The more recently articulated integrated theory of Elliott, Ageton, & Canter, 1979—see recently amplified discussion by Elliott, Huizinga, & Ageton, 1985—has attempted to synthesize and integrate these three conceptions and holds great promise as a parsimonious explanatory model for delinquency and drug use, if not the development of deviant behavior in general.) These sample theories are summarized next to illustrate how particular theoretical constructions can guide conceptual decision making in correctional interventions and their evaluation.

Strain Theory. Briefly, strain theory holds that society inadvertently encourages levels of aspiration, achievement, and material gain that are invariably beyond the socially acceptable means of some of its members to embrace and enjoy. These members, originally thought to populate primarily the lower classes (Cloward & Ohlin, 1960; Merton, 1957) but more recently viewed as extending into the middle class as well (Elliott & Voss, 1974), experience strain or frustration and resort to socially unacceptable activities to achieve the conventional goals and standards of accomplishment set by society.

Correctional interventions emanating from strain theory would, thus, be likely to focus either on strategies for minimizing or coping with the postulated frustration (e.g., stress management) or on training regimens aimed at making program clients—incarcerated adult felons, let us say—more acceptably competitive for the bounties of society. A process evaluation of an intervention taking the latter tack would carefully assess the effects of the prescribed training regimen: Did the clients learn more functional social skills or develop new and more valuable job competencies—better still, were they actually able, upon release, to land more lucrative jobs? A concomitant evaluation of program impact would center on some reliable measure of each client's postprogram offense rate.

Control Theory. Modern constructions of control theory are less concerned with social-class membership in that they postulate strain relating to unrealistically high societal goals (and some frustrations in failing to accomplish them) as characteristic of the population at large. Rather, control theory looks to the strength of the individual's connection or bond with other individuals or groups who espouse the society's conventional standards of behavior. When those bonds are weak because of inadequate childhood socialization, or stronger bonds exist with unconventional groups (e.g., gangs), or a general disintegration of the family or surrounding subculture occurs, the propensity for deviant behavior increases.

Control theory tends to lead program designers and evaluators toward clients' social environments in search of correctional remedies. As applied to adult parolees, for instance, control theory might suggest the requirement of a highly structured and actively prosocial living environment in which strong attachments to appropriate peers might be encouraged. Process evaluation here might attempt to determine the degree of the clients' actual contact with the prescribed living environments or, more ambitiously, to measure the strength or durability of the predicted attachments. Impact evaluation would, again, attempt to assess the during- or postprogram rates of deviant or criminal activities.

Social Learning Theory. Of the three major theories, social learning theory perhaps most closely matches the philosophical perspective of applied behavior analysis, though behavioral principles can be seen to underly the other theories and to present a basis for their integration (Krohn, Massey, & Skinner, Chapter 17, this volume). By contrast with strain and control conceptions, social learning theory accounts for the development of conforming and deviant behaviors within the same mechanisms. First instances of specific behaviors by the individual occur either capriciously or through the mechanism of imitation. The future likelihood of thus acquired responses then comes under the control of ongoing contingencies of reinforcement and punishment, socially or otherwise mediated, for the specific responses. The theory acknowledges that different social environments (e.g., happy families vs. delinquent gangs) both model and reinforce different categories of behaviors and it supports correctional interventions that center on either a change *of* learning environments (e.g., removal of a problem child from a dysfunctional family) or a change *in* the learning environment (e.g., effective treatment or modification of the dysfunctional family).

The tenets of social learning theory are evident in several current delinquency treatment models, for example the aforementioned TFM and a recent extension of it called foster family treatment (Hawkins, Meadowcroft, Trout, & Luster, 1985; Jones & Timbers, 1985), as well as in recent explanations of delinquency (Patterson, 1986; Patterson & Dishion, 1985). Foster family treatment, for example, attempts to redirect the behavior of delinquents by placing them, through the age of majority in some cases, with carefully selected foster families who are trained to provide continuous structure and to model and systematically reinforce appropriate social, school-related, and family behaviors. Although this intervention has not yet been formally evaluated, the process aspects of such an evaluation might assess such things as changing rates and patterns of clients' socially appropriate behaviors, client school performance, or even the simple durability of youth placements (i.e., does the intervention effectively interrupt the "revolving door cycle" from which many client referrals emanate?). Collateral impact evaluation might focus on police and court contacts, self-reported delinquency or antisocial behavior, or on in-placement rates of previously documented problem behaviors.

There are numerous variations on the theoretical constructions mentioned here as well as a range of other tenable, causal formulations (see Empey, 1978; Empey & Lubeck, 1971). Those offered here are intended to illustrate the range of viable, carefully organized, and empirically defensible rationales to which aspirant correctional program designers might look in developing their interventions.

The Evaluators and Their Questions

Let us proceed on the assumption that a perhaps novel correctional intervention has been conceived, that it can be (though not necessarily that it has been) grounded in meaningful theory, and that its designers have decided to mount the intervention on a demonstration basis. One of the first tasks facing the program's staff will be to determine who will design and conduct the required evaluation. The possibilities include existing program staff, ancillary program staff (evaluation-oriented personnel from other units or divisions within the organization mounting the new program), and evaluation specialists from outside the organization. The key issue at this point concerns the advisability of choosing an in-house versus an independent evaluator.

In-House versus Independent Evaluations

Arguments favoring the in-house evaluator center on convenience, knowledgeability about the proposed program, and the reality that specific evaluation components accompanying program support requests are often formulated by the same individuals who have proposed the program. Arguments in support of the independent or outside evaluator are concerned with the kinds of biases and potential "experimenter effects" that Rosenthal (1966) and his colleagues have cautioned about over the years in connection with experimental research in the behavioral sciences. Their points are well taken. Any time an individual charged with the evaluation of a correctional program has a proprietary or vested interest in the success of that program, doubts and concerns about the objectivity of the resulting evaluation are warranted. It is not the integrity of evaluators in these circumstances that is at issue. Rather, it is the numerous opportunities for subtle and well-intended choices by an invested evaluator to influence unintentionally the direction of evaluation results that are of concern.

A related difficulty has to do with pressures facing in-house evaluators at the level of program conception. Rossi (1972, p. 16) has observed that the major problems facing human services in general are vague goals, strong promises, and weak effects. This statement represents a particularly apt characterization of the in-house evaluator faced with the impossibility of collecting data without a program and the reality that programs are rarely funded in the absence of confident speculation that they will produce a desired outcome. This circumstance compels program developers to "promise the world" in order to attract funding for their interventions and later creates discomfort for program evaluators whose carefully collected data often fail to live up to the original promises (Jones, Timbers, & Davis, 1979).

One additional comment concerning the choice of a program evaluator relates back to the earlier discussion of the importance of grounding new interventions in theory. Theory builders are rarely the architects of new correctional approaches. Conversely, many program innovators tend (as has been intimated) to maintain only a passing and often superficial acquaintance with the theories of their time. This being at least the occasional case, most program developers would be well advised to invite the input, if not the services, of evaluation specialists who are attentive to evolving theoretical considerations.

The All-Important Questions

Whereas all evaluations emanate from questions (e.g., I wonder if this might work?), the questions that spawn evaluations are rarely the same as the formal questions to which planned evaluations are addressed. Another of the early tasks facing the individual or group responsible for the conduct of an evaluation is that of formulating and formalizing the specific questions the evaluation will try to answer. This task is more important than commonly acknowledged. If the major purpose of evaluations is to answer questions accurately—one of the premises of this chapter—then it stands to reason that the questions asked should be carefully considered. The most carefully planned and fastidiously implemented evaluation is worthless if it has addressed an irrelevant question.

Various suggestions and schemes concerning the formulation of evaluation questions have been offered. In discussing social program evaluation in general, Cronbach (1980) has recommended that "pertinent questions should be identified by examining the history of similar programs, the related social theory, and the expectations of program advocates, critics, and prospective clients" (p. 5). Concerning youth treatment evaluations, Hawkins, Fremouw, and Reitz (1982) have suggested the following minimal menu of questions for summative as well as formative evaluations: "(1) Who are the clients? (2) How does the program serve them? (3) How well does the program serve them? and (4) Under what circumstances in the natural environment does the program achieve those effects?" (p. 27).

As a useful complement to such specific recommendations, several questions about the goals of the evaluation should be considered in formulating the question or questions to be addressed. These include the following: (1) Who are the intended consumers of the evaluation? (2) Can the evaluation question(s) be cast such that the results will be of use to these consumers irrespective of the direction of the findings? (3) What breadth of generality is envisioned for the findings? (4) Can a descriptive (vs. a comparative) evaluation answer the question(s) of interest? (5) If a comparative evaluation is called for, what comparison group or groups (from the standpoint of the aforementioned consumers) might be the most relevant? and (6) What are the implications of the results—good, bad, or indifferent—for the program in question? A final point, or question, warrants special attention because it bears importantly on the ultimate utility of correctional evaluations and because it derives directly from applied behavior analysis: Does the intervention promise social significance and, if so, will the evaluation questions reveal that significance?

Social Validity. Whereas the demonstration of social validity, like other kinds of validity, must be established at the level of evaluation design and data, the concept of social validity must be considered during the formulation of evaluation questions. Conceptually, social validity refers to the degree to which the primary goals of an intervention, assuming they can be achieved, are judged to be of value to people who may be affected by the problem at hand or its proposed remedy (Wolf, 1978; see also discussion by Morris, 1980, in relation to criminal justice). Will society, for example, assign worth to a drug rehabilitation strategy that effectively interrupts its clients' addictive behavior but fails to reduce their rates of theft and assault? Are the wives and children of probationers satisfied with the quality of their family lives "now that dad isn't beating up on anyone anymore?" Does Mary, herself, feel that she is being treated fairly, humanely, and effectively in the group home where she was placed last month? The point is that correctional program designers and evaluators should approach their work sensitively and expansively, with attention to the effects of their efforts on all concerned. (The subject of measuring social validity will be addressed later under the heading "Evaluation Methods.")

Whatever sources of advice are sought, evaluators must bear in mind that the nature and scope of the questions addressed will influence major design choices (e.g., the sample or samples to be studied, the duration of data collection, the kinds of data to be collected, etc.), not to mention the overall costs of the evaluation effort. Evaluation questions can be altered, but such adjustments become increasingly problematic as the process proceeds into the design stage and are very difficult after data collection has begun. About the only thing worse than the discovery that one's evaluation has failed to answer the questions it addressed is the late revelation that one has asked the wrong questions or has cast them poorly, in the first place. Decisions about the questions to which an evaluation will be addressed are second only to key design choices in determining the overall utility of correctional evaluations.

Evaluation Methods: Design and Measurement Choices

The important work of designing a correctional evaluation ensues when a logical and, ideally, theory-based intervention has been constructed, when the parameters of that intervention have been objectively specified, and when a set of relevant and potentially answerable questions concerning its efficacy have been formulated. An evaluation design—and the various methods, measurements, and analysis strategies subsumed under it—is the *plan* for answering those questions. The overall quality of the plan is the overriding determinant of the success of the evaluation enterprise.

The molecular choices and considerations that go into the design of evaluations are almost limitless and whole volumes on the subject abound. The present comments will, therefore, focus on those design-related concepts that have evoked the most persistent debate within the corrections arena and on the methodological choices that have been most commonly blamed for deficiencies in extant evaluations. These include (1) the utility and feasibility of true versus pre- and quasi-experimental evaluation designs; (2) strengthening quasi-experimental designs through process evaluation; and (3) measurement choices in correctional evaluations.

A brief review of the more common pitfalls that effective evaluation designs seek to overcome may prove useful here. Embedded in the unique, formal questions addressed by individual evaluations is the universal query, "Did the intervention have an effect?" If the answer to that question is affirmative, second-order questions about "how much" and "compared to what" become relevant. The first concern, however, is always whether the program accounted for changes in the dependent or impact variables of concern. But even a simple "yes" answer to that basic effect question can prove problematical. The trick for evaluation designers is to ensure that apparent observed effects can be attributed to the correctional intervention and not to alternative, program-unrelated explanations or factors. The degree to which obtained changes (effects) in an evaluation's independent variable(s) can be defensibly attributed to the intervention (the independent manipulation) represent the evaluation's *internal validity,* a concept of core importance here. Unless an evaluation can be established as internally valid, the question of *external validity,* which is concerned with the generalizability of the obtained effects to other populations and environments, is rarely raised.

Campbell and Stanley's (1963) ennumeration of threats to the internal validity of educational research has stood the test of time and can be applied without significant adaptation to correctional evaluation research. Their list of factors that can rival the stated treatment or intervention in explaining obtained research/evaluation effects includes the following: (1) history effects, (2) maturation effects, (3) testing effects, (4) instrumentation or measurement effects, (5) regression effects, (6) effects of subject selection bias, (7) subject mortality effects, and (8) selection-maturation interaction effects. Although all of these factors should be understood and carefully considered prior to mounting any evaluation, three of them—sample selection difficulties, subject maturation, and statistical regression effects—have particularly and recurrently plagued correctional evaluations and will be examined here.

Artifacts

Selection Artifacts. Sample or subject selection and assignment problems tend to arise when an evaluator attempts to capture the impressive experimental control associated with true randomized designs without following the conventional rules of randomized subject assignment, that is, that each participant have an equal probability of being assigned to either (or any) of the treatment, control, or other comparison groups or conditions included in the evaluation (e.g., Blommers & Lindquist, 1960). This is not to imply that evaluators attempt to finesse their designs. Rather, the problem is associated with the practical difficulties of mounting truly randomized studies in correctional settings. We shall return to this point directly.

Maturation Artifacts. Subject maturation refers to any nonprogram effects that might occur naturally with the passage of time during the course of an evaluation. The most troublesome kind of maturation, one most commonly encountered in the evaluation of treatments with juvenile offenders, relates literally to the maturation—the "growing up"—of program subjects or clients. Certain subgroups of delinquents seem to remit spontaneously or "grow out of" their delinquent inclinations (Dinitz & Conrad, 1980, p. 147; and Wolfgang, Figlio, & Sellin, 1972, p. 253). Evaluation designs must permit these effects to be differentiated from real program effects.

Regression Artifacts. Statistical regression (toward the mean) has been called "the most persistent, complex, and insidious of all mistakes [in social research]" (Wolins, 1982, p. 13). It concerns the fact that behavior, like most other events in the universe, tends to unfold in cycles. It presents a general problem for researchers when subjects are selected for study based on extreme scores or values along any selection dimension. It creates a special problem for correctional evaluators because criminal and delinquent activity, however they are measured, logically constitute the dependent variables of many correctional evaluations and are *also* used to identify and select the subjects of such studies. That is, both adults and juveniles tend to come to the attention of the courts (and, thus, to correctional programs) during periods in which their rates of illegal activity may be unusually high. If this rate of illegal activity is designated, in the course of an evaluation employing a simple pre-post experimental design, as the pretreatment rate, posttreatment reduction in this rate (i.e., "improvement") would be expected as a function of the regression effect alone. A thoroughgoing discussion of the regression artifact and its implications for delinquency intervention research has been offered by McCleary, Gordon, McDowall, and Maltz (1979).

Experimental versus Quasi-Experimental Evaluation Designs

Perhaps one of the most empassioned debates in the evaluation literature is that concerned with the utility and feasibility of true, as opposed to pre- and quasi-experimental, designs in the evaluation of human services programs. True experimental designs, also called simple randomized designs and randomized field experiments, are distinguished from other designs by their emphasis on the randomized assignment of subjects to the groups or conditions to be compared in the evaluation. There is little disagreement on two key characteristics of true experimental designs. The first is that randomized experimental designs represent the single most powerful approach to the task of answering questions about molar program effects, impact, and outcomes (e.g., Cohen & McSweeny, 1982; Scriven, 1972). This is because they are best able to isolate actual program effects from the myriad rival, nonprogram artifacts mentioned earlier and ennumerated fully by Campbell and Stanley (1963). Although they cannot guarantee the internal validity of correctional outcome evaluations, true experiments, properly mounted, can maximize that validity. Second, there is also general agreement that randomized designs tend to present special problems and complications when used in human services evaluations and that they are, thus, typically more difficult and expensive to implement than are their less robust counterparts (e.g., Cohen & McSweeny, 1982; Rossi, 1978).

The disagreements, conversely, center on the propriety of exclusive concern with impact (vs. process) variables in correctional research and on the overall practical utility of randomized field studies in human services settings. Regarding the first of these issues, opponents of the true experiment as the only useful design argue that such designs, preoccupied as they often are with impact or outcome variables relating to the deviant client, tend to ignore larger societal factors that may be of equal or more importance in developing and refining programs that are truly responsive to society's needs. Empey (1980, p. 144) has summarized the view of several evaluation critics who have argued in favor of "process-oriented qualitative research" over randomized field evaluations (i.e., Deutscher, 1973; Rossi, 1972; Weiss & Rein, 1970) as follows:

> In programs involving real people, [true] experimental designs may not only be inappropriate but harmful. The reason is that they reinforce the belief that the problems for which corrections are sought lie not within the larger institutional structures of society but within the beliefs, personalities, and characters of aberrant individuals (Deutscher, 1973). In order to avoid reinforcing this inherent bias, therefore, evaluation research should concentrate on the problems of institutional change, and should track inevitable shifts in program implementation. The most justifiable and informative kind of research, therefore, would be that which takes into account the way social institutions, not individuals, adapt to, or resist, remedial programs.

Proponents of the true experiment as an appropriate design for correctional evaluations rejoin that properly conceived randomized evaluations can readily incorporate and elucidate the kinds of process variables that they have been accused of ignoring and that resistance to the stronger designs is, thus, not well founded (Elliott, 1980a).

Concerning the issue of the practical utility of true experimental versus quasi-experimental evaluation designs, Empey (1980, p. 143) has also nicely articulated the posture of those critical of randomized field research:

> [This] group maintains that rigorous methods of experimentation are impractical if not irrelevant (see Adams, 1975; Edwards et al., 1975; and summaries by Boruch, 1976: 160–174; Rossi, 1972:32). Not only are randomized experiments almost impossible to implement in the real world, and are excessively costly and time-consuming, but they have little payoff for administrators and policymakers. Useful evaluations are those which are devoted to improving decisions about programs and their competitors, not the testing of their relative merits. What administrators seek, and what evaluations should provide, is information which will help them make day-to-day decisions within the value contexts of their own choosing.

In addition to these distresses about the practicality of randomized evaluation designs is the frequently raised issue relating to the ethics of the "no-treatment" control group often associated with such designs. Boruch (1976) has countered that this is, at worst, a moot concern given both the availability and the advisability of alternative treatment comparison groups that can be readily substituted for the no-treatment control groups in randomized evaluations. Most applied behavior analysts would readily agree.

There appears, in any case, to be a gradually growing concensus that true experimental designs can be efficacious in many correctional evaluation situations (see discussions by Boruch, McSweeny, & Soderstrom, 1978; Cook & Campbell, 1979). Although the proponents of field experimental evaluations concede that they cannot "guarantee unequivocal evaluation findings and interpretations" (Elliott, 1980a, p. 246) and that quasi-experimental approaches may well be defensible under some circumstances (Campbell & Stanley, 1963; Cook & Campbell, 1979), they forward strong rationales supporting their contention that randomization could be applied to good effect in many more correctional evaluations than are presently attempting it.

Quasi-Experiments, Causation, and Process Evaluation

Whatever the merits of true experiments, perceived practical, ethical, and other restrictions relating to the random assignment of clients have limited their application in criminal justice settings. Far more popular among correctional program evaluators have been quasi-experimental designs, in general, and a subset of these that permit the comparison of nonequivalent groups (Grizzle & Witte, 1980). Such designs attempt to approximate the vigor of true experiments but sidestep the problem of random assignment by studying comparison groups that are not identical but that are as similar as possible to the group to be exposed to the intervention of interest (Campbell & Stanley, 1963; Cook & Campbell, 1979). The concept of process evaluation has emerged as a method of extending and strengthening these designs (Grizzle & Witte, 1980) and of broadening the focus of their inquiry.

Causality. Applied behavior analysis has brought to the field of corrections an abiding interest in the causal relationships between behavior and the stimulus environments in which it occurs (Sidman, 1960). That interest accounts, in part, for the attachment of behavior analysts to another quasi-experimental method, the reversal or counterbalanced (Campbell & Stanley, 1963, p. 50) evaluation design, in which artifactual influences are controlled, or at least minimized, by exposing all clients to all intervention and control conditions. Though not perfect, when properly executed, such designs can lead to powerful inferences about the causal relationship between the independent manipulations of interest and behavioral effects produced by them. Certainly, reversal designs far outstrip correlational analyses in their ability to identify causal relationships between events.

The emphasis in this chapter on process evaluation also relates to the previously mentioned concern with causality. As has been indicated, process evaluations monitor a program's actual implementation and seek to answer questions about the quality of that implementation and the overall content of the program. More important, the data from process evaluations can be used to address questions about observed program impact, that is, about *why* a program apparently worked or failed. In this respect, the choice to incorporate a process evaluation within a larger outcome study opens the door to establish the causal, theoretical linkages recommended in this chapter. (Mahoney, 1978,

p. 661, has offered a useful summary of the scientific requirements for causal inference in evaluation research.) Unfortunately, despite the increasingly forceful call for integrated, impact-process evaluations (Elliott, 1980b; Elliott *et al.*, 1985), such evaluations have been rare in the correctional arena. A notable exception was the Seattle Community Crime Prevention Program reported by Cirel, Evans, McGillis, and Whitcomb (1977) that, as described by Grizzle and Witte (1980, p. 262), addressed not only burglary-rate reductions as a function of the program but also concerned itself with the developmental aspects of the program, program costs, and other operational factors relating the results of the program to the needs of the community.

A Step in the Right Direction. More numerous, to date, have been correctional evaluations addressed primarily or exclusively to process variables. The architects of the behaviorally based TFM undertook numerous, process-oriented evaluations of the model during its formative stage. Although delinquency offense reduction was, and remains, the impact variable of focal interest to this group (and evaluations addressed specifically to this outcome have been conducted, e.g., Jones, Timbers, & Davis, 1982; Kirigin, Braukmann, Atwater, & Wolf, 1982—see discussion by Braukmann & Wolf, Chap. 5, this volume), early studies investigated the degree to which the individual elements or components of the model were able to accomplish their interim objectives. These included evaluations of the effectiveness of the youth motivation system that is the core of the model (Phillips, 1968); the effects of the model's approach to the development of self-government and decision-making skills (Fixsen, Phillips, & Wolf, 1973; Phillips, Phillips, Wolf, & Fixsen, 1973); the teaching procedures aimed at the development of youths' social, academic, and self-care skills (Maloney *et al.*, 1976; Minkin *et al.*, 1976; Werner *et al.*, 1975); the school–home reporting system (Bailey, Wolf, & Phillips, 1970; Kirigin, Phillips, Timbers, Fixsen, & Wolf, 1977); and the effect of specific vocational training procedures (Braukmann, Maloney, Fixsen, Phillips, & Wolf, 1974).

Despite the fact that these related investigations were not incorporated into an integrated process-impact evaluation, they have served to demonstrate the influence that process studies *per se* can have on correctional policy and local program choices. Largely on the basis of this collection of work, over 200 local replications of Teaching-Family treatment programs have been implemented in the United States and other nations.

This observation is not intended to diminish the broad recommendation favoring the combining of process *with* impact evaluations in corrections. In point of fact, neither the questions of causality nor the relation of the specified components of the TFM to an underlying theory could be addressed as part of the previously described effort because the studies were not part of a coordinated impact evaluation. New or developing programs not in a position to mount (or not sufficiently stable to warrant) vigorous impact evaluations probably should, however, consider the implementation of interim process evaluations. The "rules" guiding the conduct of such inquiries are much less well defined, and hence less rigid, than those that have evolved concerning impact or outcome evaluations. They can, thus, be readily adapted to the needs and resources of new programs and can, if they are carefully conceived and responsive to the importance of connecting the program's theoretical underpinnings with its intended impact, serve both to pave the way, and to signal the correct time, for the subsequent formalized evaluation of that impact.

Measurement Choices in Correctional Evaluations

Because this discussion has reiterated the distinction between process and impact evaluations and has emphasized the need for both in correctional evaluations, the considerations surrounding measurement decisions to be reviewed here will concern both kinds of evaluations. Because the two are aimed at somewhat different purposes, they will be addressed separately. Before proceeding to these, however, a general comment on the subject of measurement reliability is in order.

Reliability. Concern with reliability of measurement, a veritable trademark of applied behavior analysis, is a first-order task in all correctional evaluations and requires careful attention in the collection of process as well as impact data. In its broadest sense, reliability refers to the accuracy or veracity of data gathered as part of a research or evaluation effort (Fremouw, McSweeny, Fabry, & Trout, 1982). There are numerous general approaches to the problem of ensuring and demonstrating measurement reliability. One of the most common in the behavioral literature involves the use of redundant or repeated measures, or multiple observers of the behaviors or events of interest. Data so gathered can be analyzed in various ways to produce an index or coefficient of reliability (e.g., see Kent & Foster, 1977). Such devices, however, are no substitute for common sense in the choice of evaluation measures as well as care and precision in their use. Like validity, reliability can never be absolutely established. As Gottfredson and Gottfredson (1980) have observed, "Data are merely *relatively* accurate, *relatively* reliable, and *relatively* valid" (p. 98).

Client and Nonclient Process Measures. Unlike correctional impact research, whose focus is invariably on some measure of the frequency or seriousness of delinquent or criminal activity, the question of what to measure as part of interim or process evaluations can be approached more expansively. This is due only partly to the previously mentioned fact that the body of conventional wisdom surrounding process evaluations is in general less well refined than are the rules and traditions relating to impact studies. The ambiguity—or, put more positively, the flexibility—associated with process measures stems more directly from the fact that they derive from the specific parameters of the program of interest, the unique environment in which it is offered, and the tenets of the theory upon which the program is based. What this means in practice is that process variables and measures will rarely be the same for any two programs (unless, of course, one is intended as a direct replication of the other). Although process measures are often concerned with interim effects of the program on client behaviors thought to be related to delinquent or criminal activities, they are also concerned with the operational aspects of the program and should, ideally, produce a convincing assessment of the degree to which individual program components were implemented (Elliott, 1980a, p. 238). Finally, process evaluation measures may be addressed to what Shinn (1982) has described as the "social climate or personality" of the program and its effects as perceived both by its staff and its clients—what was referred to earlier as the social validity or significance of correctional interventions.

The measurement of interim program effects on the behavior and performance of clients has, to some extent, been guided by a melding of the interests and goals of professionals from two related but distinct orientations—clinical psychology and psychometry on the one hand, and applied behavior analysis on the other. Traditional clinicians have brought to the enterprise the broad-based and highly refined science of psychometric testing and measurement. For their part, the behaviorists have brought a healthy and abiding skepticism about the place and importance of attitudes (and other psychological "attributes") in correctional measurement and a still new but accumulating wisdom about how the measurement of client change might be made more objective and, thus, more useful (i.e., the developing technology of behavior assessment; see Ciminero, Calhoun, & Adams, 1977). This confluence of perspectives has produced an interesting amalgam of thought and discourse concerning which client variables should be of concern in correctional interventions and how they might best be assessed. A well-developed product of this alliance is the behavior checklist that combines the ease and convenience of the paper-and-pencil format with the objectivity and operationalization sought by the applied behavior analysts. A thoroughgoing description of the use of one such instrument, the Child Behavior Checklist, in the context of delinquency intervention has been offered by Achenbach (1982).

Process measurement of nonclient factors is usually concerned with implementation effectiveness questions. Such questions are dictated by the specifics of the intervention under study but are often answered via an assessment of staff activities and performance. Interim staff evaluations are often able to determine both whether (Patton, 1978) and how well (Daly, Wineman, Daly, & Luger, 1982) a correctional intervention has been mounted. In addition to the evaluation of program staff, the utility of program consumer evaluations has been emphasized by the proponents of behaviorally oriented correctional interventions. Consumers of programs using the TFM are, for example, formally polled at least once each year to assess their level of satisfaction with both the performance of the treatment staff and with the effectiveness of the individual program components in meeting their varied needs. Program consumers include all individuals in the community where the program is operated who have direct contact with, or interest in, the program itself or the youthful clients it serves. Consumer groups include the clients themselves, the parents or guardians of the youth, referral-agency personnel who recommended their placement, court officials, school personnel, board of directors members, and others. Consumer evaluation of this sort represents a direct assessment of the social validity of the intervention involved (Morris, 1980; Wolf, 1978). Descriptions of the method of this source of process evaluation data have been offered by Daly *et al.* (1982) and Howard (1982).

Measuring Impact. A substantially different set of considerations confronts the program evaluator faced with the choice of correctional impact measures. On the one hand, the range of traditionally acceptable measures of criminal behaviors and delinquency rates has been very narrow, usually including only recidivism, other official records or documentation of penetration into the justice system and, more recently, self-reports of criminal or delinquent activities. On the other hand, substantial criticism has been leveled at the correctional evaluation field for failing to adopt or construct—even from this very modest array of historically acceptable possibilities—sufficiently comparable methods of measurement to allow for systematic program replications or the purposive construction of theoretical generalizations (Elliott, 1980a,b). It may be instructive to review the relative merits and shortcomings of the three categories of impact measures and, against that background, return to the issue of interevaluation comparability.

Recidivism, the return of a previously adjudicated individual to the attention or custody of the court (or official documentation thereof), has been by far the most widely applied measure of correctional program impact, especially among those serving adult criminals. The most plausible, if not most compelling, explanation for the attractiveness of officially documented recidivism as an impact measure rests with its presumed objectivity, especially by contrast with self-report measures (Hawkins, Cassidy, Light, & Miller, 1977). Recidivism data are thought to be less prone to reflect evaluator biases and are presumably quantifiable—a characteristic that has enjoyed enduring appeal among social scientists. The primary criticisms of recidivism as an impact measure (and they have been voiced with increasing regularity) are that it lacks face validity and that it tends to be insensitive to real changes in criminal and delinquent behaviors.

This concern with validity relates to the judgment by many critics that recidivism is more a measure of the response of the justice system to instances of criminal activity than it is of the criminal activity itself (e.g., see Empey, 1978). The insensitivity issue reflects both the validity problem and a set of complications inherent in the nature of criminal or delinquent acts, namely that they tend to be unpredictable, of generally low frequency, and surreptitious. As Elliott (1980a) has concluded concerning both shortcomings:

> Given that official actions involve a number of factors in addition to delinquent behavior and reflect only a small fraction of delinquent acts committed, it is apparent that recidivism is neither a very pure nor sensitive measure of delinquent behavior. (p. 253)

Official records and documents can also be used with little or no emphasis on recidivism *per se* as the event of interest. A particularly systematic method of constructing youth offense histories and institutional admissions from court and police records has been reported by Kirigin *et al.* (1982) and described in detail in an unpublished manual (Kirigin, Fixsen, Phillips, & Wolf, 1974). To improve the sensitivity of this outcome measure, these researchers considered alleged offenses, whether or not formal action was taken in response to them. Although such devices can serve to attenuate the problems mentioned before in connection with recidivism, these problems are inherent in any outcome measure that depends on official documents and records as its source of data and cannot be eliminated entirely. The persisting problem as was convincingly demonstrated by Wolfgang *et al.,* (1972) is that the actual amount and frequency of illegal behavior is much greater than reported in official records.

In response to this widely acknowledged deficiency of official documentation as a means of assessing correctional outcomes, Short and Nye (1958) introduced the concept of self-reported delinquency. The concept enjoyed almost instant appeal, and early efforts to validate self-reports against polygraph results (Clark & Tifft, 1966) and informant reports (Gold, 1970) contributed to its gathering currency. The most frequently recurring criticism of the technique was that subjects were differentially likely to admit less serious offenses and that self-report measures thus consistently underestimated more serious crimes (e.g., Nettler, 1978; Reiss, 1975). Despite this criticism and the general recognition that even self-report techniques would never accurately capture all instances of actual delinquency (Hawkins *et al.,* 1977), data from several sources support the conclusion that self-report methods offer a better estimate of criminal and delinquent behaviors than do official records (e.g., Clark & Tifft, 1966; Farrington, 1973; Gold, 1970). Owing to this growing concensus, Hirschi, Hindelang, and Weis (1980) have observed that "today, self-report procedures have replaced police and court records as the most frequently used method of measuring delinquency" (p. 474).

But the problem of a lack of standard or comparable impact measures for use among different evaluations remains. Even with the increasing popularity of the self-report, no standardized self-report instrument is available (Hirschi *et al.,* 1980). Elliott (1980a) has argued that the absence of "explicit theoretical rationales" and a general "atheoretical orientation" within the correctional evaluation arena are at the core of the impact measurement problem and that these same deficiencies likely explain the field's earlier reliance on recidivism as *the* unitary "criterion variable for program success" (p. 253). The abiding absence of comparability among impact measures, Elliott (1980b) has observed in a different context, is operationally the result of few attempts to replicate earlier evaluations and the "widespread practice of researchers to develop their own unique measures of key variables" (p. 508). As a prompt in the direction of better interevaluation comparability, Elliott (1980b) has provided a comprehensive catalog of theoretically relevant impact measures developed in prior research for use by those planning new studies (pp. 516–541).

Dissemination of Correctional Evaluation Results

Any correctional evaluation worth doing and doing properly is worth disseminating. As should be clear by now, the process of constructing and carrying out a thoughtful correctional intervention evaluation, especially one that is summative and involves specific comparisons, is arduous and invariably time consuming. Such work can require years, not to mention blood, sweat, and tears by the liter. But, for all the effort, even the best evaluations accomplish nothing in and of themselves. No criminal nor delinquent youth was ever directly benefited by the evaluation of an intervention to which he or she was exposed, just as students are not taught by tests. Evaluations, like tests, are intended to answer questions. The benefit of evaluations—and this benefit can only be realized through dissemination—occurs when the answers to those questions can be effectively applied in subsequent interventions with subsequent clients.

Generality

Generality of findings, the ability of an intervention to produce similar results in settings and with populations other than those involved in its evaluation, is sometimes discussed as if it were a characteristic of (or absent from) the results of an evaluation *per se*. In fact, generality can be assessed only after the results of an intervention have been disseminated and, even then, only if the methods of the intervention have been adequately described. This is not to say that generality is accidental. On the contrary, as pointed out by Morris (1980), applied behavior analysts can and should plan for generality in constructing correctional interventions; they should not simply assume or expect it.

Replication

It is through the vehicle of replication that the generality of a particular correctional remedy is determined. And the replication of an intervention, be it direct or systematic, can only occur if that intervention is formally and thoroughly described and shared with others to whom the intervention might prove useful.

SUMMARY

This chapter has attempted to provide an introduction to program evaluation in crime and delinquency via a figurative walk through the decision-making process that typically attends the conception and conduct of such evaluations. Special attention has been given to those stages in the correctional evaluation process that have been significantly influenced by the premises and tactics of applied behavior analysis. Many of these (e.g., functional analysis, social validity, etc.) are characteristic of interventions themselves as well as of evaluations of those interventions and have been treated from different perspectives in other parts of this text.

Correctional evaluation has been depicted here as a method or tool for answering questions about the efficacy of treatment procedures in correctional settings. It is a potentially powerful tool but one that has produced less than totally satisfying results to date. The problem is that the answers to questions asked by correctional evaluators have tended to be either disappointing (the intervention did not work or its effects were not durable) or equivocal and indefinitive (the evaluation was flawed). As has been recently observed by Klein and Teilmann (1980, p. 443), society is increasingly demanding more "bang" for its correctional "buck." Program evaluators and innovators would do well to heed this demand.

The concept and application of process evaluation has been revisited, perhaps painfully often, throughout this chapter because process may represent the key, heretofore largely missing, to correctional evaluations that reveal not only whether an effect was observed but why the intervention worked or failed. Theoretical considerations have been reviewed because theory constitutes the basis of process evaluation.

Finally, encouragement has been offered for disseminating the results of all responsible evaluation efforts and, implicitly, for consuming the evaluation products of colleagues actively but critically. Science is, after all, inherently a team enterprise.

REFERENCES

Achenbach, T. M. (1982). A normative-descriptive approach to assessment of youth behavior. In J. McSweeny, W. J. Fremouw, & R. P. Hawkins (Eds.), *Practical program evaluation in youth treatment* (pp. 96–115). Springfield, IL: Charles C Thomas.

Adams, S. (1975). *Evaluative research in corrections: A practical guide.* Washington, DC: U.S. Government Printing Office.

Akers, R. L. (1977). *Deviant behavior: A social learning perspective.* Belmont, CA: Wadsworth.

Baer, D. M., Wolf, M. M., & Risley, T. R. (1968). Some current dimensions of applied behavior analysis. *Journal of Applied Behavior Analysis, 1,* 91–97.

Bailey, J. S., Wolf, M. M., & Phillips, E. L. (1970). Home-based reinforcement and the modification of predelinquents' classroom behavior. *Journal of Applied Behavior Analysis, 3,* 223–233.

Bandura, A. (1969). *Principles of behavior modification.* New York: Holt, Rinehart & Winston.

Blommers, P., & Lindquist, E. F. (1960). *Elementary statistical methods in psychology and education.* Boston: Houghton Mifflin.

Boruch, R. F. (1976). On common contentions about randomized field experiments. In G. V. Glass (Ed.), *Evaluation studies review annual* (Vol. 1, pp. 158–194). Beverly Hills: Sage.

Boruch, R. F., McSweeny, A. J., & Soderstrom, E. J. (1978). Randomized field experiments in program development and evaluation: An illustrative bibliography. *Evaluation Quarterly, 2,* 655.

Braukmann, C. J., Maloney, D. M., Fixsen, D. L., Phillips, E. L., Wolf, M. M. (1974). Analysis of a selection interview training package. *Criminal Justice and Behavior, 1,* 30–42.

Braukmann, C. J., Fixsen, D. L., Phillips, E. L., & Wolf, M. M. (1975). Behavioral approaches to treatment in the crime and delinquency field. *Criminology, 13,* 299–231.

Burchard, J. D., & Harig, P. T. (1976). Behavior modification and juvenile delinquency. In H. Leitenberg (Ed.), *Handbook of behavior modification and behavior therapy* (pp. 405–452). Englewood Cliffs, NJ: Prentice-Hall.

Campbell, D. T., & Stanley, J. C. (1963). *Experimental and quasi-experimental designs for research.* Chicago: Rand McNally.

Ciminero, A. R., Calhoun, R. S., & Adams, H. E. (Eds.). (1977). *Handbook of behavioral assessment.* New York: Wiley.

Cirel, P., Evans, P., McGillis, D., & Whitcomb, D. (1977). *Community crime prevention: An exemplary project.* Washington, DC: National Institute of Justice.

Clark, J. P., & Tifft, L. L. (1966). Polygraph and interview validation of self-reported delinquent behavior. *American Sociological Review, 31,* 516–523.

Cloward, R., & Ohlin, L. E. (1960). *Delinquency and opportunity: A theory of delinquent gangs.* Glencoe, IL: Free Press.

Cohen, S. H., & McSweeny, J. (1982). Designs for the evaluation of youth treatment programs. In J. McSweeny, W. J. Fremouw, & R. P. Hawkins (Eds.), *Practical program evaluation in youth treatment* (pp. 61–95). Springfield, IL: Charles C Thomas.

Cook, T. D., & Campbell, D. T. (1979). *Quasi-experimentation: Design and analysis issues for field settings.* Chicago: Rand McNally.

Cronbach, L. J. (1980). *Toward reform of program evaluation.* San Francisco: Jossey-Bass.

Daly, P. D., Wineman, J. H., Daly, D. L., & Luger, R. (1982). Evaluation of staff performance. In J. McSweeny, W. J. Freemouw, & R. P. Hawkins (Eds.), *Practical program evaluation in youth treatment* (pp. 144–163). Springfield, IL: Charles C Thomas.

Davidson, W. S., II, & Seidman, E. (1974). Studies of behavior modification and juvenile delinquency: A review, methodological critique, and social perspective. *Psychological Bulletin, 81,* 998–1011.

Deutscher, I. (1973). Public issues or private troubles: Is evaluation research sociological? *Sociological Focus, 9,* 231–237.

Dinitz, S., & Conrad, J. P. (1980). The dangerous two percent. In D. Shichor & D. H. Kelly (Eds.), *Critical issues in juvenile delinquency* (pp. 139–155). Lexington, MA: D. C. Heath.

Edwards, W., Guttentag, M., & Snapper, K. (1975). A decision-theoretic approach to evaluation research. In E. L. Struening & M. Guttentag (Eds.), *Handbook of evaluation research* (Vol. 1, pp. 139–182). Beverly Hills: Sage.

Elliott, D. S. (1980a). Recurring issues in the evaluation of delinquency prevention and treatment programs. In D. Schichor & D. H. Kelly (Eds.), *Critical issues in juvenile delinquency* (pp. 237–261). Lexington, MA: D. C. Heath.

Elliott, D. S. (1980b). A repertoire of impact measures. In M. W. Klein & K. S. Teilmann (Eds.), *Handbook of criminal justice evaluation* (pp. 507–544). Beverly Hills: Sage.

Elliott, D. S., & Voss, H. (1974). *Delinquency and dropout.* Lexington, MA: D. C. Heath.

Elliott, D. S., Ageton, S. S., & Canter, R. J. (1979). An integrated theoretical perspective on delinquent behavior. *Journal of Research in Crime and Delinquency, 16,* 3–27.

Elliott, D. S., Huizinga, D., & Ageton, S. S. (1985). *Explaining delinquency and drug use.* Beverly Hills: Sage.

Emery, R. E., & Marholin, D., II. (1977). An applied behavior analysis of delinquency: The irrelevancy of relevant behavior. *American Psychologist, 32,* 860–873.

Empey, L. T. (1978). *American delinquency: Its meaning and construction.* Homewood, IL: The Dorsey Press.

Empey, L. T. (1980). Field experimentation in criminal justice: Rationale and design. In M. W. Klein & K. S. Teilmann (Eds.), *Handbook of criminal justice evaluation* (pp. 143–176). Beverly Hills: Sage.

Empey, L. T., & Lubeck, S. G. (1971). *Explaining delinquency: Construction, test, and reformulation of a sociological theory.* Lexington, MA: D. C. Heath.

Farrington, D. P. (1973). Self-reports of deviant behavior predictive and stable. *Journal of Civil Law, Criminology and Police Science, 64,* 99–110.

Fitz-Gibbon, C. T., & Morris, L. L. (1978). *How to design a program evaluation.* Beverly Hills: Sage.

Fixsen, D. L., Phillips, E. L., & Wolf, M. M. (1973). Achievement Place: Experiments in self-government with pre-delinquents. *Journal of Applied Behavior Analysis, 6,* 31–47.

Fremouw, W. J., McSweeny, A. J., Fabry, B. D., & Trout, B. A. (1982). Evaluation of short-term outcomes. In A. J. McSweeny, W. J. Freemouw, & R. P. Hawkins (Eds.), *Practical program evaluation in youth treatment* (pp. 164–202). Springfield, IL: Charles C Thomas.

Glaser, D. (1977). Concern with theory in correctional evaluation research. *Crime and Delinquency, 23,* 173–179.

Glaser, D. (1980). The interplay of theory, issues, policy and data in criminal justice evaluations.

In M. W. Klein & K. S. Teilmann (Eds.), *Handbook of criminal justice evaluation* (pp. 123–142). Beverly Hills: Sage.

Gold, M. (1970). *Delinquent behavior in an American city*. Belmont, CA: Wadsworth.

Gottfredson, D. M., & Gottfredson, M. R. (1980). Data for criminal justice evaluation: Some resources and pitfalls. In M. W. Klein & Teilmann (Eds.), *Handbook of criminal justice evaluation* (pp. 97–118). Beverly Hills: Sage.

Grizzle, G. A., & Witte, A. D. (1980). Criminal justice evaluation techniques: Methods other than random assignment. In M. W. Klein & K. S. Teilmann (Eds.), *Handbook of criminal justice evaluation* (pp. 259–302). Beverly Hills: Sage.

Hawkins, J. D., Cassidy, C. H., Light, N. B., & Miller, C. A. (1977). Interpreting official records as indicators of recidivism in evaluating delinquency prevention programs. *Criminology, 3,* 397–422.

Hawkins, R. P., & Meadowcroft, P. (1983). *Practical program evaluation in a family-based treatment program for disturbing and disturbed youngsters*. Unpublished manuscript, Pressley Ridge School, Pittsburgh, PA.

Hawkins, R. P., Fremouw, W. J., & Reitz, A. L. (1982). A model useful in designing or describing evaluations of planned interventions in mental health. In J. McSweeny, W. J. Freemouw, & R. P. Hawkins (Eds.), *Practical program evaluation in youth treatment* (pp. 24–48). Springfield, IL: Charles C Thomas.

Hawkins, R. P., Meadowcroft, P., Trout, B. A., & Luster, W. C. (1985). Foster family-based treatment. *Journal of Clinical Child Psychology, 14,* 220–228.

Hirschi, T. (1969). *Causes of delinquency*. Berkeley: University of California Press.

Hirschi, T., Hindelang, M. J., & Weis, J. G. (1980). The status of self-report measures. In M. W. Klein & K. S. Teilmann (Eds.), *Handbook of criminal justice evaluation* (pp. 473–488). Beverly Hills: Sage.

Holland, J. G., & Skinner, B. F. (1961). *The analysis of behavior*. New York: McGraw-Hill.

Howard, J. R. (1982). Consumer evaluation of programs for disturbing youth. In J. McSweeny, W. J. Fremouw, & R. P. Hawkins (Eds.), *Practical program evaluation in youth treatment* (pp. 292–312). Springfield, IL: Charles C Thomas.

Jones, R. J. (in preparation). *Program evaluation in foster family treatment*. Morganton, NC: BIABH Study Center.

Jones, R. J., & Timbers, G. T. (1985, October). *Foster family treatment: Expanding the concept of professional parenting*. Paper presented at the 8th annual conference of the National Teaching-Family Association, Houston.

Jones, R. J., Timbers, G. D., & Davis, J. L. (1979). Assessing the effects of group home intervention with juvenile delinquents. *Appalachian State University Papers and Reports, 1,* 1–12.

Jones, R. J., Timbers, G. D., & Davis, J. L. (1982). *Evaluation of group homes for delinquent youth* (Final report). Washington, DC: National Institute of Mental Health, Center for Studies of Crime and Delinquency.

Jones, R. R. (1982). Using theory and precedent to design and implement follow-up evaluations. In J. McSweeny, W. J. Fremouw, & R. P. Hawkins (Eds.), *Practical program evaluation in youth treatment* (pp. 230–251). Springfield, IL: Charles C Thomas.

Kent, R. N., & Foster, S. L. (1977). Direct observational procedures: Methodological issues in naturalistic settings. In A. R. Ciminaro, R. S. Calhoun, & H. E. Adams (Eds.). *Handbook of behavioral assessment* (pp. 279–328). New York: Wiley.

Kirigin, K. A., Fixsen, D. L., Phillips, E. L., & Wolf, M. M. (1974). *An evaluation manual for collecting outcome information on youths in trouble*. Unpublished manuscript, University of Kansas.

Kirigin, K. A., Phillips, E. L., Timbers, G. D., Fixsen, D. L., & Wolf, M. M. (1977). Achievement Place: The modification of academic behavior problems of youths in a group home setting. In B. Etzel, J. M. LeBlanc, & D. M. Baer (Eds.), *New developments in behavioral research: Theory, method, and application* (pp. 473–487). Hillsdale, NJ: Lawrence Erlbaum Associates.

Kirigin, K. A., Braukmann, C. J., Atwater, J. D., & Wolf, M. M. (1982). An evaluation of Teaching-Family (Achievement Place) group homes for juvenile offenders. *Journal of Applied Behavior Analysis, 15,* 1–16.

Klein, M. W., & Teilmann, K. S. (1980). On the measurement of outcome. In M. W. Klein & K. S. Teilmann (Eds.), *Handbook of criminal justice evaluation* (pp. 443–445). Beverly Hills: Sage.

Lipton, D., Martinson, R., & Wilks, J. (1975). *The effectiveness of correctional treatment.* New York: Praeger.

Mahoney, M. (1978). Experimental methods and outcome evaluation. *Journal of Consulting and Clinical Psychology, 46,* 660–672.

Maloney, D. M., Harper, T. M., Braukmann, C. J., Fixsen, D. L., Phillips, E. L., & Wolf, M. M. (1976). Teaching conversation-related skills to predelinquent girls. *Journal of Applied Behavior Analysis, 9,* 371.

Martinson, R. (1974). What works? Questions and answers about prison reform. *The Public Interest, 35,* 22–54.

McCleary, R., Gordon, A. C., McDowall, D., & Maltz, M. D. (1979). How a regression artifact can make any delinquency intervention program look effective. In L. Sechrest, S. G. West, M. A. Phillips, R. Redner, & C. W. Yeaton (Eds.), *Evaluation studies review annual* (Vol. 4, pp. 626–652). Beverly Hills: Sage.

McCord, J. (1978). A thirty-year follow-up of treatment effects. *American Psychologist, 33,* 284–289.

McSweeny, J., Fremouw, W. J., & Hawkins, R. P. (1982). Program evaluation in youth treatment: An introduction. In J. McSweeny, W. J. Fremouw, & R. P. Hawkins (Eds.), *Practical program evaluation in youth treatment* (pp. 3–10). Springfield, IL: Charles C Thomas.

Merton, R. K. (1957). *Social theory and social structure.* Glencoe, IL: Free Press.

Milan, M. A., & McKee, J. M. (1974). Behavior modification: Principles and applications in corrections. In D. Glaser (Ed.), *Handbook of criminology* (pp. 745–776). Chicago: Rand McNally.

Minkin, N., Braukmann, C. J., Minkin, B. L., Timbers, G. D., Timbers, B. J., Fixsen, D. L., Phillips, E. L., & Wolf, M. M. (1976). The social validation and training of conversational skills. *Journal of Applied Behavior Analysis, 9,* 127–139.

Morris, E. K. (1980). Applied behavior analysis for criminal justice practice. *Criminal Justice and Behavior, 7,* 131–145.

Nettler, G. (1978). *Explaining crime.* New York: McGraw-Hill.

Palmer, T. (1975). Martinson revisited. *Journal of Research in Crime and Delinquency, 12,* 133–152.

Patterson, G. R. (1986). Performance models for antisocial boys. *American Psychologist, 41,* 432–444.

Patterson, G. R., & Dishion, T. J. (1985). Contribution of families and peers to adolescent delinquency. *Criminology, 23,* 63–79.

Patton, M. Q. (1978). *Utilization-focused evaluation.* Beveral Hills: Sage.

Phillips, E. L. (1968). Achievement Place: Token reinforcement procedures in a home-style rehabilitation setting for "pre-delinquent" boys. *Journal of Applied Behaviors Analysis, 1,* 213–223.

Phillips, E. L., Phillips, E. A., Fixsen, D. L., & Wolf, M. M. (1971). Achievement Place: Modification of the behaviors of pre-delinquent boys within a token economy. *Journal of Applied Behavior Analysis, 4,* 45–59.

Phillips, E. L., Phillips, E. A., Wolf, M. M., & Fixsen, D. L. (1973). Achievement Place: Development of the elected manager system. *Journal of Applied Behavior Analysis, 6,* 541–561.

Powers, E., & Witmer, H. (1951). *An experiment in the prevention of delinquency: The Cambridge-Somerville youth study.* New York: Columbia University Press.

Quay, H. C. (1977). The three faces of evaluation: What can be expected to work. *Criminal Justice and Behavior, 4,* 341–354.

Reiss, A. J. (1975). Inappropriate theories and inadequate measures as policy plaques: Self-reported delinquency and the law. In N. J. Demerath, III, O. Larsen, & K. F. Schuessler (Eds.), *Social policy and sociology* (pp. 211–222). New York: Academic Press.

Romig, D. A. (1978). *Justice for our children: An examination of juvenile delinquent rehabilitation programs.* Lexington, MA: Lexington Books, D. C. Heath.

Rosenthal, B. (1966). *Experimenter effects in behavioral research.* New York: Appleton-Century-Crofts.

Rossi, P. H. (1972). Testing for success and failure in social action. In P. H. Rossi & W. Williams (Eds.), *Evaluating social programs: Theory, practice, and politics* (pp. 15–58). New York: Seminar Press.

Rossi, P. H. (1978). Issues in the evaluation of human services delivery. *Evaluation Quarterly, 2,* 573–599.

Scriven, M. (1972). The methodology of evaluation. In C. H. Weiss (Ed.), *Evaluating action programs: Readings in social action and education* (pp. 123–136). Boston: Allyn & Bacon.

Sidman, M. (1960). *Tactics of scientific research: Evaluating experimental data in psychology.* New York: Basic Books.

Shinn, M. (1982). Assessing program characteristics and social climate. In J. McSweeny, W. J. Fremouw, & R. P. Hawkins (Eds.), *Practical program evaluation in youth treatment* (pp. 116–143). Springfield, IL: Charles C Thomas.

Short, J. F., & Nye, R. I. (1958). Extent of unrecorded juvenile delinquency: Tentative conclusions. *Journal of Criminal Law and Criminality, 49,* 296–302.

Skinner, B. F. (1953). *Science and human behavior.* New York: Macmillan.

Struening, E. L., & Guttentag, M. (1975). *Handbook of evaluation research.* Beverly Hills: Sage.

Weiss, R. S., & Rein, M. (1970). The evaluation of broad-aim programs: Difficulties in experimental design and an alternative. *Administrative Science Quarterly, 15,* 97–109.

Werner, J. S., Minkin, N., Minkin, B. L., Fixsen, D. L., Phillips, E. L., & Wolf, M. M. (1975). Intervention package: Analysis to prepare delinquents for encounters with police officers. *Criminal Justice and Behavior, 2,* 55–83.

Wolf, M. M. (1978). Social validity: The case for subjective measurement. *Journal of Applied Behavior Analysis, 11,* 203–214.

Wolf, M. M., Phillips, E. L., & Fixsen, D. L. (1972). The teaching-family: A new model for the treatment of deviant child behavior in the community. In S. W. Bijou & E. L. Ribes-Inesta (Eds.), *Behavior modification: Issues and extensions* (pp. 51–62). New York: Academic Press.

Wolfgang, M. E., Figlio, R. M., & Sellin, T. (1972). *Delinquency in a birth cohort,* Chicago: University of Chicago Press.

Wolins, L. (1982). *Research mistakes in the social and behavioral sciences.* Ames: Iowa State University Press.

V

ALTERNATIVE THEORETICAL CONCEPTUALIZATIONS

17

A Sociological Theory of Crime and Delinquency

Social Learning Theory

MARVIN D. KROHN, JAMES L. MASSEY, AND
WILLIAM F. SKINNER

The sociological study of crime and delinquency has focused either on the social structural factors (e.g., poverty and social disorganization) believed to generate such behavior or on the arenas (e.g., family, school, and peer groups) in which socialization to conventional or criminal values and behavior are affected. Both approaches explicitly or implicitly recognize that some form of learning takes place. For the most part, however, these approaches have not explicated the social process nor the behavioral mechanisms by which criminal behavior is produced. A notable exception is the social learning theory first proposed by Burgess and Akers (1966a) and elaborated upon by Akers (1973, 1977). The theory was originally called the "differential association-reinforcement theory" to acknowledge the two traditions that were melded to form the revision. Burgess and Akers employed the principles and vocabulary of operant conditioning to specify the learning process alluded to in Edwin Sutherland's influential theory of differential association.

In this chapter, we will review the development and current state of the theory. In so doing, we will examine the theory's relevance to other sociological perspectives on crime, the indirect and direct research evidence for the theory, and the criticisms of the theory. We will conclude the essay with some suggestions for future theoretical development and recent results from research designed to pursue some of those suggestions.

DEVELOPMENT AND STATEMENT OF SOCIAL LEARNING THEORY

Social learning theory is primarily a mixture of two intellectual traditions: the theory of differential association (Sutherland, 1947) and the princi-

Marvin D. Krohn • Department of Sociology, State University of New York, Albany, New York 12222   **James L. Massey** • Department of Sociology, University of Georgia, Athens, Georgia 30602.   **William F. Skinner** • Department of Sociology, University of Kentucky, Lexington, Kentucky 40506.

ples of operant conditioning (Skinner, 1938). Indeed, Akers forcefully stated that his intention was to revise differential association theory, not compete with or supplant it (Akers, Krohn, Lanza-Kaduce, & Radosevich, 1979; Lanza-Kaduce, Akers, Krohn, & Radosevich, 1982). We will therefore briefly summarize the differential association perspective before explicating sociological social learning theory.

Differential Association Theory

Differential association theory is perhaps the most widely known and influential perspective in criminology. Sutherland formulated his ideas about crime at a time (1924) when the dominant paradigm in criminology viewed criminal behavior as a result of some abnormality in the biological and/or psychological makeup of the individual criminal. Sutherland was adamant in his criticism of this view, stating that "many criminals are quite healthy and free from physical defects; many non-criminals are extremely defective from the physical point of view" (1924, p. 80). His alternative was to suggest that both criminal and conventional behavior are learned in association with significant others. Specifically, criminal behavior was a function of an excess of learned definitions favorable to the violation of the law over definitions unfavorable to the violation of law. By "definitions," Sutherland meant the normative evaluations about behaving in a particular manner a person has or makes in a social situation. Sutherland recognized that not all associations with patterns of behavior were equally effective in transmitting definitions. He identified the variables of frequency, priority, duration, and intensity of associations as contingencies in the learning process.

It is at this point that Sutherland's depiction of the learning process stopped. One of the statements included in the formal presentation of the theory asserted that the process of learning criminal behavior by association with criminal and anticriminal patterns involved all the mechanisms that are involved in any other learning (Sutherland & Cressey, 1974, p. 76). Those mechanisms, however, were never specified.

Primarily for this reason, the theory was criticized for being incomplete and difficult to test (Cressey, 1960; Glaser, 1956; Short, 1960). Burgess and Akers (1966a) advocated the incorporation of principles developed in behavioral psychology in order to specify the learning process to which Sutherland only alluded. By so doing, they hoped to ground the theory of differential association in a body of concepts that had established empirical referents and, thereby, produce a more testable theory.

Sociological Social Learning Theory and Criminal Behavior

The proposition that principles identified in operant conditioning could be useful in explaining social behavior was forcefully advanced by George C. Homans (1961). The groundwork laid by Homans resulted in the generation of theoretical approaches that incorporated modern behaviorism into sociological theory (e.g., social exchange and equity theory). Among these adoptions were theories to explain criminal behavior.

C. R. Jeffery (1965) was the first to suggest that modern learning theory could be used to reformulate differential association theory in order to place it in a form that was empirically testable. As Jeffery later asserted, however, his attempt did not serve the purpose of incorporating operant principles within a sociological perspective, but rather he argued that "learning theory belongs to psychology not sociology" (1980, p. 131). Jeffery outlined the principles of operant conditioning, culminating in what he called a theory of differential reinforcement:

> The theory of differential reinforcement states that a criminal act occurs in an environment in which in the past the actor has been reinforced for behaving in this manner and the aversive consequences to the behavior have been of such a nature that they do not control or prevent the response. (p. 295)

In essence, the preceding is simply a restatement of Thorndike's law of effect.

Burgess and Akers (1966a) responded to Jeffery's attempt with a more systematic and ambitious approach of directly incorporating operant principles into a restatement of Sutherland's theory. This resulted in a set of seven propositions constituting their differential association-reinforcement theory. Akers (1973, 1977) further elaborated on the theory and made minor revisions in the seven propositions (Table 1). Because the formal statement of the theory represented by these propositions does not convey the full meaning and implications of the theory, we will highlight some aspects of the theory that serve

Table 1. A Differential Association-Reinforcement Theory of Deviant Behavior

1. Deviant behavior is learned according to the principles of operant conditioning
2. Deviant behavior is learned both in nonsocial situations that are reinforcing or discriminating and through that social interaction in which the behavior of other persons is reinforcing or discriminating for such behavior
3. The principal part of the learning of deviant behavior occurs in those groups which comprise or control the individual's major source of reinforcements
4. The learning of deviant behavior, including specific techniques, attitudes and avoidance procedures, is a function of the effective and available reinforcers and the existing reinforcement contingencies
5. The specific class of behavior learned and its frequency of occurrence are a function of the effective and available reinforcers, and the deviant or nondeviant direction of the norms, and definitions which in the past have accompanied the reinforcement
6. The probability that a person will commit deviant behavior is increased in the presence of normative statements, definitions, and verbalizations which, in the process of differential reinforcement of such behavior over conforming behavior, have acquired discriminative value'
7. The strength of deviant behavior is a direct function of the amount, frequency, and probability of its reinforcement; the modalities of association with deviant patterns are important insofar as they affect the source, amount, and scheduling of reinforcement

Note. From *Deviant Behavior: A Social Learning Approach* (2nd ed., pp. 42–43) by R. L. Aicens, 1977, Belmont, CA: Wadsworth Publishing Company. Copyright 1982 by Wadsworth Publishing Company. Reprinted by permission.

to differentiate it from other learning approaches (e.g., Jeffery, 1965; Jessor & Jessor, 1977).

The theory is clearly predicated on operant principles and the meaning of the concepts (e.g., reinforcement and discriminative stimulus) are consistent with the way in which they are standardly defined (see Chapter 2, by Morris, Higgins, Bickel, & Braukmann, this volume) and need no explication here. For our purposes, it would be more fruitful to concentrate on Statements 2, 3, 5, and 6.

Statements 2 and 3 combine to present the position that, although learning takes place in nonsocial situations. the primary part of learning occurs through social interaction with the groups that comprise the individual's major source of reinforcements. Akers (1977) argued that the learning relevant to deviant behavior is in contexts wherein "other persons make reinforcers available" (p. 47). He further asserted that it is "the power and centrality of the direct and symbolic social rewards in society which lead to labeling this theory *social learning*" (p. 48). Both Akers (1981) and Jeffery (1980) concurred that this emphasis on social learning is what places Akers's theory in the realm of sociology rather than psychology.

This emphasis also led Akers to recognize the potential of imitation in the learning process—individuals clearly learn behavior from observing others engage in it (Bandura, 1977; Staats, 1975). Imitation is seen as a result of vicarious reinforcement acquired when observing a model's behavior being rewarded. Although imitation may operate at all times, Akers agreed with Bandura's emphasis on its importance in the acquisition of behavior.

Statements 5 and 6 incorporate Sutherland's emphasis on definitions. Definitions, which are verbalizations and normative statements about some aspect of behavior or the situation in which the behavior takes place, are seen as discriminative stimuli for deviant behavior. That is, they derive their meaning from having been paired with a reinforcing stimulus in the past and serve as cues for the reinforcement. It is important to recognize that Akers sees these definitions as either overt or covert behavior. People can apply these definitions to their own behavior. Akers (1977) has argued that this conceptualization remains somewhat true to the symbolic interactionism implicit in Sutherland's original formulation without being inconsistent with psychological social learning theories (cf. Platt & Prout, Chapter 18, this volume).

Two classes of definitions are seen as important to the social learning process. The first class is the positive definitions that define behavior as desirable or permissible. The second class of definitions is the neutralizing definitions. Akers borrowed this notion from an earlier statement by Sykes and Matza (1957). Essentially, these definitions make what are considered to be disapproved behaviors acceptable or at least tolerable in a given stimulus situation. For example, although car thieves may recognize that it is not right to steal, they may neutralize their behavior before the act by arguing that their victim would not lose any money because the car is insured against theft.

Statement 6 also incorporates the notion of differential reinforcement:

> Behavior (whether deviant or conforming) results from greater reinforcement, on
> balance, over punishing contingencies for the same behavior and the reinforcing-
> punishing contingencies on alternative behavior. (Akers et al., 1979, p. 638)

It is important to recognize that the probability of any behavior occurring is contingent on the relative probability of a reinforcing contingency compared with the probability of reinforcements for alternative behaviors.

Akers et al. (1979) summarized his social learning theory by describing a process whereby differential association with deviant groups provided the social environments in which definitions, imitation, and social reinforcement take place. The definitions, once learned, serve as discriminative stimuli for future behavior. After the initial behavior, social and nonsocial reinforcers and punishers should become important as imitation becomes less important. From this statement, Akers et al. identified four main concepts—imitation, differential association, definitions, and differential reinforcement—that capture the learning process identified by the theory.

Akers (1977) has demonstrated how social learning theory can be applied to various deviant activities. One such activity is occupational crime. The extant literature has made specific reference to the learning process as a way of understanding occupational crime (Conklin, 1977; Cressey, 1971; Geis, 1977; Goodman, 1963), but few studies have theoretically developed this premise. As social learning theory would suggest, occupational crime is behavior that is learned in a social environment that differentially reinforces the behavior. The learning process begins when those new to the occupation become exposed to deviant role models who provide positive definitions and rationalizations (neutralizing definitions) for the behavior. Conklin (1977) noted that when first coming to their jobs, executives convicted of price fixing found this type of behavior to be established practice. Incumbents of occupational crime learn from their associates that activities such as price fixing and bribery are, in some instances, necessary if the business is to compete in the marketplace. These and other types of occupational crime are accompanied by strong economic reward. The monetary gain and prestige for "landing a big deal" serve to reinforce business people and executives more than following legitimate business practices. As Lane (1977) reported from interviews of businessmen and government officers, "businessmen run afoul of the law for economic reasons—they want to 'make a fast buck'" (p. 103). Because business associates accept such illegal occupational practices, there is little threat of punishment; moreover, the probability of being caught is low (Akers, 1977).

Neutralizing definitions play a particularly important role in the learning of occupational deviance. Most executives are law-abiding citizens who act accordingly in many aspects of their life. It is when they are confronted with the pressures of their job and competition in the marketplace that they may turn to illegal behavior. Through differential association with others who are in a similar situation, executives and business people are exposed to and come to accept definitions of illegal behavior that neutralize or mitigate their culpability. As Akers (1977) stated, these

> rationales [involve] defining their behavior as illegal but *not really criminal,* as only *technically wrong,* as *necessary* to curb cutthroat competition and to stabilize prices, as *not really injurious to the public;* or they [define] the laws themselves as *bad laws.* (pp. 230–231)

Cressey (1971) found that one common rationalization used by embezzlers was the idea that funds were being "borrowed" rather than "stolen." Mars (1973) reported that hotel and dock workers rationalized the pilfering of property by claiming that the ownership of the property was uncertain and therefore no victim could be identified and no harm was being done.

In summary, social learning theory describes the process by which some business people can be differentially reinforced for illegal as well as legal occupational practices, mainly through economic reward. Social reinforcement for occupational deviance occurs in interaction with others who themselves have been rewarded by such activity and who provide both positive and neutralizing definitions for the behavior. The social environment set up by these behavioral contingencies constitutes the arena in which occupational deviance is learned.

Social Learning and Other Theories of Deviance

Akers (1977), as well as Feldman (1977), has stated that implicit in other etiological theories of deviant behavior are some of the same principles of operant conditioning on which Burgess and Akers built their theory. This assertion is predicated on the position that the social environment structures the probability of social and nonsocial reinforcements that, in turn, determine the probability of the behavior. Although social learning theory explains the process by which individuals acquire certain behavior patterns, it has not identified the social conditions under which it is likely that criminal behaviors will produce positive reinforcers. By identifying the implicit social learning principles in other extant theories of deviant behavior, the utility of the social learning approach will be more evident.

Strain theories posit that the inability of particular groups of people to obtain culturally prescribed goals will increase their rates of deviant behavior (Cloward & Ohlin, 1960; Cohen, 1955; Merton, 1938). From a social learning perspective, these theories are identifying the way in which the social environment limits access to salient reinforcers. For Merton and for Cloward and Ohlin, the reinforcer culturally defined is economic success, whereas for Cohen it is social status within the school. When lower-class juveniles find themselves in a situation where inequity exists in the opportunity to achieve these goals, the probability of reinforcement for conventional behavior diminishes. If these juveniles have access to illegitimate opportunities to obtain economic reinforcement (Cloward & Ohlin, 1960) or generate a new set of criteria for dispensing social reinforcement (e.g., status) (Cohen, 1955), delinquent behavior is likely to ensue.

Labeling theory (Hawkins & Tiedeman, 1975; Lemert, 1972; Schur, 1971) posits that labeling a person a deviant increases the likelihood that subsequent behavior will be deviant as a reaction to that label; this is referred to as *secondary deviance*. The fact that a person's public identity is connected with being "deviant" or "criminal" can cause others to respond differently to conventional behavior exhibited by the labeled person rather than to similar behavior by someone who has not been labeled. Hence, the labeled person may not be socially reinforced for conventional behavior. Moreover, the opportunities to pursue conventional activities for the purpose of obtaining rewards are reduced because the labeled person is viewed as untrustworthy or irresponsible. This can lead to association with groups that reinforce deviant behavior and further entrench the individual in a social context that defines deviance as acceptable.

Control theory (Hirschi, 1969) appears to be the most compatible with social learning theory. The central argument of control theory is that deviant behavior is less likely to occur the more a person is attached to conventional groups, committed to and involved in conventional activities, and believes or adheres to conventional norms and values. The efficacy of the bond people establish with conventional society is, in part, dependent upon the reinforcement and punishment contingencies of their social environment. When people are integrated into a conventional social environment that rewards conforming behavior and punishes nonconforming behavior, they are effectively controlled and consequently less likely to deviate. Deviance can occur when the bond to society is weakened. Through disassociation with conventional groups and exposure to neutralizing definitions, which mitigate the constraining influence of conventional beliefs, controls on behavior through reinforcement and punishment become ineffective. The probability that conventional behavior will occur decreases. At this point, however, control theory is mute on why one would deviate; it only tells us why conventional behavior will decrease. Hence, the control explanation needs to be supplemented with propositions that identify the source of reinforcement for deviant behavior (Conger, 1976; Krohn & Massey, 1980).

By interpreting the preceding theoretical approaches from a social learning perspective, the process by which criminal behavior is produced is made explicit. Moreover, it becomes evident that adopting any one theoretical position to the exclusion of the others may not be prudent. Instead, the strain, labeling, and control theories may be seen as explaining the generation and regeneration of reinforcing contingencies that enable the social learning process to occur.

LOGICAL AND SUBSTANTIVE ADEQUACY

The discussion of the logical and substantive adequacy of social learning theory will be centered around two controversies. The most problematic one is the question of whether the theory is tautological and hence incapable of refutation. The second controversey, which we will argue is interrelated with the first, is whether social or nonsocial reinforcers should be emphasized in the explanation of human behavior.

Although all theories based on the concept of reinforcement are subject to the criticism of being tautological, learning theories dealing with social behavior are particularly problematic. A subject's condition or state variables (e.g., deprivation level) within an experimental laboratory situation can be controlled and manipulated. Thus experimental psychologists can assume that the stimulus being presented is going to be reinforcing. When dealing with people in social relationships, however, sociologists cannot be as familiar with either the state variables or the reinforcement history of the subjects. Hence, identifying what is a reinforcer independent of the probability of subsequent behavior is more difficult. Not being able to do so can result in a circular argument.

Burgess and Akers (1966b) attempted to resolve the tautology problem by distinguishing between propositions and definitions. For example, their law of positive reinforcement states that "those events which will strengthen an operant's future occurrence include the presentation of stimuli" (p. 309). They then defined positive reinforcers as those stimuli that strengthen a behavior. The likelihood of invalidating such an "existence proposition" is so minute that their resolution is far from adequate.

Akers (1977) later conceded that his earlier resolution may not have been satisfactory. He suggested that social scientists must use their knowledge of culture and social structure to determine the arrangement of reinforcement contingencies. In so doing, he is calling for a measurement of values, at the group level as well as for individuals, separate from the measurement of the strength of the behavior. This leaves the basic principle untested but allows constructing testable hypotheses based on the principle.

Liska (1969) suggested a similar solution in his discussion of the logical properties of tautologies. He stated that although tautologies are often suggested to have no legitimate role in science, they are, indeed, basic to some of the most successful theories in physics and psychology. Liska suggested that instead of avoiding tautologies, social scientists should use them as "open concepts," that is, concepts that are empty in meaning by themselves because they are not testable but that are dependent on their empirical indexes for meaning and testing. Adopting Liska's recommendation, however, would leave one in the position of not being able to test the central proposition of learning theory but would allow for accumulating a number of empirical propositions to be integrated under one central open concept. The open concept will grow in meaning as the empirical propositions are enumerated.

In delineating empirical propositions, the question of what types of stimuli are reinforcing (or most reinforcing) for criminal or deviant behavior is inevitably raised. This question constitutes the second major controversy surrounding the social learning perspective. To some extent, the controversy reflects a debate over what is the province of sociology as contrasted with psychology. As noted before, the original presentation by Burgess and Akers (1966a) was intended to be a restatement of Sutherland's differential association theory. Sutherland's theory emphasized the influence of other people on the behavior of the actor and the actor's role in perceiving and reacting to the situation. Burgess and Akers remained true to this position, identifying social reinforcement emanating from groups with whom the individual interacts as the major source of reinforcement. They also recognized, however, that nonsocial reinforcements could affect behavior. The inclusion of nonsocial reinforcements was seen as turning what had been a sociological approach into a mere statement of psychological principles. Taylor, Walton, and Young (1973) declared that Burgess and Akers had performed a "travesty" upon Sutherland's theory. Molm (1981) distinguished behavioral psychological theories from sociological ones by whether the theories focus on dyadic or group behavior. Hence, she would concur with Taylor *et al.* in asserting that Burgess and Akers do not present a sociological theory. Akers (1981) has contended, however, that behavioral theories can focus on individual behavior and still be sociological if the independent variables are social, environmental, or interactional.

Burgess and Akers were also criticized by those who did not appreciate the emphasis on social reinforcement. Adams (1973) argued that nonsocial reinforcers were the major source of reinforcement. He restated the Burgess and Akers propositions changing the third statement to read "the principal part of learning of criminal behavior occurs in those situations which comprise the individual's major source of reinforcement" (Adams, 1973, p. 461).

Adams's critique must be evaluated in light of Liska's comments on tautologies. If we adopt Liska's resolution to the problem of tautologies, then the empirical hypotheses we generate will give meaning to the principles described by our open concept. In essence, then, our hypotheses will define the substance of our theory, with operant principles being relegated to the position of an empirically grounded vocabulary to describe the process. By changing Burgess and Akers' third proposition, Adams effectively eliminated any substantive meaning. Hence, his presentation simply represents a restatement of the open concepts with which he began. If, indeed, nonsocial reinforcers constitute the primary reinforcing stimuli for social behavior, as Adams reported, then the empirical hypotheses must so state this and identify those reinforcers.

A way to avoid the controversy over social versus nonsocial reinforcers and to circumvent the tautology problem is to make use of the concept of generalized conditioned reinforcers. A generalized conditioned reinforcer is one that has acquired its reinforcing value from being correlated with reinforcers appropriate to many different deprivation states. The tokens employed in behavior modification studies (see Kazdin, 1978), as well as money, are examples of generalized conditioned reinforcers. Kunkel (1975) stated that generalized reinforcers were the most significant in human societies and this is certainly consistent with Akers's (1977) later definition of "social" that incorporates "the whole range of tangible and intangible rewards valued in society and its subgroups" (Akers, 1977, p. 55). An advantage of working with generalized conditioned reinforcers is that knowledge of specific state variables of individuals is less important (Ferster, 1971; Kunkel, 1975), thus allowing for somewhat stronger assumptions about what may constitute reinforcement independent of behavior (Chadwick-Jones, 1976).

The tautological problem with operant principles can be circumvented if one is willing to employ the basic principles of operant behavior as open concepts and develop specific empirical hypotheses that in effect define the substance of the theory. Such an approach, however, still does not incorporate a general law about what constitutes a reinforcer (Chadwick-Jones, 1976), a problem that would seem to be endemic to the social learning approach.

RESEARCH ON SOCIAL LEARNING VARIABLES

Although a large body of experimental studies on learning principles exists with both human and nonhuman subjects, surprisingly little research has been conducted on those categories of behavior defined as deviant or criminal in order to test a social learning model. Several studies, however, are indirectly relevant in that they examine variables that could be included in a social learning model.

The research on the deterrence function of the law can be conceived of as addressing at least the cost or punishment dimension of social learning theory. Of particular significance is research that examines respondents' reports of their perceptions of the certainty and severity of informal and formal sanctions (Anderson, 1979; Anderson, Chiricos, & Waldo, 1977; Erickson, Gibbs, & Jensen, 1977; Grasmick & Bryjak, 1980; Jensen, Erickson, & Gibbs, 1978; Meier & Johnson, 1977; Silberman, 1976; Tittle & Logan, 1973; Waldo & Chiricos, 1972). The data from these studies indicate that the perceived likelihood of punishment is moderately related to deviant behavior, whereas perceived severity is either not related or only related where the perception of certainty is high. Several of these studies point out, though, that extralegal variables, most notably moral commitment and association with delinquent friends, are more strongly related to deviant behavior than perceived legal sanctions (Erickson *et al.*, 1977; Meier & Johnson, 1977; Silberman, 1976).

Another body of research has been developed around the reward–cost dimension in social learning theory (Piliavin, Hardyck, & Vadim, 1968; Piliavin, Vadim, & Hardyck, 1969; Rettig, 1964; Rettig & Pasamanick, 1964; Rettig & Rawson, 1963). These studies ask for the subjects' perception of the potential cost and rewards involved in deviant acts through questionnaire items. They then examine the propensity to deviate based on both self-report measures of delinquency and small group experiments assessing the probability of cheating. It is interesting that this research has found that expected costs are more predictive than expected rewards of committing or refraining from deviant acts.

Adams (1974) conducted a laboratory experiment designed to test the particular hypothesis that social reinforcers are more important in deviant behavior than nonsocial reinforcers. Volunteer subjects were asked to perform a difficult task within a short time span. A pretest had determined that only a limited number of problems could be completed, thus allowing the researcher to know if subjects cheated. Subjects could earn 10 cents for each completed problem (nonsocial reinforcer), or they could earn 10 cents for a peer who was at the session (presumably associated with social reinforcement), or both conditions could apply, or neither. Adams found that the nonsocial reinforcing condition was more likely to produce cheating behavior than the social reinforcing condition.

Although the Adams study is an interesting attempt at examining this controversy, it contains two problems. First, it is difficult to equate the value of the social and nonsocial reinforcers in his study. Why would subjects cheat to earn money for someone whom they may or may not have known prior to the experiment? Thus the social reinforcer employed by Adams may be an especially weak one and hence not an adequate test of the relative importance of social and nonsocial reinforcers. The second problem Adams encounters is equating money with nonsocial reinforcers. Money is a generalized condition reinforcer that has been correlated with many social as well as nonsocial reinforcers in the past. Akers (1977) recognized this in his latest statement by broadening his definition of social reinforcers to include money. The problem of distinguishing social from nonsocial reinforcers is quite complex and remains an unresolved issue in learning theory.

The variable that has been demonstrated to be most strongly related to deviant behavior is association with others who commit deviant acts. From a social learning perspective, this relationship is to be expected. It is consistent with the idea that peer groups provide cognitive or attitudinal sets toward deviance (favorable or unfavorable definitions), deviant models for imitation, direct social reinforcement for deviant behavior as well as mediation of other rewards attached to the behavior. Whether this association is considered to be indicative of imitation or reinforcement is dependent on the time ordering of association and behavior, a problem that has not been adequately addressed. In any event, studies have clearly demonstrated a strong relationship between self-reported differential association with conforming or deviant peers and delinquent behavior (Ball, 1957; Burkett & Jensen, 1975; Hirschi, 1969; Jensen, 1972; Short, 1957, 1958; Voss, 1964) and between differential association and deviant drug use (Jessor, Jessor, & Finney, 1973; Kandel, 1973; Kandel, Treiman, Faust, & Single, 1976; Krohn, 1974; Tec, 1974). Indeed, Kandel (1978) noted that this association has enjoyed the most support in the study of adolescent substance use. Some evidence also suggests that differential association precedes the onset of deviant behavior (Huba & Bentler, 1983; Jessor et al., 1973), rather than adolescents engaging in deviant behavior becoming involved in groups that induced them to engage in similar behavior. The results, however, are by no means definitive. Moreover, Conger (1976) has demonstrated that, in accordance with the principle of differential reinforcement, those youths with high reinforcement from deviant peers and low reinforcement from conventional sources (parents) are the most likely to commit delinquent behavior.

Research by Andrews and Kandel (1979) has dealt with a similar problem in an attempt to specify the relationship between attitudes and situational variables (sources of reinforcement) and their effects on deviant behavior. With survey data collected at two points in time on high-school students, the research addressed the claim that learned attitudes and associational patterns are interactive rather than additive in their effect on marijuana use. That is, the influence of attitudes on behavior is enhanced in situations that are favorable to the behavior in question and diminished in instances of low social support.

By surveying the same respondents at two points in time, Andrews and Kandel were able to show that an interactive model of attitudes and associations increases the magnitude of explained variance substantially over an additive model for students who had shifted from being nonusers of marijuana to becoming frequent users over a 6-month period. Interaction effects were not observed among attitudes and situational variables in an initiation model of marijuana use nor within a model that predicted frequency of use among continuous users. These findings are particularly important from a learning perspective because they suggest that the effects of social reinforcers are not only direct but that they may also influence the relationship between attitudes and behavior in circumstances of extreme behavioral change.

Andrews (1980) and associates (Andrews, Wormith, Kennedy, & Daigle-Linn, 1977; Andrews, Young, Wormith, Searle, & Kouri, 1973) have approached this same problem within an experimental framework. By examining interaction processes between prisoners and volunteers in group counseling, Andrews was able to test two hypotheses derived from differential association/social learning theory.

The first hypothesis, the "contingency" hypothesis, involves the assertion that criminal learning occurs as a consequence of differential exposure to criminal/anticriminal patterns. Andrews found that inmates in group counseling sessions with community volunteers were likely to report having more respect for the law than comparable individuals in nontreatment groups. Moreover, Andrews examined the "relationship principles" hypothesis, the assumption that criminal learning is a function of intimate personal relationships in which significant others (e.g., friends and counselors) control "high-quality" reinforcers and/or punishers. In this study, counseling groups were organized as before but with members randomly assigned to groups that were subsequently identified by the aggregated interpersonal skill level of group members. It was argued, and indeed discovered, that anticriminal learning was most evident within those groups that were rated by the respondents as high on openness, warmth, and understanding. In addition, experiments in different institutional settings revealed that the contingency and relationship principles interact, yielding strong procriminal sentiments among high-cohesion groups having no citizen volunteers and strong anticriminal sentiments among groups having strong socioeconomic ties and citizen volunteer participation. The findings provide strong evidence of the causal influence of criminal/anticriminal patterns and group affectivity in the learning of criminal/noncriminal conduct norms.

Although the foregoing research definitely supports social learning theory, much of it provides only an indirect examination of the theory. Studies are needed that begin with hypotheses and variables explicitly derived from social learning theory. Jessor and Jessor (1977) conducted a major research effort that approached this goal through a study of adolescent "problem behavior." This study had both a cross-sectional and longitudinal dimension; the latter was directed toward the prediction of the onset of problem behavior.

The complete Jessor model consists of four explanatory constructs with over 30 indicators of these constructs and extends beyond what is of direct relevance to social learning theory. The two theoretical constructs that include variables relevant to learning theory are the "personality system" and the "perceived environment" system. The personality system consists of personally held values, beliefs, and sources of control. The perceived environment system contains external sources of support and control (distal structures) and models and sources of approval of problem behavior (proximal structures). These systems are hypothesized to have both independent and joint effects on adolescent drinking and/or marijuana use as well as on the individual proclivity for engaging in sexual intercourse, "activist protest" (e.g., demonstrations and petitions), and general behavior (e.g., truancy, criminal trespass, theft, etc.). Although the Jessors performed a very systematic and detailed analysis of their self report data, our concern is with how the learning-related variables performed in a multivariate, cross-sectional analysis and in a longitudinal analysis designed to predict problem behavior "proneness."

In their cross-sectional analysis, the Jessors tested a number of regression models that singly, and in various combinations, estimated the explanatory power of the components of their theory. The dependent variable in this analysis was a "multiple problem behavior index" composed of an additive scale of five dichotomous variables (problem drinking, marijuana use, nonvirginity, activism, and high general deviance). The overall model accounted for over 50% of the variance in problem behavior. Although both the personality system variables and the perceived environment explained a substantial amount of the variance in problem behavior, the variables that overlap with those identified in Akers's theory were the most powerful (attitudes or definitions of deviance, friends' and parents' models and attitudes). These variables are considered more "proximal" than others and are therefore expected to be more highly related to problem behavior.

In their longitudinal analysis, the Jessors employed self report data to examine the ability of problem behavior theory to specify the onset of "age-graded, norm-departing, transition-making behaviors" (1977, p. 166). In order to keep our review succinct, we will concentrate on their findings regarding proneness toward alcohol and marijuana use. The Jessors assessed problem behavior proneness by dividing their 1971 to 1972 high-school sample into three groups: two groups whose behavior did not change between the first and second data collection time point (stable nonusers/stable users) and an onset group who initiated use between survey periods. They found that the mean differences for a majority of variables of the personality and perceived environment systems were significantly different between the stable nonusers and the transition group on the initial assessment. Although this was true for both males and females, the greatest differences among the comparison groups occurred within the female subsample. Very similar results were observed for the onset of alcohol use, although the magnitude of differences between nonusers and initiators was greatest within the male subsample.

The significance of the Jessors's longitudinal findings lies not so much in the power of their analysis but with the conceptual consistency and clarity of their results. The Jessors provide a conceptual model of problem behavior that is carefully reasoned and well-defined, lying clearly within the framework of a social learning perspective. When this is combined with the overall consistency of their empirical findings, the contribution of the Jessors to the study of adolescent development through an integrated learning perspective becomes clearly substantial.

RESEARCH TESTING SOCIAL LEARNING THEORY

The research reviewed before provides substantial evidence in support of many of the hypotheses that derive from Akers's social learning theory, yet none of those efforts specifically test the theory, and only the Jessors' work approximates the combination of variables included in the theory. Akers et al. (1979) have provided the only study that attempts to examine social learning theory as conceived by Akers (1977). That analysis consisted of an examination of the relationship between constructs of the learning process and alcohol and marijuana use and abuse among 3,065 teenageers. As stated previously, the four constructs were imitation, definitions, differential association, and differential reinforcement. The last general construct was further divided into two: differential social reinforcement and differential nonsocial reinforcement. Each construct was measured by multiple questionnaire items.

The full multiple regression equation consisting of 15 variables, explained 55% and 68% of the variance in alcohol and marijuana use, respectively, and 32% and 39% of the variance in alcohol and marijuana abuse, respectively. Although demonstrating the overall viability of a social learning explanation of substance use, Akers et al. also found that subsets of variables representing four of the five constructs were effective in explaining the variance in use patterns. The only construct that failed in this respect was imitation. They argued that the weak influence of imitation was probably due to the limited role that imitation is hypothesized to play in the maintenance of behavior as compared to the role it plays in the initiation of behavior. Akers et al. also found that variables measuring differential association were clearly the most predictive, followed by definitions, differential social/nonsocial reinforcement, and differential social reinforcement.

The relative contribution of the learning variables has generated subsequent controversy. Publication of the Akers et al. (1979) report resulted in three major responses that not only criticized the analytical approach taken but also served to question the value of social learning theory (Jacquith & Orcutt,

1983; Stafford & Ekland-Olson, 1982; Strickland, 1982). The critiques focused on Akers *et al.*'s failure to examine the causal process implied by the theory. Although Akers *et al.* did not give sufficient detail to specify a causal model and specifically discounted attempts to examine the *process* of learning with cross-sectional data, Stafford and Ekland-Olson (1982) and Strickland (1982) reanalyzed the Akers *et al.* data in order to see if the implied causal ordering was supported. Jaquith and Orcutt (1983) went one step further and examined a model specifying the predicted process involved in beginning to use marijuana and a model specifying the process of continuing use with self-report data previously collected for another purpose. The controversey was whether (1) differential association should be considered causally prior to the differential reinforcement variables in the theory or (2) whether variables tapping differential reinforcement should be incorporated. Essentially the critics were questioning whether reinforcement was the process by which differential association leads to deviant behavior. The three studies concluded that differential reinforcement measures had, at best, weak direct effects on the dependent variables and did not mediate the effect of the differential association variable.

In a rejoinder to the published critiques, Akers and associates (Lanza-Kaduce *et al.*, 1982) argued that differential association implies a process that involves imitation, reinforcement, and the acquisition of definitions. Therefore, a high degree of intercorrelation among the independent variables is expected when the theory is examined within a cross-sectional design. This multicollinearity could account for why the differential reinforcement variables had such a weak affect. Lanza-Kaduce *et al.* stated that an appropriate examination of the causal structure of the theory could only be accomplished with longitudinal data.

Although longitudinal studies examining Akers's social learning theory as an explanation of crime or delinquency do not seem to be available, findings exist on an application of the theory to adolescent cigarette use (Krohn, Skinner, Massey, & Akers, 1985). Adolescent cigarette use has been found to be related to most other forms of delinquent (Hirschi, 1969) and drug-using behavior (Jessor & Jessor, 1977). Data were collected over 3 years on the same 7th- to 12th-grade schoolchildren in a small midwestern community (population 23,000). Respondents were differentiated into groups of nonsmokers ($N=523$) and smokers ($N=379$) at Time 1. The former subsample was used to examine initiation to cigarette smoking and the latter to examine the maintenance or cessation of smoking. Separate models for initiation and maintenance were analyzed. The findings for initiation indicated that the social learning model was not effective in explaining the process by which adolescents started smoking. The results for the maintenance model were supportive of the theory and are reported in detail next.

The maintenance model is illustrated in Figure 1. The respondents' perception of definitions held by parents and friends and respondents' associated with friends who use cigarettes are predicted to be directly related to the frequency with which respondents smoke and indirectly related to smoking

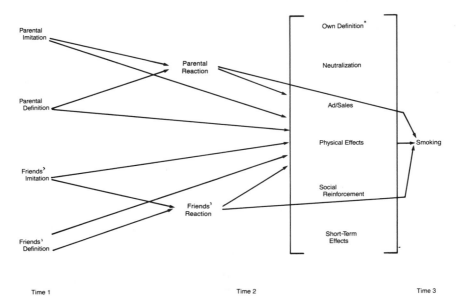

Figure 1. Path diagram for maintenance model. Asterisk (*) indicates that paths leading to and from the bracketed variables apply for all variables within the brackets.

through the Time-2 variables. The Time-2 variables include scales measuring anticipated and actual reinforcements from parents and friends, a general social reinforcement scale containing two items measuring the extent to which smoking makes one look sophisticated and like an adult, scales measuring the positive physical effects (physical effects) and the bad physical consequences (short-term effects) to be derived from smoking and scales tapping definitions used to justify or neutralize smoking, the respondent's own attitude toward smoking, and the respondent's extent of agreement that cigarette advertising and sales should be outlawed.[1]

Figure 2 illustrates the maintenance model after testing the full model and eliminating insignificant paths and variables. This respecified model was able to account for 43% of the variance in smoking at Time 3. In light of the controversy generated by the Akers *et al.* research, the direct effect of non-social reinforcement (physical effects) on smoking and the lack of effects of differential association are of particular importance. Differential association is indirectly related to smoking through friends' reaction and nonsocial reinforcement. Thus the inclusion of reinforcement variables, both social and non-social, may be essential in explaining the maintenance of smoking behavior.

This preliminary analysis indicates that the combination of principles of

[1]All scales were derived from a factor analysis using maximum likelihood procedures and oblique rotation. The factor-based scales were created by summing the standardized scores of those items that loaded .40 or above on one factor. The reliability of the scales ranged from .57 to .92. For a more extensive description, see Krohn, Skinner, Massey, and Akers (1985).

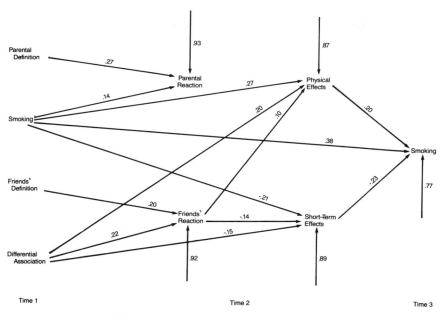

Figure 2. Respecified maintenance model.

behavioral psychology within a differential association model provides for a powerful and detailed explanation of the maintenance of smoking behavior among adolescents. That the model was not equally effective in accounting for initiation is problematic. Possibly because the measure of initiation could include experimental use of cigarettes, we may be picking up the type of activity that is so widespread as to not be a meaningful index of deviance.

The fact that the model was successful at explaining adolescent cigarette use would suggest that it would also be an effective explanation of delinquent behavior. As indicated earlier, cigarette use is highly correlated with delinquent behavior. Other theoretical approaches have been found to account for similar amounts of the variance in cigarette use as in delinquent behavior (Krohn & Massey, 1980; Krohn, Massey, Skinner, & Lauer, 1983).

FUTURE DIRECTIONS

The limitations of the research reported herein (Akers *et al.*, 1979; Krohn *et al.*, 1985) suggest the future directions that need to be pursued. To date, the theory has only been researched in regard to substance use among adolescents. We do not know whether it would also effectively explain variations in other forms of delinquent behaviors. Moreover, no research has applied Akers's theory to any form of adult crime. Akers (1977) clearly suggested that his theory should be applicable and asserted that some of the findings on certain types of adult criminality are at least consistent with theoretical expectations (e.g., white-collar crime and organized crime).

An essential feature of any research on social learning theory must be the collection of longitudinal data. Without such data, the learning processes identified by Akers cannot be empirically separated. Future efforts should also be concerned with obtaining data from younger samples with less time between observations. The learning process may begin at a younger age than the age of the youths included in most delinquency studies. In order to depict adequately the causal ordering of the variables specified in the theory, multiple observations are essential, with relatively short time intervals between them.

Conceptually, the full implications of operant or learning principles for the explanation of deviance and crime need to be explored. Insights acquired from extant theoretical perspectives in deviance can be used as the empirical propositions that give substance to the open concept. Emerson (1969) argued that conventional sociology has already done so by taking operant principles for granted. The advantage of this approach is that predictions generated from divergent theories can be integrated under the more general operant principles. Conger (1976), in discussing the similarity in the predications generated from social control and social learning perspectives, demonstrated that whereas social control propositions are deducible from operant principles, operant principles are not deducible from social control perspectives. Akers (1977) and Feldman (1977) have taken initial steps in arguing that many of the propositions generated from divergent perspectives are deducible from learning principles. To the extent that their argument is correct, operant principles can serve to integrate perspectives, many of which had previously been seen to be antithetical. This synthesizing potential may well be the most important contribution of social learning to the study of crime and deviance.

REFERENCES

Adams, R. (1973). Differential association and learning principles revisited. *Social Problems, 20,* 447–458.

Adams, R. (1974). The adequacy of differential association theory. *Journal of Research in Crime and Delinquency, 11,* 1–8.

Akers, R. L. (1973). *Deviant behavior: A social learning approach.* Belmont, CA: Wadsworth.

Akers, R. L. (1977). *Deviant behavior: A social learning approach* (2nd ed.) Belmont, CA: Wadsworth.

Akers, R. L. (1981). Reflections of a social behaviorist on behavioral sociology. *American Sociological Review, 16,* 177–180.

Akers, R. L., Krohn, M. D., Lanza-Kaduce, L., & Radosevich, M. J. (1979). Social learning and deviant behavior: A specific test of a general theory. *American Sociological Review, 44,* 636–655.

Anderson, L. S. (1979). The deterrent effect of criminal sanctions: Reviewing the evidence. In P. J. Brantingham & J. M. Kress (Eds.), *Structure, law, and power: Essays in the sociology of law* (pp. 120–134). Beverly Hills, CA: Sage.

Anderson, L. S., Chiricos, T. G., & Waldo, G. P. (1977). Formal and informal sanctions: A comparison of deterrent effects. *Social Problems, 25,* 103–114.

Andrews, D. A. (1980). Some experimental investigations of the principles of differential association through deliberate manipulations of the structure of service systems. *American Sociological Review, 45*, 448–462.

Andrews, D. A., Young, J. G., Wormith, J. S., Searle, C. S., & Kouri, M. (1973). The attitudinal effects of group discussions between young criminal offenders and community volunteers. *Journal of Community Psychology, 1*, 417–422.

Andrews, D. A., Wormith, J. S., Kennedy, D. J., & Daigle-Linn, W. J. (1977). The attitudinal effects of structural discussions and recreational associations between young criminal offenders and undergraduate volunteers. *Journal of Community Psychology, 5*, 63–71.

Andrews, K. H., & Kandel, D. B. (1979). Attitude and behavior: A specification of the contingent consistency hypothesis. *American Sociological Review, 44*, 298–310.

Ball, J. C. (1957). Delinquent and non-delinquent attitudes toward the prevalence of stealing. *Journal of Criminal Law, Criminology, and Police Science, 48*, 259–274.

Bandura, A. (1977). *Social learning theory*. Englewood Cliffs, NJ: Prentice-Hall.

Burgess, R. L., & Akers, R. L. (1966a). A differential association-reinforcement theory of criminal behavior. *Social Problems, 14*, 128–147.

Burgess, R. L., & Akers, R. L. (1966b). Are operant principles tautological? *Psychological Record, 16*, 305–312.

Burkett, S., & Jensen, E. L. (1975). Conventional ties, peer influence, and fear of apprehension: A study of adolescent marijuana use. *Sociological Quarterly, 16*, 522–533.

Chadwick-Jones, J. K. (1976). *Social exchange theory: Its structure and influence in social psychology*. New York: Academic Press.

Cloward, R., & Ohlin, L. E. (1960). *Delinquency and opportunity*. New York: The Free Press.

Cohen, A. K. (1955). *Delinquent boys: The culture of the gang*. New York: The Free Press.

Conger, R. (1976). Social control and social learning models of delinquency: A synthesis. *Criminology, 14*, 17–40.

Conklin, J. E. (1977). *Illegal but not criminal*. Englewood Cliffs, NJ: Prentice-Hall.

Cressey, D. R. (1960). Epidemiology and individual conduct: A case from criminology. *Pacific Sociological Review, 3*, 47–58.

Cressey, D. R. (1971). *Other people's money: A study in the social psychology of embezzlement*. Belmont, CA: Wadsworth.

Emerson, R. M. (1969). Operant psychology and exchange theory. In R. L. Burgess & D. Bushell, Jr. (Eds.), *Behavioral sociology* (pp. 379–405). New York: Columbia University Press.

Erickson, M. L., Gibbs, J. P., & Jensen, G. F. (1977). The deterrence doctrine and perceived certainty of legal punishments. *American Sociological Review, 42*, 305–317.

Feldman, M. P. (1977). *Criminal behavior: A psychological analysis*. New York: Wiley.

Ferster, C. B. (1971). Reinforcement and punishment in the control of human behavior by social agencies. By E. McGinnies & C. B. Ferster (Eds.), *The reinforcement of social behavior* (pp. 9–16). New York: Houghton-Mifflin.

Geis, G. (1977). The heavy electrical equipment antitrust cases of 1961. In G. Geis & R. F. Meier (Eds.), *White-collar crime* (pp. 117–132). New York: The Free Press.

Glaser, D. (1956). Criminality theories and behavioral images. *American Journal of Sociology, 61*, 433–444.

Goodman, W. (1963). *All honorable men: Corruption and compromise in American life*. Boston: Little, Brown.

Grasmick, H. G., & Bryjak, G. J. (1980). The deterrent effect of perceived severity of punishment. *Social Forces, 59*, 471–491.

Hawkins, R., & Tiedeman, G. (1975). *The creation of deviance: Interpersonal and organizational determinants*. Columbus, OH: Charles E. Merrill.

Hirschi, T. (1969). *Cause of delinquency*. Berkeley: University of California Press.

Homans, G. C. (1961). *Social behavior: Its elementary forms*. New York: Harcourt, Brace and World.

Huba, G. J., & Bentler, P. M. (1983). Causal models of the development of law abidance and its relationship to psychosocial factors and drug use. In W. S. Laufer & J. M. Day (Eds.), *Personality, moral development, and criminal behavior* (pp. 165–215). Lexington, MA: Lexington Books.

Jacquith, S. M., & Orcutt, J. D. (1983). *Social learning theory and the use of psychoactive substances: A critical and empirical assessment.* Unpublished manuscript.

Jeffery, C. R. (1965). Criminal behavior and learning theory. *Journal of Criminal Law, Criminology, and Police Science, 56,* 294–300.

Jeffery, C. R. (1980). Learning theory and modern psychobiology: A response to Halbasch. *Criminology, 18,* 130–134.

Jensen, G. F. (1972). Parents, peers, and delinquent action: A test of the differential association perspective. *American Journal of Sociology, 78,* 63–72.

Jensen, G. F., Erickson, M. L., & Gibbs, J. G. (1978). Perceived risk of punishment and self-reported delinquency. *Social Forces, 57,* 57–78.

Jessor, R., & Jessor, S. L. (1977). *Problem behavior and psychological development.* New York: Academic Press.

Jessor, R., Jessor, S. L., & Finney, J. (1973). A social psychology of marijuana use: Longitudinal studies of high school and college youth. *Journal of Personality and Social Psychology, 26,* 1–15.

Kandel, D. B. (1973). Adolescent marijuana use: Role of parents and peers. *Science, 181,* 1067–1070.

Kandel, D. B. (1978). Convergence, in prospective longitudinal surveys of drug use in normal populations. In D. B. Kandel (Ed.), *Longitudinal research on drug use* (pp. 3–38). New York: Wiley.

Kandel, D. B., Treiman, D., Faust, R., & Single, E. (1976). Adolescent involvement in legal and illegal drug use: A multiple classification analysis. *Social Forces, 55,* 438–458.

Kadzin, A. E. (1978). *The token economy: A review and evaluation.* New York: Plenum Press.

Krohn, M. D. (1974). An investigation of the effect of parental and peer associations on marijuana use: An empirical test of differential association theory. In M. Reidel & T. P. Thornberry (Eds.), *Crime and delinquency: Dimensions of deviance* (pp. 75–89). New York: Praeger.

Krohn, M. D., & Massey, J. L. (1980). Social control and delinquent behavior: An examination of the elements of the social bond. *Sociological Quarterly, 21,* 529–543.

Krohn, M. D., Massey, J. L., Skinner, W. F., & Lauer, R. (1983). Social bonding theory and adolescent cigarette smoking: A longitudinal analysis. *Journal of Health and Social Behavior, 24,* 337–349.

Krohn, M. D., Skinner, W. F., Massey, J. L., & Akers, R. L. (1985). A longitudinal examination of social learning theory as applied to adolescent cigarette smoking. *Social Problems, 32,* 455–473.

Kunkel, J. H. (1975). *Behavior, social problems, and change.* Englewood Cliffs, NJ: Prentice-Hall.

Lane, R. E. (1977). Why businessmen violate the law. In G. Geis & R. F. Meier (Eds.), *White-collar crime* (pp. 102–116). New York: The Free Press.

Lanza-Kaduce, L., Akers, R. L., Krohn, M. D., & Radosevich, M. J. (1982). Conceptual and analytic models in testing social learning theory. *American Sociological Review, 47,* 169–173.

Lemert, E. M. (1972). *Human deviance, social problems, and social control.* Englewood Cliffs, NJ: Prentice-Hall.

Liska, A. E. (1969). Uses and misuses of tautologies in social psychology. *Sociometry, 32,* 444–457.

Mars, G. (1973). Hotel pilferage: A case study of occupational theft. In P. Rock & M. McIntosh (Eds.), *Deviance and social control* (pp. 209–228). London: Tavistock Publications.

Meier, R. F., & Johnson, W. T. (1977). Deterrence as social control: The legal and extra-legal production of conformity. *American Sociological Review, 42,* 292–304.

Merton, R. K. (1938). Social structure and anomie. *American Sociological Review, 3,* 672–682.

Molm, L. D. (1981). The legitimacy of behavioral theory as a sociological perspective. *American Sociological Review, 16,* 153–165.

Piliavin, I. M., Vadim, A. C., & Hardyck, A. J. (1969). Delinquency, personal costs and parental treatment: A test of a reward-cost model. *Journal of Criminal Law, Criminology, and Police Science, 60,* 165–172.

Rettig, S. (1964). Ethical risk sensitivity in male prisoners. *British Journal of Criminology, 4,* 582–590.

Rettig, S., & Pasamanick, B. (1964). The differential judgment of ethical risk by cheaters and non-cheaters. *Journal of Abnormal and Social Psychology, 69,* 110–113.

Rettig, S., & Rawson, H. E. (1963). The risk hypothesis in predictive judgments of unethical behavior. *Journal of Abnormal and Social Psychology, 66,* 243–248.

Schur, E. M. (1971). *Labeling deviant behavior: Its sociological implications.* New York: Harper & Row.

Short, J. F. (1957). Differential association and delinquency. *Social Problems, 4,* 233–239.

Short, J. F. (1958). Differential association with delinquent friends and delinquent behavior. *Pacific Sociological Review, 1,* 20–25.

Short, J. F. (1960). Differential association as a hypothesis: Problems of empirical testing. *Social Problems, 8,* 14–25.

Silberman, M. (1976). Toward a theory of criminal deterrence. *American Sociological Review, 41,* 442–461.

Skinner, B. F. (1938). *The behavior of organisms.* New York: Appleton-Century-Crofts.

Staats, A. W. (1975). *Social behaviorism.* Homewood, IL: Dorsey.

Stafford, M. C., & Ekland-Olson, S. (1982). On social learning and deviant behavior: A reappraisal of the findings. *American Sociological Review, 47,* 167–169.

Strickland, D. E. (1982). Social learning and deviant behavior: A comment and a critique. *American Sociological Review, 47,* 162–167.

Sutherland, E. H. (1924). *Principles of criminology.* Philadelphia: J. B. Lippincott.

Sutherland, E. H. (1947). *Principles of criminology* (4th ed.). Philadelphia: J. B. Lippincott.

Sutherland, E. H., & Cressey, D. (1974). *Criminology* (9th ed.). Philadelphia: J. B. Lippincott.

Sykes, G., & Matza, D. (1957). Techniques of neutralization: A theory of delinquency. *American Sociological Review, 24,* 97–114.

Taylor, I., Walton, P., & Young, J. (1973). *The new criminology: For a social theory of deviance.* New York: Harper & Row.

Tec, N. (1974). *Grass is green in suburbia: A sociological study of adolescent usage of illicit drugs.* New York: Libra.

Tittle, C. R., & Logan, C. H. (1973). Sanctions and devance: Evidence and remaining questions. *Law and Society Review, 1,* 371–392.

Voss, H. (1964). Differential association and reported delinquent behavior: A replication. *Social Problems, 12,* 78–85.

Waldo, G., & Chiricos, T. G. (1972). Perceived penal sanction and self-reported criminality: A neglected approach in deterrence research. *Social Problems, 19,* 522–540.

18

Cognitive-Behavioral Theory and Interventions for Crime and Delinquency

JEROME J. PLATT AND MAURICE F. PROUT

The purpose of this chapter is severalfold. First, it is intended to provide the reader with some of the theoretical bases for the cognitive-behavioral interventions that have been applied recently to delinquent and criminal populations. Second, it briefly outlines some of the recent work by those cognitive-behavioral psychologists who have begun to apply their interventions to the prevention and treatment of delinquent and criminal behavior. Third, it attempts to describe the cognitive-behavioral approach in terms of target skills and/or abilities that have been identified as associated with—in some cases as underlying—other skills in which delinquent and adult offenders are deficient. As to this last point, the chapter will present some data concerning the role played by interpersonal cognitive problem-solving skills in the adjustment process of youthful offenders.

THE CONVERGENCE OF COGNITIVE AND BEHAVIORAL THERAPIES

A growing number of behavior therapists view cognitions as playing a major role in the development and maintenance of maladaptive behaviors (Bandura, 1977a; Beck, 1976; Mahoney, 1974; Meichenbaum, 1977). Those holding to this approach emphasize particularly the role of overt and covert cognitions (self-instruction) in behavior (Lazarus, 1977). The role of cognitions in mediating maladaptive behavior is not, however, readily accepted by all behaviorists, some of whom have expressed serious concerns about theories that deal with unseen entities such as thoughts and images (e.g., Rachlin, 1977). The latter emphasize principles based upon observed relationships between behaviors and environmental events (Levis, 1982). It is perhaps not surprising to find many behavior therapists reluctant, if not unyielding, when

Jerome J. Platt • Department of Psychiatry, School of Osteopathic Medicine, University of Medicine and Dentistry of New Jersey, Camden, New Jersey 08103.   **Maurice F. Prout** • Department of Mental Health Sciences, Hahnemann University, Philadelphia, Pennsylvania 19102.

considering that the roots of the behavior therapy movement are found in the reaction against cognitive, insight-oriented therapies (Levis, 1980; Wolpe, 1978). Behaviorists historically have viewed cognitive behaviors as outside the realm of behavioral research because these behaviors are not subject to direct observation, measurement, and manipulation (Rimm & Lefebre, 1981). Although behavioral approaches employ direct environmental interventions to effect changes in behavioral phenomena, cognitive approaches emphasize semantic or mediational interventions (e.g., reasoning, self-talk) to effect change in behaviors (Kendall & Hollon, 1979).

Kendall and Hollon (1979) have clearly outlined the recent theoretical integration of cognitive and behavioral interventions. They also have outlined the major elements comprising traditional, cognitive, and behavioral theories, goals, and interventions. Cognitive-behavioral interventions fall between what Kendall and Hollon see as the two extreme positions occupied by traditional cognitive and behavioral approaches. They see the cognitive-behavioral position as a purposeful combination of (a) the performance-oriented, methodologically rigorous behavioral techniques of behavior therapy and (b) clinical applications based on cognitive-mediational processes. Essentially, it is a marriage of the principles of social and developmental psychology and those of experimental-clinical psychology (Kendall & Hollon, 1979).

In the view of the cognitive-behavioral therapist, the individual is a complex product of personal, biological, and environmental forces. The individual's learning processes are seen as cognitive rather than peripherally conditioned (Mahoney, 1979). In the cognitive approach, "man is viewed as a kind of information processing machine that transforms and organizes perceptual input" (Sollod & Wachtel, 1980, p. 1). The current trend to incorporate cognitive issues within the realm of behavior therapy thus reflects an interest in internal mediating processes, including the assumptions and the attributional tendencies of patients as they impact on overt behaviors (Sollod & Wachtel, 1980, p. 4).

> Behaviorists are increasingly recognizing that behavior is not only a response to external stimuli, but rather an interactive process that includes the individual's expectations, beliefs, self-appraisals, and other cognitive factors. Particularly important in its implications for treatment is the knowledge that persons may show marked individual differences in the extent to which their behavior is controlled by internal rather than external influences. (Jesness, 1980, p. 365)

In tracing the history of cognitive-behavioral techniques, Kendall and Hollon have identified four independent influences that have led to the acceptance of a meshing of cognitive and behavioral techniques. The first of these is the position that cognitions conform to the same learning principles as overt behaviors (Cautela, 1967; Homme, 1965; Ullmann, 1970). This view permits an entry point for behaviorists into the arena of cognitive issues.

The second influence has been the growing appreciation of the role of cognitive events in affecting behavior. In this regard, Kendall and Hollon recognize the contributions of rational-emotive therapy (Ellis, 1962) and cognitive therapy (Beck, 1963, 1976). These therapies point to the effects of cognitive events on behavior and, accordingly, have implications for semantic interventions involving persuasion, reason, and logic. Those interested in the effects of cognition on behavior considered and accepted the concept of internal dialogue as a mediating factor in behavior. In a contemporaneous development, covert conditioning, which applies conditioning principles to covert events, was tested and rapidly incorporated into the practice of behavior therapy. In all this, thoughts, feelings, and images reported by patients were analyzed and employed as a means for inducing behavior change (Cautela, 1966, 1967; Homme, 1965). Once the mediating impact of cognitions upon behaviors was widely acknowledged, techniques grew to include problem solving, perspective taking, and self-verbalization. These techniques were meant to explore the relevance of social and cognitive psychology to clinical endeavors (Mahoney & Arnkoff, 1978).

The third influence has been in the theoretical integration of the behavioral paradigm and cognitive processes. Early studies on self-regulation (Kanfer, 1970) and self-efficacy (Bandura, 1977b) must be seen as a significant development in the cognitive-behavioral therapies. Studies by Kanfer (1970), Bandura (1969, 1977a), and Thoresen and Mahoney (1974) brought the focus of behavioral theory beyond simple environmental determinism, the belief that forces shaping behavior come from the external environment, to a consideration of the role the individual plays in interacting with the environment. This view is known as *reciprocal determinism* (Mahoney & Arnkoff, 1978).

Finally, a fourth influence in the meshing of cognitive and behavioral techniques is that combining contingency management techniques with cognitive treatment strategies has been found to be a viable and desirable strategy. For example, Kendall and Finch (1978) found self-instructional training via modeling together with a response–cost contingency to be an effective approach. What emerges as the result of the four influences is a cognitive-behavioral approach that reflects a flexibility of models and approaches without sacrificing assessment and evaluation (Kendall & Hollon, 1979).

COGNITIVE-BEHAVIORAL THEORY AND THE DEVELOPMENT OF ANTISOCIAL BEHAVIOR

Having traced the development of cognitive-behavioral theory, we will now apply this theory to crime and delinquency. How are social behaviors acquired? How are aggressive behaviors learned? How do internal processes impact upon delinquent and criminal behaviors?

The Acquisition of Social Behavior

The cognitive-behavioral theory that has addressed most fully the acquisition of social behavior is *social learning theory,* as the term is applied in the psychological literature (see Chapter 17 in this volume by Krohn, Massey, and Skinner concerning the use of the term in the sociological literature). Social learning theorists conceptualize social development as occurring as a result of a gradual acquisition of social knowledge through observation, imitation, and direct instructions from parents, adults, and older children. Children are selectively reinforced for correct behavior and so develop a repertoire of social behavior (Nietzel, 1979). Although acknowledging the role of selective reinforcement, social learning theory recognizes the importance of cognitive factors and the role of observational or vicarious learning. Sarason (1978) attributes many of the problems of delinquent youth to troubled early social-learning experiences, one of which is the lack of constructive modeling experiences.

Social learning theory concentrates on the behavior of individuals, but it further recognizes that different people perceive their environments in different ways and that our expectations about the results of behavior may be as influential as the actual contingencies we experience (Bandura, 1969, 1977a,b). This is in contrast to some operant and all classical conditioning views where the individual is seen as a relatively passive actor in the environment. In the social learning framework, the individual is accorded a much more active role in creating his or her own environment (Calhoun & Turner, 1981). Bandura (1969) further recognized that virtually all behavior learned through direct experience can be learned through observation. Observational learning or modeling can be an effective and efficient learning mode because it eliminates the need for trial-and-error learning and usually shortens the learning period.

Social Learning Theory and Aggression

From our own social learning orientation, extrapolated from Bandura (1973, 1976), observational learning is the most important factor in the development of aggressive behavior. The modeling of aggression by family members, frequently in the area of parental discipline, leads the child to view aggression as a style of conflict resolution. Cultural subgroups that value both aggression and symbolic models of aggression, such as those presented in the mass media, also serve as models for aggressive behavior. The child does not need to experience aggression personally to learn it. He need only view it to be influenced.

Once aggressive behaviors have been learned by modeling, they are maintained by vicarious external reinforcement and self-reinforcement. Observed successes lead observers to believe they also would succeed with the aggressive behavior.

> Observed outcomes may also result in the conditioning or the extinction of fears which would inhibit or disinhibit aggressive or transgressive behaviors. (Neitzel, 1979, p. 108)

Individuals further maintain their own aggressive behaviors if they derive a sense of self-worth or self-admiration for having succeeded in an aggressive act. If, however, their cognitions (e.g., self-directed talk) result in self-criticism of self-contempt, the behavior will likely be discontinued. According to Bandura (1976), people

tend to aggress toward persons and in contexts where it is relatively safe and rewarding to do so, but they are disinclined to act aggressively when to do so carries a high
risk of punishment. (p. 212)

Locus of Control, an Attributional Theory

The viewing of aggressive acts in the home and community or via the
media will not always result in duplicating the behavior *in vivo*. Very few
persons attempt to imitate a successful robbery or mimic an aggressive act
that went unpunished. What distinguishes the offenders from those who behave in socially acceptable ways? This is difficult to pinpoint with empirical
evidence because laboratory studies cannot approximate the social and legal
sanctions that actual offenders must risk (Nietzel, 1979). The attribution of
causality to luck, fate, or chance may result in the belief in external control of
events. Conversely, when one perceives events as contingent upon one's own
behavior, the control is believed to be internal (Rotter, 1966). The belief in
internal or external control is a mediational factor that moderates behavior
via individuals' perceptions of themselves as active causal agents rather than
passive recipients of environmental influences (Mahoney, 1974).

Some evidence suggests that delinquents who are internally oriented are
more compliant and less aggressive. For example, Ollendick and Elliott (1978)
found that a social skills training group resulted in an increase in internal
locus of control along with a reduction of disruptive behavior among delinquents. If, indeed, a causal relationship does exist between antisocial behavior
and locus of control, what might be the reason? The assumption is that in an
environment both socially and emotionally supportive of delinquent behavior,
internally oriented people should be more successful in the personal control of
whether their behavior is prosocial or antisocial than are externally oriented
people. In essence, the person with internal locus of control is less stimulus
bound to the crime-oriented environment and thus less vulnerable to acting
out.

Traditional behavioral techniques applied to correctional situations have
relied heavily on a conditioning model in which contingencies are manipulated
in the hope of changing overt performance. Cognitive-behavioral interventions would seem to support the development of an internal locus of control by
having as their goal the improvement of adaptive personal mediational processes such as self-instruction, perspective taking, and interpersonal problem
solving, all of which support self-control. These approaches seek to reorient
behaviorists to focus attention upon the internal processes and their influence
on overt behavior.

INTERVENTIONS: ADAPTIVE PERSONAL MEDIATIONAL PROCESSES, SKILL DEVELOPMENT, AND COGNITIONS

The cognitive-behavioral approach emphasizes the role of the client's cognitions (e.g., thoughts, perceptions, and beliefs) in the behavioral repertoire.

In implementing the cognitive-behavioral approach, the therapist must identify the client's cognitions (e.g., internal dialogue and images) and the relationship of those cognitions to the client's behavior and feelings. Faulty cognitions or the lack of cognitions regarding a certain behavior may interfere with adequate performance. A functional analysis of thinking processes as well as an inventory of the client's cognitive strategies is necessary to decipher which cognitions or lack thereof, and under what circumstances, are interfering with the desired behavior (Meichenbaum, 1977). For example, cognitive excesses and deficits are seen clearly as mediating factors in the theories of depression (Hollon & Beck, 1979) and in the contrasting problem of impulsivity, a common problem among delinquents (Kendall & Finch, 1979). In the cognitive view, impulsive children have cognitive deficits—they lack task-facilitating cognitions. These deficits result in an absence of problem-solving skills and verbal mediation, inaccurate responses, and excessive behavioral switching. Therapeutic techniques seek to train the impulsive individual in mediational cognitions.

Beyond identifying and correcting the client's faulty cognitions, cognitive-behavioral interventions seek to develop a repertoire of skills to facilitate adaptation in a variety of stressful situations. Self-instruction, anxiety management, stress innoculation, cognitive rehearsal, anger control, social skills training, and perspective taking are all oriented to training for coping skills and self-control. The common thread through these techniques is their attempt to induce stress and then train the clients to manage the situation effectively by providing them with coping skills (Mahoney & Arnkoff, 1978).

Self-Control and Self-Instruction

Hostile or aggressive behavior may continue because more acceptable ways of handling the demands of interpersonal relations have not been learned (Fehrenbach & Thelen, 1982). Aggressive children are often impulsive and exercise less verbal control over their behavior, using covert speech less effectively than reflective children. The aggressive child uses his or her verbal abilities far less than normal children in thinking and reasoning to reach a solution (Coates, 1979). Development of self-control is seen as emerging when the child learns to respond to his or her own verbal cues, first as response initiators, and then as response inhibitors. This self-control perspective stems from a theory of verbal mediation developed by Russian psychologists, specifically Luria (1961) and Vygotsky (1962). Luria (1961) contended that voluntary control over one's behavior is internalized by self-directed verbal commands. He described the development of self-control as occurring in three stages: (1) Children's behavior is controlled and directed by the speech of others; (2) children's own overt speech regulates behavior; and (3) the covert or inner speech of children governs their voluntary actions. These stages provide a framework for developing an approach to assist children to control their behavior. Early in the mastery of a voluntary act, overt speech serves a useful supportive and guiding function. With practice, the overt verbalizations disappear (Meichenbaum, 1977).

The internalization of verbal commands is a critical step in the child's development of voluntary behavioral control, thus suggesting that modeling and rehearsing self-instructions would be a useful therapeutic technique (Goodwin & Mahoney, 1975). These techniques aim to give children the necessary competence to deal effectively with situations in which they previously dealt in an aggressive manner.

Cognitive-behavioral techniques have been examined for application to aggressive and impulsive behaviors in adults, adolescents, and children in a number of studies. We will first discuss applications to children and adolescents. Meichenbaum and Goodman (1971) trained impulsive children to talk to themselves, facing from overt to covert statements with success. Robin, Schneider, and Dolnick (1976) used the "turtle technique" with children having trouble controlling impulsive/aggressive behavior. Children were told to imagine themselves to be a turtle, pulling in extremities, relaxing and using social problem solving when faced with the impulse to aggress. Results indicated that children can learn to regulate their own aggressive behavior.

A study by Williams and Akamatsu (1978) sought to assess the applicability of cognitive self-guidance to delinquents, a strategy described by Meichenbaum and Goodman (1971). Three treatment groups were used: an assessment-control group, a attention-control group, and a cognitive self-guidance group. Treatment for the attention-control group was limited to encouragement and social reinforcement as they performed the task. The cognitive self-guidance group had appropriate self-instructions modeled for them, were trained in overt verbalizations, and then had the overt statements faded out. Another similar task was used as a measure of generalization. No significant difference was found between the treatment and attention-control group on the primary task. The cognitive self-guidance group, however, improved significantly more than did the attention-control group on the generalization task. This generalization supports the utility of cognitive self-guidance in the treatment of delinquents.

With the goal of developing self-control, along with personal problem-solving and decision-making abilities, Thoresen et al. (1979) designed a group-home program called "learning house" to help troubled children (e.g., delinquent, unruly, truant, etc.). Initially, self-control training concentrated on the acquisition of a desired social behavior. Modeling by a trainee, role playing, and self-evaluation of videotapes of rehearsals were combined to teach the desired skill. Self-instruction and problem-solving skills were taught. Homework assignments encouraged the child to use the new skill. Children were taught to restructure their own cognitions concerning their behavior and were encouraged to make positive self-statements to others (Thoresen et al., 1979). A careful meshing of self-control skills within school, parental, counseling, and community settings was planned for and monitored in order to encourage generalization.

Kendall and Braswell (1982) wanted to evaluate the utility of the cognitive components of cognitive-behavioral treatment with children having self-control difficulties. Three treatment groups were assigned: cognitive-behavioral, behavioral, and attention control. Cognitive-behavioral subjects were trained in self-instruction via modeling and behavioral contingencies, whereas the behavioral treatment was overt modeling only with behavioral contingencies. Results indicated that the cognitive component added to the effectiveness of the behavioral intervention.

Stumphauzer (1976) reports a case study of a 12-year-old female with a history of several years of theft. A combination of self-control treatment and family contracting, along with parent bibliotherapy, resulted in the apparent cessation of stealing as well as engagement in more appropriate interpersonal and social activities for the girl at 1½ years follow-up. The patient was trained in self-control techniques geared to the past theft circumstances and her self-statements at those times (e.g., "I can't control myself"). She was taught to self-monitor, self-evaluate, and self-reinforce. On successfully refraining from stealing, she was instructed to use self-reinforcing language.

Self-instruction and self-control interventions have been used with aggressive adults, specifically with abusive parents. Work with these parents may yield the benefit of abuse cessation as well as a more appropriate role model for the children. Work on self-control and general coping skills has been done with abusive parents because, in addition to lacking information on child development processes and management, abusive parents have been found deficient in impulse control (Steele & Pollock, 1968; Wasserman, 1967). Denicola and Sandler (1980) combined training in child management techniques with cognitive-behavioral training, including self-control techniques, to teach abusive parents to manage anger. Two court-referred families participated, each receiving training in child management and self-control skills. The results, based on observation and self-report, indicated that family interactions improved and were maintained or enhanced during a 3-month follow-up. Parents attributed their improvement to learning more about child management and to improvements in their ability to cope with problem situations. A measure of self-control or learning of self-control skill would have strengthened the study and helped discern the relative effects of either treatment.

Wolfe, Sandler, and Kaufman (1981) studied eight court-referred, low-income abusive families. The families were randomly assigned to either a control or treatment group. The treatment program involved group clinic-based and individual home sessions; multiple outcome measures and a 1-year follow-up were included. The treatment program consisted of group training in parenting skills and self-control, the use of reading and practice assignments, and behavioral rehearsal of self-control skills. To facilitate generalization, criterion-based weekly training sessions were also conducted in the home. Follow-up data were presented on all the families. The outcome measures, which were taken before, immediately after, and 10 weeks following intervention, consisted of parental descriptions of child behavior problems using the Eyberg Child Behavior Inventory, weekly home observation using the Parent Child Interaction Form (Eyberg & Ross, 1978), and social service case-worker ratings of family treatment needs. The posttest results showed significant improvement in the treatment group, both in comparison to pretest data and to controls at posttest. At 1-year follow-up, no instances of child abuse were reported in the treatment families, and social service supervision was terminated. In addition, the control families that completed treatment after the comparative study were also successful, and their cases were closed by the supervising agency. One of the controls who declined treatment was cited for abuse within the follow-up period, and the other nonparticipating control family was still under active supervision.

Wolfe and his colleagues (1982) introduced a new technique for cognitive-behavioral interventions—a bug-in-ear device. They presented a case of an epileptic, single mother with low intelligence who exhibited high rates of aversive behavior with her three children. Of particular difficulty were problems of child noncompliance and joint cooperation among the children. In the clinic, simulations of these situations were developed, and a therapist gave the mother suggestions based on social learning techniques and feedback from behind a one-way mirror. Homework assignments and regular home observations were made to monitor generalizations. After 11 training sessions, the bug-in-ear device was gradually faded out over 3 sessions. Observational data in the home indicated a significant decrease in hostile parental behavior and significant increase in positive parental behavior after treatment. These levels were maintained at 1-month follow-up.

Self-instructional training has been demonstrated as having potential utility for the treatment of delinquents in two studies, by McCullough, Huntsinger, and Nay (1977) and Snyder and White (1979), respectively. In the former, a report of a case study, McCullough *et al.* demonstrated the usefulness of "thought stopping" (Wolpe, 1973), a self-instructional technique, and self-induced muscular relaxation in teaching a 16-year-old boy to control overt aggression triggered by conflict situations. In the latter study, Snyder and White (1979) trained five delinquents with histories of aggression to control their behavior. In a residential treatment setting, they used a behavior modification program with a focus upon identifying self-verbalizations and modifying them through such techniques as modeling, both overt and covert, and role playing. When compared with both attention and nonattention control groups, relatively greater change was found in the experimental group with respect to decreased class absences, decreased failure to meet social and self-care responsibilities, and decreased drug use, physical acting out, stealing, and destructive acting out. These results are very promising with respect to the usefulness of self-instructional training for delinquents.

Finally, Bowman and Auerbach (1982), who used a multimodal cognitive-behavioral training program, reported that they were able to modify impulsive behavior in adolescent youthful offenders, reducing overt antisocial behavior. The multimodal program contained relaxation training, cognitive training in problem solving, self-statement modification, and behavioral rehearsal techniques. The results were somewhat mixed. After training, youths reflected more and did not respond precipitously but did not increase in their abstract reasoning ability or in their generalized perception of the role played by personal effort, as opposed to chance, in everyday experience.

Stress Innoculation and Anger Control

Socially unacceptable behaviors are sometimes the result of maladaptive responses to stressful, anger-producing situations. Stress innoculation involves the deliberate arousal of anxiety or stress followed by practice using a variety of cognitive coping procedures in order to "develop a client's competence to respond to stressful situations so that disturbing emotions are reduced and behavioral adaptation is achieved" (Novaco, 1979, p. 265). Based on the model developed by Meichenbaum (1977), treatment advanced through three stages: educational, rehearsal, and application training. The first phase was meant to teach the client to recognize the nature of his or her response to stressful events. The rehearsal stage provided the client with a variety of coping modes, including self-statements. In the application training, Meichenbaum provided clients with a stressful situation (electric shock) in which to apply the newly acquired coping skills of relaxation and self-statements. Novaco (1979) has applied Meichenbaum's stress innoculation model to provide a theoretical framework for anger control. The model does not seek to suppress anger but rather to prevent maladaptive anger responses, to enable the individual to regulate anger arousal and concomittant cognitions, and to develop coping skills to manage the provocative situation.

The three-stage treatment process consists of cognitive preparation (education), skill acquisition (rehearsal), and application training. Applied to anger control, cognitive preparation includes (a) a study of the facets of external events that elicit anger and (b) discerning the cognitive and affective internal responses with which one responds to anger. A client instructional manual and an anger diary are used. During the skill acquisition stage, the client learns to recognize the manifestation of anger and learns about alternate coping skills. The therapist models coping skills, and the client rehearses them, with self-talk being a key skill. The application stage provides an opportunity to test acquired proficiencies in response to provocations regulated by the therapist. Because anger is difficult to generate for clinical testing, the application phase is conduced by means of imaginal and role-playing inductions of anger. Blood pressure elevation suggests the ability of the role-play procedure to induce genuine anger.

Novaco (1975, 1976) compared the effectiveness of cognitive coping and relaxation training to regulate anger in persons self-identified and assessed as having serious anger-control problems. The outcomes, measured by self-report, physiological indexes, and anger diary ratings, indicated that cognitive treatment resulted in a definite and generalized improvement in anger management. The combination of cognitive and relaxation training, however, was the most effective. In isolation, the cognitive treatment resulted in greater improvement than did relaxation treatment alone. Novaco (1979) also reports an unpublished study (Atrops, 1978) investigating, in a hospital for the criminally insane, the effects of cognitive interventions for anger based on Novaco's treatment and the effects of such interventions combined with social skills training. Results indicate that social skills training alone caused little improvement. The cognitive intervention, however, resulted in improved problem-solving skills and alternative thinking, and better anger management.

In an attempt to evaluate the effectiveness of cognitive restructuring versus the traditional technique of response cost, Forman (1980) worked with aggressive children. Those receiving the cognitive treatment discussed situations that made them angry and then developed scripts of thoughts to manage anger. They were then asked to relax and imagine themselves in an anger-provoking situation thinking the new scripts. Practice was encouraged. The response–cost group was fined 2 minutes from the group playtime for each aggressive incident. Both treatment groups showed significant reductions in aggressive behaviors with the response–cost group tending toward greatest change.

Perspective Taking

Young children operate from their own perspective, an egocentric view of the world from which they are unable to decenter (Piaget, 1926). As they mature, they can relate their behavior to the needs of others, and from this self-control develops. By adolescence, the typical individual's perspective-taking ability develops to the point of being able to take into some account the feelings, thoughts, and intentions of all involved (Schantz, 1975). Mead (1934) recognized a link between role taking and the emergence of self-concept and self-control. Gough (1948) attributed deviant thoughts and behaviors of delinquents to role-taking deficiencies and lack of impulse control. Chandler (1973) found evidence that delinquents exhibit deficiencies in role taking and that training in perspective taking addressed these deficits successfully. Little and Kendall (1979) have speculated that the self-control factor that results from the ability to take the role of another may be a covert self-statement such as "wait, the other person seems upset by what is happening." They speculate upon the possibility of direct training in such covert, self-controlling statements, while bypassing problem-solving or role-taking procedures completely.

Chandler (1973), focusing on the cognitive deficits of juvenile offenders that interfere with appropriate social behavior, explored the role of egocentrism on antisocial behavior. Chandler assumed that prosocial behavior is linked to age-appropriate role taking or perspective taking and that social deviance is often associated with persistent egocentric thought. He hypothesized a relationship between persistent social egocentrism and chronic delinquent behavior. He sought to compare the development of perspective taking (role taking) skills in delinquent and nondelinquent youths, to design a program to teach role-taking skills, and to test the effectiveness of this training on subsequent delinquent behavior. Subjects in the study consisted of 45 delinquent boys, between ages 11 and 13, each with multiple police contacts, and 45 nondelinquent boys, 15 of whom lived in the same high-crime-rate area as the delinquent boys and 30 of whom were drawn from a middle-class and upper-middle-class suburban school system. Assessments included the Peabody Picture Vocabulary Test and a measure of social egocentrism based on an assessment procedure introduced by Flavell, Botkin, Fry, Wright, and Jarvis (1968). The delinquent and nondelinquent subjects demonstrated marked and statistically significant differences in the level of role-taking skills. Delinquent subjects showed marked deficits in the ability to differentiate their own point of view from that of others, and they regularly attributed to others information only available to themselves. Delinquent subjects were then randomly assigned to one of three groups: a nontreatment control group, a placebo treatment group, and a perspective-taking skill training group. The latter group engaged in drama and film making as vehicles for helping the youths see themselves from the perspective of others and for providing remedial training in role-taking skills. The hope was to have subjects step out of their own egocentric vantages and assume roles with different perspectives. While treatment group subjects made and viewed films about age-mates in real-life situations, placebo group members made animated and documentary films about their neighborhood. Placebo group members had no viewing opportunity and were not permitted to be included as characters in the film, thus missing the opportunity for the role taking, practice, and feedback present in the treatment group. On posttest measures, the experimental treatment group members showed a significant improvement in role-taking ability over that of placebo and control groups. Eighteen-month follow-up data available on 33 of the 45 original delinquent subjects indicated that subjects in all three groups committed somewhat fewer offenses, with the most striking result being in the experimental training group. The latter group committed approximately half as many officially known delinquencies during this period. These group differences were highly significant, suggesting a relationship between intervention and the subsequent delinquencies. Although cautioning that intervening factors must be considered, Chandler's study emphasizes the importance of the acquisition of certain formal, sociocognitive operations in effectively solving human interaction problems.

Interpersonal Problem-Solving Skills

Adolescent delinquents appear to be significantly poorer in providing effective solutions to interpersonal problems than are comparable groups of nondelinquents, and the same holds true for adult offenders. For example, Spivack and Levine (1963) found that middle-class juvenile delinquents, when compared to normals, possessed less ability to plan in a stepwise fashion and provided fewer possible consequences for their actions and less prior consideration of pros and cons in considering situations involving transgression. These findings were obtained regardless of Wechsler IQ. Thus, delinquent behavior in adolescence may be, in part, a function of inadequate interpersonal problem-solving skills (Little & Kendall, 1979).

Sarason and Ganzer (1973) sought to heighten the awareness of delinquent boys concerning what constitutes socially acceptable and effective behaviors. Assuming that social behavior is the direct result of information available to and incorporated by individuals, Sarason and Ganzer sought to compare the effect of conveying such information via discussion groups and via social modeling. Results indicated that no strong, consistent differences occurred between the two treatment groups. Both groups displayed positive change in attitudes and behavior when compared to the control group. It was hypothesized that the critical factor in both treatment groups may have been the teaching of problem-solving skills. Sarason and Ganzer called for further research to clarify interactions among treatment and personal characteristics. Along this line, Coates (1979) attempted to reduce disruptive behaviors by teaching self-instruction techniques. The results indicate that the trained boys responded with fewer nondeviant solutions to staged situations.

In defining interpersonal cognitive problem-solving skills, Spivack, Platt, and Shure (1976) suggested that the following skills were necessary for successful coping in interpersonal problematic situations: (a) sensitivity to interpersonal problems, (b) causal thinking, (c) consequential thinking, (d) alternative thinking, (e) means–ends thinking, and (f) perspective-taking. Their studies indicated that there are differences in the problem-solving skills of normal and deviant populations (Platt, Scura, & Hannon, 1973; Platt, Siegel, & Spivack, 1975; Platt & Spivack, 1972a,b, 1973, 1974; Spivack et al., 1976). For example, acting-out adolescents with adjustment problems were found to be deficient in means–ends thinking, alternative thinking, and perspective taking (Platt, Spivack, Altman, Altman, & Peizer, 1974). Similarly, Freedman, Rosenthal, Donahoe, Schlundt, and McFall (1978) reported that delinquents, when presented with a list of problem situations similar to those used by D'Zurilla & Goldfried (1971), gave responses judged to be significantly less adaptive than did nondelinquents.

Other research findings further underline the relevance of interpersonal cognitive problem-solving skills in the adjustment of delinquent and offender populations. Platt (1987) has reported several sets of data in this area. First, interpersonal cognitive problem-solving scores, specifically means–ends thinking and alternative thinking, were found to relate significantly to parole success or failure in 191 treatment program "graduates" following discharge from a correctional program for youthful offenders. Second, among failures, both scores were found to relate strongly to drug use, as measured by (a) rearrests for drug-related offenses, with subsequent identification by the criminal justice system as a "narcotic user," and (b) admissions to narcotics treatment programs or identification in parole reports as a narcotic user or addict. Strengthening the study's results, the parole follow-up and other outcome data were collected by probation officers who had no knowledge of group membership of individual subjects, thus avoiding possible bias due to a "halo" effect resulting from participation in treatment. In an earlier study, drug users had significantly lower interpersonal cognitive problem-solving scores than abstainers (Platt et al., 1973).

In another study reported by Platt (1987), peer nominations of parole success were solicited as well as nominations regarding which inmates among those on a correctional housing unit were most likely to be called upon to resolve interpersonal conflicts. This study demonstrated a clear and consistent relationship between, on the one hand, frequency of being nominated by peers as someone likely to succeed on parole and to be called upon to help resolve conflicts, and on the other hand, possession of a significantly higher than average level of means–ends and alternative thinking. Peer nomination as someone likely to succeed on parole may be an important predictor of parole success. Platt and Scura (1974) demonstrated that peer ratings of parole success predicted parole status (success vs. rearrest) at 6 and 15 months following discharge. Indeed, at 15 months after discharge only 1 of 27 subjects in the "low-success-rated" group had not been rearrested. In contrast, 61.5% of the "high-success-rated" group had not been rearrested. This last finding parallels the results of a study reported by Higgins and Thies (1981) in which they found reformatory inmates rated as "misfits" by peers and staff to be significantly poorer in terms of means–ends thinking scores than inmates rated as "satisfactorily adjusted."

In exploring the development of interpersonal cognitive problem-solving skills, Spivack et al. (1976) found a progression of skills emerging at various ages. The level of expertise demonstrated by an individual of any age in a particular situation will depend upon his or her having learned the cognitive factors needed to cope with that situation. If the skill is not present, the cognitive deficit may lead to ineffectual behavior on the part of the actor. In almost all age groups, the presence of impulsive acting-out behaviors, poor academic achievement, lower peer and school adjustment status, and labeling as *behaviorally maladjusted* reflected the relative absence, when compared to appropriate control groups, of interpersonal cognitive problem-solving skills. (Although too numerous to cite here, an annotated bibliography of the interpersonal cognitive problem-solving literature, containing some 270 references, is available from the senior author of this chapter).

Interpersonal Cognitive Problem-Solving Intervention Programs

Interpersonal problem-solving group therapy is a highly structured cognitive-behavioral skill development program developed to train interpersonal problem solving and prerequisite skills (Platt & Spivack, 1977; Platt, Spivack, & Swift, 1974). Although originally designed for a psychiatric population functioning at a lower level of adjustment, this program has been useful with adolescents and young adults whose level of cognitive interpersonal skill development is poor. What is important is that 8 units of the training program that are focused upon the acquisition of interpersonal problem-solving skills are preceded by 11 sequenced units designed to train prerequisite skills. Prerequisite skills are seen as necessary to enable an individual to implement the specific interpersonal problem-solving skills taught in the second half of the program. The decision to structure the program in this manner reflects the first author's experience in pilot work with various groups, including young offenders. This experience indicated that successful acquisition of specific interpersonal problem-solving skills was dependent upon certain prerequisite skills. These prerequisite skills included imitation and group discussion skills such as those used in the successful treatment of institutionalized delinquents (Sarason, 1968; Sarason & Ganzer, 1973). The prerequisite skill training also included Meichenbaum and Cameron's (1973) technique of training self-directed speech, McFall's behavioral rehearsal techniques (McFall & Lillesand, 1971; McFall & Marston, 1970), Draughton's (1973) technique of duplicating facial expression, Camp, Bloom, Gerbert, and Van Doornick's (1977) "think aloud" technique, Spohn and Wolk's (1963) discussion task for improving social participation, Morton's (1955) use of the Thematic Apperception Test as a training device, and a modification of the Matching Familiar Figures Task (Kagan, Rosman, Day, Albert, & Phillips, 1964).

Following the units focusing upon the techniques to enhance prerequisite skills are those directed toward acquisition of the interpersonal problem-solving skills themselves. These include (a) problem recognition, (b) alternative thinking, (c) means–ends thinking, (d) perspective taking, (e) causal thinking, and (f) considering consequences.

Most recently, a new interpersonal problem-solving training manual (Platt, Taube, Metzger, & Duome, 1987) was developed for use with young adult heroin addicts. Although loosely based on the original program by Platt, Spivack, and Swift (1974), this program was developed to meet the specific needs of the heroin addict group, which is in many ways, a more sophisticated group with respect to problem-solving ability than those worked with previously. Entitled *Training in Interpersonal Problem-Solving Skills* (TIPS), this program condenses the 19 units of the earlier program into 8 "core sessions" and provides explicit instructions for leaders as well as a workbook for group members. Outcome data indicated successful acquisition and retention of skills acquired in this training (Platt, Morell, Flaherty, & Metzger, 1982). Specifically, when compared to attention ($n=29$) and no-treatment control groups ($n=94$), the treatment group's ($n=56$) interpersonal problem-solving skills, as measured by Platt and Spivack's set of measures (Platt & Spivack, 1977), were maintained up to 1 year later. It is interesting that gains in interpersonal problem-solving scores were greatest for participants initially scoring lowest on interpersonal problem-solving skills. Although heroin use following treatment participation was not examined in this study, other findings reported by Platt (1987) indicated a significant inverse relationship between level of interpersonal problem-solving skills at completion of a treatment program for incarcerated addicts and later drug use. This, of course, does not establish that the treatment program in fact had an effect on heroin use.

In a successful treatment program for incarcerated heroin addict offenders, the interpersonal problem-solving approach was utilized as one therapy element among others (Platt, Perry, & Metzger, 1980). In this case, the interpersonal problem-solving intervention was designed to provide the following skills: (a) knowing when a problem exists, (b) defining the problem by putting it into words, (c) identifying the feeling associated with the problem, (d) separating facts from opinions, (e) getting all of the necessary information, (f) generating alternative solutions, (g) considering all of the consequences, and (h) deciding and acting on the best choice.

In a 2-year follow-up study, Platt, Perry, and Metzger (1980) found treatment program participants to have a significantly lower overall recommitment rate (18%) than controls (30%); to have a significantly lower recommittment rate for nondrug offenses (15% vs. 27%); and to be more likely to be in the two "good adjustment" categories (37% vs. 20%). What is most important is that significantly more program participants than controls remained arrest-free (51% vs. 34%) and, if arrested, this occurred later during parole (at 238 days vs. 168 days). Unfortunately, these data are not by themselves proof of the effectiveness of an interpersonal problem-solving intervention because other therapy program elements were included in the treatment package and because of a quasi-experimental design, which reflects the reality of correctional research. Yet the data do suggest the possible usefulness of this approach, particularly when considered in conjunction with Platt's (1987) previously described research findings with the same general population.

In general, all interpersonal problem-solving training programs focus on acquisition of communication and problem-solving skills, with training and feedback given in therapy groups. Homework assignments are given. Training is directed toward promoting more effective resolution of interpersonal conflicts and an increased awareness of how an individual's behavior affects others. Interpersonal problem-solving training emphasizes specific coping skills that appear to be common to a wide variety of situations and life stages. The chances for durability and generalization of outcomes appear to be high following skill acquisition.

With respect to prevention, Shure and Spivack (1982) have confirmed that early prediction of social adjustment and interpersonal competence is possible, thus enabling identification of children who are deficient in facets of interpersonal problem-solving skills. Those children who exhibit either inhibited or impulsive behaviors—the latter perhaps a direct precursor of aggression— could in many cases be identified and provided treatment before behaviors become stable. What is important is that Shure and Spivack (1982) demonstrated that aberrant behaviors were less likely to persist in children identified and trained with cognitive-behavioral techniques.

Conclusions

The cognitive-behavioral approach emphasizes the remediation of cognitions that interfere with the successful attainment of personal goals, with interpersonal interactions, and with a harmonious existence within the social structure. The interventions of self-instruction, modeling and rehearsal, perspective taking, and stress innoculation as well as other cognitive-behavioral approaches seek to educate the individual in positive, productive management styles by providing models and procedures that may be adopted and modified by the individual. The coupling of cognitive skill training with performance-based behavior therapy appears to result in a powerful integration of durable and useful interventions applicable to a wide variety of situations demanding coping skills. Relying exclusively upon external contingencies would seem to often lead to poor generalization. The research presented in this chapter has suggested that attention to cognitive factors along with response contingencies results in behavior change that is durable and generalizable. With specific respect to delinquent and criminal populations, and recognizing the danger inherent in oversimplification, theorists and practitioners are becoming aware that some individuals transgress societal rules due, at least in part, to an absence of skills that are essential in reaching personal goals in a complex interpersonal environment. Furthermore, evidence indicates that remediation of specific deficiencies in terms of cognitive and behavioral skills appears to have a generally positive impact upon future performance and/or ability to conform to culturally acceptable norms. We believe that the cognitive-behavioral approach has much promise. The research touched upon in this chapter is only a brief suggestion of the significant contribution the cognitive-behavioral approach can potentially make with delinquent and criminal populations.

References

Atrops, M. (1978). *Behavioral plus cognitive skills for coping with provocation in male offenders.* Unpublished doctoral dissertation, Fuller Theological Seminary.

Bandura, A. (1969). *Principles of behavior modification.* New York: Holt, Rinehart & Winston.

Bandura, A. (1973). *Aggression: A social learning analysis.* Englewood Cliffs, NJ: Prentice-Hall.

Bandura, A. (1976). Social learning analysis of aggression. In E. Ribes-Inesta & A. Bandura (Eds.), *Analysis of delinquency and aggression* (pp. 203–232). Hillsdale, NJ: Lawrence Erlbaum.

Bandura, A. (1977a). *Social learning theory.* New York: Wiley.

Bandura, A. (1977b). Self-efficacy: Toward a unifying theory of behavioral change. *Psychological Review, 84,* 191–215.

Beck, A. T. (1963). Thinking and depression: I. Idiosyncratic content and cognitive distortions. *Archives of General Psychiatry, 9,* 324–333.

Beck, A. T. (1976). *Cognitive therapy and the emotional disorders.* New York: International Universities Press.

Bowman, P. C., & Auerbach, S. M. (1982). Impulsive youthful offenders: A multimodal cognitive behavioral treatment program. *Criminal Justice and Behavior, 9,* 432–454.

Calhoun, K., & Turner, S. (1981). Historical perspectives and current issues in behavior therapy. In S. Turner, K. Calhoun, & H. Adams (Eds.), *Handbook of clinical behavior therapy* (pp. 1–9). New York: Wiley.

Camp, B. W., Bloom, G. E., Gerbert, J., & Van Doornick, W. J. (1977). Think aloud: A program for developing self-control in young aggressive boys. *Journal of Abnormal Child Psychology, 5,* 157–169.

Cautela, J. R. (1966). Treatment of compulsive behavior by covert sensitization. *Psychological Reports, 16,* 33–41.

Cautela, J. R. (1967). Covert sensitization. *Psychological Reports, 20,* 459–468.

Chandler, M. J. (1973). Egocentrism and antisocial behavior: The assessment and training of social perspective-taking skills. *Developmental Psychology, 9,* 326–333.

Coates, K. (1979). Cognitive self-instructional training approach for reducing disruptive behavior of young children. *Psychological Reports, 44,* 127–134.

Denicola, J., & Sandler, J. (1980). Training abusive parents in child management and self-control skills. *Behavior Therapy, 11,* 263–270.

Draughton, M. (1973). Duplication of facial expressions: Conditions affecting task and possible clinical usefulness. *Journal of Personality, 41,* 140–150.

D'Zurilla, T. J., & Goldfried, M. R. (1971). Problem-solving and behavior modification. *Journal of Abnormal Psychology, 78,* 107–126.

Ellis, A. (1962). *Reason and emotion in psychotherapy.* New York: Stuart.

Eyberg, S., & Ross, A. (1978). Assessment of child behavior problems: The validation of a new inventory. *Journal of Clinical Child Psychology, 7,* 113–116.

Fehrenbach, P. A., & Thelen, M. H. (1982). Behavioral approaches to the treatment of aggressive disorders. *Behavior Modification, 6,* 465–497.

Flavell, J. H., Botkin, P. T., Fry, C. L., Wright, J. W., & Jarvis, P. E. (1968). *The development of role-taking communication skills in children.* New York: Wiley.

Forman, S. G. (1980). A comparison of cognitive training and response cost procedures in modifying aggressive behavior in elementarly school children. *Behavior Therapy, 11,* 594–600.

Freedman, B. J., Rosenthal, L., Donahoe, C. P., Schlundt, D. G., & McFall, R. M. (1978). A social-behavioral analysis of skill deficits in delinquent and non-delinquent adolescent boys. *Journal of Consulting and Clinical Psychology, 46,* 1448–1462.

Goodwin, S., & Mahoney, M. (1975). Modification of aggression through modeling: An experimental probe. *Journal of Behavior Therapy and Experimental Psychiatry, 6,* 200–202.

Gough, H. G. (1948). A sociological theory of psychopathy. *American Journal of Sociology, 53,* 359–366.

Higgins, J. P., & Thies, A. P. (1981). Social effectiveness and problem-solving thinking of reformatory inmates. *Journal of Offender Counseling, Services, and Rehabilitation, 5,* 93–98.

Hollon, S., & Beck A. (1979). Cognitive therapy of depression. In P. Kendall & S. Hollon (Eds.), *Cognitive-behavioral interventions: Theory, research, and procedures* (pp. 153–204). New York: Academic Press.

Homme, L. E. (1965). Perspectives in psychology: XXIV. Control, coverants, the operants of the mind. *Psychological Record, 15,* 501–511.

Jesness, C. (1980). Was the Close-Holton project a "bummer?" In R. Ross & P. Gendreau (Eds.), *Effective correctional treatment* (pp. 361–366). Toronto: Butterworths.

Kagan, J., Rosman, B. L., Day, D., Albert, J., & Phillips, W. (1964). Information processing in the child: Significance of analytic and reflective attitudes. *Psychological Monographs, 78*(1, Serial No. 578).

Kanfer, F. H. (1970). Self-regulation: Research issues and speculations. In C. Neuringer & J. L. Michael (Eds.), *Behavior modification in clinical psychology* (pp. 178–220). New York: Appleton-Century-Crofts.

Kendall, P. C., & Braswell, L. (1982). Cognitive-behavioral self-control therapy for children: A component analysis. *Journal of Consulting and Clinical Psychology, 50,* 672–689.

Kendall, P. C., & Finch, A. J., Jr. (1978). A cognitive-behavioral treatment for impulsivity: A group comparison study. *Journal of Consulting and Clinical Psychology, 46,* 110–118.

Kendall, P. C., & Finch, A. J., Jr. (1979). Developing nonimpulsive behavior in children: Cognitive-behavioral strategies for self-control. In P. Kendall & S. Hollon (Eds.), *Cognitive-behavioral interventions: Theory, research and procedures* (pp. 153–204). New York: Acadmic Press.

Kendall, P., & Hollon, S. (Eds.). (1979). *Cognitive-behavioral interventions: Theory, research, and procedures.* New York: Academic Press.

Lazarus, A. A. (1977). Has behavior therapy outlived its usefulness? *American Psychologist, 32,* 550–554.

Levis, D. J. (1980). Do cognitive constructs enhance or threaten the survival of clinical behaviorism? In W. W. Tryon, C. B. Ferster, C. M. Franks, A. E. Kazdin, D. J. Levis, & G. S. Tryon (Eds.), *On the role of behaviorism in clinical psychology. Pavlovian Journal of Biological Science, 15,* 15–17.

Levis, D. J. (1982). Experimental and theoretical foundations of behavior modification. In A. Bellack, M. Hersen, & A. Kazdin (Eds.), *International handbook of behavior modification and therapy* (pp. 33–56). New York: Plenum Press.

Little, V., & Kendall, P. (1979). Cognitive-behavioral interventions with delinquents: Problem solving role-taking, and self-control. In P. Kendall & S. Hollon (Eds.), *Cognitive behavioral interventions: Theory, research, and procedures* (pp. 81–115). New York: Academic Press.

Luria, A. R. (1961). *The role of speech in the regulation of normal and abnormal behavior.* New York: Liveright.

Mahoney, M. J. (1974). *Cognition and behavior modification.* Cambridge, MA: Ballinger.

Mahoney, M. J. (1979). Cognitive issues in the treatment of delinquency. In J. S. Stumphauzer (Ed.), *Progress in behavior therapy with delinquents* (pp. 22–33). Springfield, IL: Charles C Thomas.

Mahoney, M., & Arnkoff, D. (1978). Cognitive and self-control therapies. In S. L. Garfield & A. E. Bergin (Eds.), *Handbook of psychotherapy and behavior change* (pp. 689–714). New York: Wiley.

McCullough, J. P., Huntsinger, G. M., & Nay, W. R. (1977). Case study: Self-control treatment of aggression in a 16-year-old male. *Journal of Consulting and Clinical Psychology, 45,* 322–331.

McFall, R. M., & Lillesand, D. B. (1971). Behavior rehearsal with modeling and coaching in assertion training. *Journal of Abnormal Psychology, 77,* 313–323.

McFall, R. M., & Marston, A. R. (1970). An experimental investigation of behavior rehearsal in assertive training. *Journal of Abnormal Psychology, 76,* 295–303.

Mead, G. H. (1934). Mind, self, and society. Chicago: University of Chicago Press.

Meichenbaum, D. (1977). *Cognitive behavior modification: An integrative approach.* New York: Plenum Press.

Meichenbaum, D., & Cameron, R. (1973). Training schizophrenics to talk to themselves: A means of developing attentional controls. *Behavior Therapy, 4,* 515–534.

Meichenbaum, D., & Goodman, J. (1971). Training impulsive children to talk to themselves: A means of developing self-control. *Journal of Abnormal Psychology, 77,* 115–126.

Morton, R. B. (1955). An experiment in brief psychotherapy. *Psychological Monographs, 69*(Serial No. 386).

Nietzel, M. (1979). *Crime and its modification: A social learning perspective.* New York: Pergamon Press.

Novaco, R. W. (1975). *Anger control: The development and evaluation of an experimental treatment.* Lexington, MA: D. C. Health, Lexington Books.

Novaco, R. W. (1976). Treatment of chronic anger through cognitive and relaxation controls. *Journal of Consulting and Clinical Psychology, 44,* 681.

Novaco, R. W. (1979). The cognitive regulation of anger and stress. In P. Kendall & S. Hollon (Eds.), *Cognitive-behavioral interventions: Theory, research, and procedures* (pp. 241–285). New York: Academic Press.

Ollendick, D. G., & Elliott, W. R. (1978). *Locus of control as related to effectiveness in a behavior modification program for juvenile delinquents.* Unpublished manuscript, Indiana State University, Terre Haute, Indiana.

Piaget, J. (1926). *The language and thought of the child.* New York: Harcourt, Brace.

Platt, J. J. (1987). *Real-life behavioral correlates of interpersonal cognitive problem-solving skills in youthful offenders.* Unpublished manuscript, University of Medicine and Dentistry of New Jersey, Camden, New Jersey.

Platt, J. J. and Scura, W. C. (1974). Peer judgements of parole success in heroin addicts. *Journal of Counseling Psychology, 21,* 511–515.

Platt, J. J., & Spivack, G. (1972a). Problem-solving thinking of psychiatric patients. *Journal of Consulting and Clinical Psychology, 39,* 148–151.

Platt, J. J., & Spivack, G. (1972). Social competence and effective problem-solving thinking in psychiatric patients. *Journal of Clinical Psychology, 28,* 3–5.

Platt, J. J., & Spivack, G. (1973). Studies in problem-solving thinking of psychiatric patients: (I) Patient-control differences; (II) Factorial structure of problem-solving thinking. [Summary], *Proceedings of the 81st Annual Convention of the American Psychological Association, 8,* 461–462.

Platt, J. J., & Spivack, G. (1974). Means of solving real-life problems: I. Psychiatric patients versus controls, and cross-cultural comparisons of normal females. *Journal of Community Psychology, 2,* 45–48.

Platt, J. J., & Spivack, G. (1977). *Measures of interpersonal cognitive problem-solving for adults and adolescents.* Unpublished manuscript, Hahnemann Medical College & Hospital, Department of Mental Health Sciences, Philadelphia.

Platt, J. J., Scura, W., & Hannon, J. R. (1973). Problem-solving thinking of youthful incarcerated heroin addicts. *Journal of Community Psychology, 1,* 278–281.

Platt, J. J., Spivack, G., Altman, N., Altman, D., & Peizer, S. B. (1974). Adolescent problem-solving thinking. *Journal of Consulting and Clinical Psychology, 42,* 787–793.

Platt, J. J., Spivack, G., & Swift, M. (1974). *Interpersonal problem-solving group therapy* (Research and Evaluation Report #31). Philadelphia: Hahnemann Medical College & Hospital.

Platt, J. J., Siegel, J. M., & Spivack, G. (1975). Do psychiatric patients and normals see the same solutions as effective in solving interpersonal problems? *Journal of Consulting and Clinical Psychology, 43,* 279.

Platt, J. J., Perry, G., & Metzger, D. (1980). The evaluation of a heroin addiction treatment programs within a correctional environment. In R. Ross & P. Gendreau (Eds.), *Effective correctional treatment* (pp. 421–437). Toronto: Butterworths.

Platt, J. J., Morell, J., Flaherty, E., & Metzger, D. (1982). *Controlled study of methadone rehabilitation process: Final report* (Grant No. R01-DA01929). Washington, DC: National Institute on Drug Abuse.

Platt, J. J., Taube, D. O., Metzger, D. S., & Duome, M. J. (1987). Training in interpersonal cognitive problem-solving (TIPS). *Journal of Cognitive Psychotherapy.*

Rachlin, H. (1977). Reinforcing and punishing thoughts. *Behavior Therapy, 8,* 659–665.

Rimm, D. C., & Lefebre, R. C. (1981). Phobic disorders. In S. M. Turner, K. S. Calhoun, & H. E. Adams (Eds.), *Handbook of clinical behavior therapy* (pp. 12–40). New York: Wiley.

Robin, A., Schneider, M., & Dolnick, M. (1976). The turtle technique: An extended case study of self-control in the classroom. *Psychology in the Schools, 13,* 449–453.

Rotter, J. (1966). Generalized expectancies for internal versus external control of reinforcement. *Psychological Monographs, 80,* 1–28.

Sarason, I. G. (1968). A cognitive social-learning approach to juvenile delinquency. In R. D. Hare & D. Schalling (Eds.), *Psychopathic behavior: Approaches to research* (pp. 299–317). New York: Wiley.

Sarason, I. G., & Ganzer, V. J. (1973). Modeling and group discussion in the rehabilitation of juvenile delinquents. *Journal of Counseling Psychology, 20,* 442–449.

Schantz, C. U. (1975). The development of social cognition. In E. M. Hetherington (Ed.), *Review of child development research* (Vol. 5, pp. 257–323). Chicago: University of Chicago Press.

Shure, M. B., & Spivack, G. (1982). Interpersonal problem-solving in young children: A cognitive approach to prevention. *American Journal of Community Psychology, 10,* 341–356.

Snyder, J. J., & White, M. H. (1979). The use of cognitive self-instruction in the treatment of behaviorally disturbed adolescents. *Behavior Therapy, 10,* 227–235.

Sollod, R. N., & Wachtel, P. L. (1980). A structural and transactional approach to cognition in clinical problems. In M. Mahoney (Ed.), *Psychotherapy Process* (pp. 1–4), New York: Plenum Press.

Spivack, G., & Levine, M. (1963). *Self-regulation in acting-out and normal adolescents* (Report M-4531). Washington, DC: National Institute of Mental Health.

Spivack, G., Platt, J. J., & Shure, M. B. (1976). *The problem-solving approach to adjustment: A guide to research and intervention.* San Francisco: Jossey-Bass.

Spohn, H. E., & Wolk, W. (1963). Effect of group problem-solving experience upon social withdrawal in chronic schizophrenics. *Journal of Abnormal and Social Psychology, 66,* 187–190.

Steele, B. J., & Pollock, C. B. (1968). Psychodynamic factors in child abuse. In R. E. Helfer & C. H. Kempe (Eds.), *The battered child* (pp. 49–85). Chicago: University of Chicago Press.

Stumphauzer, J. (1976). Elimination of stealing by self-reinforcement of alternate behavior and family contracting. In J. Stumphauzer (Ed.), *Progress in behavior therapy with delinquents* (pp. 22–33). Springfield, IL: Charles C Thomas.

Thoresen, C. E., & Mahoney, M. J. (1974). *Behavioral self-control.* New York: Holt, Rinehart and Winston.

Thoresen, K., Thoresen, C., Klein, S., Wilbur, C. S., Becker-Haven, J. F., & Haven, W. G. (1979). Learning House: Helping troubled children and their parents change themselves. In J. S. Stumphauzer (Ed.), *Progress in behavior therapy with delinquents* (pp. 156–185). Springfield, IL: Charles C Thomas.

Ullmann, L. P. (1970). On cognitions and behavior therapy. *Behavior Therapy, 1,* 201–204.

Vygotsky, L. S. (1962). *Thought and language.* Cambridge, MA: M.I.T. Press.

Wasserman, S. (1967). The abused parent of the abused child. *Children, 14,* 175–179.

Williams, D., & Akamatsu, J. (1978). Cognitive self-guidance training with juvenile delinquents: Applicability and generalization. *Cognitive Therapy and Research, 2*(3), 205–288.

Wolfe, D. A., Sandler, J., & Kaufman, K. (1981). A competency-based parent training program for child abusers. *Journal of Consulting and Clinical Psychology, 49,* 633–640.

Wolfe, D. A., Lawrence, J. S., Graves, K., Brehovy, D., & Kelly, J. A. (1982). Intensive behavioral parent training for a child abusive mother. *Behavior Therapy, 13,* 438–451.

Wolpe, J. (1973). *The practice of behavior therapy* (2nd ed.). New York: Pergamon.

Wolpe, J. (1978). Cognition and causation in human behavior and its therapy. *American Psychologist, 33,* 437–446.

19

Neurohormonal Bases of Varying Tendencies to Learn Delinquent and Criminal Behavior

LEE ELLIS

The value of applied behavior conditioning procedures for the day-to-day management of troublesome behavior by delinquents and criminals in institutional settings (e.g., training schools), in semiinstitutional settings (e.g., group homes), and even in individual family settings has been well established (see Braukmann & Fixsen, 1975; Wood & Flynn, 1978). Nevertheless, nearly all of the most rigorously designed follow-up studies of these programs have concluded that they do not reduce recidivism, at least beyond the first few months following program completion/release (for reviews see Blakely & Davidson, 1984; Davidson & Seidman, 1974; Redner, Snellman, & Davidson, 1983).

What is proposed here is that the failure of these programs to reduce recidivism may reflect the fact that substantial variation in delinquent and criminal behavior is due to neurological variables that current behavioral conditioning procedures are poorly equipped to override. By understanding these neurological variables, behavioral procedures, either alone or in conjunction with other treatment strategies (e.g., drug treatment), eventually may be found that substantially reduce recidivism for extended periods of time.

DISTINGUISHING VICTIMFUL AND VICTIMLESS DELINQUENCY AND CRIMINALITY

Before delving into the subject of delinquency and criminality in any detail, a fundamental distinction between two major categories of offenses needs to be made. One category is called *victimful offenses,* which include aggressive-personal crimes and property crimes. The other category is called *victimless offenses,* which include status (or age-contingent) offenses and a variety of other acts in which the offender does not directly harm other people

Lee Ellis • Department of Sociology, Minot State University, Minot, North Dakota 58701.

or their property (e.g., gambling and drug offenses). Variables associated with the commission of victimful offenses may have little or no association with involvement in victimless offenses, especially when the latter occur at relatively low frequencies. Also, whereas essentially all victimful offenses are universally condemned, most victimless offenses are not. Generally, the more personal damage, property damage, or property loss involved, the greater the tendency to condemn (Burkett & White, 1974, p. 456; Westermarck, 1908, p. 103). The reader is asked to understand that references to *delinquency* and *criminality* throughout the remainder of this report will focus primarily upon *victimful* delinquency and criminality, unless otherwise stated.

UNIVERSAL CORRELATES OF DELINQUENCY AND CRIMINALITY

About 8 years ago, I began an effort to identify variables that correlated with delinquent and criminal behavior in all studies where they had been examined. Despite skepticism by some fellow criminologists that *universal correlates* of criminal behavior exist, 15 were found. They can be grouped into two distinguishable, although not entirely independent, categories: demographic correlates and personality-behavioral correlates (Ellis, 1983).

Universal Demographic Correlates

At least seven variables that governments typically collect about their citizenry (i.e., demographic variables) were found to be associated with serious delinquency and criminality in quite consistent ways (Ellis, in press-a). The first five are (a) the stability of the marital bonds of one's parents, with unstable marital relationships associated with greater delinquency/criminality; (b) number of siblings, with greater numbers associated with greater delinquency/criminality; (c) race, with blacks having the highest, orientals the lowest, and whites intermediate levels of delinquency/criminality; (d) social status, with low status associated with high delinquency/criminality; and (e) urban-rural residence, with urban residence associated with greater delinquency/criminality. In the case of these variables, fairly large numbers of studies have been conducted in diverse parts of the world. Studies based upon officially detected and recorded offenses, which largely pertained to serious and victimful offenses, were universal in indicating the just described associations. Several studies based upon self-reported offenses reported no significant associations in the previously stated directions, but these were not considered crucial tests of the relationships because they largely pertained to trivial and/or victimless offenses (e.g., truancy, marijuana use, and running away from home). Overall, although the actual references and a detailed defense for the conclusions drawn cannot be given here, the literature search strongly supported the following conclusion: Regarding even moderately serious victimful offenses, the just described five demographic variables consistently tended to be associated with involvement in delinquency and crime in every country and time period.

Two other demographic correlates of delinquency and criminality were found to have been even more firmly established than the aforementioned five—sex and age. In every country studied (some with statistics extending back over 200 years), research showed delinquency and crime to be disproportionately committed by males, particularly between 12 and 30 years of age. By and large, the more serious and victimful the offenses, the more males in this adolescent–young adult age range dominated.

Universal Personality-Behavioral Correlates

Eight universal personality-behavioral correlates of delinquency and criminality were located (Ellis, in press-b). These were as follows: (a) defiance of punishment, (b) poor school performance, (c) impulsiveness and an unstable work history, (d) childhood hyperactivity, (e) risk-taking and excitement-seeking behavior (sensation seeking), (f) recreational (as opposed to therapeutic) use of neurologically active drugs, (g) preference for active, even chaotic, social interactions, and (h) tendencies to seek broad-ranging sexual experiences and thereby form unstable bonds with sex partners and offspring. As was true of the demographic variables, the strength of the correlations between these eight variables and delinquency/criminality also seemed to increase with increasing seriousness of the offenses with which they were related.[1]

NEUROLOGICALLY SPECIFIC EXPLANATIONS OF DELINQUENT AND CRIMINAL BEHAVIOR

In the past 20 years, a few theories of delinquency and criminality have hypothesized the involvement of fairly specific neurological processes (see Elliott, 1978; Ellis, 1979). Three of the most prominant of these theories will be reviewed here—arousal theory, seizuring theory, and hemispheric functioning theory. After each theory has been described, it will be argued that they all may be predicted from knowledge of how sex hormones affect brain functioning. Finally, I will return to the universal correlates of delinquency and criminality to show that much of the reason these correlates exist could involve neurohormonal factors.

---

[1]One more universal correlate (or cluster of correlates) of delinquency and crime was located, although its complexity and somewhat more tenuous nature required that it be given special treatment (Ellis, 1985). Based upon a review of approximately 50 studies, the generalizations were drawn that low probabilities of delinquency and criminality were associated with (a) frequent church attendance, (b) belief in an afterlife as opposed to skepticism, and (c) being Jewish, as opposed to Catholic, with Protestants overall being intermediate. Unlike the other universal demographic correlates, however, at least the first two of these religiosity correlates appeared to be as strong, if not stronger, regarding victimless and/or trivial offenses as they were for serious victimful offenses.

Arousal Theory

The first theory of delinquent and criminal behavior to hypothesize the involvement of a fairly specific neurological process was suggested about 20 years ago by Eysenck (1964; for a recent version, see Eysenck, 1977), although his hypothesis was preceded by a similar explanation for psychopathy almost a decade earlier by Lykken (1955, 1957; for a recent version, see Lykken, 1982). Although complicated by the inclusion of personality variables as intervening variables, Eysenck's theory can be basically summarized by the following three propositions:

1. An animal's (including human's) tendency to be responsive to its environment is substantially dependent upon how efficient its nervous system is in detecting and processing incoming stimulation.

2. Persons who are most likely to engage in delinquent and criminal behavior seem to have inherited (or occasionally acquired through disease, injury, or malnutrition) nervous systems that are unusually well "insulated" from the environment.

3. As a result, such persons are generally more difficult to condition, are more prone to endure pain, and will seek unusually intense stimulation.

In other words, for Eysenck and other arousal theorists, delinquency and criminality are largely just one of the behavioral symptoms of nervous systems that, for genetic (and sometimes other) reasons, are unusually resistant to conditioning. According to most arousal theorists, the neurological conditions that would cause people (and other animals) to vary in their resistance to conditioning mainly appear to surround the reticular activating system (RAS) and its autonomic support network.

A model for arousal theory is provided in Figure 1. According to this model, individuals whose normal resting states are above the preferred range (illustrated by Person A in Figure 1) will try to avoid environmental encounters (social and otherwise) that arouse them further. Individuals with normal resting states within the preferred range (Person B in Figure 1) will display behavior patterns that are predictably stable with reference to their normal environment. Finally, individuals whose normal resting state hovers below the preferred range (Person C in Figure 1) will seek novel and/or intense sensory stimulation to a degree that most people would avoid. The exact behavior, of course, could vary all the way from troublesome childhood antics, poor school performance, taking a variety of neurologically active drugs, pursuing numerous types of risks, seeking unusual sexual experiences, and committing crimes—which are the types of personality-behavior traits mentioned in the previous section as being universal correlates of delinquency/criminality. Arousal theory is helpful for explaining why persons who are seriously delinquent and criminal are more likely than others to defy punishment, to be considered impulsive, and to view the typical school environment as unappealing (and consequently to perform below their intellectual abilities).

Since 1970, at least two other versions of arousal theory have been offered with regard to delinquent and criminal behavior and/or psychopathy. One

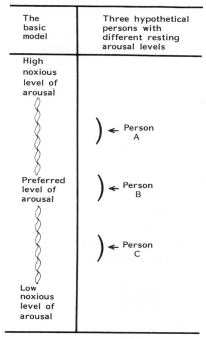

Figure 1. A model of arousal theory.

version asserts that criminals and psychopaths are unusually slow to shift from low or average arousal levels to high arousal when confronted with a threatening stimulus (see Hare, 1978, 1982; Woodman, 1979). This means that the normally noxious quality of high arousal would often fail to be paired with whatever provoked the high arousal.

The other version maintains that persons most prone toward criminal behavior and psychopathy are unusually slow to return to a preferred baseline once their arousal had been raised to a noxiously high level. This would have the effect of preventing the association of any withdrawal responses they might make with the reinforcement of a lowered arousal (see Mednick, 1975, 1977).

The three versions of arousal theory, of course, are not mutually exclusive. Although *arousal* has been difficult to operationalize, evidence has generally supported all three versions of the theory, although not without leaving much variance in delinquent and criminal behavior unexplained (see Mednick & Volavka, 1980). Nonetheless, there are several ways to operationalize *arousal,* although each has drawbacks (Humphreys & Revelle, 1984, p. 158). A useful analogy is to say that a person's arousal level is like the state of the nation's economy. Both concepts ultimately are so complex and pervasive that they must be measured with several different indexes to get a reasonably good "fix" on what one is trying to operationalize. The operational definitions for arousal basically fall into two broad categories: neurological and extraneurological.

Neurological measures include basic brain wave readings taken from electrodes attached to the scalp. Even though these electrodes primarily tap electrical activity occuring in the neocortex, rather than in the lower brain centers (which includes the RAS), neocortical activity does appear to reflect RAS functioning to at least a moderate degree. Consistent with what arousal theory would lead one to expect, studies have revealed that the most common EEG trait associated with serious criminality and/or psycopathy is unusually high percentages of slow wave (in the slow alpha or even theta range) cortical activity (Elliott, 1978; Gabrielli & Mednick, 1983; Mednick & Volavka, 1980).

Extraneurological measures of arousal include electrodermal activity (or skin conductivity) readings. Although skin conductance measures have been successful only occasionally in discriminating subpopulations of persons convicted of criminal behavior (e.g., those diagnosed psychopathic from those not so diagnosed; see Hare, 1978, p. 128), skin conductance measures have shown that, on average, persons with a history of serious delinquency and criminality have slightly lower resting levels of arousal, are less prone to arousal when provoked under standard test conditions, and recover to baseline more slowly than most other persons once they have been aroused (for reviews, see Ellis, 1983; Mednick & Volavka, 1980; Raine & Venables, 1984). In addition, some evidence suggests that criminally prone persons may simply be somewhat more volatile and unpredictable in their arousal tendencies (Blackburn, 1975; Mawson & Mawson, 1977).

Despite these average differences, however, one should quickly point out that all studies have found much overlap between persons with a history of serious criminality and persons who have no such history.

Seizuring Theory

Another type of neurologically specific theory of delinquency and criminality that has received considerable scientific attention in recent years focuses on brain seizures that are most often provoked under conditions of stress and possibly after alcohol consumption. One of the leading lines of evidence consists of numerous reports that higher incidences of epilepsy are found among criminals than among general populations (e.g., Blumer & Migeon, 1975; Derro, 1978, p. 337; Geschwind, 1975; Gunn & Fenton, 1971; King & Young, 1978; Lewis, Shanok, Pincus, & Giammarino, 1982; Roth & Ervin, 1971; Walker & Blumer, 1975; Whitman et al., 1984). Specifically, although the incidence of epilepsy among even the most serious and persistent offenders is less than 5%, rates have almost always been found to be at least twice as high as in nearly all populations at large (less than 1%) (Hauser & Kurland, 1975; Kurland, 1959; Merritt, 1973, p. 740).

In 1970, two books appeared that interpreted this and other evidence as suggesting a connection between brain seizures and criminal violence (Mark & Ervin, 1970; Monroe, 1970). A central theme in both books was that, although full-blown epileptic seizures are so debilitating as to preclude coordinated attacks upon bystanders (Delgado-Escueta *et al.*, 1981, p. 715), milder and more localized brain seizures—called *nonconvulsive seizures*—could evoke attacks upon persons in the vicinity of a seizuring individual. Many of these persons, in fact, may never be diagnosed as epileptic because their seizures are confined to subcortical brain regions beyond the detection of surface (scalp) electrodes and are subconvulsive (i.e., they do not result in epileptic fits).

The most vulnerable areas of the brain for seizures that could trigger rageful emotions are in and around the limbic system, a portion of the brain that has evolved among mammals primarily to control what might be called "social emotions" (as opposed to more basic emotions surrounding the desire for "creature comforts"). Nonhuman animal experiments indicate that the limbic system and its surrounding area are very important in controlling emotional rage (see Ingber, 1982, p. 35; McBroom, 1980, p. 41). Clinical studies have revealed that subjective experiences associated with limbic-system functioning are ones often described as profoundly meaningful and enlightening, as though the true meaning of life suddenly became apparent (MacLean, 1978, p. 331; Persinger, 1983, p. 1256).

As originally formulated, seizuring theory was seen as pertaining almost exclusively to "crimes of passion," most notably spouse and child abuse or fights among acquaintances and possibly some sexual assaults. Epilepsy, however, appears to be no less common among serious and persistent criminals generally than among criminals who have committed aggressive crimes in states of anger (Gunn, 1977; Whitman *et al.*, 1984). This implies that something about the cause of epilepsy (and, presumably, of seizuring generally) is also increasing the probability of all serious delinquent and criminal behavior, not just explosive aggressive criminality. The nature of this common cause will be proposed shortly.

Hemispheric Functioning Theory

A third neurologically specific theory of delinquent and criminal behavior started to appear about a decade ago and postulated that some aspect (or aspects) of how the two hemispheres of the neocortex functionally interrelate may predispose some persons toward criminality more than others (Andrew, 1982; Flor-Henry, 1974, 1978, 1979; Krynicki, 1978; Yeudall, 1977, 1980).

Nearly all of the pertinent evidence points away from the left hemisphere—which for most people controls most sequential-logical linguistic reasoning skills. Instead, the right hemisphere—which usually produces thoughts that are more "holistic," intuitive, and spatial in character (see Sperry, 1982, p. 1225)—has been repeatedly implicated with regard to delinquent and criminal conduct. The precise nature of such thought processes is still under investigation, but a number of studies using diverse methodologies have shown that, for most people, the right hemisphere is more involved in processing emotional information than the left hemisphere (e.g., Landis, Graves, & Goodglass, 1982; Morrow, Vrtunski, Kim, & Boller, 1981; Schwartz, Davidson, & Maer, 1975; Tucker, Watson, & Heilman, 1977). The evidence is especially strong for what might be called "negative emotions," such as hate, jealousy, cynicism, and sexual lust (Alford & Alford, 1981; Bear & Fedio, 1977, p. 465; Borod, Koff, & White, 1983; Hirskowitz, Karacan, Thornby, & Ware, 1984; Hoffman & Goldstein, 1981; Sackeim, Gur, & Saucy, 1978; Tucker, Stensile, Roth, & Shearer, 1981).

In some ways, the right hemisphere appears to be more functionally integrated with the limbic system than is the left hemisphere, at least for most people (Morrow et al., 1981). This, plus the fact that the right hemisphere is less prone to process and respond to linguistic stimuli than the left hemisphere, leads one to suspect that, for whatever reason, people who rely most on the right hemisphere in their thought processes tend to be both more emotionally "negative" and less dependent upon language for guiding their actions. Hare and McPherson (1984, p. 148) have suggested that the more people's thought processes are dominated by the right hemisphere, the more unlikely they will be to respond to linguistic rules of conduct as discriminative stimuli.

Linking the previously mentioned evidence with knowledge that the right hemisphere tends to control movement on the left side of the body and that the left hemisphere tends to control movement on the right side (Fincher, 1981, p. 32) leads to the prediction that handedness (and possibly other forms of sidedness) should be associated with delinquency and criminality. Consistent with that prediction, many studies over the years have found that, at least among males, left (and mixed) handers are more highly represented in delinquent and criminal populations than they are among general populations (Andrew, 1978; Blumer, Williams, & Mark, 1974; Ellis, 1910, p. 118; Fitzhugh, 1973; Flor-Henry, 1978; Gabrielli & Mednick, 1980; Hurwitz & Christiansen, 1983, p. 25; Krynicki, 1978; Virkkunen, Nuutila, & Huusko, 1976; Yeudall & Fromm-Auch, 1979; Yeudall, Fedora, Fedora, & Wardell, 1981; for a failure to replicate, see Hare & Forth, 1985).

Because the previously cited reports all employed official measures of delinquency and crime and confined their samples to males, an associate and I recently examined the relationship among both sexes by using a self-report questionnaire (Ellis & Ames, 1984). Our study basically confirmed previous findings of a left-handedness–criminality link for males (although all of the significant associations were of modest magnitude) but not for females. Our basic explanation for an almost complete lack of significant handedness–criminality relationships among females (despite the female sample having been nearly twice as large as the male sample) centered around a threshold concept of how sex hormones alter brain functioning. An outline of this concept is contained in the following section.

Subsuming the Three Theories under a Neuroandrogenic Theory

Evidence now is presented that arousal theory, seizuring theory, and hemispheric functioning theory may have one important feature in common:

They all appear to describe effects of exposing the nervous system to high levels of androgens (and/or its metabolite, estradiol).

Androgens encompass a variety of hormones (the main one is testosterone) that tend to masculinize animals exposed to them. Studies of humans and other mammals have shown that male levels of androgens surpass female levels at comparable stages of development (both prior to and after birth), except for shortly following birth up to the onset of puberty (when male levels on average only slightly surpass female levels) (Ellis, 1982b, p. 173; Nyborg, 1983, p. 117).

Although androgens work throughout the body, testosterone, in particular, has a chemical structure that allows it to enter the nervous system readily and thereby alter brain functioning. Testosterone (and its metabolite, estradiol) has been shown to have both permanent *organizing effects* (largely during the gestation process) and transient *activating effects* (mainly following the onset of puberty) upon brain functioning (Broida & Svare, 1984, p. 65; Coe & Levine, 1983, p. 132). The general nature of the effects is to lay down permanent chemical receptor sites for testosterone and estradiol in the brain during gestation but not to activate these sites fully until puberty. At puberty, the hormones are produced in large quantities (primarily by the testes but also by the ovaries and adrenals) and enter the brain once again en masse. To the degree that there are numerous receptor sites to be filled (which would be the case if the brain were exposed to high androgen levels before birth), brain functioning is altered substantially.

What is most interesting about androgens with respect to criminology surrounds the degree to which the so-called *pubertal surge* in testosterone parallels the rise in delinquency and crime probabilities (Ellis, 1978; see Martin, Sechrest, & Redner, 1981, p. 59). Although a causal connection between androgens and serious, persistent delinquency and criminality has been frequently postulated (e.g., Durden-Smith & deSimone, 1983, p. 86; Kruez & Rose, 1972, p. 330; Mattsson, 1981, p. 213; Mednick, Pollock, Volavka, & Gabrielli, 1982, p. 66; Rutter & Giller, 1984, p. 125; Tiger, 1975, p. 124), the question about what exactly testosterone, and its metabolites, may do to the brain to make delinquency and criminality more probable has rarely been addressed.

A search for the answer to this question gradually drew me to the three neurologically specific theories just outlined. I gradually accumulated evidence that among the effects that androgens have on brain functioning are the following: (a) they appear to lower the overall responsiveness of the brain's arousal mechanisms to stimuli; (b) they seem to increase the probability of brain seizures (at least in and around the limbic system); and (c) they are very likely to cause neocortical functioning to shift to the right hemisphere.

Detailed reviews of supportive evidence appear elsewhere (Ellis, 1983, 1986), but a summary of the evidence is worth presenting here. Regarding arousal, many studies, both in humans (e.g., Buchsbaum, Davis, Coppola, & Dieter, 1981; McGrew, 1979, p. 443; Woodrow, Friedman, Seigelaub, & Collen, 1977) and in other mammalian species (Beatty, 1978; Gandelman, 1983; except for gerbils where there are no sex differences, Beatty & Holzer 1978), indicate that males on average have higher levels of pain tolerance than females (the degree of difference is similar to the human sex difference in height, thus allowing for considerable overlap between the sexes). Experiments with rodents have shown that these average sex differences can be eliminated by elevating perinatal female androgen exposure to within the male range or by reducing perinatal male levels to within the typical female range (Beatty & Fessler, 1977; Redmond, Baulu, Murphy, Loriaux, & Zeigler, 1976, p. 322). Other indications that organizing and/or activating effects of androgens on the nervous system depress arousal comes from avoidance conditioning studies. In a wide variety of species, males have been found to be harder to train in avoidance conditioning tasks (e.g., Mactutus & Tilson, 1984; Sackett, 1974, p. 145; Shephard-Look, 1982, p. 419); in addition, several experiments have shown perinatal androgen levels to be the main factor responsible for this average sex difference (e.g., Chambers, 1982; Gray, Rickwood, Drewett, & Dunne, 1977; Meisel, Dohanich, & Ward, 1979), although postpubertal levels may augment the effects of perinatal levels.

Concerning brain seizuring, studies have repeatedly found epilepsy to be somewhat more common among males than among females, both in humans (e.g., Stedman, van Heyninger, & Lindsay, 1982, p. 69; Turner, 1973, p. 17) and in other mammalian species (Bevan, 1955, p. 482; Bielfelt, Redman, & McClellan, 1971, p. 2046; Ginsburg & Fuller, 1954; Kupke, Lewis, & Rennick, 1979). Experiments with nonhumans have demonstrated that perinatal levels of androgens and/or its metabolite, estradiol, increase seizuring susceptibility (e.g., Bevan & Chinn, 1956; Ginsburg & Fuller, 1954).

Finally, regarding neocortical functioning, considerable evidence has implicated androgens as a major cause of a "rightward shift" in hemispheric control over "higher thought." This evidence includes numerous studies documenting that males on average perform spatial-holistic reasoning tasks better than females, both in humans (e.g., McKeever, Seitz, Hoff, Marino, & Diehl, 1983, p. 665; Smail & Kelly, 1984) and in other species, as indicated by speed in error-free maze learning (e.g., Begley & Carey, 1979, p. 104; Goldman, 1976; Goy & McEwen, 1980, p. 31). Recent experiments with rodents have suggested that these sex differences in spatial reasoning are largely due to sex differences in hemispheric functioning (Biaki, 1983; Glick, Schoenfeld, & Strumpf, 1980). Other rodent experiments have shown that the sex differences can be largely eliminated by eliminating normal sex differences in organizational and activational exposure to androgens and estradiol levels (e.g., Beatty, 1979; McGivern, Claney, Hill, & Noble, 1984; Rhawn, Hess, & Birecree, 1978). Among humans, growing evidence has indicated that there are substantial sex differences in neocortical functioning centering around how the two hemispheres interrelate, although the details of these functional differences are still not fully understood (Bryden, 1979; Inglis & Lawson, 1981).

From the study mentioned earlier by Ashley Ames and myself, we hypothesized that the reason a handedness–criminality relationship was largely confined to the male sample was due to a critical threshold of perinatal androgen levels that most male brains, but few female brains, surpass sufficiently to enhance one's victimful criminal tendencies. If such a hypothesis should be confirmed, it may be worthwhile to look for other critical threshold requirements for androgens to increase susceptibility to brain seizuring or to lower arousal levels.

None of this is to suggest that androgens are the only cause of variations in arousal levels, seizuring thresholds, or a "rightward shift" in neocortical functioning, or that many other variables are not involved in causing delinquent and criminal behavior. There are likely to be hundreds of causes for each aspect of brain functioning and many of these causes are bound to be experiential in nature. Nevertheless, the evidence suggests that the primary cause of the *average sex difference* in these three aspects of brain functioning has to do with the neurological effects of androgens and some of the key metabolites of androgens (primarily estradiol). If so, androgen infiltration of the nervous system both before birth and after puberty is likely to alter brain functioning in ways that increase the probability of delinquency and criminal behavior.

RECONSIDERING THE UNIVERSAL CORRELATES OF DELINQUENCY AND CRIMINALITY

The theory that androgenic effects upon at least three different aspects of brain functioning increase the likelihood of delinquency and criminality leads to the expectation that a number of variables would be universally associated with delinquency and criminality.

First and foremost, males should be more delinquent and criminal than females and, because a sharp rise in testosterone marks the onset of male puberty, it is not surprising that male offense probability would rise rapidly in the early teenage years. Nevertheless, these associations are only true at an aggregate level, and one cannot conclude that the measurement of an *individual's* androgen levels will predict his or her delinquency probability.

Regarding the eight personality-behavioral correlates of delinquency and criminality, the theory would explain such behavior tendencies as defiance of punishment, impulsiveness, risk taking and excitement seeking, nontherapeutic drug use, preference for chaotic social interactions, and unstable bonding with sex partners and offspring as primarily reflecting attempts to compensate for suboptimal arousal levels. Regarding poor school performance, both suboptimal arousal and shifting away from left hemispheric domination in higher thought processes could be responsible for a number of so-called *learning disabilities* and for why these disabilities are more common in criminal populations than in the general population.

The neurohormonal theory outlined here fails to explain directly why such traits as parental marital stability, number of siblings, race, social status, and urban-rural residency would be universally correlated with delinquency and criminality. A new hypothesis recently advanced by Rushton

(1985), however, surrounding the concept of *r–K selection* may be integrated with the theory to help account for these statistical associations. Basically, *r-selection* refers to reproductive processes that emphasize numbers of offspring produced and, at the same time, that deemphasize parental investment in each offspring. *K-selection,* on the other hand, refers to approaches to reproduction that place a premium value (from a natural selection standpoint) on high parental investment and, in the process, that sacrifice maximal fecundity (Daly & Wilson, 1978, p. 124; Gadgil & Solbrig, 1972). At least in large urban populations, natural selection may favor r- over K-selection. As Rushton suggests, such variables as marital instability, large family size, social status, race, and criminality may be all crude proxy variables for these natural selection effects. Such a hypothesis would imply that males, especially soon after reaching puberty, are more r-selected than females and that androgens essentially have evolved to promote r- over K-selection (Ellis, 1987).

This line of reasoning implies that genetic factors play a causal role in delinquency and criminality. Since the 1970s, especially, strong evidence has accumulated to support the conclusion that genetic factors do contribute to a propensity toward such behavior (for reviews, see Ellis, 1982a, Mednick *et al.*, 1982; Rowe & Osgood, 1984; Van Dusen, Mednick, Gabrielli, & Hutchings, 1983; see also Cadoret, Cain, & Crowe, 1983; Mednick, 1985). The strongest evidence has come from studies of adoptees. Even though they were adopted near birth by nonrelatives and have had no significant contact with their genetic parents, adoptees with serious criminal records (e.g., a felony arrest or conviction) tend to more closely resemble their genetic parents regarding such behavior (using the same measures) than they resemble their rearing parents.

The neurohormonal theory sketched out here eventually may help to explain how some of the genetic influences operate, although whatever the final processes may be, they are bound to be complex, even without the confounding effects of experiential variables. The basic Darwinian perspective under which the neurohormonal theory may be subsumed also could help account for why purely social approaches to the prevention and treatment of delinquency and criminality have been fairly ineffective. In the future, manipulating both neurohormonal *and* social environmental variables simultaneously may eventually yield effective prevention and treatment approaches to delinquency and criminality.

SUMMARY AND CONCLUSIONS

Three neurologically specific theories of delinquent and criminal behavior have been discussed to demonstrate recent efforts at developing a better understanding of how brain functioning appears to alter the probability of delinquent and criminal behavior at various points in human development. Such theories in no way deny the role of learning in such behavior but maintain that some persons, at least at some periods in their lives, more readily learn and/or are more easily provoked into delinquent and criminal conduct by the social environments they confront than other persons.

First, arousal theory asserts that behavior often can be understood as an effort to maintain an optimal level of arousal and that delinquents and criminals may be unusually prone to have suboptimal arousal levels, thus inclining them to seek new stimulation in a variety of ways and to tolerate more pain in the process of doing so. Second, seizuring theory contends that explosive aggression and other forms of emotionally impulsive acts of a criminal nature may be triggered by subconvulsive brain seizures localized in or around major emotion-motivation control centers in and around the limbic system. Third, hemispheric functioning theory holds that involvement of the more impulsive, "nonlinguistic" right hemisphere in higher thought may prevent persons from attending to linguistic commands and otherwise to be more cynical and defiant of environmental control efforts.

Following a discussion of these three theories, evidence was reviewed indicating that the effects of androgens on the mammalian brain may be a common denominator for all three theories. Both human and nonhuman animal data indicate that androgens alter brain functioning in ways that increase the probability of (a) suboptimal arousal, (b) seizuring, and (c) a rightward shift in neocortical functioning.

Like social scientists generally, most criminologists still work from a rationalistic (or mentalistic) perspective (Ellis, 1977, p. 78). From this perspective, the fundamental driving force behind most human behavior is conscious, rational thought that is considered irreducible to neurochemistry and is a feature of behavior control believed to distinguish humans from all other animals. Such a perspective allows one to conclude that knowledge of the brain and how it works is superfluous to understanding delinquent and criminal behavior.

The approach represented in the present chapter may be called a *genetic-environmental, neurologically mediated interactionist (GENMI)* approach. It stands in opposition to the rationalist perspective in at least three important respects. First, it assumes that the physical-chemical functioning of the brain is directly responsible for all behavior and, second, that this is just as true for human behavior as it is for the behavior of other animals. Third, the physical-chemical functioning of the brain is assumed to be the result of the interaction of genetic and environmental factors, not simply the result of environmental factors (Ellis, 1982a, p. 44). Environmental factors not only include "tangible" factors that are known to alter brain functioning (drugs, poisons, physical injuries, etc.) but also innumerable experiential factors (causing what is known as *learning*). Thought (rational or otherwise), according to the GENMI perspective, is essentially just another thing that functioning brains do in the course of controlling behavior.

Behaviorism essentially constitutes a third approach to the study of complex human behavior. Behaviorism and the GENMI perspective both tend to regard the rationalist assumption that human motives, roles, and customs are irreducible causes of human behavior as incorrect. Unlike those with an GENMI perspective, however, behaviorists have tended to avoid conjecture about how specific brain functioning patterns may alter behavior. In addition, most behaviorists seem to concur with rationalists that experiences following birth—not genetic endowment, exposure of the brain to hormones, and the like—are largely responsible for human variations in behavior. Thus, most behaviorally oriented criminologists have traditionally sided with rationalists in the assumption that, except for their different social environmental experiences, everyone would be more or less equally disposed toward delinquency and criminality.

Despite this essential agreement with rationalism regarding the importance of social environmental variables in regulating human behavior, behaviorism developed out of a philosophical and methodological tradition that assumed human behavior was governed by the same basic laws (in a scientific, not legalistic sense) as those governing the behavior of other animals (Wyers et al., 1980, p. 958). In this respect, behaviorism is more consistent with the GENMI perspective than with rationalism. In addition, Darwinian evolutionary theory, which can be seen as subsuming the GENMI perspective—in which behavior is seen as part of the adaptive "strategies" that organisms (and the genes they carry) have made to their environments (Ellis, 1982c)—is considered by many behaviorists as consistent with their perspective (Skinner, 1984; Smith, 1983).

Overall, differences between behaviorism and the GENMI approach are largely ones of emphasis. Behaviorists emphasize the importance of learning and the degree to which learning is independent of genetics. They also have championed, more than any other group of social/behavioral scientists, the need to demonstrate in empirical terms that specific techniques for changing behavior are actually effective.

Those taking a GENMI approach emphasize the need to understand how the brain functions in order to understand and change behavior. To date, this emphasis has caused them to concentrate primarily upon relatively gross "hard-wired" brain functions than upon brain functions surrounding complex learning processes. Presumably, this is because learning, and the behavior accompanying it, typically involves physical-chemical changes in brain functions that are still extremely difficult to detect. Nevertheless, as the neurologically specific approach develops, more and more of its attention should focus upon brain processes accompanying the conditioning procedures that behaviorists have led the way toward elucidating.

Behaviorists can point to many areas of human conduct in which effective conditioning procedures for changing behavior have now been developed (Peterson, 1976, p. 577); and all must agree that these accomplishments have been made with little or no understanding of the underlying neurological functioning. However, now that shortcomings to the behaviorist approach have appeared regarding the production of enduring reductions in recidivism among delinquents/criminals, the GENMI perspective may be able to help. Integrating applied behavioral procedures and programs with discoveries about how people may neurologically differ in their conditionability may provide important leads to effective treatment and prevention. In other words, by working together, both behaviorism and the GENMI perspective may benefit, and criminology could be an ideal field in which to try.

ACKNOWLEDGMENTS

Helpful comments on drafts were provided by Heather Ellis and M. Ashley Ames.

REFERENCES

Alford, R., & Alford, F. (1981). Sex differences in asymmetry in the facial expression of emotion. *Neuropsychologia, 19,* 605–608.

Andrew, J. M. (1978). Why can't delinquents read? *Perceptual and Motor Skills, 47,* 640–642.

Andrew, J. M. (1982). Memory and violent crime among delinquents. *Criminal Justice and Behavior, 9,* 364–471.

Bear, D. M., & Fedio, P. (1977). Quantitative analysis of interictal behavior in temporal lobe epilepsy. *Archives of Neurology, 34,* 454–467.

Beatty, W. W. (1978). DRL behavior in gerbils and hamsters of both sexes. *Bulletin of the Psychonomic Society, 11,* 41–42.

Beatty, W. W. (1979). Gonadal hormones and sex differences in non-reproductive behaviors in rodents: Organizational and activational influences. *Hormones and Behavior, 12,* 112–163.

Beatty, W. W., & Fessler, R. G. (1977). Gonadectomy and sensitivity to electric shock in the rat. *Physiology and Behavior, 19,* 1–6.

Beatty, W. W., & Holzer, G. A. (1978). Sex differences in shock thresholds in rats and gerbils and the day-night cycle. *Bulletins of the Psychonomic Society, 11,* 71–72.

Begley, S., & Carey, J. (1979, November). The sexual brain. *Newsweek,* (Nov. 26) pp. 100–105.

Bevan, W. (1955). Sound-precipitated convulsions: 1947–1954. *Psychological Bulletin, 52,* 473–504.

Bevan, W., & Chinn, R. M. (1956). Audiogenic convulsions in male rats before and after castration and during replacement therapy. *Physiological Zoology, 29,* 309–313.

Biaki, V. L. (1983). Factors of the vertebrates' brain lateralization. *Fiziologicheskii Zhurnal SSSR, 69,* 865–875.

Bielfelt, S. W., Redman, H. C., & McClellan, R. O. (1971). Sire- and sex-related differences in rates of epileptiform seizures in the purebred beagle dog colony. *American Journal of Veterinary Research, 32,* 2039–2048.

Blackburn, R. (1975). Aggression and the EEG: A quantitative analysis. *Journal of Abnormal Psychology, 84,* 358–365.

Blakely, C. H., & Davidson, W. S. (1984). Behavioral approaches to delinquency: A review. In P. Karoly & J. J. Steffen (Eds.), *Adolescent behavior disorders: Foundations and contemporary concerns* (pp. 241–271). Lexington, MA: Lexington Books.

Blumer, D. P., & Migeon, C. (1975). Hormone and hormonal agents in the treatment of aggression. *Journal of Nervous and Mental Disease, 160,* 127–137.

Blumer, D. P., Williams, H. W., & Mark, U. H. (1974). The study and treatment, on a neurological ward, of abnormally aggressive patients with focal brain disease. *Confinia Neurologica, 36,* 125–176.

Borod, J. C., Koff, E., & White, B. (1983). Facial asymmetry in posed and spontaneous expressions of emotion. *Brain and Language, 2,* 165–175.

Braukmann, C. J., & Fixsen, D. L. (1975). Behavior modification with delinquents. In M. Hersen, R. M. Eisler, & P. M. Miller (Eds.), *Progress in behavior modification* (Vol. 1; pp. 193–231). New York: Academic Press.

Broida, J., & Svare, B. (1984). Sex differences in the activity of mice: Modulation by postnatal gonadal hormones. *Hormones and Behavior, 18,* 65–78.

Bryden, M. P. (1979). Evidence for sex-related differences in cerebral organization. In M. A. Wittig & A. C. Petersen (Eds.), *Sex-related differences in cognitive functioning* (pp. 121–143). New York: Academic Press.

Buchsbaum, M. S., Davis, G. C., Coppola, R., & Dieter, N. (1981). Opiate pharmacology and individual differences. I. Psychophysical pain measurement. *Pain, 10,* 357–366.

Burkett, S. R., & White, W. (1974). Hellfire and delinquency: Another look. *Journal for the Scientific Study of Religion, 13,* 455–462.

Cadoret, R. J., Cain, C. A., & Crowe, R. R. (1983). Evidence for gene-environment interaction in the development of adolescent antisocial behavior. *Behavior Genetics, 13,* 301–307.

Chambers, K. (1982). Failure of ACTH to prolong extinction of conditioned taste aversion in the absence of the testes. *Physiology and Behavior, 29,* 915–919.

Coe, C. L., & Levine, S. (1983). Biology of aggression. *Bulletin of the American Academy of Psychiatry and the Law, 11,* 131–148.

Daly, M., & Wilson, M. (1978). *Sex, evolution and behavior.* North Scituate, MA: Duxbury.

Davidson, W. S., & Seidman, E. (1974). Studies of behavior modification and juvenile delinquency: A review, methodological critique, and social perspective. *Psychological Bulletin, 31,* 998–1011.

Delgado-Escueta, A. V., Mattson, R. H., King, L., Goldensohn, E. S., Spiegel, H., Madsen, J., Crandall, P., Dreifuss, F., & Porter, R. J. (1981). The nature of aggression during epileptic seizures. New England Journal of Medicine, 305, 711–716.

Derro, R. A. (1978). Admission health evaluation of inmates of a city-county workhouse. *Minnesota Medicine, 61,* 333–337.

Durden-Smith, J., & deSimone, D. (1983). *Sex and the brain.* New York: Warner.

Elliott, F. A. (1978). Neurological aspects of antisocial behavior. In W. H. Reid (Ed.), *The psychopath: A comprehensive study of antisocial disorders and behaviors* (pp. 146–189). New York: Brunner/Mazel.

Ellis, H. (1910). *The criminal.* New York: Walter Scott.

Ellis, L. (1977). Rejoinder. *American Sociologist, 12,* 77–80.

Ellis, L. (1978, November). *Androgens and criminality: Recent research and theoretical implications.* Paper presented at the meeting of the American Society of Criminology, Dallas, TX.

Ellis, L. (1979). Toward neurologically-specific theories of criminal behavior. *Contemporary Sociology, 8,* 372–376.

Ellis, L. (1982a). Genetics and criminal behavior: Evidence through the end of the 1970s. *Criminology, 20,* 43–66.

Ellis, L. (1982b). Developmental androgen fluctuations and the five dimensions of mammalian sex (with emphasis upon the behavioral dimension and the human species). *Ethology and Sociobiology, 3,* 171–197.

Ellis, L. (1982c). Back on the path toward an evolutionary-biological approach to political theory. *Politics and the Life Sciences, 1,* 69–71.

Ellis, L. (1983). *Androgens, the nervous system and criminal behavior.* Unpublished doctoral dissertation, Florida State University, Tallahassee.

Ellis, L. (1985). Religiosity and criminality: Evidence and explanations of complex relationships. *Sociological Perspectives, 28,* 501–520.

Ellis, L. (1986). Evidence of neuroandrogenic etiology of sex roles from a combined analysis of human, nonhuman primate and nonprimate mammalian studies. *Personality and Individual Differences, 7,* 519–552.

Ellis, L. (1987). Criminal behavior and r/K selection: An extension of gene-based evolutionary theory. *Deviant Behavior, 8,* 149–176.

Ellis, L. (in press-a). The victimful-victimless crime distinction, and seven universal demographic correlates of victimful criminal behavior. *Personality and Individual Differences.*

Ellis, L. (in press-b). Criminality, psychopathy and eight other apparent behavioral manifestations of sub-optimal arousal. *Personality and Individual Differences.*

Ellis, L., & Ames, M. A. (1984, November). *Sex differences in sidedness and delinquency: A test of the androgen hypothesis.* Paper presented at the meeting of the American Society of Criminology, Cincinnati, OH.

Eysenck, H. J. (1964). *Crime and personality* London: Routledge & Kegan Paul.

Eysenck, H. J. (1977). *Crime and personality* (3rd ed.). London: Routledge & Kegan Paul.

Fincher, J. (1981). *The brain.* Washington, DC: U.S. News Books.

Fitzhugh, K. B. (1973). Some neuropsychological features of delinquent subjects. *Perceptual and Motor Skills, 36,* 494–496.

Flor-Henry, P. (1974). Psychosis, neurosis, and epilepsy: Developmental and gender-related effects and their etiological contribution. *British Journal of Psychiatry, 124,* 144–150.

Flor-Henry, P. (1978). Gender, hemispheric specialization, and psychopathology. *Social Science and Medicine, 12,* 155–162.

Flor-Henry, P. (1979). On certain aspects of the localization of the cerebral systems regulating and determining emotion. *Biological Psychiatry, 14,* 677–698.

Gabrielli, W. F., Jr., & Mednick, S. A. (1980). Sinistrality and delinquency. *Journal of Abnormal Psychology, 89,* 654–661.

Gabrielli, W. F., Jr., & Mednick, S. A. (1983). Genetic correlates of criminal behavior. *American Behavioral Scientist, 27,* 59–74.

Gadgil, M., & Solbrig, O. T. (1972). The concept of r- and K-selection: Evidence from wild flowers and some theoretical considerations. *American Naturalist, 106,* 14–31.

Gandelman, R. (1983). Gonadal hormones and sensory function. *Neuroscience and Biobehavioral Review, 7,* 1–17.

Geschwind, N. (1975). The clinical setting of aggression in temporal lobe epilepsy. In W. S. Fields & W. H. Sweet (Eds.), *Neural bases of violence and aggression* (pp. 273–281). St. Louis: Warren H. Green.

Ginsburg, B. E., & Fuller, J. L. (1954). A comparison of chemical and mechanical alterations of seizure patterns in mice. *Journal of Comparative and Physiological Psychology, 47,* 344–348.

Glick, S. D., Schonfeld, A. R., & Strumpf, A. J. (1980). Sex differences in brain asymmetry of rodents. *Behavioral and Brain Sciences, 3,* 236–238.

Goldman, P. S. (1976). Maturation of the mammalian nervous system and the ontogeny of behavior. In *Advances in the study of behavior* (Vol. 7). New York: Academic Press.

Goy, R. W., & McEwen, B. S. (1980). *Sexual differentiation of the brain.* Cambridge, MA: M.I.T. Press.

Gray, J. A., Rickwood, L., Drewett, R. F., & Dunne, E. (1977). Gonadal hormones and effects of partial reinforcement on appetitive behavior in the rat. *Physiology and Behavior, 19,* 41–45.

Gunn, J. (1977). *Epileptics in prison.* London: Academic Press.

Gunn, J., & Fenton, G. (1971). Epilepsy, automatism, and crime. *Lancet, 1,* 1173–1176.

Hare, R. D. (1978). Electrodermal and cardiovascular correlates of psychopathy. In R. D. Hare & D. Schalling (Eds.), *Psychopathic behaviour* (pp. 107–143). New York: Wiley.

Hare, R. D. (1982). Psychopathy and the personality dimensions of psychoticism, extraversion, and neuroticism. *Personality and Individual Differences, 3,* 35–42.

Hare, R. D., & Forth, A. E. (1985). Psychopathy and lateral preference. *Journal of Abnormal Psychology, 94,* 541–546.

Hare, R. D., & McPherson, L. M. (1984). Psychopathy and perceptual asymmetry during verbal dichotic listening. *Journal of Abnormal Psychology, 93,* 141–149.

Hauser, W. A., & Kurland, L. T. (1975). The epidemiology of epilepsy in Rochester, Minnesota 1935 through 1967. *Epilepsia, 16,* 1–66.

Hirskowitz, M., Karacan, I., Thornby, J. I., & Ware, C. (1984). Nocturnal penile tumescence and EEG asymmetry. *Research Communications in Psychology, Psychiatry and Behavior, 9,* 87–94.

Hoffman, E., & Goldstein, L. (1981). Hemispheric quantitative EEG changes following emotional reactions in neurotic patients. *Acta Psychiatrica Scandinavia, 63,* 153–164.

Humphreys, M. S., & Revelle, W. (1984). Personality, motivation, and performance: A theory of the relationship between individual differences and information processing. *Psychological Review, 91,* 153–184.

Hurwitz, S., & Christiansen, K. O. (1983). *Criminology.* London: Fairleigh Dickinson University Press.

Ingber, D. (1982, April). The violent brain. *Science Digest,* pp. 34–35, 105, 114.

Inglis, J., & Lawson, J. S. (1981). Sex differences in the effects of unilateral brain damage on intelligence. *Science, 212,* 693–695.

King, L. N., & Young, Q. D. (1978). Increased prevalence of seizure disorders among prisoners. *Journal of the American Medical Association, 239,* 2674–2675.

Kreuz, L. E., & Rose, R. M. (1972). Assessment of aggressive behavior and plasma testosterone in a young criminal population. *Psychosomatic Medicine, 34,* 321–332.

Krynicki, V. E. (1978). Cerebral dysfunction in repetitively assaultive adolescents. *Journal of Nervous and Mental Disease, 166,* 59–67.

Kupke, T., Lewis, R., & Rennick, P. (1979). Sex differences in the neuropsychological functioning of epileptics. *Journal of Consulting and Clinical Psychology, 47,* 1128–1130.

Kurland, L. A. (1959). Incidence of epilepsy in a small urban community. *Epilepsia, 1,* 143.

Landis, T., Graves, R., & Goodglass, H. (1982). Aphasic reading and writing: Possible evidence for right hemisphere participation. *Cortex, 18,* 105–112.

Lewis, D. O., Shanok, S. S., Pincus, J. H., & Giamarino, M. (1982). The medical assessment of seriously delinquent boys: A comparison of pediatric, psychiatric, neurologic and hospital record data. *Journal of Adolescence and Health Care, 3,* 160–164.

Lykken, D. T. (1955). *A study of anxiety in the sociopathic personality.* Unpublished doctoral dissertation, University of Minnesota, Minneapolis.

Lykken, D. T. (1957). A study of anxiety in the sociopathic personality. *Journal of Abnormal and Social Psychology, 55,* 6–10.

Lykken, D. T. (1982, September). Fearlessness. *Psychology Today,* pp. 20–28.

MacLean, P. D. (1978). A mind of three minds: Educating the triune brain. In National Society for the Study of Education (Ed.), *Education and the brain, 77th yearbook* (Part II, pp. 308–342). Chicago: University of Chicago Press.

Mactutus, C. F., & Tilson, H. A. (1984). Neonatal chlordecone exposure impairs early learning and retention of active avoidance in the rat. *Neurobehavioral Toxicology and Teratology, 6,* 75–83.

Mark, V. H., & Ervin, F. R. (1970). *Violence and the brain.* New York: Harper & Row.

Martin, S. E., Sechrest, L. G., & Redner, R. (1981). *New directions in the rehabilitation of criminal offenders.* Washington, DC: National Academy Press.

Mattsson, A. (1981). Psychoendocrine aspects of male delinquency and aggression. In D. O. Lewis (Ed.), *Vulnerabilities to delinquency* (pp. 205–219). New York: S. P. Medical and Scientific Books.

Mawson, A. R., & Mawson, C. D. (1977). Psychopathy and arousal: A new interpretation of the psychophysiological literature. *Biological Psychiatry, 12,* 49–74.

McBroom, P. (1980). *Behavioral genetics* (NIMH monograph). Washington, DC: U.S. Government Printing Office.

McGivern, R. F., Claney, A. N., Hill, M. A., & Noble, E. P. (1984). Prenatal alcohol exposure alters adult expression of sexually dimorphic behavior in the rat. *Science, 224,* 896–898,

McGrew, W. C. (1979). Evolutionary implications of sex differences in chimpanzees' predation and tool use. In D. A. Hamburg & E. R. McCowen (Eds.), *The great apes* (pp. 440–462). Menlo Park, CA: Benjamin/Cummings.

McKeever, W. F., Seitz, K. S., Hoff, A. L., Marino, M. F., & Diehl, J. A. (1983). Interacting sex and familial sinistrality characteristics influence both language lateralization and spatial ability in right handers. *Neuropsychologia, 21,* 661–668.

Mednick, S. A. (1975). Autonomic nervous system recovery and psychopathy. *Scandinavian Journal of Behavior Therapy, 4,* 55–68.

Mednick, S. A. (1977). Preface. In S. A. Mednick & K. O. Christiansen (Eds.), *Biosocial bases of criminal behavior* (pp. ix–x). New York: Gardner.

Mednick, S. A. (1985). Crime in the family tree. *Psychology Today, 19,* 58–61.

Mednick, S. A., & Volavka, J. (1980). Biology and crime. In N. Morris & M. Tonty (Eds.), *Criminal justice: An annual review of research* (Vol. 2, pp. 85–158). Chicago: University of Chicago Press.

Mednick, S. A., Pollock, V., Volavka, J., & Gabrielli, W. F. (1982). Biology and violence. In M. E. Wolfgang & N. A. Weiner (Eds.), *Criminal violence* (pp. 21–80). Beverly Hills: Sage.

Meisel, R. L., Dohanich, G. P., & Ward, I. L. (1979). Effects of prenatal stress on avoidance acquisition, open-field performance, and lordotic behavior in male rats. *Physiology and Behavior, 22,* 527–530.

Merritt, H. (1973). *A textbook of neurology.* Philadelphia: Lea and Febiger.

Monroe, R. (1970). *Episodic behavioral disorder: A psychodynamic and neurological analysis.* Cambridge: Harvard University Press.

Morrow, L., Vrtunski, P. B., Kim, Y., & Boller, F. (1981). Arousal responses to emotional stimuli and laterality of lesion. *Neuropsychologia, 19,* 65–71.

Nyborg, H. (1983). Spatial ability in men and women: Review and new theory. *Advances in Behavior Research and Therapy, 5,* 89–140.

Persinger, M. A. (1983). Religious and mystical experiences as artifacts of temporal lobe function: A general hypothesis. *Perceptual and Motor Skills, 57,* 1255–1262.

Peterson, D. R. (1976). Is psychology a profession? *American Psychologist, 31,* 572–581.

Raine, A., & Venables, P. H. (1984). Tonic heart rate level, social class, and antisocial behaviour in adolescents. *Biological Psychology, 18,* 123–132.

Redmond, D. E., Baulu, J., Murphy, D. L., Loriaux, D. L., & Zeigler, M. G. (1976). The effects of testosterone on plasma and platelet monoamine oxidase (MAO). *Psychosomatic Medicine, 38,* 315–326.

Redner, R., Snellman, L., & Davidson, W. S. (1983). A review of behavioral methods in the treatment of delinquency. In R. J. Morris & T. Kratochwill (Eds.), *Practice of therapy with children: A textbook of methods.* New York: Pergamon Press.

Rhawn, J., Hess, S., & Birecree, E. (1978). Effects of hormone manipulations and exploration on sex differences in maze learning. *Behavioral and Neural Biology, 24,* 364–377.

Roth, L. R., & Ervin, F. R. (1971). Psychiatric care of federal prisoners. *American Journal of Psychiatry, 127,* 424–430.

Rowe, D. C., & Osgood, D. W. (1984). Heredity and sociological theories of delinquency: A reconsideration. *American Sociological Review, 49,* 526–540.

Rushton, J. P. (1985). Differential K theory and race differences in E and N. *Personality and Individual Differences, 6,* 769–770.

Rutter, M., & Giller, H. (1984). *Juvenile delinquency: Trends and perspectives.* New York: Guilford Press.

Sackeim, H., Gur, R. C., & Saucy, M. C. (1978). Emotions are expressed more intensely on the left side of the face. *Science, 202,* 434–436.

Sackett, G. (1974). Comment cited in discussion: Stress and early life experiences in nonhumans. In R. C. Friedman, R. M. Richart, & R. L. Vande Wiele (Eds.), *Sex differences in behavior* (pp. 143–45). New York: Wiley.

Schwartz, G. E., Davidson, R. J., & Maer, F. (1975). Right hemispheric lateralization for emotion in the human brain: Interactions with cognition. *Science, 190,* 286–288.

Shepherd-Look, D. L. (1982). Sex differentiation and the development of sex roles. In B. B. Walman (Ed.), *Handbook of developmental psychology* (pp. 403–433). Englewood Cliffs, NJ: Prentice-Hall.

Skinner, B. F. (1984). The evolution of behavior. *Journal of the Experimental Analysis of Behavior, 41,* 217–221.

Smail, B., & Kelly, A. (1984). Sex differences in science and technology among 11-year-old school children. I. Cognitive. *Research in Science and Technical Education, 2,* 61–76.

Smith, T. L. (1983). Skinner's environmentalism: The analogy with natural selection. *Behaviorism, 11,* 133–153.

Sperry, R. (1982). Some effects of disconnecting the cerebral hemispheres. *Science, 217,* 1223–1226.

Stedman, J., van Heyninger, R., & Lindsay, J. (1982). Educational underachievement and epilepsy. A study of children from normal schools, admitted to a special hospital for epilepsy. *Early Child Development and Care, 9,* 65–82.

Tiger, L. (1975). Somatic factors and social behavior. In R. Fox (Ed.), *Biosocial anthropology.* New York: Wiley.

Tucker, D. M., Watson, R. T., & Heilman, K. M. (1977). Discrimination and evocation of affectively intoned speech in patients with right parietal disease. *Neurology, 27,* 947–950.

Tucker, D. M., Stensile, C. E., Roth, R. S., & Shearer, S. L. (1981). Right frontal lobe activation and right hemisphere performance. *Archives of General Psychiatry, 38,* 2–9.

Turner, W. A. (1973). *Epilepsy.* New York: Raven.

van Dusen, K. T., Mednick, S. A., Gabrielli, W. F., & Hutchings, B. (1983). Social class and crime in an adoption cohort. *Journal of Criminal Law and Criminology, 74,* 249–254.

Virkkunen, M., Nuutila, A., & Huusko, S. (1976). Effect of brain injury on social adaptability. *Acta Psychiatrica Scandinavica, 53,* 168–172.

Walker, A. E., & Blumer, D. (1975). Long term effects of temporal lobe lesions on sexual behavior and aggressivity. In W. S. Fields & W. H. Sweet (Eds.), *Neuronal bases of violence and aggression* (pp. 392–400). St. Louis: Warren H. Green.

Westermarck, E. (1908). *The origin and development of the moral ideas.* London: Macmillan.

Whitman, S., Coleman, T. E., Patmon, C., Desai, B. T., Cohen, R., & King, L. N. (1984). Epilepsy in prison: Elevated prevalence and no relationship to violence. *Neurology, 34,* 775–782.

Wood, R., & Flynn, J. M. (1978). A self-evaluation token system versus an external token system alone in a residential setting with predelinquent youth. *Journal of Applied Behavior Analysis, 11,* 503–512.

Woodman, D. (1979). Biochemistry of psychopathy. *Journal of Psychosomatic Research, 23,* 342–360.

Woodrow, K. M., Friedman, G. D., Seigelaub, A. B., & Collen, M. F. (1977). Pain tolerance: Differences according to age, sex and race. *Psychosomatic Medicine, 34,* 548–556.

Wyers, E. J., Adler, H. E., Carpen, K., Chiszar, D., Demarest, J., Flanagan, O. J., Jr., Von Glasersfeld, E., Glickman, S. E., Mason, W. A., Menzel, E. W., & Tobach, E. (1980). The sociobiological challenge to psychology. *American Psychologist, 35,* 955–979.

Yeudall, L. T. (1977). Neuropsychological assessment of forensic disorders. *Canada's Mental Health, 25,* 7–15.

Yeudall, L. T. (1980). A neuropsychosocial perspective of persistent juvenile delinquency and criminal behavior: Discussion. *Annals of the New York Academy of Sciences, 347,* 348–355.

Yeudall, L. T., & Fromm-Auch, D. (1979). Neuropsychological impairments in various psychopathological populations. In J. Gruzelier & P. Flor-Henry (Eds.), *Hemisphere asymmetries of function in psychopathology* (pp. 401–428). Amsterdam, The Netherlands: Elsevier.

Yeudall, L. T., Fedora, O., Fedora, S., & Wardell, D. (1981). Neurosocial perspective on the assessment and etiology of persistent criminality. *Australian Journal of Forensic Science, 13,* 131–159, *14,* 20–44.

VI

PROFESSIONAL ISSUES IN BEHAVIORAL APPLICATIONS

20

Psychologists in Adult Correctional Institutions

Getting Off the Treadmill

CARL B. CLEMENTS

> A psychologist should not be part of any prison treatment program that coerces inmate participation.
> —Nietzel (1979)
> It seems clear that psychotherapy should not be routinely practiced in the prison system as we know it today.
> —Schlesinger (1979)
> If we persist in the negative view of correctional treatment, we are encouraging the correctional system to escape its own responsibility.
> —Gendreau and Ross (1979)
> To . . . unnecessarily restrict [behavioral] research is to freeze our state of knowledge and quality of [correctional] programming at its present impoverished level.
> —Ayllon and Milan (1979)

Nineteen seventy-nine was a good year—a year for debate on the efficacy, value, logic, and, indeed, the ethics of psychological intervention in correctional settings. Stemming from this same climate of healthy and sometimes heated dialogue were important sets of standards and recommendations promulgated by the American Association of Correctional Psychologists (AACP, 1980) and the American Psychological Association (APA) (Monahan, 1980). In addition, the mid-to-late 1970s and early 1980s saw a wave of prison litigation that featured, in part, attacks on the widespread failure to provide minimally adequate psychological services and environments (Clements, 1982).

Within criminal justice settings—and particularly adult prisons—psychologists have been portrayed as part of the problem, hailed as part of the solution, or viewed with stark indifference. Each of these diverse characterizations has its proponents; however, the most accurate resolution to this riddle is "all of the above." When psychologists engage in routine psychological testing with little hope of contributing to differential treatment or management plans, they waste valuable time and resources (American Psychological Asso-

Carl B. Clements • Department of Psychology, University of Alabama, Tuscaloosa, Alabama 35487-2968.

ciation, 1978). Worse, if psychologists are co-opted by deficient systems into routinely making extravagant predictions (e.g., regarding risks) or using coercive means to force inmate participation in treatment programs, they may indeed have become part of the problem. Whether limiting themselves to familiar, traditional duties of assessment and treatment, or pursuing new and expanded roles, psychologists in correctional settings must confront Judge David Bazelon's (1972) long-standing challenge to do "good" for the offenders, while doing "well" for themselves.

Until very recently, organized psychology has had a relatively minor impact on adult corrections. Roles were limited, and little influence on the basic structure or operation of prisons was enjoyed. Often working in isolation from other behavioral scientists, sometimes poorly paid, and usually not trained specifically to work with offenders or in secure institutional settings, many psychologists employed in prisons have attempted nevertheless to establish the legitimacy of their methods and perspectives, which often run counter to prevailing correctional philosophy. These "pioneers" (Megargee, 1982) and the many who followed have attempted to introduce an open, research-based approach to the problems facing corrections—problems to which applied behavioral science has direct relevance.

Thus, despite an uneven history and the potential for compromised application, there remains much promise in psychological contributions—contributions that can withstand ethical, judicial, and scientific examination. These applications may include well-reasoned, data-based, behavioral treatment activities that truly involve offender-clients as voluntary, fully informed participants. Other applications may reach into basic decision-making processes in an effort to improve the allocation of scarce prison resources (Clements, 1985, 1986; Palmer, 1984; Quay, 1983). Still other applications grow from a behavioral community psychology model in which prison environments are examined and modified in order to minimize negative impact and promote prosocial living.

The scope of behaviorally oriented applications to prison settings has expanded greatly. These developments parallel the ever-broadening position that behavioral principles and practices occupy in mainstream American psychology. Advances in knowledge in the areas of behavioral assessment, well-focused treatment paradigms, and person–environment interplay will facilitate a more integrated, comprehensive approach to correctional treatment. This chapter focuses principally on that integration and attempts to place behavioral approaches in the context of the opportunities and constraints of the prison environment.

The diverse activities of psychologists in correctional institutions also will be highlighted. Although much promising work has already been done in community-based justice settings as is evidenced by a number of chapters in this volume, a clear bias may be detected in this chapter, namely that traditional "mental health" functions are too often narrowly conceived and thus fail to address many important needs of offenders and prison systems. Whatever the scope of psychological activities, they must be performed with professional competence and ethical sensitivity. Ultimately, however, the choice of roles and practices may determine whether correctional psychologists get off the "treadmill" (Schlesinger, 1979, p. 307) or continue with "business as usual" (Nietzel, 1979, p. 147).

THE BASIS FOR PSYCHOLOGICAL INTERVENTION IN CORRECTIONS

By the early 1960s, psychologists were viewed, at least hypothetically, as integral members of the "treatment team" concept in corrections (American Correctional Association, 1964). During that era, offenders were seen as candidates for an elaborate classification analysis designed to embrace every facet of their makeup. Presumably, treatment formulations would be developed that targeted offenders' criminopathic features.

Because most early psychological perspectives viewed criminal behavior *per se* as psychopathological, the attractiveness of a medical model, curative approach naturally followed. For a variety of reasons, the availability of professional workers in corrections was so limited that such an ambitious goal became a hollow promise. Of course, the very assumptions that underlay this early treatment thrust were themselves shown to be somewhat naive, perhaps even counterproductive (American Friends Service Committee, 1971; Milan & McKee, 1974).

Efforts to establish crime-related psychopathology models, broadly applicable to offenders, have not been particularly successful. Psychiatric nomenclature (i.e., *Diagnostic and Statistical Manual* [DSM-III-R] of the American Psychiatric Association), among other trait-centered formulations, provides little assistance in comprehending either the behavioral variability observed across offender populations or the existence of otherwise symptom-free law violators. Behaviorists and radical criminologists are not surprised at this failure, sharing as they do a recognition of the power of the social context in promoting and/or labeling illegal behavior (Schur, 1973). In turn, some behavioral and economic/political models have shortcomings based on their exclusion of psychologically predisposing factors (Nietzel, 1979). A broader interactionist perspective that, by contrast, recognizes person-centered factors, situation-centered factors, and unique person-by-situation interactions may be more comprehensive and fruitful in accounting for the acquisition and maintenance of criminal behavior (Lillyquist, 1980). Feldman (1977) has proposed a similar model that integrates learning theory, individual psychological predisposition, and the influence of social labeling.

These more contemporary models, supported directly or indirectly by research, appear to have important implications for the applicability (and limitations) of psychological intervention in correctional settings. Of any group, psychologists ought to, and by training are best equipped to, anchor their efforts in a sound theoretical context and upon well-developed principles. Too often, correctional settings have witnessed weak applications of poorly specified interventions (Quay, 1977; Sechrest, White, & Brown, 1979). Shotgun, half-hearted attempts at correctional treatment have too often been the norm. Single-mode efforts are also destined to fail. It is no more logical that one type of intervention should be prescribed for offenders than for any other hetero- geneous group—for example, students, mental health clients, or medical patients.

A more rigorous application of current and, admittedly, more complex interactionist models would emphasize efforts to target specific subgroups with tailored treatments (Palmer, 1984). Behavioral approaches, especially those that embrace interactionist perspectives, seem particularly compatible with this larger principle. The "nothing-works" mentality (Martinson, 1974) can be comfortably rebutted with the search for what works with which people for what kinds of problems (Gendreau & Ross, 1979; Palmer, 1975). Why it should have ever been thought otherwise is now increasingly unclear.

The potential for applying psychology to the total correctional environ- ment is self-evident. Psychologists, however, have historically, and perhaps predictably, focused major attention on offenders who meet traditional defini- tions of mental illness. Although the estimates vary greatly, the presence of such individuals has been consistently documented in the literature (Brodsky, 1972) and in past prison litigation (Clements, 1982). In addition, there is evidence that mental health deinstitutionalization has pushed more "disor- dered" individuals toward the justice system (Teplin, 1984). The harsh real- ities of prison overcrowding and the correlated shortage of normalizing work, training, and recreational opportunities also makes offenders potential candi- dates for maladjustment (Toch, 1985). The increased number of traditionally labeled *mental health* clients in the correctional setting need not result, though, in an excessive reliance on traditional one-to-one intervention models. Indeed, sensitive and creative applications of a variety of psychological ap- proaches appears to be called for.

In fact, a number of developments of psychological science in the broad fields of human performance and adjustment are mirrored in correctional settings. This reflection is not without distortion, however, as criminal justice applications are often filtered through competing sets of values and political demands (Brodsky, 1980). Moreover, incarcerated clients may be less able than other groups to exercise individual choice in selection of treatment options. Truly voluntary participation may be difficult to achieve because the scarcity of prison resources makes any inducement appear attractive. Nevertheless, as psychology has reached beyond its partnership with psychiatry and mental health, so have its applications in corrections, often with quite positive results. The unifying theme of these diverse efforts has been a reliance on objective data and on a robust combination of interactionist-behavioral theory and eco- logical psychology.

By contrast, some writers have argued that psychologists have little to offer in the correctional setting. They contend, for example, that the nature of prison confinement precludes establishing the conditions necessary for change (Schlesinger, 1979) or that psychologists' efforts are inappropriately directed toward the goals of institutional management and/or are disproportionately reliant on prisoners' subservience (Nietzel, 1979). These cautions are well-taken and are addressed, at least in part, by the ethical guidelines and standards noted earlier (AACP, 1980; APA, 1978).

Cognizant of the potential role diversity in corrections, Brodsky (1972) has developed a helpful framework in which a psychologist's activities and beliefs are said to vary along a system–professional/system–challenger continuum. In the extremes, the system–professional consistently accepts and follows the company line, whereas the challenger questions the very basis of the structure and practices of the prison system. Staying with extremes, the former plays out a functionary role with little thought of the larger social and ethical context. The later may refuse play at all. Moderated somewhat, these opposing attitudes have given rise to well-developed standards for professional practice, on the one hand, and critical scrutiny of ethical implications, on the other. In the main, psychologists practicing in corrections ought to have a firm grasp of both points of view.

THE INSTITUTIONAL ENVIRONMENT

Work Settings

Psychologists in corrections are found in three primary settings and several secondary worksites with correspondingly different roles and functions. First, of the some 700 doctoral- and master's-level psychologists employed in U.S. prisons (Otero, McNally, & Powitzky, 1981), a sizable proportion are located in assessment/reception centers that operate centrally or regionally to screen and classify newly received offenders. Depending on the configuration of associated prisons, these staff may also provide treatment-oriented services. Second, in many states and in the federal prison system, psychologists are stationed at specific prison units and provide a range of services, some of which will be described later. A third and increasingly frequent place for psychologists in corrections is the specialized mental health treatment facility (or unit within a larger prison). In this last kind of setting, the client population is typically described as mentally disordered; here, psychologists function primarily as mental health practitioners.

Alternative locations and functions occupy substantially fewer psychologists, but these roles are nevertheless important. For example, some psychologists have roles within the central (state-level) administration involving management, research, planning, and evaluation. Psychologists may also direct larger-scale "treatment" networks that encompass a full range of services and programs (e.g., education and recreation). Finally, some prison systems employ consulting psychologists to provide specific kinds of interventions and/or to bolster the supervision needed for other personnel.

Psychologists comprise approximately half of the professionally trained mental health staff in prisons. They outnumber psychiatrists by at least 5:1 (Otero et al., 1981); indeed, in some states, psychiatrists are used as consultants only. Employment of psychologists in corrections, however, appears to have barely kept pace with the increasing population of incarcerated offenders. Thus, despite growth in absolute numbers, psychologists are available in approximately the same staff–inmate ratio (1:375) now as a decade ago (Gormally & Brodsky, 1973).

One impediment to recruitment and retention of prison psychologists is the minimal provision for affiliation with academic institutions or other consultative agencies. Also rare are opportunities to collaborate in training future psychologists via internship programs, clerkships, and the like. (The federal prison system and the Wisconsin Bureau of Corrections are two notable exceptions.) Similarly, specialized graduate-level training that connects psychology to corrections is offered in only a few university programs (Fowler & Brodsky, 1978; Melton, 1983).

As Powitzky (1981) notes, recruiting and retaining well-trained practitioners, enhancing professional collaboration, and increasing the production of research are important objectives for psychologists in corrections. Despite relatively underdeveloped linkages with the broader academic-professional community, psychologists in corrections have made considerable progress in defining roles, in providing valuable services, and in promulgating standards for their work. The climate seems supportive of continued growth and improved quality.

Legal Issues

Legal and ethical issues facing psychologists in criminal justice are reviewed elsewhere in this volume (see Chapter 21, by Sheldon). A brief overview, however, is provided here, describing specific prison-based legal considerations (e.g., overcrowding, deficient assessment and classification practices, inadequate mental health services, and limited behavioral opportunities) that directly affect the existing work environment and the challenges facing psychologists.

Prison Crowding

Overcrowding has been the principal systemic factor driving most recent prison litigation and, in turn, prompting a closer review of all prison programs. In several suits, federal courts have addressed the deleterious impact of severe prison crowding. A number of researchers have attempted to evaluate specific indexes of this psychological fallout (e.g., Cox, Paulus, & McCain, 1984; D'Atri & Ostfeld, 1975; McCain, Cox, & Paulus, 1980; Nacci, Teitelbaum, & Prather, 1977) and to describe the broader influence of crowding in prisons (Clements, 1979; Ellis, 1982; Toch, 1985). The negative impact on health status, aggression, and self-reported stress levels has been consistently documented.

Far-reaching court orders, which have sought to reduce crowding and/or neutralize its impact, also recognize a not-so-subtle influence of overcrowding on the availability and quality of prison services and programs. When staff and physical resources are stretched thinly, needed services do not get delivered. Indeed, the major cases reviewed by the U.S. Supreme Court (*Hutto v. Finney,* 1978; *Rhodes v. Chapman,* 1982) have focused less on crowding *per se* than on its tendency to magnify all other deprivations. The Court has apparently supported the "totality of conditions" concept whereby the accumulation of several negative systemic factors is sufficient to warrant judicial intervention (Angelos & Jacobs, 1985). Among the main psychological issues considered by courts in such an analysis are assessment and classification, mental health services, and behavioral opportunities. Each of these issues is summarized next.

Assessment and Classification

Courts have suggested that the failure to distinguish among the widely heterogeneous offender population leads to a chaotic mismatching of offender needs and correctional responses. That such failures are prevalent in corrections should be no news to behaviorally oriented practitioners. Global, shotgun, nondifferential approaches to assessment, treatment, and management are familiar themes that we face in every institutional setting. Two deficiencies in particular have been cited in legal opinions: (1) the absence of screening efforts to identify those with special needs or vulnerabilities and (2) the use of arbitrary, often invalid prediction schemes that assign "risk" designations to offenders. Especially in prisons with scarce resources, such approaches often result in curtailing offender access to needed programs and limiting their movement to less restrictive, more appropriate alternatives. Prison-based screening programs also typically fail to assess important personal-social deficits that are particularly amenable to behavioral intervention.

In several court decisions (e.g., *Ramos v. Lamm,* 1981) and in out-of-court consent decrees, states have been required to provide comprehensive consideration of inmate characteristics and to articulate and consistently apply more "objective" bases for decision making. Nationally, much attention is now being devoted to offender classification models and techniques. These efforts stem less from a rehabilitation perspective than from the now-obvious need to manage and develop prison resources more rationally (Clements, 1985). Innovations in this area are reviewed in a subsequent section.

Mental Health Services

Courts (and practitioners) have also noted the failure to deliver needed services for those experiencing pronounced psychological distress or long-term maladjustment. Even in state prison systems having specialized mental health units, the capacity and the available staffing of those programs are often too limited to address the mental health needs of offenders adequately (Comptroller General, 1979; Toch, 1982). To begin with, services are rarely available for the marginally adjusted. The more seriously disordered offenders, by contrast, are often sequestered in highly restrictive units and have little access to "normalizing" prison activities. Even within a narrowly defined "clinical" area of mental health treatment, presumably characterized both by humane values and clinical expertise, little can be pointed to with pride. There are exceptions, certainly, but the record to date is not a good one.

Behavioral Opportunities

A popular belief about American prisons is that offenders are well-occupied with daily work and/or training activities. Unfortunately, idleness is too often the rule. Recognizing the common-sense value of meaningful work and opportunities for self-improvement (as well as the negative implications of enforced idleness for inmate welfare), courts have been particularly critical of overcrowded state systems that fail to provide more than "warehousing." To be sure, there are political and economic realities associated with such deficiencies. Regardless of their source, we are ethically bound to assess the impact of limited resources. For example, we can estimate the influence of idleness as it potentially magnifies the stress associated with crowded, unstable, often tension-ridden living environments (Cox et al., 1984). Second, policies can be identified that limit opportunities for prosocial experience and development, that foster regimentation, and that curtail opportunities for self-reliance. Third, we can assess the degree to which existing or created programs (e.g., educational, vocational, and skills training) are of adequate quality. A behavioral analysis is particularly appropriate in evaluating the environmental support (or lack thereof) for such activities (Ayllon & Milan, 1979).

Roles and Functions

A number of writers have identified major functional areas of activity for psychologists in criminal justice and corrections (e.g., Megargee, 1982; Twain, McGee, & Bennett, 1972). A composite analysis suggests differing points of focus on offenders, staff, and system variables. Table 1 outlines these functions.

Although often disconnected in practice, these functional areas are by no means mutually exclusive. Indeed, the quality and relevance of much traditional psychological work would be enhanced by a broadened interrelatedness. Perhaps recognizing this need, psychologist-respondents to Otero et al.'s (1981) survey indicated a lack of involvement in larger, systems-overview issues. Moreover, the presumably natural linkage between assessment and treatment is particularly vulnerable to disruption in the prison environment.

This latter shortcoming may result from an overreliance on psychodiagnostic testing that becomes "ritualistic and pointless" (Brodsky, 1980, p. 65), especially when it provides so little on which to base treatment or management decisions. This failure, in turn, relates to the absence of an empirical approach in which the reliability and validity of assessment might be evaluated and improved. More recently, a number of empirically based classifica-

Table 1. An Outline of Psychological Functions
in Prison Settings

Function	Target	Examples
Assessment/referral	Offenders	Intellectual; behavioral; mental status screening; needs assessment; treatment recommendations
Treatment	Offenders	Crime-related psychopathology; survival in prison; psychological adjustment; life-style, skills training
Crisis intervention	Offenders	Self-injurious behavior; acute stress; intergroup tensions; victimization
Training and consultation	Staff	Human relation skills; stress management; environmental analysis
Planning, development, and evaluation	System	Needs analysis; program design, monitoring, and supervision; evaluation of service delivery; projections and trends; administration; environmental design

tion systems and typologies have been devised (Megargee, 1982; Quay, 1984). Coupled with behaviorally oriented approaches to assessment (Hersen & Bellack, 1981) and the as-yet underutilized work on objective measurement of institutional environments (Moos, 1975), more ethical and practical assessment/classification/treatment paradigms are likely to result. Examples of these developments and their application are reviewed in a subsequent section.

Psychological Applications: Direct and Indirect

Efforts by psychologists in correctional settings have for too long been piecemeal and disjointed. Although often delivering high-quality assessment and/or treatment services, many psychologists give little attention to an overall systems perspective. Quality work, if misdirected, is wasted effort. The broader view demands that we periodically reassess the focus, the rationale, and the objective of our work. We must ask the question: Are we working on the right problem?

In prison settings, power has accrued to psychologists to do those things that psychologists presumably do best, such as diagnosis and intervention with clinical populations. Although this domain of activity has been fruitful, it has also been artificially restrictive; psychologists are often allowed only to serve in a specialist, one-on-one role, and in many instances their treatment and assessment activities appear to operate outside of the institutional mainstream. Increasingly though, psychologists are being pulled into (or permitted access to) partnerships within the larger correctional structure to add expertise and perspective on the broader problems facing contemporary American prisons. Given the necessary mixture of humility, political sensitivity, and ethical safeguards to accompany their skills and competencies, behavioral science practitioners may be able to realize an important, more systemic type of contribution than has been previously attained.

A necessary first step toward this goal of more effective contribution is to define the scope and rationale of psychological activity in prison settings. As implied earlier (see Table 1), psychological attention can be focused on different aspects of the offender: (1) traditional "mental health" needs, (2) deficits or behavioral patterns that interfere with prosocial adjustment, (3) and situational and person-by-situation factors that relate to overall institutional living and adjustment. These focuses, in turn, are roughly comparable to traditional clinical, behavioral, and community approaches to assessment and intervention. Moreover, the number of target offenders subsumed under these headings progressively increases from narrowly defined client groups to the entire offender population. And, as has been characteristic of behavioral and community psychology, the latter two approaches necessarily involve correctional staff and significant others. The activities carried out under the behavioral and community orientations may, in turn, soften the environmental stressors associated with more acute disorders and disruptions. The implication to be underscored in this analysis is that psychological contributions must become integrated into the organizational structure of prison systems.

This broader view should not be taken to minimize the direct contribution of behavioral and community-oriented practitioners to traditionally defined mental health problems. Particularly important is the development of treatment environments and the arrangement of staff responsiveness. Whether or not acutely and chronically disordered offenders ought to be in regular prison settings, they, in fact, are (Comptroller General, 1979). Current efforts to treat them are too often inadquate.

Assessment and Classification

Assessment *per se* has little justification or value unless it is translated to differential treatment or management (APA, 1978) or applied to a systemwide planning process. Indeed, some writers have suggested that the failure to specify the purpose of assessment (or prediction) directly impedes accuracy and value (Monahan, 1981). In the context of such cautions and with adherence to basic psychometric principles, assessment may still be profitably viewed as a distinct function. A brief review is presented next of several attempts, all behaviorally oriented to some degree, to increase the quality and applicability of offender assessment and classification. For the most part, these efforts exemplify a partnership with other correctional practitioners.

Needs Assessment

As psychologists in prison settings have broadened the scope of their concerns, innovative approaches to assessment have followed. Some of these are specifically offender-focused; others are adaptations from developments in related areas. Although many well-known standard psychological tests are routinely administered to inmates, assessment procedures that are directly linked to programmatic goals and offender assignments hold more promise. Choice of assessment instruments and techniques is obviously important. But the development of an assessment program should also adhere to basic organizing principles (Clements, 1986). These include (1) clear definitions and rationale for the focal area (deficits or skills) to be assessed (e.g., drug-abuse patterns, vocational skills, depression, and personal-social skills); (2) assessment of needs and deficits relevant to both institutional and community settings; (3) the construction of a resource map or matrix that identifies the location of appropriate treatment resources; (4) the use of data management techniques that allow systemwide analysis of offender profiles, so that treatment resources can be intelligently developed and utilized; and (5) the use of ecologically relevant follow-up measures to assess change as a function of intervention.

The organization of assessment efforts in most prison settings encompasses a range that includes broad, initial screening of all offenders; more detailed assessment for a substantial proportion; and, finally, highly focused assessment for selected individuals. In turn, the outputs associated with these levels of assessment are, respectively, a broad subdividing of inmate groups (i.e., those with deficits or needs in selected areas versus those without such deficits or needs); program or treatment assignments based on the nature and extent of deficits/needs; and, in selected instances, highly individualized treatment plans resulting from more intensive assessment.

An analogous view of assessment from the behavioral perspective has been noted by a number of writers (e.g., Hawkins, 1979; Nelson & Hayes, 1981) who describe a "funnel" process. For example, Nelson and Hayes (1981) describe this process:

> At the wide mouth of the funnel, screening procedures may be employed to determine which persons would profit from treatment. Since a large number of people usually undergo screening, these procedures should be relatively inexpensive in terms of both cost and time. . . . Once the client has been selected, a broad range of information should be gathered. . . . Interviewing, self-report questionnaires, ratings by others, and self-monitoring may be techniques particularly appropriate for this broad assessment. Eventually, the assessment funnel narrows and more specific information is sought . . . [through] techniques [that] may include observations in naturalistic situations, self-report questionnaires, self-monitoring, physiological measurement, intelligence or achievement testing, or behavioral by-products. (p. 20)

It should be apparent that as one approaches the narrower end of the funnel, assessment probably requires more involvement from individuals who have a direct role in intervention and treatment.

Unfortunately, present assessment activities in most prisons are heavily focused on the screening function (Clements, McKee, & Jones, 1984). To be sure, an initial basis for assigning offenders to mental health units, educational programs, and the like is critically needed. A robust and comprehensive assessment system, however, requires much more specificity and, if nothing else, direct linkages to intervention. The history of poorly defined offender assessment practices mirrors directly the same ambiguous approach to correctional treatment. Ironically, even behaviorally well-defined institutional intervention programs such as token economies, aversive conditioning, and contingency management have not regularly included an individualized assessment component. Rather, target offenders are often categorized fairly globally (e.g., poorly adjusted, sex offenders, etc.). Thus both assessment without follow-up and treatment without assessment too often occur. A few of the isolated efforts that do not succumb to these shortcomings are reviewed next.

Assessment for Internal Management

The most frequently used psychological inventory in corrections is the Minnesota Multiphasic Personality Inventory (MMPI) (Clements et al., 1984; Otero et al., 1981). Until recently, however, no offender-based norms were available (Fowler, 1979). Additionally, practitioners often attempted to stretch the applicability of the MMPI (and other such tests) beyond its known validity limits. In reaction to these deficiencies, as well as general inadequacies in offender classification, Megargee and his colleagues invested a decade of research in developing an MMPI-based offender typology (Megargee & Bohn, 1979). In this system, offenders are identified as 1 of 10 types. Management and treatment recommendations are then based on differential behavioral and adjustment profiles. A flurry of studies has followed, some of which suggest an instability of the types over time (e.g., Simmons, Johnson, Gouvier, & Muzyczka, 1981). In a review of these studies, however, Zager (1983) has pointed to the failure to gather collateral behavioral data against which to compare typology changes. Quite properly, she notes that offender changes over time ought to be reflected in typological shifts. Despite these unanswered questions, the approach to date seems to have met at least one set of published criteria for developing a "good" classification system (Megargee, 1977).

Application of the Megargee system to offender management has been reported in one federal prison—the Federal Correctional Institution in Tallahassee, Florida. Based on MMPI typology, staffing patterns were shifted, and units were realigned to accommodate inmates of similar profiles (Bohn, 1979). In particular, the objective was to separate the more predatory inmates from those most prone to victimization. Differential management strategies were also developed. The institution was a fairly open one, and thus the usual temptation to put vulnerable inmates in restrictive, so-called "protective custody" was avoided. In 1- and 2-year follow-ups, assault rates were reduced by nearly 50% with no increase in staffing.

Another assessment paradigm based on treatment subtypes has been developed by Arlen and his associates (Wisconsin Bureau of Corrections, 1982). This system—client management classification (CMC)—uses structured information gathering, specific selection criteria, and five differential treatment/management strategies. Offenders are assigned to management categories based on the composite results of a semistructured interview, objective demographic data, and behavioral ratings. At present, Wisconsin's CMC system has reported positive results with probationers and parolees; moreover, the staff report improved knowledge of offenders, more efficient use of program resources, and better anticipation of client difficulties. Feedback from institutional applications is incomplete.

Such systems should be viewed as second-order assessment. In other words, the assessment is integrated with other basic considerations such as security/custody ratings and the needs offenders may have in the areas of health, mental health, education, and the like. Most inmates, however, spend considerable proportions of time in their living/housing units; hence the ability to place them into units that are reasonably responsive and consistent seems quite attractive. Other efforts to achieve more homogeneous inmate groupings (e.g., with respect to needs for structure, support, etc.) are a natural companion to this line of work (Toch, 1979).

A not dissimilar approach and one based on substantial research is Quay's (1984) Behavioral Classification System for Adult Offenders (BCSAO). In use at selected state and federal prisons, the BCSAO subdivides offenders into five management categories. Assignments are made on the basis of scores on a correctional adjective checklist (behavioral observations) and an analysis of adult life history. The latter is dependent on an accurate social history, typically based on a presentence investigation. Quay notes that, ideally, five separate housing units would be available within a given institution to accommodate the subtypes. In the major evaluation of the system, its implementation was found to dramatically reduce the rates of violence relative to that in four control institutions (Quay, 1983; Smith & Fenton, 1978). Other kinds of misconduct rates and even inmate grievances apparently decrease as a function of homogeneous groupings.

It is clear that these approaches are not highly focused in their specification of target behaviors, nor do the management/treatment protocols rely on particularly behavioral paradigms (see Chapters 6 and 7, by Milan, this volume). These efforts, however, provide stable milieus that are reasonably responsive to important subgroup differences. And they may, as one prison warden has observed, increase the viability of other psychologically based efforts (see Quay, 1983).

In these examples, assessment takes on a lively sense of meaning. The techniques are neither esoteric nor mystical (although much sophisticated research may be at their base), and nonpsychologists can assume equal responsibility and credit for implementation. Shared involvement with subsequent treatment activities is also a promising possibility.

Assessment for Treatment Planning

The prevailing imbalance between assessment and intervention in many correctional settings has been previously noted. On the surface, this situation seems to imply that current assessment efforts should be postponed until treatment becomes a realistic option. Yet, without basic assessment information, the development and selection of treatment resources is left to speculation or, worse, is neglected. To return to an earlier point, a system of needs assessment should be able to identify for all offenders the presence of and extent of needs or deficits relevant to their adjustment, survival, or reintegration. And these assessments, even at a screening level, should provide some implications for management and treatment (Megargee, 1977).

Among the behaviorally oriented assessment areas that appear most readily linked to treatment intervention are depression (Beck, 1972; Rehm, 1981), social skills (Arkowitz, 1981; Curran & Wessberg, 1982). sexual deviation (Abel, Barlow, Blanchard, & Guild, 1977; see Chapter 13, by Quinsey, Chaplin, Maguire, & Upfold, in this volume), alcohol and drug abuse (Jenkins, Muller, deValera, & Kelly, 1977; see Stitzer & McCaul, Chapter 12, this volume), environmental support (Jenkins, deValera, & Muller, 1977) and occupational skills (Mathews, Whang, & Fawcett, 1980, 1981). Somewhat less well established are methods for assessing offenders with respect to family discord or their potential for victimization within the prison setting (Clements, 1986). The assessment of adaptive behaviors, though rarely discussed in the context of prison survival, is an additional important area and is readily accessible in the work of Meyers, Nihira, and Zetlin (1979) and the American Association on Mental Deficiency (1983).

Treatment

Though little data exist from which to draw confident conclusions, psychologists seem to be becoming proportionally more active in providing treatment and intervention services in corrections. Evaluation and assessment functions remain important, but the Otero *et al.* survey (1981) suggests that up to 30% of staff time is devoted to treatment-oriented activities. Moreover, psychologists view this role as having high priority. Interestingly, a similar trend exists in the functioning of psychologists in institutions for the mentally retarded. Baumeister and Hillsinger (1984) have reported a shift in emphasis from evaluative to treatment activities. Specifically, behaviorally oriented treatment is given high value. And, of the traditional evaluation activities in institutions for the retarded, only adaptive behavior assessments remain a high priority.

Treatment in correctional settings ranges from the poorly specified (e.g., group therapy) to the highly structured (e.g., biofeedback). In this regard, the variety of treatment approaches that have been attempted mirrors that of the psychological field in general and, as such, shares its strengths and weaknesses. Especially troubling in any setting, but particularly in corrections, is the failure to specify the nature of the intervention and to document its delivery. Lapses in "treatment integrity" are a too frequent occurrence (Johnson, 1977; Sechrest *et al.*, 1979).

By contrast, a trend is evident in the delivery of more behaviorally oriented interventions that are inherently more conducive to specification, systematic delivery, and outcome measurement. Psychological staff have developed modular or focalized treatment packages with distinct behavioral components. These include behavior therapy, biofeedback, rational-behavior therapy, sex-offender therapy (focusing on coping skills and impulse control), interpersonal skills training, assertiveness training, job skills training, and the like. Both the Otero *et al.* survey (1981) and the one by Clingempeel, Mulvey, and Reppucci (1980) indicate a strong endorsement of behavioral approaches by practitioners in criminal justice.

In a 1979 article, Schlesinger argued that offering traditional psychotherapy was virtually an unethical practice in prison settings. He cited the inherent inability to provide the necessary conditions of trust, confidentiality, and voluntariness. If offenders are indeed coerced into therapy (as a real or perceived condition of parole, for example), if their disclosures are broadcast to third parties, or if therapists seek to gain information only for purposes of institutional control, then Schlesinger rightly denounces such practices. It has been argued alternatively, however, that ethical guideposts can accommodate the therapist–client relationship in prison (Brodsky, 1980). Moreover, strong momentum is developing to make participation in rehabilitative programs voluntary (Morris, 1974). To minimize the perceived link between mere participation and the positive consequences that could accrue to the offender, decisions about housing, parole, and other privileges would have to be independently arrived at. Of course, treatment might still lead indirectly to offender gains that in turn could be a factor in determining their security risk, amenability for other programs, and similar kinds of decisions.

Schlesinger (1979) also dismisses behavior modication approaches in prisons because of the unfavorable professional and legal reviews given to a few early and well-publicized attempts. In contrast, the message of the current volume, particularly the chapters by Milan, emphasizes the viability of behavioral approaches in institutions. The potential ethical issues are numerous (Nietzel, 1979 see Sheldon, Chapter 21, this volume), but avoidance of coercion remains the principal safeguard. In addition, behavioral psychologists need not focus exclusively on offender-clients. Few ethical concerns, for example, would be raised in providing interpersonal skills training to correctional officers or in arranging the institutional environment to support prosocial behaviors.

As an additional sign of maturity, behavioral efforts in prison and reformatory settings appear to have moved away from a heavy preoccupation with contingencies and consequences. The broad social learning model now, more clearly than a decade ago, acknowledges environmental settings, antecedent conditions, and unique person-by-situation interactions. In turn, behavioral treatment in prison reflects an increased stress on self-control, private mediators, and collaborative treatment planning (see Chapter 18, by Platt and Prout, this volume).

Staff Training

Treatment efforts need not be exclusively focused on offenders. Indeed, the relative scarcity of psychologists in corrections, coupled with concerns about cost-effectiveness, demands that psychological knowledge and skills be transmitted to other front-line staff. The fact that behavioral principles can be effectively taught to and applied by paraprofessionals has long been noted (Brown, 1971). Basic mental health training has been successfully provided to jail officers (Morgan, 1978), and behavioral principles have been taught to prison guards (Milan & McKee, 1974), as have communication and facilitation skills (e.g., Katrin, 1974; Menard, 1978). The work of Hosford and his colleagues is also well known in the area of providing behavioral counseling training to correctional staff (e.g., Hosford, George, Moss & Urban, 1975). Such efforts are consistent with an objective of establishing a more positive institutional milieu, as well as increasing concrete interpersonal skills that facilitate staff–inmate interaction.

Other factors that potentially disrupt the institutional environment may also be addressed through psychological methods. For example, the stress experienced by prison guards has been described as chronic and costly (Gardner, 1981). Turnover, absenteeism, and aggression are often cited as symptoms. Not unexpectedly, stress management programs for prison staff have become increasingly popular (e.g., Cheek & Miller, 1983; Dahl, 1979). Placing these issues in a social learning model, Stalgaitis, Meyers, and Krisak (1982) have provided an excellent review and analysis of correctional officer stress. Their recommendations include the kind of differential assessment described earlier so that, for example, officers with adequate coping skills need not participate in program components.

CONCLUSION

The assessment and treatment approaches and related issues highlighted in this chapter point to some common themes. First, psychologists are increasingly involved in a widening range of activities. Roles are not limited to assessment of and intervention with disturbed offenders. Indeed, staff and systems focuses are seen as both promising and mandatory components of psychological practice in corrections. Second, treatment activities are increasingly guided by empirical approaches to assessment and problem specification. Similarly, treatment regimes and packages ought to be delivered with adequate strength and with adherence to previously established literature. The psychologist in corrections must struggle, perhaps more than colleagues in other settings, to stay current with research-based methods and well-grounded principles. Third, and perhaps what is most obvious, practitioners must operate within increasingly well-formulated standards and guidelines that apply both to criminal justice settings and to psychological activity at large (e.g., AACP, 1980; APA, 1978, 1979, 1981). Given the inherent political and social pressures to compromise such standards, the justice system particularly requires very careful delivery of the science of psychology.

Despite some optimism as to the increasing specificity and power of assessment and treatment strategies, psychologists in corrections are always faced with the dilemma of where to focus their efforts. A corollary concern is the measurement of impact. Some critics have hinted that correctional psychologists are good at trivial matters but inconsequential to the important concerns (Bazelon, 1972). Psychological treatment no doubt was, in the minds of many, lumped into Martinson's (1974) overstated conclusions regarding the failure of rehabilitation. Although Martinson's methodology and analysis have been effectively criticized (e.g., Adams, 1977; Quay, 1977), the current movement in penology is toward punishment, plain and simple. This leaves efforts to treat, to intervene, or to curb the excesses of harsh prison environments on less sure footing (Cullen & Gilbert, 1982).

Such pessimism should not go unchallenged. Megargee (1982) has pointed out that discouraging figures on recidivism rates (a narrow criterion at best) are often exaggerated, typically because of methodological shortsightedness. The "do-nothing" attitude associated with such reports of poor outcome is self-defeating. Although recidivism rates cannot be ignored as one yardstick of success, other responses to the prison experience must also be measured, especially within presumably treatment-oriented programs. Megargee and Cadow (1980), in one such example, report that over half of the offenders in a federal prison showed positive improvements from intake to discharge on blindly rated test–retest personality inventories. The prison experience does not have to be a uniformly negative one.

Quite aside from recidivism and globally assessed improvement measures, other worthwhile points may be focused on. Adaptive behavioral change can be associated with a host of important intrainstitutional factors: reduced victimization and aggression, acquisition of interpersonal coping skills, specific vocational and academic competencies, self-monitoring and self-regulation, to name just a few. Moreover, as a "community," the prison environment yields readily to an analysis of both deficiencies in and opportunities for promoting mutually rewarding behaviors. This joint tack—meaningful self-change technologies and the necessary environmental support—provides virtually limitless opportunities for the behaviorally oriented psychologist in corrections.

Finally, it must be noted that generalization of gains to community settings is critical to the ultimate value of correctional intervention. Although we have argued that institution-based approaches can be creative and efficacious, we should not expect resulting gains to withstand powerful competing influences, especially those in the community. Nor should we blame poor outcomes solely on prison practices (any more that we would blame poor occupational adjustment of college graduates solely on their college experience). A balance must be achieved; we must insist on high-quality institutional interventions and at the same time appraise those efforts within the constraints of other factors that influence outcome. As is apparent, both in this volume and in the accumulating literature, a behavioral approach to community-based correctional treatment is highly viable. Psychologists in corrections should thus add their expertise and energy to establishing and strengthening linkages across settings.

References

Abel, G. G., Barlow, D. H., Blanchard, E. B., & Guild, D. (1977). The components of rapists' sexual arousal. *Archives of General Psychiatry, 34,* 895–903.

Adams, S. (1977). Evaluating correction treatments: Toward a new perspective. *Criminal Justice and Behavior, 4,* 323–339.

American Association of Correctional Psychologists. (1980). Standards for psychology services in adult jails and prisons. *Criminal Justice and Behavior, 7,* 81–127.

American Association on Mental Deficiency. (1983). *Classification in mental retardation.* Washington, DC: Author.

American Correctional Association. (1964). *Handbook on classification in correctional institutions* (rev. ed.). New York: Author.

American Friends Service Committee. (1971). *Struggle for justice.* New York: Hill & Wang.

American Psychological Association. (1978). Report of the task force on the role of psychology in the criminal justice system. *American Psychologist, 33,* 1099–1113.

American Psychological Association. (1979). *Ethical standards of psychologists.* Washington, DC: Author.

American Psychological Association (1981). Ethical principles of psychologists. *American Psychologist, 36,* 633–638.

Angelos, C., & Jacobs, J. B. (1985). Prison overcrowding and the law. *The Annals of the American Academy of Political and Social Science, 478,* 100–112.

Arkowitz, H. (1981). Assessment of social skills. In M. Hersen & A. S. Bellack (Eds.), *Behavioral assessment: A practical handbook* (pp. 296–327). New York: Pergamon Press.

Ayllon, T., & Milan, M. A. (1979). *Correctional rehabilitation and management: A psychological approach.* New York: Wiley

Baumeister, A. A., & Hillsinger, L. B. (1984). Role of psychologists in public institutions for the mentally retarded revisited. *Professional Psychology: Research and Practice, 15,* 134–141.

Bazelon, D. L. (1972). Psychologists in corrections: Are they doing good for the offender or well for themselves? In S. L. Brodsky (Ed.), *Psychologists in the criminal justice system* (pp. 149–154). Urbana: University of Illinois Press.

Beck, A. T. (1972). *Depression: Causes and treatment.* Philadelphia: University of Pennsylvania Press.

Bohn, M. J. (1979). Management classification for young adult inmates. *Federal Probation, 43*(4), 53–59.

Brodsky, S. L. (Ed.). (1972). *Psychologists in the criminal justice system.* Urbana: University of Illinois Press.

Brodsky, S. L. (1980). Ethical issues for psychologists in corrections. In J. Monahan (Ed.), *Who is the client?* (pp. 63–92). Washington, DC: American Psychological Association.

Brown, D. G. (1971). Behavior analysis and intervention in counseling and psychotherapy. In H. C. Rickard (Ed.), *Behavioral intervention in human problems* (pp. 27–34). New York: Pergamon Press.

Cheek, F. E., & Miller M. D. (1983). The experience of stress for correctional officers: A double-bind theory of correctional stress. *Journal of Criminal Justice, 11,* 105–120.

Clements, C. B. (1979). Crowded prisons: A review of psychological and environmental effects. *Law and Human Behavior, 3,* 217–225.

Clements, C. B. (1982). Psychological roles and issues in recent prison litigation. In J. Gunn & D. P. Farrington (Eds.), *Abnormal offenders, delinquency, and the criminal justice system* (pp. 37–59). London: Wiley.

Clements, C. B. (1985). Prison resource management: Working smarter, not harder. *The Annals of the American Academy of Political and Social Science, 478,* 173–182.

Clements, C. B. (1986). *Offender needs assessment.* College Park, MD: American Correctional Association.

Clements, C. B., McKee, J. M., & Jones, S. E. (1984). *Offender needs assessment: Models and approaches.* Washington, DC: National Institute of Corrections.

Clingempeel, W. G., Mulvey, E., & Reppucci, N. D. (1980). A national study of ethical dilemmas of psychologists in the criminal justice system. In J. Monahan (Ed.), *Who is the Client?* (pp. 126–153). Washington, DC: American Psychological Association.

Comptroller General (1979). *Report to the Congress of the United States: Prison mental health can be improved by better management and more effective federal aid.* Washington, DC: General Accounting Office.

Cox, V. C., Paulus, P. B., & McCain, G. (1984). Prison crowding research. *American Psychologist, 39,* 1148–1160.

Cullen, F. T., & Gilbert, K. E. (1982). *Reaffirming rehabilitation.* Cincinnati: Anderson Publishing.

Curran, J. P., & Wessberg, H. (1982). The assessment of social inadequacy. In D. H. Barlow (Ed.), *Behavioral assessment of adult disorders* (pp. 405–438). New York: Guilford Press.

Dahl, J. J. (1979). *Management of stress in corrections* (participant's handbook). Washington, DC: University Research Co.

D'Atri, D. A., & Ostfeld, A. M. (1975). Crowding: Its effects on the elevation of blood pressure in a prison setting. *Preventive Medicine, 4,* 550–566.

Ellis, D. (1982). *Crowding and prison violence: An integration of research and theory.* Toronto: York University Press.

Feldman, M. P. (1977). *Criminal behavior: A psychological analysis.* London: Wiley.

Fowler, R. D. (1979). Use of the computerized MMPI in correctional decisions. In J. N. Butcher (Ed.), *New developments in the use of the MMPI* (pp. 325–340). Minneapolis: University of Minnesota Press.

Fowler, R. D., & Brodsky, S. L. (1978). Development of a correctional-clinical psychology program. *Professional Psychology, 9,* 440–447.

Gardner, R. (1981). Guard stress. *Corrections Magazine, 7*(5), 6–14.

Gendreau, P., & Ross, B. (1979). Effective correctional treatment: Bibliotherapy for cynics. *Crime & Delinquency, 25,* 463–489.

Gormally, J., & Brodsky, S. L. (1973). Utilization and training of psychologists for the criminal justice system. *American Psychologist, 28,* 926–928.

Hawkins, R. P. (1979). The functions of assessment: Implications for selection and development of devices for assessing repertoires in clinical, educational, and other settings. *Journal of Applied Behavioral Analysis, 12,* 501–516.

Hersen, M., & Bellack, A. S. (Eds.). (1981). *Behavioral assessment: A practical handbook.* New York: Pergamon Press.

Hosford, R. E., George, G. O., Moss, C. S., & Urban, V. E. (1975). The effects of behavioral counseling training on correctional staff. *Teaching of Psychology, 2,* 124–127.

Hutto v. Finney, 437 U.S. 678 (1978).

Jenkins, W. O., de Valera, E. K., & Muller, J. B. (1977). The Behavioral Evaluation Treatment and Analysis (BETA) System in the prediction of the criminal and delinquent behavior. *Quarterly Journal of Corrections, 1,* 44–50.

Jenkins, W. O., Muller, J. B., deValera, E. D., & Kelly, J. V. (1977). *An evaluative follow-up study of the Birmingham treatment alternatives to street crime (TASC) drug program.* University, AL: Rehabilitation Research Foundation.

Johnson, V. S. (1977). Behavior modification in the correctional setting. *Criminal Justice and Behavior, 4,* 397–428.

Katrin, S. E. (1974). The effects on women inmates of facilitation training provided correctional officers. *Criminal Justice and Behavior, 1,* 5–12.

Lillyquist, M. J. (1980). *Understanding and changing criminal behavior.* Englewood Cliffs, NJ: Prentice-Hall.

Martinson, R. (1974). What works? Questions and answers about prison reform. *The Public Interest, 35,* 22–34.

Mathews, R. M., Whang, P. L., & Fawcett, S. B. (1980). Development and validation of an occupational skills assessment instrument. *Behavioral Assessment, 2,* 71–85.

Mathews, R. M., Whang, P. L., & Fawcett, S. B. (1981). Behavioral assessment of job-related skills. *Journal of Employment Counseling, 18,* 3–11.

McCain, G., Cox, V. C., & Paulus, P. B. (1980). *The effects of prison crowding on inmate behavior* (Final Report, LEAA Grant No. 78-NI-AX-0019). Arlington: University of Texas at Arlington.

Megargee, E. I. (1977). A new classification system for criminal offenders. *Criminal Justice and Behavior, 4,* 107–114.

Megargee, E. I. (1982). Reflections on psychology in the criminal justice system. In J. Gunn & D. P. Farrington (Eds.), *Abnormal offenders, delinquency and the criminal justice system* (pp. 9–35). London: Wiley.

Megargee, E. I., & Bohn, M. J. (1979). *Classifying criminal offenders: A new system based on the MMPI.* Beverly Hills, CA: Sage Publications.

Megargee, E. I., & Cadow, B. (1980). The ex-offender and the monster myth. *Federal Probation, 44*(1), 24–37.

Melton, G. B. (1983). Training in psychology and law: A directory. *Division of Psychology and Law Newsletter, 3*(3), 1–5.

Menard, J. M. (1978). Preparing correctional officers and inmates for their interaction. In S. Moore-Jochums (Ed.), *Tools for trainers* (pp. 121–137). Carbondale: Southern Illinois University.

Meyers, C. E., Nihira, K., & Zetlin, A. (1979). The measurement of adaptive behavior. In N. R. Ellis (Ed.), *Handbook of mental deficiency: Psychological theory and research* (2nd ed., pp. 431–481). Hillsdale, NJ: Lawrence Erlbaum.

Milan, M. A., & McKee, J. M. (1974). Behavior modification: Principles and applications in corrections. In D. Glaser (Ed.), *Handbook of criminology* (pp. 745–776). Chicago: Rand McNally.

Monahan, J. (Ed.). (1980). *Who is the client? The ethics of psychological intervention in the criminal justice system.* Washington, DC: American Psychological Association.

Monahan, J. (1981). *Predicting violent behavior: An assessment of clinical techniques.* Beverly Hills, CA: Sage Publications.

Moos, R. (1975). *Evaluating correctional and community settings.* New York: Wiley.

Morgan, C. H. (1978, October). *Service delivery models.* Paper presented at the Special National Workshop on Mental Health Services in Jails, Baltimore, MD.

Morris, N. (1974). *The future of imprisonment.* Chicago: University of Chicago Press.

Nelson, R. O., & Hayes, S. C. (1981). Nature of behavioral assessment. In M. Hersen & A. S. Bellack (Eds.), *Behavioral assessment: A practical handbook* (pp. 3–37). New York: Pergamon.

Nacci, P. L., Teitelbaum, H. E., & Prather, J. (1977). Population density and inmate misconduct rates in the federal prison system. *Federal Probation, 41*(2), 26–31.

Nietzel, M. T. (1979). *Crime and its modification.* New York: Pergamon.

Otero, R. F., McNally, D., & Powitzky, R. (1981). Mental health services in adult correctional systems. *Corrections Today, 43*(1), 8–18.

Palmer, T. (1975). Martinson revisited. *Journal of Research in Crime and Delinquency, 12,* 133–152.

Palmer, T. (1984). Treatment and the role of classification: A review of basics. *Crime & Delinquency, 30,* 245–267.

Powitzky, R. (1981). Mental health professionals: Becoming viable in corrections. *Corrections Today, 43*(1), 4–6.

Quay, H. C. (1977). The three faces of evaluation: What can be expected to work. *Criminal Justice and Behavior, 4,* 341–354.

Quay, H. C. (1983). *Technical manual for the behavioral classification system for adult offenders* (Grant No. FB-6). Washington, DC: National Institute of Corrections.

Quay, H. C. (1984). *Managing adult inmates.* College Park, MD: American Correctional Association.

Ramos v. Lamm, 520 F. Supp. 1059 (D. Colo. 1981).

Rehm, L. P. (1981). Assessment of depression. In M. Hersen & A. S. Bellack (Eds.), *Behavioral assessment: A practical handbook* (pp. 246–295). New York: Pergamon.

Rhodes v. Chapman, 452 U.S. 337 (1982).

Schlesinger, S. E. (1979). Therapy on a treadmill: The role of the prison psychotherapist. *Professional Psychology, 10,* 307–317.

Schur, E. M. (1973). *Radical non-intervention: Rethinking the delinquency problem.* Englewood Cliffs, NJ: Prentice-Hall.

Sechrest, L., White, S. O., & Brown, E. D. (1979). *The rehabilitation of criminal offenders: Problems and prospects.* Washington, DC: National Academy of Sciences.

Simmons, J. G., Johnson, D. C., Gouvier, W. D., & Muzyczka, M. J. (1981). The Meyer-Megargee inmate typology: Dynamic or unstable? *Criminal Justice and Behavior, 8,* 49–54.

Smith, W. A., & Fenton, C. E. (1978). Unit management in a penitentiary: A practical experience. *Federal Probation, 42*(3), 40–46.

Stalgaitis, S. J., Meyers, A. W., & Krisak, J. (1982). A social learning theory model for reduction of correctional officer stress. *Federal Probation, 46*(3), 33–40.

Teplin, L. A. (1984). Criminalizing mental disorder: The comparative arrest rate of the mentally ill. *American Psychologist, 39,* 794–803.

Toch, H. (1979). *Living in prison: The ecology of survival.* New York: Free Press.

Toch, H. (1982). The disturbed disruptive inmate: Where does the bus stop? *Journal of Psychiatry and Law, 10,* 327–350.

Toch, H. (1985). Warehouses for people? *The Annals of the American Academy of Political and Social Science, 478,* 58–72.

Twain, D., McGee, R., & Bennett, L. A. (1972). Functional areas of psychological activity. In S. Brodsky (Ed.), *Psychologists in the criminal justice system* (pp. 15–24). Urbana: University of Illinois Press.

Wisconsin Bureau of Corrections (1982). *Client management classification: Institution treatment outline.* Madison: Author.

Zager, L. D. (1983). Response to Simmons and associates: Conclusions about the MMPI-based classification system's stability are premature. *Criminal Justice and Behavior, 8,* 310–315.

21

Legal and Ethical Issues in the Behavioral Treatment of Juvenile and Adult Offenders

JAN SHELDON

In the last several years, almost every book on the application of behavioral procedures and programs has included a chapter on legal and ethical issues (e.g., Bellack, Hersen, & Kazdin, 1982; Craighead, Kazdin, & Mahoney, 1981; Kazdin, 1980; Lutzker & Martin, 1981; Martin & Pear, 1983; Redd, Porter-field, & Anderson, 1979; Spiegler, 1983; Walker & Shea, 1980; Wood, 1975). One may wonder whether those involved in behavioral research or those using behavioral techniques engage in more illegal or unethical behavior than other personnel in the human service field. This is not likely to be the case. It is clear that although behavior therapists have often been zealous in their attempts to correct any ethical abuses of behavior therapy and to protect clients' rights (Spiegler, 1983), legal and ethical issues arise in any therapeutic endeavor; many books have been written specifically addressing these issues (e.g., Fields & Horwitz, 1982; Gutheil & Appelbaum, 1982; Hannah, Christian, & Clark, 1981; Koocher, 1976; Martin, 1975; Melton, 1982; Sadoff, 1982; Schetky & Benedek, 1980; Schwitzgebel & Schwitzgebel, 1980; Slovenko, 1973). Nonetheless, those writing about behavioral approaches continue to be concerned that others in the behavioral field are cognizant of the relevant legal and ethical issues.

This concern is well taken for several reasons. First, those using behavioral procedures generally focus on changing observable behaviors by establishing specific goals, and this often involves intervening in a person's life. Whenever one person intervenes in another's life with any type of therapy or treatment, legal and ethical issues may arise. Unfortunately, as Spiegler (1983) has pointed out, behavior therapy is

> especially vulnerable to ethical dilemmas [since it] emerged at a time of heightened concern about external control . . . the invasion of personal privacy . . . and the abuse of civil liberties. (p. 325)

Thus many people seem to be extremely concerned about techniques that are specifically designed to change behavior, especially when the goals are specific

Jan Sheldon • Department of Human Development and School of Law, University of Kansas, Lawrence, Kansas 66045.

and concrete (e.g., a decrease of a child molester's penile erection in the presence of pictures of children) as opposed to therapies where the goals are vague (e.g., becoming a more socially acceptable citizen). Along these same lines, most behavioral techniques have been demonstrated to be effective; thus, the procedures used do change behavior. People are generally not concerned about issues of control with procedures that produce little, if any, effects, but concerns arise with techniques that do produce change (Friedman, 1975). Many people argue that those who can change behavior can thereby control behavior, and the ability to control behavior raises additional legal and ethical issues (Brown, Wienckowski, & Stolz, 1975).

A second reason for addressing legal and ethical issues is that practitioners in the behavioral field may employ certain techniques that draw public attention and raise concern about potential abuse or misuse. For example, those attempting to treat severe behavior problems or severely debilitated people might, with good intentions, utilize aversive procedures such as time-out or the application of electric shock or motivational systems that restrict access to certain rights. Additionally, the general public often mistakenly believes that any procedure that changes behavior is a behavior modification technique. Thus people assume that individuals who perform psychosurgery or who use electroconvulsive shock therapy or psychotropic drugs, for example, are behavior therapists even though those procedures are not considered part of behavior therapy (Spiegler, 1983). Therefore behavior therapists continue to have to address unrelated issues because of a definitional problem.

Finally, this is the era of consumer protection, and consumers are those receiving any type of goods or services, including human services. In the last 15 years, hundreds of lawsuits have addressed the legal rights of people receiving care and treatment from mental health providers (see the American Bar Association's *Mental and Physical Disability Law Reporter,* 1976–present). In addressing the issues raised in these lawsuits, the courts and legislatures have established certain standards that professionals must follow when working with particular populations in institutions or in the community, including persons with mental illness, mental retardation, or physical disabilities, persons seeking psychological counseling, and juvenile and adult offenders. Professionals using behavioral approaches have often focused their attention on these populations; thus, the court and legislative mandates are particularly relevant to persons in the behavioral field. Although many of these concerns are not idiosyncratic to behavioral approaches, to work effectively in the human service field today, behaviorists must be well aware of the legal and ethical issues that can potentially arise in their treatment, training, and research efforts.

For the most part, human service professionals have been concerned with the legal rights and ethical considerations involved with dependent populations, that is, those people who are unable to care for themselves adequately, such as children or mentally ill or mentally retarded individuals. This concern reflects court and legislative decisions that have focused on the rights and safeguards that must be provided when the state intervenes to care for someone who has not committed a crime and then essentially deprives that person of his or her liberty. It is easy to see how judges and legislators can look benevolently on persons with mental illness or mental retardation or abused and neglected children and thus be zealous in their protection of these persons' rights.

Protecting the rights of individuals who have committed illegal acts and who are thought to be justly deprived of liberty is not as easily argued. People often are not as concerned about the legal rights of incarcerated offenders within the judicial system. Generally the primary concern has been whether there were adequate safeguards in the process that allowed the offender to enter the system; that is, were there adequate due process protections guaranteed by the Constitution such as notice, right to an attorney, and right to a jury trial, to name a few. Until recently, once a determination of guilt had been made, courts and legislatures were not especially receptive to issues raised about the treatment of those legally placed within the judicial system. This trend has changed somewhat over the last several years, and in this chapter, the ethical and legal considerations that arise when working with juvenile and adult offenders will be discussed.

ETHICAL ISSUES

This chapter is divided into two major sections—one on ethical issues and one on legal issues. It is difficult to determine which topics should be covered in each section because there is no clear-cut definition as to what constitutes a legal issue versus an ethical issue. Most writers generally discuss those topics that courts and legislatures have addressed under a section on legal issues, while discussing topics that reflect rules of moral or professional conduct under a section on ethical issues. The difficulty with this distinction is that new legal rights emerge each year, and many of those rights originally may have been thought of as ethical considerations. In addition, the possibility always exists that a professional may be sued for negligence for failure to conform with ethical guidelines. Legal and ethical issues are closely intertwined, and professionals should consider all topics with equal importance.

Although there are many definitions of the term *ethics,* the term is difficult to define because it involves individual attitudes, judgments, and values. When defining ethics, one can talk about rules of conduct with respect to human actions, or moral principles, or the human character in its ideal state (Barnhart, 1970). Yet, all of these definitions are vague. In *Beyond Freedom and Dignity,* Skinner (1971) attempted to define morals, ethics, and values. Values, according to Skinner, merely refer to reinforcing contingencies, whereas ethical or moral judgment refers to the customary practices of a group. As Stolz (1978a) points out, ethical statements usually refer to controlling contingencies. Thus the situation exists whereby "good" behavior leads to positive reinforcement because it reflects the norms of society. There is some conflict over whether ethical issues can be reduced to a mere description of contingencies and, therefore, to questions of fact (Stolz, 1978a). In any event, it appears that many people (as reflected by lawsuits, the development of ethical guidelines, and the establishment of professional review boards) are concerned with the way people should behave with respect to other people in certain situations.

As Skinner (1971) pointed out, the technology of behavior modification is "ethically neutral" (p. 150). It is the way it is implemented by the person using the technology that is critical. Therefore, it may be useful to discuss the important issues that therapists and researchers should address when working in crime and delinquency to encourage these professionals to conform their behavior to a desired standard of conduct, which may change over time and differ from culture to culture but is nonetheless reflected in laws and professional ethical standards. Thus, the intertwining of the law and ethics goes on. Due to page limitations, several issues will be discussed only briefly; the reader is referred to other references cited herein for more in-depth discussion of these topics (e.g., Martin, 1975; Stolz, 1978a,b).

Balancing the Enforcement of Legal Conduct and the Protection of Offender Rights

When a therapist is asked to intervene with offenders in the juvenile or criminal justice system, he or she may be placed in an ethical dilemma for a variety of reasons. In most programs, it is normally suggested that the client be involved in the treatment process, especially in terms of deciding the goals and the type of treatment procedures to be used (Stolz, 1978b). When working with offenders, however, the therapist often has more clients than just the offender whose behavior is to be changed—these include the staff and administrators who may pay the therapist's salary or fee (Brown *et al.*, 1975; Friedman, 1975; Stolz, 1978a,b). Although therapists may believe that their intervention and therapy program will be beneficial to both the program staff and the offender, it may not be viewed that way by the parties involved because one party's desires and goals may be very different from another's. On the one hand, for example, staff may want a resident's "aggressive" behavior replaced with docile and compliant behavior. The offender, on the other hand, may not want to have his or her "assertive" behavior modified. As another example, the staff in a residential program for juveniles may want the youths placed on a contracting program in which they will be required to earn "privileges" each day (e.g., TV time, telephone time, extended bedtime); the youths may be opposed to any infringements on what they consider to be "rights." Thus, as Stolz (1978b) has pointed out:

> The most basic decisions made by the behavioral mental health worker—whether to modify, which response to modify, and how to modify—involve value judgments . . . and raise ethical issues. (p. 40)

Ethically, then, what should a therapist do when working with offenders? One of the first considerations might be to ensure that all the guidelines relating to legal issues are followed; these will be discussed in a section later on. An example, however, of one of these guidelines is that there are certain procedures (e.g., the use of vomit-inducing drugs to reduce an inappropriate behavior) that the therapist would not want to advocate using without the offender's consent, irrespective of staff preference. The Association for the Advancement of Behavior Therapy (AABT) (1977) has suggested a number of additional ethical considerations for therapists. These, along with others, will be outlined later.

At the onset of any therapy or research program, therapists should explicitly discuss with everyone involved what the therapist's role is; that is, what they are there to do and what course of action therapists may have to take in order to accomplish their goals. This needs to be clearly stated so that there is no misunderstanding about whom the therapist is working for or what the therapist is attempting to accomplish. For example, if the therapist was hired by a social service agency to operate a diversion program for truant youths and their families, the therapist should, at the outset, inform the social service agency, the schools, all youths, and the youths' families that the therapist was hired in an attempt to correct truancy problems so that the youths and their families will not have to go to court. Therefore, the primary task that the therapist will address is helping youths go to school. The school needs to know that attendance is the main concern, not necessarily the youth's academic performance or demeanor while at school. The family needs to know that it may choose not to participate in the program but that a likely consequence will be referral to court. The family should also know that although the therapist will be working closely with the youth and the family, the therapist will have to inform the social service agency about the youth's attendance. Thus, all parties should know at the outset of any intervention, therapy, or research exactly what the role of the therapist is to be.

Next, the therapist should consider the goals of the therapy or intervention and whether the offender's behavior selected by the staff should be modified (AABT, 1977; Brown *et al.,* 1975; Davison & Stuart, 1975; Feldman & Peay, 1982, Stolz, 1978a,b; Wexler, 1975). This task is much easier if the target behavior is in violation of a law because it is then clear that society considers the behavior deviant and inappropriate. In the example described previously, the therapist was hired to work on the problem of truancy. Truancy is normally defined by state statute, and the laws governing truancy reflect a societal consensus that children should go to school. The goal of going to school, therefore, has already been selected by elected representatives who wrote the law. Another example might be the goal of eliminating child sexual abuse by adults. Again, the legislature has in essence stated that this is an appropriate goal because the target behavior has been designated as a crime. A more difficult situation arises when staff target other behaviors of offenders that are not illegal but that they feel are inappropriate. For example, the staff may want an offender to become more compliant, to stop drinking alcohol, or to refrain from engaging in homosexual relations. Here, the therapist must consider whether this is a behavior that society considers deviant and, thus, would lead to negative consequences for the offender. The therapist should examine the short- and long-term interests of the offender as well as of society or significant others (Martin, 1975). The therapist should ensure that the goals are explicitly stated to the offender and any other persons who might be involved and that everyone, especially the offender, clearly understands these goals. Stolz (1978a,b) and her colleagues (Brown *et al.*, 1975) have also suggested that a review committee be constituted to review and pass on proposed goals of the program. This review committee could be comprised of offender representatives as well as representatives from the community. Although the review committee may not provide a total safeguard against choosing unethical goals, the regular meeting of people with conflicting viewpoints, at the very least, sensitizes administrators, staff, and therapists to the conflicting interests involved.

Once the goals have been decided on and explicitly described, the intervention procedure must be considered. The AABT (1977) has suggested that the therapist should decide whether the procedure is appropriate; that is, does the published literature indicate that it is effective with the target behavior? If there is no literature, the therapist should determine whether the procedure is a generally accepted one and whether it is the least intrusive one that can provide the most effective treatment. If the procedure is controversial, the therapist should ensure that alternative treatment procedures have been considered and that a protective mechanism, such as a review committee or a human rights committee, has been consulted.

Therapists, when selecting either goals or procedures, should also recognize that when they are hired by someone other than the person whose behavior is to be changed, the employer is in control of a powerful reinforcer (i.e., money) for the therapist. The person whose behavior is being modified may offer the therapist few, if any, reinforcers and, therefore, have little countercontrol over the behaviorist (Stolz, 1978a,b). This type of situation has powerful implications for deciding what behaviors should be changed and what procedures should be used. As Stolz (1978b) has pointed out:

> When the client is not the same as the person whose behavior is to be modified, special precautions are required. The less directly the participants in the program are involved in the initial determination of the goals and means of the program, the more protections for them should be built into the system. (p. 41)

As mentioned previously, one way of providing more protections for offenders is to have a protective or advisory committee that is established to safeguard the offenders' rights by reviewing the goals for change as well as the procedures selected.

Finally, therapists should ensure that they are qualified to work with offenders and to provide the type of treatment that is needed. In determining this, one would consider the therapist's training or experience in treating offenders or other people with similar problems (AABT, 1977). Therapists in the human service field need to be extremely cognizant of the fact that behavioral training (e.g., a master's or doctoral degree in the behavioral sciences) does not qualify the therapist to work with all problems. Similar to the specialization requirements in many psychology certification laws, therapists should be able to show specialized education, training, or experience with offenders or the types of problems being exhibited in order to consider themselves qualified to work with the offender.

Providing Information and Obtaining Consent

Any time a therapist intervenes in the lives of other people, those persons have a right to be informed about what is going to happen to them. Also, consent should be obtained before any intervention takes place (see, e.g., Ayllon, 1975; Christian, 1983; Friedman, 1975; Hare-Mustin, Marecek, Kaplan, & Liss-Levinson, 1979; Meisel, Roth, & Lidz, 1977; Schwitzgebel, 1979; Schitzgebel & Schwitzgebel, 1980; Sheldon-Wildgen, 1982; Stolz, 1978a,b; Timbers, Jones & Davis, 1981; Turnbull et al., 1977). With offenders, it may not always be legally necessary to obtain consent before proceeding with an intervention because many interventions are court ordered. Nonetheless, the therapist has an ethical duty to inform the offender about the program. This information should include a description of proposed goals and the procedures that will be used. Offenders should also be told (a) what will be expected of them (i.e., what the offender will be required to do in the program); (b) the anticipated results, including the positive results as well as any negative side effects; (c) the duration of the program; and (d) the expected timetable for progress (Schwitzgebel, 1979; Sheldon-Wildgen, 1982).

If procedures are to be used with the offender that legally require consent, then the therapist must obtain consent before proceeding. Consent normally requires that three elements be present: capacity, information, and voluntariness (Friedman, 1975; Turnbull et al., 1977). The people who are to give consent must have the mental ability to make and communicate rational decisions, and if they do not have this ability, another person, group, or judicial body should be asked to consent for them (Sheldon-Wildgen, 1982). The "information" component consists of providing the items listed in the previous paragraph, and this information should be given in a manner that can be easily and fully understood by the offender. Finally, the consent must be "voluntary"; that is, the person giving consent must be able to exercise free power of choice and not be functioning under some form of coercion, duress, force, fraud, overreaching, or deceit (Friedman, 1975; Kaimowitz v. Department of Mental Health, 1973; Turnbull et al., 1977). This last element may present the most difficulty for persons working in programs serving adult and juvenile offenders. Some courts have held that certain penal environments are so coercive that consent cannot freely be given (Kaimowitz v. Department of Mental Health, 1973). The Kaimowitz case, however, involved a criminally insane offender who was to be the sole subject of an experimental psychosurgery procedure; thus the facts of the case involved a very intrusive procedure to be conducted with a person in a mental hospital for the criminally insane who could not competently consent for himself. The more intrusive, irreversible, and experimental the procedure, or the less mentally able the offender is to consent, the more the consent will be scrutinized (Davison & Stuart, 1975;

Turnbull *et al.*, 1977). Even in a situation not resembling the *Kaimowitz* case where the offender is competent to consent and the procedure is not extremely intrusive or irreversible, the therapist should be cognizant that the penal environment may be coercive (Brown *et al.*, 1975; Friedman, 1975). Offenders are in a restrictive environment and may feel that in order to be released earlier than the legally required date, they should comply with any intervention procedure or participate in any research. The therapist might protect against this by having a human rights committee review any controversial or experimental procedure.

Therapists should note that it is therapeutically important to obtain consent and a commitment to participate in the therapy from offenders. If offenders feel they are being coerced into a program and do not see the justification for the program, they can subtly, yet easily, sabotage all the work the therapist does. In addition, it is unlikely that any treatment changes will generalize outside of the treatment setting if the offenders have not voluntarily consented to the program and understood the rationales as to why the treatment should help them. Thus, for example, offenders may attend every treatment session but may not actively participate. Or, they may participate in the treatment session, especially if release is contingent on performance in those sessions, but may behave outside the treatment session contrary to what was taught in treatment (Ayllon, 1975).

Confidentiality, Privacy, and Privileged Communications

Therapists need to be knowledgeable about the laws and ethical guidelines relating to information obtained from the people with whom they are working (see, e.g., DeKraai & Sales, 1982; Everstine *et al.*, 1980; Gutheil & Appelbaum, 1982; Jagim, Wittman, & Noll, 1978; Noll & Hanlon, 1976; Rachlin & Appelbaum, 1983; Schwitzgebel & Schwitzgebel, 1980; Shah, 1970; Sheldon-Wildgen, 1982; Siegel, 1979; VanBiervliet & Sheldon-Wildgen, 1981). There are two primary concepts that are relevant in this area. The first is confidentiality, that is, not disclosing information about a person with whom one is working without that individual's consent. Confidentiality is normally considered an ethical issue because it is covered under professional principles and guidelines (e.g., American Psychological Association, 1979, 1981). Divulging information without the proper consent would be a violation of an ethical principle and could result in a sanction being imposed by the relevant professional organization of which the behaviorist is a member. In addition, a client or research participant could potentially sue a therapist for invading the person's right to privacy if the therapist divulged confidential information (*Doe v. Roe,* 1977; VanBiervliet & Sheldon-Wildgen, 1981). Therefore, a therapist should only talk about the offender with other professionals who have a relevant need to know information about the offender (APA, 1981). The offender should be told about any disclosures, and this should normally be done in advance of the disclosure (for example, the offender should be told if a treatment team will discuss the offender's program).

Another issue related to communications with offenders involves "privileged communications." A privileged communication is a statutory exception to the general rule of law that holds that every person testifying in court must answer all questions posed to him or her. These exceptions are given in order to encourage relationships between a client and a professional (e.g., a physician or an attorney) so that the client will feel free to divulge all necessary information. In a statutorily recognized relationship, anything the client says in confidence to the professional is considered a privileged communication, and the client can prohibit the professional from disclosing that information in court. Only professionals designated by statute are allowed the right to engage in legally recognized privileged communications. If the professional does not meet the qualifications required by statute, then the professional would be required to testify in court if called upon to do so.

Exceptions to Confidential and Privileged Communications

There are certain types of information that are not protected by the ethical concept of confidentiality or the legal concept of privileged communication (Everstine et al., 1980; Schwitzgebel & Schwitzgebel, 1980), and therapists should inform those with whom they are working about these at the outset of any intervention, therapy, or research program (Everstine et al., 1980; Sheldon-Wildgen, 1982). First, for public policy reasons, some statutes require that certain types of information must be reported to authorities. The most common type of information that is required to be reported involves any known or suspected child abuse or neglect. Thus, for example, if therapists are working with an offender or with offenders and their families and they become aware of suspected child abuse, that would have to be reported immediately.

Second, if therapists have good reason to believe that an offender is dangerous to an identifiable third party, they may have a duty to warn that third party and, therefore, divulge confidential information. (This duty will be described in more detail later.)

Finally, therapists who work with juvenile or adult offenders may be required to report to the legal authorities any specific criminal activities that offenders state they are going to perform (Everstine et al., 1980). This, like the duty to warn third parties, must be based on specific information such as the following: statements by offenders indicating that they are going to engage in a specific illegal act or harm an identifiable third party; behaviors emitted by offenders that indicate a high probability of following through; and the means and ability to carry out an act, based on such factors as having a plan with a purpose and having access to materials needed to carry out the plan. In all the previously mentioned cases, the policy of protecting innocent community members outweighs the offenders' right to have information remain confidential.

Ethical Issues in Conducting Research with Offenders

Many of the issues discussed previously are pertinent when conducting applied research with juvenile or adult offenders. As with aversive or intrusive procedures, special care must be taken when using experimental procedures. Therefore, information such as the goals of the research, the treatment procedures to be used, the anticipated duration of the research, any risks or benefits, as well as the prospect for success, should be given to the offender, who in turn must be competent to consent and must do so voluntarily. Offenders must also be informed about the right to withdraw from the research at any time without penalty (Schwitzgebel & Schwitzgebel, 1980; Stolz, 1975). Researchers also need to remember that the consent of an offender may need to be strictly scrutinized, especially if the offender is confined because he or she may be agreeing to participate in research with the hope that participation will lead to the provision of more privileges or even release from the facility (Friedman, 1975). One court held that involuntarily confined individuals live in an inherently coercive environment where voluntary consent may be impossible to give (*Kaimowitz v. Department of Mental Health,* 1973). As previously mentioned, however, the *Kaimowitz* case involved experimental psychosurgery with a mentally ill offender. Courts would most likely be less zealous in their protection of mentally competent offenders from less intrusive procedures. Nonetheless, because of the potential coercion that exists, and especially with juvenile offenders who may not be able to give legal consent, researchers would be wise to receive approval from a review committee prior to implementing any research. In addition, research funded by certain agencies (e.g., the Department of Health and Human Services) must be approved by a review committee (Curl, 1982).

When conducting research, the therapist should attempt to use a design that exposes the offender to the least amount of injury or harm while at the same time demonstrating experimental control. Because one cannot make a general statement that one type of design (e.g., multiple baseline) is ethically "better" than another type of design (e.g., a reversal design), each design, along with the target behavior(s) and treatment procedures, must be considered individually. There is some question, however, about the ethical responsibility to the control group subjects in an experimental group–control group design. Stolz (1975) suggests that the control group subjects could be exposed to (a) accepted therapy while the experimental group receives the experimental procedure or (b) the therapist for the same amount of time but without receiving the experimental procedures. Doing either of these two things would mean that the control group receives some form of treatment while allowing the researcher to address certain issues such as how the accepted therapy compares with the experimental therapy or what the role of the therapist's presence is. If the experimental procedure is shown to be effective, the control group could be offered the experimental therapy after completion of the study.

LEGAL ISSUES

As mentioned previously, legal and ethical issues are closely intertwined with one another and it is often difficult to determine which is which. The topics in this section are discussed here rather than under ethical issues primarily because courts or legislatures have made some statement on the topic. It should be noted that many practices and procedures mentioned in this section would *not* be condoned by therapists. They are nonetheless important to consider because they have been used in programs for juvenile and adult offenders. Therapists consulting or working with these types of programs may encounter administrators and staff who wish to use certain procedures. Thus the therapist should be aware of the legal considerations surrounding various procedures.

Before going into the specific substantive legal issues, one should note that professionals in the legal system view and respond very differently to adult offenders than to juvenile offenders. The state is allowed to intervene in the lives of adult offenders under the doctrine of police power that gives the state certain powers necessary to protect society. Constitutional requirements must be met, but there is no affirmative duty to provide rehabilitation once the adult offender is incarcerated. The juvenile courts, however, were developed under the doctrine of *parens patriae* that allows the state to intervene to care for and treat children and dependent persons (this is the same doctrine that allows the state to intervene and care for mentally ill and mentally retarded persons) (Kittrie, 1971). In fact, one court stated that the juvenile justice system has features of both the criminal justice system and the mental health process (*Nelson v. Heyne,* 1974). Under the *parens patriae* doctrine, the emphasis is on the state's provision of rehabilitation and treatment when it intervenes and takes custody of a person. Because of this emphasis on treatment and rehabilitation, one can more easily argue for certain substantive rights for juveniles that may not exist for adults in the criminal justice system where the goals may include punishment, deterrence, and retribution (*Inmates of Boys' Training School v. Affleck,* 1972; *Morales v. Turman,* 1974). Nonetheless, many rights applicable to juveniles may be relevant for adult offenders in light of recent judicial decisions. Therefore, the legal issues will be presented in general, with any distinctions between juveniles and adults highlighted.

Placement

One of the first issues that a therapist may need to address when treating offenders is that of determining the most appropriate disposition or placement. Courts operating within the juvenile justice system (and some adult criminal justice systems) generally have a bifurcated hearing system: The first hearing is to decide whether the juvenile should be adjudicated (i.e., whether the youth engaged in a behavior that would bring him or her under the juvenile court's jurisdiction) and, once adjudicated, at the second hearing, a judge decides the appropriate disposition or treatment. At the second hearing, a therapist may be asked to testify about what might constitute the most appropriate placement. There are also many situations where the court recommends that an offender may be placed in a particular treatment program. A therapist working for that program may need to decide if the offender would be an appropriate candidate for treatment.

In order to know whether an offender is appropriate for a particular treatment program, two things must be done. First, the treatment personnel must decide the type of individuals with whom they can work and the type of services that can be provided. This generally involves specifying the problems that the program personnel feel they can treat and the type of environment that can be provided (e.g., secure, open, outpatient, etc). For example, the board of directors of a community-based group home for court-referred juveniles may feel that they can offer treatment for runaway and truant youths, youths having problems within the family, and even youths who commit minor criminal offenses. The board, however, may legitimately believe that they cannot offer treatment in their program to the more serious juvenile offender. Likewise, a program serving adults who engage in substance abuse is probably not appropriate for adults who engage in sexual abuse. Program personnel must, therefore, decide on the type of offenders to be treated and make these criteria public. It should be noted that program personnel should never discriminate against an individual on the basis of illegal criteria (e.g., race or origin) or criteria that do not relate to the purpose of the program.

Second, in order to place an offender appropriately, one may need to perform some type of assessment. If an assessment instrument is used, the items on this instrument should relate to the person's problem(s) and the treatment provided by the program. Assessment instruments that are used should be valid and reliable and administered in a manner that invades one's privacy to the least extent possible (VanBiervliet & Sheldon-Wildgen, 1981).

Once the offender is placed, program personnel have to specify the criteria for release if they have the power to do so. These criteria may include amount of time spent in the program as well as behavioral changes to take place or goals to be met. All persons involved should be informed of these criteria so that it is clear to everyone from the outset what goals are being worked toward.

Providing Appropriate Treatment

As previously discussed, there is no presumption of providing treatment for adult offenders, whereas there is a presumption under the *parens patriae* doctrine that juveniles should be provided with treatment (*Inmates of Boys' Training School v. Affleck*, 1972). Several cases regarding institutionalized juveniles have mandated that treatment be provided (e.g., *F. E. v. Hensley*, 1978; *Gary W. v. Louisiana*, 1976; *Inmates of Boys' Training School v. Affleck*, 1972; *Martarella v. Kelley*, 1972; *Morales v. Turman*, 1973, 1974, 1983; *Morgan v. Sproat*, 1977; *Nelson v. Heyne*, 1974). These courts usually argued that treatment must be given as the quid pro quo for allowing society to exercise *parens patriae* jurisdiction over juveniles without providing all the due-process safeguards that adults have. Whereas the cases all mandated that treatment be provided, the courts differed in terms of defining what constituted treatment and the discretion staff would be given in determining how best to implement it.

Some courts have required adequate treatment (*Martarella v. Kelley,* 1972), individualized treatment (*Nelson v. Heyne,* 1974), or appropriate and adequate treatment (*Inmates of Boys' Training School v. Affleck,* 1972). Most courts, however, do not like to define specifically what constitutes adequate, appropriate, or individualized treatment because they feel that invades the province of the professionals in the corrections or mental health fields. For example, the *Affleck* (1972) court pointed out that the court's judgment did not reflect on the staff's choice of rehabilitative techniques. Another court, however, felt comfortable in stating that the mere establishment of a behavior and personality classification system did not constitute treatment (*Nelson v. Heyne,* 1974). The court, however, did not state what would constitute treatment. Finally, some courts have been willing to go into more specific detail about what is to be included in each youth's educational or treatment program. For example, in *F. E. v. Hensley* (1978), the court required a written treatment plan with the parents or guardians participating in the formulation of the plan; comprehensive testing; a statement of the reason for institutionalization; the problems and needs of the youth; the treatment modalities necessary; long-term goals and a method and timetable for meeting them; a description of the staff person responsible for implementing the plan; the proposed family involvement; the criteria for release to a less restrictive placement or discharge; a form to be used to detail each youth's progress; and a comprehensive review to be held at least every 90 days. This court also discussed educational, vocational, and aftercare plans. These requirements are consistent with what most behavior therapists do when treating juveniles, so the requirements should not impose a hardship on many persons in the behavioral field.

Before leaving the topic of treatment, one should note that over the last few years, many states have been attempting to crack down on the more serious juvenile offender, that is, those juveniles committing misdemeanors and felonies, especially on a repeated basis. Some states have addressed this issue by having two separate codes to handle juveniles: (a) one code for the status offender (i.e., youths who commit acts that are illegal only because of the offender's status as a juvenile, such as truancy, running away, buying alcohol, etc.) and dependent, neglected, or abused children and (b) a second code for youths committing criminal acts. In the latter type of code, there are more severe sanctions for the youths. If the state legislatures continue in the direction of providing more severe sanctions for the serious juvenile offender, one may see a statutory and judicial trend away from providing treatment for those particular youths.

Basic Rights

One issue that arises in residential programs serving adult and juvenile offenders concerns the minimum conditions that must be provided for the residents. Considering these minimum conditions often becomes especially relevant when one is using a token economy or employing a tier or phase system whereby offenders, contingent on their behavior, can progressively gain a greater amount of freedom and access to more privileges.

Several years ago, courts and legislatures began examining the conditions that existed in institutions where mentally ill and mentally retarded persons were being housed. Judges and legislators were appalled by the dehumanizing conditions they found (e.g., residents locked in overcrowded wards with minimal supervision; persons, without clothes, lying in their own feces; children being fed a mushlike food with only 2 to 3 minutes to eat). These investigations led to court and legislative mandates essentially stating that when the government deprives people of their liberty, a certain level of care must be provided. A famous case in Alabama, *Wyatt v. Stickney* (1972), was one of the first cases to enumerate the minimum rights that had to be provided mentally ill and mentally retarded residents. For one of the first times, these minimum rights were viewed as things that program personnel had a duty to provide noncontingently to a resident; only in extreme cases and after procedural safeguards were provided, could one infringe upon an individual's basic rights. Basic rights included such things as nutritionally adequate meals; physical activity both inside and outdoors; appropriate sleeping facilities; access to personal closets and lockers; the right to have personal belongings such as clothes and possessions; room dividers to maintain privacy; appropriate toilet and shower facilities; a right to send and receive mail; a right to religious worship; a right to engage in activities with members of the opposite sex; a right to visitation and telephone communications; and access to television and recreational activities (*Wyatt v. Stickney*, 1972).

The issue of basic rights and minimum conditions has also been addressed in cases concerning adult prisoners and juvenile offenders. Four years after the *Wyatt* decision, the same court established minimum conditions for the Alabama penal institutions. Some of the basic rights that were specified for adult inmates in Alabama included three wholesome and nutritious meals per day; a bed, a clean mattress, linen, blankets, and towels; adequate and clean clothing; a storage locker with a lock; toiletry items; the right to send or receive mail; a right to receive visitors on at least a weekly basis; the right to participate in a meaningful job, taking into consideration the inmate's abilities and interests as well as institutional needs; the opportunity to participate in educational, vocational, recreational, and transitional programs; and the right to be protected from violence (*Pugh v. Locke*, 1976).

A variety of courts have mandated certain basic rights for juveniles incarcerated in residential facilities, including the following: a nutritionally adequate, well-prepared, and well-served diet; sufficient clothing to meet seasonal needs; appropriate bedding supplies, including blankets, sheets, pillows, pillow cases, and matresses; personal hygiene supplies, including soap, toothpaste, towels, toilet paper, and a toothbrush; a change of undergarments and socks every day; daily showers; daily access to medical facilities; prescription eyeglasses, if needed; access to books, periodicals, and reading materials; a room equipped with lighting sufficient for the juvenile to read until 10:00 P.M.;

minimum writing materials; right to be visited by persons (especially parents) from outside the facility; opportunity for free communication with persons outside the institution by mail and telephone; opportunity for adequate recreation, exercise, and leisure-time activities; freedom from unnecessary confinement or restriction of legitimate activities; freedom from unnecessary or arbitrary invasions of privacy; liberty to exercise freedom of choice in personal matters; and appropriate educational or treatment plan (*F. E. v. Hensley*, 1978; *Gary W. v. Louisiana*, 1976; *Inmates of Boys' Training School v. Affleck*, 1972; *Martarella v. Kelley*, 1972; *Morales v. Turman*, 1973, 1974, 1983; *Morgan v. Sproat*, 1977; and *Nelson v. Heyne*, 1974, with the most specific rights being delineated by the *Affleck, Gary W.*, and *Morales* courts). Additionally, in 1974, the *Morales* court gave extensive yet sometimes vague rights to juveniles (e.g., freedom from unnecessary and arbitrary invasions of privacy) and did not attempt to define them specifically because the court felt that the rights might vary according to the nature of the living environment. The court stated the following:

> At this point, the court does not attempt to delimit more specifically the boundaries of the above rights. Such an attempt would be fruitless, since much must depend upon the nature of the child's living environment. A rule of conduct that may be entirely laudable in a group home for six children may be completely inappropriate in an institution for thirty; practices may be justified for an intensive care facility that are unacceptable in a halfway house. (*Morales v. Turman*, 1974, p. 101)

It is interesting to note that as late as 1983, the *Morales* case was still not settled. An extensive agreement between the plaintiffs and defendants that detailed the youths' rights was not automatically approved by the court. Rather, the court appointed an expert to inspect the Texas youth correctional facilities and report back to the court on her factual findings. The court was concerned about the "debased, execrable institutions in which juveniles were tortured and terrorized" (p. 334) as little as a decade ago and that these conditions might occur again if monitoring did not continue. Thus the court held that even if the agreement was subsequently approved, the agreement would be repudiated and the dismissal order vacated if it became impossible to monitor or enforce the agreement (*Morales v. Turman*, 1983).

The "rights" outlined here reflect society's view (as stated by judges and legislatures) of what should humanely be provided for incarcerated persons. A presumption exists that the offenders should always have access to these basic minimum rights and that staff should not be allowed to deprive individuals of their rights. That is not to say, however, that certain restrictions might not be placed on some of these rights (Budd & Baer, 1976). To do this, however, one would likely have to follow very stringent procedural safeguards and document why this restriction is in the best interest of the offender. For example, a youth in a residential program may be receiving mail that is disturbing to him or her, and the staff may want to place some restrictions on incoming mail in order to prevent serious harm to the youth. This restriction should only be imposed after documentation of the problem and a determination of the least intrusive way to remedy it. In addition, the restriction should last for a short period of time (e.g., 1 month) with a review at the end of that month (*Gary W. v. Louisiana,* 1976). In fact, the Supreme Court has commented on mail restrictions for adult prisoners in *Procunier v. Martinez* by stating:

> [Prison officials] must [first] show that a regulation authorizing mail censorship furthers one or more of the substantial governmental interests of security, order, and rehabilitation. Second, the limitation of First Amendment freedoms must be no greater than is necessary or essential to the protection of the particular governmental interest involved. (p. 413)

In addition, approval of a restriction on a basic right should first receive the approval of a committee established to protect the offender's rights, and the offender should be allowed a hearing to determine if the restriction is justified.

The law generally states that unless specific problems are occurring with a basic right, the right should be provided noncontingently. For example, an offender in a treatment program may have the right to have visitors such as family members. The staff generally cannot use visitation from the family as a contingent reinforcer that the offender must earn; rather, the staff must find nonbasic items or new possessions that the offender might find reinforcing. If, however, the offender always schedules family visits during the time when the staff are providing treatment, the staff may be able to restrict family visits during these treatment times while ensuring that adequate family visitation is allowed at other times. In addition, depriving a person of basic rights for the purpose of punishment, restitution, or the convenience of the staff would be illegal.

One should also note that a person may voluntarily waive his or her rights, often in exchange for participation in a special treatment program. To do this, however, the offender must be accurately informed about the details of the program being offered and should be free of any outside coercion. Usually, the waiver of basic rights will be scrutinized with respect to the type and extent of intrusion into these rights.

Finally, although courts have mandated that these basic rights be provided, they have also recognized that certain privileges may be restricted (*Inmates of Boys' Training School v. Affleck,* 1972). "Privileges" are usually considered nonbasic or special items that program personnel are not required to provide or that could be provided contingently to the residents. Privileges might include such things as a choice of food, commissary goods, special outings, creative ways of providing basic rights (e.g., an offender may have the right to use a telephone, but the privilege of having a telephone in one's room could be earned) or any idiosyncratically preferred, but nonbasic, activity or item (Budd & Baer, 1976; Martin, 1975; Schwitzgebel, 1979; Sheldon-Wildgen, 1976; Wexler, 1973, 1974). Nonetheless, one court specifically stated that there were "floors" on the power of administrators and staff to deprive inmates of certain "privileges" and that the minimal conditions set forth by the court were rights rather than privileges (*Inmates of Boys' Training School v. Affleck,* 1972).

Motivational Systems

Many behavioral programs utilize motivational systems to increase appropriate behaviors (see Milan, Chapter 7, on token economies). Indeed, such systems are often the cornerstone of a behavioral change program. Personnel in the correctional field have become aware of the importance of motivating people and have created programs attempting to use and adapt motivational systems. Unfortunately, some motivational programs in the crime and delinquency area that have received judicial attention have been programs that may, on the surface, resemble a behavioral motivational program but that are inappropriately designed and carried out. Some of these programs have involved an initial severe deprivation of basic rights or placement in an environment where minimal rights and humane conditions are denied. Offenders are then allowed to work their way out of this environment or are allowed to earn back certain basic rights (see also Milan, Chapter 7).

One prison program that received much publicity was a program in Missouri called the Special Treatment and Rehabilitation Program (START). Federal prisoners were selected for this program according to the number of their aggressive acts that had resulted in segregation. The program utilized a tier system in which levels differed with respect to responsibilities and privileges. One could "move up the system" by increasing the number of desirable behaviors exhibited within the institution. The first level had the fewest privileges, with little access to reinforcing items or events; the deprivations at this level were severe. Prisoners were involuntarily transferred into this program without consent being obtained. Although the court did not state that the substantive program, which had been discontinued, could not be used, it did hold that before a prisoner could be transferred into the program, procedural safeguards, including a hearing, had to be provided (*Clonce v. Richardson,* 1974). Schwitzgebel (1979) commented that therapists should take note of this court decision and ensure that any program they operate meets certain guidelines: voluntary participation, no limitations on basic rights, and treatment goals that are clearly specified and relevant to success outside the correctional facility, as opposed to behaviors that relate to desired performance within the institutional setting only (as was the case with the START program).

Other cases in the juvenile justice system have addressed the use of motivational systems involving levels that differ according to the number of privileges available (*Morgan v. Sproat,* 1977; *Nelson v. Heyne,* 1974). Although focusing on the right to treatment rather than an evaluation of motivational systems *per se,* the courts did not view favorably the way in which these tier or level systems had been designed. In *Morgan v. Sproat* (1977), for example, the court noted that a behavior modification specialist, who evaluated the institution's Progressive Phase Program, found that the program violated many of the basic principles of behavior modification. There was a lack of consistency, a failure to specify concrete goals, an absence of positive incentives to generate appropriate behavior, and a long delay in giving positive rewards following appropriate behavior. The system appeared to be based solely on avoiding unacceptable behavior. In addition, in *Nelson v. Heyne,* (1974), the court noted that often these programs are standardized in such a way that youths do not receive individualized treatment pertinent to their needs.

Persons in the behavioral field who are working with court-adjudicated youths should be sensitive to certain issues when designing a motivational system. First, all responsibilities should be clearly defined and easily and reliably monitored. Youths should be informed from the beginning of the program about the expected and desired behavior and what behaviors must be exhibited in order to earn privileges or to be released from the program. Although some general responsibilities may be required by the program (such as personal grooming and housekeeping), the programs should include responsibilities that are tailored to each individual youth's problems. Thus, for example, if a youth is having problems with aggressive outbursts, the staff should address the problem by providing consequences for it in the motivational system. Also, the issues and recommendations discussed in the section on basic rights should be considered. When using motivational systems, it is best to attempt to find idiosyncratic and nonbasic reinforcers for youths. Only in extreme cases and after procedural safeguards are followed should any deprivation of basic rights occur. Finally, consequences should be given immediately and consistently following either appropriate or prespecified inappropriate behaviors with a great emphasis on rewarding appropriate behavior.

Employing Aversive Techniques

In the past, program personnel often have used certain aversive techniques and labeled the use of these procedures as behavior modification. Those techniques that are aversive in nature normally recieve the most public attention and can, thereby, give the term *behavior modification* a negative connotation. Although many of the procedures used would not be considered behavior modification by professionals in the field, therapists need to be aware of what procedures have been used and what restrictions have been placed on their use in order to design programs adequately and correct any mininterpretations about behavioral procedures.

The Eighth Amendment prohibits "cruel and unusual punishment." In attempting to define what might constitute cruel and unusual punishment, Schwitzgebel and Schwitzgebel (1980) pointed out that

> [a] procedure may constitute cruel and unusual punishment if it violates minimal standards of decency, is wholly disproportionate to the alleged offense, or goes beyond what is necessary. (p. 84)

Many procedures, even some labeled as treatment, have been scrutinized under the cruel and unusual punishment prohibition of the Eighth Amendment. The most common procedures are briefly discussed next.

Drugs

Although few therapists use drugs as part of their behavior change programs, Budd and Baer (1976) at least consider that "the contingent delivery of drug dosages for particular responses is within the scope of behavior modification" (p. 222). The use of drugs in a variety of ways has been employed when working with incarcerated adult and juvenile offenders. For example, inmates in an Iowa prison were given injections of apomorphine in order to induce vomiting. The injections were supposedly to be given for behaviors such as swearing, lying, talking, not getting up, and giving cigarettes against orders. Apparently, the injections were inconsistently given and did not always immediately follow the target behaviors. The court, in *Knecht v. Gillman* (1973), found that this procedure was not a recognized and accepted medical procedure and that its use without the consent of the inmate constituted cruel and unusual punishment. The court, however, did not rule out the use of apomorphine; rather, extensive consent requirements were mandated. This decision should be compared with the decision in *Kaimowitz v. Department of Mental Health* (1973) where the court did not allow a mentally ill prisoner (or his parents) to consent to experimental psychosurgery that had irreversible results.

In another case, *Mackey v. Procunier,* (1973), a prisoner consented to shock treatment but instead was given a respiration-inhibiting drug, succinycholine, that also produces temporary paralysis. This was to be administered contingent on aggressive episodes, destruction of property, self-mutilation or suicide attempts, or sniffing toxic substances. The inmate did not consent to the use of this drug. Although the lower court dismissed the prisoner's case, the Ninth Circuit reversed, stating that the use of this drug could raise questions regarding cruel and unusual punishment.

Therapists advising personnel who may wish to use drugs in a manner similar to the previously described cases should ensure that informed and voluntary consent is first obtained and that the offender is competent to give consent. In addition, the more experimental the procedure is, the more the consent will be scrutinized. Finally, therapists should consider the ethical issues involved in using drugs in this manner and determine whether less intrusive and more socially acceptable procedures might produce the desired change.

Other courts, especially in juvenile cases, have addressed the issue of the use of tranquilizing drugs (*Morales v. Turman,* 1983; *Nelson v. Heyne,* 1974; *Pena v. New York State Division for Youth,* 1976). For example, in *Nelson v. Heyne* (1974), the court found that tranquilizing drugs were being administered intramuscularly to the juveniles in order to control their behavior. Physicians merely gave standing orders, and the custodial staff recommended to nurses that injections should be given. The juveniles were never examined to determine their tolerances. The court held that this practice constituted cruel and unusual punishment because physical harm to the juveniles (e.g., collapse of the cardiovascular system, asphyxiation, jaundice, hematological disorders, and sore throat and ocular changes) could occur. The court ordered less intrusive procedures to be used first and medical safeguards followed when drugs were given. Likewise, the court in *Pena v. New York State Division for Youth* (1976) found that the administration of thorazine or other tranquilizing drugs as punishment or as a behavior control device violated the juveniles' constitutional rights. The court held that these drugs could only be used as part of an ongoing treatment program authorized and supervised by a physician, and that, when used, the youths be given the option of taking the drug orally.

Drugs have often been used for the convenience of staff or as a substitute for treatment, and therapists must safeguard the rights of offenders by ensuring that tranquilizing medication, whenever given, is indeed necessary (*Gary W. v. Louisiana,* (1976). In addition, one should monitor the levels of any drugs used to be confident that the person is still able to make progress toward targeted goals while on medication.

Corporal Punishment

Although most therapists do not condone the use of physical punishment, some correctional facilities, in the past, have openly used the infliction of physical punishment on inmates. Therapists, therefore, should be aware of related issues in the event that they are advising administrators or staff about the use of physical punishment. In *Nelson v. Heyne* (1974), the court held that the supervised beating of juveniles residing in a correctional facility, with a long, thick paddle constituted cruel and unusual punishment. The court noted that the defendants had not shown that a less severe punishment would not accomplish the same disciplinary aim. In another institutional case concerning juveniles, *Morales v. Turman* (1973), the court prohibited the use of physical abuse, including beating, kicking, and slapping residents, without the staff's demonstration of exigent circumstances. A court in another juvenile case, *Gary W. v. Louisiana* (1976), prohibited the use of corporal punishment under any circumstances. The Supreme Court, however, did not find the use of corporal punishment a violation of the Eighth Amendment with juveniles in the public school setting (*Ingraham v. Wright,* 1977). The Court did state, though, that juveniles and their parents might be able to pursue a civil suit against the school personnel if corporal punishment were used. Therapists should realize that much potential for misuse and abuse exists when using corporal punishment because it is difficult to monitor the force that is used when the punishment is administered. Here again, therapists should attempt to find less intrusive techniques to control behavior.

Seclusion

Although not a procedure advocated by most behaviorists, one of the most common procedures used with incarcerated juvenile and adult offenders has been the process of separating them from other inmates and activities by placing them in solitary confinement or seclusion. This has the effect of removing the person from the environment, thereby creating a situation in which staff do not have to deal with that person for a period of time, thus making their job easier. In addition, placement in seclusion often results in removing a person from reinforcing items or activities. Unfortunately, the conditions of solitary confinement have often been deplorable. For example, offenders have been held in cells with inadequate heat, ventilation, light, clothing, and bathroom facilities for extended periods of time. Although seclusion and solitary confinement may be used with adult inmates, minimum conditions must be met (Budd & Baer, 1976), and certain procedural due process requirements may be required (*Wolff v. McDonnell,* 1974).

Courts have also considered the issue of seclusion and solitary confinement with respect to incarcerated juveniles. In one case, *Inmates of Boys' Training School v. Affleck* (1972), the court prohibited the defendants from reopening a building where youths had been placed in isolation for periods ranging from a few hours to 2 ½ months. Youths placed in this building were rarely allowed to go outside and were almost never allowed out of their cells. Although the court was not willing to forbid the use of solitary confinement in other less restrictive buildings, the court did mandate that minimum conditions (e.g., access to adequate lighting, reading and writing materials, clothing, bedding, personal hygiene supplies, daily showers) be met while the youths were in confinement. Several of the professionals who were called to testify about this procedure stated that isolation could never constitute rehabilitation and, in fact, could result in the worsening of a youth's condition. For example, when a youth is in isolation, it is impossible to teach appropriate behaviors because, by definition, no one can have contact with the youth. Other courts have held that isolation can only be used when youths engage in such violent behavior that they represent a threat to themselves or others and only after less restrictive methods of restraint have failed. These courts have also placed limits on the length of time a youth can remain in isolation (e.g., 3 to 6 hours) and have required periodic checking of the youth (e.g., every 15 minutes) and detailed reports to be kept by the staff (*Morales v. Turman,* 1983; *Pena v. New York State Division for Youth,* 1976).

The behavioral analog of seclusion and solitary confinement is time-out (see Milan, Chapter 6). Time-out, however, is normally thought of as removing a person from a reinforcing setting or environment for a short period of time (e.g., a few minutes) contingent on a predetermined inappropriate behavior being exhibited. Although courts have distinguished between seclusionary practices and the use of "legitimate time-out procedures" (e.g., *Gary W. v. Louisiana,* 1976), many states require the approval of the executive director of the program or a human rights committee before time-out can be used, especially in community-based programs. Therapists considering the utilization of time-out should document that less restrictive procedures have been tried and have failed, that the time-out is for a brief period of time, and that the person is to be continually monitored. In addition, if data indicate that the time-out program is unsuccessful in eliminating the undesirable behavior, the program should be discontinued.

Physical Restraints

Although the use of physical restraints is normally not advocated by behaviorists, courts have addressed the issue of staff physically restraining prisoners or juvenile offenders by handcuffing them or strapping them down in some manner. Courts have held that this type of restraint can be unconstitutionally excessive and highly antitherapeutic (*Pena v. New York State Division for Youth,* 1976). Although the staff may be allowed to restrain an inmate physically in an attempt to prevent danger to self, others, or physical property and when less restrictive procedures have failed, the restraint should be for a very brief period (e.g., no more than 30 minutes) and never used for the convenience of the staff, for retribution, or as a substitute for treatment (*Gary W. v. Louisiana,* 1976). In addition, staff should be trained in procedures whereby they can physically restrain an aggressive person without injury or harm to that person.

Overcorrection

Overcorrection is a behavioral procedure developed by Azrin and Foxx (1971) and their colleagues to decrease inappropriate behavior. Contingent on exhibiting a behavior targeted for change, a client is first required to correct anything in the environment that has been harmed by the inappropriate behavior; this is often called *restitution.* Restitution can easily be used in the criminal or juvenile justice system by requiring the offender to attempt to compensate a victim by paying money for damages or performing services such as community work. For less serious crimes, this may provide a more useful consequence for illegal behavior than incarceration alone because the offender must engage in appropriate behavior in order to make restitution and the victim, who is often ignored, receives some compensation (Spiegler, 1983).

A second part of overcorrection usually involves requiring the client to practice repeatedly an appropriate or postive behavior that could be substituted for the inappropriate behavior. Although this procedure can be useful in reducing many inappropriate behaviors, therapists must ensure that the procedure is not misused. For example, some correctional facilities have required inmates to engage for hours in certain repetitive, nonfunctional, and unnecessary tasks as punishment. For example, in one case, juveniles were required to pull grass without bending their knees, to move dirt from one place to another and then back again repeatedly, or to buff a small area on the floor for long periods of time. The court held that these procedures constituted cruel and unusual punishment (*Morales v. Turman,* 1973). Most therapists would agree that the procedure used in the preceding example would not be considered overcorrection, although it is easy to see how it could be mislabeled as such. Therapists should, therefore, ensure that when using overcorrection procedures, the offender is required to make restitution and is then taught to engage in an appropriate behavior. Overcorrection tasks should be functional, and a limit should exist on the length of time the person is required to engage in the positive-practice aspect of the overcorrection procedure.

Conclusion

If a therapist wants to use any aversive technique or deprive a person of basic rights, he or she should obtain consent and demonstrate that the procedure is justified with respect to the target behaviors to be decreased or increased; no less intrusive or restrictive procedures will accomplish the same purpose; procedural safeguards will be provided to the offender, such as a hearing and/or review before a committee designed to protect the offenders' rights; the procedure is professionally justified as evidenced by the professional literature; the benefits outweigh the risks of using the procedure; and the program will be continually monitored to determine if it is working and that it will be discontinued if it is not successful within a reasonable amount of time.

Right to Refuse Treatment

The right to refuse treatment generally arises with respect to procedures that are intrusive or invasive, that is, that intrude into one's body or mental functioning or invade one's right to privacy. Most law in this area concerns procedures described in the section on aversive techniques. Because of the problems discussed with these procedures, one could argue that offenders would have a right to refuse any treatment involving those techniques. These or any technique that involves the deprivation of a basic right should only be used with consent from the offender. In the absence of consent, where treatment personnel feel strongly that one of these techniques should be used, it would be wise to ensure that procedural safeguards are provided for the offender. These safeguards might include a review by a committee designed to protect the offenders' rights, for example, a human rights or review committee; a hearing with the offender present where the staff present their reasons for wanting to utilize a particular technique; and an appeal procedure to a court of law.

In the mental health field, the right to refuse treatment has received the most attention in the area of psychotropic drugs. Two major judicial decisions exist in this area (*Rennie v. Klein,* 1983; *Rogers v. Okin,* 1984). Both held that staff may employ psychotropic drugs with involuntarily committed patients in emergency situations without the consent of the patient. Use in other than an emergency situation requires procedural due process within either the institution (*Rennie v. Klein,* 1983) or the judicial system (*Rogers v. Okin,* 1984). Therapists working with juvenile or adult offenders may want to establish similar procedural safeguards.

Normally, a juvenile or adult offender does not have the right to refuse treatment that does not involve a deprivation of basic rights, the use of aversive techniques, an invasion of privacy, or, in the case of juveniles, the use of involuntary servitude.

Involuntary Servitude

Involuntary servitude refers to requiring people to work without just compensation and is prohibited by the Thirteenth Amendment that states:

> Neither slavery nor involuntary servitude, except as a punishment for crime whereof the party shall have been duly convicted, shall exist within the United States, or any place subject to their jurisdiction.

Obviously, adult prisoners would not be protected by this amendment. It can be argued, however, that juveniles fall under the protection of this prohibition because they normally are not regarded as having been "convicted;" rather, the language in most juvenile codes refers to juveniles being "adjudicated." One reason that the term *conviction* is not used is to avoid the criminal connotations because the purpose of the juvenile justice system is rehabilitation. In addition, one could argue that the Thirteenth Amendment allows involuntary servitude only as a punishment for a crime. Because punishment is not one of the goals of the juvenile justice system and juveniles are not convicted of "crimes," involuntary servitude would be prohibited with juveniles.

Therapists who work with juveniles who are placed in residential programs should be aware of the relevant concerns regarding involuntary servitude or forced work. As previously mentioned, it is clear that repetitive, nonfunctional work should not be required (*Morales v. Turman,* 1973). Other forms of work, however, may be required. Before discussing other forms of work, it is important to note that courts have distinguished between facilities serving mentally ill or mentally retarded persons and correctional facilities serving juvenile offenders.

Courts have forbidden residential staff from requiring mentally ill and mentally retarded residents to engage in nontherapeutic tasks that are solely for the purpose of maintaining the facility or that are contract work. Only personal housekeeping tasks (e.g., cleaning one's own bedroom) and therapeutic tasks that do not involve the operation of the facility may be required of residents. The opportunity to complete tasks involving the maintenance of the facility may be offered to residents, but if they accept, they must be justly compensated (*Jobson v. Henne,* 1966; *Wyatt v. Stickney,* 1972).

Although requirements enumerated for mentally ill and mentally retarded residents could be extended to facilities serving juveniles, especially those who have not committed criminal acts (i.e., the status offender who engages in behaviors that are injurious to self, such as truancy, running away, being habitually disobedient, etc.), most courts that have addressed the issue have allowed facilities to require juveniles to engage in certain tasks. For example, in *Gary W. v. State of Louisiana* (1976), the court stated that children could be required to perform housekeeping tasks that would be similar to those performed by children in a natural home, foster home, or group home, although in no case could a child be required to perform housekeeping tasks for more than 12 other people. In the 1983 *Morales v. Turman* decision, the tentative agreement between the parties stated that

> students in TYC facilities shall not be required to perform work of any kind (other than academic school work) unless (1) the work is reasonably related to the student's housekeeping or personal hygienic needs and is equitably shared by the other students in that program or facility, (2) the work is part of an approved vocationally oriented program for the students, (3) the work is in furtherance of the maintenance of the facility and is in lieu of restitution for property damage committed by the student or is routine clean-up which is equitably shared by all of the students, (4) the student volunteers for the work assignment, or (5) the student is being compensated for the work assignment. (p. 349)

With these statements in mind, the following guidelines might be useful for therapists working in facilities serving juveniles. First, it may be useful to designate housekeeping skills as part of each youth's therapy plan and specifically define them. An active instructional program should exist to ensure that the youths are taught the skills correctly. No one youth should ever be solely responsible for one task; rather, the housekeeping tasks should be rotated and equitably shared. Housekeeping or cooking tasks that a youth is asked to learn and perform should be for the entire group, not just for one other person. For example, it might be acceptable to require a youth to help clean the living room but not be acceptable to require a youth to clean another youth's room. Tasks that would benefit the facility for a longer period of time than the average tenure of a youth's stay in the program (e.g., painting the outside of the house) should probably not be required. Finally, youths should never be required to do work solely for the benefit of the staff. For example, staff should not require youths to do such things as clean the staff's living quarters, wash the staff's cars, or baby-sit the staff's children. Although the *Morales* agreement appeared to allow juveniles to volunteer for work, the work being described was for the facility's benefit rather than the personal benefit of the staff. In addition, one could argue that there is an inherently coercive nature that exists in any correctional facility, either institutional or community-based, with the possibility of overreaching on the part of the staff. Thus juveniles may "volunteer" to do personal work for staff in order to win favor with them. To avoid this possibility, staff should never require juveniles to do any work that benefits the staff member personally. Staff may offer those types of jobs to juveniles, but the staff must then justly compensate the juvenile for the work with the staff member's personal money rather than program funds.

Search and Seizure

An enormous amount of law exists on search and seizure. Most of that law pertains to the Fourth Amendment protection against unreasonable searches prior to incarceration in a correctional facility. Once in a correctional facility, the staff has great latitude in searching inmates' or residents' belongings for contraband in order to maintain a secure and safe environment.

It is not the purpose of this section to review all the law on search and seizure because most of it is not relevant to those working in the behavioral field. Many therapists, however, work in or consult with schools or community-based programs serving juveniles. Therefore, the primary search and seizure issues to be discussed in this chapter relate to the search of juveniles in the school system and in community-based programs. The Fourth Amendment protects people against unreasonable searches made by the government—not searches made by private individuals. When interpreting the Fourth Amendment, courts have generally required that either (1) a search warrant be obtained that is based on probable cause that evidence or contraband exists in a particular place (the warrant requirement can be waived in certain exigent circumstances) or (2) the individual involved must consent to the search.

When school officials search students or their lockers, one initial question that arises is whether the school official is a governmental officer such that the Fourth Amendment requirements are invoked. Many people have argued that school officials are not law enforcement or governmental officials because they are acting *in loco parentis* (i.e., in the place of the parent) while the child is at school. Others have maintained that school officials should be considered governmental officers because they often report any evidence of criminal liability to the law enforcement officers, sometimes under statutory requirement.

The Supreme Court of the United States recently decided a school search and seizure case, thus partially ending the long controversy on the issue (*New Jersey v. T. L. O.*, 1985). The Court held that school personnel are to be considered governmental officials and that the Fourth Amendment is, therefore, applicable. A search warrant is not required, however, because

> requiring a teacher to obtain a warrant before searching a child suspected of an infraction of school rules (or of the criminal law) would unduly interfere with the maintenance of the swift and informal disciplinary procedures needed in schools. (p. 743)

In addition, the standard for determining the reasonableness of the search is lower than the "probable cause" standard normally used. This lower standard was judged necessary to insure that education can be provided in an atmosphere free from danger or disruption. The legality of a search in the school will "depend simply on the reasonableness, under all the circumstances, of the search" (pp. 743–744).

Therapists working in or advising administrators and staff of community-based nonresidential programs should also be aware of the search and seizure issues. Staff should not go into a private home and search for contraband. Although not a governmental officer, the staff member could be sued for trespassing for engaging in such behavior. In addition, although a parent can search a child's room, it is not clear that a parent can consent to a search conducted by another person of a child's room or child's belongings.

If therapists are working as staff members in or consulting with a community-based residential facility for adult or juvenile offenders, they should consult an attorney or the court to determine the law in that particular jurisdiction concerning searches or finding and reporting contraband. One case on this topic involved the issue of whether the Fourth Amendment prohibition against unreasonable searches and seizures applied to a foster parent who was licensed and paid by the state (*J. M. A. v. State*, 1975). In this case, a foster parent became concerned that her foster child, J. M. A., was involved in the trafficking of drugs. She therefore searched his room and listened to phone conversations without his permission. She found marijuana in one of his pockets and then called J. M. A.'s social worker, who called the police. The Alaska court held that the foster parent was partially acting as a substitute for a natural parent and should, therefore, not be subjected to constitutional restraints. In addition, the court also held that because J. M. A. had been declared a delinquent and placed in the foster home as an alternative to placement in a correctional facility, the foster parent had the same right to search his room as the correctional facility staff would have had. This decision appears to give foster parents (and group home staff) the ability to search resident's rooms. The decision was from the Supreme Court of Alaska and is, therefore, law only for Alaska.

Providing Adequate Supervision and Trained Staff

Therapists working in any type of program should ensure that enough properly trained staff are available to supervise participants adequately. In a correctional program, one must have enough staff to prevent routine problems such as fights or attacks on other inmates or staff, leaving the program without authorization, and offenders being involved in accidents. In the mental health field, a large number of lawsuits arise yearly due to a staff's failure to supervise clients adequately (VanBiervliet & Sheldon-Wildgen, 1981). In these cases, liability has been imposed on staff and administrators for injuries due to this failure. Imposing liability could also occur in programs serving offenders, especially juvenile offenders, because a court might hold that juveniles did not have the ability to perceive a dangerous situation or protect themselves. Thus adequate staff is important for security and liability reasons. Staff should also be properly trained in carrying out the procedures used by the facility, in legal and ethical issues, and, for juveniles, in implementing treatment. Proper staff training probably should include ongoing inservice instruction, consultation, and observation of performance with feedback based thereon.

Releasing Appropriately

Once a juvenile or adult offender is properly placed in a program and has met the goals or requirements of the program, the professional staff often will be called on to make a decision regarding release. In the mental health field, administrators and treatment staff can be held liable for improperly releasing a resident who subsequently harms another. Liability is imposed in cases where the courts conclude that the staff knew or should have known that the resident was dangerous. In addition, staff might be held liable for failing to release people who have met their treatment goals. With juvenile and adult offenders, liability only arises if the facility has some discretion in the release of the offender. This may arise quite frequently, however.

To ensure that offenders are released properly, therapists should specify the requirements for release in advance; document an offender's progress in meeting these requirements; base any decision regarding release on data taken on these requirements; select requirements for release that relate to the skills and behaviors necessary for successful living in the community; and document any belief that an offender will be dangerous and then ensure that the offender is not released. If the program personnel have no control over a release (e.g., the offender was placed in the program for a set amount of time by a court) and the staff feel the person is dangerous, staff would be wise to inform the court that placed the offender as well as the police about the possibility of this person being dangerous to others. (In some cases, as discussed later, the staff may be required to warn a third party.)

Finally, when offenders are placed in a program and the program staff is given the discretion to decide when the person leaves, the staff should not keep the person beyond the time when the original goals are met. In other words, once goals have been set, the program staff should not continually change them with the result of not releasing the offender. This is especially relevant in programs serving juveniles, where the program may have the ability to keep a youth until the age of 21 in order to provide individualized and appropriate treatment. Some programs provide inadequate treatment, yet refuse to release the juvenile in an apparent attempt to keep revenue from the state to support the staff. This can be avoided by establishing goals, specifying procedures, and evaluating program success. Thus the evaluation of treatment programs may be a critical factor in safeguarding offenders' rights.

Duty to Warn Third Parties

Therapists working in the field of crime and delinquency need to be aware of the current judicial and statutory law regarding a therapist's duty to warn third parties about a client's threat of violence to that third party. In a famous case, *Tarasoff v. Regents of the University of California* (1976), the California Supreme Court held that

> once a therapist does in fact determine, or under applicable professional standards reasonably should have determined, that a patient poses a serious danger of violence to others, he [or she] bears a duty to exercise reasonable care to protect the foreseeable victims of that danger. (p. 345)

In the *Tarasoff* case, a university psychologist was working with a young man who threatened to kill a female friend of his. The psychologist was concerned about the man's threats and contacted the university police who questioned him but released him because they did not feel that he was dangerous.

The man subsequently stabbed and killed his female friend. The woman's parents sued the psychologist, his supervising psychiatrist, the university, and the Board of Regents. The court gave the previously cited holding and also stated that therapists cannot discharge their duty to warn the third party by informing the police; rather, the information must be given directly to the potential victim.

Other courts have held that this duty applies only if a foreseeable victim exists. If a therapist believes a person is a danger to society at large, for example, there is no victim to contact. In such a situation, the therapist should contact law enforcement officers. Although not all jurisdictions have adopted the *Tarasoff* ruling, therapists working in the crime and delinquency area may want to err on the safe side by following this decision. Although warning third parties raises issues about divulging confidential information, many courts have held the duty to protect confidential communications is often outweighed by the duty to protect society from harm when therapists clearly believe that a person is dangerous (*McIntosh v. Milano,* 1979). It is clear, though, that therapists must be prudent regarding decisions to warn others and ensure against indiscriminate disclosure of personal information (VanBiervliet & Sheldon-Wildgen, 1981).

Protective Mechanisms: Human Rights and Review Committees

Throughout this chapter, I have recommended the use of protective mechanisms, such as an advisory, review, or human rights committees, that can be used to protect the offender and the therapist. In the last 10 years, courts and legislatures have begun mandating the establishment and utilization of these committees, especially in residential programs (e.g., *Wyatt v. Stickney,* 1972). The use of these committees is desirable whenever a person is under the supervision or control of another individual(s) (Friedman, 1975; Mahan, Maples, Murphy, & Tubb, 1975; May et al., 1976; Sheldon-Wildgen, 1976; Sheldon-Wildgen & Risley, 1982; Stolz, 1978a,b; VanBiervliet & Sheldon-Wildgen, 1981).

These committees normally consist of a group of people from the community, in addition to members of the target class (e.g., offenders), who review the treatment of individuals in a program to guard against inhumane or improper treatment. Sheldon-Wildgen and Risley (1982) have suggested that the committee members should function much like a jury in terms of reviewing and evaluating information and evidence in order to protect those who are unable to protect themselves adequately. These committees generally review the use of any aversive procedure, any experimental procedure, or any procedure that involves a deprivation of rights or an invasion of privacy. Sheldon-Wildgen and Risley (1982) also encourage committees to review the treatment and progress of each client continually to ensure that appropriate treatment is being provided. This is especially relevant for juvenile offenders. Staff are required to present information regularly to this committee and to receive committee approval before proceeding with certain types of procedures. The independent review by this type of committee serves three functions: it protects the rights of the clients; it reassures others that the program personnel are behaving in an appropriate manner; and, if the therapists and program personnel follow the recommendations of the committee, it offers some protection against legal or ethical sanctions being imposed against the therapist or program administrators.

CONCLUSION

Ethical and legal topics have concerned society for centuries, but only recently have human service professionals become so critically aware of these issues and the ramifications of their professional actions. Therapists working in the correctional field are no exception. Treating people humanely and ethically is an important and valid consideration in the criminal and juvenile justice system, and this importance is exemplified not only in the protection of both offender and therapist rights but also in the ability to treat and rehabilitate both juvenile and adult offenders successfully. It is very likely that those individuals who believe that they have been treated fairly, ethically, and legally within the correctional system may be better candidates for successful behavioral change. If their rights have been protected while in the correctional system, they may feel little need to engage in illegal behavior toward society as retribution for mistreatment they received. Obviously, providing legally safe and ethically humane environments will not ensure that offenders will decrease their illegal behavior, but it may greatly aid in helping provide the appropriate environment for treatment to occur. Addressing the issues outlined in the chapter may set the stage for effective treatment to take place and, thus, offenders, therapists, and society will reap the benefits.

REFERENCES

American Bar Association. (1976–present). *Mental and Physical Disability Law Reporter*. Washington, DC: Author.
American Psychological Association. (1979). *Ethical standards of psychologists* (rev. ed.). Washington, DC: Author.
American Psychological Association. (1981). Ethical principles of psychologists. *American Psychologist, 36*, 633–638.
Association for the Advancement of Behavior Therapy. (1977). *Ethical issues for human services*. New York: Author.
Ayllon, T. (1975). Behavior modification in institutional settings. *Arizona Law Review, 17*(1), 3–19.
Azrin, N. H., & Foxx, R. M. (1971). A rapid method of toilet training the institutionalized retarded. *Journal of Applied Behavior Analysis, 4*, 89–99.
Barnhart, C. L. (Ed.). (1970). *The American college dictionary*. New York: Random House.
Bellack, A. S., Hersen, M., & Kazdin, A. E. (Eds.). (1982). *International handbook of behavior modification and therapy*. New York: Plenum Press.
Brown, B. S., Wienckowski, L. A., & Stolz, S. B. (1975). *Behavior modification: Perspective on a current issue* (DHEW Publication No. ADM 75-202). Washington, DC: U.S. Government Printing Office.

Budd, K. S., & Baer, D. M. (1976). Behavior modification and the law: Implications of recent judicial decisions. *Journal of Psychiatry and Law,* Summer, 171–244.

Christian, W. P. (1983). Protecting clients' rights in mental health programs. *Administration in Mental Health, 11*(2), 115–123.

Clonce v. Richardson, 379 F. Supp. 338 (W.D. Mo. 1974).

Craighead, W. E., Kazdin, A. E., & Mahoney, M. J. (1981). *Behavior modification: Principles, issues, and applications* (2nd ed.). Boston: Houghton Mifflin.

Curl, R. M. (1982). Adherence to the legal and ethical requirements of human research. *The Behavior Therapist, 5*(4).

Davison, G. C., & Stuart, R. B. (1975). Behavior therapy and civil liberties. *American Psychologist, 30*(7), 755–763.

DeKraai, M. B., & Sales, B. D. (1982). Privileged communications of psychologists. *Professional Psychology, 13*(3), 372–388.

Doe v. Roe, 400 N.Y.S.2d 668 (Sup. Ct. 1977).

Everstine, L., Everstine, D. S., Heymann, G. M., True, R. H., Frey, D. H., Johnson, H. G., & Seiden, R. H. (1980). Privacy and confidentiality in psychotherapy. *American Psychologist, 35*(9), 828–840.

F. E. v. Hensley, Civ. No. 73-CV 43-4-1 (W.D. Mo. 1978).

Feldman, M. P., & Peay, J. (1982). Ethical and legal issues. In A. S. Bellack, M. Hersen, & A. E. Kazdin (Eds.), *International handbook of behavior modification and therapy* (pp. 231–262). New York: Plenum Press.

Fields, F. R. J., & Horwitz, R. J. (Eds.). (1982). *Psychology and professional practice.* Westport, CT: Quorum Books.

Friedman, P. R. (1975). Legal regulation of applied behavioral analysis in mental institutions and prisons. *Arizona Law Review, 17*(1), 39–104.

Gary W. v. Louisiana, 437 F. Supp. 1209 (E.D. La. 1976), *aff'd and remanded,* 622 F.2d 804 (5th Cir. 1980).

Gutheil, T. G., & Appelbaum, P. S. (1982). *Clinical handbook of psychiatry and the law.* New York: McGraw-Hill.

Hannah, G. T., Christian, W. P., & Clark, H. B. (Eds.), (1981). *Preservation of client rights.* New York: The Free Press.

Hare-Mustin, R. T., Marecek, J., Kaplan, A. G., & Liss-Levinson, N. (1979). Rights of clients, responsibilities of therapists. *American Psychologist, 34*(1), 3–16.

Ingraham v. Wright, 430 U.S. 651 (1977).

Inmates of Boys' Training School v. Affleck, 346 F. Supp. 1354 (D.R.I. 1972).

J. M. A. v. State, 542 P.2d 170 (Ala. 1975).

Jagmin, R. D., Wittman, W. D., & Noll, J. O. (1978). Mental health professionals' attitudes toward confidentiality, privilege, and third-party disclosure. *Professional Psychology, 9*(3), 458–466.

Jobson v. Henne, 355 F.2d 129 (2d Cir. 1966).

Kaimowitz v. Department of Mental Health, Civ. No. 73-19434-AW (Mich. Cir. Ct., Wayne County, 1973).

Kazdin, A. E. (1980). *Behavior modification in applied settings* (rev. ed.). Homewood, IL: The Dorsey Press.

Kittrie, N. N. (1971). *The right to be different.* Baltimore: Johns Hopkins Press.

Knecht v. Gillman, 488 F.2d 1136 (8th Cir. 1973).

Koocher, G. P. (Ed.). (1976). *Children's rights and the mental health professions.* New York: Wiley.

Lutzker, J. R., & Martin, J. A. (1981). *Behavior change.* Monterey, CA: Brooks/Cole.

Mackey v. Procunier, 477 F.2d 877 (9th Cir. 1973).

Mahan, S., Maples, S., Murphy, S., & Tubb, G. (1975, spring). A mechanism for enforcing the right to treatment: The human rights committee. *Law & Psychology Review,* 131–149.

Martarella v. Kelley, 349 F. Supp. 575 (S.D. N. Y. 1972).

Martin, G., & Pear, J. (1983). *Behavior modification: What it is and how to do it* (2nd ed.). Englewood Cliffs, NJ: Prentice-Hall.

Martin, R. (1975). *Legal challenges to behavior modification.* Champaign, IL: Research Press.

May, J. G., Risley, T. R., Twardosz, S., Friedman, P., Bijou, S. W., Wexler, D., *et al.* (1976).

Guidelines for the use of behavioral procedures in state programs for retarded persons. Arlington, TX: National Association of Retarded Citizens.

McIntosh v. Milano, 403 A.2d 500 (N.J. Sup. Ct. 1979).

Meisel, A., Roth, L. H., & Lidz, C. W. (1977). Toward a model of the legal doctrine of informed consent. *American Journal of Psychiatry, 134*(3), 285–289.

Melton, G. B. (Ed.). (1982). Legal reforms affecting child & youth services [Special issue]. *Child and Youth Services, 5* (1/2).

Morales v. Turman, 364 F. Supp. 166 (E.D. Tex. 1973); *aff'd,* 383 F. Supp. 53 (E.D. Tex. 1974); *rev'd & remanded,* 535 F.2d 864 (5th Cir. 1976); *rev'd & remanded,* 430 U.S. 322 (1977); *rehearing denied,* 430 U.S. 988 (1977); *remanded,* 562 F.2d 993 (5th Cir. 1977); *aff'd with requirements to meet before approval of settlement,* 569 F. Supp. 332 (E.D. Tex. (1983).

Morgan v. Sproat, 432 F. Supp. 1130 (S.D. Miss. 1977).

Nelson v. Heyne, 491 F.2d 352 (7th Cir. 1974) *cert. denied,* 417 U.S. 976 (1974).

New Jersey v. T. L. O. 469 U.S. 325 (1985).

Noll, J. O., & Hanlon, M. J. (1976). Patient privacy and confidentiality in mental health centers. *American Journal of Psychiatry, 133*(11), 1286–1289.

Pena v. New York State Division for Youth, 419 F. Supp. 203 (S. D. N. Y. 1976).

Procunier v. Martinez, 416 U.S. 396 (1974).

Pugh v. Locke, 406 F. Supp. 318 (M.D. Ala. 1976).

Rachlin, S., & Appelbaum, P. S. (1983). The limits of confidentiality. *Hospital and Community Psychiatry, 34*(7), 589–590.

Redd, W. H., Porterfield, A. L., & Anderson, B. L. (1979). *Behavioral approaches to human problems.* New York: Random House.

Rennie v. Klein, 462 F. Supp. 1131 (D.N.J. 1978); *aff'd* 476 F. Supp. 1294 (D.N.J. 1979); *aff'd., modified & remanded,* 653 F.2d 836 (3rd Cir. 1981); *vacated & remanded,* 458 U.S. 1119 (1982); *aff'd & remanded,* 720 F.2d. 266 (3rd Cir. 1983).

Rogers v. Okin, 478 F. Supp. 1342 (D. Mass. 1979); *aff'd in part, rev'd in part, & remanded,* 634 F.2d 650 (1st Cir. 1980); *vacated & remanded,* 457 U.S. 291 (1982); *aff'd & remanded,* 738 F.2d 1 (1st Cir. 1984).

Sadoff, R. L. (1982). *Legal issues in the care of psychiatric patients.* New York: Springer.

Schetky, D. H., & Benedek, E. P. (Eds.). (1980). *Child psychiatry and the law.* New York: Brunner/Mazel.

Schwitzgebel, R. K. (1979). *Legal aspects of the enforced treatment of offenders* (DHEW Publication No. ADM 79-831). Washington, DC: U.S. Government Printing Office.

Schwitzgebel, R. L., & Schwitzgebel, R. K. (1980). *Law and psychological practice.* New York: Wiley.

Shah, S. A. (1970). Privileged communications, confidentiality, and privacy: Confidentiality. *Professional Psychology, 1,* 159–164.

Sheldon-Wildgen, J. (1976). Rights of institutionalized mental patients: Issues, implications, and proposed guidelines. *Kansas Law Review, 25*(1), 63–85.

Sheldon-Wildgen, J. (1982). Avoiding legal liability: The rights and responsibilities of therapists. *The Behavior Therapist, 5*(5), 165–169.

Sheldon-Wildgen, J., & Risley, T. R. (1982). Balancing individual rights: The establishment of peer review and human rights committees. In A. Bellack, M. Hersen, & A. E. Kazdin (Eds.), *International handbook of behavior modification* (pp. 263–259). New York: Plenum Press.

Siegel, M. (1979). Privacy, ethics, and confidentiality. *Professional Psychology, 10,* 249–258.

Skinner, B. F. (1971). *Beyond freedom and dignity.* New York: Knopf.

Slovenko, R. (1973). *Psychiatry and law.* Boston: Little, Brown.

Spiegler, M. D. (1983). *Contemporary behavioral therapy.* Palo Alto, CA: Mayfield.

Stolz, S. B. (1975). Ethical issues in research on behavior therapy. In W. S. Wood (Ed.), *Issues in evaluating behavior modification* (pp. 239–256). Champaign, IL: Research Press.

Stolz, S. B. (1978a). Ethics of social and educational interventions: Historical context and a behavioral analysis. In A. C. Catania & T. A. Brigham (Eds.), *Handbook of applied behavior analysis: Social and instructional processes* (pp. 652–676). New York: Irvington.

Stolz, S. B. (1978b). Ethical issues in behavior modification. In G. Bermant, H. C. Kelman, & D. P. Warwick (Eds.), *The ethics of social intervention* (pp. 37–60). Washington, DC: Hemisphere.

Tarasoff v. Regents of the University of California, 131 Cal. Rptr. 14, 551 P.2d 334 (1976).

Timbers, G. D., Jones, R. J., & Davis, J. L. (1981). Safeguarding the rights of children and youth in group-home treatment settings. In G. T. Hannah, W. P. Christian, & H. B. Clark (Eds.), *Preservation of client rights* (pp. 246–277). New York: The Free Press.

Turnbull, H. R., Biklen, D. P., Boggs, E. M., Ellis, J. W., Keeran, C. V., & Siedor, G. R. (1977). *Consent handbook.* Washington, DC: American Association on Mental Deficiency.

VanBiervliet, A., & Sheldon-Wildgen, J. (1981). *Liability issues in community-based programs.* Baltimore: Brookes.

Walker, J. E., & Shea, T. M. (1980). *Behavior modification: A practical approach for educators* (2d ed.). St. Louis: C. V. Mosby.

Wexler, D. (1973). Token and taboo: Behavior modification, token economies, and the law. *California Law Review, 61,* 81–109.

Wexler, D. (1974). Of rights and reinforcers. *San Diego Law Review, 11,* 957–971.

Wexler, D. B. (1975). Behavior modification and legal developments. *American Behavioral Scientist, 18*(5), 679–684.

Wolff v. McDonnell, 418 U.S. 539 (1974).

Wood, W. S. (Ed.). (1975). *Issues in evaluating behavior modification.* Champaign, IL: Research Press.

Wyatt v. Stickney, 325 F. Supp. 781, *aff'd on rehearing,* 334 F. Supp. 1341 (M.D. Ala. 1971), 344 F. Supp. 373, *aff'd in separate decision,* 344 F. Supp. 387 (M.D. Ala. 1972), *aff'd sub nom,* Wyatt v. Aderholt, 503 F.2d 1305 (5th Cir. 1974).

22

Social and Political Challenges to Behavioral Programs with Delinquents and Criminals

JOHN D. BURCHARD

Considerable attention has been focused on social and political challenges to behavior therapy or behavior modification (Atthowe, 1973; Goldiamond, 1978; Jason, 1977; Liberman, 1979; Norley, 1977; Reppucci, 1973; Reppucci & Saunders, 1974; Rozynko, Swift, Swift & Boggs, 1973; Wray, 1980).[1] Much of this focus has been on social and political forces within family, group, community, and institutional settings that pose resistances and constraints on the administration of traditional behavior modification programs. For example, in declaring optimism for the future of behavior therapy, Liberman (1979) warned that

> we should pay some attention to the problems we face in applying our knowledge, and to the limitations that hamper or impair our work, and slow our progress. These limiting factors lie primarily outside the domain of behavior therapy. It is often not behavioral technology as such, but rather political and social issues that make or break an innovative program. (p. 370)

Certainly, social and political variables can impair and even prevent behavior therapy programs, particularly behavior therapy programs for delinquents and criminals. Liberman and others (Burchard & Harig, 1976; Burchard & Lane, 1982; Laws, 1974; Nietzel, 1979) have cited many examples of administrators, legislators, attorneys, judges, and even program staff posing insurmountable obstacles to such programs. The number of unreported casualties must be immense.

We must learn from these experiences. Program administrators must become more adept at obtaining compliance from significant others who function outside the realm of behavior therapy. Some behavior therapists also need to become more sensitive to relevant ethical issues (e.g., informed consent and

---

[1] *Behavior modification* and *behavior therapy* have frequently been used interchangeably in the literature. The terms are used synonymously in this chapter.

John D. Burchard • Department of Psychology, University of Vermont, Burlington, Vermont 05405.

excessive and unnecessary aversive control) that have prompted much justifiable legal concern and action (Nietzel, 1979; see Sheldon, Chapter 21, this volume).

But, is Liberman correct in implying that we have the technology to rehabilitate delinquents and criminals and that the forces that most limit our progress are the social and political resistances to our programs? First, the data do not appear to support such a claim. Long-term positive outcomes do not tend to covary with social and political program resistance. Rather, long-term positive outcome data are difficult to obtain under any social and political circumstances. Second, the biggest social and political challenge is not resistance to behavior therapy programs. A more critical challenge is the vast array of other social and political contingencies that are designed to modify delinquent and criminal behavior, either directly or indirectly.

Contingency management involves the rearrangement of the environment so that desirable behavior is strengthened and/or undesirable behavior is weakened. It is important to understand that when it comes to contingency management, behavior therapy is not the only game in town. In addition, behavior therapists are not the only players of the game. The criminal and juvenile justice systems are comprised of complex contingency management systems that are designed to modify delinquent and criminal behavior. Social and political contingencies that make up those justice systems are established by politicians and bureaucrats, not behaviorists.

The focus of this chapter is on social/political contingencies, how they differ from the more therapeutic contingencies designed by professionals, and how they influence the offender as well as the behavior therapist. Several specific examples will be provided. Because the primary thesis of this chapter is that behavior therapists should become more involved in the development and modification of social/political contingencies, there will also be a discussion of the barriers to such involvement and how those barriers might be overcome.

The architects of professional, therapeutic contingencies and of social/political contingencies live almost in two separate worlds. At present, the world of those who construct social/political contingencies is in tremendous conflict. For the past several years, a battle has been waged between two distinctly different ideologies with respect to social/political contingencies for juvenile and criminal offenders. On one side are those who believe that the juvenile justice system is ineffective at best, and harmful at worst. They have been promoting such concepts as prevention, diversion, and deinstitutionalization (Burchard & Burchard, 1987). The other side wants to reform the system by making it more restrictive and punitive, particularly for serious offenders. In addition, they want government to get out of the business of delinquency prevention (Regnery, 1986).

More of the specifics of this particular dispute will be discussed later. The question to be raised here is: Where are the behaviorists? Although some may argue that the issues are beyond the realm of behavior therapy, those issues are clearly not beyond the realm of social learning theory (Bandura, 1973,

1974). Behaviorists are supposed to be the experts on such issues as the relationship between behavior and environment, the effects of punishment and restriction on behavior, and the generalization of behavioral change from an artificial to a natural environment.

The ideological battles that are taking place are not merely battles of rhetoric. The outcomes have had, and will continue to have, a very powerful effect on the behavior of both the offender and the behavior therapist. It is not in the best interests of either the offender or the behavior therapist to wait until the dust settles and then administer behavior therapy programs in the midst of the political fallout. In fact, the message in this chapter is that the longer we wait, the less likely there will be any behavior therapy programs to administer.

THERAPEUTIC VERSUS SOCIAL/POLITICAL CONTINGENCIES

In his classic introduction to the science of human behavior, B. F. Skinner described a social system as being comprised of controlling agencies and of individuals who are controlled by those agencies (Skinner, 1953). His examples of the controlling agencies were government, law, religion, psychotherapy, economic control, and education. Psychotherapy was regarded as a special agency that was concerned with helping people adjust to their environment. Unlike government, psychotherapy was not a large organized agency, but a profession, the members of which developed and applied their controlling techniques to their clients. Had behavior therapy been in existence in 1953, it probably would have been regarded in a similar fashion.

According to Skinner (1953), the controlling techniques of government are much different than those of psychotherapy.

> The techniques available to government agencies are extremely powerful, and they are frequently misused with disadvantageous results both to the individual and to the group. Some degree of counter control on the part of psychotherapy or some similar agency is therefore often needed. Since the variables under the control of the therapist are relatively weak, and since he must operate within certain ethical, religious and legal limits he can scarcely be regarded as a serious threat. (p. 373)

The statement characterizes the existing relationship between behavior therapy and the criminal justice system. This can be seen most clearly by focusing on the distinction between therapeutic and social/political contingencies and their effects on unlawful behavior.

Therapeutic contingencies are those contingencies that are designed and administered by persons trained in the technology of behavioral change. They are contingencies designed to modify the behavior of juvenile and adult offenders and are derived systematically from social learning theory and behavioral research. In short, they are the contingencies administered by behavior therapists.

Therapeutic contingency management tends to be administed in the context of a *program* where similar contingencies exist for a group of offenders. If the program takes place in a closed or total environment (e.g., prison, detention center, or training center), a greater proportion of the daily contingencies are therapeutic contingencies. The therapeutic contingencies in a closed environment, however, are usually quite different from the contingencies that exist once the offender leaves the program; moreover, there is usually little opportunity or effort to modify the contingencies in the nonprogram environment. If the program is operated in a more open environment (e.g., group home, foster home, probation, parole, diversion program), a smaller proportion of day-to-day contingencies are therapeutic contingencies, and the contingencies are more similar to those that will exist once the offender leaves the program.

Social/political contingencies are laws, regulations, and policies that are designed to change or influence the frequency of unlawful behavior. They are developed and administered by policymakers and lawmakers who tend not to be trained in the technology of behavioral change. Like therapeutic contingencies, social/political contingencies change the relationship between behavior and environment in ways that are supposedly designed to weaken undesirable behavior and strengthen desirable behavior.

Social/political contingencies can have either a direct or indirect influence on behavior. Those contingencies with a direct influence establish a specific behavior-consequence relationship. Examples of direct social/political contingencies involving unlawful behavior in a community setting include expulsion from school, fines, consequences specified in probation conditions, and placement in more restrictive living environments such as foster homes, group homes, wilderness camps, detention centers, training schools, or prisons.

Indirect social/political contingencies establish the parameters for direct contingencies, whether they are therapeutic or social/political. This would include laws, regulations, and policies that have a significant influence on the offenders' environment, including the behavior of the people within it. Some examples are regulations or policies prohibiting the use of aversive control, legislation to build additional correctional facilities, policies that change resident/staff ratios, and legislation that establishes or eliminates funding for prevention or rehabilitation programs.

Although therapeutic and social/political contingencies are both designed to prevent or eliminate unlawful behavior, they differ significantly in terms of power and influence. The power differential is obvious. Behavior therapists are not able to change the total environment contingent upon a particular behavior.

With respect to influence, the therapeutic and social/political contingencies also differ significantly. Whereas a multitude of therapeutic contingencies may reach a few offenders, a few social/political contingencies will reach a multitude of offenders. In 1982, there were 1,630,226 arrests involving juveniles (Federal Bureau of Investigation, 1983), and the nation's juvenile courts disposed of an estimated 1,296,000 delinquency and status offense cases (Krisberg, Schwartz, Litsky, & Austin, 1986). Although each of these offenders experienced several powerful social/political contingencies, less than 1% of the offenders probably came in contact with therapeutic contingencies.

That therapeutic contingencies reach so few offenders would be less of a problem if it could be shown that behavioral technology was having a positive impact on the criminal/juvenile justice system. Unfortunately, that is not the case. Behavioral research rarely finds its way into the political debates regarding the need for systems change; moreover, the work of the behavior therapists within the system has had little influence on the programs administered by nonbehaviorists. In fact, the generalization of behavior therapy programs appears to be as difficult to achieve as the generalization of the behavioral change that occurs within them. Programs tend to terminate shortly after the departure of the program initiator and fewer new programs are being initiated. If the present trend in correctional facilities continues, there will soon be more reviews of behavior therapy programs in institutions than programs to review (see Milan, Chapters 6 and 7, this volume).

In order to facilitate the use of behavior therapy with the offender, behavior therapists must focus more attention and action on social/political contingencies. Whereas the consequences used in therapeutic contingencies are program-specific (e.g., time-out, response cost, token reinforcement, etc.), the consequences of social/political contingencies determine who goes to the program and, what is more important, whether or not there will even be a program.

The following four social/political contingencies will be discussed: (a) the training school contingency, (b) the diversion program contingency, (c) the intensive supervision contingency, and (d) the funding contingency. The first three contingencies are direct contingencies, whereas the fourth is indirect. Most of the emphasis will be placed on the training school contingency, which will serve as a prototype for analyzing social/political contingencies in general. The presentation of the other three contingencies will be briefer and more general. Although the selection of these four contingencies was not arbitrary, it should be clear that many other social/political contingencies could have been chosen.

The Training School Contingency

This contingency is self-explanatory. If juveniles engage in a sufficient amount of unlawful behavior, they will be sent to some form of institution, generally referred to as a training school. The individuals who administer the contingency are usually judges or public agency administrators. The contingency is always authorized by legislation, the specifics of which may vary considerably from one state to another. Although much has been written about the training school contingency, the focus here will be on three characteristics: (a) the benefit to the offender, (b) the utilization of the contingency, and (c) ways the contingency has been modified.

Benefit to the Offender

Social scientists have struggled for many years to try to determine the rehabilitative effect of training schools. Although it is not within the scope of this chapter to analyze that literature, some general impressions are necessary in order to better understand the training school contingency.

On the basis of several reviews in the 1970s, it was concluded that training schools have no appreciable impact on the rate at which the offender returns to crime (Lipton, Martinson, & Wilks, 1975; Robinson & Smith, 1971; Romig, 1978). No good comparative data to refute such a claim exist. Although it has been argued that training schools do have a beneficial "suppression effect" for the more chronic, violent offender (Murray & Cox, 1979), more recent studies have placed that finding in doubt (Lundman, 1986). Based on available data, it would seem that the search for alternatives to training schools should continue and the training school contingency should be used with extreme caution.

Utilization and the Training School Contingency

Two dimensions of the utilization of the training school contingency deserve discussion: the recent increase in the per-capita frequency of its use on a national basis and the inconsistency of its use across legal jurisdictions (e.g., states or counties within states).

Both of these characteristics were documented in a recent report released by the Hubert H. Humphrey Center for the Study of Youth Policy at the University of Minnesota (Krisberg et al., 1986). Table 1 shows the increase in training school admissions based on data from the U.S. Census Bureau's biannual survey (also referred to as the Children in Custody Survey). Although the absolute number of admissions declined between 1971 and 1982, the rate per 100,000 age-eligible youth increased by 5%. The increase in per-capita admissions in the midst of a decline in absolute admissions is due to a significant decrease in the birth rate during the 1960s.

For those who have a negative view of the training school contingency, the Minnesota report also contains the following alarming trends. First, an even greater increase has occurred in the admission of juveniles to private correc-

Table 1. U.S. Public Training School Admissions

	Year				% Change
	1971	1974	1979	1982	1971–1982
Number of admissions					
Total	67,775	67,406	63,901	65,401	−3.5
Male	53,089	53,737	55,457	57,472	+8.3
Female	14,686	13,669	8,444	7,929	−46.0
Rates per 100,000 age-eligible youths					
Total	226	228	222	238	+5.3
Male	354	364	386	418	+18.0
Female	98	93	59	58	−40.8

Table 2. 1979 Admissions to Training Schools per 100,000 Age-Eligible Youths

State	Rate	Admissions
States with highest admission rates		
Delaware	605	510
Oregon	532	1,739
Wyoming	518	358
Arizona	472	1,700
California	447	13,578
States with lowest admission rates		
New Jersey	59	605
Michigan	53	630
New York	38	661
Massachusetts	2	15
Vermont	0	0

tional facilities. Second, between 1979 and 1983 the per-capita length of stay in training schools increased 7.5% (e.g., 238 days in 1979 to 256 days in 1982). Third, the proportion of minority youth in the nation's training schools has increased. In 1977, 53% of the public training school population was white; by 1982 that proportion had declined to 46%. And fourth, many jurisdictions, including Illinois, Colorado, and California, are reporting severe crowding in their training schools.

All of these trends led the authors of the Minnesota report to conclude that

> despite a declining youth population, declining serious juvenile crime rates, and the relatively high costs and limited benefits of institutional care, the number of juveniles incarcerated on a given day in detention centers and schools is increasing. Also, juveniles are being confined in such facilities for longer periods of time. There is no solid evidence that these policies of increased juvenile incapacitation are positively affecting public safety. Incarceration policies are largely unrelated to rates of serious youth crime. (Krisberg et al., 1986, pp. 32–33)

The consistency with which the training school contingency is applied is shown in Table 2, which displays 1979 training school admission rates in the five states with the highest and lowest rates (Krisberg, Schwartz, & Litsky, 1984). The differences are dramatic even when considering states of comparable population. For example, with respect to two of the smallest states, Vermont had an admission rate of 0 (actually a few offenders were admitted to out-of-state training schools), whereas Wyoming had 358 admissions out of 144,692 age-eligible youths (a rate of 518 per 100,000 age-eligible youths). As for the two largest states, the rate per 100,000 youths in California (447) was almost 12 times as great as the rate in New York (38).

Why the huge differences in admission rates? Is there that much more delinquent behavior in California and Wyoming? Are the juvenile justice systems in Vermont and New York much worse at detecting offenders or much better at rehabilitation? Probably not, at least not to that extent. Differences in the application of the training school contingency are mostly due to differences in public policy and politics. In their article on justice by geography, Krisberg and his colleagues concluded that very little of the variation in admission rates could be attributed to the frequency or severity of juvenile crime. In fact, the only variable for which there was a correlation was the number of training school beds. Obviously, the number of training school beds is the product of the political process.

From a research standpoint, the inconsistency in the training school contingency offers promising opportunities. Every separate governmental jurisdiction has its own unique laws, regulations, and/or policies that make up the training school contingency. In many states, the contingency is administered at the county level. This means the training school contingency is administered in hundreds of different ways to tens of thousands of youths each year. As we improve our ability to categorize those interventions and monitor their outcomes, our understanding of the effects of the training school contingency should increase. More research is needed to determine differential effects with respect to the extreme variation in the training school contingency. The fact that one state incarcerates youth at a rate 12 times greater than another creates a social/political experiment that should not be ignored.

Modification of the Training School Contingency

The training school contingency is developed through the political process with input from all three branches of government. The same is true with respect to its modifications. Several examples involving dramatic change will be described briefly.

At the executive level, significant change has resulted from closing training schools. In 1974, Vermont's training school admission rate was 187 per 100,000 age-eligible youths (Krisberg *et al.*, 1986). By 1979, the rate had declined to zero. The change occurred very abruptly when the governor and the commissioner of the Department of Social and Rehabilitation Services closed the only training school in the state. Similar change also occurred a few years earlier in Massachusetts. More gradual but substantial reductions in the reliance on the training school contingency have resulted from administrative policy changes in West Virginia, Michigan, Pennsylvania, Kentucky, Utah, and Alabama.

Obviously, changes at the executive level are not restricted to reductions in the use of training schools. On a national basis, the utilization is increasing, not decreasing. Increased utilization (at least through the construction of new training schools) usually requires the combined effort of both the executive and legislative branches of government.

The federal Juvenile Justice and Delinquency Prevention Act of 1974 (JJDPA) is an example of a legislative change in the training school contingency. The JJDPA should be of interest to behaviorists because it employed a reinforcement contingency to produce the change. In order to obtain federal funds through JJDPA, states had to make policy and/or legislative changes that would effectively remove status offenders from secure facilities that also contained delinquents. Most training schools were defined as secure facilities.

Although the financial incentive for the JJDPA was relatively small, the impact was significant with all but five states qualifying for the program (Nevada, North Dakota, Oklahoma, South Dakota, and Wyoming). According to the Office of Juvenile Justice and Delinquency Prevention, the population of 5,000 status offenders held in public facilities in 1977 decreased to slightly more than 2,000 in 1982, a decline of approximately 60% (Martin, 1985). This decline, however, should be treated with caution. Although the JJDPA did in fact result in specific and/or policy changes in 45 states, the actual impact on the status offender is less clear. Further research is needed to determine how many youths (a) were adjudicated delinquent and remained part of the training school population, (b) were transferred into other secure institutional facilities (e.g., mental hospitals or minitraining schools for status offenders), (c) were placed in less restrictive, community-based programs, and (d) were not placed into any program (Logan & Rausch, 1985).

Unlike the executive and legislative branches of government, the judicial branch does not establish social/political contingencies. Nevertheless, the judicial interpretation of laws, regulations, and policies can have a considerable impact on whom the laws, regulations and policies apply, and how they are applied. An example of the former is the Supreme Court decision in *Schall v. Martin* (Schall, 1984), a decision that upheld New York's preventive-detention law. Basically, the preventive-detention law permits alleged offenders to be confined in a secure institutional setting not simply to ensure appearance at a trial but because they are regarded as at serious risk to commit new crimes while awaiting trial. Not only is the decision likely to increase the detention population, but it is also likely to facilitate the use of more long-term placements in training schools. Examples of judicial influence over how the training school contingency is applied include recent prohibitions over the use of excessive isolation, the use of physical restraints (e.g., hog tying and shackling to fixed objects), and dirty, unsanitary conditions (*Bobby M.* 1983, 1985; *Gary Hegstrom,* 1984).

In summary, the training school contingency is one of the most powerful social and political contingencies that exists. In essence, it constitutes a total and prolonged change in the offender's environment. Unfortunately, it is also one of the least understood contingencies. In the absence of any convincing scientific data pertaining to cost-effectiveness, there has been a huge discrepancy in its utilization from one legal jurisdiction to another. Several examples were provided showing how the training school contingency has been modified through all three branches of government. The next three examples of social and political contingencies will be discussed in less detail.

The Diversion Contingency

The diversion contingency provides community-based services to an offender that are designed to divert the offender from the juvenile justice system (see Chapter 9 by O'Donnell, Manos, and Chesney-Lind, this volume). The diversion program was conceptualized by the President's Commission on Law Enforcement and the Administration of Justice in 1967 and implemented through federal funds provided by the Law Enforcement Assistance Administration (LEAA).

Although the diversion contingency produced a multitude of programs in every state, the outcome was largely negative in that (a) most of the clients who were served by diversion were juveniles that previously would have been lectured and released, (b) even with this less serious population the evidence regarding recidivism is equivocal, and (c) the vast majority of the programs was terminated soon after the federal resources were eliminated (Dunford, Osgood, & Weichselbaum, 1982; Klein, 1979; Osgood & Weichselbaum, 1984).

In Vermont, a diversion program has been developed that appears to be more successful, although it does differ significantly from most other diversion programs. The Vermont program, which is logically consistent with social learning theory (though not designed by behavior therapists), has two main components. First, offenders are not referred to the program until after a delinquency petition has been filed in court. This condition of "postcharge" referral provides a safeguard against widening the net of the juvenile justice system and provides motivation to the participant to comply with the program. Noncompliance can and frequently does result in subsequent adjudication.

The second important component of the Vermont diversion program is the formulation of a time-limited behavioral contract by a board of interested citizens from the community. The contracts specify behavioral commitments that typically focus on victim restitution, community service, school or job performance, and curfew conditions. In essence, the contract represents a specific opportunity for offenders to make up for their mistakes rather than participate in diffuse, nonspecific counseling and other services that are usually associated with the more traditional diversion programs.

Although the data are correlational, they strongly suggest that the Vermont diversion program has had a positive impact. As shown in Table 3, at the beginning of 1981, a total of 496 delinquents were under the jurisdiction of the state—348 on probation and 148 in state custody (e.g., the more serious delinquents that usually reside in foster homes, group homes, or the wilderness camp). During 1981, the state legislature appropriated funds for 13 separate diversion programs serving almost the entire state. By 1985, the total number of delinquents under state jurisdiction had declined to 387, a decrease of 22%. The decrease was accounted for by the reduction (46%) in delinquents placed on probation, the population that was most likely to be referred to the diversion program by the prosecuting attorneys. The decline in the population of delinquents between 1981 and 1985 is especially significant, given a marked increase in public sentiment to get tough with delinquents in the summer of 1981 following the tragic murder of a 12-year-old girl by two juveniles. That event, which resulted in a special session of the legislature, was most likely responsible for the corresponding 28% increase in delinquents in custody.

At this time, a comprehensive assessment of the Vermont diversion pro-

Table 3. The Number of Adjudicated Delinquents in the State of Vermont at the Beginning of Each Calendar Year

	Year					% Change
	1981	1982	1983	1984	1985	1981–1985
Total delinquents	496	473	434	376	387	−22
Custody	148	164	190	207	200	+28
Probation	348	309	244	169	187	−46

gram is not available. Although the program coordinator reports a contract completion rate of 94% and a recidivism rate of 8% (e.g., subsequent adjudication into the juvenile justice system), the actual program impact on delinquent behavior is unknown. It is certain, however, that the program has not resulted in an increase in the total number of youth who enter the Vermont juvenile justice system; it also offers a viable explanation for the actual decline in that population. Finally, it provides a promising way to prevent delinquency from the standpoint of social learning theory.

The Intensive Supervision Contingency

A contingency that has been an encouraging alternative to adult incarceration is the intensive supervision contingency (Petersilia, 1985, see Nietzel & Himeline, Chapter 4, this volume). Similar in some ways to the Vermont diversion program, the contingency represents an intermediate consequence in the criminal justice system—it is a more restrictive form of punishment than probation but not as severe (or expensive) as prison. The contingency is usually administered by a court, although some correctional agencies are using it as a variation of probation.

Participants in an intensive supervision program are typically supervised on a daily basis by two-person teams made up of a probation officer and a law enforcement officer. Most programs require curfews, job attendance, victim restitution, and community service, with serious noncompliance or transgressions resulting in incarceration.

The intensive supervision contingency is promising for several reasons. First, it is compatible with social learning theory. Instead of placing the offender in an extremely artificial environment that shapes dependency and forces an external control of behavior, the offender stays in the community where more realistic learning can occur. Offenders are required to make amends for their mistakes in an environment where reinforcement and punishment contingencies are administered on a daily basis (compared to a monthly basis for traditional probation). A second promising aspect of the intensive supervision contingency relates to some preliminary outcome data suggesting that the participants do much better than their counterparts on probation or in prison (Conrad, 1985; Pearson, 1985). In addition, one comparison study, involving random assignment, indicates that pretrial released felony offenders who received intensive supervision did better than those who participated in other forms of pretrial release (Austin, Krisberg, & Litsky, 1985). An interesting subcomponent of that study involved a comparison of supervision alone with supervision plus agency services (e.g., counseling from professional social workers and employment specialists). Both types of supervision were equally effective in keeping the subsequent pretrial arrest and fugitive rates at about 10%. The final point to be made on behalf of the intensive supervision contingency relates to cost. According to officials in Georgia, their program costs the state $4.50 per day per participant compared to $30.43 per day to keep a person in prison (Clendinen, 1985). Others point out that the greatest potential for savings is through a reduced need for prison expansion or renovation in the capital construction budget (Austin *et al.,* 1985).

Although the intensive supervision contingency is a logical consequence of social learning theory, its origin had little to do with either theory or research. The contingency was created through the pressure of the federal courts to solve the problem of prison overcrowding and increasing prison costs. Although overcrowding seems to have spawned a desirable alternative to incarceration, it can hardly be regarded as a desirable strategy for systems change. In fact, it can be associated with deadly side effects. For example, for the 38,000 inmates who live in the overcrowded and understaffed Texas prison system, the homicide rate is so high that a person living in prison is six times more likely to be murdered than a person living outside prison (Clendinen, 1985).

Like the training school contingency, the intensive supervision contingency is subject to considerable variation across state and county jurisdictions. The rate of incarceration can account for a significant proportion of that variation. The contingency was developed in the South where it is used much more extensively than in other parts of the country. The rate of incarceration in the South is also the highest in the country. In Massachusetts, for example, where the incarceration rate is 80 per 100,000 people, intensive supervision occurs less frequently than in Georgia, Florida, and Texas where the incarceration rates per 100,000 are 260, 242, and 226, respectively (Bureau of Justice Statistics). Based on the encouraging data that have been accumulated thus far, the intensive supervision contingency should be expanded, and its use with even more serious offenders should be explored.

The Funding Contingency

The funding contingency is an indirect social/political contingency that enables all direct professional and social/political contingencies to exist. It results from the political process that determines laws and public policies.

Although the funding contingency is intended to enable the implementation of policies and programs, the contingency has considerable influence over conceptualization and development. An example already discussed is the diversion contingency. In 1975, it would have been difficult to find a major city that did not have some sort of diversion program. At the present time, few of those programs are in existence. Although some professionals would like to believe the changes were a function of research and evaluation, two more likely variables are a reduction in resources and changes in the ideology of the lawmakers and policymakers who authorize funding.

Another example of how funding, or the lack of it, can influence the development of policies and programs is the intensive supervision contingency. Because of prison overcrowding and a "get-tough" ideology, policymakers and lawmakers were faced with two choices: build more prisons or develop a less expensive "get-tough" program. The fact that intensive probation makes more sense from a social learning standpoint appears to be coincidental. In the previously mentioned two examples, changes in a funding contingency were associated with positive results. In one case, a program that did not seem to be working was reduced; in the other case, a less expansive and possibly more effective alternative to incarceration was initiated.

Obviously, however, a major change in funding does not necessarily produce desirable results. The following examples forecast some ominous consequences. One of the fundamental beliefs of the Reagan administration is that there is too much government, particularly at the federal level and most particularly with respect to social programs (Regnery, 1986). Each year the president has sent to Congress a budget that calls for a sharp reduction in domestic programs. For example, the administration's 1987 budget would eliminate more than 40 separate social programs including the Office of Juvenile Justice and Delinquency Prevention. Although Congress has not endorsed all of the administration's budgetary requests, it has produced changes in two major funding contingencies designed to eliminate or reduce social programs. One was the Omnibus Reconciliation Act of 1981 that is estimated to have cut 10 billion dollars from services to at-risk, low-income children (Children's Defense Fund, 1982). The other is the Gramm-Rudman-Hollings Act (Public Law 99-177) that, if not declared unconstitutional, could result in automatic annual reductions of services to many social programs.

Although a reduction in funding is relatively easy to document, the ultimate impact on unlawful behavior is a much more complex question that takes considerable time and research to resolve. Nevertheless, there are two aspects of recent or proposed changes in funding contingencies that appear especially noteworthy. One is that most of the program reductions are likely to come from the prevention/early intervention end of the continuum of services, and the second is that the number of at-risk children who are the targets of many of those programs is increasing.

With respect to the differential impact that the funding contingencies will have on the continuum of rehabilitation services, it has already been noted that a greater proportion of convicted juvenile offenders are going to the more restrictive (and more expensive) programs, namely training schools. Not only has there been 5% increase in the use of the training school contingency (Table 1), the national prison population has increased from 229,000 in 1974 to 438,000 in 1983, a 91% increase (Petersilia, 1985). Given the prevailing public and political demand for more restrictive and punitive responses to unlawful behavior (e.g., just desserts and selective incapacitation), program cuts are not likely to come from this end of the continuum of services.

As for the increase in the population of children that are at risk of becoming unlawful offenders, consider the following (Children's Defense Fund Budget, 1985). First, 13.3 million children were living in poverty in 1983, a 35.6% increase over 1979. Second, 55% of all children living in female-headed houses live in poverty, a 14% increase since 1977. Third, over 80% of all children living in poverty in 1973 were living in families receiving federally subsidized welfare benefits (e.g., Aid to Families with Dependent Children or AFDC). By 1983, however, that percentage had declined to 53%. Fourth, 95% of all children living in poverty in 1974 were receiving federally subsidized health care benefits (Medicaid). By 1983, that percentage had declined to 70%. Finally, in 1970, 30% of all teengagers who gave birth to children were unmarried. By 1982, that percentage had increased to 55%.

Although the offender population comes from all socioeconomic levels, a disproportional number of juveniles living in poverty self-report that they have engaged in crime (Elliott, Ageton, Huizinga, Knowles, & Canter, 1983), and an even greater proportion penetrate well into the juvenile justice system. For example, in Vermont, approximately 45% of the delinquents in state custody come from families receiving welfare benefits, yet only 15% of all Vermont children reside in such families.

A need exists for more and better data with respect to the existing ideological dispute over whether limited resources are better spent on incarceration programs or prevention programs. The point is that the architects of social/political contingencies cannot wait for such data. In fact, all too often they are not influenced by the best data that are available. In addition to improving their base of scientific knowledge, behavior therapists also need to address the barriers to the modification of social/political contingencies.

Barriers to the Modification of Social/Political Contingencies and Recommendations for Change

Earlier in this chapter, the architects of professional and social/political contingencies were described as coming from two different worlds. The schism between the two becomes clearer if one visualizes the social policymakers as social architects and behavior therapists as plumbers. Using this analogy, the architects and the plumbers have to work together to ensure a well-designed and functioning house. The plumbers need some understanding of the overall design of the house, and the architects need specific technical information that only the plumbers can provide. There is increasing concern that the current social architects are building a house in which the pipes just will not fit.

It is likely that public policies that increase poverty, homelessness, hunger, and the like will result in more crime, thereby increasing the demand for more jails and training schools. Behavior therapists must resist the pressures to serve the social architects and their conceptualization of a well-designed house. Although incarceration may provide necessary temporary relief, in and of itself, it is a barrier to rehabilitation. To carry the analogy a step further, it makes no sense to ask the social architects to make the pipes fit. Viable solutions are more apt to come from professionals who devote their careers to the science and art of behavioral change.

The silence of the professionals is quite evident. Behavior therapists spend little time or effort trying to influence social/political contingencies, yet little evidence exists that behavior therapist are enamored with the present system. If a close relative of a behavior therapist were arrested on a charge of breaking and entering and the state made available $30,000 for rehabilitation, would the behavior therapist choose to spend it for a year of residency at the state training school? Would it matter if the training school had a behavior therapy program? Given complete discretion on the expenditure of $30,000, most behavior therapists would probably believe they could piece together a program that would be more effective than the training school. In fact, most behavior therapists would probably resist the training school placement even without that discretion. But how many behavior therapists would actively resist the state (or its policymakers) if there were an effort to build another training school? Or how many behavior therapists would resist social policies that move us toward a two-class society in which services to the underclass are only provided to the most severely disabled and disadvantaged? Although the barriers to such actions are profound, they are not insurmountable.

Many of the barriers to the influence of social/political contingencies by behavior therapists fall into two categories: (a) training and education and (b) the contingencies that presently maintain the behavior of behavior therapists. In general, training and education for the behavior therapist have been similar to that experienced by persons engaging in most other forms of psychological and psychiatric interventions. Most of the emphasis has been on training them in the treatment of individual clients or the administration of intervention programs for relatively small groups of clients. Although this form of intervention is easily justified in terms of science and humanity, it is unlikely to have a significant impact on the prevalence or the incidence of unlawful behavior. In a very persuasive argument on behalf of prevention, George Albee has documented the ultimate futility of traditional therapeutic intervention (Albee, 1985). A landmark epidemiological study estimated that there are 43 million adults in this country who are "mentally ill" (not including the institutionalized and the homeless, most of whom are also mentally ill). To combat this problem, we have a therapy force of approximately 45,000 psychiatrists, clinical psychologists, and counseling psychologists delivering mental health services at any one time. The ratio is even more skewed with respect to the offender, who typically rejects or resists any form of counseling or individual therapy. It is clear that the vast amount of unlawful behavior that

occurs in this country cannot be brought under control by the direct administration of therapy or counseling. Albee stresses the need for more and better
programs in the field of primary prevention. Also important is the need to
establish more cost-effective social/political contingencies.

In recent years, several professional organizations affiliated with the
training and education of behavior therapists have begun to focus on the field
of public policy (Morris, 1985). The Society for the Advancement of Behavior
Analysis (AABT) has established a research action committee with a public
relations subcommittee; the Association of Behavior Analysis now has a subcommittee on public policy; and the Association for the Advancement of Behavior Therapy has recently established a committee on legislative affairs
that is designed to (a) monitor state and federal policy initiatives, (b) provide
information to policymakers via policy analyses, position papers, briefs, and
expert testimony, and (c) develop a comprehensive national social-policy information network with AABT members serving as policy liasions in each state.
In addition, there have been several articles focusing on the need to bridge the
gap between the professional and the social policymaker and on the ways to do
it (Carey, Carey, & Turkat, 1983; Gonzales, 1984; Masters, 1984; Morris,
1985). Many of the recommendations involve the application of good behavioral principles to the policymaker instead of the client. Examples include the
need to target specific persons such as key legislative committee members
and/or staff and the importance of communicating to policymakers in a concise, readable format.

Although the recent focus on public policy has been encouraging, it is
doubtful that sufficient change will occur unless there is also substantial
modification in the contingencies that affect behavior therapists. At the present time, behavior therapists are paid to conduct traditional programs in
traditional settings, not to engage in political advocacy. Most of the political
advocacy in which we do engage relates to social/political contingencies that
affect our ability to conduct therapy (e.g., third-party payments) rather than
to social/political contingencies that directly affect our clients.

Although social/political contingencies could be changed in many ways to
facilitate both the offender and the behavior therapist, two specific examples
will be provided. Both will be conceptualized in terms of new legislation, which
can create the broadest impact. The first example is legislation that would
require a professional, human impact statement prior to the consideration of
any bill that might effect the offender or the potential offender. The legislation would be similar to the environmental impact statement presently required for legislation that might adversely affect the environment. It would
require an impartial body of professional experts to provide their best estimate
about any adverse effects the proposed legislation might have on the prevalence or incidence of unlawful behavior.

Although a human impact statement will not guarantee the best decision,
it will help bridge the gap between the social scientist and the social policymaker. It will cause the social scientists to address the vast, uncontrolled
social experimentation that takes place in the political arena by requiring

specific estimates as to how a change in a social/political contingency will affect behavior. If social scientists were reinforced for providing such information, it might also increase their motivation to conduct research on these more complex but pervasive variables. At the same time, it will force the social policymakers to consider the "best guess" of those who spend their careers addressing the subject of human impact.

Two recent books on the subject of crime (Currie, 1985; Wilson & Herrnstein, 1985) take the position that no matter how we might transform the criminal justice system, it will have little impact on criminal or delinquent behavior. According to that position, no differences exist between a reprimand, restitution, incarceration, or intensive vocational training. The implication is that consequences do not make a difference, an untenable position from a social learning perspective. Although behavior therapists have labored intensively in their own programs to determine what works and what does not, they have not addressed adequately the behavioral impact of the juvenile/criminal justice systems. Requiring assessments of the human impact of potential changes in relevant social/political contingencies would be a step in that direction.

The second example of a change in a social/political contingency that would be beneficial to the offender and the behavior therapist involves legislation promoting more innovative and potentially beneficial alternatives to incarceration. In essence, the legislation would require that before a *nonviolent* offender could be placed in a more restrictive, more expensive placement, the equivalent cost would have to be spent on the offender in the less restrictive placement for a period of at least 6 months.

This cost-equivalency legislation would be designed to separate two variables that tend to be confounded in our efforts to rehabilitate the offender— cost of services and security. In most jurisdictions, a continuum of services is available for the offender. In the juvenile service system in Vermont, probation is at the least restrictive end of the continuum. Probation officers have an average caseload of 40 to 50 offenders and privde minimal supervision. The next step is foster care where the annual residential cost per youth is about $3,000. Most youths who cannot adjust to foster homes are placed in group homes where the annual cost is about $20,000. The more restrictive end of the continuum consists of a wilderness camp ($25,000) followed by placement in an out-of-state institution ($25,000–$50,000). The system usually starts with the least restrictive and least expensive placement. If that fails, there is almost invariably a significant increase in both restrictiveness (security) and cost of service. For example, if a youth in a foster home breaks into someone else's house and steals property, he or she would most likely be placed in a group home (add $17,000 per year) or a training schoold (add $22,000 to $47,000 per year). The question is, what if $17,000 to $47,000 in services had been added to the foster home placement? It is very conceivable that more offenders could be rehabilitated by wrapping additional services around offenders in less restrictive settings rather than by placing them into increasing degrees of incarceration (and cost).

The problem with the equivalency-of-cost contingency strategy is that unless (or until) it replaces some of the more expensive, restrictive programs, it will cost more money. A minor reduction in a training school population saves almost nothing. When Vermont closed its only training school in 1979, however, more than a million dollars was shifted into community-based programs. Although this may not be the best time to close training schools, overcrowded facilities, together with severe budget cuts, may force policymakers to consider alternatives that in the long run will be less expensive. As in the case with intensive supervision, some of those alternatives may also be more effective.

CONCLUSION

The primary objective of this chapter is to encourage behavior therapists working in the field of crime and delinquency to adopt a more *ecological* perspective (Rogers-Warren & Warren, 1977). In referring to such a perspective as ecobehavioral technology, Willems (1983) has stated the problem as follows:

> In looking to psychology for ways to deal with complex behavior problems, society is looking to a discipline with narrow vision. The subtle interdependency of phenomena that is taken for granted by ecologists in other disciplines has not impressed the scientists and practitioners of behavior, and the conceptual scope of these scientists and practitioners is too restricted to take account of the larger contexts or systems in which persons and their behavior are embedded. Thus, while demonstrating ever greater mastery of units of behavior, behavior therapists continue to disregard demonstrable effects of larger systems and their interdependencies, even though those phenomena are very likely to affect the success of failure of therapeutic work. (p. 427)

In order to advance the behavioral technology for the prevention and modification of delinquent and criminal behavior, behavior therapists must expand their vision beyond traditional therapeutic interventions under "given" environmental circumstances. The most significant social and political challenge to behavioral programs for delinquents and criminals is the creation of more effective social/political contingencies. Behaviorists have an effective technology for changing behavior. It is time to incorporate that technology into the everyday contingencies that affect all delinquents and criminals and not merely to apply it to those few who are the recipients of our behavior therapy programs.

REFERENCES

Albee, G. W. (1985, February). The answer is prevention. *Psychology Today, 19*, 60–64.
Atthowe, J. M. (1973). Behavior innovation and persistence. *American Psychologist, 28*, 34–41.
Austin, J., Krisberg, B., & Litsky, P. (1985). The effectiveness of supervised pretrial release. *Crime and Delinquency, 31*, 519–537.
Bandura, A. (1973). *Aggression: A social learning analysis*. Englewood Cliffs, NJ: Prentice-Hall.

Bandura, A. (1974). Behavior theory and models of man. *American Psychologist, 29,* 859–869.

Bobby M. (1983). Court order on use of security units and lock-ups, No. TCA 83-7003 (N.D. Fla. July 5).

Bobby M. (1985). Court order on preliminary injunction, No. TCA 83-7003, (N.D. Fla. July 14).

Burchard, J. D., & Burchard, S. (Eds.). (1987). *The prevention of delinquency.* Beverly Hills: Sage.

Burchard, J. D., & Harig, P. T. (1976). Behavior modification and juvenile delinquency. In H. Leitenberg (Ed.), *Handbook of behavior modification and behavior therapy* (pp. 405–452). Englewood Cliffs, NJ: Prentice-Hall.

Burchard, J. D., & Lane, T. W. (1982). Crime and delinquency. In A. S. Bellack, M. Hersen, & A. E. Kazdin (Eds.), *International handbook of behavior modification and therapy* (pp. 613–652). New York: Plenum Press.

Carey, K. B., Carey, M. P., & Turkat, I. D. (1983). Behavior modification in the media: A five year follow-up. *American Psychologist, 38,* 498–500.

Children's Defense Fund Budget (1982). Washington, DC: Children Defense Fund.

Children's Defense Fund Budget (1985). Washington, DC: Children Defense Fund.

Clendinen, D. (1985, December 18). Crowded prisons in South lead to tests of other punishments. *New York Times,* p. 18.

Conrad, J. P. (1985). The penal dilemma and its emerging solution. *Crime and Delinquency, 31,* 411–422.

Currie, E. (1985). *Confronting crime: An American challenge.* New York: Pantheon Books.

Dunford, F. W., Osgood, D. W., & Weichselbaum, H. F. (1982). *National evaluation of diversion projects.* Washington, DC: U.S. Government Printing Office.

Elliott, D. S., Ageton, S., Huizinga, D., Knowles, B. A., & Canter, R. J. (1983). *The prevalence and incidence of delinquent behavior: 1976–1980* (National youth survey report no. 28). Boulder: C/A Publications.

Federal Bureau of Investigation. (1983). *Crime in the United States.* Washington, DC: U.S. Government Printing Office.

Gary Hegstrom (1984). Pocket No. 77-1039-BV (D. Oregouk, unpublished opinion).

Goldiamond, I. (1978). The professional as a double agent. *Journal of Applied Behavior Analysis, 11,* 178–184.

Gonzales, H. B. (1984). Scientist and congress. *Science, 244,* 127–129.

Jason, L. A. (1977). Behavioral community psychology: Conceptualizations, and applications. *Journal of Community Psychology, 5,* 302–312.

Klein, M. W. (1979). Deinstitutionalization and diversion of juvenile offenders: A litany of impediments. In N. Norris & M. Tonry (Eds.), *Crime and justice: An annual review of research.* Chicago: University of Chicago Press.

Krisberg, B., Schwartz, I., & Litsky, P. (1984). Youth in confinement: Justice by geography. *Journal of Research in Crime and Delinquency, 21,* 153–181.

Krisberg, B., Schwartz, I. M., Litsky, P., & Austin, J. (1986). The watershed of juvenile justice reform. *Crime and Delinquency, 32,* 5–38.

Laws, D. R. (1974). The failure of a token economy. *Federal Probation, 38,* 33–38.

Liberman, R. P. (1979). Social and political challenges to the development of behavioral programs in organizations. In P. O. Sjoden, S. Bates, & W. S. Dockens, III. (Eds.), *Trends in behavior therapy* (pp. 369–398). New York: Academic Press.

Lipton, D., Martinson, R., & Wilks, J. (1975). *The effectiveness of correctional treatment: A survey of treatment evaluation studies.* New York: Praeger.

Logan, C. H., & Rausch, S. P. (1985). Why deinstitutionalizing status offenders is pointless. *Crime and Delinquency, 31,* 501–517.

Lundman, R. J. (1986). Beyond probation: Assessing the generalizability of the delinquency suppression effect measures reported by Murray & Cox. *Crime and Delinquency, 32,* 134–147.

Martin, E. (1985). *Deinstitutionalization of status offenders: A national perspective.* Paper presented at the First Annual Conference for Children and Youth Councils, Boise, Idaho.

Masters, J. (1984). Psychology, research, and social policy. *American Psychologist, 39,* 851–862.

Morris, E. (1985). Public information, dissemination, and behavior analysis. *The Behavior Analyst, 8,* 95–110.

Murray, C. A., & Cox, L. A., Jr. (1979). *Beyond probation*. Beverly Hills, CA: Sage.

Nietzel, M. T. (1979). *Crime and its modification: A social learning perspective*. New York: Pergamon Press.

Norley, D. B. (1977). The care and feeding of legislators. *Defiance Mentale/Mental Retardation, 27*(3), 25–27.

Osgood, D. W., & Weichselbaum, H. F. (1984). Juvenile diversion: When practice matches theory. *Journal of Research in Crime and Delinquency, 21,* 33–56.

Pearson, F. S. (1985). New Jersey's intensive supervision program: A progress report. *Crime and Delinquency, 31,* 393–410.

Petersilia, J. (1985). Community supervision: Trends and critical issues. *Crime and Delinquency, 31,* 339–347.

Regnery, A. S. (1986). A federal perspective on juvenile justice reform. *Crime and Delinquency, 32,* 39–54.

Reppucci, N. D. (1973). Social psychology of institutional change: General principles for intervention. *American Journal of Community Psychology, 1,* 330–341.

Reppucci, N. D., & Saunders, J. T. (1974). Social psychology of behavior modification: Problems of implementation in natural settings. *American Psychologist, 29,* 649–660.

Robinson, J., & Smith, G. (1971). The effectiveness of correctional programs. *Crime and Delinquency, 17,* 67–80.

Rogers-Warren, A., & Warren, S. (Eds.). (1977). *Ecological perspectives in behavior analysis*. Baltimore: University Park Press.

Romig, D. (1978). *Justice for our children: An examination of juvenile delinquency rehabilitation programs*. Lexington, MA: Heath.

Rozynko, V., Swift, K., Swift, J., & Boggs, L. J. (1973). Controlled environments for social change. In H. Wheeler (Ed.), *Beyond the punitive society—Operant conditioning: Social and political aspects*. San Francisco: W. H. Freeman.

Shall, M. (1984). *United States Law Review, 52,* 4681–4696.

Skinner, B. F. (1953). *Science and human behavior*. New York: The Free Press.

Willems, E. P. (1983). Training for ecobehavioral technology. In M. Rosenbaum, C. Franks, & Y. Jaffe (Eds.), *Perspectives on behavior therapy in the eighties* (pp. 416–429). New York: Springer.

Wray, L. D. (1980). Social, political, and cultural challenges to behavioral programs in the community. In G. L. Martin & J. G. Osborne (Eds.), *Helping in the community: Behavioral applications* (pp. 355–369). New York: Plenum Press.

Wilson, J. Q., & Herrnstein, R. J. (1985). *Crime and human nature*. New York: Simon & Schuster.

Author Index

Subject Index